Reviews for *VMware vSphere™ 4 Implementation*

"Mike Laverick is true to form in this, his latest effort. He provides a wealth of information along with a dash of humor, making his work a joy to read. Mike is a well-known and well-respected member of the VMware community—a VMware Certified Instructor, a VMware vExpert, and the author of the must-visit blog site, www.rtfm-ed.co.uk. You will not find anyone better qualified to tell this story!"

–Ken Cline
Sr. Consultant, VMware Professional Services

"Mike Laverick's *VMware vSphere 4 Implementation* provides a practical, step-by-step approach to all the elements of vSphere 4. Mike does this in a way that makes the most multifaceted topics seem simple, and breaks down complex sequences into steps that everyone can follow. This book covers everything from installation and networking to storage and advanced vSphere 4 features, enabling you to get the most out of your infrastructure."

–Chad Sakac
P.Eng, vExpert VP, VMware Technology Alliance EMC Corporation,
and author of http://virtualgeek.typepad.com

"Mike Laverick has been a stellar resource for VMware education for a long time, so it is no surprise that his latest book is more of the same. I find his tone very enjoyable and easy to read. As an author myself, I know how much of a challenge it is to make a technical manual something that does not put people to sleep! I was excited to read that Mike considers PowerCLI (VMware's PowerShell scripting toolkit) to be as important to the vSphere admin as I do. He has included a nice overview of the technology, and has plenty of great code samples. I cannot wait to get a bound copy of this for my own bookshelf."

–Hal Rottenberg
Author of *Managing VMware Infrastructure with Windows PowerShell: TFM®*,
and co-host of the PowerScripting Podcast

"Mike's RTFM Education website has always been a shining beacon of virtualization wisdom for mere mortals like me and now he continues that tradition in his latest book. Mike talks you through vSphere implementation in his knowledgeable and witty way. Instead of pushing his opinion, Mike shows you all the possible alternatives and how you should chose your ideal path. Reading this book is like having him sit right at your desk to teach you this noble art."

–Luc Dekens (LucD)
vExpert 2009

"Mike's conversational writing style brings *VMware vSphere 4 Implementation* to life. His skills gained as a VMware trainer show in his ability to break down complex theories and procedures into bite-size, easily digestible portions. Whether you are an absolute beginner with virtualization or a guru, you will find plenty of use for this book so I thoroughly recommend it to everyone."

–Tom Howarth
Owner of PlanetVM.Net and Analyst with the Virtualisation Practice

About the Author

Mike Laverick is a professional instructor with 15 years of experience in technologies such as Novell, Windows, Citrix, and VMware. Mike first became active in the VMware community in 2003. He is a VMware forum moderator and member of the London VMware User Group steering committee. Aside from his teaching duties, Mike is the sole owner/author of the popular RTFM Education web site (and blog), where he publishes a range of free guides and utilities aimed specifically at VMware users. In 2009, Mike help found the Irish and Scottish VMware User Groups. Mike has been recognized for his outstanding contribution to the VMware community and was granted vExpert status by VMware.

About the Technical Editor

Gabrie van Zanten has been working in IT for more than 12 years. Currently, he works as a consultant/architect of virtual environments for Logica. In February 2009, he was awarded vExpert status by VMware. Gabrie regularly writes on his blog gabesvirtualworld.com, and for other Web sites and magazines.

VMware | vSphere™ 4 Implementation

Mike Laverick

Mc
Graw
Hill

New York   Chicago   San Francisco
Lisbon   London   Madrid   Mexico City
Milan   New Delhi   San Juan
Seoul   Singapore   Sydney   Toronto

The **McGraw·Hill** Companies

Cataloging-in-Publication Data is on file with the Library of Congress

McGraw-Hill books are available at special quantity discounts to use as premiums and sales promotions, or for use in corporate training programs. To contact a representative, please e-mail us at bulksales@mcgraw-hill.com.

VMware vSphere™ 4 Implementation

234567890   DOC DOC   109876543210

ISBN   978-0-07-166452-3
MHID   0-07-166452-1

 The pages within this book were printed on paper containing 100% post-consumer fiber.

Sponsoring Editor	**Technical Editor**	**Production Supervisor**
Jane K. Brownlow	Gabrie van Zanten	George Anderson
Editorial Supervisor	**Copy Editor**	**Composition**
Janet Walden	Marilyn Smith	Glyph International
Project Manager	**Proofreader**	**Illustration**
Ekta Dixit,	Carol Shields	Glyph International
Glyph International	**Indexer**	**Art Director, Cover**
Acquisitions Coordinator	Robert Swanson	Jeff Weeks
Joya Anthony		**Cover Designer**
		Jeff Weeks

This book is dedicated to my partner, Carmel, who puts up with me droning on and on about virtualization.

Contents at a Glance

Contents

Foreword

Choosing the right virtualization platform to build your virtualized datacenter, private or internal cloud infrastructure, is an important one. A large number of providers now claim to offer virtualization products, but not all virtualization offerings are created equal. The fact you are reading this foreword suggests you have made a wise decision to implement VMware vSphere within your business.

The problems we set out to solve with virtualization were not new (ask anyone with a mainframe background), but we believe virtualization has made a bigger impact on these problems than any other technology in the past 20 or more years. For those of us working in the virtualization space, we sometimes forget that the challenges that drove this market are still around today:

- Low infrastructure utilization
- Increasing physical infrastructure costs
- Increasing IT management costs
- Insufficient failover and disaster protection
- High-maintenance end-user desktops

You might ask, "What does all this mean? Can I use vSphere to solve these common challenges? Or is it only for building cloud computing environments I am hearing so much about?"

To address this question, let us consider some current common phrases often used to describe VMware vSphere and its capabilities—"it makes the IT plumbing disappear," "vSphere is a virtualization platform," or "vSphere is the first true cloud platform."

The point is, whether you are new to virtualization and tasked with implementing it for the first time or an experienced consumer of virtualization looking to build out a large-scale cloud computing platform, VMware vSphere is the right choice. As our CEO likes to say, "Cloud is not a destination, but a way of doing computing."

Everyone should be able to achieve the benefits of "cloud" computing. The closer you get to 100 percent virtualized, the closer you get to achieving the benefits of "cloud" computing.

When all is said and done, someone needs to implement this vision. Usually it is at this point that people such as myself, who work on the technical side of things, will start having frequent dialogue with customers asking for documentation references, best practices, case studies, or hints and tips.

During my early career at VMware, one of the resources I most often referred customers to were the RTFM-ed guides (www.rtfm-ed.co.uk) written by Mike Laverick. What I liked about these guides was the crystal-clear explanation of every step, usually accompanied with a variety of screenshots and descriptions of exactly what was going on.

As a VMware certified instructor and independent author, Mike drew on his wealth of experience from VMware teaching to describe things in a way that makes even the most complex concepts simple to understand. The guides were written in the form of a firsthand account or diary of an administrator's own real-world experience implementing the product. The hands-on examples, best practices, hints, tips, and pitfalls made them unique. And this style and quality of content has been used expertly in *VMware vSphere 4 Implementation*.

Whether you are new to VMware or an experienced VMware administrator, I honestly believe this book will prove an invaluable resource during your implementation of VMware vSphere and will assist you in achieving your goal of a successful deployment—first time. Happy reading!

—Lee Dilworth
Principal Systems Engineer, VMware UK

Acknowledgments

I would like to reiterate my thanks to my partner, Carmel Edwards. She helped me do the initial proofreading of the book before it was submitted to a commercial proofreader. She also puts up with me talking excitedly about my adventures in virtualization, which must be very tedious for her.

I would also like to thank all of the people on the VMware Communities forums whom I have helped and who have helped me in the last six to seven years of using VMware products. Special thanks must go to Steve Beaver, Ken Cline, Alex Mittel, Thomas Bryant, and William Boyd.

I would also like to thank Adam Carter of LeftHand Networks for providing me with access to their Virtual SAN Appliance (VSA). I would like to thank Chad Sakac and Alex Tanner of EMC for providing me with two Celerra and Clariion systems for my work on Fibre Channel SANs. Additionally, I would like to thank Vaughn Stewart of NetApp for the contribution of two NetApp FAS storage units. EMC's and NetApp's contribution in this respect will enable me to continue my work on VMware Site Recovery Manager.

I would also like to thank Richard Garsthagen and Andy Stevens at VMware for providing access to VMware's remote lab environment in EMEA. This enabled me to write the chapter on VMware Fault Tolerance. Without this assistance, this book would have been greatly delayed.

I would like to thank John Troyer and Robert Dell'Immagine, who collectively manage and maintain the VMware Communities forums. They have created a community of technical experts, of which I am part and regularly depend on, to fix problems I have never seen before, as well as a forum for asking my peers their collective opinions on new features and functionality.

Finally, I would like to thank Gabrie van Zanten. I first met Gabrie at this year's VMware Europe in Cannes, France. By chance, McGraw-Hill contracted him to be my technical editor. It was a pleasure to work with Gabrie, and I found someone taking a look over my work invaluable.

Introduction

The purpose of this book is to guide you though the most popular and recommended configurations of vSphere 4, with particular emphasis on VMware's ESX and VirtualCenter (now officially called vCenter). It is not intended as a complete reference, but does cover associated products and features, such as VMware High Availability (HA), Distributed Resource Scheduler (DRS), Fault Tolerance (FT), and VMotion.

When writing this guide, I used a mix of hardware—some old and some new. My equipment has two CPUs, four network interface cards (NICs), and connectivity to a fibre-channel storage area network (SAN). In some cases, I had a fully redundant connection to the SAN for the purposes of capturing a real-world configuration in dialog boxes and command-line tools. Midway through the writing process, both EMC and NetApp made very generous donations of their storage arrays.

How This Book Is Structured

The structure of this guide was taken roughly from the VMware authorized course "Install, Configure and Manage," which I teach on a regular basis, with the idea that this guide could act as a companion to the course manual (which you might have if you attended the class). I offer additional information and tips and tricks along the way. I've tried to explain various features and options in a new light, which might assist you in making the VMware software work optimally for your environment. I also point out problems that can arise and suggest ways to resolve them.

I thought that mimicking the structure of the official VMware course might help people whose aim is to use this guide as part of their preparation for the VMware Certified Professional (VCP) exam. I wouldn't say this book is an exam cram guide. For the most part, I don't reproduce streams of endless facts that are subject to change, and that can be looked up easily in VMware's own product documentation. Additionally, I thought that this structure might be of benefit to those studying the product on their own, without the benefit of official VMware training.

In this book, I've included a "What's New?" section at the beginning of chapters. This is intended to be a 1,000-foot view of the new features in vSphere 4. Those folks who have been using VMware ESX and vCenter for some time can refer to these lists for a quick check of the important changes.

I do intend to add updates during the lifetime of this book. After all, it's not uncommon for procedures to change and for new features to be added to ESX or vCenter within a release. I'm committed to producing a second edition of the book if VMware make a major update.

In the meantime, you might like to keep an eye on my blog, where I will be releasing videos and guides on aspects of the vSphere 4 product that did not make it into this edition.

Disclaimer

During the lifetime of the Beta program, VMware made the decision to rebrand its flagship product from Virtual Infrastructure 4 to vSphere 4. By this time, I had already created screen grabs with the fully qualified domain name (FQDN) of vi4book.com. In the end, I decided that an FQDN is an FQDN, and rather than generating unnecessary work, I retained the domain name. However, the text of this book refers to the correct product name of vSphere.

You might wonder why on earth VMware would decide to change the name of its core enterprise product. Well, putting aside the usual jokes about overpaid marketing guff, I believe the reason is that a term like *Virtual Infrastructure* is difficult to copyright and trademark. A term like *vSphere* is easier to protect.

I recall that almost a year before this rebranding, I joked that, with the rise and rise of the cloud computing concept, the next thing we would see would be vRainbows (you can read my vRainbows blog post at http://www.rtfm-ed.co.uk/?p=598). Who knows, maybe when version 5 is released, we will see another rebranding exercise.

What Is Virtualization: Do I Really Need to Spell It Out?

In the training courses I teach for VMware, "What Is Virtualization: Do I Really Need to Spell It Out?" is the title of one of the PowerPoint slides. Interestingly, it wasn't introduced into the slide deck until 2008. Whenever I hit the SPACEBAR and the "What Is Virtualization" slide appears, a wry smile crosses my face, because it really is a bit "Johnny come lately." This slide would have been a lot more useful in 2003. Back then, most people didn't know what the term meant. With *virtualization* being the IT buzzword of the current decade, I often jokingly say to my students that the slide should read "What stone have you been living under that you don't know what virtualization is?"

However, virtualization *is* new to some people, and I meet plenty of them in the training courses I teach. Very often, this is the "fast track" course, which is a little worrying—because by Wednesday or Thursday, these folks have generally reached saturation point. Sometimes I wonder if vendors like VMware should also develop "slow track" course for people with little experience who want to go through things very, very slowly!

What I do like about the "What Is Virtualization" slide is that it debunks some myths, and it seeks to explain what virtualization is not. Many people who are experienced with virtualization *think* they know what it is, but when they are asked to describe it, I find that they confuse it with other similar, but different, technologies.

It's Not Emulation or Simulation—It's Virtualization

Virtualization is *not* simulation or emulation. When you install Windows, Linux, Novell, or Solaris into a VMware virtual machine, the guest operating system inside the virtual machine has *no idea* what's going on. It honestly thinks it is running inside a *physical* machine, even though you and I know it's running inside a *virtual* machine. This is similar to how some folks in the Second Life virtual world honestly believe their Second Life avatar is a true reflection of their inner self. (Like many, I've concluded I barely have time for my first life, never mind a second one.)

A virtual machine has a BIOS just like a physical machine, and VMware use the Phoenix BIOS, which is popular within a lot of Dell hardware. A virtual machine also has virtual interrupts, as it addresses devices like storage controllers and NICs, which it presumes to be physical, but you and I know are virtual. The ESX server that starts up the VM must intercept these virtual interrupts and redirect them to a real physical device inside the ESX host, in a process called *binary translation*.

Simulation and emulation work entirely differently from virtualization. With simulation, all we get is the *appearance* of a system, as opposed to the system itself. So a Cisco simulator or an HP EVA simulator provides an environment within which you can learn Cisco or HP without having the actual expensive physical equipment—much in the way that a flight simulator gives the appearance of flying from London to New York, but the pilot's feet never leave *terra firma*. This distinction is sometimes hard to maintain, as the term *simulation* is often misused by vendors in our industry. For example, some storage vendors allow you to run their storage appliances inside a virtual machine, and they call these *simulators*, as a way of keeping them distinct from the physical storage appliances. They should really call these downloadable virtual machines by the correct name: *storage virtual appliance*.

In contrast to simulation, emulation is very easy to define. Emulation is the process of getting one process or system to work in an environment for which it was never designed. An example of this is the old Atari game of strategy called Combat, or as I called it in my early teens, "invisible tanks." The Atari system didn't use Intel processors; it used solid-state cartridges to hold the programs that made up the games people played. So, if I wanted to play the original "invisible tanks" on a PC or Mac, some kind of emulator would have to be created, which emulated the instruction set of the Atari game on the instruction set of the PC or Mac. What I didn't know at the time was that I was playing a game that would become reality. They are called "stealth tanks" in the military. However, as in the game, they suffer from a major flaw: as soon as you fire your cannon, you're not particularly "stealthy" anymore! (If all this talk of Combat and invisible tanks has brought back memories, then head off to one of these URLs, where you can download an emulator for Atari on the PC: http://stella.sourceforge.net/, http://www.whimsey.com/z26/z26.html, or http://pcae.classicgaming.gamespy.com/.)

Emulators have performance issues, because the instructions are always being translated into a nonnative system, and that translation comes with overhead. The overhead varies, depending on how well assembled the emulator is. The reason for carrying out emulation is that in some cases, it is cheaper to create an emulator (that would run every Atari game, for example) than reencode and rewrite all those applications from scratch.

At this point, you might have picked up on my use of the word *translation* in the description of emulation and ask, "Well, how is this different from binary translation?" You have a fair point. Binary translation in virtualization is not without overhead, but it is a very mature method, which goes a long way back into the world of UNIX and other kernels. Also, wherever possible, most virtualization vendors like VMware will use instructions sent directly to the processor, in a process called *direct access*.

Even though you will read terms like *virtual CPU* (vCPU) in this book and elsewhere, the vCPU of the virtual machine isn't *truly* virtualized. A VMware virtual machine knows if it's running on an Intel or AMD processor and can speak directly to these physical CPUs. Sometimes this is for standard calls; other times, it utilizes particular features of the CPU such as Streaming SIMD Extensions (SSE), an attribute you might know better as Intel Multimedia Extensions (MMX).

In recent years, CPU vendors have developed new attributes specifically aimed at virtualization workloads. Within a single decade, we have come a long way from 32-bit Intel Xeon processors with hyperthreading enabled. We now have multicore CPUs with their own bus to memory and so-called virtualization hardware assist features, such as Intel Virtualization Technology (Intel VT) and AMD Virtualization (AMD-V).

Virtualize Now!

I feel I have been rambling around the question of "What is virtualization?" in a desperate bid not to answer it, mainly for fear of totally patronizing you. So let me cut to the chase.

Virtualization allows you to run on x86 hardware multiple copies of Windows, Linux, Novell, or Solaris on single physical machine. Most operating systems do not use all their hardware when they are in use, which is effectively a waste of computer power. A better use of that physical server would be to run 5, 10, 20, or 30 virtual machines, which all share the underlying physical resources of the host. This allows for the server consolidation of rack upon rack of 1U, 2U, and even 4U physical servers into a much smaller number of physical nodes.

The end result is that businesses need less physical hardware to offer the same services. This represents substantial savings in space, heat, and cooling. Additionally, as virtual machines are encapsulated (contained in) files, creating a new virtual machine is nothing more than a fancy file-copy process. This can massively reduce your deployment time for bringing a new service onstream. Beyond the initial benefits, a whole panoply of other applications of virtualization beckons.

Virtualization Applications

Two applications really, really light my fire (as Jim Morrison might have said). The first one is virtualized disaster recovery. Since a virtual machine is just a file on a block of storage, if we have the appropriately supported storage array, bandwidth, and licenses, it's very easy to replicate or copy virtual machines from one site (the primary/protected site) to another (the secondary/recovery site). VMware has a technology that allows you to pair the protected and recovery site together, and automate a great deal of the manual tasks involved in disaster recovery. It's called VMware Site Recovery Manager, and I wrote a book on that.

Another popular virtualization application is virtual desktops. Ever since Microsoft added the Remote Desktop Protocol (RDP), there has been the possibility of replacing or augmenting the end-user PC with a desktop environment delivered remotely and thinly to the user's client device. That device could be a conventional desktop PC or a dumb terminal, which now can come in cigarette-packet-sized units replete with a USB, PS2, and UTP connections—and a big fancy monitor. (As we all know, the bigger the screen, the faster the computer will go!)

The idea is to replace PCs and/or Terminal Services/Citrix with a virtual desktop that is exclusive to the end user. The concept of virtual desktops isn't restricted to corporate environments. Pretty soon, we will have a virtualization layer for the PC that goes beyond the concept of VMware Workstation or VMware Player, and also a virtualization layer in a mobile phone such that you can have one physical phone with many virtual phones (desktops) within it. Heck, one day you might be able to VMotion a virtual machine from one mobile phone to another, without needing a gigabit backbone.

The virtual desktop is rapidly developing before our very eyes, and it *could* be the next big gravy train. It seems that every software vendor has some kind of virtual desktop offering. Generally, the spin on this is that they are an OEM (so they can supply the dumb terminal and virtual desktop system, which will work with VMware, Citrix, or Microsoft), or they are a virtualization vendor like VMware, Microsoft, and Citrix (so they can sell you the virtualization layer and virtual desktop system).

Personally, I find the virtual desktop space is a still a *little* immature. I speak as a former Citrix Certified Instructor (CCI) and Citrix Certified Enterprise Administrator (CCEA). The problem with the virtual desktop space is that it's highly fragmented, and no one vendor seems to have an offering that knocks all the others into a cocked hat at the right price point. I think with VMware's "ownership" of the underlying virtual layer that allows virtual desktops to function, it is in a very strong position. (I have a feeling that my next book is likely to be about the virtual desktop offering from VMware called View.)

Other applications of virtualization deal with workflow automation, and are of interest to large companies that have substantial IT lab and testing facilities. And yes, you've guessed it, VMware has a product for them, which is called Lab Manager.

Even with all the automation offered by virtualization, there may still be a need for workflow management. The most common workflow is the process a virtual machine might take from testing, staging, deployment, upgrading, decommissioning, and archiving. And as you might expect, VMware has management products called Stage Manager, Orchestrator, and Lifecycle Manager.

I think it's only fair to tell you that I will not be touching on these technologies in this book. My main agenda is to take you through the core platform, rather than additional layers of management.

A Virtualization Analogy: Hotel Virtualization

One of the occupational hazards I face occurs when I'm attending a party or some other event. I'm asked, "So what do you do?" Generally, I respond, "I'm in IT." The average person will just raise her eyebrows and say nothing. Of course, you do realize that IT people are for the most part universally hated by everyone else in the business—and they wonder why we lock our offices or hide in the server room! Occasionally though, people want to know more, and a response of, "You really don't want to know" sometimes doesn't shake them off. So, sometimes I just say, "I work in the field of virtualization." And, in some cases, this stimulates the other party to say excitedly, "Oh, virtualization, that sounds cool—please tell me more."

Another occupational hazard of "being in IT" is explaining to your manager or some other C class executive what the heck virtualization is. Indeed, you might be forced to explain this in an effort to get some hard cash out of these guys for your virtualization project.

Frequently, students ask me if I have an analogy for what virtualization is, without going too technical, so it can be understood by people who know nothing about IT.

I have two such analogies: one to do with an airline and the other to do with a hotel. Some years ago, VMware's term *reservation* got me thinking about hotel and airline reservations as a means of explaining the term. Like all analogies, they are not perfect, but as Kurt Vonnegut once said, "So it goes." I use the airline analogy in Chapter 11, which covers resource management. Here, I'll outline the hotel one. I will keep this very brief, because we are in *Sesame Street* territory.

Welcome to the Hotel Virtualization (sing this to the "Hotel California" tune).

In the past, the server was like a very expensive hotel. It was the worst kind of hotel. It had only one big room, and only one person could stay there. However, each employee—whether he was the CEO or copyboy—had to stay there when he was away on business. This is like the guest operating system being installed on a physical server.

Half the time, the hotel occupant was out doing other things, asleep, or just lying on the bed surfing up and down the channels looking for pornography. This is like when Linux or Windows is idling and using only 5% to 10% of CPU or memory. It became too costly to build such hotels, considering that filling them with one occupant was very wasteful. That occupant consumed heat, water, and power and, most of the time, either wasn't there or was asleep!

So some bright spark thought of a better hotel—one divided into a series of rooms that could be of different sizes and offer different qualities of service. It didn't matter what one guest did in one room, as it could not affect other guests. This hotel had really thick sound insulation, so you couldn't hear the wedding party downstairs or the newlyweds consummating their nuptials next door. On the top floor beyond the bridal suite were the penthouse suites, which were reserved for the high rollers, specifically for Mr. Exchange, Miss SQL, and Mrs. SAP. On other floors, the rooms were barely large enough to swing a small furry animal. These rooms were where Mr. DHCP and Dr. DNS resided.

The old hotel was so expensive that only people like Howard Hughes could afford a room there. But this new, more efficient, hotel cost the same to build and maintain, and everyone could find a room that was suitable for their needs—from the odd billionaire to the businessman on an overnight stay before catching a flight. It also meant we had to build fewer hotels. The other thing we discovered was when Mr. Exchange or Miss SQL weren't around or sleeping—when they were consuming fewer resources—the resources could divvied up among the other residents in the hotel to improve their experience. It was easier to get that table in the fancy restaurant, and it was quicker to get served in the bar.

The old hotel model became increasingly regarded as a luxury few companies could afford. Finally, it died a swift and untimely death when the economy fell off the end of a cliff. The Hotel Virtualization model ruled the roost, because it offered the most flexible way of accommodating guest operating systems with their wildly different resource demands.

And with that, it's time to take off my "Big Bird" suit and get down and technical.

CHAPTER 1 | Install and Configure ESX 4 Classic

Currently, two versions of ESX are available: ESX 4.*x* and ESXi 4. Functionally, they offer the same hypervisor and kernel. The ESX 4.*x* version ships with an installer, which copies the source code to disk. ESXi is generally distributed on a USB stick held inside the physical server. The front end of the physical console of the two versions differ substantially. ESX 4.*x* management's front end is called the Service Console, and it is based on Red Hat Linux. ESXi offers a configuration shell based on a system called BusyBox.

VMware's stated long-term plan is eventually to discontinue the 4.*x.x* version in preference to ESXi, which offers a smaller footprint, simplifies patch management, and provides other advantages (discussed in the next chapter). However, for the moment, we have two versions available: the "full-fat" ESX 4.*x* version, which comes with the Service Console. I refer to this as *ESX Classic*. Additionally, we have the "skinny latte" ESXi 4 version, which has a more appliance-based front end, rather than an interactive command-line shell.

Despite the advantages of ESXi, the Classic edition of ESX with the Service Console is still the dominant platform, which is why I've started with its installation and configuration. Chapter 2 covers ESXi installation and configuration.

In this book, I will be using both versions to validate the technical content against the two flavors, and show you how to manage the ESXi 4 host in practically the same way as ESX Classic. Although they may be managed by the same vCenter server, I will deliberately separate them into different VMware clusters. Blending ESX Classic and ESXi together is not recommended; you risk creating surprising new features. (I'm using "features" in the same way as Microsoft!)

Before we get to the installation ESX Classic installation procedure, let's take a moment to consider just what ESX is.

What's New in ESX?

- 64-bit only
- Support for 512GB of RAM, 64 cores, and any combination up to a maximum 512 vCPUs includes1-, 2-, 4-, and 8-way virtual machines. There is experimental support for 1TB of memory. To configure a VM with 8 vCPU you will need an Enterprize Plus license.
- Support for up to 512 vCPUs on single ESX host with an increase of supported number of VMs to 320
- Native SATA disk support
- Support for IPv6
- Service Console as a virtual machine that uses a virtual disk
- Memory increased to 300MB for the Service Console
- Setting of NTP in the installation
- Built-in scripted installation option for the installer
- No longer licensed by a .lic file; licensed through locally held license strings or licenses held in the VMware vCenter database

What Is ESX?

As the years roll by, the function of the server platform, VMware ESX, has been subtly changing. When I first started teaching ESX (we didn't even formally cover Virtual Center back then), we had a PowerPoint slide that clearly stated what ESX wasn't. This slide said that ESX wasn't just Linux with bells on or an operating system. This distinction has been somewhat muddied in recent years, even by VMware. If you take a look at the new VMware architecture and "big-picture" PowerPoint slides, you'll see they have inserted the concept of the Virtual Datacenter Center Operating System (VDC-OS).

With the advent of cloud computing and the introduction of vSphere and VDC-OS, there has been a significant repositioning of the VMware offering. Additionally, the ESX host now has an increasing number of APIs that other organizations can plug into—projects like VMsafe, vNetwork, and vStorage, which allow companies like McAfee, Cisco, and EMC to plug into ESX. This increasingly makes ESX more like an operating system than it has been in the past.

So, is ESX actually an operating system? Personally, I don't think it is. ESX does carry out one aspect of an operating system, which is to be the arbitrator to hardware. ESX "owns" the physical hardware and sits at ring 0, the most privileged ring that exists in most x86 processors. Fundamentally, if any process needs access to hardware resources (CPU, disk, network, memory, and so on), it must liaise with ESX's VMkernel for that resource.

However, ESX is not an operating system in the sense that it does not provide a rich collection of programming APIs such that an independent software vendor (ISV) could develop an application to run inside the VMkernel as a process. ESX will not run Microsoft Word or Microsoft Exchange Services—well, not directly. Apart from its own internal processes and drivers, the only thing ESX executes is the virtual machine, sometimes referred to as the virtual machine monitor. Now, of course, you could install any supported guest operating system on the virtual machine, and then run any supported application within it. For ESX, a virtual machine is just another process, albeit a very important one. Everything that ESX does is an attempt to make that process more stable, reliable, and faster than the competition offers.

Of note is that the guest operating system's role has been depreciated significantly. Applications that can run as the guest operating system now manage only *virtual* hardware, not *physical* hardware. VMware terms this depreciated guest operating system JeOS (pronounced "juice"), which stands for Just Enough Operating System. The concept basically is one of stripping down a fat operating system to a much slimmer one, leaving behind just enough to run the application. The point is that it's a mistake to take a general-purpose operating system and retrofit a virtualization piece to a kernel that is decades old. You inherit all the vulnerabilities and design flaws of the original, and try to make it do a job for which it wasn't designed. It is better to start from scratch with a brand-new file system designed for storing virtual machines. For many, ESX represents a return to that super-skinny, super-efficient coding of the past that we lost somewhere between an operating system needing 64KB of memory to run to one needing 2GB.

Let's get back to the question of what ESX *is*. ESX is what is called a *hypervisor*. The hypervisor—ESX's VMkernel—sits between the hardware and the virtual machine. Its primary task is to run virtual machines, as well as carry out other important ancillary tasks such as monitoring the performance of the processes it manages. This VMkernel is incredibly slim, leaving less of a "surface" area for vulnerabilities that could make it unstable or open to attack by intruders.

So, ESX is like an appliance that sits in your rack. Indeed, VMware could have taken the original equipment manufacturer (OEM) model of buying servers with truckloads of CPU and RAM, and then yanked the bezels off the front, attached a VMware bezel, and sold ESX as a VMware appliance. Fortunately, VMware didn't use this hardware route to market. Instead, the company partnered with existing OEMs and leveraged the OEMs pre-sale, support, and access to clients. For example, ESX is shipped on a USB stick inside certain IBM servers. To boot from the ESX USB stick, you merely enable it in the BIOS. This is done with all servers of this type, despite the fact that the customer might not use ESX. It's a good indication of how ESX has become the de facto platform in the corporate datacenter for running virtual machines.

I guess the safest thing to say about ESX is like a lot of systems, it's a work in progress. From its very creation, it has been endless evolving. And by the end of this book, you might indeed regard it as the VDC-OS.

Now let's get ready to install ESX.

Preparing for ESX Installation

You will be pleased to know that ESX is very easy to install. You are asked even fewer questions than for the ESX 3.x installation, and the biggest part of the installation is the file-copy event.

You can download ESX 4.x from VMware's web site once you have been provided with the correct serial numbers and logins.

Confirming Physical Settings

Before you install ESX, you should check the physical configuration of the server. To be more specific, you should run updates against your main system BIOS and firmware upgrades for devices such as host bus adapters (HBAs). As you know, servers tend to ship with factory software that isn't always up to date, and you may encounter unpredictable performance and lack of stability without the prerequisite updates to your system.

Additionally, I recommend that you check your BIOS settings to make sure additional features are enabled. Certain advanced features of vSphere 4 require special options to be enabled in the BIOS. For example, for VMware fault tolerance to work, you must have "virtualization hardware assist" options like Intel Virtualization Technology (Intel VT) or AMD Virtualization (AMD-V) enabled. Enabling these options before you begin your installation will save you time in the long run.

Finally, check that all your cables and connections are good by using the LEDS that appear on network interface cards (NICs) and HBAs. I know this sound very obvious—indeed, even patronizing to anyone who has worked in IT for some time—but in reality, the obvious is frequently overlooked.

Checking Your Source Code ISO

After downloading the source ISO file, you should check that file before you burn it to a CD. You can do this by confirming the MD5 checksum. An md5sum program allows you to confirm your ISO file has not been corrupted by the download process. The source MD5 sum value is normally put under the link to the ISO or file you are downloading.

If you are running Linux on your desktop PC, you already have access to md5sum on the command line. If, you are running Microsoft Windows, you can use a free tool, such as the one available from Nullriver Software (http://www.nullriver.com/) to check that your file is not corrupted.

Using an ILO

The installation medium is a DVD, rather than a CD-ROM ISO image. As such, the installation with virtual media can be incredibly slow. If you are using virtual media to start the boot process, I recommend that you use your ISO with the "virtual media" features of your server's ILO, if it has one. In the past, users have had problems with the installer engine and ILOs; however, these issues appear to have been resolved in this release.

To use this method, first copy the contents of the ISO file to a web server accessible to your ESX hosts. At the install prompt, press F2 on the keyboard to pipe a value to the installer engine, called askmedia.

This will allow you to boot from the virtual media, but midway through the installation process, specify the path to the web server for the file-copy process.

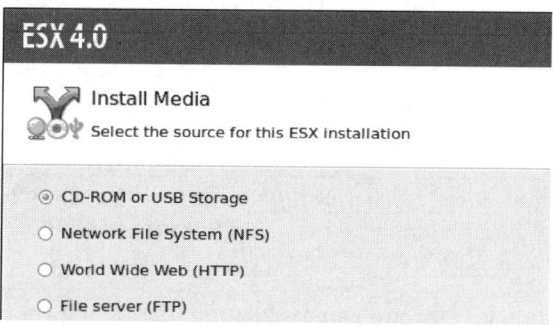

This significantly reduces the time to install ESX.

NOTE *You may as want to investigate a totally scripted installation, perhaps using Pre-boot Execution Environment (PXE) booting together with a web server. Chapter 17 covers PXE-based deployment.*

If you are using an ILO to do your installation, you may find that the mouse pointer is simply not there or does not operate correctly. This is due to the limitations of some ILOs, as opposed to the ESX installer itself. If you do use the graphical installer and your mouse does not work, you can use the keyboard. as follows:

- TAB moves forward.
- SHIFT+TAB moves backward.
- The spacebar opens pull-down lists.
- The cursor keys navigate lists.
- ENTER selects items.

Installing ESX 4 Locally

The installation engine behind ESX is "weasel," which is a modified version of the Anaconda installation engine used for Red Hat Linux. When the system boots to the installer, it actually runs a very slim Linux distribution called BusyBox. BusyBox's job is to load the files required to install ESX, including Python scripts used by the weasel installer engine.

The first major task the BusyBox environment carries out is to load the VMkernel, which allows you to configure an ancillary virtual machine called the Service Console. The Service Console used to be very much a physical system, and was not completely virtual. For example, in previous releases, the Service Console could see a physical drive; however, in this release, it sees a virtual disk. The Service Console's virtual disk is created on a Virtual Machine File System (VMFS) volume and can be seen by using the Datastore Browser.

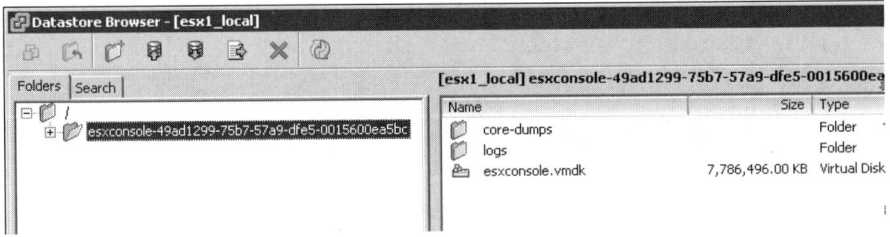

NOTE *The Service Console is just a management front end that allows you to log in to the ESX Classic host, and carry out task through a command-line interface (CLI). It does not own or manage the virtual machines.*

In this example, I guide you through an installation to local logical unit numbers (LUNs). Later in the chapter, I will show you how to set up to boot from a storage area network (SAN). If you are installing ESX to the local storage, I recommend disconnecting the SAN cables if you can. This prevents any chance of installing ESX to SAN unintentionally, as well as reduces your chances of accidentally destroying terabytes of data on the SAN while installing ESX! If physical access is limited—perhaps your hardware is miles away in a colocation—you could use the BIOS of the physical host to temporarily disable the Fibre Channel card. In the installer, this level of access should be there already. However, if you also manage the storage layer, by far the easiest way to prevent access to the storage array is by using your vendor's array management software.

As I've said, ESX installation is easy. Only two areas could cause you problems: selecting the correct network card for use with the Service Console and building a robust and reliable partition table. I'll talk more about these areas as we step through the procedure.

Starting the Installation

Begin by booting to the ESX 4.*x* CD. The opening installation screen presents six choices for completing the installation.

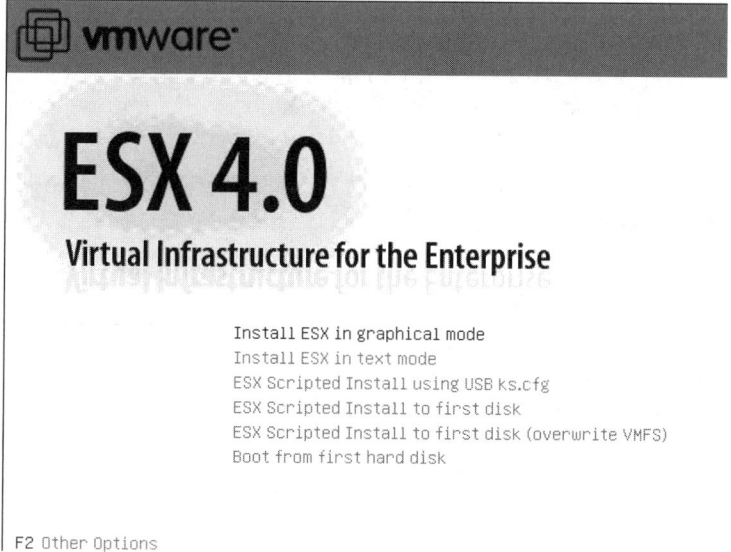

NOTE *Notice the banner reads "Virtual Infrastructure for the Enterprise." The old name Virtual Infrastructure survives!*

The text mode option is very different from that in the ESX 2.*x* and 3.*x* installation program. It is a purely CLI-based installation, with each choice confirmed by a 1 for yes or 0 for no type of response. In many respects, the graphic installation is *much* more friendly and intuitive.

The third option can be used for a scripted installation with the script file held on a USB stick. The options for scripted installations from to the first disk are dangerous if you are connected to a SAN. They may actually pick out a SAN LUN, rather than local storage. The final option merely bypasses the installer altogether and boots whatever operating system is located on the first hard drive. You would use this option if you accidentally left the ESX CD in the drive, for example.

Pressing F2 from this screen allows you to pass custom weasel variables to any one of the first five installation options.

Follow these steps to install ESX in graphical mode:

1. At the initial screen, press the ENTER key to choose the graphical installation. (If you simply wait 60 seconds, the installer will enter the graphical mode by default.)

2. The installer will proceed to the Load ESX screen. Click Next.

3. Agree the end user license agreement (EULA).

4. Select your keyboard type.

5. When prompted to select custom drivers, choose No, and then select Yes to allow the installer to load the built-in drivers supplied on the ESX CD. In the rare case that the hardware you are using is so new that you need to supply a driver that is not on the ESX CD, you will then need to select custom drivers (this is like pressing F6 during a Windows installation). Once the status is 100% complete, click Next.

6. Optionally, enter your serial number. As stated earlier, VMware has abandoned the use of license files (.lic) adopted in VMware Infrastructure version 3 (Vi3), and reverted back to using license strings. If you are not using vCenter, you should enter your ESX host license now. If you are using vCenter, you can choose the "Enter a serial number later" option. Your ESX host will continue to function in an evaluation mode up to 60 days until you license it with vCenter.

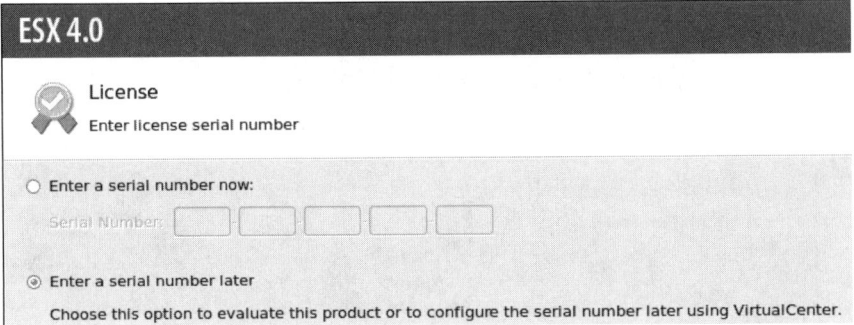

Specifying Your Network Configuration

Next, the installer asks you to select a network adapter for ESX and optionally set the virtual local area network (VLAN) ID, which will be used by the Service Console.

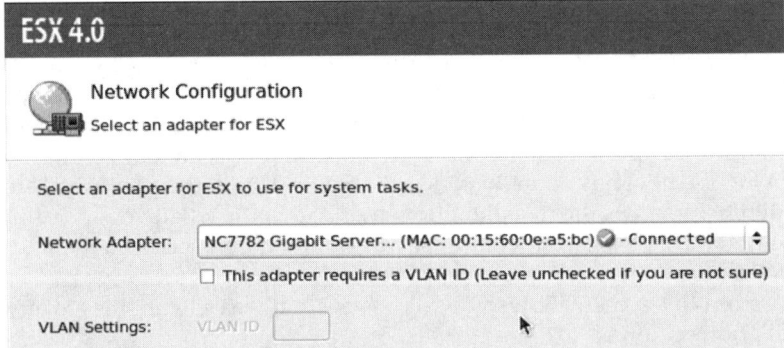

CAUTION *If you select the wrong network interface card (NIC), you will not be able to communicate with the ESX host after the installation.*

How do you know you have selected the correct NIC during the installation? If after installing the ESX product, you find you cannot even ping the Service Console interface, it could be that you selected the wrong NIC during the install. If this happens to you, you may wish to consult the end of Chapter 4 entitled "Managing Service Console Networking." We used to see PCI information (Bus, Slot and Function numbers) and Speed/Duplex settings. Unfortunately, this is no longer displayed, however what is being displayed is whether the NIC is connected (there's little point in selecting a disconnected NIC now is there?) and the MAC address of the physical NIC. In fact you might prefer this data to PCI Bus:Slot :Function numbers as it is generally easier to find out the MAC address of NICS.

You should set the VLAN ID only if you're using VLAN tagging, and trunk ports have been set up on the physical switch. (If none of this makes sense, it will once you have read Chapter 4.)

Next, set your IP address, subnet mask, default gateway, primary DNS, secondary DNS, and fully qualified domain name (FQDN) for the host name.

ESX 4.0

Network Configuration
Enter the network configuration information

Network Adapter: vmnic0

Adapter Settings

○ Set automatically using DHCP

◉ Use the following network settings:

IP Address:	192.168.2.101
Subnet Mask:	255.255.255.0
Gateway:	192.168.2.199
Primary DNS:	192.168.2.199
Secondary DNS:	192.168.2.200
Host name:	esx1.vi4book.com

Enter a fully qualified host name (e.g. host.example.com)

Test these settings

An FQDN and DNS name resolution are required for many key features. I recommend that you have your DNS infrastructure set up and in place before beginning the ESX installation. I also recommend using a static IP address, rather than using DHCP with "client reservations." This is pretty much a universally accepted standard in Europe, the Middle East, and Africa (EMEA) for server-based operating systems, although this convention may differ in different regions.

New in ESX 4.x is a method to test your IP configuration. It's by no means foolproof. The test button checks only for syntax, such as accidentally typing a comma instead of a period in the fields. It does not check if the IP address of your default gateway or DNS are pingable. The result you want to see is "No problems detected with the network settings."

Setting Up Your Storage and Datastore

After completing your network settings, select Advanced as your partition scheme, and then select the LUN/disk on which you wish to install ESX. The installer will then enumerate your LUNs.

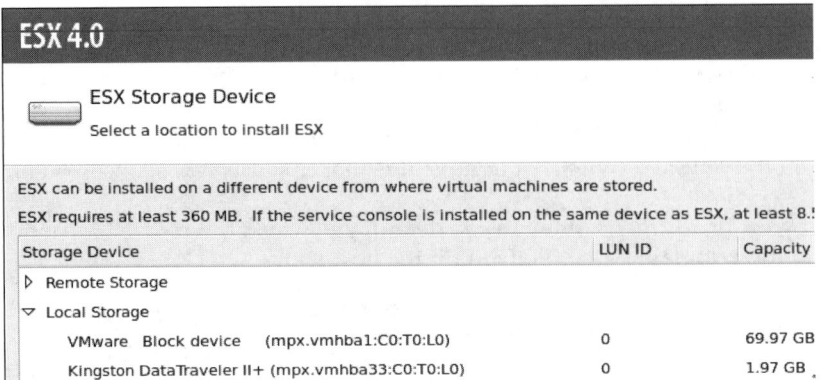

If you left the SAN connected (which is not best practice), you will see both remote and local storage. In the screenshot shown here, the "VMware block device" is actually a Smart Array P600 SAS controller inside a HP ProLiant G1 DL385. C0-T0-L0 is the first controller (C0), first target (T0), and first and only LUN (L0). The Kingston DataTraveler is a copy of ESXi 4, which is held on a USB memory stick. I will be booting to this in Chapter 2 to show you how the ESXi product is configured.

At this stage, you are selecting a physical disk that will hold your first VMFS volume. This is mainly necessary to give ESX a location in which to create the virtual disk of the Service Console.

You may receive a warning that the /dev/sdN is unreadable. This reference to /dev/sdN indicates the SCSI disk (SD), which is found first (A, B, C). Also, the dialog box should indicate on which controller this disk was found. Additionally, if you have previously installed ESX and are trying to reinstall the product, you will receive this warning message:

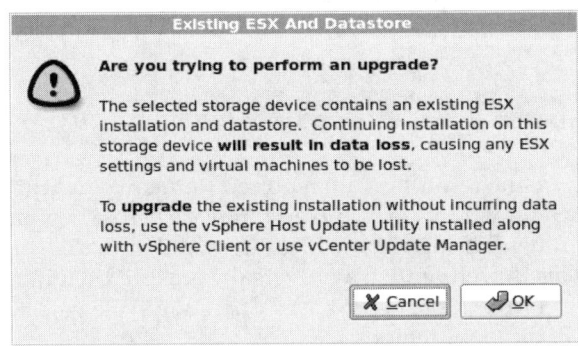

As the dialog box indicates, VMware no longer supports using the DVD media to upgrade an ESX host. Instead, you must use either the vSphere Host Update Utility (which is limited to ESXi only) or vCenter Update Manager (which can upgrade both ESXi 3 and ESX 3).

After selecting your storage device, specify a datastore for ESX. By default, the installer will assume you require a VMFS volume, and that this volume will be created on the same LUN as selected in the previous part of the installation, because of the default option "Create on the same device as ESX." The default volume name of "storage" is not a good one. I suggest that you use a more unique naming convention, something like local_ *hostname* (such as local_ esx1).

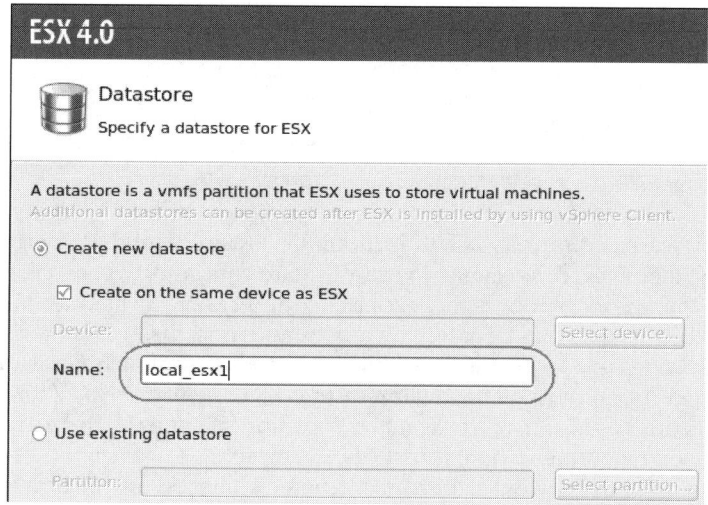

As the partition table doesn't exist, the installer will wish to initialize the disk. This operation is potentially dangerous if there is data on the drive. It is fine to do this if you know the LUN is blank. If your ESX host is connected to a SAN, be very careful in accepting yes!

Creating the Partitions

Like most operating systems, the reliability of the build will come from the installer's decisions. It's critical that your partition scheme be able to protect itself from rapidly filling event log files and users copying large files to the wrong location.

Rather than using drive letters (C:, D:, E:, and so on) to address these partitions, folders are used as mounting points, because ESX is based on Linux/UNIX, where this is a standard. (You have been able to do something similar to this with Microsoft operating systems since Windows 2000 was released.) As for the physical disks themselves, I usually recommend two 36GB or 72GB disks in a mirror.

Remember that now that the Service Console is fully virtualized, you have no control over the partitions that are created on the physical disk (in particular, the /boot and vmkcore partitions). You can control only the destination of these partitions and the VMFS volume used to hold the Service Console's virtual disk. If you use autopartitioning, the installer will place the first three partitions (boot, vmkcore, and local vmfs) on a physical drive selected earlier in the installer. The remaining partitions (swap, var/log, and /) are created inside a virtual disk. Table 1-1 summarizes the physical and virtual disk partitions and their purposes.

Physical Disk	Purpose
/boot	Holds boot .img files called by the GRUB boot loader
vmkcore	Used to collect diagnostics information in the event of a VMkernel crash or PSOD
extended partition	Takes up the whole of the volume selected during the installation
vmfs	Creates a VMFS volume within the extended partition using all remaining free space
Virtual Disk	**Purpose**
swap	Areas of swap space used by the Service Console
/var/log	Used to keep your log files out of the / partition
/	Main "operating system" partition, which is where the Service Console is installed

TABLE 1-1   Physical and Virtual Disk Partitions

Few in the VMware community use the automatic, "Recommended" partition scheme offered by the installer. Nearly everyone in the VMware community uses their own manual partition scheme, based on their personal experience and company standards.

The VMware community has debated the advantages and disadvantages of various partitioning approaches in a long and interesting forum thread, which was started by Steve Beaver, a very good friend of mine. If this interests you, check out http://communities .vmware.com/thread/46345. There are as many partition schemes as there are people on this forum. The one I recommend here is just one example.

Table 1-2 shows a summary of the partition scheme I suggest for the Service Console virtual disk. This partition scheme uses about 13GB of space. You could easily increase these values and add more partitions. Generally, I create three primary partitions, and the rest are treated as logical drives in an extended partition. The disk management utility (called Disk Druid) automatically creates an extended partition for you using the remainder of the disk, once the installer has created the /boot and vmkcore partitions.

Here are some notes on the size and purpose of each partition:

- **ext3**   EXT3 is the primary file system of Linux, which is an appropriate choice, since the Service Console is based on Red Hat Linux. Also available are two proprietary file systems, which are accessible only by the VMkernel: vmkcore and VMFS version 3 (VMFS is covered in the Chapter 6).

Mount Point	File System	Size in MB	Purpose
N/A	swap	1600	Swap for Service Console
/	ext3	5120	Main OS location
/var	ext3	2048	Log files
/tmp	ext3	2048	Temporary files
/opt	ext3	2048	VMware HA logging
/home	ext3	2048	Location of users' storage

TABLE 1-2   Recommended Partition Scheme for the Service Console Virtual Disk

- **/boot**   This is where core boot files with an .img extension (bootable image files; analogous to ISO files, which can also be bootable) are stored. After powering on ESX, the master boot record (MBR) is located and the boot loader is run. In the case of ESX 4.*x*, this is now the Grand Unified Bootloader (GRUB). GRUB then displays a menu that allows you to select which .img file to execute. The /boot mounting point is automatically created and is reserved by the installer. You cannot create this partition or change its size.

- **/swap**   This is where the Service Console swaps files if memory is low. I've chosen to overallocate this partition. The default amount of memory for the Service Console is 300MB. VMware usually takes this number and doubles it to calculate the swap partition size (600MB). The maximum amount of memory you can assign to the Service Console is 800MB. This is how I derived the 1600MB value. This means if you ever choose to change the default amount of memory assigned to the Service Console, you do not need to worry about resizing the swap partition. It doesn't have a mounting point, as no files from the administrator are copied there.

- **/**   Referred to as the root partition, this is the main location where the ESX operating system and configuration files are copied. If you have a Windows background, you can see it as a bit like the C: partition and folders on that drive, like C:\Windows or C:\Program directory. If this partition fills, you may experience performance and reliability issues with the Service Console, just as you would with Windows or any other operating system.

- **/var**   This is where log files are held. I generally give this a separate partition just to make sure that excessive logging does not fill the / file system. Log files are normally held in /var/log, but occasionally hardware vendors place their hardware management agent log files in /var. Another reason to use a separate partition is that agents or processes that crash dump their crash information into /var/core, which can sometimes fill quite rapidly when you have a bad agent installed.

- **/tmp**   In the past, VMware has recommended using a separate partition for /tmp, which I have always done. As I have plenty of disk space, I have made this larger than it really needs to be.

- **/opt**   Several forum members reported that they had seen the /opt directory fill up very rapidly in ESX 3.*x*, and as a consequence, fill the / partition. This location is also sometimes used as a logging location for hardware agents. In VMware, the High Availability feature generates logging data here as well, so I created a separate partition for it to make sure it does not fill the / partition.

- **/home**   Technically, you don't need a separate /home partition. In the past, VMware recommended one for ESX 2.*x* in production systems. This was due to the fact that the virtual machine's configuration files (.vmx, .nvram, and .log) were stored in the /home location. In ESX 4.*x*, all the files that make up a virtual machine are more likely to be located on external storage. I still create this partition for consistency purposes, and any users on the local ESX server are more likely to create files here than in a directory in the / partition.

- **vmkcore**   This is a special partition used only if the ESX VMkernel crashes, commonly referred to as the Purple Screen of Death (PSOD). If that happens, ESX writes debugging information into this partition. After a successful boot, the system will automatically run a script to extract and compress the data to a zip file in /root.

This file with a tar.gz extension can be sent to VMware Support, who will work to identify the source of the problem. In ESX 4.*x*, VMware automatically creates a vmkcore partition for you with a fixed size of 100MB. It is no longer possible to create the vmkcore partition type from the installation routine, since this partitioning routine is now being carried out within a virtual disk. (Remember that the Service Console is just a virtual machine, and as a consequence, it sees only a virtual disk; the VMkernel sees the physical disk.)

NOTE *PSODs are normally caused by failures of RAM or CPU. You can see a rogue's gallery of PSODs at http://www.rtfm-ed.co.uk/?page_id=246.*

- **/vmimages**   In ESX 2.*x*, a /vmimages partition or mounting point to a network location was used primarily for templates and ISOs. This partition is no longer required, as we now have more effective and easier ways of storing this data. Of course, if you are an ESX 2.*x* veteran who wishes to keep using /vmimages for consistency purposes, then that is fine. It's just no longer required or recommended. Personally, I still like to have a portion of disk space given over to this partition location as a "working area" when I am dealing with large files, although I've found that with my recent purchase of a SAN, this is something I use much less. If you have done a clean install, you will have a directory called /vmimages, even if you haven't created a /vmimages, which contains files used internally by VMware ESX. I will discuss this more in Chapter 7, which covers creating virtual machines.

The following screenshot shows the installer window for configuring the Service Console virtual disk image and the dialog box for creating a new partition. In this case, I selected / home from the pull-down list (you can also type in this area), chose ext3 as the partition type, and entered 2048MB as the size.

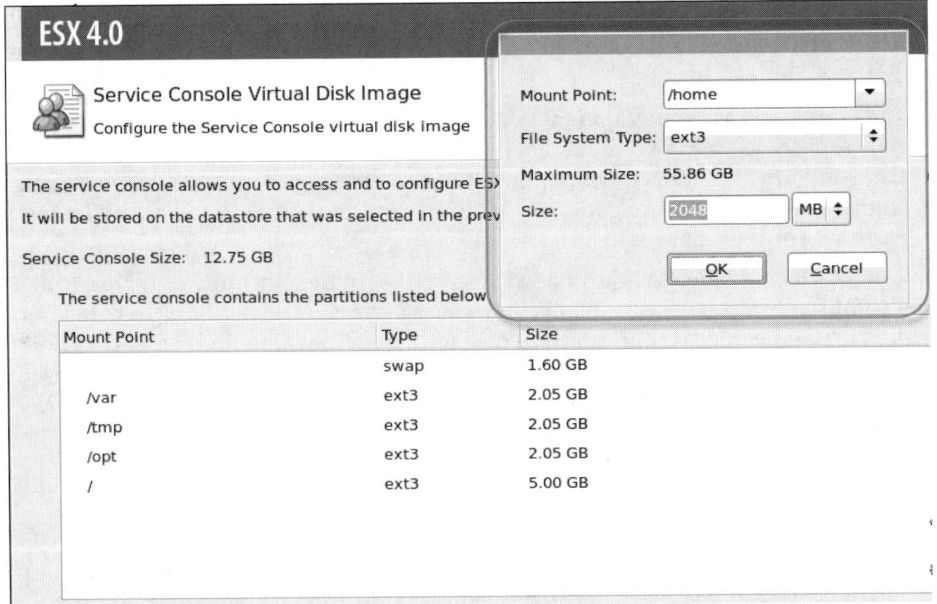

After you have built the partition table, take a few moments to confirm you created the correct number of partitions of the appropriate size. The partition table is not committed to the disk until you click Next. This would be an ideal opportunity to spot an error and correct it. Partition errors can be corrected afterward using fdisk, but it's much easier to get it right the first time. In my experience, a bad partition scheme usually results in wasted time spent reinstalling ESX.

Completing the Installation

Once you have partitioned the virtual disk, the remainder of the installation procedure is very simple. It asks you many ancillary but important questions, such as your time configuration and user account configuration. Follow these steps to complete the installation:

1. Set your time zone. You can set the time by clicking the map. This interface can be difficult to use via an ILO because of mouse latencies. You might find it easier to click the Advanced button and use the PAGE DOWN key to set your time zone.

2. Set your time and date. In ESX 4.*x*, you can now set the Network Time Protocol (NTP) settings during the installation. This can save some time in the postconfiguration phase. Select the option Automatically, and type the name or IP address of your NTP server. The Synchronize button will attempt to sync your local time to the NTP service. If it cannot communicate, you will see an alert:

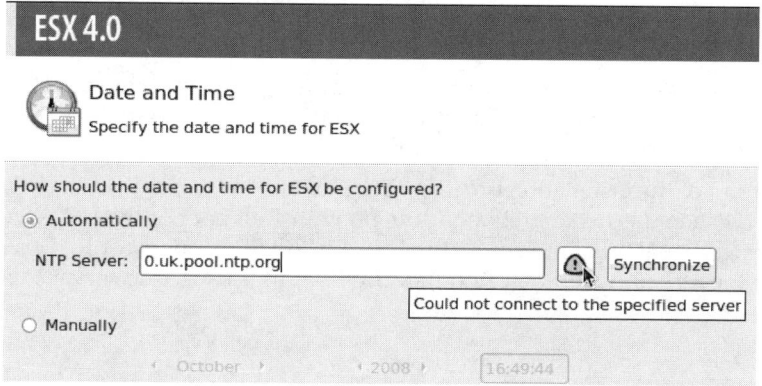

3. Set the root password. The root account is the user with highest privileges. You can create other ESX users within the installer. It's good practice to create a user for yourself now, as you will then be able to use a Secure Shell (SSH) client like

PuTTY immediately, without the need to load the vSphere Client to create a user account first. (Using PuTTY and installing the vSphere Client are discussed in the next section.)

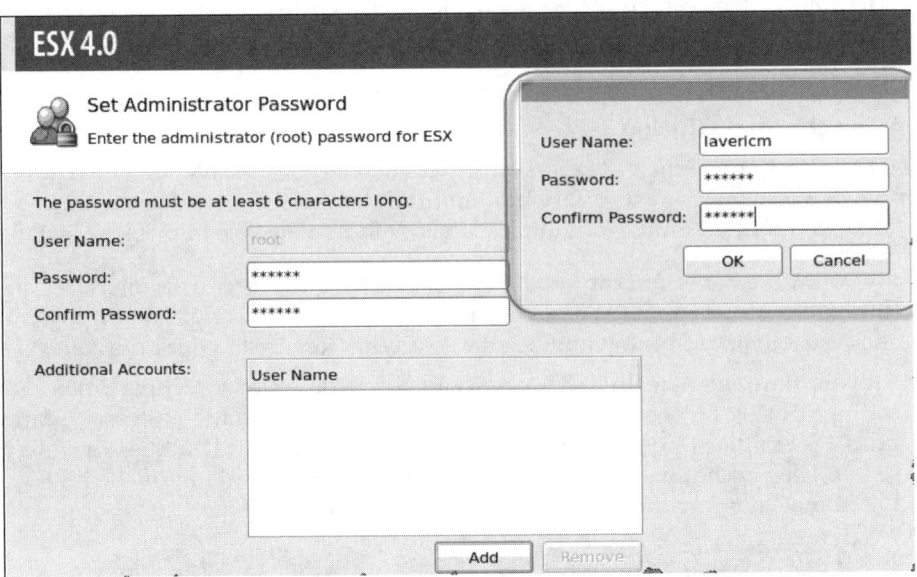

4. You will see a summary of your choices. At this stage, you can go back and change some settings, such as your IP address, if you feel you have set them incorrectly. Clicking Next initiates the copy process.

5. At the end of the installation process, click Finish. This normally causes the CD-ROM to eject. When the system reboots, you get your first boot of the ESX server. If you are using virtual media to access the ESX 4.x ISO file, remember to disconnect it before the reboot. You might find that BIOS settings cause the server to boot to the CD again.

Connect and Manage the ESX host

You can use an SSH client to access ESX's command line. For access to the graphical user interface (GUI), you use the vSphere Client.

Gaining Command-Line Access

The SSH protocol allows you to gain access to ESX's CLI without the use of an ILO. A very popular tool used to create a remote SSH session is PuTTY, created by Simon Tatham. This tool is available from http://www.chiark.greenend.org.uk/~sgtatham/putty/.

Why would you want this command-line style access to ESX? One reason is that there are some tasks that can be done only via the command line. In other situations, because you have a mix of CLI and GUI tasks, it is easier to choose one interface rather than work with two.

However, in ESX 4.*x*, some new security settings disable SSH access to the root account. By default, in a clean install, there is no access to the ESX Service Console for the root account except via the ILO. This security change was introduced to enforce more user account traceability and an audit trail. User activity such as logons and changes in privilege are logged in /var/log/messages.

To get around this limitation, you can create a local account on ESX, use PuTTY to gain access, and then finally switch to the root account. To gain command-line access as root with SSH, open a SSH/PuTTy session to the ESX host and log in with your recently created account. To levitate to a higher plane of privileges type **su** -. Enter the root account password assigned during installation.

The su command allows you to "switch user" and assumes, unless otherwise specified, that you would like to change to root. The minus sign indicates you would like to use the root account's environmental settings, such as path variables. This is very important if you want to run commands properly and not receive "command not found" error messages.

A more sophisticated way to allow elevated access without using the su command or having knowledge of the root account's password is to use the sudo utility, which allows you to specify which commands an ordinary user can run. This allows you to avoid disclosing the root password to allow a user to run commands normally used by root. I present a simple sudo configuration in the free PDF guide on the ESX Classic command-line available from my web site:

http://www.rtfm-ed.co.uk/docs/vmwdocs/ESX4.x-VC4.x-ServiceConsole-Guide.pdf

Installing the vSphere Client

The main graphical tool used to administer an ESX server directly or via vCenter is the vSphere Client. You can download and install this tool from the ESX host. You can then use this tool to create additional ESX users that can log in remotely with SSH. You will need to do this if you neglected to create a user during the installation.

To download the vSphere Client, from your management PC, open a web browser and type in the FQDN of your ESX host (such as https://esx1.vi4book.com). Choose Yes to continue to access the ESX host, despite the fact its certificate is not trusted. (ESX creates a server certificate for each installation you do. These are autogenerated using OpenSSL and are not signed from a recognized root certificate authority.) Finally, select the link to download the vSphere Client.

Now you can run the VMware-viclient.exe file to install the client to your management PC. Select your required language. Next, enable the option to "Install vSphere Host Update Utility 4.0." This is a utility that allows you to patch your ESX hosts, even if you don't have vCenter and VMware Update Manager.

After installing the vSphere Client, you should be able to open it from the shortcut on your desktop by logging on to your ESX host by its FQDN as the root user. You'll notice in this release that VMware has added "pass-through" authentication to the vSphere; that is, if you enable the option, it will attempt to use the credentials you supplied to your management PC and pass them through to the vSphere. This is great if you're using vCenter, but it's not valid if you're logging in to the ESX host directly, where only the root account exists by default. ESX does automatically resolve your Windows users to the ESX users.

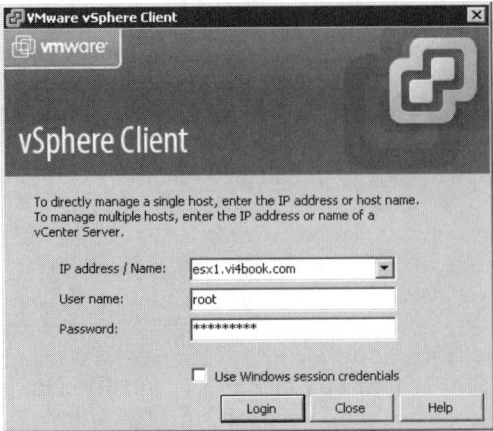

Until you license the ESX host, you will always receive a message stating how many days you remaining in the evaluation period.

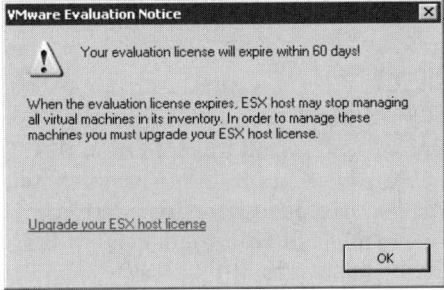

Creating Additional Local Users on an ESX Host

When the new vSphere Client opens, you might not immediately see your ESX host, but see the Inventory view instead.

Select the Inventory icon, and you will then see your ESX host, in a view that looks very similar to the previous version of VMware Virtual Infrastructure client.

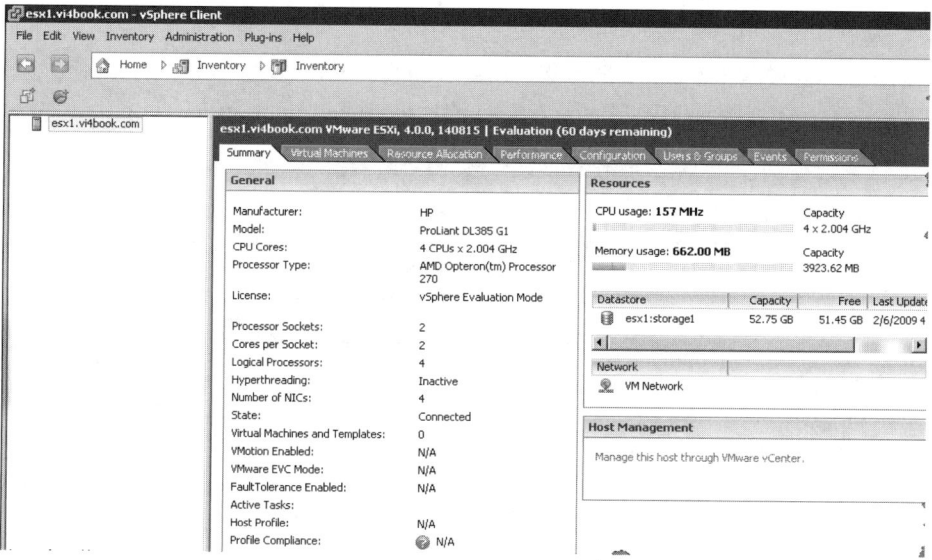

From this view, click the User & Groups tab, right-click the window, and choose Add. Fill in the dialog box to create the new user.

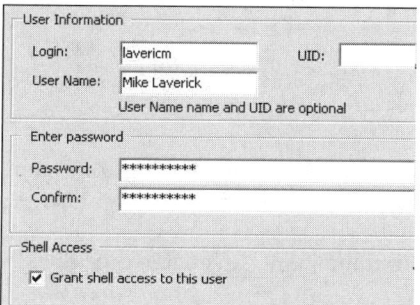

You must enable "Grant shell access" to allows this user to have access to the Service Console via SSH. Otherwise, the user will have access to the ESX host only with vSphere. (In ESXi 4, this "Grant shell access" option is not available, as technically, there is no command-line shell available.)

Enabling SSH from Your ESX Host to Other Hosts

I like to connect to one ESX host and then use SSH from that session to get to my other servers. This saves me from needing to open repeated PuTTY sessions. However, you will be unable to use the scp (Secure Copy) command to copy files to ESX servers from an ESX server. Under the default settings, this is not allowed in ESX 4.*x*, as the firewall denies the client (although every ESX host is an SSH server), with an error like "ssh: connect to host esx2.vi4book.com port 22: Connection refused."

To enable this kind of access, you need to adjust the firewall settings, as follows:

1. In the vSphere Client, click the Configuration tab.
2. Under the Software panel, select Security Profile.
3. Click the Properties link in the far-right corner.
4. In the Firewall Properties dialog box, enable the SSH Client option, and then click OK.

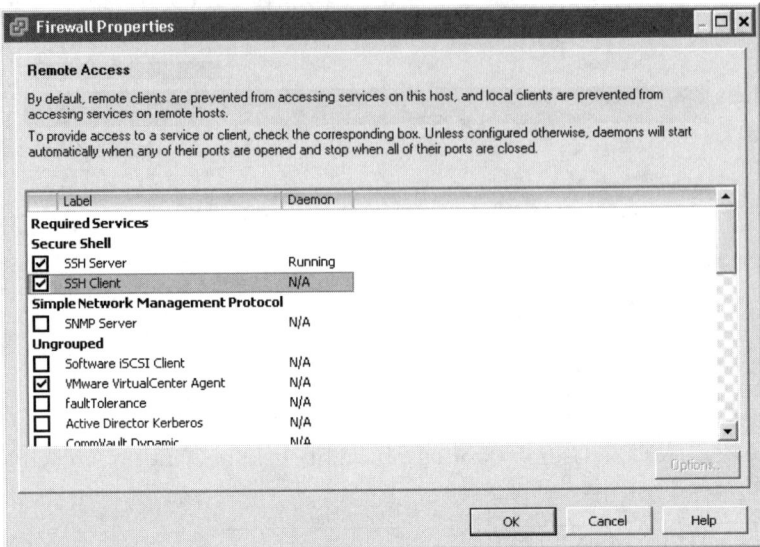

This is all that's required for SSH. Now you could type something like `ssh -l lavericm esx2.vi4book.com` and then use `su -` to elevate your privileges to root rights, as described earlier.

If you ever get confused about who you are, try the command `whoami`. If you are unsure which host you're connected to, try the command `hostname`. You can use the command `exit` to leave SSH sessions.

If you are using the command line, you can enable the SSH client using the command-line version of the ESX firewall:

```
esxcfg-firewall -e sshClient
```

Note that this command, like all ESX CLI commands, is case sensitive.

Configuring NTP

Whether your virtual machines do or don't get their time from the ESX hosts is separate and distinct from the time configuration of the ESX host itself. Even if your Windows virtual machines still receive time updates from a physical domain controller, time still needs to be correctly configured for the ESX host. Without a correct time configuration of an ESX host, your log files will have incorrect date and time stamps relative to actual events themselves, and performance statistics will be skewed at best; at worst, they simply not be displayed at all. You can configure NTP from the GUI from the VSphere Client, as follows:

1. In the vSphere Client, click the Configuration tab.

2. Under the Software panel, select Time Configuration.

3. Click the Properties link in the far-right corner.

4. In the Time Configuration dialog box, click the selection box to choose NTP Client Enabled.

5. Click the Options button.

6. In the NTP Daemon (ntpd) Options dialog box, select NTP Settings in the list on the left.

7. Click the Add button to add the name or IP address of an NTP service/server. Ideally, you should be able to point to an internal NTP server, which in turn synchronizes its time with an external time source with a public NTP server.

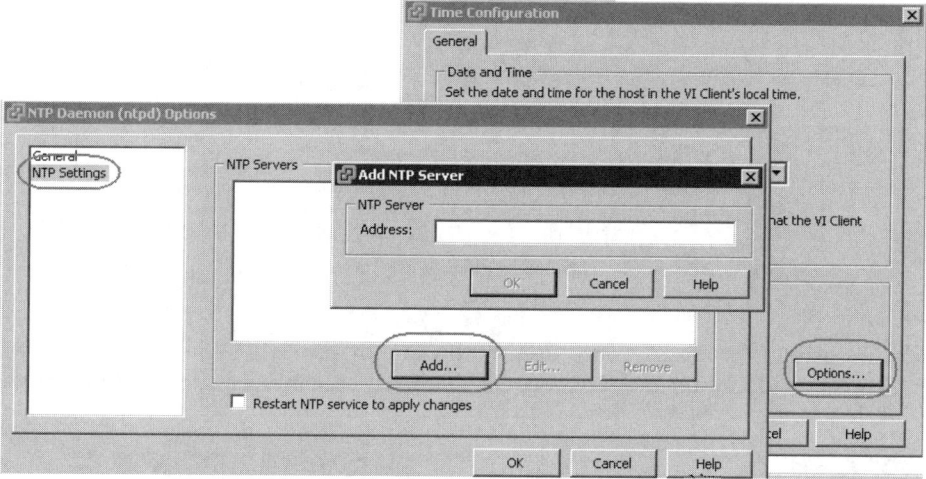

8. Click OK to close all the dialog boxes.

Monitoring Hardware

Historically, we have needed to install hardware monitoring agents (commonly referred to as vendor CIM agents) to allow us to monitor the physical server in the hardware vendor's management and monitoring tools. For example, it's not unusual to install the HP Insight Management Agents to an HP ProLiant Server so we can monitor the hardware in HP management tools. We would do the same with Dell (OpenManage) and IBM (Director). Since Vi3.5, we have also been able to monitor the hardware status of an ESX host using the Health Status option.

Viewing Health Status

The Health Status feature first came into being specifically for ESXi 3, but it is also available to the ESX Classic edition as well. ESXi doesn't have the Service Console environment to allow this functionality to be installed, and so VMware partnered with the OEMs to "embed" the Common Information Model (CIM) into the ESXi product. This allows you to monitor the status of the hardware either from the vSphere Client or from your vendor's proprietary monitoring system.

To view your physical server's health status, in the vSphere Client, click the Configuration tab. Under the Hardware panel, select the Health Status option. The example shown here is taken from an HP ProLiant Blade. The health status tab only appears when you connect directly to an ESX host, and it does not appear if you manage the ESX host with vCenter. However, you do have a "Hardware Status" tab which reports very similar information.

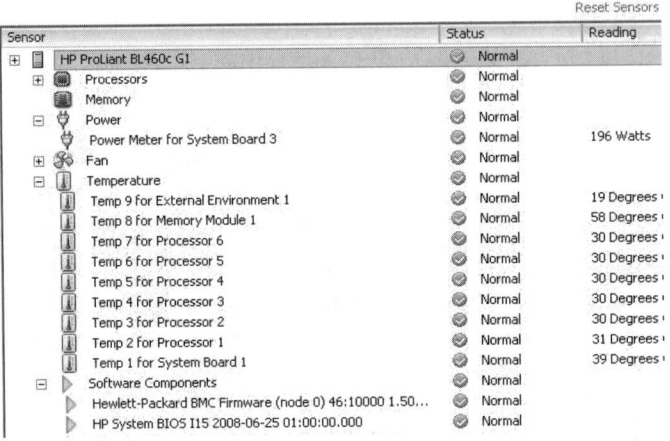

If you are using ESX Classic configured with vCenter, you will see a Hardware Status page, which you will find on each ESX host. This can offer some very detailed information about your hardware.

Installing Hardware Management Agents

Despite the existence of the Health Status feature in the ESX product, you might still wish to install the full hardware management agent to your ESX hosts. One reason is just to reduce their noise—most servers will run at their maximum fan speeds until you install the management agent. Perhaps that is deliberate, because you will certainly know if you haven't installed the agent!

As an example, I've chosen to document the installation of the HP Insight Management Agent for ESX 4. The procedures for other vendors' agents will vary.

I've often found locating the correct version of the hardware agent tricky. Start with a search on something like, "HP Management Agents for VMware ESX Server 4.x." At the time of writing, the latest HP Insight Management Agent isn't available on the main hp.com domain, but on the ftp site instead at this location:

ftp://ftp.hp.com/pub/softlib2/software1/pubsw-linux/p332370759/v49789/

Download the agent, and upload it to the ESX Classic host using the DataStore Browser.

Log in to the Service Console as root, and extract the download package with the `tar` command:

```
tar -zxvf hpmgmt-N.N.N-vmware4x.tgz
```

Change directory into the hpmgmt directory created via the extraction process. Execute the installer. With the HP Insight Management Agent, this is generally called installvmNNN.sh:

```
./installvmNNNvibs.sh
```

Most installers of this type can run silently with the script. This usually requires a couple of switches on the .sh file, together with some kind of answer or unattended text file. HP has a sample unattended file in its agent called hpmgmt.conf.example, which could be run as follows:

```
installvmNNNvibs.sh --silent --inputfile hpmgmt.conf.example
```

The HP installer engine checks the version of ESX you are running and will alert you if you are installing a version of the agent that is incompatible with the version of ESX you are using. At the end of the installation, you will be asked to reboot the ESX host.

Increasing Memory Allocation to the Service Console

The Service Console in ESX Classic is given an allocation of resources in precisely the same way as a virtual machine. More specifically, the Service Console is given an allocation of memory. In ESX 3, this was 272MB of RAM. In ESX 4, it is given 300MB of RAM.

Some environments may use a more customized ESX classic installation, which includes additional agents and daemons to the base installation. These additional agents and daemons may consume more memory than was originally expected by VMware. If necessary, you can increase the amount of memory allocated to the Service Console as follows:

1. Select the ESX host, and then click the Configuration tab.

2. In the Hardware pane, select the Memory link.

3. On the far-right side of the vSphere Client window, select Properties.

4. In the dialog box, type in the new amount of memory.

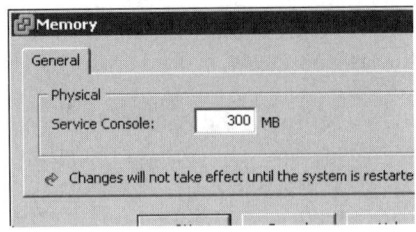

The option to increase the memory allocated to the Service Console appears only in ESX Classic, and is not available or relevant to the ESXi 4 platform.

As the dialog box clearly states, you will need to reboot the ESX host for this change to take effect. For this reason, if you do think you will need to increase the amount of memory to the Service Console, then you may wish to factor in this configuration change during the roll-out phase.

Configuring ESX4 Classic for SAN Booting

If you are unfamiliar with SAN technology, you might wish to read Chapter 6, which covers storage, and then return to this section. It's also worth noting that with the advent of ESXi 3 and 4, the attractiveness of the configuration for SAN booting might decline. After all, if you want a diskless ESX host, you can use the embedded version of ESX. However, if your organization wants to keep on using the ESX Classic edition and has a diskless server, you can follow the instructions in this section.

Since ESX 2.*x*, VMware has supported booting from both local storage and from SAN-based storage. SAN-based booting is a tempting option, especially if you run ESX servers from blades. It allows you to quickly replace a failed blade with a working one, and bring that ESX host back online quickly. Another advantage is that you can leverage your SAN snapshot features as a way of backing up your ESX server build. One of the appeals of booting from a SAN is that nothing about the ESX host itself is physically stored locally. This makes the ESX product more like an appliance—merely an engine for running virtual machines. But as I've just noted, that same goal can be achieved with ESXi 4, and with a much simpler configuration.

SAN-Based Booting Restrictions and Requirements

Before preparing ESX for SAN-based booting, it's important to know some key restrictions and what is actually supported by VMware:

- In previous releases booting from an SAN and using virtual machine clustering (clustering software from Microsoft or Veritas, for example) was not supported. If you want to set up clustering software, you needed local storage on the server. This restriction has now been removed and VMware does now support virtual machine clustering with the boot disks of the virtual machines stored on the SAN.

- The ESX server can see up to a maximum of 256 LUNs (0–255). (Previous versions of the ESX installer displayed only the first 128 LUNs; this limitation no longer exists.)

With ESX 2.x, you could not use a feature called Raw Device Mappings (RDMs). RDMs allow a virtual machine access to native LUNs on the SAN for existing data or storing your data using the guest operating system's native files system on an SAN LUN, rather than creating a virtual disk on VMFS partition. RDM files and SAN booting are now supported together. Also, in ESX 2, VMware supported booting only for the "lowest order" LUNs, so if an ESX host had access to LUNs 10, 12, and 15, the LUN selected as the boot LUN would be 10. This restriction was ended with the release of ESX 3.

Additionally, there are a number of physical hardware requirements for a SAN-based booting configuration:

- The Fibre Channel card used should sit highest in the PCI bus for performance reasons and should be plugged into an "active" storage processor on the SAN.

- Correct LUN masking and zoning should be implemented so only the ESX host can see the correct LUN. This has some implications when you replace a blade in the enclosure. The new blade might present a different World Wide Name (WWN) value, unless you have moved up to the modern blades, for which this issue has been resolved by virtualizing the HBA connection. The SAN will need reconfiguring to present this LUN to the new ESX host.

- Booting from the SAN is supported only in conjunction with a Fibre Channel switch. Direction conenction without a fibre-channel switch may not be supported with all storage vendors. I would consult the VMware SAN Configuration Guide and the VMware HCL if you are considering configuring this setup to confirm it is properly supported.

- IBM eServer BladeCenters that ship with IDE drives onboard need these drives disabled on each blade.

- If you intend to configure booting from a SAN using iSCSI, this is supported only with hardware iSCSI HBAs from vendors like QLogic and Emulex.

Preparing for Installing a SAN-Based Booting Configuration

Before beginning the installation, I recommend that you set the main system BIOS to boot from the CD-ROM. In the main BIOS, you set the Fibre Channel storage controller to be above the internal RAID controller card. This stops the server from booting to local internal storage.

Once the main BIOS has been correctly configured, you will need to enter the configuration tool for your Fibre Channel card. The Fibre Channel device will need to be enabled as a boot device, and the LUN where installation files were copied selected as the boot LUN. Clearly, these settings are very hardware-specific. The instructions in this section are based on using HP ProLiant DL 385 with a QLogic 2340 Fibre Channel card. You should consult your vendor's procedures for enabling SAN-based booting on your specific hardware.

Finally, before you begin, I recommend either removing physical disks or using your RAID controller card to remove any LUNs. This will ensure that the only storage you see during the installation procedure is SAN-based.

Configuring the Fibre Channel BIOS Options

Here are the steps for configuring the BIOS options:

1. Power on your server.

2. Press ALT+Q to enter the QLogic card's BIOS settings.

3. Choose Configuration Settings and press ENTER.

4. Choose Host Adapter Settings and press ENTER.

5. Set the Host Adapter BIOS option to Enabled.

6. Press ESC to exit the Host Adapter Settings menu.

7. In Configuration Settings, choose Selectable Boot Settings.

8. Set Selectable Boot Device option to Enabled.

9. Cursor down to select Current Boot Node Name and press ENTER.

The following diagram shows the disks displayed to my server.

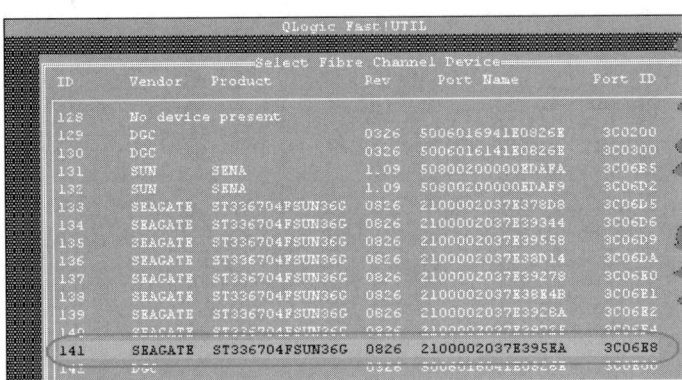

Here, my ESX host can see many LUNs/disks. You might find it much *safer and easier* to mask all LUNs away from the server except the SAN boot LUN. This will make selecting the correct LUN much clearer.

1. Select the appropriate LUN or disk from the list. I will use ID1, which has the NAA name that ends with 20nnnnnnnnnnnn95EA.

NOTE *A Network Address Authority (NAA) name is a special address that uniquely identifies a disk or a LUN in Fibre Channel- or iSCSI-based SANs. VMware still refers to disks by the vmhba syntax in the vSphere Client, but also shows the NAA values. You will learn more about these addressing schemes in Chapter 6.*

---

2. Press ENTER to select the target LUN, which will then be set as the Primary Boot Port Name and LUN.

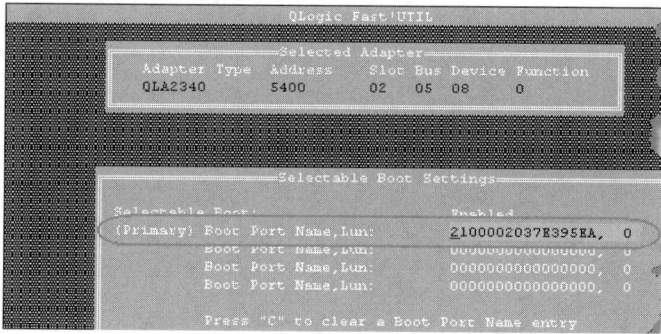

3. Press ESC and choose to save your changes.

4. Finally, exit the utility and choose to reboot the system.

When you reboot, you will see that the QLogic card reports different settings, indicating that the BIOS is enabled and that the target LUN is selected.

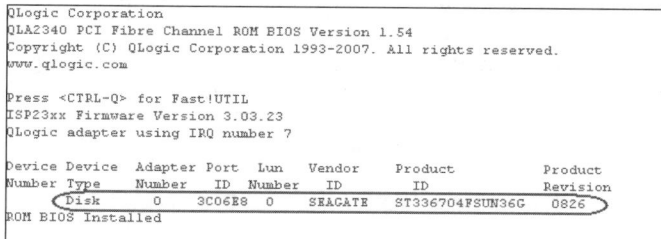

Configuring the Main System BIOS

Different systems use different BIOS providers and different keyboard strokes to gain access to the main keyboard settings. For example, on most HP systems, you press F10 to enter the BIOS, but on Dell systems, it is normally F2.

The following is the procedure for configuring the BIOS on a HP ProLiant Server:

1. Press F10 at the prompt.

2. Choose the Setup Utility option and press ENTER.

3. Choose Boot Controller Order (IPL) and press ENTER.

4. Select the QLogic card and press ENTER. (On my system, this appears as Ctlr:3 PCI Slot 3 SCSI Mass Storage Controller.)

5. Choose Control Order 3. The following screenshot shows configuring the QLogic card to be the primary device for boot purposes.

NOTE *If you were doing this in a Dell BIOS, you would choose the option called Hard Drive Sequence and use the +/– keys to move the QLogic card to the top of the list.*

6. Press ESC and then F10 to save your changes.

Boot Order

Normally, I have a personal preference for the boot order on my ESX hosts, which is as follows:

- Hard drive
- CD-ROM
- Floppy
- USB key drive
- PXE

This is to prevent me from accidentally leaving a CD, floppy disk, or USB key in a drive and finding a reboot boots to removable media. You might notice that the ESX CD does not ask you to "Press any key to boot from this CD," as some operating systems do.

When it comes to booting from SAN setups, I change this order to the following:

- CD-ROM
- Hard drive
- Floppy
- USB key drive
- PXE

This is to ensure that when I reboot the server, I get to the CD the first time, and the system doesn't try to boot from a blank LUN before I have had the opportunity to install ESX there.

Installing ESX to a SAN LUN

Generally, the ESX installation procedure for a boot-from-SAN configuration differs little from an installation to local storage. The only real difference is that rather than selecting local storage when you partition the disk or set the location of the MBR, you select a LUN on the SAN.

To install ESX to a SAN LUN, insert the ESX CD, and then press the ENTER key to enter the graphical installation. During the installation, choose the correct LUN from the SAN when you partition the LUN, and remember to put the MBR on the same LUN.

Summary

By now, I hope you are fully *au fait* with the ESX installation procedure. In time, you will probably do a few ESX installations, and all of this will become second nature to you. Eventually, you will get truly bored with the idea of performing manual installations from a CD-ROM. Manual installations take time and address only a small part of the overall configuration of the ESX host for use in a live environment. You'll learn more about that configuration in Chapters 4 and 6, which cover networking and storage.

You'll be pleased to hear that much of this configuration can be automated with deployment tools, some of which are free. However, before you consider automating the process, I advise reading the chapters that cover networking and storage if you are new to the product, so you are completely familiar with the postconfiguration of an ESX host. Then, if you're interested in this subject, you may wish to proceed to Chapter 17 entitled "Advanced Configuration Tools," which covers scripted installations with "kickstart" scripts, with the source code delivered across the network with a free PXE "virtual appliance."

CHAPTER 2 | Install and Configure ESXi 4

SXi (Integrated) 4 is a version of ESX that ships with hardware. You can see it as an OEM edition of the product. In this guise, ESX is embedded into your hardware in memory chips or read-only memory (ROM). ESXi 4 has a much smaller footprint than the initial release of ESX 4.*x*, as it does not include the Service Console piece. As I noted in the previous chapter, the future of ESX lies with this embedded version.

If you're upgrading from the previous version of ESXi, as you might have hoped, there isn't much difference between ESXi 3 and ESXi 4. ESXi 4 now supports IPv6, as well as all the new features of ESX Classic, as noted in the previous chapter.

What's New in ESXi 4?

- Support for IPv6
- 64-bit only
- Support for 512GB of RAM, 64 cores, and any combination up to a maximum 256 vCPUs includes 1-, 2-, 4-, and 8-way virtual machines
- Native SATA disk support
- No longer licensed by a .lic file; licensed through locally held license strings or licenses held in the vCenter database

---

Advantages of ESXi 4

ESXi 4 offers a number of advantages, including the following:

- **Reduced patch burden** Most of the patches issued for ESX 4.*x* address problems in the Service Console, rather than VMkernel. By removing this part of the platform, VMware have instantaneously made your life easier. Additionally, as many of these patches address security vulnerabilities in the Service Console, ESXi 4 should be more secure, as these weaknesses simply don't exist.

- **Restricted access** The ESXi 4 system has a lockdown mode, which prevents access by using the vSphere Client directly from the ESX host. Once lockdown mode is enabled, the ESX host can then be managed only via the ILO (often referred to as the local console) or vCenter. This effectively makes users in Active Directory the only valid centralized account database for managing the ESXi host. ESXi presents a smaller "surface area," so does not need the same bolting-down procedures required to meet internal corporate or external compliance requirements than the older ESX "Classic" version.

- **Rapid provisioning** Rather than requiring you to install the ESX product to disks or invest some time in automating the ESX installation, ESXi 4 simply does away with the installation process, and eliminates many of the operator decisions required to deploy ESX. However, your networking and vSwitches still must be created, although this process could be automated with remote CLI scripts. ESXi 4 also ships with an .ISO which allows you to install it either to disk or USB memory sticks. So it is possible to install it to conventional mirrored disks. Currently ESXi does not support a boot-from-SAN configuration.

- **Greater reliability**   With ESXi 4 being integrated with solid-state components rather than on hard drives, you no longer need to worry about the failure rate of physical disks, unless you are creating local VMFS volumes.

- **Hardware monitoring**   Currently, after installing ESX "Classic," the operator will, in many cases, install vendor-specific hardware management agents such as the HP System Insight Management or the IBM Director agents. When ESX "Classic" is upgraded from one release to another, generally you will find that you need to download and install a new hardware agent. With ESXi 4, hardware monitoring is integrated into the system. Therefore, you do not need to manually install any hardware monitoring agents. However, with this said there are "intergration packs" from IBM Director and HP SIM.

As with all products, ESXi 4 is not without disadvantages, and these generally present themselves to businesses that have been using ESX for some time. These businesses may have become dependent on the Service Console for various operations, such as scripting various tasks. With the removal of the Service Console, it is very unlikely that these console scripts will continue to work in ESXi. However, the main ESX commands that begin with the `esxcfg-` prefix are still available. Additionally, many people in the community are not yet completely satisfied with the quality of hardware monitoring provided by the built in CIM of ESXi 4.

Installing ESXi 4

Since ESXi 4 is the embedded version of the VMware hypervisor, in an ideal world there should be nothing to install—it sits in memory embedded on your motherboard. Most vendors revise the BIOS utilities to enable the booting from this device. All this leaves you to perform are the configuration steps, such as setting an IP address and specifying your password for the root account.

However, you may have a server that is on the hardware compatibility list (HCL) for ESXi 4, but did not ship with it embedded. All is not lost. There is an installable version of the ESXi 4 product, too. In fact, the installer for this has been available since August 2007, when VMware released ESXi 3 to download for free.

The installation procedure is straightforward:

1. Boot to the ESXi 4 CD.

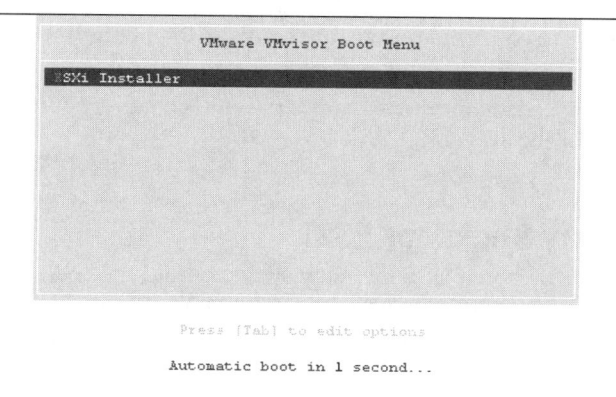

2. Choose the Install option by pressing the ENTER key. (You also have the a Repair option, which reinstalls the ESXi 4 software without affecting your settings.)

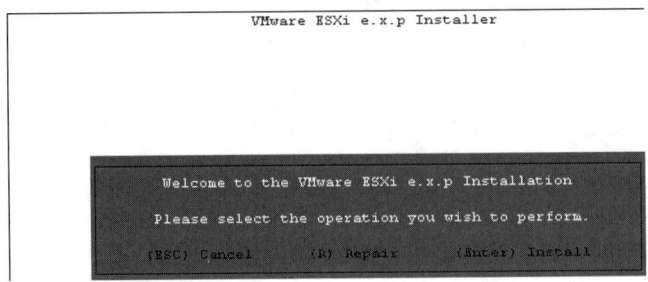

3. Press F11 to accept the EULA.

4. Select a disk on which to install ESXi 4. If you have a memory stick connected to the system, you can select it as a target for installing ESXi 4.

Disk	Vendor	Model	Type	Size	Empty
Disk0	Kingston	DataTraveler II	USB	1GB	N
Disk1	VMware	Blocks Device	Block	67GB	N

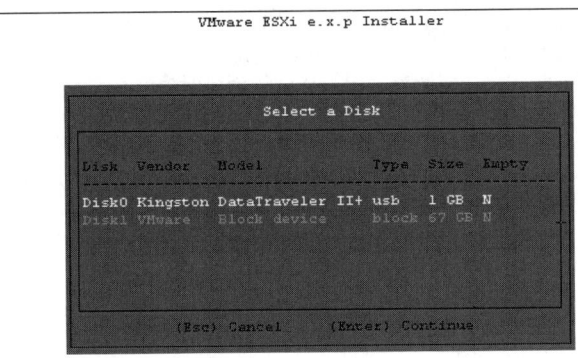

5. Press F11 again to confirm you wish to start the installation.

6. At the end of the installation (which takes a fraction of the time of ESX Classic installation procedure described in the previous chapter), when prompted, press ENTER to reboot the server.

Creating USB Memory Sticks for ESXi

It is possible to create your own USB memory sticks to hold the ESXi 4 software, even if your vendor hasn't supplied them to you. You might have noticed in the previous section, that is a possible to set a USB Memory stick as a installation location. However, if whatever reason that process is unsuccessful, it is possible to manually transfer the image of ESXi 4 to a memory stick. You should first try the installation to the memory stick, as it is much easier. The following instructions are intended as Plan B, just in case Plan A doesn't work out for you. This process has been tested on the following memory sticks:

- Kingston DataTraveler II
- Lexar JumpDrive
- SanDisk Cruzer Micro (SDCZ4)
- SanDisk SADUFD2AA-4096

If you cannot gain access to these memory sticks, any 1GB or 2GB USB device that is USB 2.0 certified and labeled with the Certified Hi-Speed USB logo should work. My memory sticks are the Kingston DataTraveler II type (they were issued for free to delegates to the VMware Europe in Cannes in 2008). It is possible to use USB 1.0 ports, but these are not recommended.

To carry out the following steps, you will need access to the ISO file for the installable version of ESXi 4. This version has a .dd image file, which you can use to "image" a USB memory stick. Unfortunately, it's held within a number of files: a zip file using the bzip2 format, which in turn is packaged in a .tgz file, which in turn is in held on the installable ISO image!

The following instructions describe how to create a memory stick for ESXi software using Linux (or an existing ESX Classic host using the Service Console). A Windows method that uses a dd utility (available from http://www.chrysocome.net/dd) works in the same way, but with a different syntax to address the disk.

1. Create a mounting point for the ISO image:

   ```
   mkdir /mnt/isocd
   ```

2. Using the `mount` command, mount the .ISO image of the installable version of ESXi 4:

   `mount -o loop -t iso9660 -r` /vmfs/volumes/local_esx2/VMware-VMvisor-Installer-4.0.0-140815.x86_64.iso **`/mnt/isocd`**

3. Copy the image.tgz file to /root:

   ```
   cp /mnt/isocd/image.tgz /root
   ```

4. From the image.tgz, extract the .bz2 file, which contains the .dd file:

   ```
   tar -zxvf mnt/isocd/image.tgz *.dd.bz2
   ```

5. Unzip the .bz2 file:

   ```
   bunzip2 /root/usr/lib/vmware/installer/VMware-VMvisor-big-NNNNNN-x86_
   64.dd.bz2
   ```

6. Identify the Linux device name (/dev/sda, dev/sdj) for the USB memory stick. You can do this by using the `esxcfg-scsidevs` command if you are carrying out this task at the ESX Classic Service Console:

   ```
   esxcfg-scsidevs -l | more
   mpx.vmhba32:C0:T0:L0
   Device Type: Direct-Access
   Size: 1967 MB
   ```

```
Display Name: Local USB Direct-Access (mpx.vmhba32:C0:T0:L0)
Plugin: NMP
Console Device: /dev/sda
Devfs Path: /vmfs/devices/disks/mpx.vmhba32:C0:T0:L0
Vendor: Kingston Model: DataTraveler II+ Revis: PMAP
SCSI Level: 2 Is Pseudo: false Status: on
Is RDM Capable: false Is Removable: true
Is Local: true
Other Names: vml.0000000000766d68626133323a303a30
```

You can use `fdisk -l | more` in a similar way, which will produce the following kind of output. Here, you can see the disk is a 2048MB USB memory stick:

```
Disk /dev/sda: 2062 MB, 2062548992 bytes
64 heads, 62 sectors/track, 1015 cylinders
Units = cylinders of 3968 * 512 = 2031616 bytes
```

For greater accuracy, you might prefer to use the Linux `dmesg` command, which will give you this output:

```
[ 4.592387] scsi1 : usb-storage
[ 6.655678] scsi2 : vml0
[ 6.656066] Vendor: Kingston Model: DataTraveler II+ Rev: PMAP
[ 6.656074] Type: Direct-Access ANSI SCSI revision: 02
[ 6.666590] SCSI device sda: 4028416 512-byte hdwr sectors (2063 MB)
```

7. Use the command `dd` to transfer the image file to the device:

```
dd if= VMware-VMvisor-big-NNNNN-x86_64.dd of=/dev/sda bs=500MB
```

CAUTION *If you have any other device present and you specify /dev/sdn incorrectly in this command, you will have an unpleasant surprise at the end: a very blank disk. Spot the man who is speaking from personal experience at 10:30 PM a couple of months ago!*

This will take about 15 minutes, resulting in this output:

```
1+1 records in
1+1 records out
838860800 bytes (839 MB) copied, 1001.89 seconds, 837 kB/s
```

8. You can confirm whether the USB stick is an exact image of the .dd file by knowing the size of the .dd image file and using the `md5sum` command:

```
ls -l VMware-VMvisor-big-NNNNNN-x86_64.dd
md5sum VMware-VMvisor-big-NNNNNN-x86_64.dd
dd if=/dev/sda bs=838860800 count=1 2> /dev/null | md5sum
```

Setting Up ESXi 4

As you will see when you're using ESXi 4, most of the configuration is done once the VMkernel has been loaded and ESX has fully booted. When you first boot a server with ESXi 4, it will default to a number of key settings:

- A default virtual switch called vSwitch0 is created with two port groups, called VM Network and Management Network. The Management Network port group replaces vswif0 and holds the IP settings of ESXi.

- The root account has no password assigned to it.
- The default FQDN is localhost.localdomain.
- If the local disks are blank, a local VMFS volume called datastore1 will be created. You may wish to rename this volume to reflect a more unique naming convention.

CAUTION *My experience has shown that ESXi 4 will not wipe an existing server of its partition table. However, it is not recommended to use ESXi 4 with an existing server with local storage. The VMware documentation does not promise that your files will still be there after booting to the ESXi system!*

I recommend setting a static IP configuration for ESXi. It is tempting to use DHCP with client reservations (where the same IP is leased to the ESX host based on the MAC address) to reduce the configuration to just naming your ESX host and setting a password for the root account. However, I personally feel uncomfortable with server-based systems using a DHCP server, as it then becomes the single point of failure in the environment. I speak as someone who worked in a location where the DHCP server was restarted on weekly basis. With this caveat in place I must admit I have been using DHCP to set the IP configuration of my ESXi 4 servers. I'm pleased to report that I've found this to be very reliable. I guess that many people will have an ideological position on whether or not ESXi 4 should be configured using DHCP. Indeed, there are many people who will find they simply cannot get approval for the use of DHCP in their server rooms.

This configuration can be done via your server's ILO or remotely using the vSphere Client.

If you are using the ILO, you should know that the colors currently used at the ESXi 4 console can sometimes be difficult to read. The images in this book have been manipulated to allow them to be reproduced properly. Normally, these screens are in yellow-mustard and bright-aqua colors. When an ESX host is left idle for a short time, the colors default to a black background with yellow text.

To configure ESXi 4, from the initial setup screen, press F2 to choose Customize Settings.

```
        VMware ESXi e.x.p build-113880

        HP ProLiant DL385 G1

        2 x AMD Opteron(tm) Processor 270
        4 GB Memory


        Download tools to manage this host from:
        http://192.168.2.37/ (DHCP)




<F2> Customize System                          <F12> Shut Down/Restart
```

The Customize Setup screen displays the configuration options.

To navigate the ESXi 4 Customize Setup screen, you can use keyboard keys:

- The cursor keys move up and down.
- Press ENTER to make and save changes.
- Press ESC to save your changes, exit, and log out.
- Press the spacebar to select items in a list.

You should find the configuration of ESXi 4 simple to accomplish. For completeness, I will walk you through the typical configuration changes required.

Setting the Root Password

Follow these steps to set the root password:

1. From the initial setup screen, press F2 to choose Customize System.

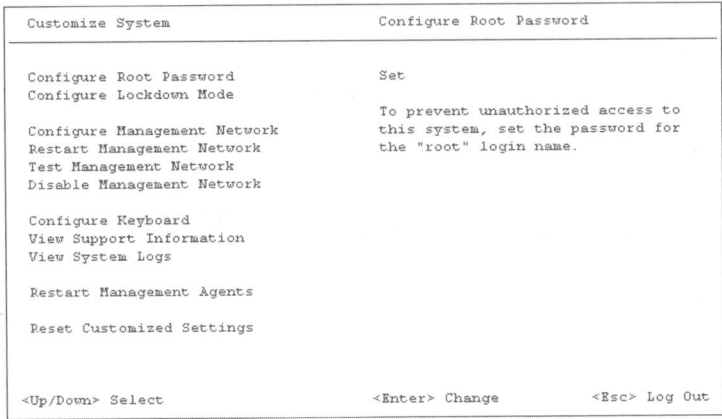

2. Under Customize System, ensure Configure Root Password is selected, and then press ENTER to set a root password.
3. The root password is currently blank. Press ENTER to accept the Old Password field.
4. In the New Password and Confirm Password fields, type your preferred password.

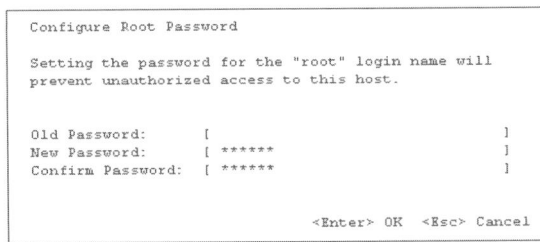

Although little in the way of password complexity is enforced since the Release Candidate of ESXi 4, simple passwords such as "vmware" are not allowed. Using a password that has a mix of character cases and numbers should be acceptable.

Once a password has been set, you will be challenged for it to gain access to the Customize System screens. ESXi 4 hosts left unattended will eventually log out the root account and leave the system at the welcome screen.

Configuring Management Network

The Configure Management Network option allows you to change five main settings:

- VLAN settings
- IP settings
- DNS configuration
- Custom DNS suffixes
- Network adapters

To display this screen, from the initial setup screen, press F2 to choose Customize System. From the Customize System screen, select Configure Management Network and press ENTER.

Setting Your Network Adapter

As in the older ESX releases, by default ESXi 4 selects the first NIC for which it has a valid driver as your management console network connection. This might not be the correct NIC for the network or VLAN from which you carry out management tasks. To set your network adapter, follow these steps:

1. From the Customize Management Network screen, select Network Adapters and press ENTER. The Network Adapters screen lists the current vmnic devices used and the MAC addresses of each of the NICs. The following example shows four NICs. These are two dual-port cards. My server has one dual-port on-board Broadcom NIC (00:15) and an external dual-port Intel card (00:02).

```
Configure Management Network              Network Adapters

 Network Adapters

 Select the adapters for this host's default management network
 connection. Use two or more adapters for fault-tolerance and
 load-balancing.


       Device Name   Hardware Label (MAC Address)   Status
 [X] vmnic0          N/A (00:15:60:aa:6f:7c)        Connected
 [ ] vmnic1          N/A (00:15:60:aa:6f:7b)        Connected
 [ ] vmnic2          N/A (00:02:a5:49:1b:a2)        Connected
 [ ] vmnic3          N/A (00:02:a5:49:1b:a3)        Connected





 <D> View Details  <Space> Toggle Selected      <Enter> OK  <Esc> Cancel
```

2. Use the cursor keys and the spacebar to select the NIC(s) you would like to use.

3. Press ENTER to save your changes.

Setting the VLAN Identity

Optionally, you can set your VLAN ID. Select the VLAN (Optional) option from the Configure Management Network screen and press ENTER. Set the VLAN value using the appropriate value, from 1 to 4094.

```
VLAN (optional)

If you are unsure how to configure or use a VLAN, it is safe to
leave this option unset.


VLAN ID (1-4094, or 4095 to access all VLANs):          [      ]


                                         <Enter> OK  <Esc> Cancel
```

For this to work, you first need to enable VLAN trunk ports to allow the VLAN tagging method. This will be discussed in greater detail in Chapter 4.

Configuring IP and DNS

To configure your IP and DNS settings, follow these steps:

1. From the Customize Management Network screen, select IP Configuration and press ENTER.

2. Cursor down to select "Use the following IP address and network settings" and press the spacebar.

3. Modify the IP, subnet mask, and default gateway as appropriate for your network ranges.

```
IP Configuration

This host can obtain network settings automatically if your network
includes a DHCP server. If not, you must specify these settings.


( ) Use dynamic IP address and network configuration
(o) Set static IP address and network configuration:

IP Address                              [ 192.168.2.103   ]
Subnet Mask                             [ 255.255.255.0   ]
Default Gateway                         [ 192.168.2.199   ]


<Up/Down> Select  <Space> Mark Selected      <Enter> OK  <Esc> Cancel
```

4. Press ENTER to confirm your changes.

5. Select DNS Configuration and press ENTER.

6. Modify the fields to set your primary and secondary DNS configuration.

```
DNS Configuration

This host can only obtain DNS settings automatically if it also obtains
its IP configuration automatically


( ) Obtain DNS server addresses and a hostname automatically
(o) Use the following DNS server addresses and hostname:

Primary Server        [ 192.168.2.199                              ]
Alternate Server      [ 192.168.2.199                              ]
Hostname              [ esx3.vi4book.com                           ]


<Up/Down> Select   <Space> Mark Selected          <Enter> OK   <Esc> Cancel
```

Currently, it is not possible to set a tertiary DNS from the local console. Additionally, ESXi 4 must be completely statically configured or use DHCP. Unlike Microsoft Windows. an ESXi host cannot be a DHCP client for its IP, subnet, and default gateway addresses and statically configured for DNS.

7. Press ENTER to save your changes.

8. Select Custom DNS Suffixes and press ENTER.

9. Type the appropriate DNS suffix search domain for your ESX host.

```
Custom DNS Suffixes

DNS queries will attempt to locate hosts by appending the
suffixes specified here to short, unqualified names.

Use spaces to separate multiple entries.

Suffixes:          [ vi4book.com                                  ]

                                        <Enter> OK   <Esc> Cancel
```

10. Press ESC to save your changes, and choose Yes at Configure Management Network: Confirm screen to restart the ESXi 4 network layer. Whenever you make major changes to the ESXi management network settings, you will always be prompted to restart the network layer to put your settings in effect.

```
Configure Management Network: Confirm

You have reconfigured this host's management network.
Before your changes take effect, they must be applied.

Note: Applying these changes may disconnect remote management
software.


  Save changes and restart management network?


<Y> Yes  <N> No                              <Esc> Cancel
```

Testing the Management Network

The ESXi 4 Customize System screen offers an option to perform network tests to confirm that the default gateway is up (and therefore checks that your IP and default gateway settings are good, too) and checks that your DNS configuration works correctly. (Although the tests are similar to the Test Network options available when you install ESX 4.x, I think that ESXi does a better job of confirming your IP configuration.)

To run the tests, from the Customize System screen, choose Test Management Network and press ENTER. Press ENTER again to confirm you would like to test all your settings.

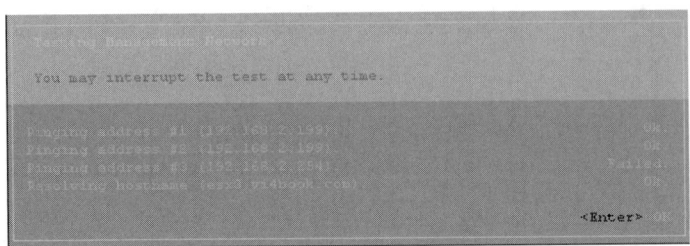

In this example, I deliberately typed a bogus IP address (192.168.2.254), which I know does not exist on my network, just to verify the tests are rigorous and to show you what a failure would look like. Interestingly, in this case, the test results screen never times out and changes color, so it's difficult to read. Here's what it says:

Pinging address #1 192.168.2.199	Ok.
Pinging address #1 192.168.2.200	Ok.
Pinging address #1 192.168.2.254	Failed.
Resolving hostname (esx3.vi4book.com)	Ok.

You don't *need* to test the management network from the ESXi 4 management console. You can instead use conventional methods from your workstation to confirm these changes have been effective.

Setting Other ESXi 4 Options

The other options on the Customize System screen allow you to configure your system as follows:

- **Configure Lockdown Mode**   This option prevents access to the ESXi 4 host directly via the vSphere Client. Normally, you enable this when you add an ESXi host to vCenter. This effectively makes vCenter the only GUI management system available. You can see this as a "hardening" of the ESXi 4 platform. Of course, it can always be disabled by the root administrator at the physical server. So the buck really stops with your physical and ILO security!

- **Restart Management Network**   This restarts the management network, which normally happens whenever you change any network settings.

- **Disable Management Network**   This stops the management network and will prevent anyone from managing the ESXi 4 host via the vSphere Client. It's hard to imagine a usage case for this feature, unless you are facing some major security breach or you want to isolate the ESX host from the network due to some severe maintenance requirements (although ESXi has had a Maintenance Mode feature since version 3, so this shouldn't be necessary). The use of this feature requires confirmation by pressing the F11 key. Additionally, it also toggles the option from Disable Management Network to Enable Management Network.

- **Configure Keyboard**   This currently allows you to switch from English (the default) to French, German, Japanese, or Russian. This is not a regional setting, and does not change the ESXi console to use a different language. It merely sets your keyboard type. Admittedly, the selection options are not great. For example it doesn't allow you to set a UK keyboard as opposed to US keyboard. However, ESXi 4 is not intended to be used with interactive prompt at the server itself but with remote CLI tools such as the RCLI, vMA or PowerCLI where your locale keyboard settings will apply.

- **View Support Information**   This will show your serial number and license number if you have set one. More usefully it will also show the SSL thumbprint (SHA1), which can be used to check when you connect the ESXi 4 host with the vSphere Client that you are connecting to a genuine ESX host, as opposed to some man-in-middle spoofed ESX host. The usefulness of this is directly related to your level of paranoia!

Viewing the System Logs

ESXi 4 currently has three system logs: Messages, Management Agents (hostd), and vCenter Agents (vpxa). These are rolling logs, which are very similar to the logging screen that appears when you press ALT+F12 on a conventional ESX 4 host.

From the Customize System screen, you can select View System Logs to see these logs. Each log is allocated a number from 1 to 3. (At this stage, you may see only two logs, as the vpxa log appears only after the ESXi 4 system has been added to vCenter.) From the log view, press Q to return to the main initial setup screen.

ESXi logs are always in UTC time, whereas ESX Classic logs are in your local time. This can sometimes produce some strange results when comparing logs to other system logs.

Some other logs are available during the boot process itself. When you see the message "Loading VMware Hypervisor" it is possible to press ESC to see "hidden" aspects of the boot process.

Rebooting an ESXi 4 Host

The local console does state very clearly that reboots and shutdowns should ideally be triggered from the vSphere Client. However, you can also do this from the local console, which is useful in cases where communication via the vSphere Client may not be possible. Here is the procedure:

1. At the main splash screen, press F3.
2. Press ENTER to accept the use of the root account.

3. Supply the root password and press ENTER. You will see a warning screen.

```
Shut Down/Restart

We recommend using remote management software such as
VMware Infrastructure Client to safely shut down or
restart this host.

Shutting down or restarting now will power off,
suspend, or shut down running virtual machines
according to the current system shutdown policy. By
default, virtual machines will be powered off.




<F2> Shut Down  <F11> Restart              <Esc> Cancel
```

4. Press F11 to trigger a reboot or F2 to shut down.

Enabling the Tech Support Command-Line/PuTTY Access

The official line is that there is no interactive command-line shell available for ESXi 4 (or ESXi 3, for that matter). One of the goals of the embedded versions of ESX is to wean you from your dependency on the Service Console command-line environment, and make ESX effectively an appliance—albeit one that has an OEM's bezel on the front of it, rather than a VMware one. If you want to interact with ESXi from a CLI, a number of remote command-line shells are available for that purpose. These include a virtual appliance that provides a CLI, a "remote" CLI that can run on Windows or Linux, the VI Toolkit for Windows (PowerShell), and a VI Perl Toolkit.

However, if you must persist in using PuTTY and commands executed at the physical ESX host, there is a way. Be warned that it is unsupported and could be removed by VMware at anytime, so I wouldn't grow too dependent on its use. This method is referred to as Tech Support Mode, although BusyBox provides the CLI. As with the Service Console, BusyBox is an ancillary system that merely acts as a front end to the ESXi system. It is still VMware's VMkernel that runs virtual machines.

BusyBox is often regarded as being ideal for special distributions of Linux or for embedded devices. If you want to learn more about BusyBox check out its entry at http://en.wikipedia.org/wiki/BusyBox.

Core Linux-style commands like `ls` and `df`, and utilities like VI are present on an ESXi 4 host. There are even some ESX commands, such as `esxcfg-vswitch`, and utilities like esxtop. But don't expect all the utilities you might know, say from ESX 3.*x*, to be available from the Tech Support CLI, or for them to behave in exactly the same way.

To enable SSH on ESX 4i you will need to use the Linux text editor VI, because nano is not included in BusyBox (nano is available on only Red Hat Linux distributions). I wouldn't recommend taking the following steps unless you're familiar with VI.

If you wish to enter into the Tech Support CLI, follow these steps:

1. At the splash screen of an ESXi 4 host, press ALT+F1.

2. Type the word **unsupported**. This is not a joke! It's just there to remind you every time that what you're doing is unsupported!

3. At the password prompt, type the root password. You will then gain access to an interactive CLI.

```
ESXi 4.0 http://www.vmware.com
Copyright 2007-2008 VMware Inc.,

Password:

Tech Support Mode successfully accessed.
The time and date of this access have been sent to the system logs.

WARNING - Tech Support Mode is not supported unless used in
consultation with VMware Tech Support.
```

4. Type `vi /etc/inetd.conf`.

5. Press ESC to enter text edit mode.

6. In the file, locate the line that begins with `#ssh` and remove the #.

7. Press ESC again to enter command mode.

8. Type `:wq` to save the file and exit VI. (If you make a mistake, you can press ESC and then type `:q!` to quit vi without saving the file.)

9. Reboot the ESXi 4 host for these changes to take effect.

Summary

In this chapter, you have seen how much quicker it is to get started with the ESXi 4 edition, compared to the older ESX Classic. ESXi is the way forward, and my sources inside VMware tell me that ESX 4.*x* will be the last version of ESX that will have the full Service Console. So, I warn new customers of becoming overly reliant on the ESX Classic edition.

If you watch the VMware community forums, you might find some hostility toward the embedded version of ESX. Typically, these are hard-core COS (community speak for the Service Console) users, who have been using ESX since version 1 or 2. Some of this hostility could be dismissed as being RTC (resistance to change), but it would also be fair to say that some of it is based on losing access to certain tools and utilities that administrators expect to find from previous editions. (Note that, as VMware has yet to make an official public announcement declaring the end of the Classic edition, I might be a bit premature in writing its obituary.)

Personally, I grew up with the COS and will to some degree miss it. In fact, a few years ago I was at the forefront of writing free PDF guides to both ESX 2 and 3 Service Consoles. But I also know that the new remote CLIs, especially the PowerCLI (VMware additions to Microsoft PowerShell) and the VI Perl Toolkit, are much more powerful APIs, mainly because they are vCenter-aware. We might find that just as old-school DOS-based batch files gave way to much richer APIs such as VBSScript and Windows Management Instrumentation (WMI) in Windows, the same will happen to my old friend, the Service Console.

CHAPTER 3 | Install vCenter

This chapter covers the setup and configuration of VMware's vCenter and licensing your ESX hosts. vCenter is the most common method of managing many ESX servers and the virtual machines that run on them. I will also explain how vCenter enables you to organize your virtual infrastructure in a way that facilitates administration and delegation of responsibility. Additionally, I will discuss the configuration of vCenter in terms of its own fault tolerance. I will cover a number of best practices and address the most common questions surrounding the implementation of vCenter.

What's New in vCenter?

- Brand-new look and feel, but essentially the vCenter product remains the same

- Linked mode, which allows the administrator to consolidate multiple vCenter instances together into a single view and log in once via the vSphere Client

- A massively increased number of alarms and alerts

- Reporting and search feature

- A version of vCenter based on Linux (currently in beta)

- No more license server; just license strings with consumption monitored by vCenter and held in its back-end database

---

What Is vCenter?

vCenter is a management application that allows you to manage several ESX hosts in a single window. It has a number of key features that make it a must-have for even modest-sized implementations. Without vCenter, some tasks can be completed, such as making a copy of a virtual machine and delegating tasks using Microsoft Active Directory users and groups, but they are much harder to execute and less flexible. Beyond this entry-level management, there is a whole list of features that are available only if you have vCenter and the appropriate add-ons:

- Distributed virtual switches
- Microsoft user accounts
- Templates and template management
- Cold and hot migrations (VMware VMotion and Storage VMotion)
- VMware Distributed Resource Scheduler (DRS)
- VMware High Availability (HA)
- VMware Fault Tolerance (FT)

Currently, the supported version of vCenter runs solely on Windows. However, a free download of the Linux version of vCenter is available. Note that it's currently not supported in production, works with only VI3.5, and is available only as a technology beta download (from http://communities.vmware.com/community/beta/vcserver_linux).

vCenter is a database application, in that it stores its information in a database back end. The following database engines have full support from VMware:

- Microsoft SQL Server 2005 and 2008 (supported with vCenter 2.0.1 or higher)
- Oracle 10g and 11g
- IBM DB2

Additionally, Microsoft SQL Server Express is offered for test and development environments. SQL Server Express is freely distributable and has been copied to the vCenter CD, so there is no need to download it from Microsoft's web site.

CAUTION *One big reason to avoid Microsoft SQL Server Express at all costs (even in a test and development environment) is that it has a maximum database size of 4GB, which may be too small for some production implementations. Also, in previous editions of vCenter, such free database formats often got heavily modified during upgrades—for example, in an upgrade from vCenter 2.0.0 to vCenter 2.0.1. The database was reinitialized, meaning your previous work in vCenter was lost, and you needed to re-create everything by hand.*

Where's vCenter 3?

You might notice that VMware has done some subtle changes around version numbers, as well some less-than-subtle product name changes! We have had vCenter 1, vCenter 2, and now vCenter 4. So what happened to vCenter 3?

Historically, the hypervisor (ESX) came out as a release 1 product, with vCenter 1 not being released until ESX 2. So the product numbers have historically been out of sync. To correct this, VMware have opted to change the release numbers to avoid confusion about production versioning and marketing. VMware is not the first to do this. Citrix has for many years rebranded very well-known products that do exactly the same job (WinFrame, MetaFrame, Presentation, XenApp, and so on). And at the time of this writing, the next release of Windows is slated to be called Windows 7, and there is healthy (some might say tedious) debate about whether that is technically true.

My opinion is this: I don't care! What I care about is whether a product works reliably, performs well, and is a significant improvement on the previous release—whatever product name the marketing team decides on!

What Is VMware vCenter Web Access?

Web Access is another service that can be installed alongside vCenter. It offers a basic user interface that allows operator-style access to virtual machines, without the need for the vSphere Client. It is also required if you wish to develop your own applications with the vCenter Software Development Kit (SDK).

Of course, you could manage your Windows-based virtual machines with Microsoft Remote Desktop Protocol (RDP) and your Linux virtual machines with PuTTY, but some corporate environments prohibit these protocols (especially Microsoft's RDP) because of security concerns. The nice thing about Web Access is that all the communication is encrypted with SSL certificates on firewall-friendly 443 TCP ports.

What Are vSphere Modules, Extensions, and Plug-ins?

As with everything in IT, if vendors can think of three words to describe essentially the same thing, they will. I find this helps to keep an air of mystery around the things I do, and gives management the impression that I must be a clever guy—merely because they haven't a clue about what any of the words mean! Seriously though, *modules*, *extensions*, and *plug-ins* are the same thing. They are usually (but not always) back-end services that extend the functionality of vCenter.

Normally, a plug-in can be installed to the vSphere Client to allow for additional management features. This functionality was first added in the VI3.5 release in December 2007. At that time, there were only two extensions: VMware Update Manager (a patch management service and plug-in) and the VMware Converter (essentially a physical-to-virtual service and plug-in).

The VMware community has responded favorably to plug-ins, and some of the more developer-minded members of the community have written their own plug-ins. A good site to check for vSphere plug-ins is http://www.lostcreations.com.

The popularity of these plug-ins seems to suggest that VMware's master plan is working—vCenter will become an extensible management platform that its own developers and third parties can hook into. A good example of a plug-in (which is, in fact, a product in its own right) is VMware's Site Recovery Manager, which has a disaster recovery planning management service and plug-in to vCenter.

What Happened to VMware License Server?

In VI3, VMware's license server was a Macrovision FLEXnet License Server, which is used by many vendors to license their products. The VI3 licensing service was quite poorly received by the VMware community when VI3 was launched in 2006. There were issues with .lic files not being delivered quickly and efficiently, and occasionally bad license files were generated. It was often difficult to see this, because many customers would open their .lic files with Microsoft Notepad. This would add hidden line-feed (LF) characters to the .lic file and subsequently corrupt it!

Although the license server was meant to assist in the licensing process, quite frequently, it merely got in the way. Additionally, it introduced a potential single point of failure, with license files expiring after a 14-day grace period.

For these various reasons, the VMware license server has now been removed, and replaced with license strings or numbers. For those with ESX 2.*x* experience, this will be nothing new, since this is how licenses were dealt with in the past. So now you can either license the ESX host directly with an ESX serial number or you can license it with a vCenter license number.

Should vCenter Run on a Virtual or Physical Machine?

Answer: I don't care.

Well, actually I do. This old chestnut has been around for some time. Back in VI2 days (ESX 2 and vCenter 1), VMware explicitly stated that vCenter should run on a physical machine. This both confused the pro-virtualization lobby and delighted the anti-virtualization camp. The reason back then was that ESX 2 was quite modest—it could offer only 3GB of RAM and two virtual CPUs (vCPUs). For larger environments of hundreds of ESX hosts and thousands of virtual machines, the vCenter virtual machine couldn't cope with the I/O load.

Since VI3, VMware's position has been a neutral one, offering to support a virtual vCenter or a physical vCenter. It's interesting that VMware is neutral, because this is actually quite a political decision. So, the best response is to sit on the fence and avoid the politics!

I was quite shocked by recent research by VMware that showed that 60% of its customer base runs vCenter on a physical server. I think this has largely to do with customers continuing to follow now out-of-date recommendations from back in the days of vCenter 1.*x*.

Personally, I am all for virtualizing vCenter. Here are my arguments:

- If virtualization is good enough for production virtual machines that support your business operations and are connected by end users, why isn't it good enough for you?

- You can put vCenter into a DRS/HA-enabled cluster. Then it can be moved to another ESX host to improve its performance or because the ESX host it was running on crashed.

- You can snapshot and clone your vCenter with a click of a mouse.

I don't see this functionality being extended to physical machines any time soon!

Join vCenter Servers in to "Linked Mode"

New in vSphere 4 is the capability to join together multiple vCenter servers in a vCenter connection group to allow them to be managed using a single vSphere Client connection. VMware calls this *linked mode*, and it uses Microsoft Active Directory Application Mode (ADAM) to store the vCenter linked mode configuration data. If you have ever used VMware's Virtual Desktop Manager, you will be familiar with this concept, because it's exactly the same type of back end.

The important thing to know about ADAM is that it does not touch or modify anything about your domain-based Active Directory, which you use to manage users, groups, and computers. They are totally separate from each other. The only relationship that vCenter has with your Active Directory structure is that, like any Windows system, it can be joined to the domain. This means that you have access to those users and groups for the purpose of setting permissions and rights with the vCenter Inventory.

Remember that ADAM is not currently a replacement for the supported Microsoft SQL Server, Oracle, or IBM DB2 database. It is merely used to maintain the linked-mode state.

CAUTION *Despite vCenter ADAM providing multiple-master replication, this does* not *mean that you don't need to back up vCenter.*

This new linked mode provides a more aggregated view of vCenter and allows for a single logon to multiple vCenter instances (depending on your rights and privileges). For example, you could have two vCenter instances—one for your two ESX Classic hosts and another for your two ESXi hosts—and join them together into a single connection group.

Be aware that an ESX host can be a member of only one vCenter at one time. It isn't possible for an ESX host to be managed by two different vCenter instances at the same time. The linked mode feature is simply a way to aggregate the view of many vCenter instances into one view.

TIP You can obtain a management tool for VI3.5 installations that works similarly to linked mode, without ADAM, called the vCenter Admin Portal. It's currently a beta product, but it's a free and open beta. You can find this on the Beta Community portion of the VMware Communities forums, at http://communities.vmware.com/community/beta/vcadminportal.

Configure Your Database for vCenter

Before you run the installation CD for vCenter, you must first set up your database back end. Here, I will walk you through the procedures required to get up and running. You should know that the vCenter database expands incrementally over time, as it continually collects performance data. Care should be taken to make sure that the database has enough free disk space into which it can grow.

The database I will use for this example is Microsoft SQL Server 2005. For your implementation, ensure that the SQL Server Agent service is installed and enabled, as this service is required for background tasks carried out in vCenter, including rolling up performance statistics.

Setting SQL Server Authentication

Your organization most likely has its own rules about how user accounts are configured for services. It is common to have datacenter policies that decree that local accounts are not allowed, and that only domain-based user accounts can be used.

In Microsoft SQL Server, authentication comes in two flavors: SQL Server authentication and Windows authentication. Windows authentication is the strongest method.

With vCenter 4, VMware now supports both Windows authentication and SQL Server authentication. I recommend using Mixed Mode in SQL Server to support both types of authentication, and use Windows authentication wherever possible.

If you are installing SQL Server for the first time, you can set the system to support both SQL Server and Windows authentication. If you are using an existing SQL Server implementation, you can change its authentication type using the Management Studio console.

Create the Database and Setting Permissions

During installation, the vCenter installer needs DB_OWNER access to the internal MSDB database. This access is required *only* during an installation or upgrade; it is not required for day-to-day operations. The following procedure includes setting up the necessary DB_OWNER permissions.

To create the database in SQL Server 2005 and set the permissions, follow these steps:

1. Create a local user with Active Directory, called, for example, **vc1_dbuser**. Additionally, make this user a member of the local Administrators group on your vCenter server.

2. Open Microsoft SQL Server Management Studio.

3. Log in to SQL Server.

4. Right-click Databases and choose New Database.

5. In the New Database dialog box, enter a database name, such as **vc1-db**. Also, it's a good idea to store the database somewhere other than on the C: drive (as you know, the C: drive is quite possibly the worst location to hold any data that is important to you).

6. Click OK to create the database.

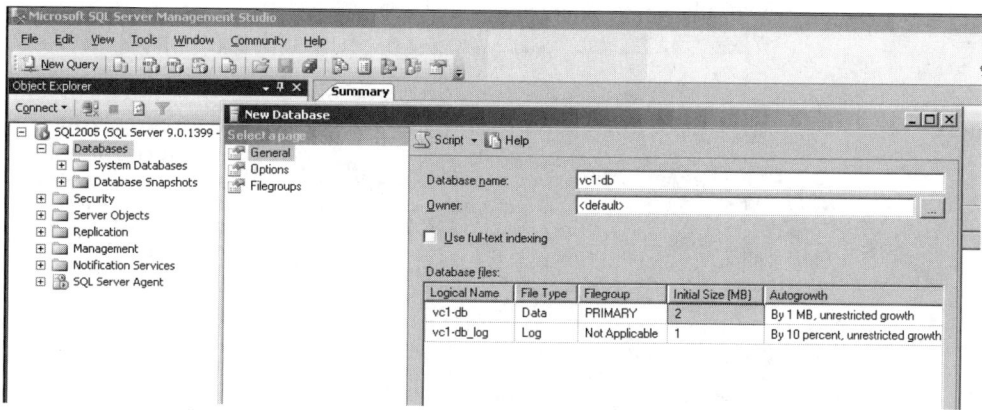

7. Expand Security, right-click Logins, and choose New Login.

8. In the Login – New dialog box, click the Search button and locate your database user account. Select the Windows authentication radio button. Set the default database to the new database you just created.

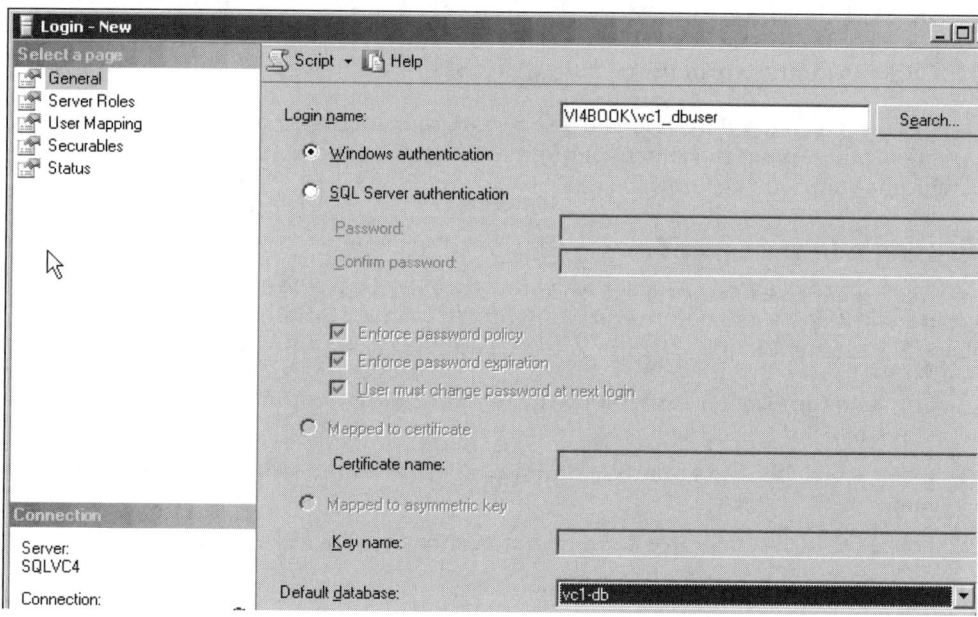

9. Click User Mapping on the left side of the dialog box.

10. Select the MSDB and vc1-db databases. Enable the permission db_owner. Click OK to create the new login.

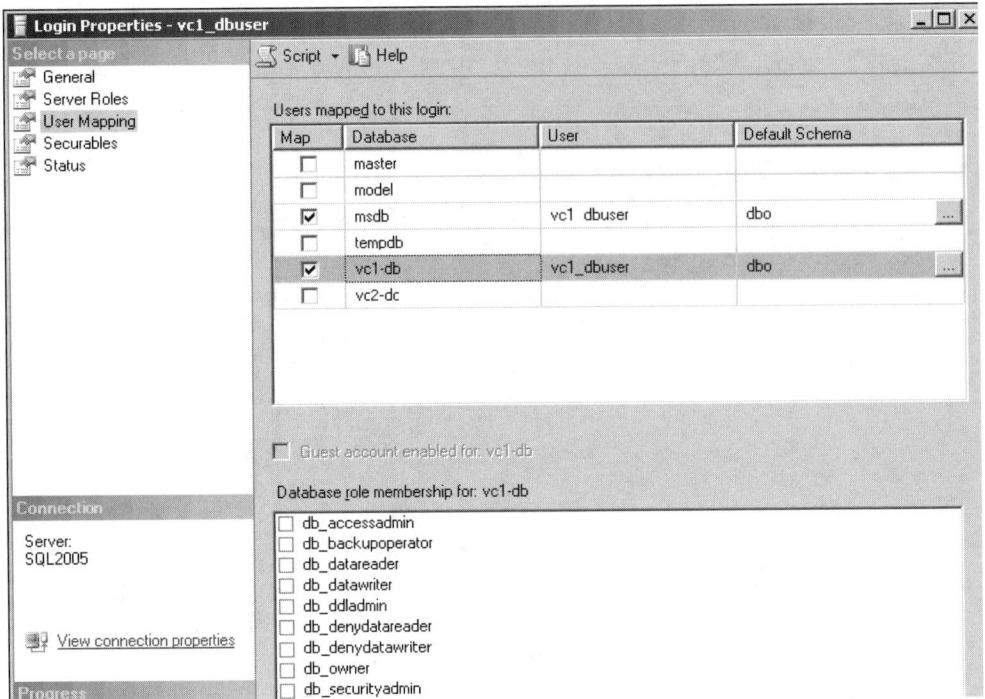

11. Click OK, and confirm the password again.

Later in this chapter, I'll describe how to repeat this process for a second vCenter server, so you can install vCenter twice to two different databases, and then run them in linked mode with the connection groups feature.

Configuring a DSN Connection

It's a good idea to have your Data Source Name (DSN) set up before you begin and to resolve any database issues before you crank up the vCenter installer engine. You must install the SQL Server Native Client to your vCenter server for this part to work.

1. Log in to the vCenter server with the database user account you created in Active Directory.

2. Open the ODBC Data Source Administrator from Administrative Tools on the Start menu.

3. In the ODBC Data Source Administrator, choose the System DSN tab.

4. Click the Add button.

5. From the end of the list, choose SQL Server Native Client, and then select Finish.

6. In the Create a New Data Source to SQL Server dialog box, type **VMware VirtualCenter** in the Name field.

7. From the Server drop-down list, select your SQL Server 2005 server, and then click Next.

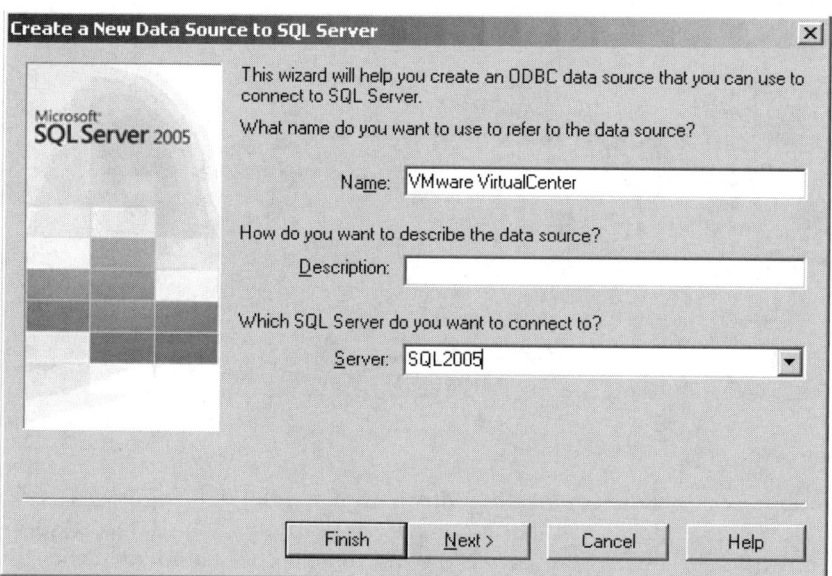

8. Select the "With Integrated Windows authentication" option, and then click Next.

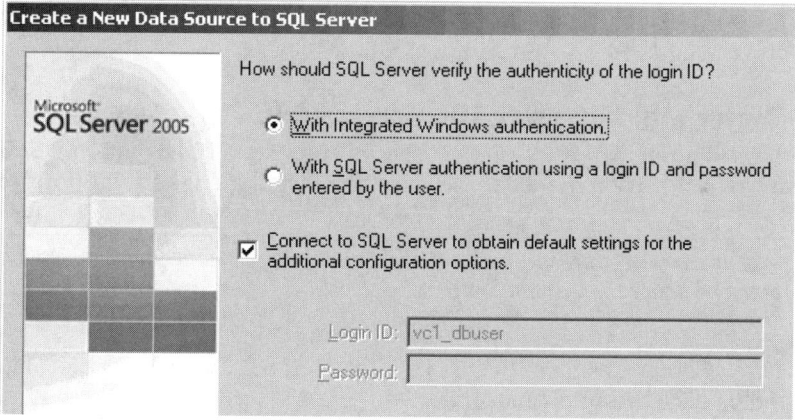

9. Select "Change the default database to" and select the database you created earlier.

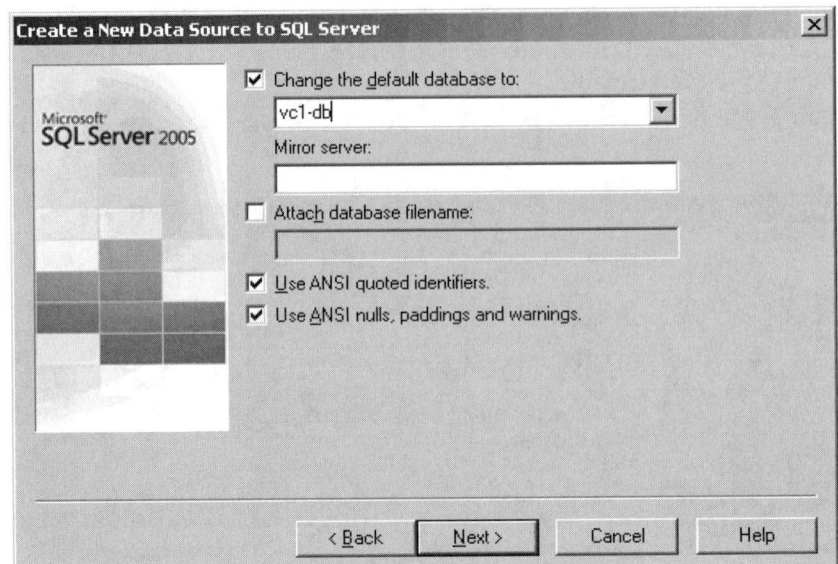

10. Click Next, and then click Finish.

You should now be able to confirm the information in all the dialog boxes associated with the ODBC setup, and also test that you have connectivity to the database server. This test is nearly always successful. It does *not* test your user account credentials.

Setting Up vCenter

After you've configured your database for vCenter, the next step is to install the vCenter server. Then you can add ESX Classic and/or ESXi hosts.

Installing vCenter with Microsoft SQL Server 2005

In this section, I will guide you through the basic vCenter server installation. For the most part, once you have addressed the database issue, the installation is straightforward.

CAUTION *Remember the account you use for the vCenter database needs to be a member of the local Administrators group for the installation to be successful.*

---

1. Insert the vCenter CD or connect to its ISO file. If the CD fails to autorun, then you can double-click the autorun.exe file.

2. Select vCenter Server, and then move through the welcome screen and accept the EULA.

3. In the Customer Information dialog box, enter your name and organization, and if you have it, your vCenter license number.

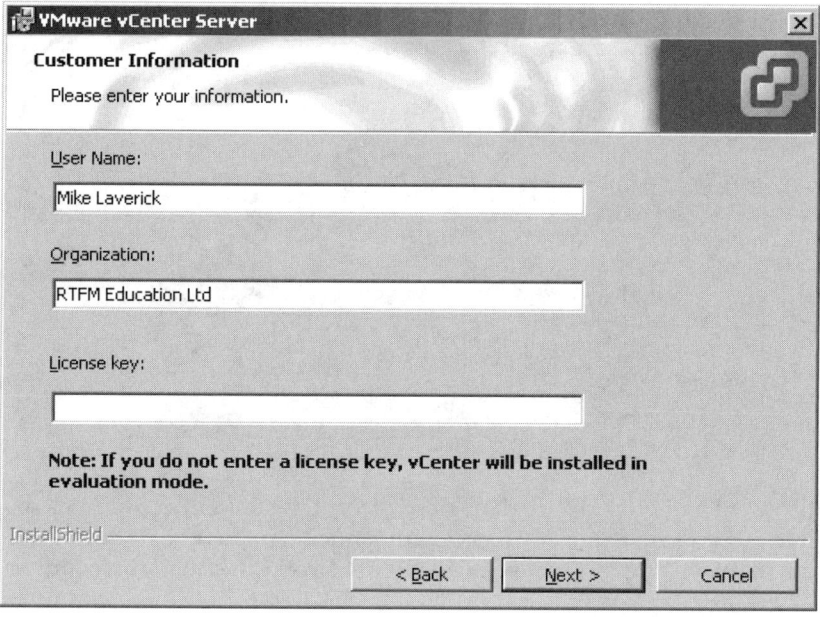

4. In the Database Options dialog box, select the option to "Use an existing supported database." From the drop-down list, select the DSN you created earlier.

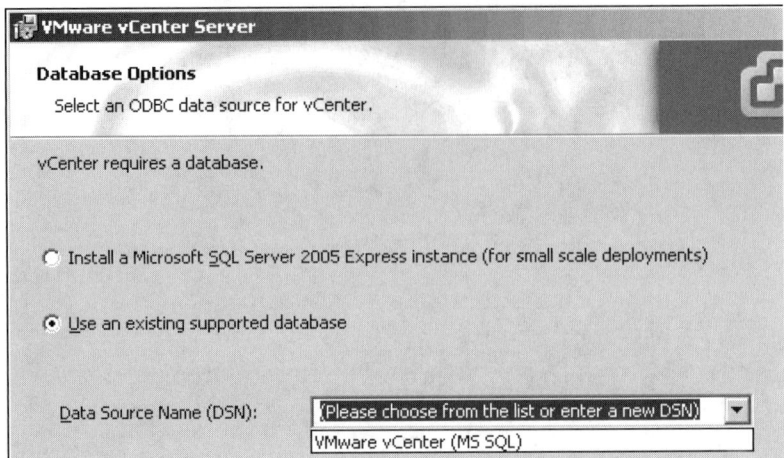

5. Type in the username and password used by the DSN to access the vCenter database.

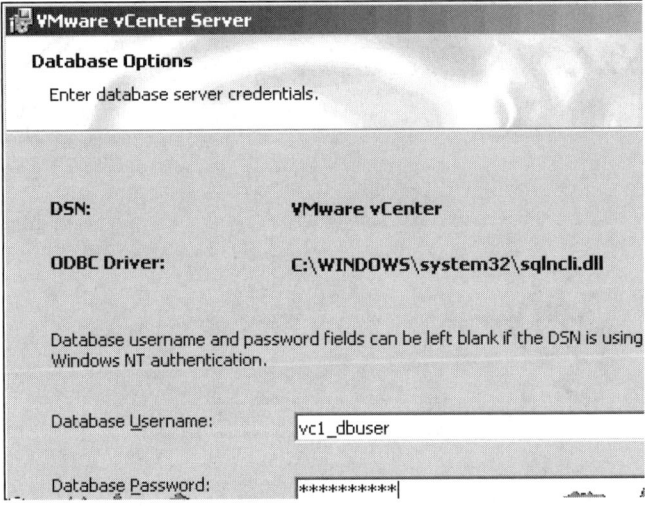

6. In the vCenter Server Service dialog box, accept the default account for running vCenter. (If you are using SQL Server authentication, the Use SYSTEM Account option in this dialog box will be available, and you can enter an account name and password.)

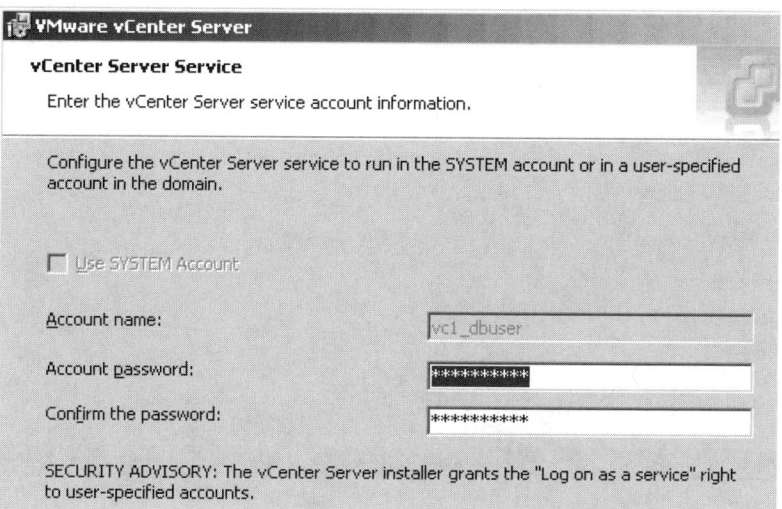

NOTE *Security policies are likely to prohibit the use of local accounts for SQL Server authentication. If I am using SQL Server authentication, I create a user in Active Directory called something like vc1_serviceaccount, with the options "User cannot change password" and "Password never expires" enabled. This domain account does need to be a member of the local Administrators group on the vCenter server for the installation to proceed.*

7. Accept the default path for the installation, C:\Program Files\VMware\ Infrastructure.

8. As this is the first vCenter 4 installation in this example, in the vCenter Linked Mode Options dialog box, select "Create a standalone VMware vCenter Server instance."

9. Accept the default port numbers for the vCenter services.

10. Start the installation by clicking the Install button. (The installation will take some time to complete.)

Other components can be installed to the vCenter server, and if I were setting up the system for a client, I would generally install them now. However, for this book, I will cover installing these additional components on chapter-by-chapter basis.

If you have a PC with the vSphere Client already installed, as described in Chapter 1, there is no need to install the client to the vCenter desktop. The vSphere Client can be used directly at an ESX host (log in in with root and a password), or it can be opened against a vCenter server using the built-in administrator account of the local vCenter server or a domain.

Creating Datacenters and Folders

By default, the Administrators group within Windows is used to allow access to vCenter. If your user account is a member of this group, then you will also be a full administrator in the vCenter environment. If the vCenter server is part of the domain, then the Domain

Admins group will be added to the local Administrators group automatically. Therefore, if your user account is a member of the Domain Admins group, you will also be a full administrator in vCenter.

VMware's friendly name for everything that vCenter stores is the Inventory. There are five main vCenter Inventory views:

- Hosts and Clusters
- VMs and Templates
- Networking
- Datastores
- Search

Click the Home icon to see the views available.

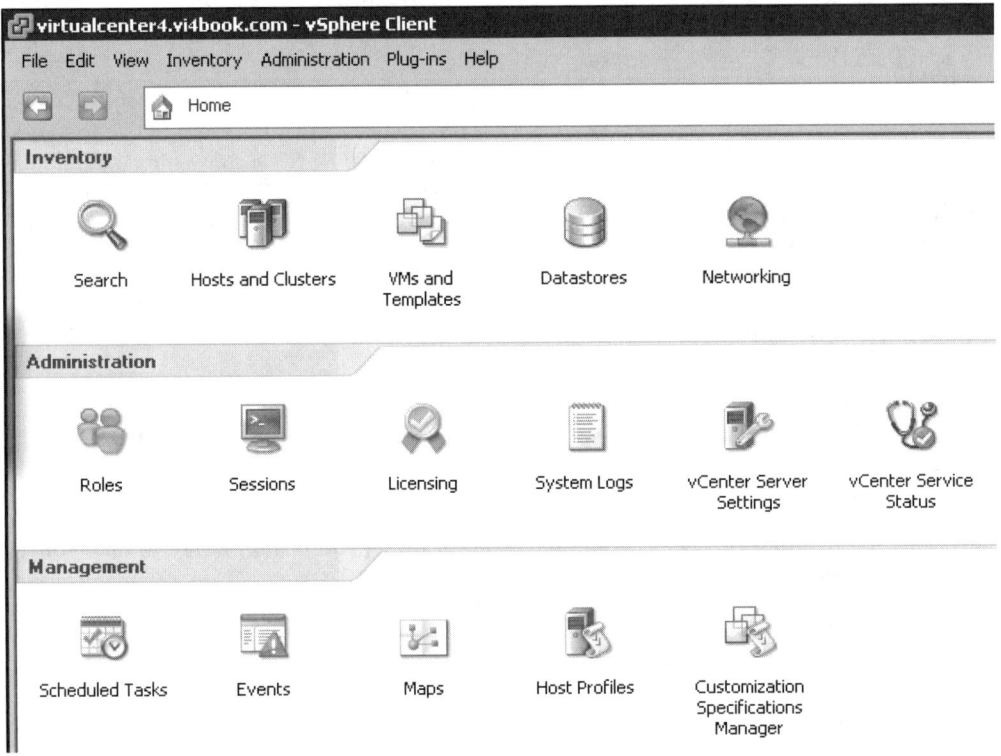

The Hosts and Clusters view is a very physical view that allows you to see stand-alone ESX hosts, ESX hosts in DRS, or HA clusters, together with the virtual machines that they are running. The VMs and Templates view is a very logical view that shows just virtual machines and templates, not the physical hosts on which they are running. The folder structures in the VM and Templates view can be totally different from the structures you create in the Host and Clusters view. The Datastores and Networking views show you the vSwitch port group names currently in use and the datastore names (SAN, iSCSI, and NAS), respectively. All four views share the common object called the *datacenter*.

vCenter has a hierarchical format that is similar to Active Directory's domains and organizational units. The container types available are datacenter and folder. The primary container in vCenter is the datacenter. (Previous versions of vCenter used the term *farm* instead.) Generally, these management units reflect distinct collections of ESX servers that share common SAN, iSCSI, or network-attached storage (NAS) storage and common LAN connectivity.

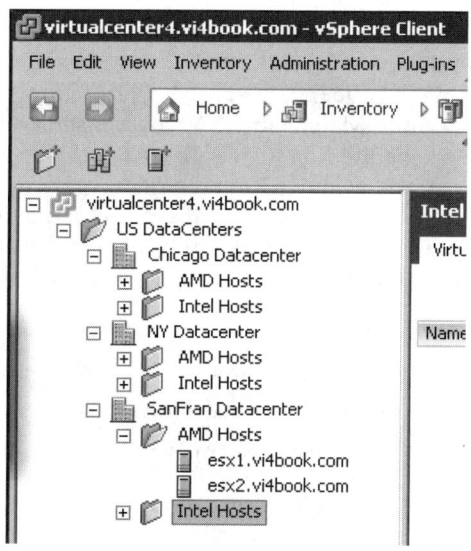

Only a datacenter can contain ESX hosts. If you wish to put an ESX host into a folder, you must first create a folder with a datacenter. Folders can contain practically anything—other folders, virtual machines, datacenters, and ESX hosts. The example to the right illustrates some of the possible permutations of datacenters and folders.

Similarly, in the VMs and Templates view, you can create folders that more accurately reflect the structure of your organization from an IT perspective. For example, you can create folders based on department (such as Accounts, Management, and Distribution), by location (New York, Paris, London, and so on), or by function (Web, DB, AD, File and Print, and so on). The following folder structure is used in many of the examples in this book. Occasionally, I will change it to suit the topic or as the chapter dictates.

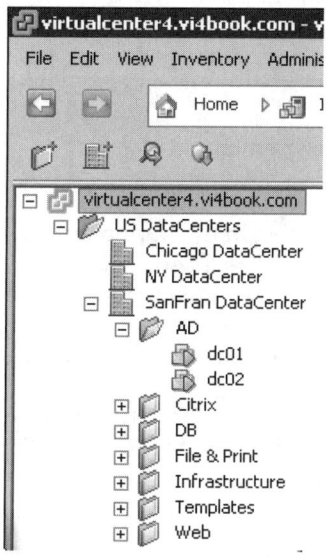

CAUTION *You cannot create a folder in the Hosts and Clusters view where the parent object is a VMware DRS or HA cluster.*

Adding ESX and ESXi Hosts to vCenter

When you first add an ESX host to vCenter, the process can take some time to complete. While your ESX host is being added to vCenter, two critical changes are taking place: the vCenter Management Agent is installed to your ESX host, and a user account called vpxuser is generated on the ESX host.

The vCenter Management Agent allows vCenter to communicate with the ESX host being added and therefore manage it. The agent communicates with the primary management service in ESX called *hostd* (its service name is mgmt_vmware) and has four main tasks:

- Relay ESX host configuration changes to hostd.
- Relay virtual machine create and change requests to hostd.
- Relay resource allocations to virtual machines to hostd.
- Gather performance information, alarms, and alerts from hostd.

The vpxuser user account is used by the vCenter service to authenticate to the ESX host when it sends instructions; you can regard it as a service account. The actual actions themselves are executed by the root account at the ESX host. VMware uses this method to make sure that the root account credentials are never transmitted across the network during normal operations. You need only the root account and password when you first add an ESX host to vCenter. This event happens only once, and the credentials of root are not stored either on the vCenter server or in the database. It is therefore entirely safe to reset the root user's password without fear of complications or problems in vCenter.

When you add an ESX host to the list, you can use IP addresses instead of an FQDN. However, I do not recommend this. Historically, many VMware products require name resolution, and without reverse lookups on DNS, this can cause complications. It is well worth resolving any name resolution problems at this stage, rather than bypassing them with an IP address.

Finally, you should know that is possible to add both ESX 2.*x.x*, ESX3.*x.x* and ESX 4.*x.x* into vCenter 4.0 and manage them from window.

Enabling Check Host Certificates

In the beta release, adding the ESX host in the normal way caused issues with VMware FT. A more rigorous method of adding an ESX host can be enabled where the ESX host must confirm its identity to the operating system using its self-signed certificate generated during the installation process. In the light of how intrusive it is to modify this setting *after* ESX hosts have been added and clusters created, this was changed in the final release of the product. To check this setting, follow these steps:

1. In the Administration menu of vCenter, select vCenter Server Settings.
2. Select Configuration.
3. Select SSL Settings.
4. Make sure the Check Host Certificates option is enabled.

Adding an ESX Classic Host

Follow these steps to add an ESX Classic host to vCenter:

1. Log in to the vCenter server using the vSphere Client.
2. Select the Host and Clusters view.

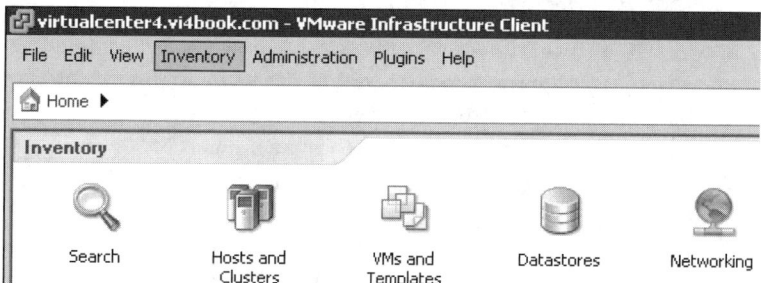

3. Select the New Datacenter icon.

4. Type in a name for your datacenter.
5. Select the datacenter (or folder contained in the datacenter), and then click the Add Host icon.

6. In the first page of the Add Host Wizard, type the name of your ESX host, and enter the root and root account's password. Then click Next.

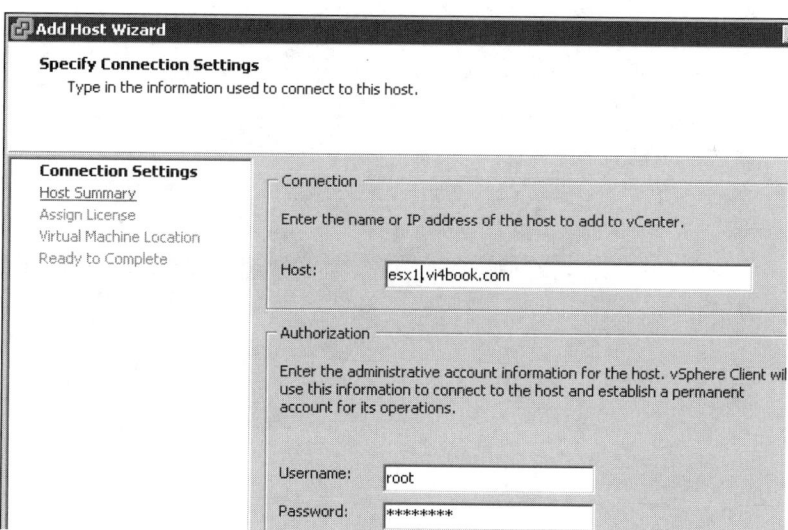

7. Click Yes to accept the SHA1 thumbprint in the Security Alert dialog box.

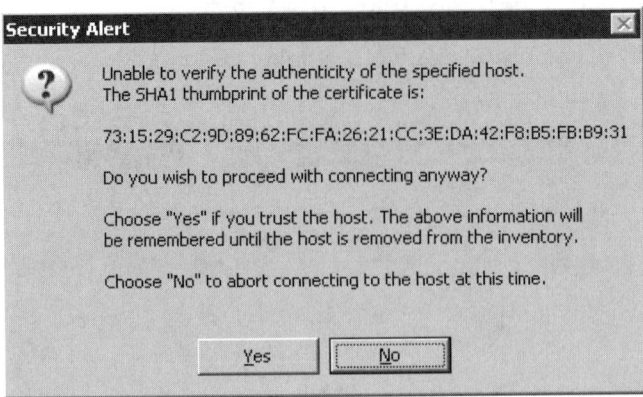

8. In the Assign License dialog box, select "Assign a new license key to this host." Then click the Enter Key button and enter your ESX host license in the Add License Key dialog box.

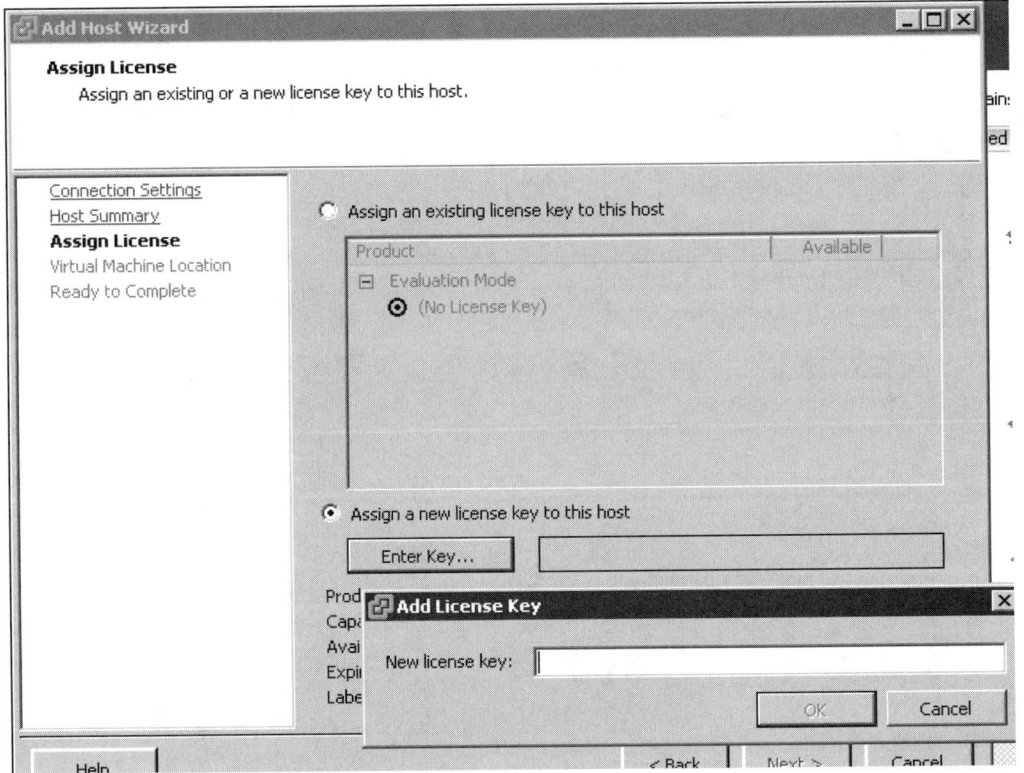

9. Click Next, and then click Finish.

After adding the first ESX host, you will see the license key you entered appear. As you probably know, ESX is still licensed for management by the number of CPUs it has. So when you add an ESX host, the amount of licenses available will decrement by the number of CPUs the server has. The following example shows how initially I had 50 CPU licenses, and after adding my second ESX host (which has only two sockets dual-core), I had 46 CPU licenses left over in my bundle.

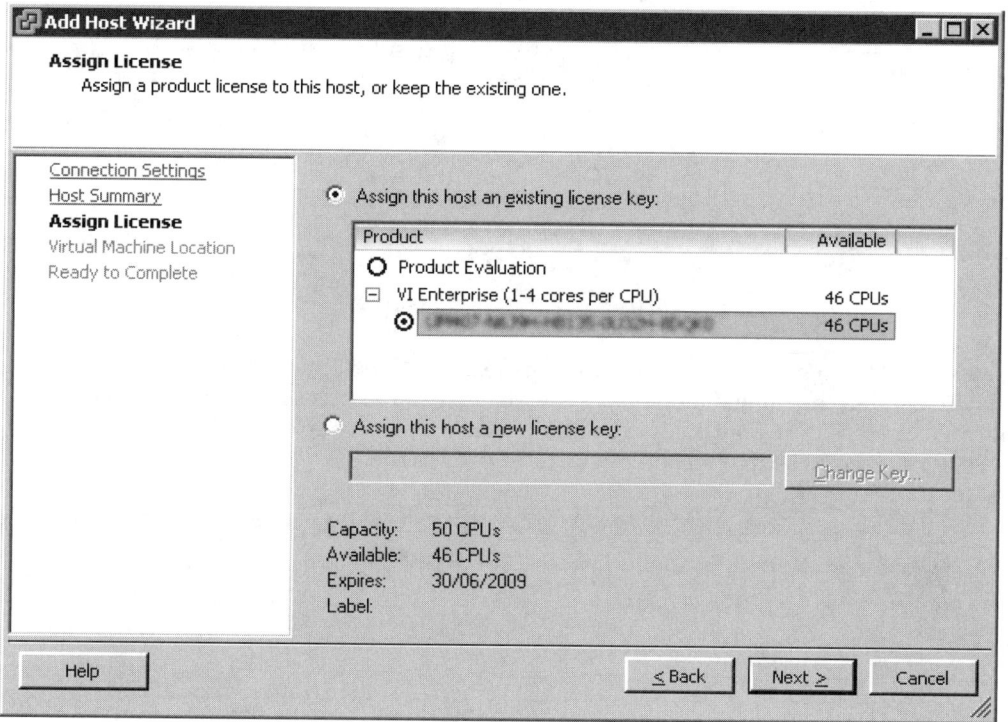

Adding an ESXi Host to vCenter

Adding an ESXi 4 host to vCenter does not differ much from adding an ESX Classic host, except in one respect: lockdown mode can be enabled to prohibit the use of the vSphere Client directly at the host. This is used to harden the ESXi host. In lockdown mode, the only way to manage the ESXi host graphically is via vCenter. In this case, your vCenter permissions (governed by Active Directory) are enforced. The only way to switch off lockdown mode once it has been enabled is through the physical ESXi 4 console.

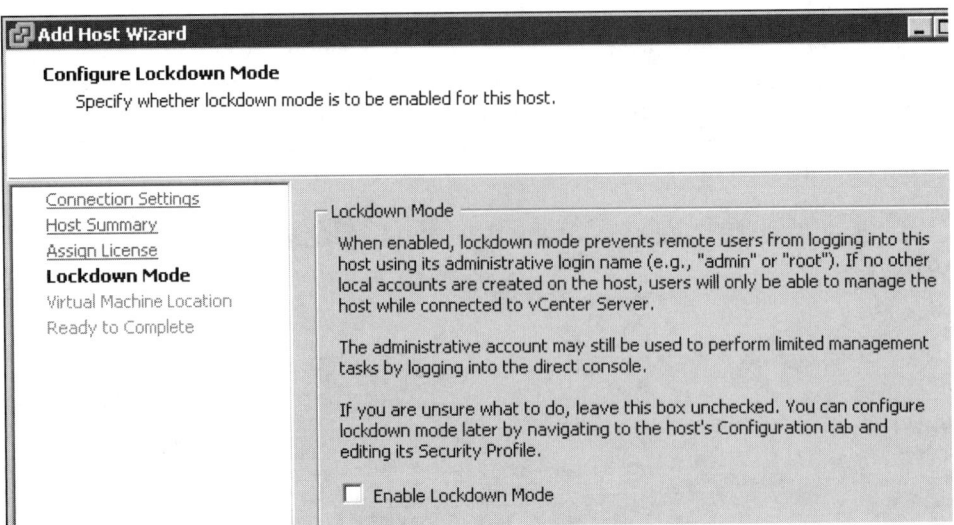

After lockdown mode is enabled, attempts to access the vSphere Client directly from the host will result in the same dialog box as seen by an ordinary user with no privileges trying to log in to an ESX host. So it's not immediately clear if it's a case of using the wrong logon details or root access being blocked by the lockdown mode.

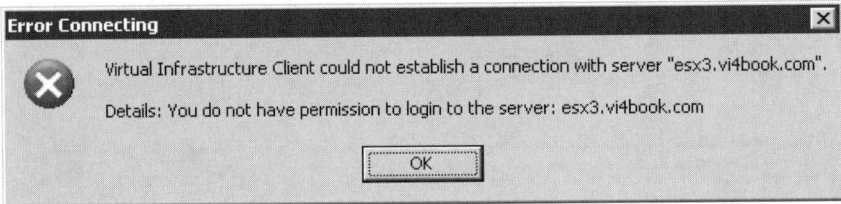

If you forget to enable lockdown mode while adding the host to vCenter, you can enable it from the ESXi host's Configuration tab, in the Security Profile section.

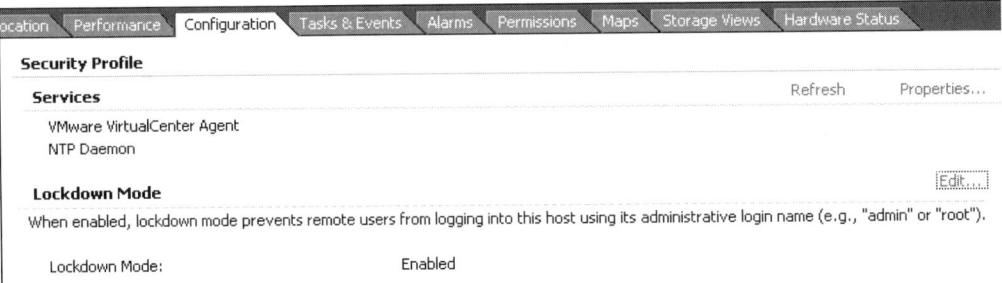

Alternatively, you can configure lockdown mode from within the Configuration front end of the ESXi host directly.

```
Configure Lockdown Mode

When enabled, lockdown mode prevents remote users from logging
into this host using the "root" login name.


[ ] Enable lockdown mode

<Space> Toggle Selected                    <Enter> OK  <Esc> Cancel
```

Configuring vCenter Linked Mode

As discussed earlier in the chapter, a new feature of vCenter, called linked mode or connection groups. allows you to aggregate multiple vCenters into one manageable view. Of course, if you have more than one vCenter server, it's by no means mandatory to couple them together into linked mode. You may require separate vCenters for security, political, geographical, or compliance reasons.

NOTE   *In order for linked mode to be successful, the user account used with the joining vCenter must be an administrator on both of the vCenters.*

If you wish to install a second instance of vCenter as a member of a linked group, when you get to the Virtual Center Group Options dialog box of the installation routine, choose the Join Group option.

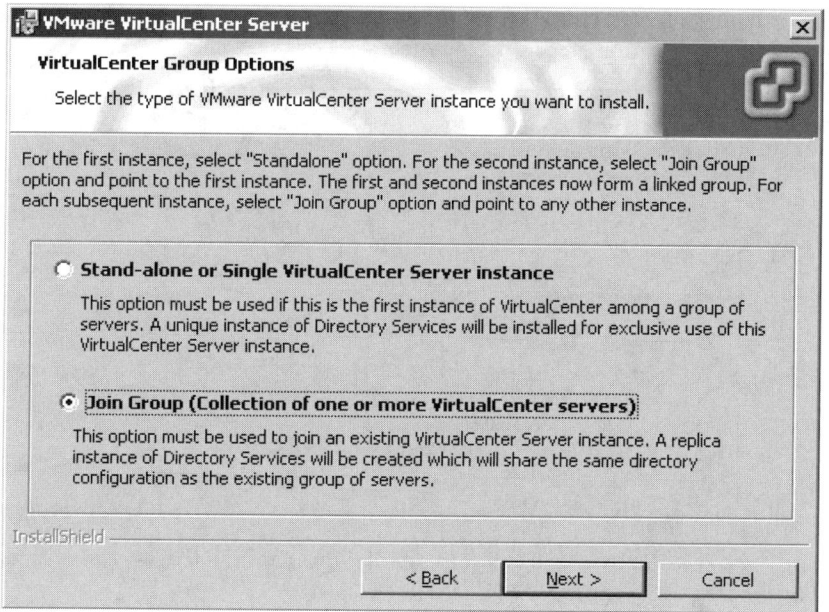

After clicking Next, in the Join Group dialog box, type in the name of any existing vCenter 4 server.

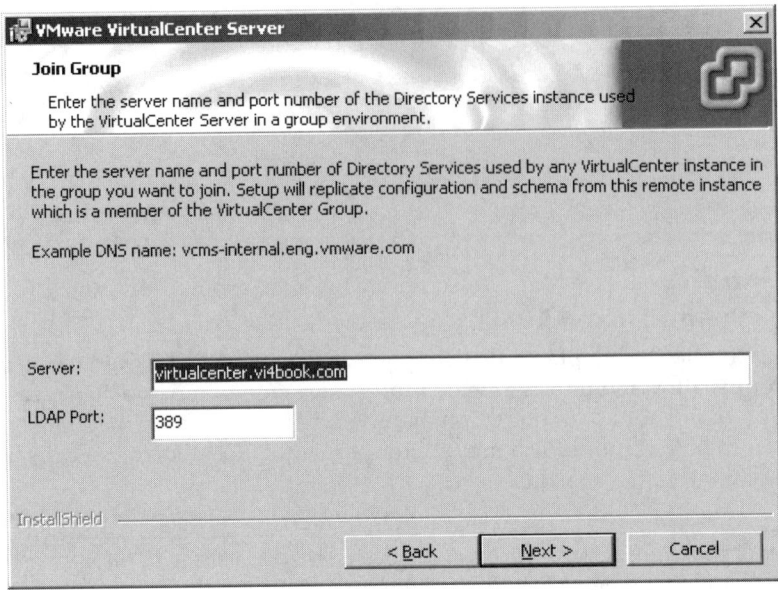

After the installation, you will get the display of multiple vCenter systems, without having to worry about which vCenter you log in to. As long as you have rights to one, you will see the other Inventory. In the following example, you can see two vCenter environments (VirtualCenter4 and VirtualCenter4i). I've chosen to put my ESX Classic hosts in the SanFran Datacenter, and the ESXi 4 hosts into the London Datacenter. So that's two different vCenters using entirely different versions of ESX in a single view.

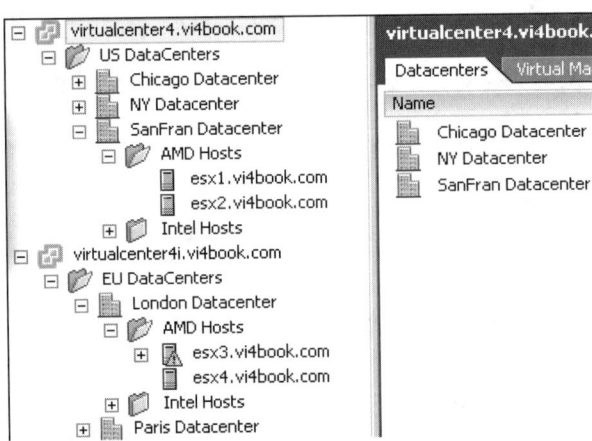

If either of your vCenter systems is not available, the vSphere Client will still load, but will display a warning message on the Recent Tasks bar.

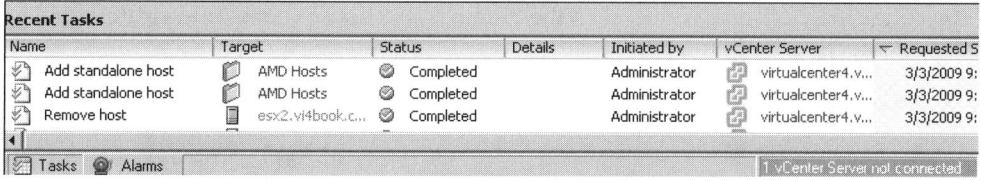

You can easily add or remove vCenter instances from linked groups after the installation. From the Start menu of the vCenter server, open the VMware program folder to access the vCenter Server Linked Mode Configuration Wizard, which essentially reruns the linked mode part of the installation routine.

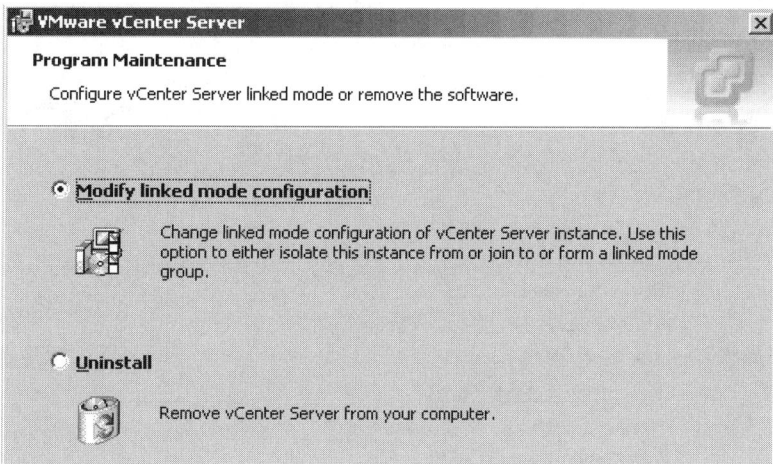

Monitoring vCenter

If the vCenter service fails, you will soon know about it, as your vSphere Client will probably become disconnected. If you are disconnected from the vCenter server, the vSphere Client will try to reconnect to the service automatically.

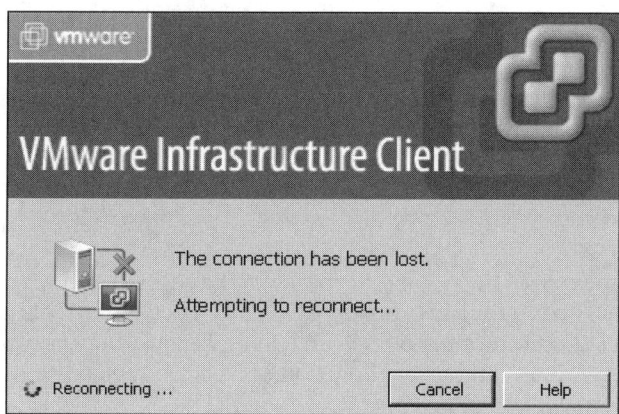

To monitor the vCenter service, click the Home icon, choose the Administration tab, and click the vCenter Service Status icon.

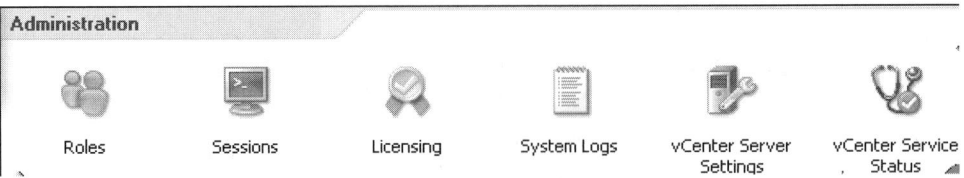

You will see the vCenter Service Status window.

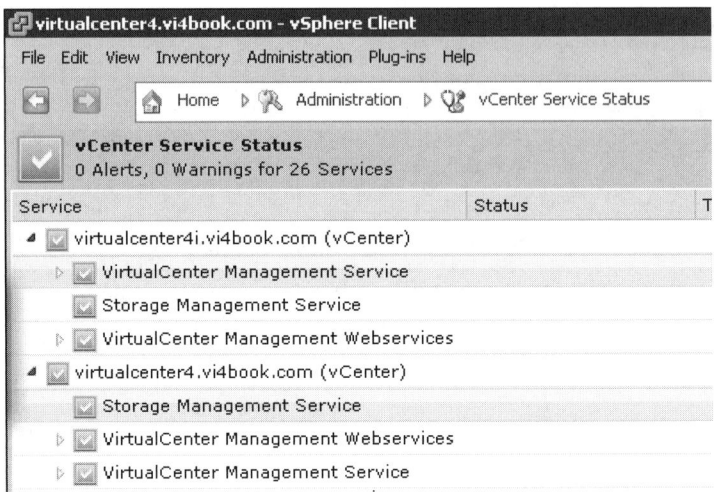

Viewing vSphere 4 License Usage

As you can see, we have license strings to license vCenter and separate license strings to manage ESX hosts. The license strings for vCenter decrement by a factor of how many vCenter systems you build, whereas the ESX licenses decrement by the total amount of CPU sockets your ESX hosts contain. You can quickly view your license usage from vCenter. To do so, click the Home button, choose the Administration tab, and click the Licensing icon.

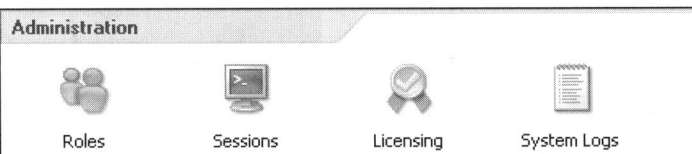

You will see a summary of how many licenses you have used and how many remain. In the following example, I have four ESX hosts with two sockets, each dual-core. This makes a total of 8 CPU licenses used out of my 50, which leaves 42 socket licenses. I have only two instances of vCenter running, out of my allocation of five, so three remain. My licenses are evaluation ones, which will expire on the date shown.

Licensing

Report	View by:	⦿ Product	⦿ License key	⦿ Asset			

Product	Assigned	Capacity	Label	Expires
⊟ vCenter Server	2 instances	5 instances		
⊟ N300h-390Ht-H80J-C3382-2DQ74	2 instances	5 instances		6/30/2009
virtualcenter4.vi4book.com	1 instances			
virtualcenter4i.vi4book.com	1 instances			
⊟ vSphere Enterprise (1-6 cores per CPU)	8 CPUs	50 CPUs		
⊟ C400h-N620H-400GE-0U1FK-29M60	8 CPUs	50 CPUs		6/30/2009
esx1.vi4book.com	2 CPUs			
esx2.vi4book.com	2 CPUs			
esx3.vi4book.com	2 CPUs			
esx4.vi4book.com	2 CPUs			

Protect Your vCenter Server

One concern you will have will be protecting the vCenter server and its database back end. The biggest single point of failure for vCenter is its database. Depending on the cost you wish to invest and the level of your concern, there are a number of options to protect your vCenter system. This said, it's worth remembering that if the vCenter database or server fails, the ESX hosts continue to run and so do the virtual machines. Even advanced features such as VMware HA operate independently from vCenter; in fact, VMware HA is an ESX host service. However, the loss of your management system is not a very pleasant experience. The more dependent you become on vCenter, the more time you will need to spend thinking of the best ways to protect it. Here are some suggestions:

- **Back up the database (highly recommended)**   You can back up vCenter using your backup software. This has two advantages: as well protecting your database files from corruption, it will keep the transaction logs maintained by the database nice and slim. Although the database files that make up vCenter are relatively small (their actual size depends on the number of ESX hosts and virtual machines), many people have found the transaction logs can grow to a very large size, very quickly. In most database systems, running a backup will merge the transaction logs into the database file.

- **Run vCenter in a DRS/HA cluster (highly recommended)**   This is my preferred approach. It is easy to do, but it does require you to run vCenter in a virtual machine. Setting up DRS/HA is a relatively simple task and the setup is very easy to maintain.

- **Virtualize vCenter (recommended)**   With vCenter running on a virtual machine, you can protect it along with your other virtual machines, using VMware HA or FT.

- **Use a hot standby (not recommended)**   You can use a second vCenter server to act as a hot standby should the primary vCenter server fail. This is an older method; it will work, but it's not very sophisticated. The easiest way to create a hot standby is to clone the existing vCenter, which is simple to do if you are running vCenter in a virtual machine. The other benefit of cloning is that it will preserve the certificates that make up the vCenter system.

- **Use network replication of database files (neutral)**   By far, the cheapest way to configure protection is to use some kind of network replication of the database files with a second database server. I'm neutral on this approach—I don't think it's the best way of protecting the vCenter databases, but there's no reason why it wouldn't work.

- **Use Microsoft Cluster Service (MSCS) for SQL Server and vCenter (not recommended)**   You could set up your database to be protected by MSCS, which has been possible since vCenter 1.4.1 patch level 4. I don't recommend this method, as it's costly from a financial, setup, and long-term management perspective. (Of course, you shouldn't be surprised to hear from a VMware guy like myself that I don't recommend using MSCS!)

- **Use the VMware vCenter Server Heartbeat service**   VMware has acquired a license to a technology called Neverfail, which has been in existence for some time. It's not unlike VMware HA, and is actually a licensed version of the Legato AAM software. The VMware vCenter Server Heartbeat service installs to two vCenter instances, and will protect the vCenter system from ESX host failures, guest operating system failures, and vCenter service outages. I believe the main intention of VMware in developing this solution is to offer protection for vCenter when customers install the product on a physical server.

Technology Preview: vCenter Mobile Access

With more and more people connecting to the Internet via personal digital assistants (PDAs) and smartphones, administrators want to be able to manage their environment from these handheld devices. For this purpose, VMware developed the vCenter Mobile Access virtual appliance. At its heart, this appliance is merely a web server that communicates with the vCenter. This web server renders the information in plain HTML, formatted to work with a standard screen of a modern handheld device, with the data entry reduced to small amounts and text and single-click actions. Currently, the Mobile Access virtual appliance is regarded by VMware as a power toy and is not officially supported; it was issued as a Technology Preview in early 2009. Here, I'll outline how to download, configure, and use Mobile Access.

Downloading and Configuring Mobile Access

The Mobile Access virtual appliance ships zipped in the Open Virtualization Format (OVF) format and needs 512MB of RAM, 1 vCPU, and about 7GB of free disk space.

Before powering on the appliance, you need to make sure it is configured for a virtual switch port group. If you are unsure how to do this, you may wish to skip this section and return after you've read Chapters 4 and 5, which cover networking.

Follow these steps to obtain and configure Mobile Access:

1. Download the zip file that contains the OVF file(s) and extract the contents of the zip file. At the time of writing, Mobile Access is still a public beta, and can be downloaded from http://communities.vmware.com/community/beta/vcmobileaccess.

2. In the vSphere Client, select the ESX host as the target to run Mobile Access.

3. From the File menu, select Deploy OVF Template.

4. In the wizard, select the option to deploy from a file, and use the Browse button to locate the OVF file.

5. Accept the OVF template details and the EULA.

6. In the Name and Location dialog box, set a name for the appliance, such as **vMA**.

7. Select a datastore location to store the files of the virtual appliance.

8. If your ESX host has more than one virtual machine port group for networking, you will be asked to set which network the deployed template should use.

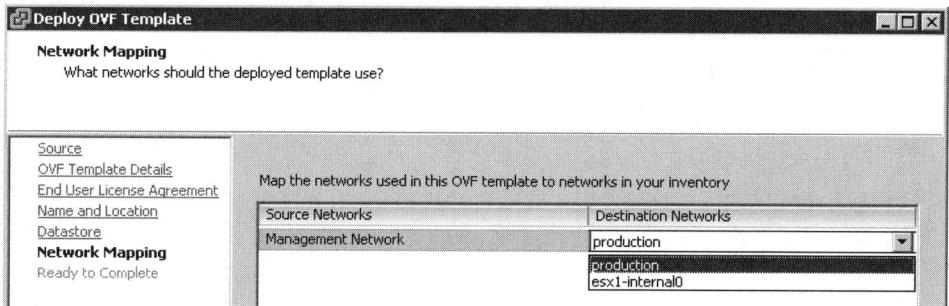

9. Power on Mobile Access.

10. During the boot process, you have the choice to use DHCP or to configure the IP address of the virtual applicance statically. I prefer to use a static IP. Choose N to indicate you do not want to use DHCP.

11. Set the virtual appliance's IP, subnet mask, and DNS server settings.

12. Set the host name/FQDN of the virtual appliance. For this example, I used vma.vi4book.com.

13. At the end of the procedure, type **yes** and press ENTER to confirm your settings.

```
Starting snmpd:                                             [  OK
Starting network configuration ...
Configuring eth0...
Use DHCP to configure the network (yes/no) [yes]: no
Enter IP Address: 192.168.2.165
Enter Subnet Mask: 255.255.255.0
Enter Gateway Address: 192.168.2.199
Enter Primary DNS Address(Press Ctrl-D to clear existing value)

Enter Hostname [marketing15.vdmdomain.com]: vma.vi4book.com

You have selected the following settings
-----------------------------------------------
Configure interface eth0 statically with
IP Address: 192.168.2.165
Subnet Mask: 255.255.255.0
Gateway Address: 192.168.2.199


Primary DNS:
Secondary DNS:
Hostname: vma.vi4book.com
-----------------------------------------------
Are the above settings correct (yes/no)?: yes_
```

14. Set a password for the vi-admin account, which is used to administer the virtual appliance.

These configuration changes can be handled through a friendly web page if you prefer. I'm assuming that there is no DHCP server on the network, and therefore that option may not be available. This web page is available at https://192.168.2.165:5480. After completing the logon process, the web page allows you to reconfigure the appliance as you see fit.

And that's it for the configuration of Mobile Access.

Using Mobile Access

As long as the Mobile Access virtual appliance is accessible via the Internet or your wireless network and can communicate with your ESX hosts, it should be browsable with *any* web browser—whether it's on a PC/Mac or smartphone. Clearly, Mobile Access is not intended to duplicate all the functionality of the vSphere Client, but it's a powerful tool that allows you to do the following:

- Search
- Migrate virtual machines
- View ESX hosts and clusters, alarms, and events
- Trigger host tasks such as shutdown, standby, reboot, maintenance mode, and performance information
- Ping ESX hosts and virtual machines
- Trigger Tracert tests
- Send messages
- Run scheduled tasks

You can test Mobile Access using a smartphone simulator. For example, RIM has a BlackBerry simulator that can be installed on a Windows system. For the BlackBerry simulator to establish an HTTP connection, you will also need to download the BlackBerry MDS Services Simulator package. This is regarded by BlackBerry as a "premium resource," and you will need a developer account to acquire it. It's available from the following URL:

http://na.blackberry.com/eng/developers/browserdev/devtoolsdownloads.jsp

For the screenshots in this section, I downloaded and installed the BlackBerry Device Simulators v4.7.0.75 (9530 Vodafone) package.

To access vCenter Mobile Access as an end user, rather than go to the configuration web pages, enter the URL such as http://mobileaccess.vi4book.com/vim/. Input the name or IP address of your vCenter server, together with your username and password, and then click Login button.

Once you're logged on, you will be presented with a very simple and easy-to-use interface.

Summary

Since VI3, we have observed how vCenter has quickly evolved from a "nice-to-have" application to being an absolute must-have for any serious VMware implementation. The pundits were right. The hypervisor (in our case, ESX) has become a commodity, and the real action and money are in the advanced management layer.

In this chapter, we looked at the setup and configuration of VMware's vCenter. I also demonstrated how vCenter will enable you to organize your virtual infrastructure in a way that facilitates administration. The new linked mode will be attractive to very large installations that work in a multiple vCenter environment.

As you've learned, the introduction of Microsoft ADAM does not yet replace the Microsoft SQL Server, Oracle, or IBM DB2 database. In the longer term, I think many of us hope to see vCenter become merely a downloadable Linux virtual appliance, primarily so we need to worry only about our VMware licenses, rather than Microsoft ones as well. Once vCenter is a Linux virtual appliance, we could hope to see Microsoft ADAM supplanted by open-source LDAP multiple-master replica. It's not that VMware guys like me have it in for Microsoft. How could we when 90% of virtual machines are running Windows? It's just that many of us would like to see VI liberated from any dependence on Microsoft platforms to make deployment and licensing easier. In fact, in years to come, perhaps this chapter will be only a couple of pages long, as the vCenter installation routine will be replaced by a download routine.

CHAPTER 4 | Standard Networking

Improvements in VMware networking open many possibilities in ESX, and make certain network tasks much simpler than they have been in the past. This chapter covers standard VMware networking, focusing on creating and managing virtual switches. I'll also describe how to enable IPv6 on a VMware system.

What's New in VMware Networking?

- Up to 4088 ports on a standard vSwitch
- Support for IPv6 in the Service Console and VMkernel IP stacks
- Distributed virtual switches, which can be managed centrally and picked up by every ESX host with support for private VLANs (covered in Chapter 5)
- Cisco Nexus, a virtual appliance that allows you to create and manage distributed switches using Cisco commands

---

What Are Standard vSwitches?

The VMkernel is a very sophisticated kernel. Not only can it create and run virtual machines, but it can also create virtual switches, called *vSwitches*. The virtual machine's virtual NICs are plugged into vSwitches, which are then mapped to physical NICs on the ESX host. This allows many virtual machines to be networking from a single ESX host with relatively few NICs.

When two virtual machines communicate with each other on the same vSwitch, no physical network traffic is generated. The VMkernel moves the data in memory seamlessly from one virtual machine to the other, without ever hitting a physical NIC. In this respect, you're not limited by the Ethernet access method Carrier Sense Multiple Access with Collision Detection (CSMA/CD). If you have two network-intensive virtual machines, you may want to locate them on the same ESX host on the same vSwitch. However, network performance is only one critical resource—it's demands must be balanced against the other key resources such as CPU and Memory.

Standard vSwitches are not full-fledged HP ProCurve or Cisco Catalyst switches, so don't expect all the features of physical switches. Nonetheless, they are VLAN-aware and can control outbound traffic using a technology VMware calls *traffic shaping*. They can also impose certain security settings.

You can create a vSwitch without any NICs mapped to it, with one physical NIC mapped to it, or with two or more NICs mapped to it.

A vSwitch without any NICs mapped to it is often referred to as an *internal* vSwitch, as it allows communication only within the ESX host. The internal switch could be used as a staging area where you build a virtual machine before "patching" it to a production network. Alternatively, you can use internal vSwitches to emulate a sophisticated network environment. As one vSwitch cannot "auto-magically" communicate with another vSwitch, you could use internal vSwitches to create what VMware calls a "firewall-in-the-box," linking the various switches together through virtual machines with more than one NIC containing Network Address Translation (NAT) software or with firewall products, such as Microsoft Internet Security and Acceleration Server or Check Point.

The only drawback of internal switches is that you cannot carry out VMotion events without first disconnecting users from the virtual machine. Since they are internal to the

ESX host, we cannot guarantee that users would have a continuous connection to the virtual machine during the VMotion event.

A vSwitch with one physical NIC mapped to it gives you basic connectivity to the outside world. This might be suitable for the VMotion network or one that doesn't require fault tolerance, such as a network for testing and developing virtual machines. It could be used to allow connectivity to IP-based storage such as NAS, if that storage location is not offering anything mission-critical, such as access to ISO files or virtual machine templates.

A vSwitch with two or more NICs mapped to it gives you fault tolerance and load balancing. This is ideal for virtual machines and IP storage where greater redundancy might be required.

You can have up to 20 physical NICs in an ESX host of any link speed. There are now 56 ports by default on a vSwitch, and this is configurable for up to 4,088 ports. (ESX 2.*x* users were limited to 8 gigabit or 16 100Mbps NICs on an ESX host and just 32 ports per vSwitch.)

What Are Port Groups?

vSwitches can be subdivided into smaller units called *port groups*. While this technology has been in ESX since version 2.*x*, it has now been expanded. ESX 2.*x* port groups were just a method of allowing virtual machines to interact with VLANs. Since ESX 3, they still have this functionality, but their purpose includes much more.

There are three types of port groups, each relating to a different type of traffic:

- Virtual machine port group
- Service Console port group
- VMkernel port group (for VMotion, VMware FT logging, and IP storage)

Theoretically, you could have one big "über" vSwitch that all your NICs are attached to, with many port groups, each configured for the Service Console, VMkernel IP storage, VMotion, and virtual machines. It is likely you will still want to physically separate network traffic for performance and security. VMware recommends keeping different types of traffic (management, VMotion, storage, and virtual machine) on separate VLANs, serviced by separate NICs.

What Is VMotion?

VMotion allows you to move a virtual machine from one ESX host to another in real time, without powering off the virtual machine. VMotion is essentially a network event, involving cloning virtual machine memory from one ESX host to another until they are in the same state. Once both virtual machines are identical, the original one can be switched off. This requires a VMkernel port to be configured and gigabit networking between the hosts in question.

Although the VMotion process that executes in the background is quite complicated, actually enabling VMotion is easy. If you can type in an IP address, subnet mask, and put a check in a box, you can set up VMotion. (I must say that when I'm teaching VMware, this frequently appears to be the one thing that my students forget to do!) What's necessary for getting VMotion working correctly is knowing the physical and virtual machine requirements to make it reliable.

Port Group Naming

When you are creating a port group for a vSwitch, its name is very important. Port groups must be named consistently from one ESX host to another; otherwise, you will have problems during VMotion and cold migration. Additionally, although the vSphere Client is a Windows application, the definition of a virtual switch is stored on the ESX host in a text file (/etc/vmware/esx.conf). As such, they are also case-sensitive.

In the past, many people used scripted installations to make sure they achieved consistency in their port names. vSphere 4 offers some new features that can help you maintain consistent names, such as distributed switches and host profiles, so such scripted installations are less useful.

One way of resolving a port group naming consistency problem would be to rename port groups. However, this approach is not without consequences. When you rename a port group—just changing case, for example—virtual machines become orphaned from the switch because the name of the switch to which the virtual machine is attached is held in the virtual machine's configuration file (.vmx). If you have 32 virtual machines on one ESX host, they would each need to be told the new vSwitch port group name. Some enterprising VMware Communities forum members have written looping scripts to handle this, but it's easiest to avoid this situation in the first place. In Chapter 17, I will present some handy PowerShell scripts that can be used to address some of these issues.

The following examples illustrate the problem with renaming port groups. Here, I renamed one of my vSwitch port groups from Production to production. This made the virtual machine orphaned from its port group. The effect isn't catastrophic—my virtual machine was still able to communicate with the outside world, and users were not disconnected. It just isn't neat or pleasant to see in the vSphere Client.

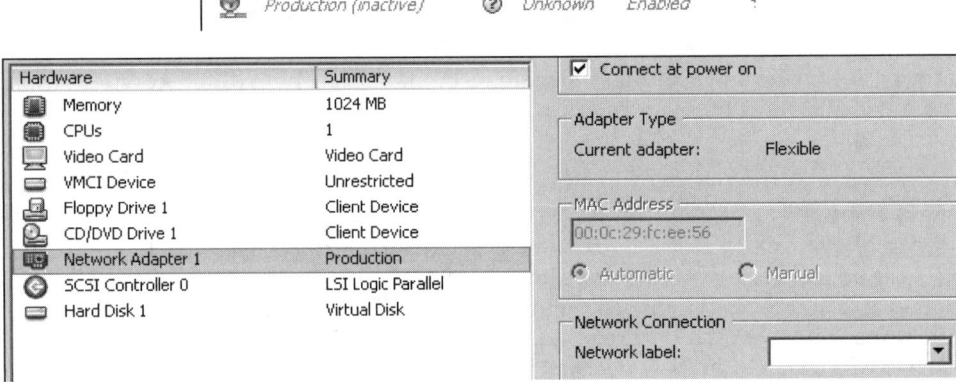

Port group name consistency is not an issue if you use distributed virtual switches, which are covered in the next chapter.

Creating Standard vSwitches

Using the vSphere Client, you can easily create standard vSwitches. Here, we'll look at creating the following types of vSwitches:

- Internal vSwitch
- Teamed vSwitch
- vSwitch with VLAN support
- VMkernel vSwitch for VMotion

Creating an Internal Standard vSwitch

Unlike vSwitches that might be utilized across ESX hosts, the port groups for internal vSwitches don't need to be named the same from one ESX host to another. However, it's still good practice to adopt a unique naming convention, so that when you are viewing your networks in the vSphere Client, you can easily identify the vSwitch type and location. In this example, I'll use the name internal0-esx1 for an internal vSwitch located on the first ESX host.

Follow these steps to create an internal standard vSwitch:

1. In the vSphere Client, select your ESX host.
2. Select the Configuration tab.
3. In the Hardware pane, select Networking.
4. Click the Add Networking link.
5. Choose Virtual Machine and click Next.

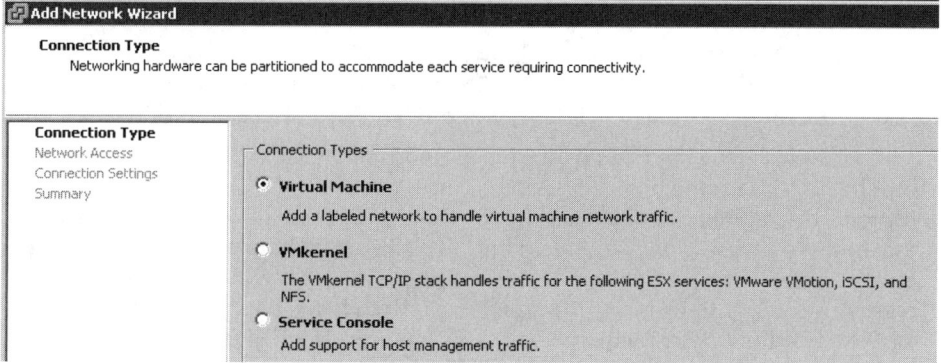

NOTE *If you are working with an ESXi 4 host, only the virtual machine and VMkernel connection types are available (since ESXi does not have a Service Console). VMkernel ports in ESXi are used for VMotion.*

6. Make sure no network adapters are selected, and then click Next.

7. In the Port Groups Properties dialog box, type a descriptive and unique name for this connection, such as **internal0-esx1**.

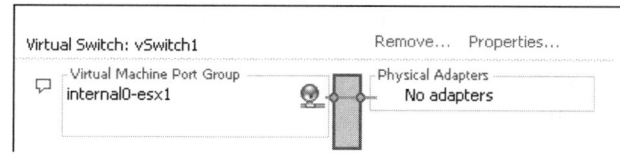

8. Click Finish. The internal vSwitch will be created.

Creating a Teamed Standard vSwitch

Creating a vSwitch with multiple NICs is as simple as checking a couple boxes. By doing this, you will grant every virtual machine on that switch the attributes of fault tolerance and load balancing. The VMkernel configures this feature for you now, avoiding the use of proprietary wizards in Windows for Intel or Broadcom cards.

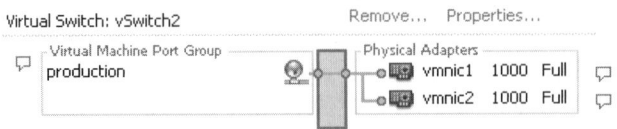

Creating a Standard vSwitch with VLAN Support

in ESX 4.x, port groups can be used for adding VLAN support. In this case, multiple virtual machines connect to a single switch containing multiple port groups, each representing one of the available VLANs.

Actually, ESX supports two main methods of enabling access to VLANs, which are referred to as follows in the VMware documentation:

- **External switch tagging (EST)**   This method is to simply plug in the relevant NICs to the relevant VLANs and set the virtual machine's IP settings for that network. However, this method consumes a lot of NICs. For each VLAN you have, you need at least one NIC. If you also factor in the requirement for fault tolerance, that means you need at least one vSwitch per VLAN, with two NICs for each vSwitch. Once you get beyond a couple of VLANs, you quickly begin to run out of NICs.

- **Virtual switch tagging (VST)**   In this method, the network interfaces are plugged into *trunk ports* on the physical switch. Trunk ports allow many VLAN packets to traverse them. Even with just one or two NICs, ESX can allow multiple virtual machines to access many VLANs. There is a slight CPU burden on the VMkernel, but the overhead is so tiny that this is insignificant. As each virtual machine communicates with its port group and is about to leave the physical server, the VMkernel adds 4 bytes to the packet. This includes the flag indicating this is a VLAN packet and its VLAN number. This packet traverses the trunk port and is intercepted by the physical switch. The physical switch then directs the packet to the appropriate VLAN broadcast domain.

The port group method requires the fewest NICs and the smallest amount of administration. As with NIC teaming, no special work is required of your given guest operating system (Windows, Linux, Novell, or Solaris); the clever stuff is done by VMkernel, leaving the virtual machine totally unaware that it's on a VLAN. The downside of this method is that you must persuade your switch administrators to enable IEEE 802.1Q, or VLAN Tagging, on their physical switches.

However, if you have a small number of VLANs, the physical approach has some benefits. One is that it removes the need to speak to the physical switch administrator. Unfortunately, sometimes avoiding politics and change management requests might be your overriding criteria, above and beyond choosing the best technological method.

Here, I will demonstrate how to use the port group method to support VLANs. In this example, as I am running out of network ports, I will first remove the production port group to create new port groups with the VLAN information.

I like to name my port groups after the VLAN ID. Even though a description displays in this interface (of VLAN 96, for example), when you plug a virtual machine into the port group, all you will see is its friendly name, such as vlan97. If you have hundreds of VLANs, you should select a naming convention that includes a leading zero in the port group name, such as vlan097 and vlan098. Then your port groups will be correctly sorted by the vSphere Client. Again, whatever naming convention you choose, it should be meaningful and consistent.

Follow these steps to remove a port group, and then create a vSwitch to support a VLAN:

1. In the vSphere Client, select the Configuration tab.

2. In the Hardware pane, select Networking.

3. Click Properties of vSwitch2 (the production port group).

4. In the vSwitch2 Properties dialog box, click the production port group, click the Remove button, and confirm that you want to remove this port group.

5. Click Add, and in the Add Network Wizard, choose Virtual Machine.

6. In the Port Group Properties dialog box, type a friendly name, like **accounts** or **vlan96**.

7. In the VLAN ID (Optional) field, type **96**.

8. Click Next, and then click Finish.

Repeat this procedure for other VLAN IDs by adding more port groups.

The following examples show this configuration after adding two more port groups, called sales and distribution, for a total of four port groups, representing VLANs 96, 97, 98, and 99.

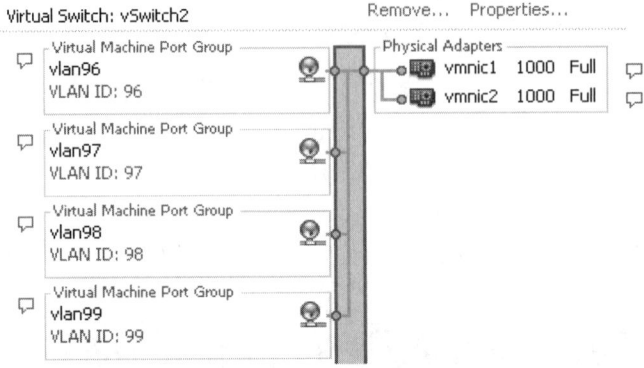

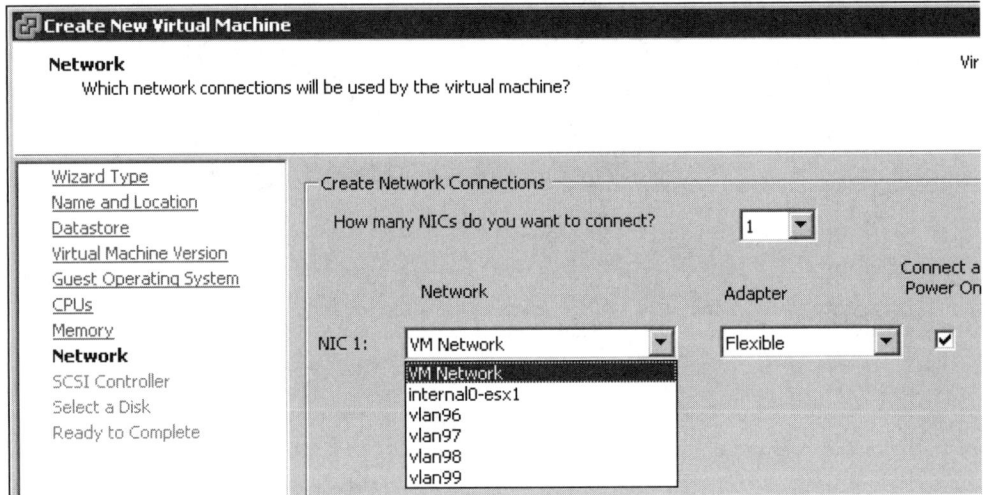

Creating a VMkernel Standard vSwitch for VMotion

A very popular configuration is enabling a VMkernel port group for use with VMotion. When you create a VMkernel port group on a vSwitch, you will be asked to enter an IP address, a subnet mask, and, optionally, a default gateway. You may wonder why you're doing this again, since you already set these values during the ESX installation. Here, you are setting up an IP configuration for the VMkernel, whereas in the installation, you configured the IP address of the Service Console merely for management purposes.

Follow these steps to create a vSwitch to support VMotion:

1. In the vSphere Client, select the Configuration tab.
2. In the Hardware pane, select Networking.
3. Click the Add Networking link.
4. Choose VMkernel and click Next. In this example, three of the four NICs are assigned (vmnic0 to the Service Console vSwitch; vmnic1 and vmnic2 to the production vSwitch). The dialog box gives you the option of using NICs assigned to other switches.

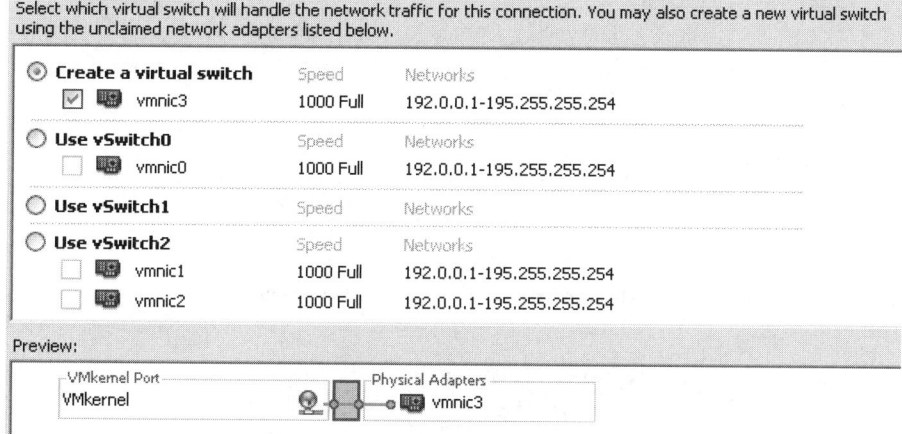

5. For this example, choose the "Create a virtual switch" option, and then click Next.
6. In the Port Groups Properties dialog box, type a friendly name for this connection, such as **vmotion**. Select "Use this port group for VMotion."

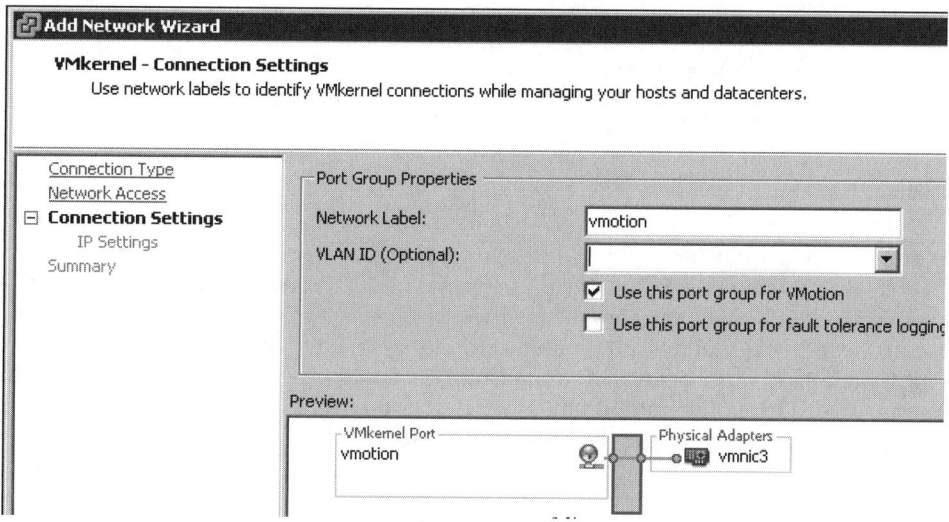

7. Set an IP address and subnet mask for VMotion. For this example, I used 10.0.0.1/ 255.0.0.0 for esx1.vi4book.com, 10.0.0.2/255.0.0.0 for esx2.vi4book.com, and so on.

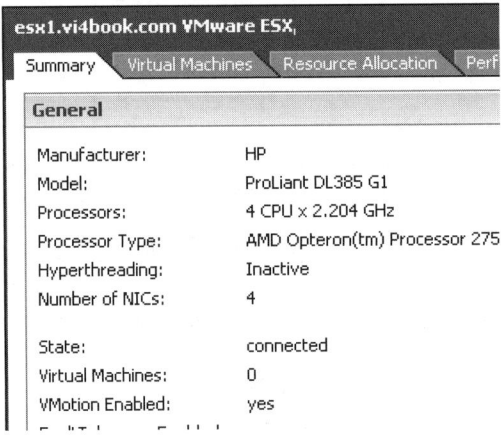

8. You can tell whether VMotion has been enabled by checking the Summary tab of the ESX host.

It's unusual to want to carry out VMotion events across large distances, as normally these events are between two ESX hosts on the same LAN. For this reason, it would be unusual to set a default gateway for a VMkernel port group for VMotion. However, you may need to set a VMkernel default gateway, for example, if the vSwitch is being used to access iSCSI and NAS/NFS devices that the ESX host is separated from by a router. In that case, you may need to set the default gateway to cross the router. (VMware does not recommend driving storage traffic though a router, but it is certainly possible to do so.)

If you do need to set a default gateway, you can find the relevant location by clicking the DNS and Routing link in the Software pane of the Configuration tab in the vSphere Client.

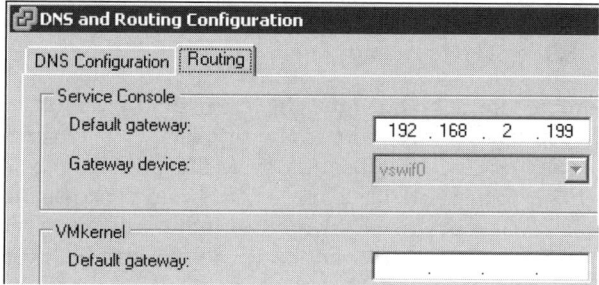

Broken Network Links

Network links can be broken for many reasons, such as a damaged NIC, broken cable, or switch/port failure. Just like many popular operating systems, the vSphere Client will show you if you have network failure by flagging an interface with a red X in the network section.

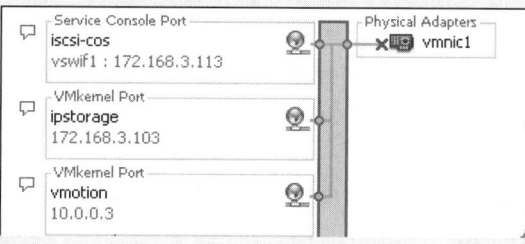

Configuring Standard vSwitches and Port Groups

You have many choices for the configuration of your vSwitches. The settings you can adjust range from the number of ports to security, traffic shaping, and NIC teaming options.

Increasing the Number of Ports on a vSwitch

ESX 2.*x* allowed only 32 virtual machines per vSwitch. ESX 3.*x* raised the maximum number of ports to 1016. In ESX 4.*x*, you can change the number of ports to 24, 56, 120, 248, 504, 1016, 2040, or 4088. What might seem odd about these numbers is they are exactly eight digits less than what you might expect (32, 64, 128, 256, 512, 1032, 2048, and 4096). So what happened to the other eight ports? Well, those eight ports are there, but they are used by the VMkernel for background monitoring processes.

You might wonder why you would need to change this value. Here are two reasons:

- You are using vSphere 4 to run a Virtual Desktop Infrastructure (VDI) environment. In a VDI environment, you expect to see a much larger number of virtual machines, simply because their resource demands in terms of memory tend to be much lower than with server consolidation. (I think I will gloss over here what the memory requirements are for Windows Vista!)

- As you move up to a much larger amount of physical memory in the ESX host, it is likely that you will see an increase in the number of virtual machines you can run per ESX host. ESX 4.*x* introduces support for a terrifying amount of ESX host memory: 512GB. (Well, that sounds daunting now, but it will be chicken feed when we've reached 1TB or 2TB of memory.)

I personally wouldn't recommend changing the number of ports on a vSwitch unless you have come up against these usage cases. There is no published data from VMware of the overhead for either memory or CPU if you configure to the maximum. Also, a configuration change like this needs to be documented as part of your build process, and then automated as part of that build process, or reproduced if you need to rebuild a lost ESX host. I've never been a fan of unnecessary configuration changes for no discernable performance, functionality, or stability benefit. I can think of only one good reason to configure to the maximum, which would be to avoid an unwanted reboot for the sake of a pull-down list!

Caution *Changing the number of ports on a vSwitch requires a reboot of the ESX host to take effect.*

Here is the procedure for increasing the number of ports on a vSwitch:

1. In the vSphere Client, select your ESX host.
2. Select the Configuration tab.
3. In the Hardware pane, select Networking.
4. Click Properties for the vSwitch you wish to modify (vSwitch2 in this example).
5. In the Properties dialog box, click the Edit button.
6. On the General tab, click the pull-down list for the number of ports.

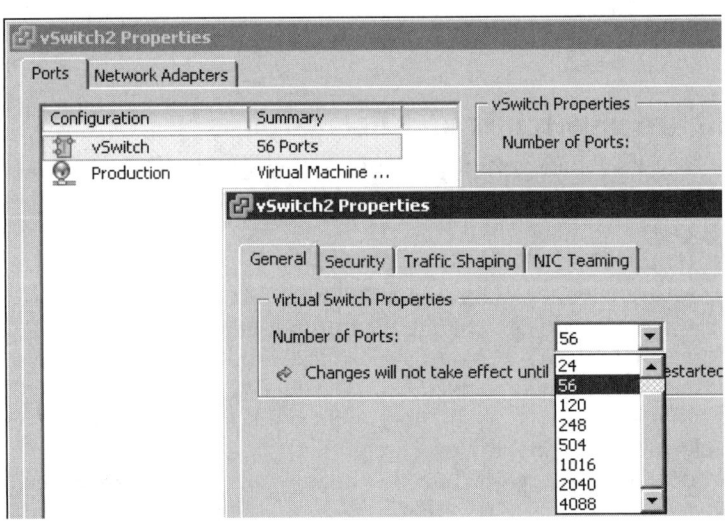

7. Click OK. As the message in the dialog box says, your changes will not take effect until you restart the system.

Setting Speed and Duplex on Physical NICs

The IEEE recommends setting the gigabit-to-gigabit to auto-negotiate. In fact, if you want to adjust the speed and duplex in gigabit environments, this is usually done at the switch, not at the NIC. Even if you change the speed and duplex settings of a gigabit card, it will still auto-negotiate. So these settings are really only relevant perhaps in the Service Console's vSwitch (vSwitch0), where you may still be using 100Mbps.

Here's the procedure for adjusting the speed and duplex settings on a NIC:

1. In the vSphere Client, select your ESX host.
2. Select the Configuration tab.
3. In the Hardware pane, select Networking.
4. Click Properties of the vSwitch for which you wish to adjust the settings.
5. On the Network Adapters tab, select the NIC adapter and click the Edit button.
6. In the Configured Speed, Duplex drop-down list, select your preferred settings, and then click OK.

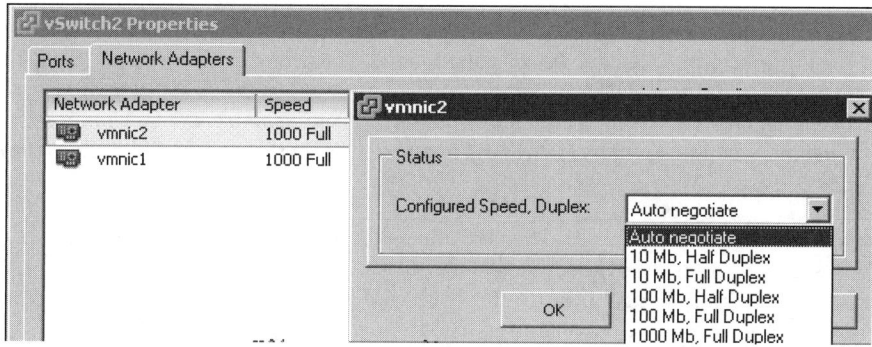

TIP *ESX 2.x people might be interested to know that since ESX 3, you can adjust the speed and duplex settings for the Service Console NIC without editing the modules.conf file. From the Service Console, use the command* `esxcfg-nics -s 100 -d full vmnic1` *to set the speed and duplex, and use* `esxcfg-nics -a vmnic1` *to set the NIC to use auto-negotiate.*

Setting vSwitch and Port Group Policies

If you look at the properties of a vSwitch and the properties of a port group, you will see very similar tabs: Security, Traffic Shaping, and NIC Teaming. You might ask why they appear twice. Well, the settings on the vSwitch form a "global policy," or rule, if you prefer, whereas the settings on the port group act as exceptions to that global policy. Put another way, you could have settings on a vSwitch where "one size fits all," or have per port group settings to give your configuration more flexibility. The settings themselves don't differ; they merely adjust the scope of your changes. As with all security settings, before you decide to close the door, you must first be sure that none of the traffic you are disabling is legitimate, so you don't break one of your applications or services. It's worth saying that these settings are, to some degree, unique to the virtualization world, as they are usually not available in the physical world.

Let's look at the options available on each of these tabs, starting with the Security tab.

Security Settings

VMware had an audit of security that formed the basis of its security settings. Back in ESX 2.*x*, most of these settings weren't configurable, and for those that were, you needed to manually edit a virtual machine's configuration file (.vmx) to make changes. Now you can configure several security settings from the GUI.

VMware's default settings are a compromise (as are all security settings) between security and usability. This is why you don't see all of the Security tab's options set to Reject.

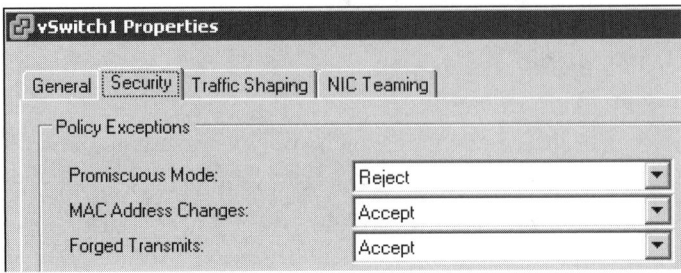

> **CAUTION** *Just as port groups need to be consistent, so must your security settings. Inconsistent security settings will cause VMotion errors. It makes sense if you think about it. If this wasn't enforced by using VMotion, you would have the ability to adjust a virtual machine's security settings just by moving it from one ESX host to another. Now that wouldn't be very secure, would it?*

The following sections discuss the three options on the Security tab: Promiscuous Mode, MAC Address Changes, and Forged Transmits. For the most part, the default settings for these options are acceptable, and if in doubt, leave them alone. Make sure you thoroughly test your virtual machines if you do change the default settings.

Promiscuous Mode   As you might know from your "networking essentials" days, promiscuous mode describes a NIC that can collect all network packets, even ones not intended for it. It is generally used in network-sniffing applications, which you may use against a firewall to troubleshoot networking and such. Usually, you will find the promiscuous mode in Windows or Linux by looking at the NIC settings. In VMware's networking architecture, this behavior is not allowed, so the default for this setting is Reject. VMware wants to stop a compromised virtual machine from being used as a tool by a potential hacker to attack the rest of the system.

Of course, you could be carrying out packet-capturing for legitimate purposes. In that case, you could configure a special port group called "network-analysis" or something equally descriptive, and put a single virtual machine on it. Another reason you might need to enable this feature is so you can run intrusion-detection software inside a virtual machine.

You should also be aware that setting a VLAN ID of 4095 is an All setting that allows a virtual machine to sniff all the network traffic on the vSwitch.

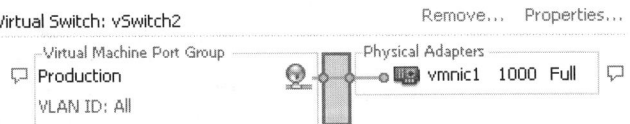

MAC Address Changes Under normal operations, the MAC address of a virtual machine does not change. Of course, hackers may try to spoof the MAC address, as they do with an IP address, to make other systems assume they are sending legitimate traffic.

A virtual machine's virtual MAC address is automatically created by an algorithm to ensure its uniqueness (the algorithm uses a combination of the UUID and unique location of the virtual machine's configuration file). This allows changing the MAC from within the guest operating system, even if the MAC address stored in the configuration file (.vmx) of the virtual machine is different.

I had this situation arise when using Fedora Core 5. I created a brand-new .vmx file for an existing virtual disk. As the Fedora Core 5 operating system loaded, it complained that the MAC address of my virtual NIC was different from the one stored in the operating system. The MAC address of the Fedora Core 5 is also stored in /etc/sysconfig/network-scripts/ifcfg-eth0. Fortunately, I had not altered the default security settings, and communication did work, despite the warnings from the guest operating system. If I had changed the default setting of the MAC Address Changes option from Accept to Reject, so all inbound frames were rejected, I would have been dropped by the ESX host. Later, in the lifetime of this virtual machine, I made the MAC address in the .vmx file the same as the MAC address held in ifcfg-eth0. This resolved the warning messages in my virtual machine.

In some special cases, the MAC address of a virtual machine does change. MSCS and Microsoft's Network Load Balancing (NLB) are two examples of services running inside a virtual machine where MAC addresses must be manipulated to create cluster addresses to which these initially connect.

Forged Transmits The Forged Transmits option, which is set to Accept by default, controls whether a virtual machine is allowed to send traffic under a MAC address that is different from that of the virtual machine. Again, some networking technologies, such as Microsoft's NLB, could break if you prevent forged transmits. If this option is set to Reject, all outbound frames generated by the virtual machine are dropped by the ESX host.

Traffic Shaping Settings

Traffic shaping is the ESX method of controlling outbound traffic generated by virtual machines heading from the server to your wider physical network. You might ask, "Why doesn't VMware have a method of controlling inbound network traffic to the ESX host?" The answer is simple: for the VMkernel to analyze the traffic, it must arrive at the network interfaces, which would cause a performance hit. By then, the damage is already done, so to speak, and limiting can happen only on outbound traffic (where the VMkernel has control). With that said, it's worth mentioning that the newer distributed virtual switch, discussed in the next chapter, does indeed support ingress and egress controls on network traffic.

Outbound traffic limits aside, traffic shaping is an interesting feature. First, it allows us to whittle down network performance to incredibly small amounts—even to kilobits per second! Second, it acts as a "soft cap" to network performance; the hard cap being the maximum bandwidth your physical NICs can provide before being saturated. Even if the bandwidth is there, traffic shaping continues to adjust the amount you have given it. This has some tempting possibilities, such as the ability to emulate wide area network (WAN) speeds between two ESX hosts. However, this wouldn't truly reflect the latency and retransmits that typify WAN communications.

Traffic shaping also comes with some downsides. It's not dynamic—it can't react to changes in circumstances. Once you have set the configuration, some burst rules are allowed, but limiting bandwidth based on time, for example, is not available.

Another interesting question is "What traffic management do we currently do on our LAN?" The answer to this question is almost none. Most LANs operate on a first-come, first-served basis, and we don't do any traffic management at all. Far from throttling our network, we try to give our virtual machines as much bandwidth as we possibly can, within reason.

Another worry might be that during the hours of 9:00 AM to 5:00 PM, you might wish to throttle network bandwidth used by your virtual machine, but what if you are still running backup agents within the virtual machine, and running network backups between 6:00 PM and 6:00 AM? There isn't any built-in way to indicate when the traffic shaper module is active.

So, with these caveats in place, let's see how the traffic shaping feature works. You set three values: an average, a peak, and the burst size. The following example shows the standard settings for traffic shaping.

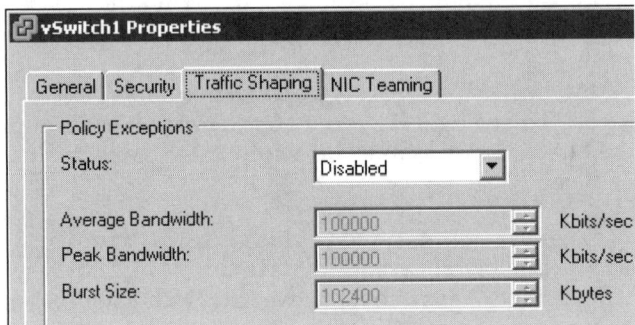

The peak acts as a cap—an upper maximum over which the virtual machines cannot rise. The burst acts a little like a window size. As all bandwidth is measured by time over the amount of data you can send (for example, 57Kbps or 512Kbps), the burst size basically controls this. When the burst size is full—that is, you have used all of your allocation—the ESX pushes the virtual machines back down under their average value. In this respect, peak is always more than average, and it's actually the average value that acts as a throttle on network bandwidth.

NOTE *Personally, I have never seen anyone use traffic shaping in a production environment. Perhaps customers cannot find a good usage case for this feature. After all, most people's bandwidth restrictions are imposed by physical limits to the Internet or to branch offices.*

NIC Teaming Settings

The NIC Teaming tab is a busy dialog box that has a lot of interesting settings. Some of the options, such as Network Failover Detection and Notify Switches, are Boolean, with only two choices. Some of the other settings, such as Load Balancing, have four options associated with them.

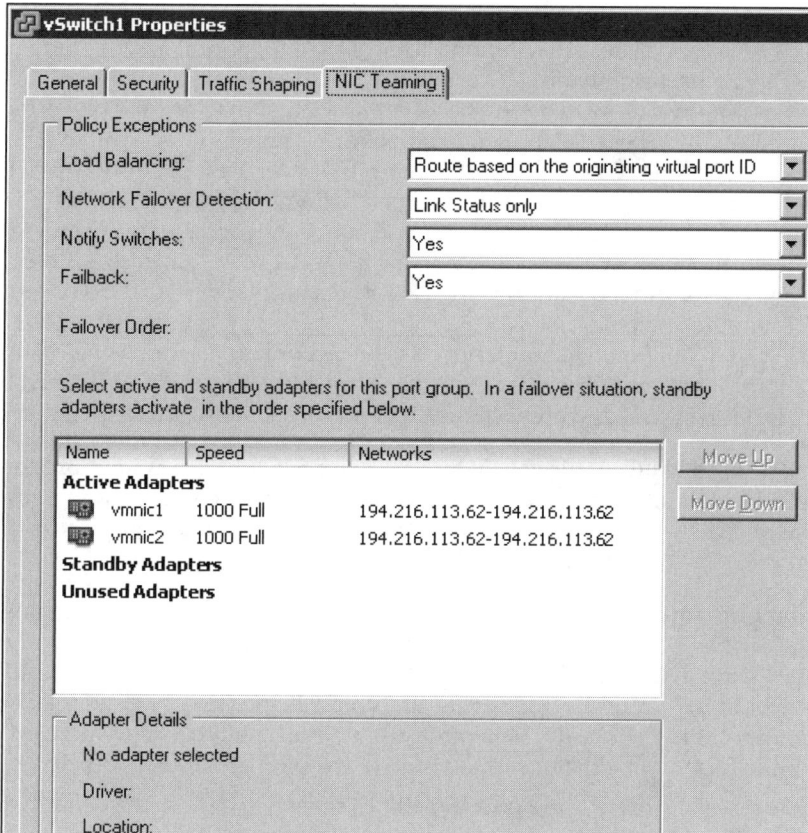

The following sections address the simpler settings on the NIC Teaming tab first, before moving onto to those that are more complex.

Network Failover Detection   The Network Failover Detection option controls how ESX detects a network failure, thus triggering the movement of packets from one adapter to another in a vSwitch with more than one NIC attached to it.

The default of Link Status only is similar to the guest operating systems you run. It will detect a failed NIC, cable, or switch/hub to which the server is directly attached, but cannot detect whether other paths are valid.

In contrast, the Beacon Probing setting is able to see beyond the first uplink to the physical switch by sending a packet between the NICs in the vSwitch. This setting has some issues. A dropped packet, regardless of the reason, can make the system think a NIC is down when it isn't. Beacon Probing is rarely used in production ESX environments, and I don't recommend it.

NOTE *Currently, some Cisco documentation indicates that switching to Beacon Probing in some of its switch architectures has little effect.*

Notify Switches The Yes default setting for the Notify Switches option indicates that when failures occur, a Reverse Address Resolution Protocol (RARP) packet is sent out to physical switches. (ARP is the protocol that relates your MAC address to an IP address.) This updates the lookup tables on physical switches to indicate that virtual machine packets must be sent to different physical NICs, because the original network path is now unavailable.

The default is a good setting, because it ensures that packets will be successfully delivered and reduces the chance of losing packets during a VMotion event. In VMotion, the virtual machine's virtual MAC address remains unchanged; once the virtual machine has been moved from one ESX host to another, the physical MAC addresses have most definitely changed. Additionally, notifications are issued whenever you add or remove a physical NIC from the vSwitch.

For the most part, this setting should not be changed unless you are using Microsoft's NLB within a virtual machine. The default setting is incompatible with NLB when NLB is set to unicast mode. However, if you are using NLB in multicast mode, this is not a problem.

Load Balancing Within a Standard vSwitch Once you create a vSwitch with more than one NIC, you have, by default, created a format of load balancing. On the NIC Teaming tab, you can tweak the network settings considerably. The Load Balancing option gives you four different ways of configuring multiple NICs with a vSwitch:

- **Originating port ID** Basically, this algorithm makes each virtual machine use the next available NIC in the bundle. It's a bit like a round-robin effect. If you had a virtual switch with three NICs mapped to it, this method would cycle among them: VM1 would use vmnic1, VM2 would use vmnic2, and then VM3 would use vmnic3. After that VM4, VM5, and VM6 would use vmnic1, vmnic2, and vmnic3. The effect is a crude form of load balancing on each of the NICs. Sounds good, doesn't it?

  In most cases, the originating port ID setting is just fine, and as the default, it is used in at least 90% of environments. It works out of the box with no special configuration, and puts zero load on the ESX host. Its main merit is its compatibility with all physical switches, and it reduces complexity on the networking side. This is especially true if you decide to split your physical NICs across more than one physical switch to protect your system from physical switch failure. Its downsides are that it lacks awareness of link speeds, how heavily saturated a link is, and the latency on a given uplink. Weighing all these pros and cons, I still recommend leaving the default setting if you want a quiet life.

- **Source MAC address hash** This method uses an algorithm that does a computation via the MAC address, which generates a value or hash that can be used for load-balancing decisions. This is somewhat more intelligent than the originating port ID setting. However, as routers (and some switches) hide the MAC address of the source, it is load balancing with limits. The algorithm simply isn't intelligent enough to work out the best trip for the packet. The problem isn't so much a faulty algorithm, but the limited amount of information it has at its disposal. What is there in a MAC address that tells you anything about performance? The answer is nothing. And ARP is limited to broadcasts only.

NOTE *The source MAC address hash setting was the default in ESX 2.x. I suspect its persistent presence in the ESX product is primarily for backward compatibility.*

- **IP hash**   On paper, academically speaking, the IP hash algorithm is the "Rolls Royce" of load balancing. It uses the source and destination IP address to work out the best trip for the packet to take. It is aware of latency because it is IP-based, and it's also aware when a link is saturated. Additonally, the IP hash is aware of clients that have communicated across a router to the virtual machine running on an ESX host. With all of this information at its disposal, the IP hash is aware of the effect of network traffic on overall performance. The trade-off is a more complex configuration that needs to be maintained, which may not be worth it weighed against the needs of the virtual machines. Have you looked at network utilization on 95% of your servers? They often average below 5MB.

  To use this method, 802.3(AD) Link Aggregation should be enabled on the physical switch. No vendor-specific enhancement from the switch vendor should be enabled, as the virtual switch will not be able to interpret these protocols properly. The success of this method also depends on the quality of the firmware in the switch. Many customers report they end up returning to the originating port ID setting, because they have reverse NIC teaming errors in a multiple-switch environment. With reverse NIC teaming errors, packets leave the ESX host from one NIC, but then try to return via a different NIC. The appearance is of packets leaving the host, but never returning. In other words, there is either no network communication or it is unreliable.

CAUTION   *Like some of the other security settings, the IP hash method is incompatible with Microsoft's NLB in unicast mode. If you have NLB working in multicast mode, there is no problem.*

- **Explicit failover**   In reality, this option allows you to manually configure how multiple cards are used and works in conjunction with the rolling failover setting and the active/standby feature. It provides a stricter way of controlling what happens when NICs fail. If you enable it, you have two other settings: Failback and the Active/Standby Adapter section of the dialog box. As the name suggests, this setting allows you to set so many adapters as active and so many adapters as standby. The active ones can have load-balancing features (as long as there is more than one listed!), and the standby NICs engage only if the active ones fail.

  The Explicit failover setting does not wait for all the active adapters to fail before engaging the standbys. As soon as one active NIC fails, a standby is selected from the order in the list and is used.

- **Failback**   This option controls what happens when a failed NIC becomes available again. If you set it to Yes, when a failed NIC comes onstream again, the active adapter can be used immediately, taking over the role of the standby adapter. If Failback is set to No, the NIC that comes back onstream is not used until another active adapter fails. The assumption here is that if you have lost a NIC, you may begin to distrust its reliability, and setting No here would prevent it from being used again, unless you had another failure. For example, you might use this feature when you have a team of two NICs, one 1000Mbps and the other 100Mbps. You would make the 1000Mbps card active, and put the 100Mbps card on standby. With Failback set to Yes, if the 1000Mbps card failed, it would failover to the 100Mbps card. When the 1000Mbps card was active again, ESX would return to the "home" adapter. (But note that many switch vendors do not support mixed speed/duplex cards in the same NIC team or bond.)

NOTE *Using the Explicit failover setting allows you to have more control over which virtual machines use which NICs, because you now set these parameters on port groups. In the past, these settings were available only on a vSwitch. This was a bit "one size fits all." The downside of this kind of per-port group configuration is that it could get very complicated. You might prefer to follow the KISS (keep it simple, stupid) principle.*

As an example, you could create one vSwitch with three port groups—vlan10, vlan11, and vlan12—each with a separate VLAN ID. However, the vSwitch could have four physical NICs set up with trunk ports. That way, any one of these NICs could be used to send data to the correct VLAN, as long as the correct virtual machines are plugged into the right port groups. You could use the Explicit failover setting to assign their preferred NIC, like this:

- **vlan11 port group**   Active: vmnic1; Standby: vmnic2, vmnic3
- **vlan12 port group**   Active: vmnic2; Standby: vmnic1, vmnic3
- **vlan13 port group**   Active: vmnic3; Standby: vmnic1, vmnic2

The following example shows this particular configuration. Here, I've inherited the defaults from the virtual switch (for the Load Balancing, Network Failover Detection, and Notify Switches settings), but I've created an exception to those rules using the "Override vSwitch failover order" option.

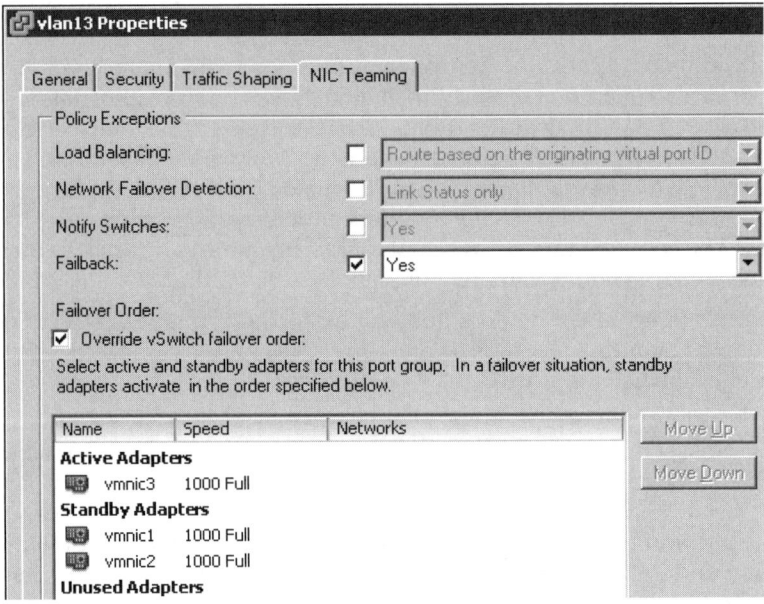

Under normal operations, the vlan13 port group would prefer to use vmnic3. This means that a lot of network activity within the vlan11 or vlan12 port groups would have no impact, as they prefer to use vmnic1 and vmnic2, respectively. I get excellent redundancy, because three NICs could possibly be used at any one time. Failover has been set to Yes, so if vmnic3 went offline and then came back onstream again, I would get the separation of network traffic. This configuration also allows for specific security and traffic shaping settings to be applied to accounts (and the virtual machines configured to use it), without it affecting the vlan11 and vlan12 port groups.

Using a Master vSwitch

One example of vSwitch design is a single configuration that uses just one virtual switch for all the networking tasks of an ESX host. This is in marked contrast to the approach of using a single switch for each task. The main advantage of this "über" vSwitch approach is that it offers fault tolerance to every part of the ESX host: the management network, virtual machine network, VMkernel storage network (for iSCSI and NAS), and VMotion network. The downsides of the configuration is that it becomes increasingly harder to interpret the configuration (unless you make it your organization's standard), and it becomes less easy to predict and control where the network traffic will travel unless you use the active/standby options available through the properties of a port group.

In the über-vSwitch approach, you have a single vSwitch with multiple port groups using the VLAN tagging method to keep the traffic on different VLANs. The following example illustrates this configuration.

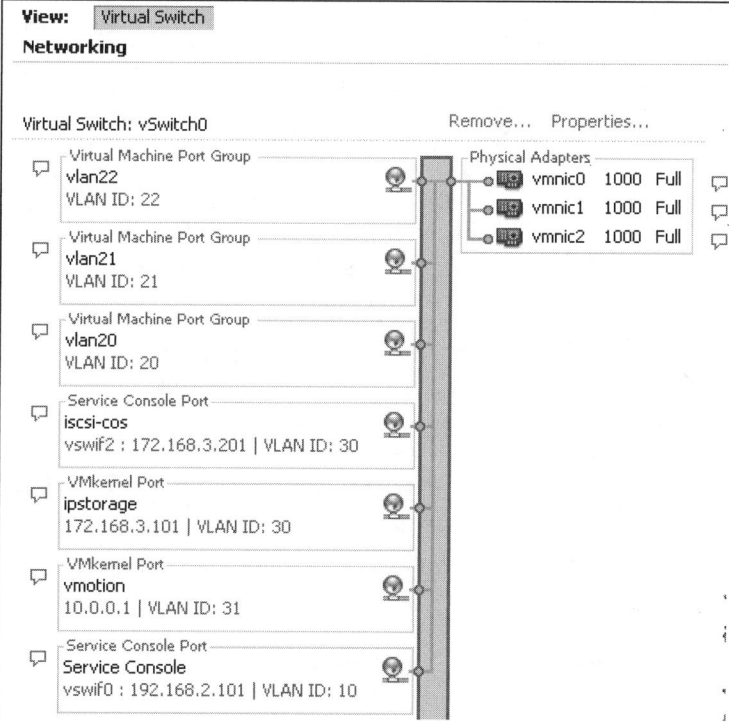

Creating Standby vSwitches

It is possible to configure a vSwitch with multiple NICs so that some of the NICs are active and some are standby. The idea behind this is to guarantee a degree of quality of service. So, if you lost one NIC, you could replace it with the same level of bandwidth. Additionally, it allows you to control the direction that network traffic will take under normal operations, as the preference will always be the active adapter.

For this configuration, after you set some of the NICs on the vSwitch to be active and others to be standby, you set the Load Balancing setting on the NIC Teaming tab to "Use explicit failover order."

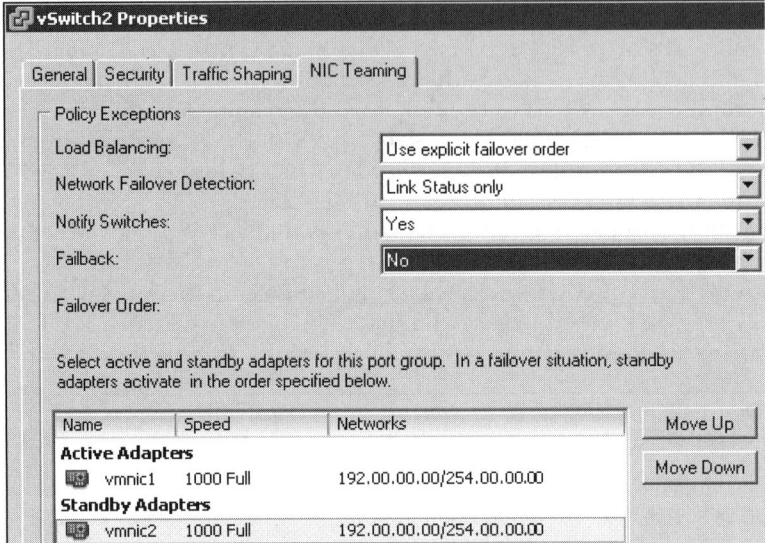

After clicking OK, the vSphere Client will refresh and indicate which NIC is active and which is standby. Notice how the Failback option is set to No. This is because as both NICs are of the same link speed, I don't care which one is in use; in fact, I would prefer to use the one that has the best uptime.

The following examples show this configuration when the vmnic1 is functioning and when failover has occurred because it has malfunctioned, respectively.

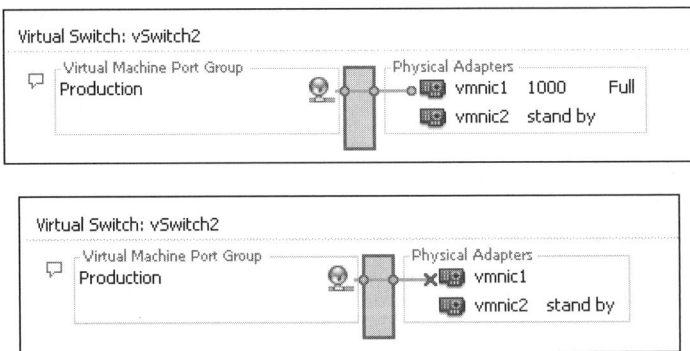

As illustrated, it is very easy to see the settings if active and standby NICs are configured at the vSwitch level. It is less clear in the vSphere Client if you enable active and standby at the port group level. By clicking the small blue speech bubble icon next to each port group, you can view each setting.

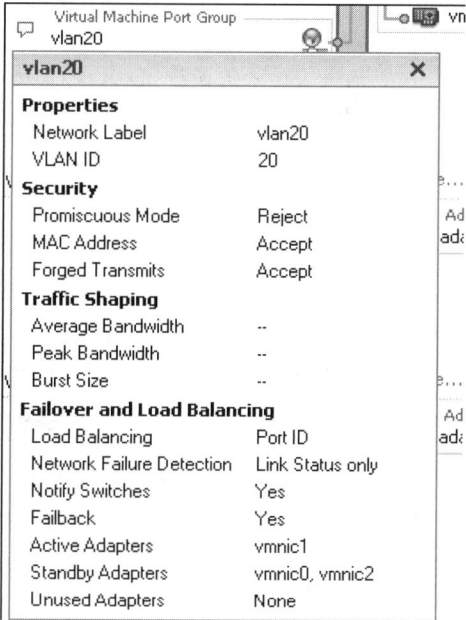

So, you don't need to navigate through layers of dialog boxes, properties options, and edit options to view your settings.

Managing Service Console Networking

This section describes configuration settings related specifically to the Service Console. I'll explain how to add a backup Service Console connection and how to modify the original IP settings configured during the installation.

Creating a Backup Port Group for the Service Console

Up until ESX 4.x, there has always been a single point of failure on the ESX host: the Service Console network. If the single NIC (vmnic0) on vSwitch0 failed, we would have no management over the ESX host except by its ILO card. Remember that if our virtual machines were on a different vSwitch configured with many virtual NICs, they would remain unaffected.

In ESX 4.x, the networking architecture treats the Service Console as if it were just another virtual machine connected to a virtual switch. This default switch is called vSwitch0. (Incidentally, the default number of ports on the vSwitch is just 24, rather than 56.) These Service Console ports have a special name: vswif, which stands for virtual switch interface. They are serialized as you create them, with the first vswif0, the second vswif1, and so on.

If you have spare network adapters, it's very easy to protect the Service Console network by adding another vSwitch within the Service Console port group or by adding another Service Console port group to an existing vSwitch.

In Chapter 6, you will learn that a second Service Console network is often required to configure the iSCSI software adapter. Additionally, in Chapter 15, you will learn that this backup Service Console network can mitigate an unwanted event called the "split-brain" phenomena in VMware HA.

It's quite common to put this second Service Console connection on the VMotion vSwitch, as this is one that all ESX hosts are plugged into, and this is the approach taken in the following steps. This is safe because the VMotion switch is not typically the primary network for managing virtual machines, and VMotion is not an event that happens very frequently.

Follow these steps to create a backup port group for the Service Console:

1. In the vSphere Client, select the Configuration tab.

2. In the Hardware pane, select Networking.

3. Click the Properties link next to the VMotion vSwitch.

4. Click the Add button to add another port group to the vSwitch.

5. Select Service Console. As you already have a Service Console port, the system names this Service Console 2. In this example, I renamed the port group calling it the Backup Service Console Connection. Click Next.

6. Enter the IP settings appropriate for your network infrastructure. Click Next.

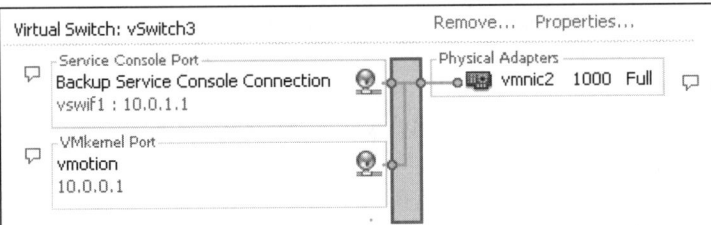

It's a good idea to confirm you can connect to this new port with ping/PuTTY and by pointing the vSphere Client to this IP address/name.

As another way of protecting the Service Console network, try just adding another NIC vSwitch. By doing so, you will create a bond for the Service Console. However, most people would agree this is a waste of bandwidth. If you have spare NICs, you should allocate them to the virtual machines. After all, they are the ones that require bandwidth and fault tolerance.

Adding a second NIC is also a safer procedure than switching the NIC on the Service Console switch. For example, if you add the second NIC (100Mbps) and remove the first NIC (1000Mbps), you shouldn't lose connectivity to the Service Console.

Changing the Service Console Network Settings

One reason to change your Service Console's settings is to change your IP address, subnet mask, or default gateway. One of the dangers is if you make a mistake, it's a bit like sitting on a tree branch with a saw and sawing your way through the very branch that is holding you there!

If you are going to modify the primary connection for the Service Console, this could cause a disconnection. If this change goes horribly wrong, it is not the end of the world—you will be able to use the backup Service Console network connection. If you don't have a backup connection, you will receive a warning.

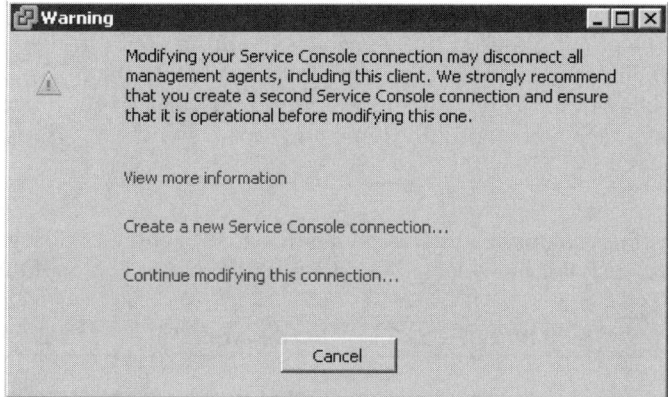

The safest method is to connect your backup Service Console 2 network to the ESX host and then change Service Console properties. This way, you will not be disconnected in the process of changing the IP address. If you do make a mistake, you still have your backup connection in place. Here are the steps:

1. Close your vSphere Client.
2. Open the vSphere Client using the backup Service Console IP address of the ESX host.
3. Select the Configuration tab.
4. In the Hardware pane, select Networking.
5. Select Properties of vSwitch0 with the port group name of Service Console.
6. In the dialog box, select the port group of the Service Console, and then click Edit.
7. In the Service Console Properties dialog box, you can change your IP settings.

Troubleshooting Service Console Networking

As discussed in Chapter 1, during ESX installation, you select the NIC used for the Service Console and also configure its IP settings. Occasionally, people get this wrong and select entirely wrong NIC and IP values. When this happens you have three options:

- Reinstall and try again.
- Walk to the server room and reroute the network cables to the correct switch.
- Connect via the ILO, and use command-line tools to correct your mistakes.

As you might gather, using command-line tools to fix the problem is the recommended method.

CAUTION *Remember that the command line is case-sensitive.*

Correcting Your NIC Selection

If you chose the wrong NIC during installation, you can rectify this problem by gradually adding in NICs while pinging the Service Console's IP address (assuming that the IP settings are correct). I normally use `ping -t` to do this. As I add the NICs, I can judge by whether I get a reply as an indication that I have found the correct NIC. First, I type the command that lists my vSwitch configuration using the `-l` switch.

```
esxcfg-vswitch -l
```

In this example, there is one vSwitch, which is vSwitch0, with one port group called Service Console. The installer has selected, by default, the first NIC it could find: vmnic0.

Switch Name	Num Port	Used Ports	Uplink
vSwitch0	32	3	vmnic0

NOTE *You might notice that the CLI often shows different values than what you see in the vSphere Client. For example, in the vSphere Client, vSwitch0 may be shown to have 24 ports, whereas the Service Console reports 32. In the CLI, the number is showing* all *the ports on the vSwitch, including the eight ports that are normally reserved by the VMkernel.*

If you want see which NICs are available, including their settings such as vmnic name, PCI bus details, driver, link speed, duplex, and vendor make and model, you can use this command:

```
esxcfg-nics -l
```

To link another NIC to the switch, use the `-L` switch:

```
esxcfg-vswitch -L vmnic1 vSwitch0
```

I keep on doing this until I have a response. Once I have worked out, by a process of elimination, the correct NIC, I unlink the NICs that were patched to vSwitch0/vswif0 using the `-U` switch:

```
esxcfg-vswitch -U vmnic0 vSwitch0
```

Using the `esxcfg-vswitch -l`, `-L`, and `-U` commands, you can quickly change the preferred NIC for vSwitch0 and be up and running with the vSphere Client quickly.

Correcting IP Settings

Occasionally, people type the wrong IP address or subnet mask during ESX installation. And many people don't notice that the ESX installer does some work for you by automatically setting the default gateway based on the IP address and subnet mask.

If you set 192.168.3.101 and 255.255.255.0 as your IP address and subnet mask, respectively, the installer will fill in 192.168.3.254 as your default gateway and 192.168.3.1 as your primary DNS server.

Fortunately, if you have ILO or physical access to the server, these settings are very easy to correct, either with `esxcfg` command-line tools or with a text editor to modify the configuration files. Again, you could use `ping -t` against the IP address of the Service Console to confirm you get valid responses.

To view your current IP address and subnet mask, you can use the `-l` switch on the `esxcfg-vswif` command, like so:

```
esxcfg-vswif -l
```

To change them, you can use the command with `-i` and `-n` switches. You also need to indicate which vswif interface you are changing (as you know, you can have more than one for backup purposes).

```
esxcfg-vswif vswif0 -i 192.168.3.104 -n 255.255.255.0
```

If your problems reside with your default gateway or you incorrectly set the DNS settings, these can be fixed with a text editor, such as vi or nano. Linux users prefer to use vi, as it is on every single Linux distribution; nano exists only on Red Hat Linux. If you do use nano, remember to use the `-w` switch, which switches off the word-wrap feature (which could corrupt the file if you're not careful).

To correct your default gateway, you need to edit the network file. Here's how to do this with nano:

```
nano -w /etc/sysconfig/network
```

Modify your default gateway. Then press CTRL+X to exit nano, type **Y** to accept changes, and press ENTER to overwrite the original file. To make this change take effect, you need to restart the networking for the Service Console with Red Hat Linux's `service` command (the `service` command is not available on all Linux distributions, but it is available within the ESX Service Console).

```
service network restart
```

If your problems reside with the DNS settings, you can edit these with the following command:

```
nano -w /etc/resolv.conf
```

Generally, if you have basic connectivity to the Service Console, many of these settings can be altered through the vSphere Client. However, knowing how to use the `esxcfg` commands will help in extreme cases where you simply cannot connect to your ESX host with the vSphere Client.

To change your default gateway, ESX host name, or DNS settings using the vSphere Client, navigate to the Configuration tab, then the Software pane. Select DNS and Routing and choose Properties. One of the downsides of using the GUI is that for some operations, you will need to reboot the ESX host for changes to take effect.

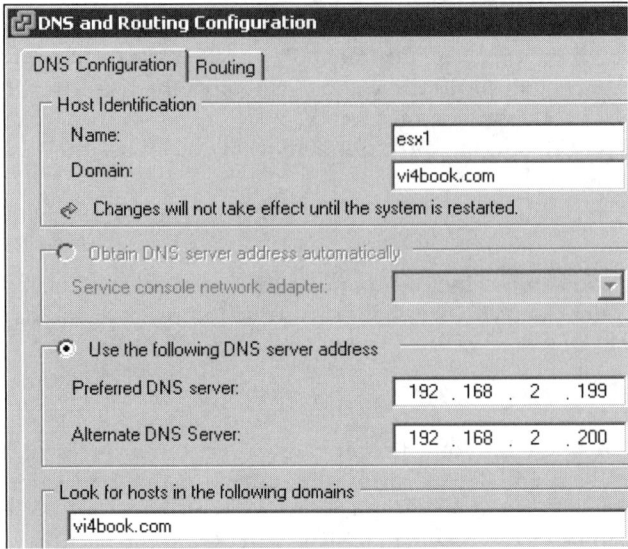

Advanced Switch Settings

This section discusses a couple switch configurations that may be useful for some networks: enabling support for the Cisco Discovery Protocol (CDP) and changing the maximum transmission unit (MTU) size.

Configuring the Cisco Discovery Protocol

CDP allows for sharing of both physical and virtual switch configurations. Clearly, this is of use to you only if your switch supports CDP. Although CDP may not actually assist in troubleshooting complex network problems, additional information is always handy, especially when you do not manage the underlying physical switch layer.

In a standard vSwitch, you must use command-line tools to configure CDP. The configuration allows for four modes:

- The listen mode allows a vSphere Client to display CDP data of the physical switch. This is the default.
- The advertise mode allows the ESX host to publish vSwitch data to the Cisco administrator.
- The both mode is a combination of Listen and Advertise.
- When CDP is set to disabled, no inbound or outbound CDP communication is allowed.

If you want to use CDP, you will need to enable it on each and every standard vSwitch. (It is much easier to configure with the new type of virtual switch, which is covered in the next chapter.)

To configure CDP, open a SSH session, and switch to root. Type the following command to retrieve a list of your vSwitches:

```
esxcfg-vswitch -l
```

```
Switch Name       Num Ports    Used Ports   Configured Ports   MTU     Uplink
vSwitch0          64           3            64                 1500    vmnic0

  PortGroup Name           VLAN ID   Used Ports   Uplinks
  Service Console          0         1            vmnic0
```

To view your current CDP settings, use the following command:

```
esxcfg-vswitch -b vSwitch0
```

This should return the value `Listen` if you have not made any changes.

If you wish to make the vSwitch bidirectional to both listen for physical vSwitches CDP data and also advertise its own CDP information, issue the following command:

```
esxcfg-vswitch -B both vSwitch0
```

As I've noted earlier, CLI commands are case-sensitive. In this case, a lowercase b retrieves the current configuration, and an uppercase B sets a new configuration.

Once CDP is enabled, at the Cisco switch, you can use this Cisco command:

```
show cdp neighbors
```

For the ESX host, you can use the following command to display CDP data:

```
esxcfg-info | more +/CDP\ Summary
```

From the vSphere Client, click the small information icon that appears on the right side of every switch to see switch information.

Configuring the Maximum Transmission Unit Size

As you know, networking isn't for free, and both Ethernet data and IP data significantly encroach on the amount of true data throughput. The MTU value is the size of the largest datagram that can be placed on a network segment. The larger the MTU value proportionally, the more data transmitted as a ratio of the overhead of the network layer. The more common term for large MTU datagrams is *jumbo frames*, and VMware has been supporting them since VI3.5

Cisco Discovery Protocol

Properties

Version	2
Timeout	0
Time to live	141
Samples	836
Device ID	esx2.vi4book.com
Address	0.0.0.0
Port ID	vmnic0
Software Version	Releasebuild-140815
Hardware Platform	VMware ESX
IP Prefix	0.0.0.0
IP Prefix Length	0
VLAN	0
Full Duplex	true
MTU	1500
System Name	esx2.vi4book.com
System Oid	
Management Address	0.0.0.0
Location	

CDP Device Capability

Router	false
Transparent Bridge	false
Source Route Bridge	false
Network Switch	true
Host	false
IGMP Enabled	false

Increasing the MTU value can have significant performance improvements, especially for those systems that experience high network throughput. The MTU value on a standard vSwitch can be change with the command utility esxcfg-vswitch –m. A good example is if you are using IP storage such as iSCSI/NAS-based systems. Increasing the MTU value *might* improve performance for virtual machines, but much depends on what level of I/O they generate. For example, systems like DNS and Active Directory are not especially bandwidth-intensive and they rarely saturate network interfaces. Indeed, the doubling up of gigabit interfaces on a standard vSwitch often is more for fault tolerance than it is to increase bandwidth, because most people find they are not using those links at anything near than 20% to 30% of their capacity.

Additionally, care must be taken in setting the MTU value for two main reasons:

- Large packets can get choked when they traverse a slow link for some time. This will actually increase lag and latency.

- Fragmentation of large MTU packets can occur. When a system configured with a 9000 MTU communicates unexpectedly with a 1500 MTU system, the 1500 MTU system will need to break up each packet into six separate packets (9000/1500). This can cause unexpected network connectivity problems.

Arbitrarily changing the MTU value on physical switches and virtual switches can cause difficult-to-troubleshoot network connectivity problems. I know this from personal experience, which I'll recount here as an example of how sudden, uncoordinated, untested, and unannounced changes can cause unintended consequences.

One weekend, I couldn't gain access to my online banking. I tried three times to log in, forgetting that on the third attempt, my bank automatically locks the account. After locking myself out, I realized that something was wrong. I began to see a pattern emerging. If any web site was accessed with http:// and demanded an HTTP style of username and password, I could log in. But if I visited a web site with https://, I was bounced out. All the usual suspects were discounted; it wasn't the web browser, the date on the machine, or the router. At this point, I submitted a query to my Internet Service Provider (ISP). Then the truth emerged. Without informing its customers, over the weekend, my ISP reconfigured its Cisco network to use a much large MTU value, increasing it from 1500 to 9000. My old router was configured for 1500. Unfortunately, reconfiguring my router to take the higher MTU value did not fix the problem. In the end, my ISP solved the problem by merely putting me on its older 1500 MTU network.

Enabling IPv6 Support

As you probably know, IPv4 is rapidly running out of addresses, and it is due to be replaced by IPv6, which has much bigger pool of addresses. Although firewalls, proxy servers, and NAT have extended the lifetime of IPv4 by allowing multiple clients to use a valid IP for the Internet, this approach has in turn increased the likelihood of bottlenecks and barriers to some types of communication. Additionally, as more and more devices other than servers and PCs are connected to the network, we will need a more robust system of addressing than IPv4 and DHCP currently allow. Although IPv4 has been retrofitted to improve its security and quality of service (QoS), which were never in the design of TCP/IP, a protocol upgrade is inevitable.

Support for IPv6 has been in existence for number of years. For example, you might be surprised to know that Windows NT 4 DNS included an AAAA record for storing IPv6 addresses. We are now moving rapidly to the point where servers and workstations support both IPv4 and IPv6 addresses.

The IPv6 address space is so huge that everyone should be able to get a public IP address for every device they will ever own. Theoretically, it shouldn't be necessary to have private IPv6 addresses like the 192.168.x.x and 10.x.x.x addresses in IPv4. Nonetheless, the Internet societies have allocated a block of IPv6 addresses for internal use, and I will be using that range throughout this section to avoid employing genuine routable Internet IPv6 addresses.

IPv6 addresses can be configured either statically or with DHCP, and routers can intercede to move packets from an IPv4 network to an IPv6 network.

NOTE *If you just want to give your virtual machines IPv6 addresses, you do not need to change the ESX host configuration whatsoever. Enabling IPv6 support in ESX 4.x allows you to use an IPv6 address for the Service Console management network and for the VMkernel; for example, to give the ESX host access to an IPv6-enabled NAS or iSCSI system.*

Introduction to IPv6 Addressing

IPv4 has a 32-bit address space, which allows for 2^{32}, or 4,294,967,296, possible addresses. IPv6 is a 128-bit address space that allows for 2^{128}, or 340, 282, 366, 920, 938, 463, 463, 374, 607, 431, 768, 211, 456, possible IP addresses.

This is what an IPv6 address looks like:

```
3ffe:1900:4545:3:200:f8ff:fe21:67cf
```

The first time you see an IPv6 address, a shudder of fear might ripple down your spine. As you can see, these addresses are very different from the familiar IPv4 addresses. However, at the heart of IPv6 is the same numbering system as IPv4: binary.

IPv4 uses up to 32 ones and zeros to make up the address. IPv6 uses 128 ones and zeros to make up the address. In IPv4, the 32 bits are broken up into four blocks separated by a period. IPv6 addresses are 128 bits long, written in hexadecimal, and separated by colons. The colon separates the 128 bits into a series of eight 16-bit fields (8 × 16 = 128), just like the period used in IPv4. The leading zeros can be omitted in each field, as in the preceding sample address, where the field :0003: is written as :3: and 0200: is written as :200.

If a field is not in use (all zeros), a double colon (::) can be used once in the address to replace that fields. This is sometime referred to as *zero compression*. The preceding IPv6 address when converted from hexadecimal into binary looks like this:

```
1111111111110:1100100000000:100010101000101:11:1000000000:1111100011111111
: 1111111000100001:110011111001111
```

With IPv6 addresses, the use of subnet masks to separate the network ID and host ID is no longer required. Instead, we use the Classless Inter-Domain Routing (CIDR) notation, as follows:

```
3ffe:1900:4545:3:200:f8ff:fe21:67cf/64
```

This indicates that the first 64 bits of the IPv6 address are the network ID, or "prefix," and the remaining 64 bits are for allocating to hosts within that network. Indeed, the whole notion of Class A, Class B, and Class C addresses that dominated the era of IPv4 does not apply in IPv6. With IPv6, there are merely addresses and the CIDR notation. In essence though, the principles remain. So, in the preceding IPv6 address, the first 64 bits represent the subnet, and the remaining bits are the unique identifier for the NIC itself.

Additionally, while the concept of unicast and multicast still exist, there is no concept of broadcast in IPv6. All broadcast addresses are treated as multicast addresses instead. There is, however, a concept of *anycast*, which represents the nearest (from a routing perspective) IP address in a given range.

IPv6 addresses are truly hierarchical, because the first four blocks of 16 bits represent a discrete network path, with each block leading closer and closer to the destination of a specific IP-enabled device. As such, they include not just if a node is on the Internet or private, but also the location of the device. You can consider the IPv6 address as a very qualified path statement that uniquely describes the location of all IPv6 devices on the network.

All unicast addresses in IPv6 can be broken down into the following six types (which are present in the IPv6 IP address in the eight blocks of 16 bits):

- **Global**   Routable and reachable on the IPv6 Internet.
- **Link-local**   Used with node-to-node communications, without a router.
- **Site-local**   Removed in RFC 3879, but still in use in existing implementations.
- **Unique-local**   Unique address for each location in a business.
- **Special addresses**   Loopback addresses and no IPv6 addresses represented by zeros.
- **Transition addresses**   Allow for transition from IPv4 to IPv6 addresses.

Within an IPv6 address, the first 64 bits of each of the eight blocks are divided as follows:

- The first 3 bits are the format prefix (FP).
- The next 13 bits are the top-level aggregation identifier (TLA ID).
- The next 8 bits are reserved for future use.
- The following 24 bits are the next-level aggregation identifier (NLA ID).
- The final 16 bits are the site-level aggregation identifier (SLA ID).

The remaining 64 bits are the interface ID.

For simplicity, we can break down these identifiers into three types: a prefix, a globally unique ID, and subnet ID. The prefix ID and global ID together represent your entire organization, and the subnet ID represents all of your networks. The Internet societies have allocated a prefix ID for internal use, which is akin to the older Class A (10.), Class B (172.), and Class C (192.) addresses, which lie in the fd: range.

If you intend to roll out IPv6, it is recommended that you claim a public prefix and global ID for your organization, which is just like registering your Internet .com domain with the Internet societies. For testing purposes, you can use the fd: prefix. Many web sites will generate a valid pool of IPv6 addresses. For the examples in this section, I used the Simple DNS Plus web site (http://www.simpledns.com/private-ipv6.aspx) to generate a block of valid IPv6 addresses from the fd: range.

Private IPv6 address range

Here is a unique private IPv6 address range generated just for you (refresh page to get another one):

Prefix/L: **fd**
Global ID: **597417adc4**
Subnet ID: **b36e**
Combined/CID: **fd59:7417:adc4:b36e::/64**
IPv6 addresses: **fd59:7417:adc4:b36e:xxxx:xxxx:xxxx:xxxx**

If you have multiple locations/sites/networks, you should assign each one a different "Subnet ID", but use the same "Global" ID for

This gave me a globally unique ID of fd59:7417:adc4, with a subnet of b36e. Within that subnet, I have four blocks of 16-bit addresses—64 bits per subnet to allocate to my computers. To make my life simpler, I made each of the four blocks hold the equivalent of an IPv4 address. This is my convention:

- IPv4: 192.168.2.201

- IPv4: fd59:7417:adc4:b36e:0**192**:0**168**:000**2**:0**201**

Tip *You can find many resources for learning about the details of IPv6. One I heartily recommend is the Microsoft TechNet article "IPv6 Transition Technologies," located at http://technet.microsoft .com/en-us/library/bb726951.aspx.*

Transitioning to IPv6

Once I got started on this subject, I became very interested in getting my Windows and VMware environment working on IPv6. (Technically, this has absolutely nothing to do with VMware and virtualization in general.)

The transition to IPv6 can be achieved by a number of different strategies—and yes, you've guessed it—each one has its own advantages and disadvantages.

One technique is to run IPv4 and IPv6 side by side. Most Windows systems actually support IPv4 and IPv6, so as long as your routers can route IPv6 packets, you're good to go. The downside of this is that you have doubled the number of IP addresses you must manage. Some care needs to be taken in the way these protocols are bound to a single network adapter. When you have two protocols, you will need to decide which one gets used and when. This dual-protocol configuration will work quite well for clients, as a DHCP server in Windows 2008 can serve both IPv4 and IPv6 addresses to Windows Vista and Windows 7 clients.

(continued)

Another approach is to create a tunnel via a gateway from IPv4 to IPv6. This allows your IPv4 network to remain unchanged, and means that for modern operating systems, you don't need to worry about configuring both IPv4 and IPv6. In my experience, when moving from one protocol (such as Novell's IPX/SPX) to another (such as TCP/IP), protocol gateways or tunnels can become both single points of failure and bottlenecks. There are many ways to get IPv4 to IPv6 tunnels working, including through an IPv4/IPv6 enabled hardware router, Intra-Site Automatic Tunnel Addressing Protocol (ISATAP), 6to4, and a project called Teredo (which uses a NAT process).

It is possible with Windows to run an entirely pure IPv6 environment, but with caveats. The older Windows operating systems are significantly harder to configure. Frequently, the only way to set a valid IPv6 address is by using command-line tools.

Additionally, although Windows 2003 supports IPv6, and some services have been updated to listen for inbound IPv6 requests, you may be (un)surprised to hear that while services like DNS on Windows 2003 are supported, the Active Directory service is not. This means that if you want to configure a Windows Vista or Windows 7 system to a pure IPv6 environment, it could never be a member of a Windows 2003 Active Directory environment. If this is of concern to you, then consult the Microsoft TechNet article "Exploring IPv6," at http://technet.microsoft.com/en-us/library/cc776103.aspx, which outlines what is and is not supported with Window 2003 IPv6.

Enabling IPv6 Support in Windows 2003 with DNS

To enable IPv6 support in Windows 2003, you need to install the protocol, and then configure it with the Microsoft `netsh` command (with Windows 2003, you are able to set a IPv6 address only from the command line). If Windows 2003 is running DNS, then you must use the dnscmd utility to tell the DNS service to listen for inbound IPv6 DNS queries.

First, in the Local Area Connection Properties dialog box, click the Install button, select Protocol, and select Microsoft TCP/IP Version 6.

Next, open a command prompt and use `netsh` commands to configure IPv6. The following are examples of setting the IP, default gateway, and DNS values for a statically configured host:

```
netsh interface ipv6 set privacy disabled
netsh interface ipv6 add address interface="Local Area Connection"
address=fd59:7417:adc4:b36e:0192:0168:0002:0160 store=persistent
netsh interface ipv6 add dns interface="Local Area Connection"
address=fd59:7417:adc4:b36e:0192:0168:0002:0160
```

Now that the IPv6 address is configured, you will need the dnscmd.exe utilty to inform DSN that it should listen for IPv6 queries. The dnscmd utility can be found in the /support/tools/support.cab on the Windows CD. Type the following command:

```
dnscmd /config /enableIPv6  1
```

Finally, restart the DNS service to make this take effect, as follows:

```
net stop dns
net start dns
```

You might wish to issue the command `ipconfig /flushdns`, and then check in DNS to see that an AAAA record is created. The AAAA record is used to store IPv6 addresses for host name resolution, so that when a client queries the DNS server, an IPv6 address is returned.

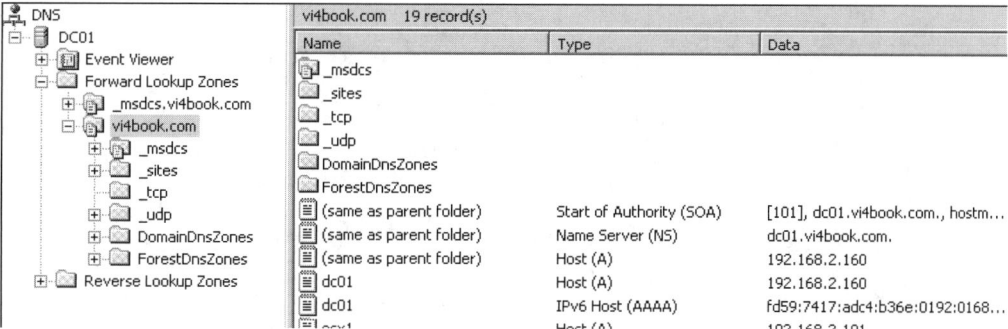

You can see your complete IPv6 configuration with the `netsh` command.

```
Interface 5: Local Area Connection

Addr Type   DAD State   Valid Life   Pref. Life   Address
----------  ----------  -----------  -----------  -------
Manual      Preferred     infinite     infinite   fd59:7417:adc4:b36e:192:168:3:16
2
Link        Preferred     infinite     infinite   fe80::20c:29ff:fee9:a7be

Interface 4: Teredo Tunneling Pseudo-Interface

Addr Type   DAD State   Valid Life   Pref. Life   Address
----------  ----------  -----------  -----------  -------
Link        Preferred     infinite     infinite   fe80::ffff:ffff:fffd

Interface 2: Automatic Tunneling Pseudo-Interface

Addr Type   DAD State   Valid Life   Pref. Life   Address
----------  ----------  -----------  -----------  -------
Link        Preferred     infinite     infinite   fe80::5efe:192.168.3.162

Interface 1: Loopback Pseudo-Interface

Addr Type   DAD State   Valid Life   Pref. Life   Address
----------  ----------  -----------  -----------  -------
Loopback    Preferred     infinite     infinite   ::1
Link        Preferred     infinite     infinite   fe80::1
```

Notice that the fe80 addresses are all auto-generated addresses associated with tunneling or routing methods of handling IPv6/IPv4 communications, such as using the Teredo Tunneling Pseudo-Interface.

Enabling IPv6 Support in Windows 2008 with an IPv6 DHCP Server

For DHCP to work in Windows 2008, you will need *both* static IPv4 and IPv6 addresses on the local area connection.

First, from the Local Area Connection Properties dialog box, select Internet Protocol Version 6 (TCP/IPv6), and then select Properties. Complete the dialog box as fits your IPv6 scheme.

In the following example, I'm using the IP range provided to me from the Simple DNS web site (http://www.simpledns.com/private-ipv6.aspx).

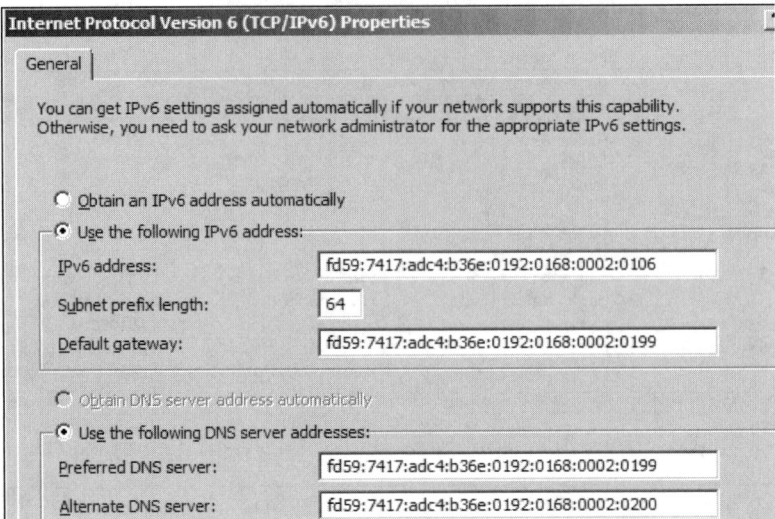

Next, configure an IPv6 DHCP Server on the Windows 2008 server as follows:

1. From Administration Tools, select Server Manager.
2. Select Roles and click the Add Roles button. Click Next.
3. Select the role of DHCP server, and then click Next.
4. Select the default NIC that will service the DHCP requests.
5. Set your DNS domain name and IP addresses for your DNS server(s).

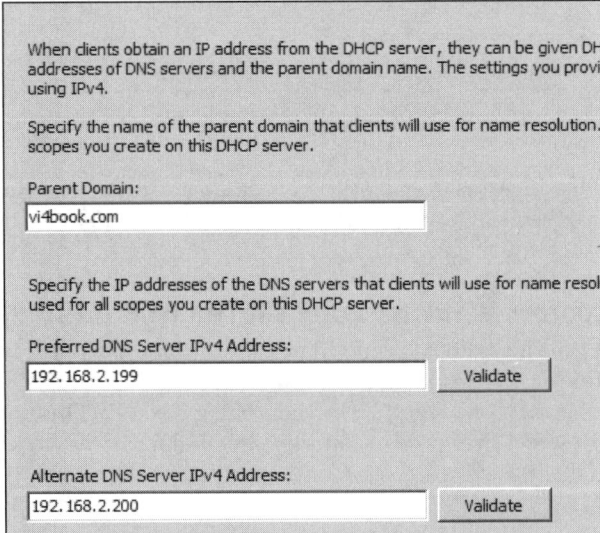

6. Specify the IP start and end range for the IPv4 scope, setting the default gateway and lease duration periods.

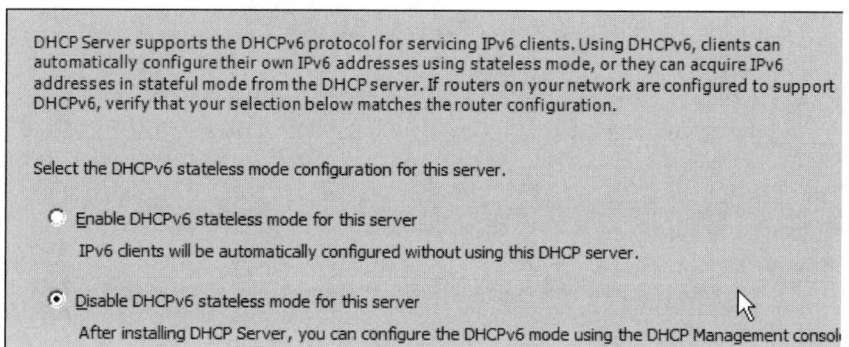

7. Choose the option to disable stateless mode for this server.

NOTE *In stateless mode, clients use DHCP only to obtain network configuration parameters other than an IPv6 address. In this scenario, clients configure an IPv6 address through a non-DHCP based mechanism (such as IPv6 prefixes included in router advertisements). In stateful mode, DHCP clients acquire both the IPv6 address, as well as other network configuration parameters through DHCPv6.*

8. Click Finish.
9. From the Administration Tools, open the DHCP Management Console.

10. Right-click the IPv6 node and choose New Scope.

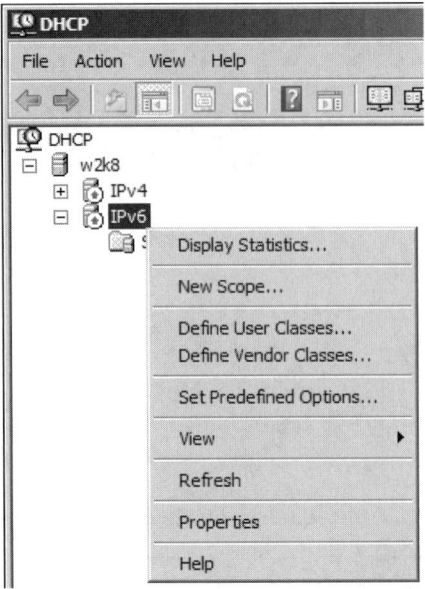

11. Type in a name for the scope (VI4BOOK Network in this example).

12. Type in your IPv6 prefix, using a syntax of 0:0:0:0 to represent the bits used for the host ID.

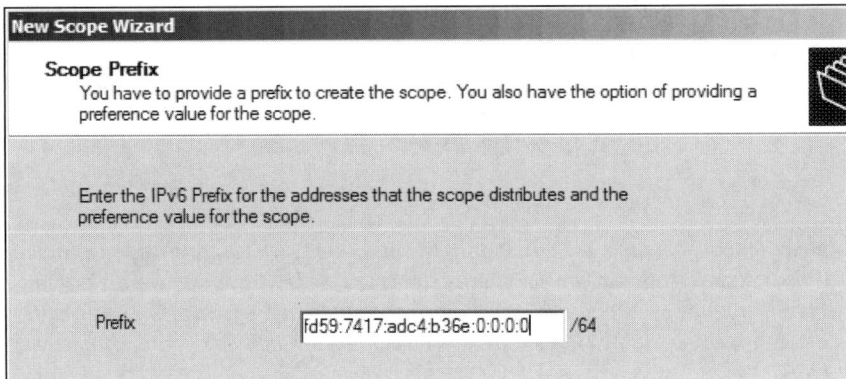

13. Add exclusions to the range, if necessary.

14. Set the lease duration.

15. Accept that the scope will be activated by default.

16. Click Finish.

Enabling IPv6 Support in vCenter

Enabling IPv6 within vCenter is just a matter of setting a valid IPv6 address if you are running on Windows 2008, or installing and configuring IPv6 if you are running on Windows 2003, as described in the previous sections. After configuring IPv6 for the first time, be sure to restart the vCenter services. In practice, because there are so many services that run on vCenter, it's sometimes easier to claim a maintenance window and carry out one of the Windows three-fingered salutes to reboot the system.

On the surface, merely being able to communicate to vCenter with IPv6 will give a workable environment. This is because an IPv6-enabled vCenter can also have a IPv4 configuration. Effectively, what happens is that the IPv6 client connects to vCenter on IPv6, which in turn communicates with the ESX host using its IPv4 address.

However, there are some actions for which the vSphere Client connects directly to an ESX host, even when it is loaded against a vCenter environment. A case in point is the redirection of mouse, keyboards, and screen (mks) that is delivered by the Remote Console feature, which allows you to interact with a virtual machine. The Remote Console feature requires name resolution, and in the case of a pure IPv6-only client, needs a valid AAAA record in DNS with an ESX host with a valid IPv6 address. One way of emulating a pure IPv6 client (a client that has no IPv4 awareness) is simply to disable the protocol in Windows Vista or Windows 7. The following two examples illustrate this point.

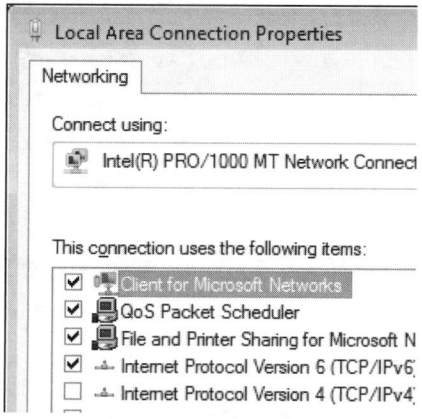

Enabling IPv6 Support on ESX

Enabling IPv6 support on ESX is easy, but you must reboot the ESX host in order for it to take effect. If you are using ESXi, you can enable IPv6 support at the host.

Follow these steps to enable IPv6 support on ESX:

1. In the vSphere Client, select your ESX host.

2. Select the Configuration tab.

3. In the Hardware pane, select Networking.

4. Select the Properties link in the top-right corner.

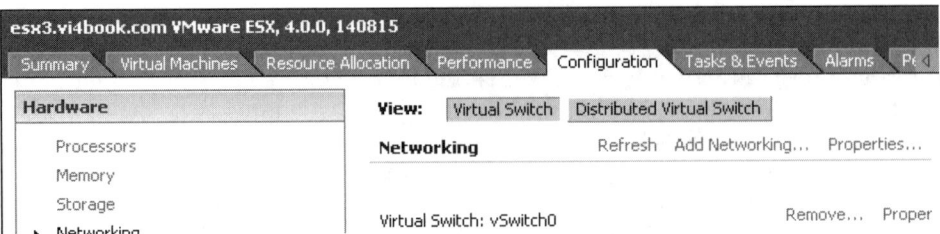

5. Select the option "Enable IPv6 support on this host."

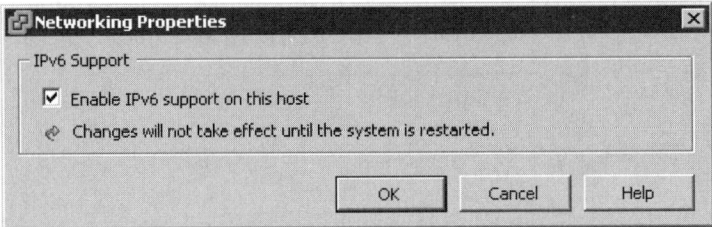

6. Set the IPv6 address for the VMkernel.

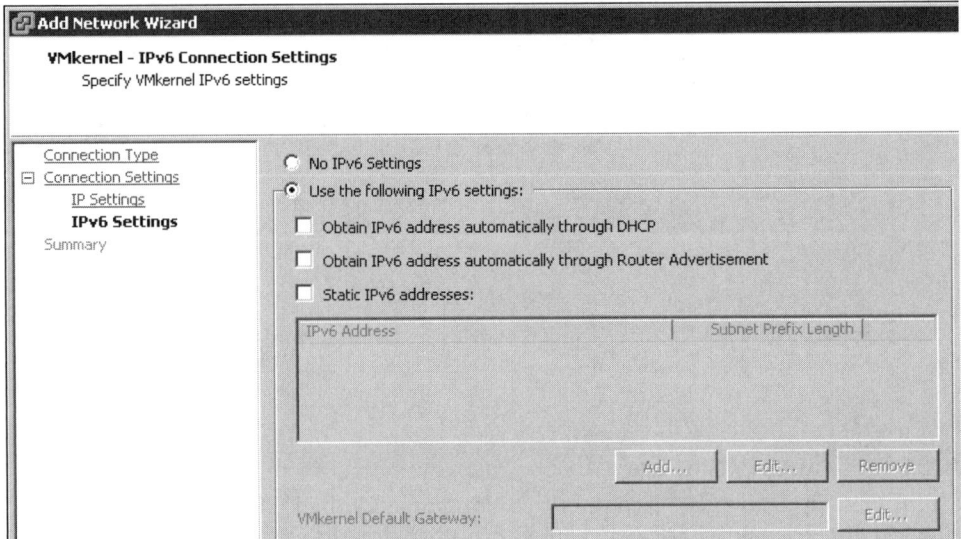

7. To set a static IPv6 address for the Service Console, select Static IP addresses.

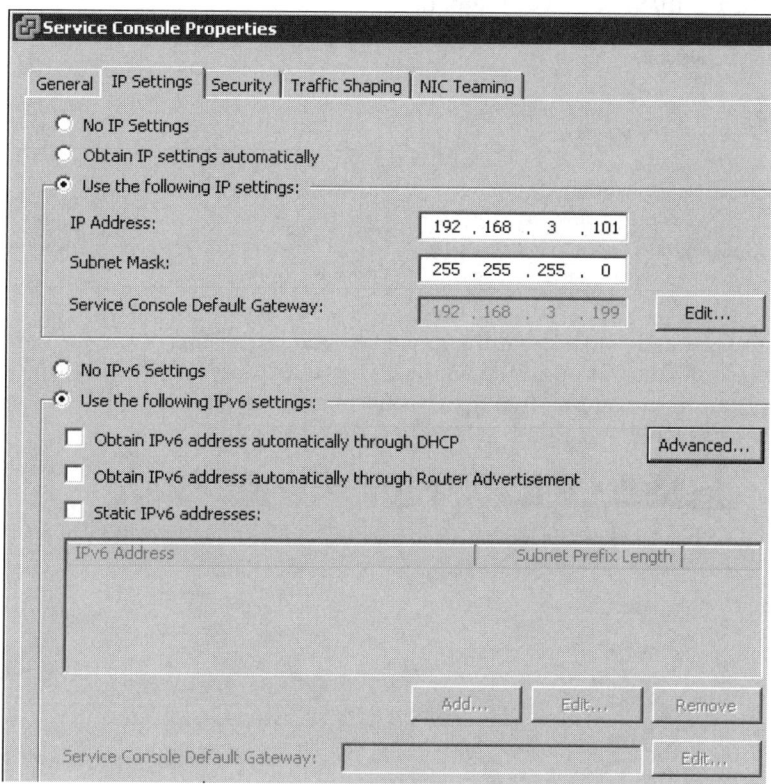

8. Click Add, and type in a valid IPv6 address for the ESX host.

After completing the dialog box, the view of vSwitch0 will update to show the static IPv6 address that you have assigned.

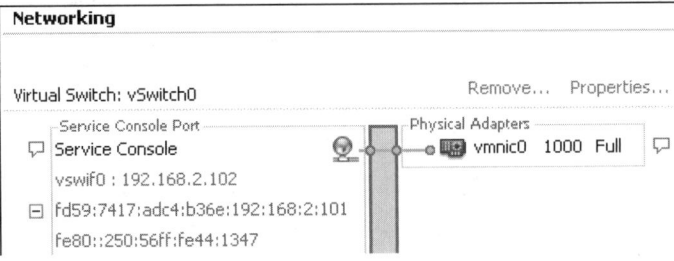

9. You can set a valid IPv6 default gateway on the properties of the port group for the Service Console or through the vSphere Client, by opening the DNS and Routing Configuration dialog box (navigate from the Software pane of the Configuration tab, click the DNS and Routing link, and then click Properties).

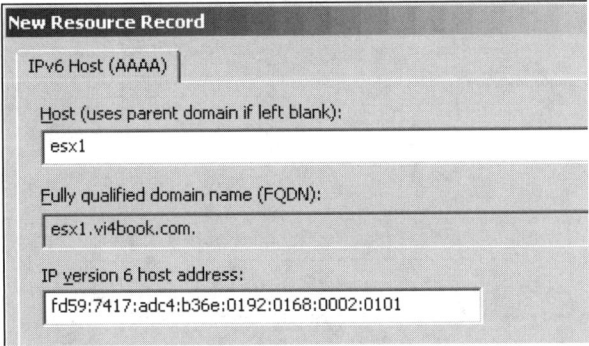

10. After completing this process, you will need to update DNS with the correct AAAA record for the ESX host in question.

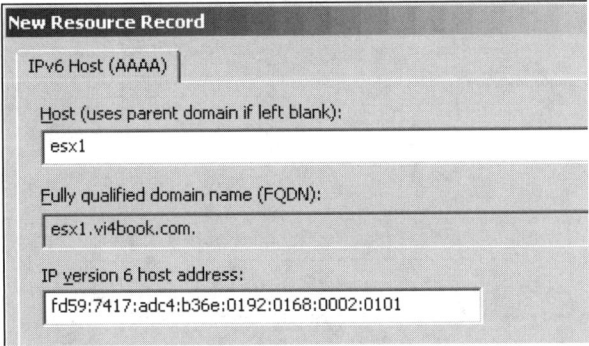

Summary

As the NIC vendors have caught up with the demands of virtualization, and as VMware improves its hardware support, we have witnessed the introduction of support for such features as 10 Gigabit Ethernet, InfiniBand, jumbo frames with larger MTU values, and TCP Segmentation Offload (TSO). It's likely that these I/O performance enhancements will benefit people who have adopted IP storage (iSCSI/NAS) over Fibre Channel SANs. It will also benefit virtual machines if they are bandwidth-intensive, and possibly allow for VMotion to cope with much larger memory sizes in the virtual machines with ease.

Standard vSwitch networking is a very mature and well-understood method of connecting your virtual machines and ESX host to the outside world. For many smaller environments, vSwitches offer perhaps the easiest way of getting up and running. However, as your infrastructure grows, you might find that very limiting settings are locked to each individual host. A more attractive approach might be to adopt the newer distributed virtual switch, which is described in the next chapter.

This chapter also covered how to use IPv6 addresses. While you may not have immediate plans to roll out IPv6 in your network, the time is right to make sure you are familiar with the basics of its usage. If nothing else, it will demonstrate to your colleagues and managers that you are keeping up to date with new technology changes coming through in the next decade.

CHAPTER 5 | Distributed Virtual Networking

Completely new to vSphere 4 is distributed virtual networking (DVN). On the surface, DVN is a project within VMware (sometimes called vNetwork) that enhances the network layer of the VMkernel. It introduces new features such as private VLANs, Network VMotion, and API support for third parties like Cisco to introduce their own vSwitch management tools. DVN also includes new features and initiatives such as VMDirectPath I/O (native access to the PCI bus) and new NIC drivers within the guest operating system using vmxnet3.sys.

One critical part of DVN is the distributed virtual switch (DvSwitch). This chapter covers how to create and configure DvSwitches for your ESX hosts.

What Are DvSwitches?

At the most basic level, a DvSwitch can be considered a global switch. Rather than needing to configure vSwitches for each ESX host, you can create a DvSwitch that is applied to every ESX host. Instantaneously, you have a vSwitch that is the same across multiple ESX hosts. If you are familiar with the concept of resource pools in VMware, a DvSwitch is analogous to a resource pool on a cluster, whereas a standard vSwitch is like a resource pool on a stand-alone ESX host.

DvSwitches represent not just a global switch, but also an implementation of private VLANs (PVLANs) within the VMware product. PVLANs can help you address some of the complexities of networking that large hosting providers have and issues pertaining to disaster recovery (of special interest to me, given the fact that I wrote a book about administering VMware's Site Recovery Manager).

With DvSwitches, you can do all the things you can do with standard vSwitches, and DvSwitches are easy to set up. Even if you use DvSwitches in exactly the same way as you use standard vSwitches, you will still get benefits.

A DvSwitch offers more ports than a standard vSwitch. The standard vSwitch has 4088; a DvSwitch has 6000. This increased scalability does not apply to all virtual switch attributes, however. For example, a single ESX host can have up to 248 standard vSwitches, whereas an ESX host can have a maximum of 16 DvSwitches. But 16 DvSwitches are a lot, and most VMware implementations will not need that many.

> **TIP** *VMware publishes a helpful PDF guide that outlines all the maximum configurations currently supported. You can find this guide at http://www.vmware.com/pdf/vsphere4/r40/vsp_40_config_ max.pdf.*

What Are Distributed Virtual Uplinks?

DvSwitches use distributed virtual uplink (dvUplink) ports. You can think of a dvUplink as merely a container for holding a reference to a physical NIC, such as vmnic1.

When you create a DvSwitch, the system attempts to set the correct number of dvUplink ports for you. It does this by looking at all your ESX hosts in the selected datacenter, searching for the ESX host with the most uplinks. For example, if you have three ESX hosts with four NICs and three ESX hosts with six NICs, the wizard would set six dvUplinks. Your DvSwitch would take all of the NICs from the three ESX hosts with six NICs and just use as many NICs as possible from the ESX hosts that had only four NICs. In other words, find the ESX host in the datacenter with the most NICs, and that will be the one that sets the maximum number of dvUplinks.

The nice thing about dvUplinks is that they can be renamed, unlike the device name (vmnic1), which is hard-coded and cannot be changed. This allows for a more meaningful and logical configuration to be constructed. This is analogous to renaming Local Area Connection in Windows to be more meaningful, which is especially helpful in a multihomed Windows server. When you do this, the device ID in Windows stays the same, but the friendlier name is displayed in the interface.

Creating Distributed vSwitches

You must have vCenter to create DvSwitches. Their settings are stored centrally in the vCenter database, If the vCenter system becomes unavailable, the DvSwitches will continue to function, because operationally, they reside inside the VMkernel. In this respect, vCenter is not a single point of failure. However, if you had problems with vCenter, your control over the DvSwitch would be limited until the vCenter server was brought back online. When DvSwitches are created the system will create a DvSFolder on shared storage, additionally a local database is created on each of the ESX hosts. This DvSFolder and local database ensure the switch is operates even if vCenter is unavailable.

DvSwitches are created in the datacenter level in vCenter. You'll notice that in the Hosts and Clusters view, the DvSwitch icon is dimmed and unavailable. This is an anomaly in the vSphere Client interface, and not a lack of user rights.

You must be in the correct view in vCenter for this icon to become available. To create a DvSwitch, click the Home icon, click the Networking icon, and then select your datacenter. The DvSwitch icon will now be available.

You can create DvSwitches for virtual machine, VMkernel, and management networking. Let's begin with a virtual machine networking example.

Creating a DvSwitch for Virtual Machine Networking

To create a new DvSwitch, in vCenter, navigate to the Networking view. Select your datacenter, and click the DvSwitch icon. In the dialog box, type in a friendly name for your DvSwitch.

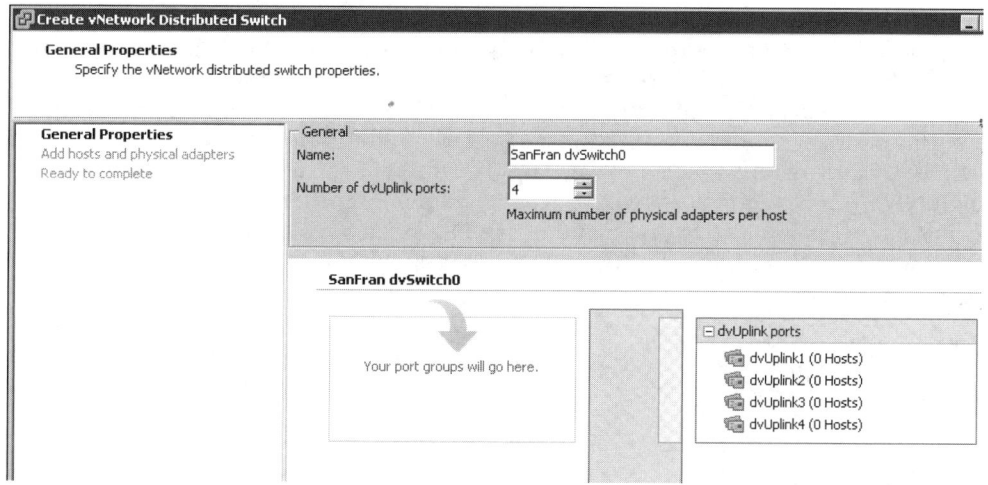

Unlike standard vSwitches, DvSwitches do not impose their own naming convention. However, I recommend using names that follow a similar convention, but are unique to the datacenter where they reside, such as DvSwitch SanFran-AMD Cluster DvSwitch0.

As noted earlier, the wizard fills in the number of dvUplinks for you automatically, but you can change this value. In this example, each of my ESX hosts has four NICs.

Notice how no hosts have yet been assigned to the DvSwitch, hence the dialog box says 0 hosts. Click Next and select which ESX hosts will use the DvSwitch, and which *physical* NICS will be used by each ESX host.

When do you want to add hosts and their physical adapters to the new vNetwork distributed switch?

◉ Add now
○ Add later

Host/Physical adapters	In use by switch	Physical adapter details
☐ ☑ 🖥 esx1.vi4book.com		
Select physical adapters		
☑ 🖳 vmnic1	--	View details...
☑ 🖳 vmnic2	--	View details...
☐ 🖳 vmnic3	--	View details...
☐ ☑ 🖥 esx3.vi4book.com		
Select physical adapters		
☑ 🖳 vmnic1	--	View details...
☑ 🖳 vmnic2	--	View details...
☐ 🖳 vmnic3	--	View details...
☐ ☑ 🖥 esx2.vi4book.com		
Select physical adapters		
☑ 🖳 vmnic1	--	View details...
☑ 🖳 vmnic2	--	View details...
☐ 🖳 vmnic3	--	View details...

You can see here that vmnic0 is not available in the list. This is because it is in use by the standard vSwitch0 created during the installation. In this example, I selected vmnic1 and vmnic2, because I want this DvSwitch to support fault tolerance and load balancing. This will create an *uplink group*, which is a collection of NICs (group) associated with the DvSwitch.

You should try to make sure this NIC assignment is correct at the time of DvSwitch creation, because changing this physical NIC assignment via the GUI is not especially friendly. You would think that if vmnic1 and vmnic2 are bundled together to create an uplink group for each and every ESX host selected, it would be easy to change from the DvSwitch. Unfortunately, this is not the case. As you will see later, if you wish to reassign NICs—say, to move a physical NIC from one DvSwitch to another—you must perform that task manually for each and every ESX host. So, although there's a quick and easy way to *assign* physical NICs to DvSwitches, there is no quick and easy way to *reassign them*.

When you complete the wizard, you will see a diagram of your new DvSwitch.

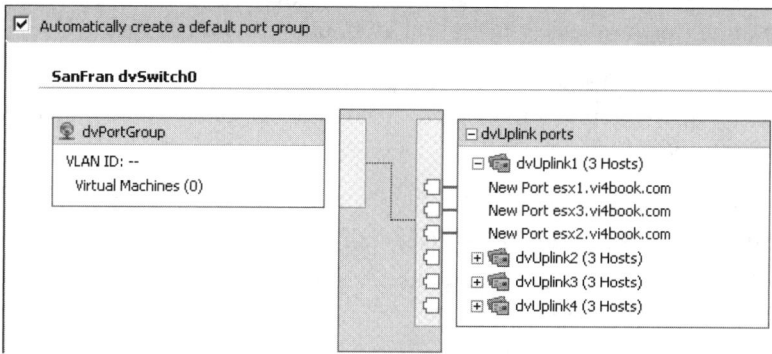

You can see that three hosts are assigned to this DvSwitch. Notice how the wizard has automatically added a port group called dvPortGroup. If you would rather the wizard didn't do this, remove the check next to "Automatically create a default port group." You can rename DvSwitch port groups, as well as create new ones, as described in the following sections.

In the Networking view, you will see your new DvSwitch, uplink group, and port group (unless you chose not to create a default port group).

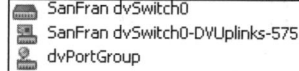

In this example, SanFran dvSwitch0 is the DvSwitch, SanFran dvSwitch0-DVUplinks-575 is a uniquely created name for the uplink group, and dvPortGroup is the port group created by the wizard.

Selecting the DvSwitch gives you access to a Hosts tab, which shows on which ESX hosts the DvSwitch is created. From here, you can add ESX hosts, if you failed to do that during the creation of the DvSwitch or if you have new ESX hosts to configure.

Additionally, you can see the DvSwitch on every ESX host to which it was applied. In the Hosts and Clusters view, select the ESX host, and choose the Configuration tab. In the Hardware pane, select Networking, and then click the DvSwitch icon.

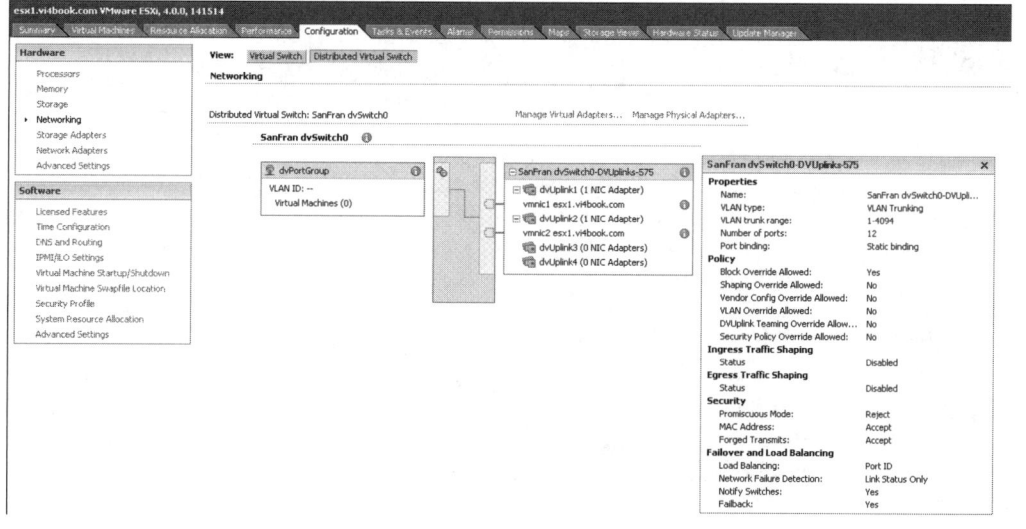

Finally, it's important to note that there is no concept of an "internal" only DvSwitch. Any DvSwitch created must have at least one DvLink added to it. It's not possible to create DvPort Group unless there is least one DvLink defined on the DvSwitch.

Renaming a DvSwitch Port Group and Setting Its VLAN ID

Next, you can rename the port group created during the creation of the DvSwitch, and also set its VLAN attribute, as follows:

1. Click the Home icon, and then click the Networking icon.

2. Select the port group called dvPortGroup, right-click it, and choose Edit Settings.

3. In the Name field of the General section, type a new name for the port group, such as **dvPortGroup-VLAN10**.

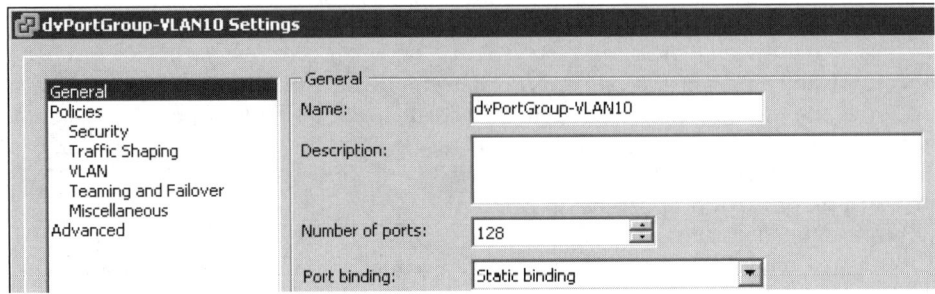

4. Select Policies in the list on the left, and then select VLAN.

5. From the VLAN Type pull-down list, select VLAN. In the VLAN ID field, enter the ID, such as **10**.

NOTE *The VLAN Type pull-down list includes a VLAN Trunking option. This is the same as using 4095 in a standard vSwitch. Additionally, you can set a PVLAN value here if your physical switch has been configured for a PVLAN.*

6. Click OK to save your changes.

Adding Port Groups to a DvSwitch

To create additional port groups, right-click the DvSwitch and choose New Port Group. In the dialog box, type a new port group name, such as **dvPortGroup-VLAN11**. From the

VLAN Type pull-down list, select VLAN and set the VLAN ID, such as **11**. Click OK to create the new port group.

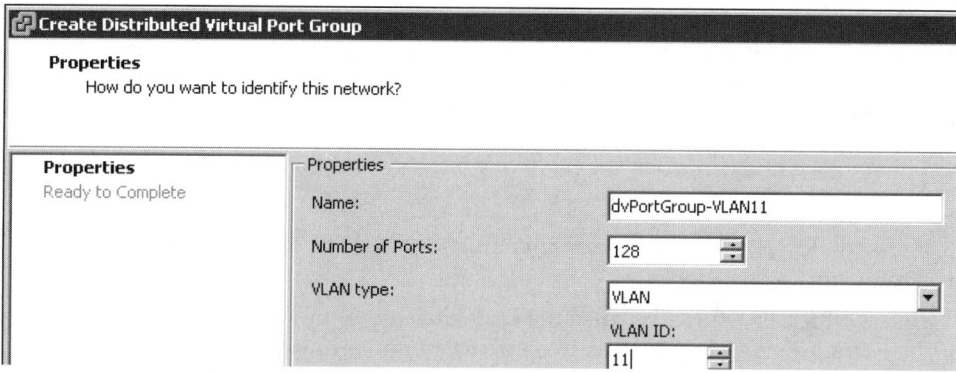

After repeating this process a few times, you will have setup that is very similar to VLAN tagging with standard vSwitches.

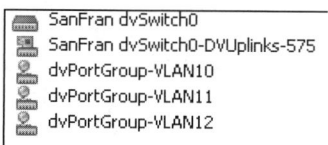

The dvPortGroup labels appear in the pull-down list when you create a new virtual machine, just as they would if you were using standard vSwitches.

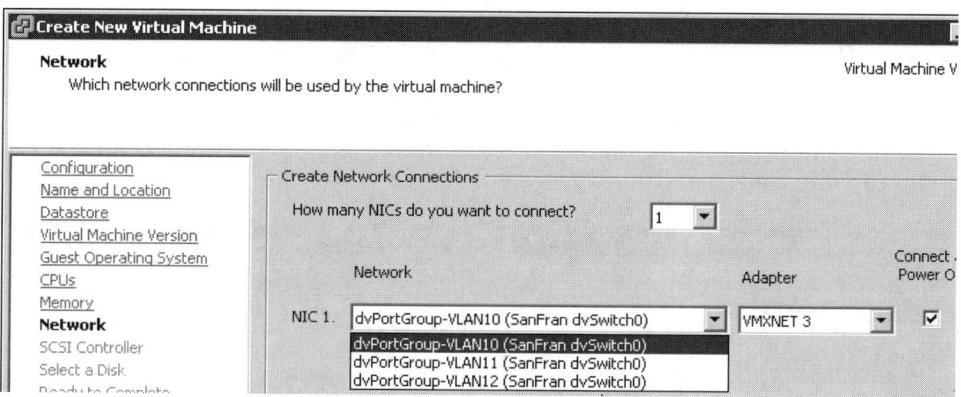

Creating a VMkernel DvSwitch for VMotion

As with a standard vSwitch, you can create a DvSwitch for VMotion using VMkernel port groups. DvSwitches for VMkernel networking are interesting because they constitute a global switch that crosses many ESX hosts, but at the same time, each ESX host needs its own unique IP address, subnet mask, and default gateway. One way to deal with these per-ESX settings with vCenter is to use host profiles to handle these settings. We will look at host profiles in Chapter 17. Here, I will show you how to handle these per-ESX host settings manually.

To create this type of DvSwitch, you need to move from one view to another to complete the job. Initially, you will be in the Networking view, where you will create the DvSwitch across many ESX hosts. Then you will switch to the Hosts and Clusters view to add a VMkernel port.

1. Click the Home icon, click the Networking icon, and then select your datacenter.

2. Click the DvSwitch icon.

3. In the dialog box, type in a friendly name for your DvSwitch, such as **SanFran DvSwitch1**. Click Next.

4. Select which ESX hosts will use the DvSwitch and which *physical* NICs will be used by each ESX host. In this example, vmnic0, vmnic1, and vmnic2 are unavailable because they are in use by the standard vSwitch0 or the SanFran DvSwitch0.

When do you want to add hosts and their physical adapters to the new vNetwork distributed switch?		
⦿ Add now		
○ Add later		
Host/Physical adapters	In use by switch	Physical adapter details
☐ ☑ ▤ esx1.vi4book.com		
Select physical adapters		
☑ ▥ vmnic3	--	View details…
☐ ☑ ▤ esx3.vi4book.com		
Select physical adapters		
☑ ▥ vmnic3	--	View details…
☐ ☑ ▤ esx2.vi4book.com		
Select physical adapters		
☑ ▥ vmnic3	--	View details…

5. To rename the port group created by the wizard, select the port group named dvPortGroup, right-click, and choose Edit Settings. Enter a new name for this port group, such as **dvPortGroup-VMotion**.

🔲 dvPortGroup-VMotion Settings		
	General	
General	Name:	dvPortGroup-VMotion
Policies		
Security	Description:	
Traffic Shaping		
VLAN		
Teaming and Failover		
Miscellaneous		
Advanced	Number of ports:	128

6. Optionally, select Policies, select VLAN, and choose VLAN from the VLAN Type pull-down list. Enter the VLAN ID, such as **14**.

7. To set the IP details required to enable the VMotion feature for each ESX using the DvSwitch, click the Home icon, and then click the Hosts and Clusters icon. Choose your datacenter and your ESX host.

8. On the Configuration tab, in the Hardware pane, select Networking.

9. Click the DvSwitch icon.

10. Scroll down to locate the DvSwitch, and then select the Manage Virtual Adapters link.

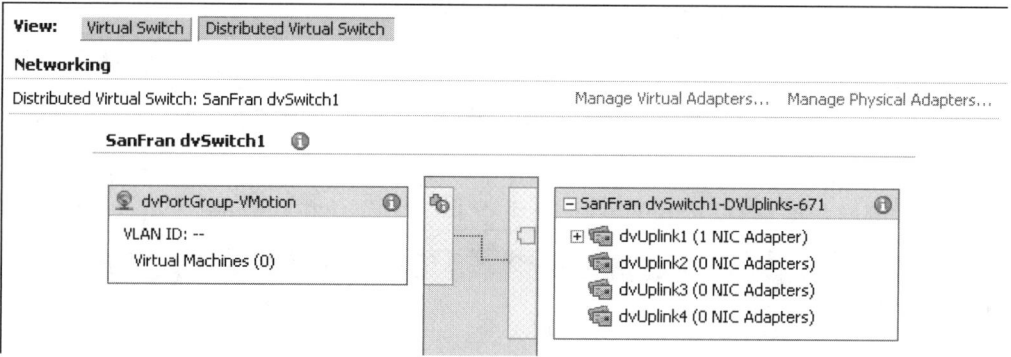

11. In the Manage Virtual Adapters dialog box, click Add. (If you are using ESXi 4, the Service Console type will not be present in the Manage Virtual Adapters dialog box.)

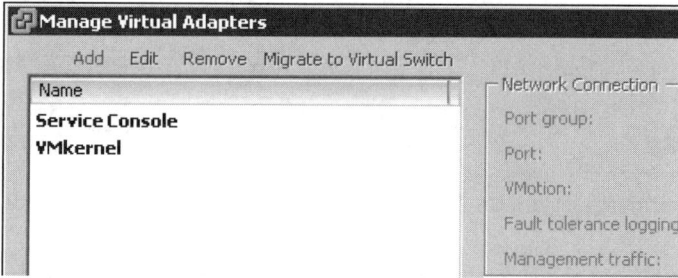

12. Choose the "New virtual adapter" option. The migration option is used when you migrate all the settings on an existing standard vSwitch to the DvSwitch type, as discussed later in this chapter.

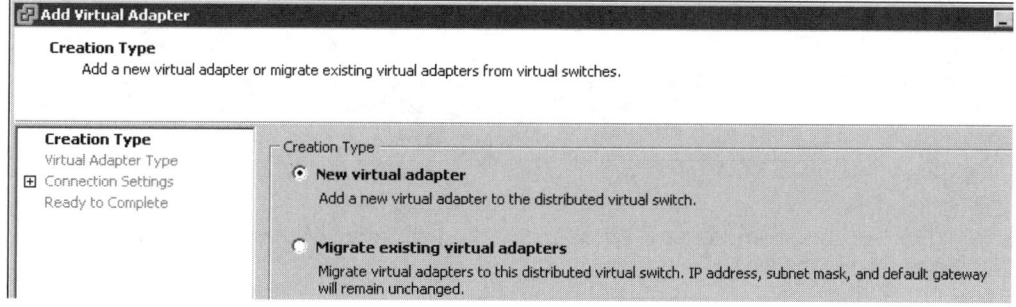

13. Choose the VMkernel option.

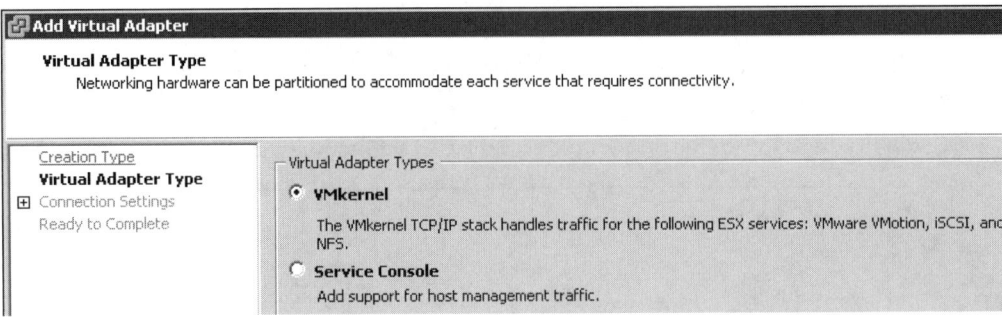

14. In the next dialog box, select the "Use this virtual adapter for VMotion" option. Then select the port group you created for this DvSwitch from the pull-down list.

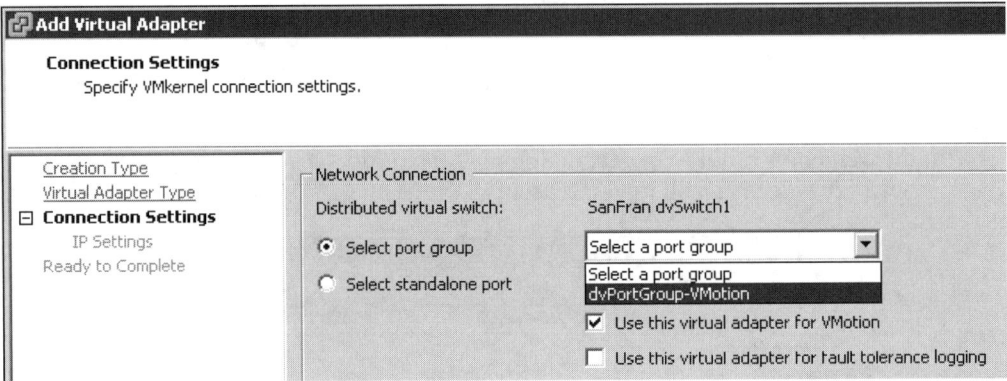

15. Set the IP address, subnet mask, and (optionally) default gateway for the VMkernel port.

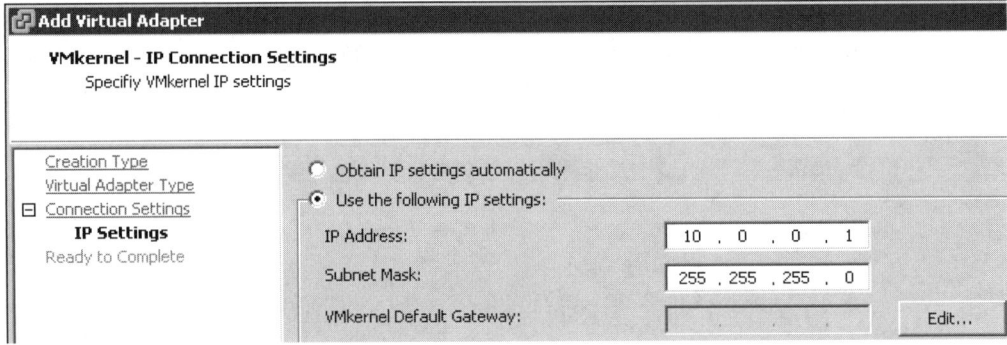

16. Click Finish to complete the wizard, and then close the Manage Virtual Adapter dialog box.

As with a standard vSwitch, this will create a VMkernel port called vmk0. In the Manage Virtual Adapters dialog box, you will see the IP address used and that this vmk0 port is enabled for VMotion.

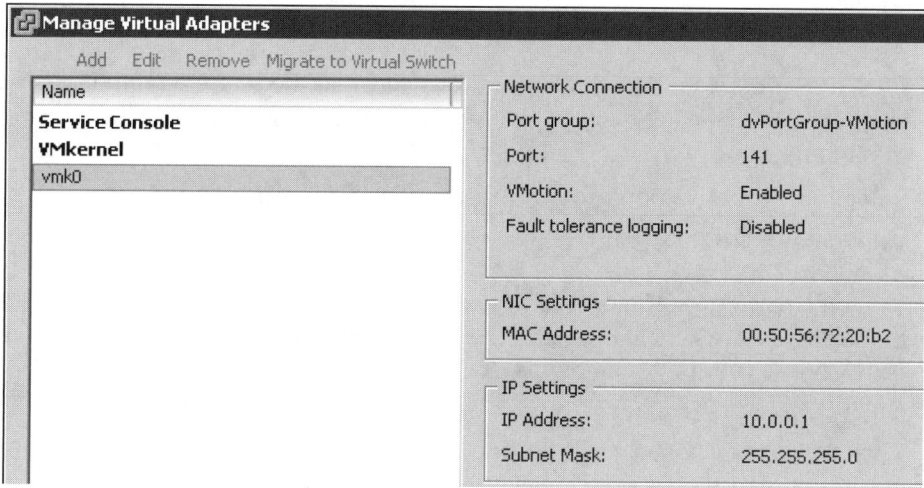

The main view of the DvSwitch will be refreshed, and from here, you can see the vmk0 port settings and which physical NIC is being used by the DvSwitch.

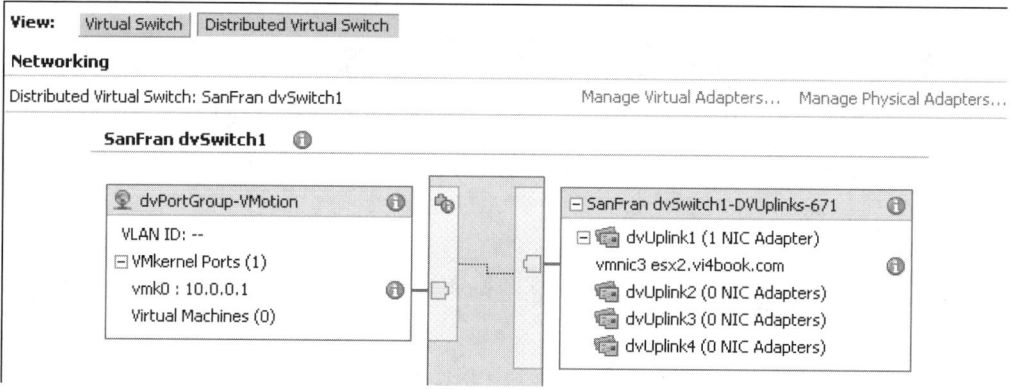

Creating a DvSwitch Port Group for the Service Console

You may want to add a DvSwitch port group for the Service Console. As with creating a DvSwitch for VMkernel networking, you need to move from one view to another view to complete the job, starting in Networking view and switching to the Hosts and Clusters view. In this example, I will name the second Service Console connection dvPortGroup-HA-Heartbeat. (I will explain the use of heartbeat information to prevent the phenomena of "split-brain" in Chapter 15, which covers VMware HA.)

NOTE *If you are using ESXi 4, the Service Console type is not available for virtual adapters, since the ESXi product does not have a Service Console component. If you want to create another management network for ESXi 4, choose to create a VMkernel type, and then provide valid IP data.*

1. Click the Home icon, click the Networking icon, and then select your datacenter.
2. Right-click the DvSwitch (SanFran DvSwitch1 in this example) and select New Port Group.
3. Enter a name for this port group, such as **dvPortGroup-HA-Heartbeat**.
4. Optionally, select Policies, select the VLAN option, and choose VLAN from the VLAN Type pull-down list. Then specify the VLAN ID, such as **14**.
5. To set the IP details required to create an additional Service Console port for each ESX using the DvSwitch, click the Home icon, and then click the Hosts and Clusters icon. Choose your datacenter and your ESX host.
6. On the Configuration tab, in the Hardware pane, select Networking.
7. Click the DvSwitch icon.
8. Scroll down to locate the DvSwitch, and the select the Manage Virtual Adapters link.
9. In the Manage Virtual Adapters dialog box, click Add.

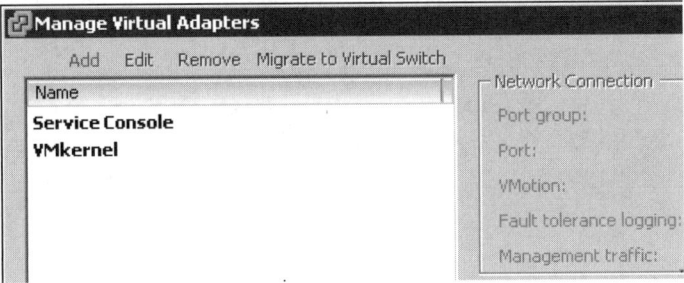

10. Choose the "New virtual adapter" option.
11. Choose the Service Console option.
12. Select the port group you created for this DvSwitch from the pull-down list.

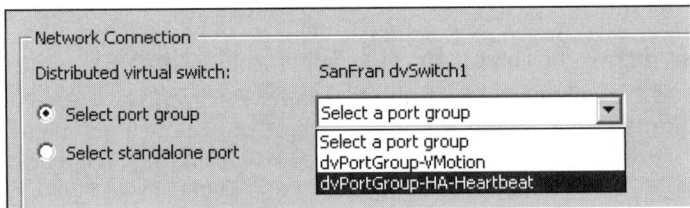

13. Set the IP address, subnet mask, and (optionally) default gateway for the new Service Console port.

14. Click Finish to complete the wizard, and close the Manage Virtual Adapter dialog box,

As with a standard vSwitch, this will create a Service Console port called vswif1, and in the Manage Virtual Adapters dialog box, you will see the IP address used.

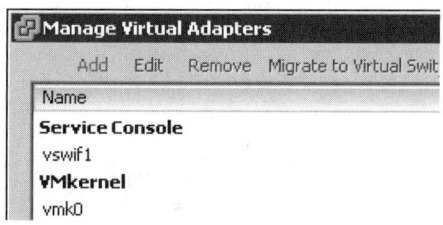

Adding and Removing Physical NICs

Unfortunately, once you have created a DvSwitch, you must visit each ESX host to add or remove a physical NIC. As an example, I will walk through the steps to remove the vmnic3 from the DvSwitch for VMotion, and then allocate this NIC to my DvSwitch for virtual machine networking. The result is not good—with only four NICs, my VMotion and HA Heartbeat service will not work—so I will soon be undoing this process.

NOTE *Technically, you do not need to remove a physical NIC from one DvSwitch to add it to another. You can move it from one DvSwitch to another if you so wish.*

1. In the Hosts and Clusters View, select your ESX host and click the Configuration tab.

2. Locate the DvSwitch from which you wish to remove a physical NIC (SanFran DvSwitch1 in this example).

3. Select the Manage Physical Adapters link.

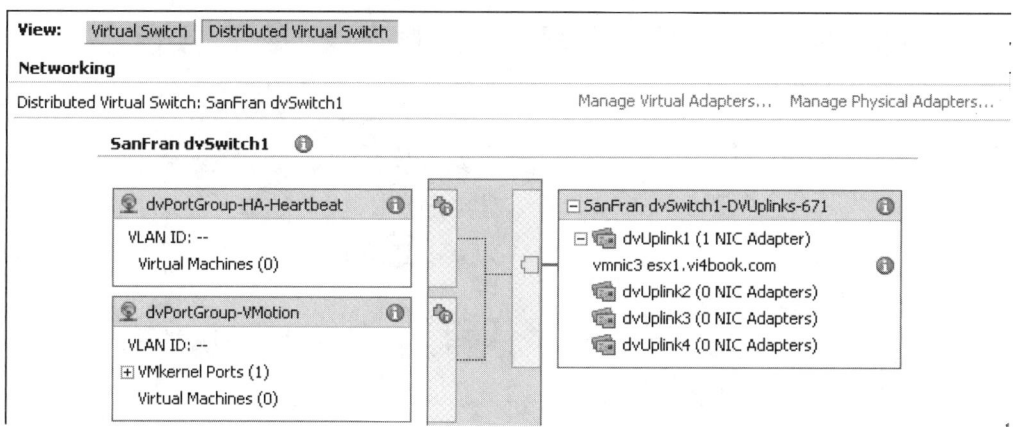

4. Select the NIC associated with the dvUplink group and choose Remove.

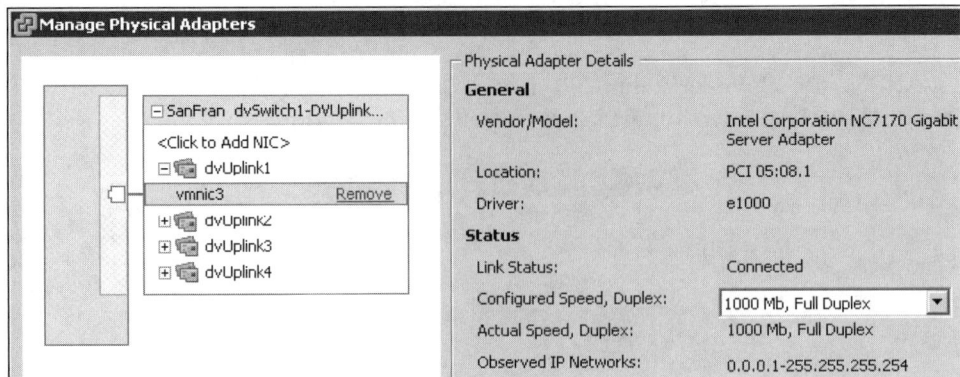

5. Click OK to confirm your removal. You will see a warning alerting you that no physical NICs are assigned to this DvSwitch and that virtual machines attached to it may have networking issues. Effectively, this DvSwitch is very like an internal standard vSwitch; if virtual machines were attached to it, they would not be able to communicate with the outside world (unless some other device—such as a firewall, router, or NAT—bridges the network for those virtual machines).

Distributed Virtual Switch: SanFran dvSwitch1   Manage Virtual Adapters...   Manage Physical Adapters...

⚠ No physical adapters from this host are connected to this distributed virtual switch. Virtual machines running on this host, which are connected to this distributed virtual switch will have some networking issues. To resolve these issues, add at least one physical adapter to this distributed virtual switch.

---

6. To allocate this freed physical NIC to another DvSwitch on the same ESX host, locate that other DvSwitch (SanFran DvSwitch0 in this example) and then select the Manage Physical Adapters link.

7. In the list of dvUplinks, locate a free dvUplink and select the "Click to Add NIC" option.

8. In the dialog box that appears, allocate the free NIC to this DvSwitch.

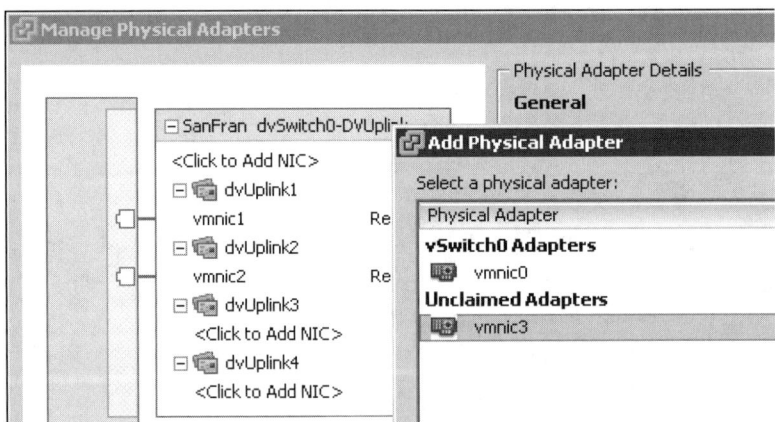

Once the physical NIC has been added, it will appear in the main window. Expanding the values and selecting a virtual machine patch to a port group will give you a much better view of how a single-NIC virtual machine is actually allowed to use the many NICs that make up a DvSwitch.

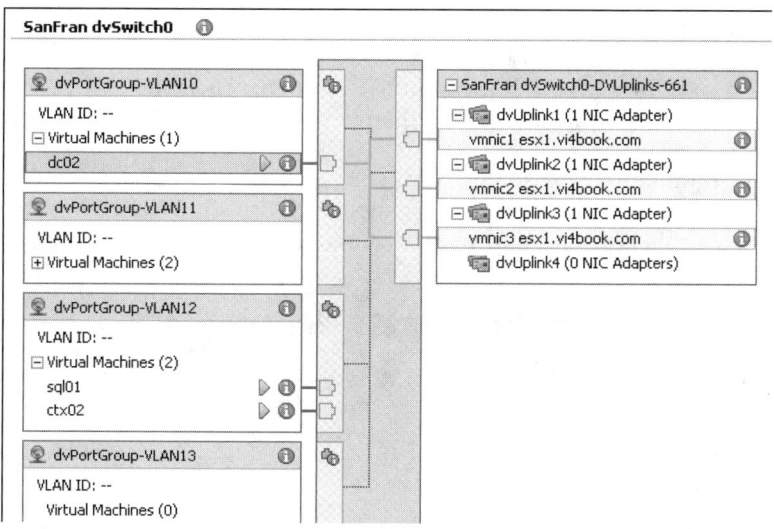

Removing a DvSwitch from an ESX Host

Removing an ESX host from a DvSwitch has the result of removing the DvSwitch from that host, just as adding an ESX host to a DvSwitch has the result of creating the DvSwitch on the ESX host.

To remove an ESX host, navigate to the Networking view, select the DvSwitch in the relevant datacenter container, and select the Hosts tab. Locate the relevant ESX host, right-click, and choose Remove from Distributed Virtual Switch.

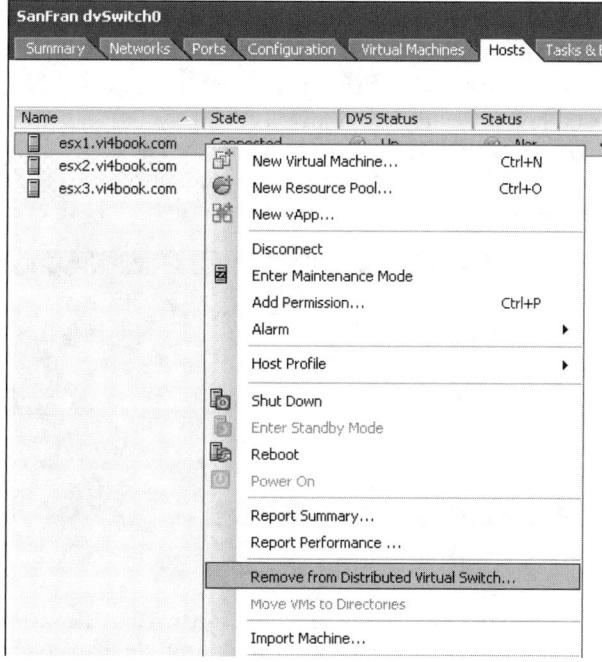

If you try to remove an ESX host when one of the ports on the DvSwitch is in use by a powered-on virtual machine, you will receive an error message.

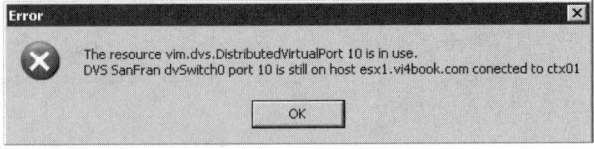

This same message can appear if you try to delete a DvSwitch when it's in use by a virtual machine.

Once you are sure the DvSwitch is not in use, or its functionality is being delivered by another DvSwitch or standard vSwitch, then you can right-click the DvSwitch and choose Remove.

Additionally, removing an ESX host from vCenter without first removing it from the DvSwitch will generate an error message for each and every DvSwitch it is using. This includes DvSwitches used for management, the VMKernel (iSCSI, NAS, VMotion, FT, and HA), and virtual machines.

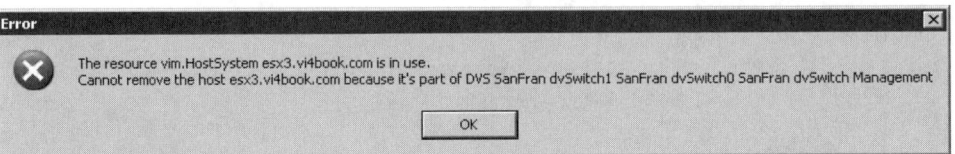

Advanced DvSwitch Settings

Like most advanced settings you can find these on the properties of the DvSwitch, dvUplink Group or DvPort Group. These settings are very like the Standard vSwitch setting we covered earlier. So I want to focus on the unique settings that are new or only available on the properties of each of the DvSwitch components.

Configuring and Viewing DvSwitch Settings

On the Properties tab of the DvSwitch's Settings dialog box, the Advanced section allows you to set the CDP settings and the MTU value. This is a vast improvement over the standard vSwitch configuration, which requires the use of command-line utilities to set these values for each and every vSwitch on each and every ESX host.

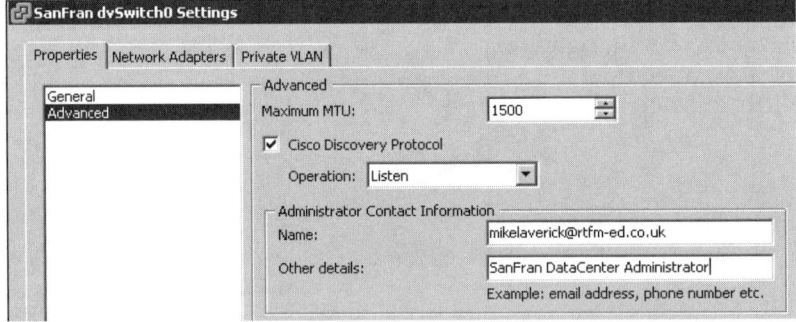

The General section of the Properties tab allows you to rename the DvSwitch, as well as set the number of dvUplinks. Additionally, you can change the default name of the dvUplinks.

The Network Adapter tab of the DvSwitch's Settings dialog box shows you which ESX hosts have been added to the DvSwitch, and which physical NICs have been assigned to them. The Private VLAN tab allows you to set up the PVLAN configuration for the DvSwitch.

The tabs of the DvSwitch's window display a lot of information. The Ports tab shows you the ports on the DvSwitch (524 by default). From here you can see which port on this switch the respective virtual machines use. In the following example, the ports have been sorted by runtime MAC address to show the virtual machine's port usage.

SanFran dvSwitch0

Summary | Networks | **Ports** | Configuration | Virtual Machines | Hosts | Tasks & Events | Alarms | Permissions

Time since last refresh: 03:28

Port ID contains

Port ID	Name	Connectee	Runtime MAC add...▽	Port group	State	Blo
132	--	fileserver02	00:50:56:b1:52:74	dvPortGroup-VLAN12	Link Up	No
385	--	dc02	00:50:56:b1:36:e4	dvPortGroup-VLAN10	Link Up	No
129	--	sql01	00:50:56:b1:2f:32	dvPortGroup-VLAN12	Link Up	No
257	--	web01	00:50:56:b1:25:45	dvPortGroup-VLAN13	Link Up	No
10	--	ctx01	00:50:56:b1:1f:c0	dvPortGroup-VLAN11	Link Up	No
133	--	web02	00:50:56:b1:1f:72	dvPortGroup-VLAN12	Link Up	No
131	--	ctx02	00:50:56:b1:1c:d1	dvPortGroup-VLAN12	Link Up	No
258	--	fileserver01	00:50:56:b1:1c:c6	dvPortGroup-VLAN13	Link Up	No
130	--	sql02	00:50:56:b1:16:bb	dvPortGroup-VLAN12	Link Up	No

The Configuration tab of the DvSwitch's window is probably the richest location for checking the configuration settings of *all* the parts that make up a DvSwitch. Almost every component has an information icon that you can click to see the advanced settings on the DvSwitch. Additionally, there are quick links for common tasks such as adding a host or creating a new port group. On the far-right side of the tab, the Pan and Zoom option allows you to zoom in and out (similar to the Maps feature in VI3).

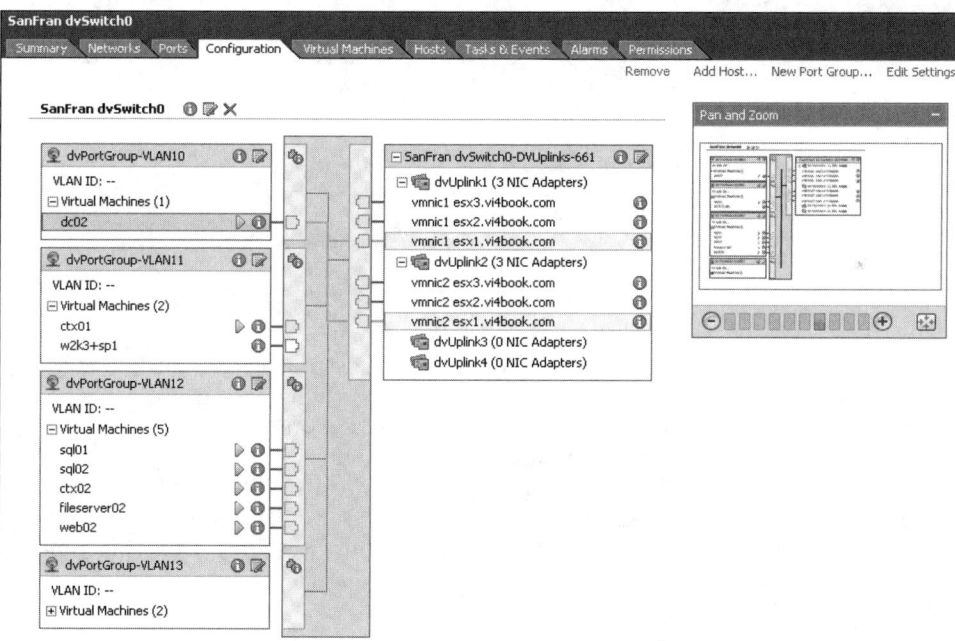

Configuring DvSwitch Port Group Settings

In the General section of the DvSwitch port group Settings dialog box, you can change the number of ports and the port binding options. As you saw on the Ports tab, a DvSwitch has many ports, and each virtual machine's virtual NIC is bound to a port on the DvSwitch within the port group. Three binding options are available:

- **Static binding**   With static binding, the virtual machine is allocated to a port on the DvSwitch at the time it is created. The virtual machine is bound to the port and always reuses it. No other VM can use the port even when the owning VM is powered off. This is the default binding used in DvSwitches and will only allow a set number of VMs to be powered on at any one time. Static bind is useful if you apply per-port settings. It ensures each time a VM is powered on it returns to the same port and gains the same settings.

- **Dynamic binding**   With dynamic binding, the virtual machine is allocated to the port on the DvSwitch when it is powered on. When the virtual machine is powered off and then on, it continues using the dynamically allocated port. It allows you to have more VMs connected to the DvSwitch than you have ports available. The assumption is that you only need the right number of ports for the number of VMs concurrently powered on at one time.

- **Ephemeral**   This represents no binding. As you might suspect, the virtual machine is allocated a port when it is powered on, but when it is powered off and on again, it is allocated to any free port. Ports are created on demand, so as you create more VMs more ports are generated.

As with a standard vSwitch, you can set various policies for the DvSwitch port group. The security parameters are the same as those for a standard vSwitch. Traffic shaping is also possible for a DvSwitch port group, but here you can set both ingress and egress settings. Ingress traffic is network activity that comes from outside the ESX host, and can be regarded as *inbound traffic management*. This is the same as the standard vSwitch traffic shaping settings. The egress traffic-shaping settings are unique to DvSwitch port groups. Egress traffic is network activity that comes into the ESX host from either the virtual machines or the ESX host itself, and can regarded as *outbound traffic management*.

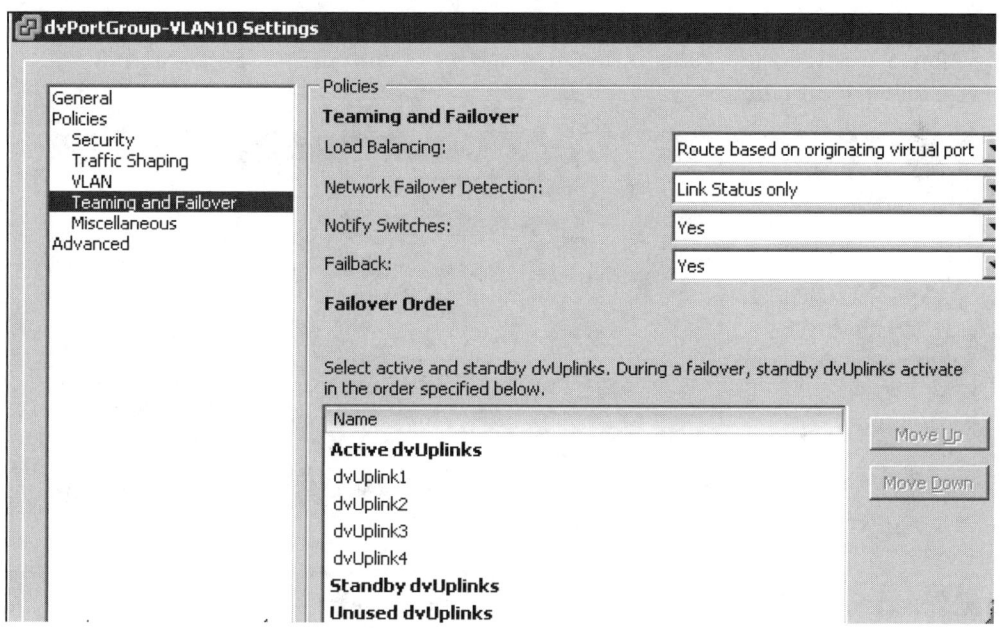

The VLAN policy settings allow you to configure VLAN tagging, VLAN trunking, and the private VLAN. The Teaming and Failover policy settings are similar to those for a standard vSwitch. The difference here is that the NIC references are not directly related to the physical NIC, but to the dvUplink port values.

The Miscellaneous settings allow you to enable port blocking. This is a single Yes or No choice. It's possible to block network traffic to and from a VM by locating it in the "port tab" of a DvS Port group. When you right-click a VM in the port tab this will allow you set per-VM port settings one of which includes the option "block all ports" in the dialog box.

In the Advanced settings, you can set the following options:

- **Override port policies**   Overrides the settings on the dvUplink group. The Edit Override Settings link lets you allow the dvUplink group settings to apply on individual policies.

- **Live port moving**   Allows stand-alone ports to be moved to distributed port group even when they are in use. Stand-alone ports can currently only be created using the vSphere SDK.

- **Configure reset at disconnect**   Means that when a port is disconnected from a virtual machine, the configuration of the port is reset to the DvSwitch's port group settings such that any per-port overrides are discarded.

- **Port name format**   Allows you to change the default naming convention for DvSwitch port groups.

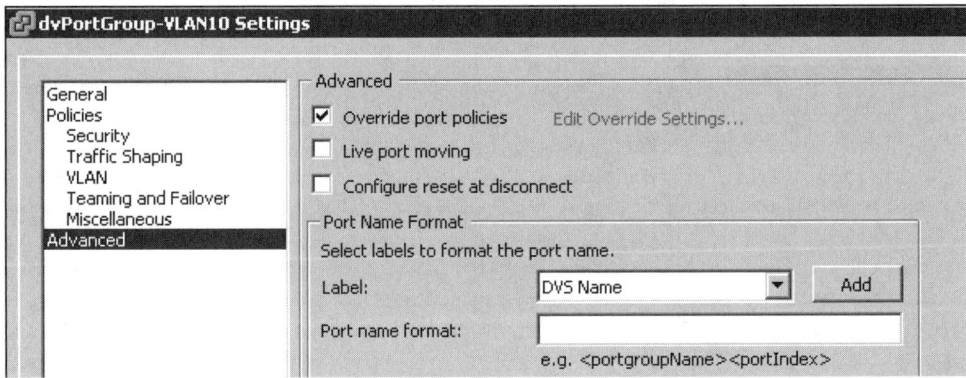

Migrating from Standard vSwitches to DvSwitches

There may be cases where you wish to move from using a standard vSwitch to using DvSwitch. For example, you may want to do this after an upgrade from ESX 3 to ESX 4, or if a change in your physical network allows for some of the advanced features of DvSwitches, such as PVLANs. Perhaps you have been following along with the instructions in this book, and you have an ESX host with a whole bunch of standard vSwitches that you don't want to destroy (especially if you have already proceeded to populate them with dozens of virtual machines!).

The migration process can be accomplished in five general steps:

- Create a DvSwitch and port groups.
- Transfer the physical NICs to the DvSwitch.
- Migrate virtual machines from the standard vSwitch to the DvSwitch.
- Migrate other hosts to the DvSwitch.
- Decommission the old standard vSwitches.

The process is relatively simple, but care must be taken to avoid a situation where virtual machines, the VMkernel, or the management network become orphaned from the network, resulting in user disconnects or management woes. You may also suffer a temporary loss of bandwidth or fault tolerance, depending on the number of NICs associated with the affected standard vSwitches. For example, if you have four port groups on one standard vSwitch with two physical NICs, as you move just one (because to move all of them would disconnect users from the virtual machines!), until the migration process is completed, you will half the bandwidth and no fault tolerance. The work-around for this situation is to have a standard vSwitch with four physical NICS assigned to it, so that you can move two physical NICs to the DvSwitch, leaving two behind on the standard vSwitch, ready for the migration of the virtual machines from one switch type to another.

To illustrate this migration process, I set up my ESX hosts to have a blend of many Service Console interfaces, VLAN tagging for the virtual machines, and a VMKernel port for VMotion. The following screenshot shows the configuration I used for this part of the book.

I also had to wrestle with the issue of not having a lot of physical NICs available. So occasionally, I would move vmnic1 or vmnic12 to a different vSwitch to protect the network I was working with during the migration process. While this is not mandatory, I heartily recommend you do the same if you have a limited number of NICs.

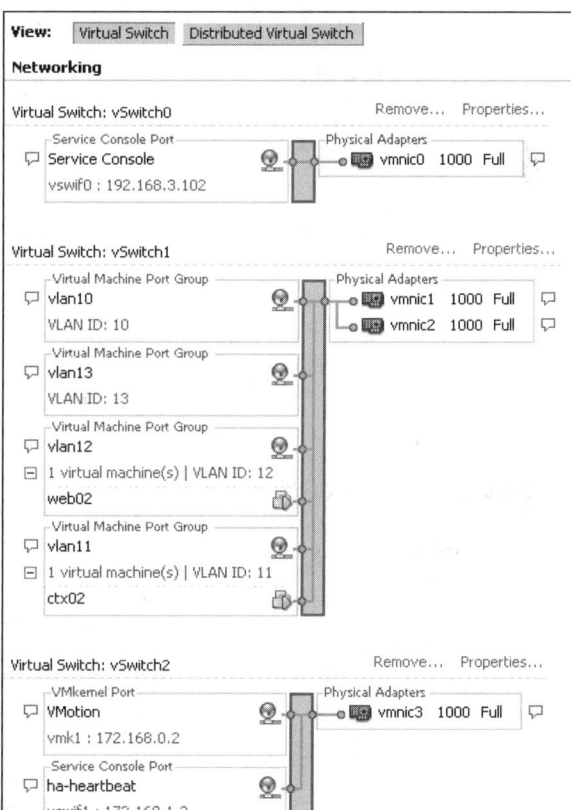

Migrating to a Virtual Machine Networking DvSwitch

We'll begin with the process of migrating from an existing standard vSwitch for virtual
machines. This involves creating the new DvSwitch and its port groups, adding ESX hosts,
transferring the virtual machines to the new DvSwitch, and removing the old standard
vSwitches.

Creating the DvSwitch

Create a new DvSwitch as described earlier in the chapter in "Creating
Distributed vSwitches," but in the Add Hosts and Physical Adapters
dialog box, select Add Later. Although your ESX hosts will be listed here, if all the physical
NICs are in use, you cannot allocate any to the DvSwitch yet. If you chose the Add Now
option, you would see a warning.

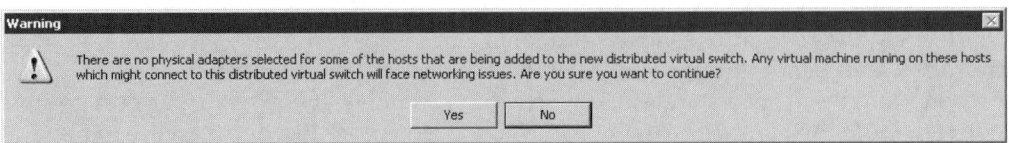

After the wizard completes, you will see a diagram of the DvSwitch.

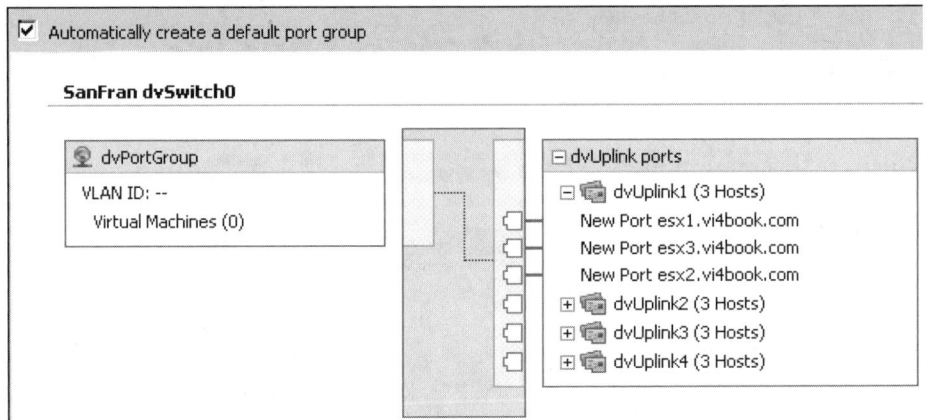

Setting Up the Port Groups

Next, rename the built-in port group and create new port groups reflecting your VLAN
configuration, as follows:

1. Select the port group called dvPortGroup, right-click, and choose Edit Settings.

2. Enter a new name for the port group, such as **dvPortGroup-VLAN10**.

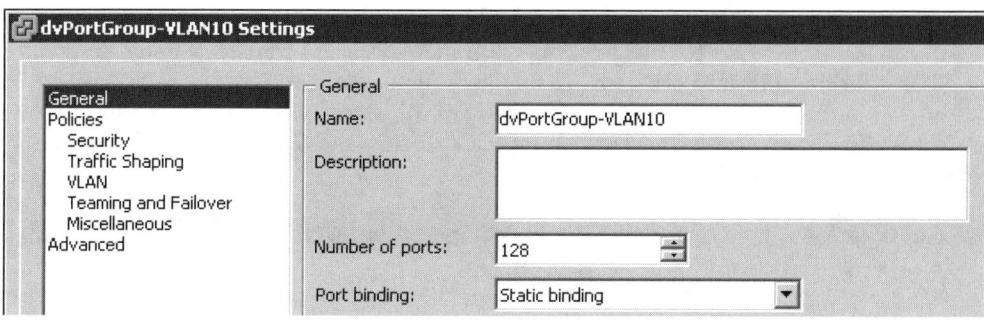

3. Under Policies, select VLAN. Choose VLAN from the VLAN Type pull-down list, and then type the VLAN ID. Then click OK.

4. Right-click the DvSwitch and choose New Port Group.

5. In the dialog box, type a new port group name, such as **dvPortGroup-VLAN11**.

6. From the VLAN Type pull-down list, select VLAN. Set the VLAN ID. Click OK.

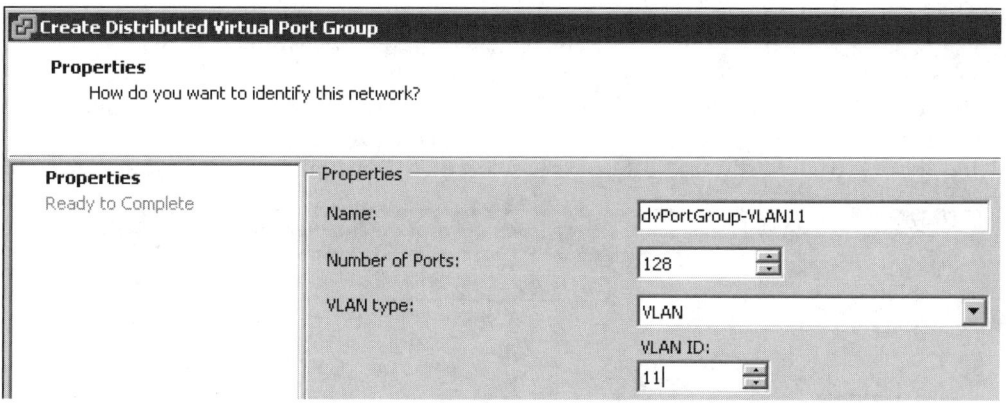

After repeating this process a few times, you will have a setup very close to VLAN tagging with standard vSwitches.

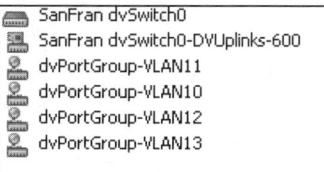

Adding ESX Hosts

Now you can add ESX hosts to the DvSwitch, and in the process transfer some (but not all) of the NICs from the standard vSwitch1 to the DvSwitch.

Right-click the DvSwitch (SanFran DvSwitch0 in this example) and select Add Host. Select an ESX host from the list, and select the NIC(s) you wish to move from the standard vSwitch to the DvSwitch.

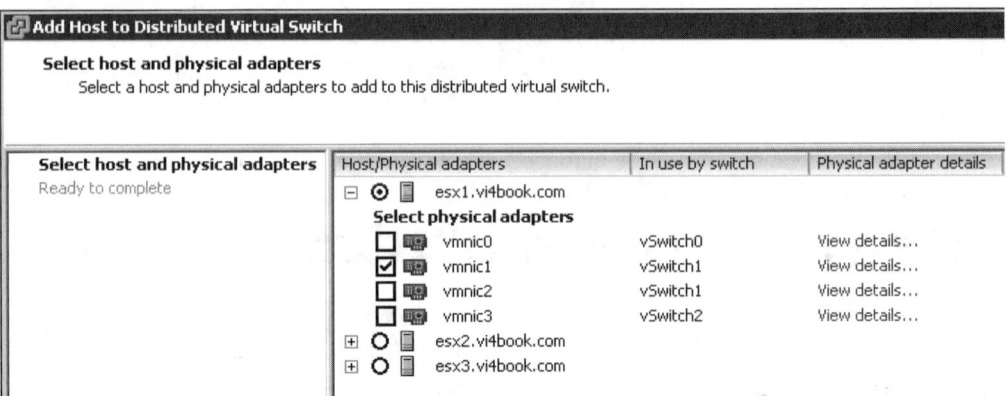

This will trigger two major changes in the network layer: the DvSwitch will have the NIC(s) assigned to it, and the standard vSwitch will have the NIC(s) deallocated from it.

You can repeat this process for each ESX host, being careful to transfer only the correct number of NICs to the DvSwitch. Remember that your precious virtual machines are still connected to the network under the existing standard vSwitch. As you do this gradually, the number of ESX hosts in the Add Host list will reduce.

Transferring the Virtual Machines

The next task is to transfer all the virtual machines from their existing standard vSwitch port groups to the DvSwitch port groups.

Right-click the DvSwitch (SanFran DvSwitch0 in this example) and select Migrate Virtual Machine Networking. Select from the list a source network and destination network, and click the Show Virtual Machines button. Now select all the virtual machines to be migrated.

Repeat this process until all your virtual machines affected by the change have been migrated to the new DvSwitch port groups.

Completing the Migration

Finally, you can finish the migration process by destroying the old standard vSwitches and transferring the remaining physical NICs to the DvSwitch, as follows:

1. In the Hosts and Clusters view, select your ESX hosts.

2. On the Configuration tab, select the Networking link in the Hardware pane, locate the standard vSwitch, and click Remove. It is safe to remove vSwitches when no virtual machines are configured for any of its port groups.

3. Click the Distributed Virtual Switch button, and select the Manage Physical Adapters link.

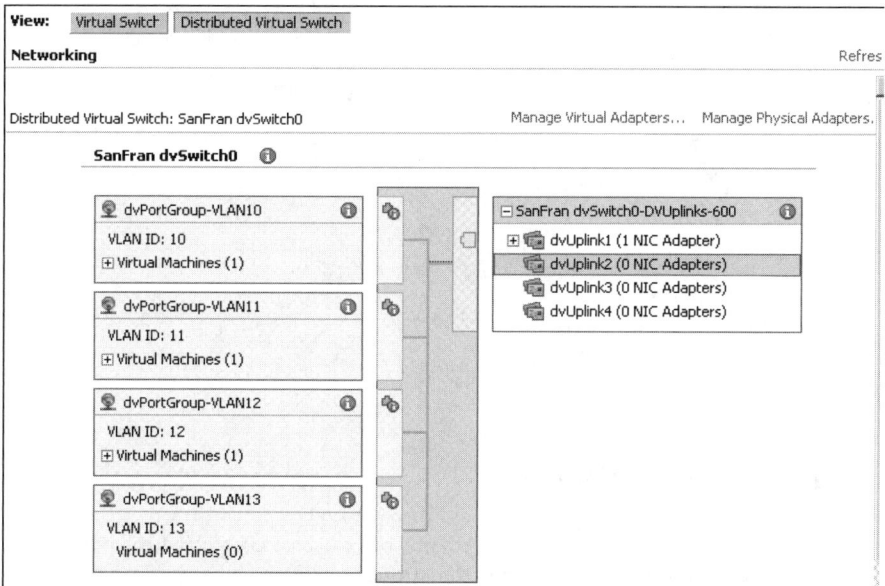

4. In the Manage Physical Adapters dialog box, select the next free dvUplink slot (dvUplink2 in this example).

5. In the Add Physical Adapter dialog box, select an unclaimed adapter.

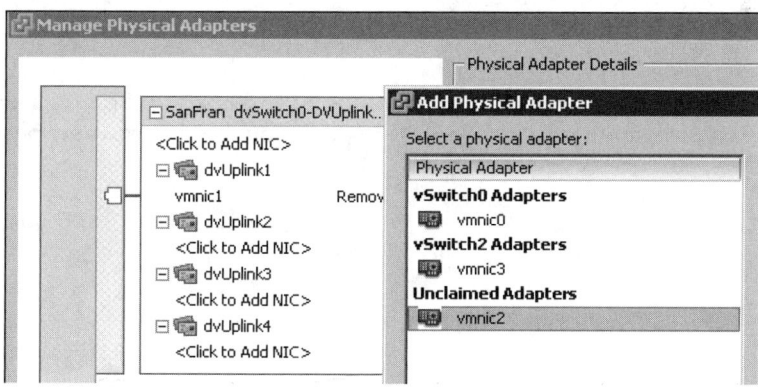

6. Click OK in the Add Physical Adapter and Manage Physical Adapters dialog boxes. The window will refresh to show the physical NIC assignment.

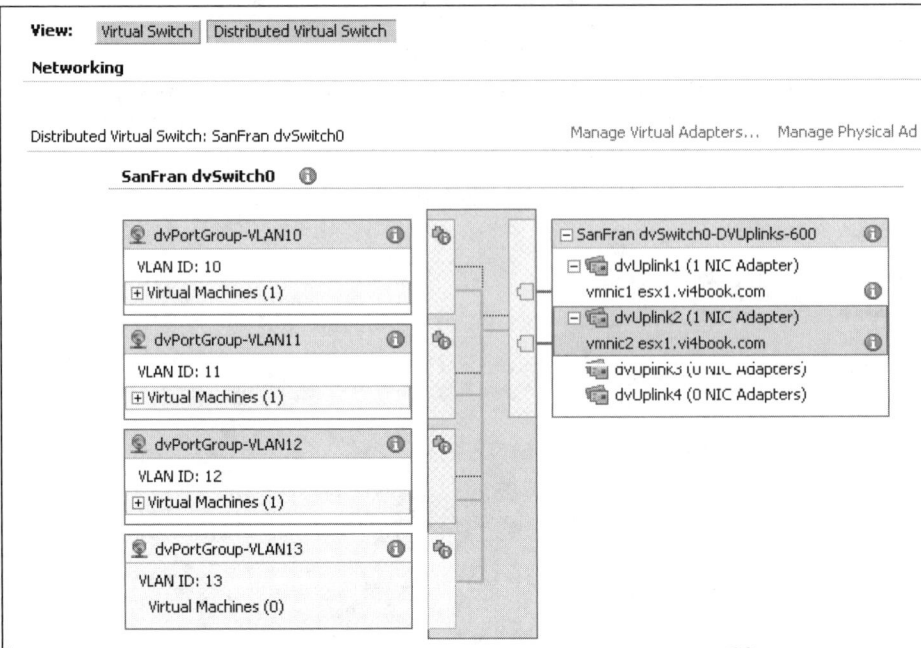

Migrating to a VMkernel DvSwitch

Just as with virtual machine networking, you can use a DvSwitch to replace standard vSwitches you created for management and VMkernel networking (VMotion, iSCSI, NAS, HA, and FT). The process of migrating from the standard vSwitch to the DvSwitch is similar to that described in the previous section, but there is more work to do, because each ESX server has its own unique settings for VMotion, iSCSI, HA, and FT, which must be migrated to the new DvSwitch.

As with our previous example, you will need to be cautious in transferring VMkernel ports to the DvSwitch. During the period of migration, you might find that features like VMotion, DRS, HA, iSCSI, NAS, and FT fail because of broken network connectivity.

Here's the general procedure:

1. Begin by creating a new DvSwitch, choosing to add hosts and physical adapters later. Next proceed to rename the built-in port group and create new port groups reflecting your VLAN configuration.

2. Set VLAN IDs as required.

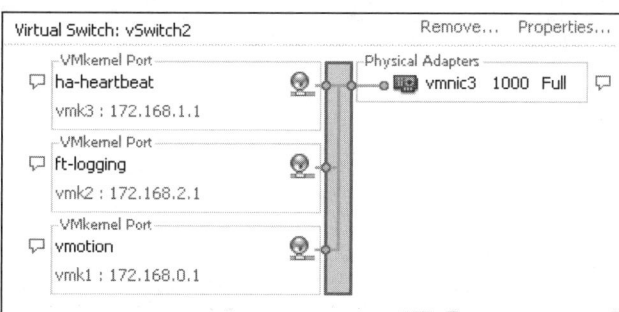

3. Create additional DvSwitch port groups as required. Much depends on whether you want to create one VMkernel DvSwitch with just one port group for each task, such as a DvSwitch for VMotion and a separate DvSwitch for iSCSI.

NOTE *Remember that VMware recommends keeping VMotion, FT, and IP-based storage on different physical NICs to prevent network contention and to enhance security. In this example, because of a lack of NICs and for simplicity, I created just one standard vSwitch for all VMkernel communications. This is not best practice, but allows me to illustrate this functionality.*

4. Add ESX hosts to the DvSwitch and transfer all of the NICs from the standard vSwitch1 to the DvSwitch, as described in the previous example.

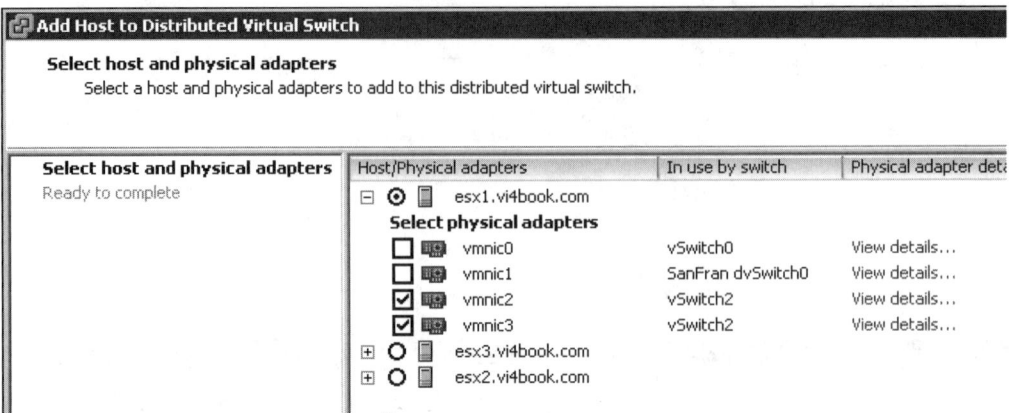

During this process, VMkernel processes that require ESX host-to-host communications will remain unaffected. However, if you do try a manual VMotion operation from an ESX host with a standard vSwitch to an ESX host with a DvSwitch, you will receive a warning.

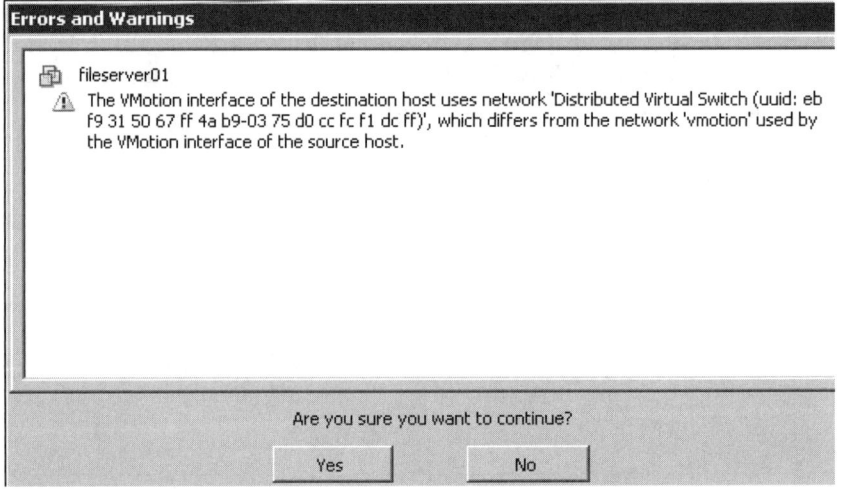

The warning can be ignored, and the VMotion operation will be successful. Warnings are ignored by other features dependent on VMotion, such as Distributed Resource Scheduler (DRS), Distributed Power Management (DPM), and Update Manager.

5. Select the port group(s) on the standard vSwitch and map them to the DvSwitch.

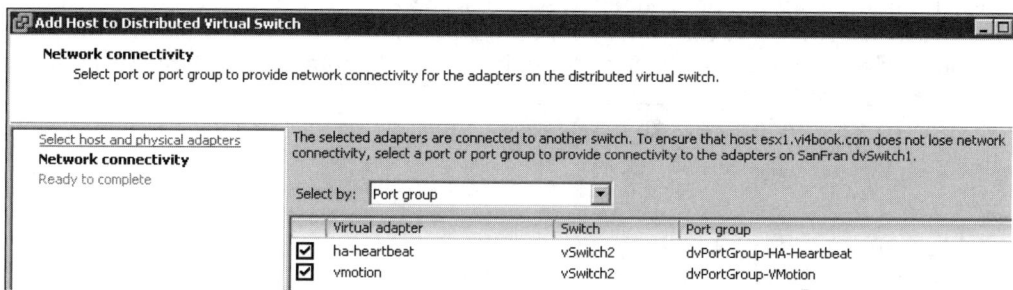

When the wizard completes, you will see a view of the final configuration. This process can be repeated for each ESX host. At the end of the process, each ESX host will have a standard vSwitch that has no port groups or NICs attach to it. The standard vSwitches can safely be removed from each ESX host.

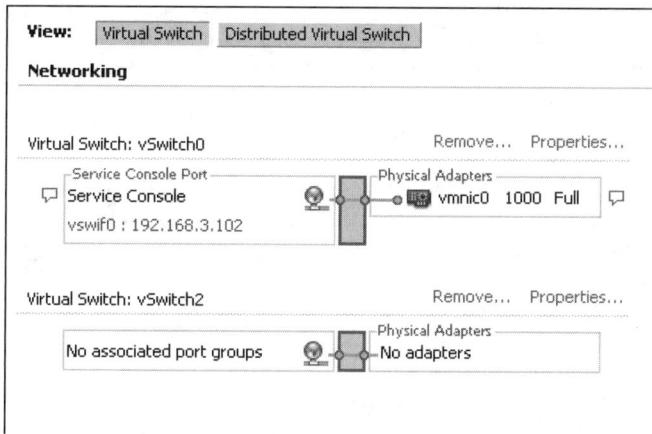

Migrating to a Management DvSwitch

Although an ESX host (regardless of flavor) starts its life with a standard vSwitch0, it is possible to migrate these standard vSwitches to a DvSwitch.

The migration process for management networking for an ESXi 4 host is subtly different from that for an ESX 4.x (Classic) host. Remember that in ESXi, there is no Service Console. With ESX Classic, networking for management is still delivered by the Service Console, which is a Linux distribution. So, this version offers three types of port groups: Virtual Machine, VMkernel, and Service Console. In contrast, ESXi 4 has only two types of port groups: Virtual Machine and VMkernel. VMkernel ports can be used for management, VMotion, IP storage, and other VMkernel features such as FT and HA. Generally, the process of migrating a standard vSwitch0 for ESXi is much the same as it is for ESX Classic, but expect to see references to vmk0 rather than vwif0 in the wizards and dialog boxes, depending on which distribution of ESX you are using.

As in the previous examples, you need to be cautious in transferring NICs to the DvSwitch. During the period of migration, you might see your ESX hosts become disconnected from vCenter. To avoid problems, you could temporarily adjust your networking to allocate an additional NIC to standard vSwitch0, and take just one NIC from the standard vSwitch.

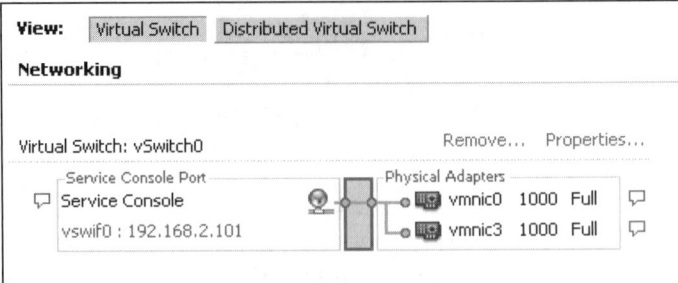

In this example, I migrated from standard vSwitch0 with just one NIC to the DvSwitch without taking any such precautions. I found it to be very reliable, and it did not lead to any disconnections in vCenter. The ESX host triggered an alarm for a moment's worth of slight network outage. I did not need to use the Connect option or force a reconnection from vCenter to the ESX host.

As in the previous migration examples, create a new DvSwitch, this time for use by your management network, choosing to add hosts and physical adapters later. Then set up the required port groups for the DvSwitch.

Add ESX hosts to the DvSwitch and transfer all of the NICs from the standard vSwitch0 to the new management networking DvSwitch (SanFran dvSwitch Management in this example).

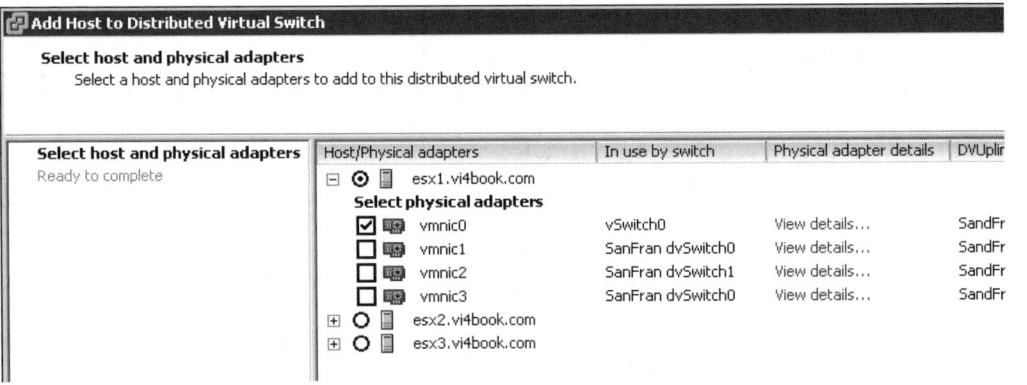

Select the port group(s) on the standard vSwitch and map them to the DvSwitch.

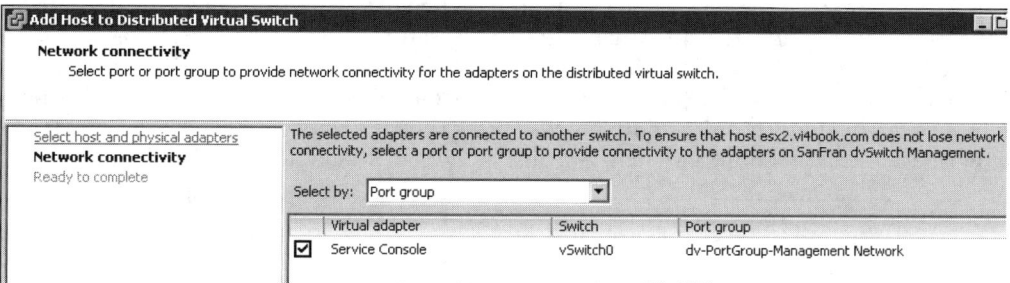

This process can be repeated for each ESX host. At the end of the process, each ESX host will have a standard vSwitch without any port groups or NICs attached to it, and this vSwitch can be safely removed from the ESX host.

Recovering from Lost NICs

Migrations of virtual switches can be quite dangerous if you don't engage your brain. For example, in my experiments, I wanted to return from a DvSwitch back to vSwitch0. As I tried to reverse the migration process by simply migrating from the DvSwitch to the standard vSwitch, the wizard allowed me to destroy the management port on the DvSwitch and move it over to the standard vSwitch, which promptly caused a disconnection from the ESX hosts, because the standard vSwitch *was without NICs*. It was a Homer Simpson "Doh!" moment I won't be repeating again, which is a bit like PuTTYing into an ESX host and then using the `esxcfg-vswitch -U` command to remove the very NIC the session is working from!

It took me a short time to work out how to unlink a physical NIC from the DvSwitch and then link it to a standard vSwitch:

```
esxcfg-vswitch -Q vmnic0 -V 129 'Sanfran Dvswitch Management'
esxcfg-vswitch -L vmnic0 vswitch0
```

The –Q switch is used to remove a physical NIC when it's in use by a DvSwitch port ID of 129. This port ID was discovered by using `esxcfg-vswitch -l`.

Migrating from a DvSwitch to a Standard vSwitch

The migration process from standard vSwitches to DvSwitches is not a one-way, no-reverse-gear process. It is possible to undo the DvSwitch migration process and return to standard vSwitches if you wish. Most likely, if you have created or migrated to DvSwitches, you will not want to return to the older format. However, for the sake of completeness, I will show you how it can be done. In this example, I will walk through returning the management network back to the standard vSwitch, starting without any standard vSwitches.

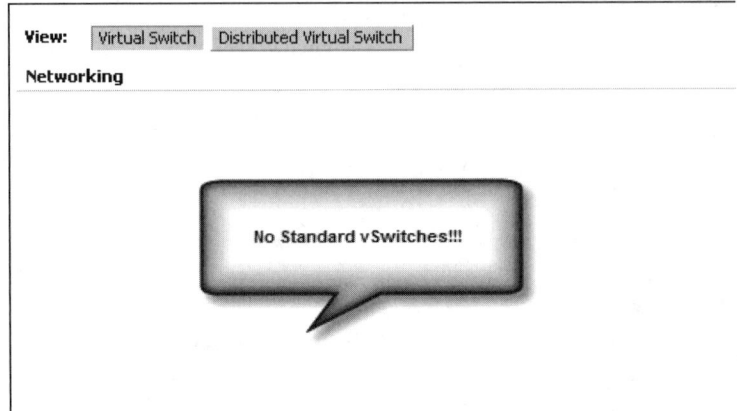

The process is quite straightforward. In fact, DvSwitches have a Migrate to Virtual Switch option—here, virtual switch means standard vSwitch. However, as with migration from standard vSwitches to DvSwitches, care must be taken to avoid disconnecting the virtual machines, the VMkernel, or the management network.

Begin by making sure that there is a free NIC your management PC will be able to use to communicate with the ESX host. In this example, I added vmnic1 to the DvSwitch for management and removed the vmnic0 NIC, using the Manage Physical Adapters option. I did this because I prefer vmnic0 to be allocated to vSwitch0. This is safe to do, as long as all the NICs are patched into the same network or VLAN tagging is in place for the Service Console. It doesn't matter which NIC you allocate, as long as there is one NIC attached to the DvSwitch and another NIC attached to standard vSwitch. Otherwise, you run the risk of totally disconnecting the ESX host.

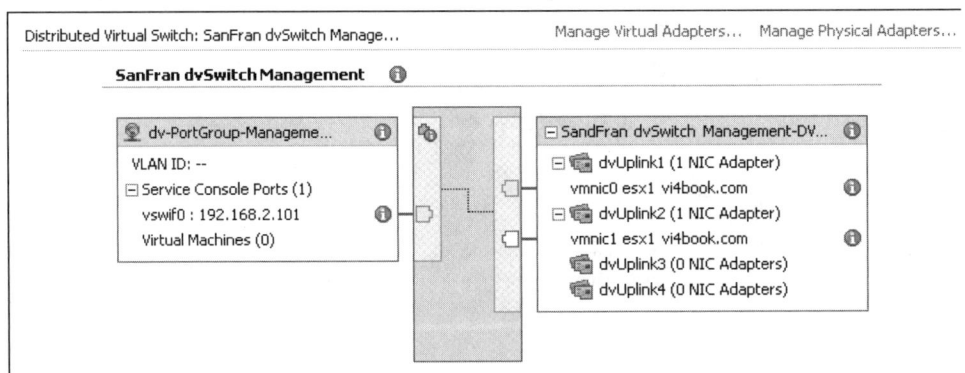

Next, create a standard vSwitch using the vmnic0. Unfortunately, the GUI will not allow you to create a standard vSwitch without a port group. If you are using the GUI, you can just create a temporary port group (named temp in this example) to complete the wizard.

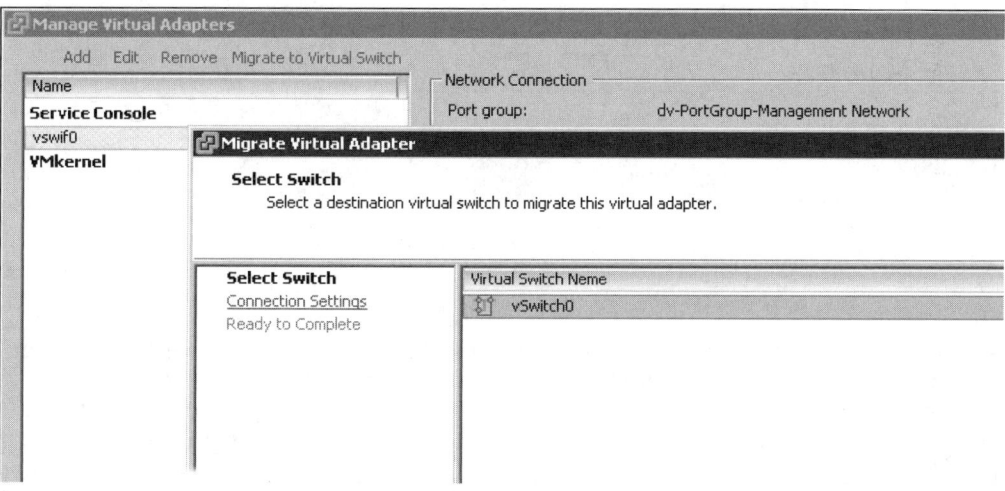

It is possible to create a vSwitch without a port group via the Service Console with the following commands:

```
esxcfg-vswitch -a vSwitch0
esxcfg-vswitch -L vmnic0 vSwitch0
```

Next, click the DvSwitch icon on the Configuration tab of the ESX host. Locate the DvSwitch created for management, and select the Manage Virtual Adapters link. Under the Service Console category, select the vwif0 option, and then choose the Migrate to Virtual Switch option. In the next dialog box, select the standard vSwitch that will be the target for migrating the Service Console settings back to a standard vSwitch.

This will migrate the Service Console settings away from the DvSwitch to the standard vSwitch. You can now remove the temporary virtual machine port group you created.

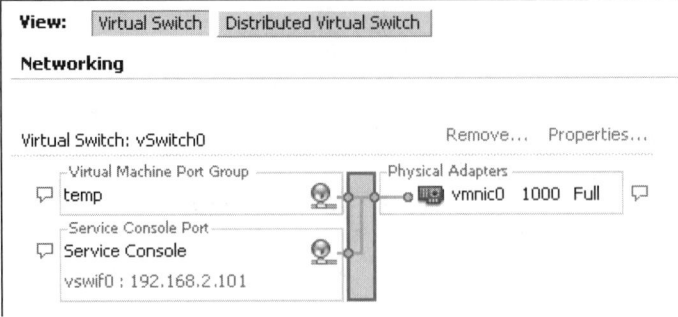

You can use the Migrate to Virtual Switch option for all management and VMkernel port groups. However, virtual machines must be migrated from the DvSwitch using the Migrate Virtual Machine Networking wizard used in earlier examples. The difference in this case is the source and destination options are inverted to allow virtual machines to migrate from a DvSwitch port group to a standard vSwitch port group.

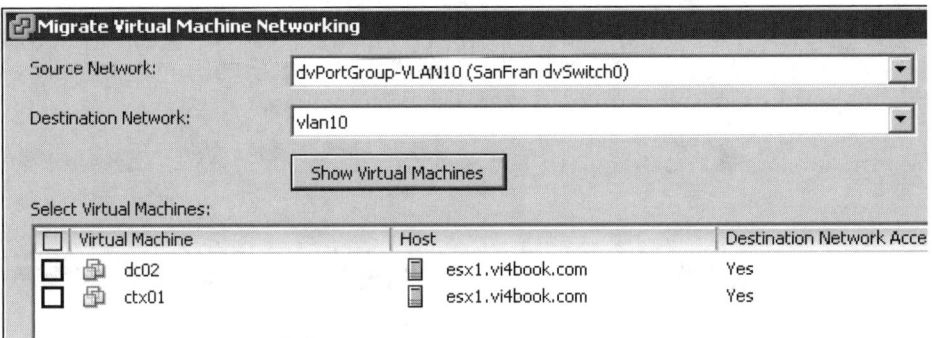

Summary

Distributed virtual switches are a leap forward for ESX. I recommend them for all large organizations that want to lower their total cost of ownership (TCO). Even with good scripting and host profiles, standard virtual switch configurations represent one of the major administrative overheads of the previous version. DvSwitches eliminate much of that burden.

As you have seen, migrating the standard vSwitch environment does take some thought and planning, but compared to other migration routines, it is painless and seamless to the end users. If like me, you grew up on ESX 2 and then ESX 3 networking, you might be a bit RTC (resistant to change). Don't be. For years, people bellyached about the per-ESX network settings being an administrative burden. In years to come, I imagine a future edition of this book that dispenses with standard vSwitches altogether.

CHAPTER 6 | Storage

In this chapter, we will look at the three primary ESX 4.x storage options: storage area network (SAN), Internet SCSI (iSCSI), and network-attached storage (NAS). Additionally, we will take a look at VMware's file system (VMFS) and explain how to format and extend a VMFS volume.

By their nature, SAN and iSCSI systems are very proprietary. Here, I will not go into the details of configuring HP, IBM, or EMC storage. Rather, I will explain and demonstrate how VMware can leverage this storage.

What's New in VMware Storage?

- Improved user interface for multipathing
- Improved storage views in vCenter
- A built-in Increase option to expand a VMFS volume size to take up available free space
- Pluggable Storage Architecture (PSA) support, which allows storage vendors, such as NetApp and EMC, to add plug-ins to vCenter
- Ability to organize datastores in folders and set permissions to filter virtual machine administrator's access to storage
- Improvements in the VMFS resignature process; access to VMFS volume signature writable snapshots without requiring resignaturing

---

Configuring SAN-Based Storage

It is extremely unlikely that anyone would buy a SAN and use it with only an ESX server. It is very likely that existing physical servers running an array of different operating systems would have access to the same SAN. Since ESX, Linux, Novell, Windows, and Solaris do not share a common file system, corruption of data is possible.

SAN administrators use the World Wide Name (WWN)—a 64-bit address, which is stamped on every HBA that has a connection to the SAN—to allow or deny access to LUNs on the SAN. (A WWN is akin to the MAC address on a NIC.) This way, they can mask, or hide, LUNs to make sure the right operating system sees the right LUNs. Usually, SAN vendors will have their own product-specific term for this feature. For example, HP calls their technology Selective Storage Presentation.

If your SAN does not support firmware-based LUN masking, you might be interested to know that ESX server can mask the LUNs through an ESX server configuration setting (on the Configuration tab, in the Software pane, select Advanced Settings and set the Disk.MaskLUNs parameter in the Disk section). However, most production SANs will support LUN masking, and their built-in support should always be preferred over any other software method.

Some organizations go an extra step in SAN configuration. Along with LUN masking, they might also create zones, similar to Ethernet's VLAN, for SAN switches to configure the switches into smaller networks. This zoning can be carried out for each and every HBA in an ESX host. Some people regard this as excessive, but it can significantly improve performance. Additionally, if an HBA malfunctions, it cannot affect the other HBAs on the same switch. Although zoning every HBA involves quite a bit of administration, it does deliver long-term benefits.

Discovering Your HBA's WWN

As an ESX administrator, you might be required to provide the WWN of your server or servers, so that the storage administrator will be able to set up LUN masking. Alternatively, if you are fortunate enough to manage your own SAN, you may require this information personally.

As with NICs, storage adapters are labeled vmhba0, vmhba1, and so on. Usually, the internal RAID controller card has a HBA number of 0, because this naming convention works by merely looking at the PCI bus and serializing the storage adapters as they are found during the installation. So in most cases, your first Fibre Channel HBA is likely to be vmhba1.

To find out an HBA's WWN, in the vSphere Client, select your ESX host, click the Configuration tab, and from the Hardware pane, choose Storage Adapters. The following example shows two Fibre Channel HBAs and their WWNs.

Configuration	Tasks & Events	Alarms	Permissions	Maps	Storage Views

Storage Adapters

Device	Type	WWN
QLA2340-Single Channel 2Gb Fibre Channel to PCI-X HBA		
vmhba2	Fibre Channel	20:00:00:e0:8b:0b:1b:6b 21:00:00:e0:8b:0b:1b:6b
ISP2312-based 2Gb Fibre Channel to PCI-X HBA		
vmhba1	Fibre Channel	20:00:00:e0:8b:85:2e:54 21:00:00:e0:8b:85:2e:54
Smart Array 6i		
vmhba0	Block SCSI	

Rescanning HBAs

After new LUNs have been made available, or the storage people have done their work, you will need to force a rescan of the HBA from the vSphere Client. On bootup, ESX scans all the LUNs it is able to see, but you really don't want to do unnecessary reboots of the ESX server itself just to see a new LUN. This is why the rescan feature exists.

ESX server can see up to a maximum of 256 LUNs, from LUN0 to LUN255. On some systems, LUN0 is a management LUN and should not be used, unless you want to run SAN management tools within your virtual machine. You should consult your documentation if you are not sure whether LUN0 is available.

NOTE *ESX 2.x had a setting called Disk.MaxLUN that would stop the LUN scanning once an ESX host had scanned from LUN0 to LUN7. This value was been changed from ESX 3 onwards, mainly to reduce the number of support requests generated by VMware customers not knowing about the Disk.MaxLUN value! The current setting for Disk.MaxLUN is 256, with a starting and scanning position of 1.*

The Rescan option allows you to rescan for new LUNs and also check if they contain VMFS volumes. To force a rescan, in the vSphere Client, select your ESX host, click the

Configuration tab, and from the Hardware pane, choose Storage Adapters. Then choose to rescan a single HBA or all HBAs, as follows:

- To rescan a particular HBA, select the HBA you wish to rescan, right-click, and choose Rescan.

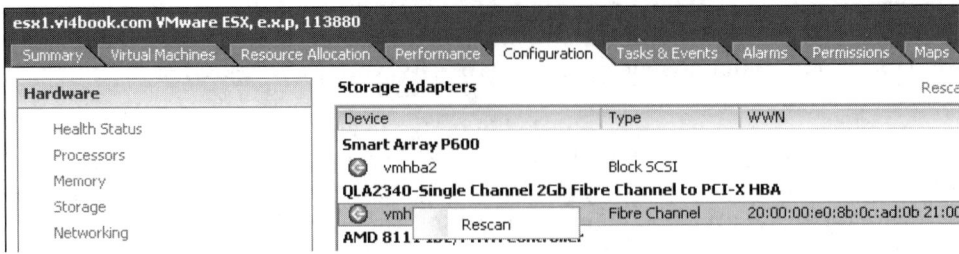

- To rescan all HBAs, click the Rescan link in the top-right corner of the vSphere Client window.

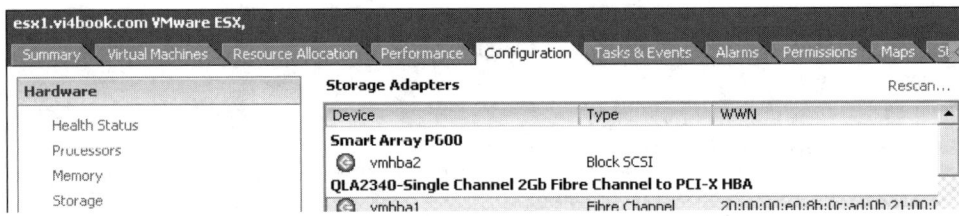

You will see the Rescan dialog box. Click OK to force the rescan.

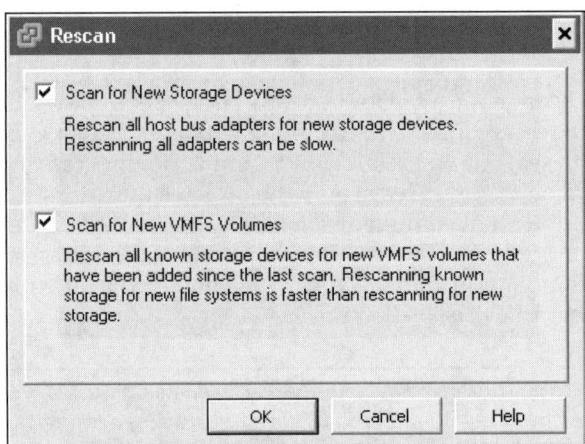

You can also force a rescan using the command-line tool esxcfg-rescan. It takes the following form:

```
esxcfg-rescan vmhbaN
```

vmhba*N* is the HBA used for the rescan process. Its ability to show you the LUN discovery process in more detail can be useful, especially if you print to the console the contents of the vmkernel log afterwards, with the following command:

```
tail -f /var/log/vmkernel
```

As you might imagine, if you create a new LUN and you have 32 ESX hosts, navigating to each ESX host configuration and issuing the Rescan command is quite time-consuming. Many VI3.5 users began to use utilities like the VI ToolKit for Windows (PowerShell for VMware) to carry out bulk administration tasks like rescanning multiple ESX hosts. VMware has improved vSphere 4 by adding the option to rescan many ESX hosts with a single click. To use this option, right-click a vCenter object that contains many ESX hosts, such as folder (the AMD Hosts folder in this example), and select Rescan for Datastores.

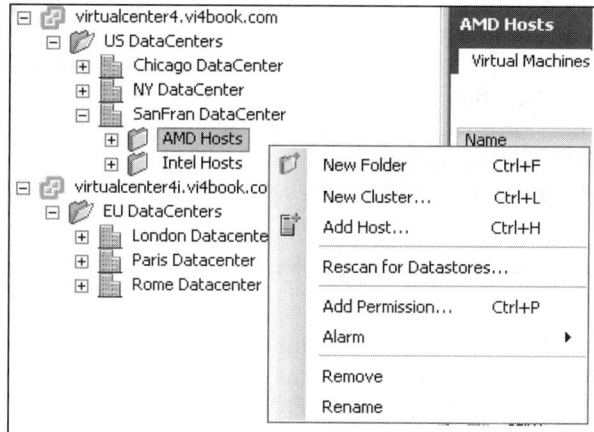

You will see a warning about the rescanning process possibly taking a long time.

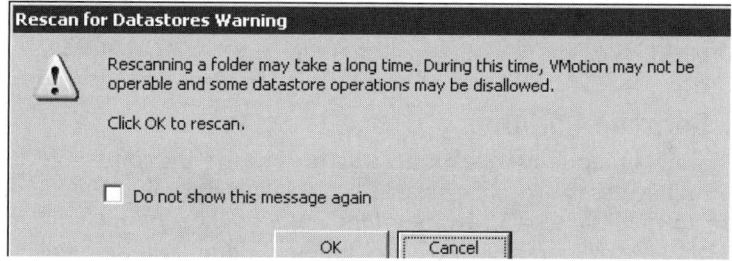

After you click OK in the warning dialog box, you will see the standard Rescan dialog box, and can click OK to start the rescanning process.

Understanding the vmhba Syntax

ESX server uses a special syntax so that the VMkernel can find the storage it is using. This syntax is used by local storage, SAN, and iSCSI systems. This syntax is not unique to ESX servers; it has been used in UNIX for many years.

The vmhbaN:N:N:N syntax includes a sequence of numbers that tells the VMkernel how to navigate to the specific storage location. This syntax has slightly changed in vSphere4 compared in previous releases. Previously, the numbers represent the adapter, target, LUN, and volume, respectively. People tried to remember by the acronym A:T:L:V. The target in SAN or iSCSI environments represents the storage processors on the disk array. The first three digits (A:T:L) begin their numbering at 0; the last digit (V) starts with 1.

For example, vmhba2:1:18:3 indicates the third HBA (0,1,2) connected to the second storage processor (0,1) using the LUN 18, and the volume (or partition) is the third one (3). Remember that LUN 18 is actually the nineteenth LUN, as LUN counting starts from 0.

In vSphere 4 the HBA syntax is now set to enumerate vmhbaN:C:T:L:V. The C option now displays what "channel" is currently in use. This is particularly relevant to environments that use iSCSI. Some iSCSI vendors use a channel identify to enumerate volumes that are using the same connection, but referenced by different channels. Not all iSCSI vendors adopt this convention preferring instead to present one volume per channel. If you are using fibre-channel connections this number will always be zero.

In day-to-day operations, you usually won't need to know this syntax. Most people use volume and datastore labels, which are available when you format a LUN as VMFS. However, you will need to know this syntax when formatting VMFS volumes and to configure other advanced storage options, such as Raw Device Mapping (RDM) files. (RDM files allow the ESX administrator to give a virtual machine direct access to LUNs on a SAN or iSCSI system, as discussed in Chapter 7.)

Configuring iSCSI SAN-Based Storage

iSCSI is a competitor to Fibre Channel SANs. This said, frequently the people who make SANs make iSCSI equipment, too. iSCSI is similar to SAN technology in that it is capable of presenting a LUN to a server. What makes iSCSI different is the transport used to carry the SCSI commands. It uses TCP port 3260 for this communication. If you work in a restrictive firewall environment, you may find that this port is not open. Additionally, the ESX server has its own firewall, which may prevent iSCSI communication. Currently in ESX 4.x, when you enable VMware's software iSCSI, it automatically opens TCP port 3260 to allow communication. In ESX 3.x, VMware kept changing this behavior, so I now manually enable firewall ports to be sure they are not the source of blocked communication.

Hardware and Software Initiators

iSCSI uses your normal Ethernet network infrastructure to carry the commands themselves. This means you don't necessarily need special HBAs and switches. You can use a conventional NIC to connect to an iSCSI system. VMware refers to this as the *software initiator*. VMware's software iSCSI is actually part of the Cisco iSCSI Initiator Command Reference. In previous release the software intiator inside the VMkernel worked together with an vmkiscsi deamon in the Service Console environment. This is no longer the case, and the entire iSCSI stack resides inside the VMkernel. Alternatively, you can buy an adapter that is designed for iSCSI communication from companies like QLogic. VMware refers to this as a *hardware initiator*.

As the name suggests, an initiator is the side that begins the communication (the client) to the iSCSI target (the disk array). Hardware initiators have what is called a TCP Offload Engine (TOE) chip, which improves performance by removing the load from the main CPUs. In the future, all systems will have a TOE chip, which will be enabled/disabled in the BIOS. In fact, the new HP ProLiant G5 Servers already support this multifunctionality.

In this chapter, I will focus on the use of a software initiator, as this is a method everyone can configure.

iSCSI Qualified Names

Another unique iSCSI feature is its use of a different naming convention. iSCSI does not use WWNs. Instead, it uses the iSCSI Qualified Name (IQN). You can regard the IQN as a DNS name, or reverse DNS. It's a convention rather than something that is hard-coded. The IQN looks something like this:

```
iqn.2008-11.com.vi4book:esxhost1
```

New to vSphere4 VMware now additionally support the IEEE "Extended Unique Identifier" (EUI). A sample EUI would look like this:

```
eui.fedcba9876543210
```

In many ways they serve the same purpose as the WWN in fibre-channel or like a MAC address in Ethernet networking used to control access to storage.

The first part is always the letters *iqn*, followed by the domain name registration date, and ending in the name itself. In reality, it is only used to ensure uniqueness. After all, a domain name can't be registered by more than one organization at the same time. The next part is your domain in reverse—com.vi4book in this example (this might look like uk.co .rftm-ed or com.vmguru). After that, you can specify a colon and alias; in the example, the alias has been set to esxhost1. As with all aliases, the intention is to allow you to use short names instead of specifying the full IQN in software interfaces.

With the software adapter, the IP address, subnet mask, and default gateway are specified in a VMkernel port group on vSwitch. The IQN itself is specified when you configure the software adapter for the first time. If you are working with a hardware adapter such as a QLogic iSCSI card, you will probably find these settings are held in the card's BIOS settings.

You will generally want to have an isolated network for your iSCSI traffic, not only for performance, but also because the traffic generated, as in SANs, is not currently encrypted. VMware's iSCSI implementation does support authentication with the Challenge Handshake Authentication Protocol (CHAP) for an additional tier of security, in addition to the IQN value.

Limitations on iSCSI Use

While iSCSI systems can do all the things SANs can do, you should be aware of three current limitations in terms of VMware support:

- You can install ESX to iSCSI LUN for iSCSI booting purposes, but you must use a supported hardware initiator.

- Only the hardware initiator supports a static discovery of LUNs from the iSCSI system. This is not very limiting, since dynamic discovery is much easier to set up and works with both software and hardware initiators.

- There is no support for running clustering software within a virtual machine using iSCSI storage. However, as of VI3.5, there is now support from VMware for iSCSI used in conjunction with VMware's Consolidated Backup.

Emulating an iSCSI System

A number of free virtual appliances can emulate an iSCSI system for you. While I wouldn't recommend these for a production environment, they are perfectly fine for your test and development labs or for your own personal development in the process of learning VMware, perhaps as part of your preparation for a VMware Certified Professional (VCP) test. As with all things in life, book learning is one thing, but hands-on experience is quite another.

You might want to look at Openfiler (http://www.openfiler.com), which is a Linux build designed for storage that includes iSCSI support. Alternatively, iSCSI Virtual SAN, created by the scarily named user reaper007, is available from the VMware Virtual Appliances site (http://www.vmware.com/vmtn/appliances/directory/364).

Along with these free but unsupported virtual storage appliances, many commercial SAN and iSCSI vendors now offer their technologies as virtual appliances. For example, EMC offers the Celerra storage system as a virtual appliance, and FalconStor and LeftHand Networks (recently acquired by HP) also have storage solution virtual appliances. Often, these vendor-specific virtual appliances are fully supported. They are an investment, but can often be evaluated at no cost, usually for 30 to 60 days. What's great about these virtual appliances is that they will frequently have advanced features such as replication. Using them, you can learn more about storage, as well as other technologies, such as VMware's Site Recovery Manager.

To give you a feel for how iSCSI works, I will show you how to configure a software-based iSCSI emulator, or target, in case you don't happen to have an iSCSI system currently installed. This way, you will be able to see both sides of the storage equation and understand how ESX communicates with an iSCSI array (after all, your ESX initiators need something to communicate with). As an example, I have chosen to use the HP LeftHand iSCSI Virtual SAN Appliance software (VSA). Note that this doesn't mean that I prefer the HP LeftHand software, but it is easy to acquire and configure, so it works for demonstration purposes here.

What's a Virtual Appliance?

A virtual appliance is a downloadable virtual machine that already contains an operating system supported by a virtualization vendor and a ready-to-run application or service. Some virtual appliances are completely free, especially when they are based on Linux. Some vendors offer evaluation versions of their virtual appliances, which you can use before parting with hard cash.

Many virtual appliances can be downloaded from the Internet in a zip format, and then once extracted, imported via vCenter to then execute on a selected ESX host. Vendors are gradually updating their virtual appliances to be compatible with VMware's Open Virtual Machine Format (OVF) files. This is a format that VMware has made open source to allow virtual machines to be moved around, stored on the Internet, and then downloaded by anyone who is interested.

Importing VSA

Follow these steps to download, unzip, and import the HP LeftHand VSA:

1. Browse to the HP LeftHand SAN solutions web site at https://h20392.www2.hp .com/portal/swdepot/displayProductInfo.do?productNumber=LHNSW8.1

2. Download two packages: CMC Windows (.exe), which is the Management Console for the VSA (a Linux version is also available), and VSA Full Evaluation Version (.ovf), which is the VSA virtual appliance. In order to download the evaluation version, you must provide an email address.

TIP *As the CMC package is smaller than the VSA package, it will probably take a much shorter time to download. So while the VSA downloads, you might want to install the CMC to your management PC. The Management Console will need to connect to the VSA over the network, so you will need to think about which network and IP range the VSA will reside on, whether there is a route from your ESX hosts to it, and whether there is a route from your management PC to the VSA. The CMC is a very simple application and is not difficult to install; a typical install will meet the requirements for the examples in this chapter. Although you can install the CMC now, there is little point in executing the CMC until you have downloaded, extracted, imported, and configured the VSA.*

---

3. After the packages are downloaded, extract the vsa.zip file with your preferred unzip utility to some temporary location.

4. To import the file into the vCenter/ESX environment, from vCenter's File menu, select Deploy OVF Template.

TIP *Selecting Browse VA Marketplace from vCenter's File menu allows you to visit the portion of VMware's Web site that hosts virtual appliances, many of which are free to evaluate or even completely free.*

---

5. In the OVF Template Wizard, select the "Deploy from file" option, browse to the VSA.ovf file, and then click Next.

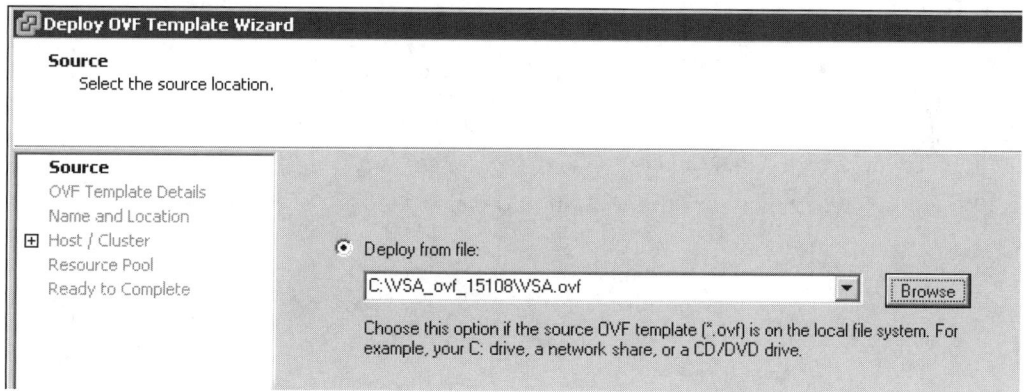

6. Accept the EULA and click Next.

7. Enter a friendly name and virtual machine folder location for the VSA.

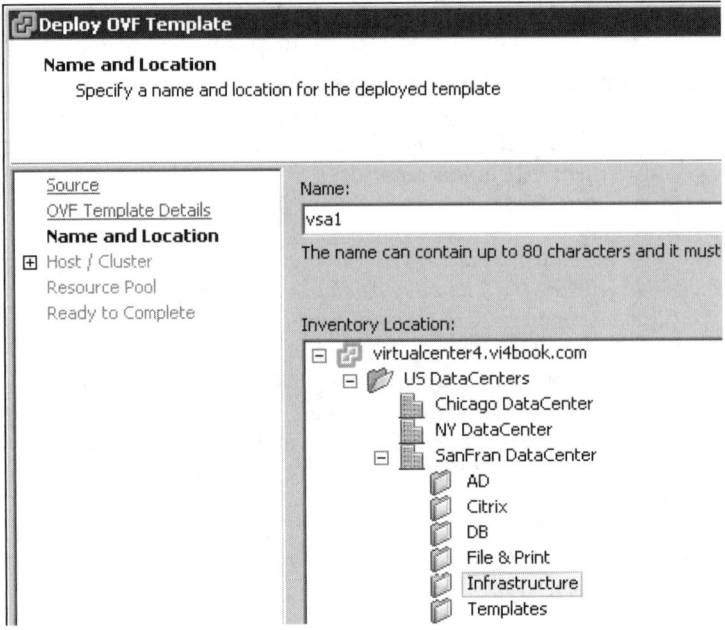

8. Select the ESX host (or cluster) on which you wish to run the VSA.

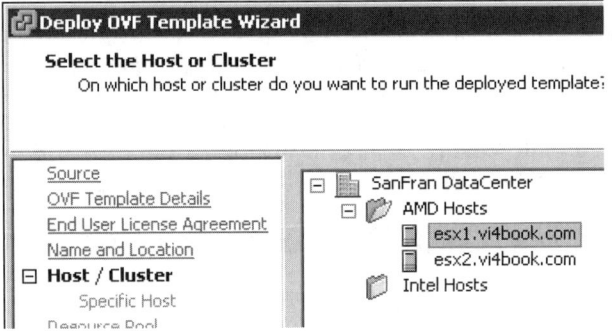

9. Select on which datastore you wish to locate the VSA.

10. Select on which network the VSA should reside.

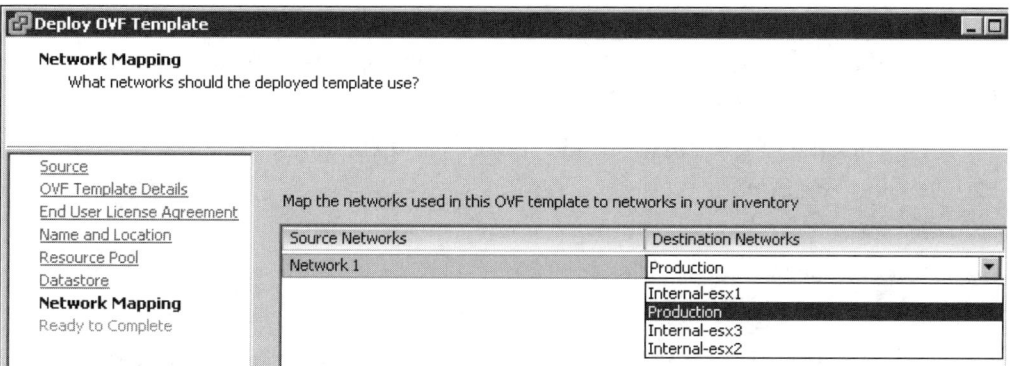

11. Click Finish to start the import process.

Modifying the Virtual Machine's Network Settings

By default, the VSA may be patched to a virtual machine network. This is the virtual machine port group created by default in an ESX installation. However, if you choose to manage the VSA, it must be patched to a network accessible to the ESX host that has iSCSI LUNs presented to it by the VSA.

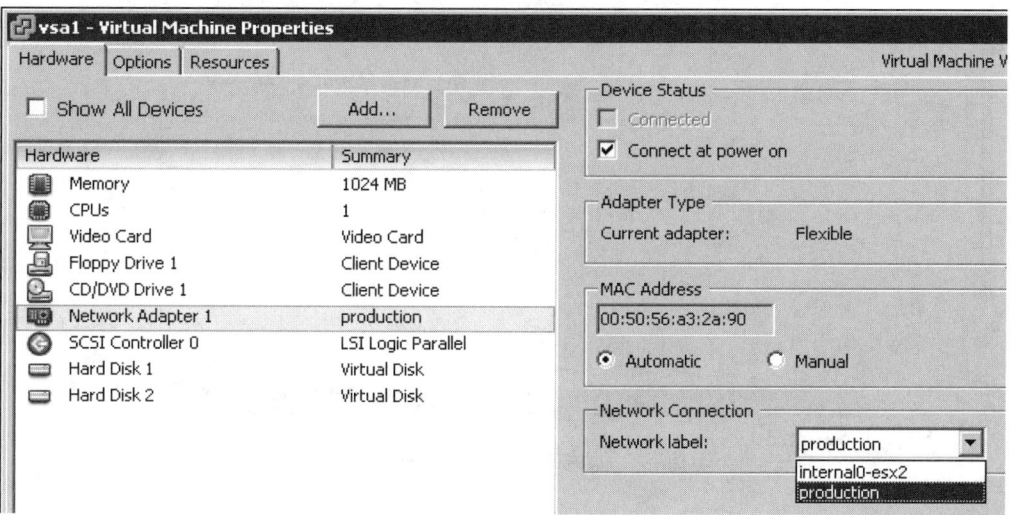

Adding a Third Virtual Disk

Next, add a third disk. This disk will be a volume presented to your ESX hosts. You will want to make it as big as possible, as you will create virtual machines here. Additionally, it must be located on SCSI 1:0. The following steps outline the process. You'll learn more about the specifics of these settings in Chapter 7, which covers creating virtual machines.

NOTE *Currently, the VSA can contain only three virtual disks, including the two provided in the zip file. Future versions of the VSA will allow for more virtual disks to be added as storage demands change.*

1. Right-click the VSA virtual machine and select Edit Settings.
2. Click the Add button.
3. Select Hard Disk.
4. Select "Create new virtual disk."
5. Set the size of the virtual disk.

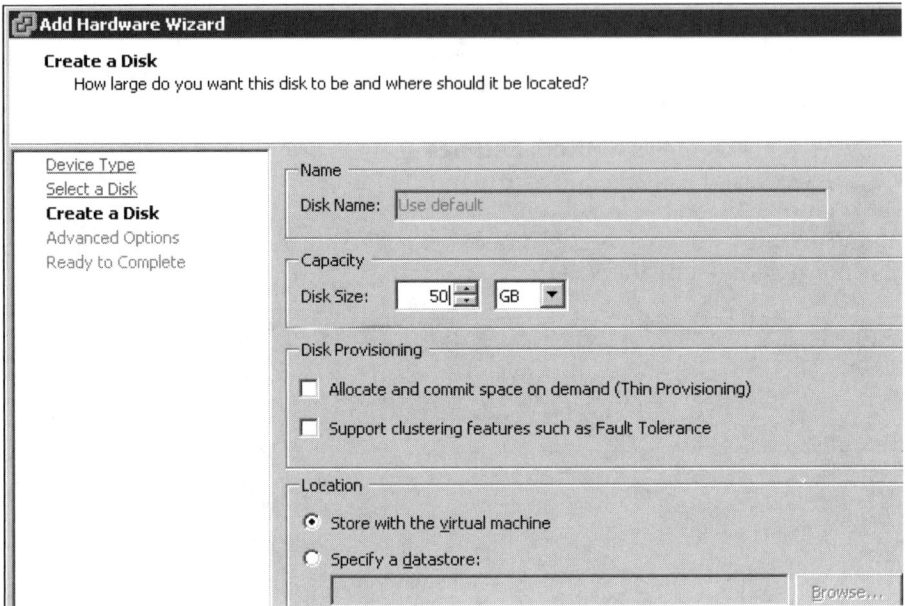

6. Select SCSI 1:0 as the SCSI adapter and SCSI ID for the virtual machine.

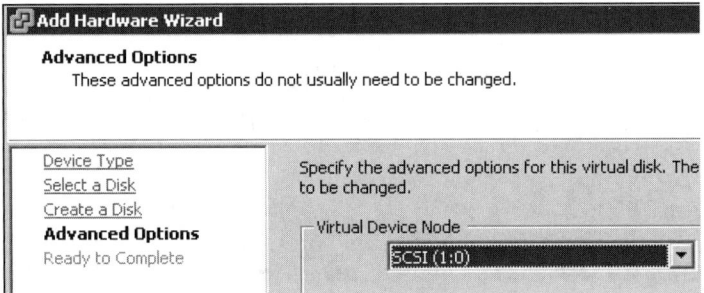

7. Click Next, then Finish, and then OK.

Later, when I describe how to create volumes in the VSA, I will use thin provisioning to present this disk a 1TB LUN. Even so, the larger this third disk is, the more space you will have for your virtual machines.

Using a Static or Dynamic Virtual MAC Address

Before you power on the VSA for the first time, you might want to consider how the product is licensed should you wish to use VSA beyond the 60-day evaluation period. VSA is licensed by the virtual MAC address of the virtual machine generated by VMware at power on. This auto-generated MAC address typically won't change, but it may if you manually register and unregister a virtual machine from one ESX host to another. Additionally, if you fail to back up the VMX, you could lose this information forever. And if you clone the VSA with the vCenter cloning facility, a brand-new MAC address is generated at that point.

Depending on your circumstances and requirements, you might prefer to set and record a static MAC address to your VSA. (HP LeftHand recommends setting a static MAC address.) You can set a static MAC address in the range provided by VMware. Since VI3.5, we have been able to set a static MAC address in the GUI, and no longer need to edit the VMX file directly to set this value, as was necessary in ESX 2.x.

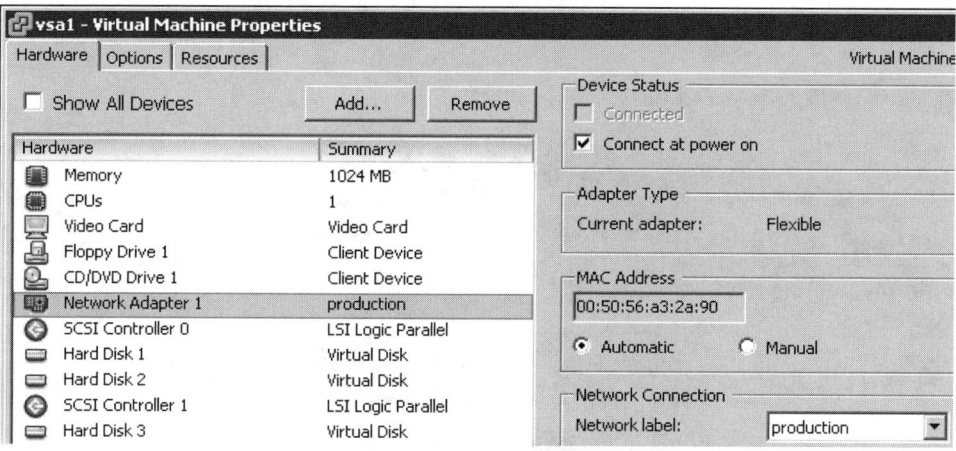

Whether you use a static or dynamic MAC address, be sure to make a record of that address so your license key (if you have purchased one) will be valid if you need to completely rebuild the VSA from scratch.

Considering a Second VSA

Before you first power on the VSA and configure it, you might want to consider your options for creating a second VSA, if you wish to add one. A second VSA could be configured as replication partner, which would be suitable for development work with, say, VMware's Site Recovery Manager.

You currently have a VSA in a clean and unconfigured state. To rapidly create a second VSA, you could run a vCenter cloning operation to duplicate the current VSA virtual machine configuration. You can do this even if the virtual machine is located on local storage, as is the case with my first VSA. HP LeftHand does not support cloning the VSA once it is in a management group set up with the client console used to manage the system.

Configuring the VSA Host

The primary configuration involves setting the host name and IP settings for the VSA from the VMware Remote Console window. You can navigate this utility using a combination of keystrokes, such as the cursor keys, TAB key, SPACEBAR, and ENTER/RETURN keys. It is very simple to use.

1. Power on the VSA virtual machine.

2. Open a virtual machine Remote Console window.

3. At the login prompt, type **start** and press ENTER.

```
                    Welcome to SanIQ

Loading vmlinuz....................................
Loading initrd.gz..................................................
..........................
Ready.
Uncompressing Linux... Ok, booting the kernel.
Loading keymap: us [  OK  ]

Type in "start" and hit enter at the login prompt.
none login: start_
```

4. Press ENTER to select Login.

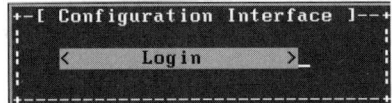

5. In the menu, select Network TCP/IP Settings and press ENTER.

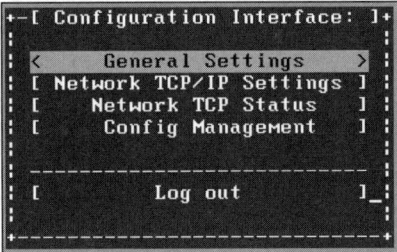

6. Cursor up, select <eth0>, and press ENTER.

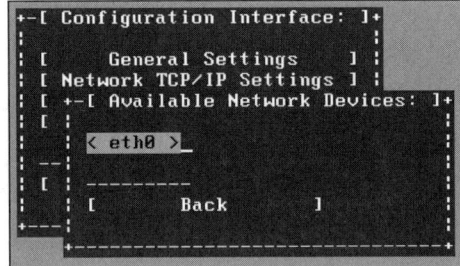

7. Change the host name and set a static IP address.

```
+-[ Network Settings: ]----------------------------------+
:                                                        :
: Specify the network settings for the Advanced Micro    :
: Devices [AMD] 79c970 [PCnet32 LANCE] port. Be sure the :
: ethernet cable is plugged into the selected port.      :
:                                                        :
: Hostname:    vsa1.vi4book.com                          :
:                                                        :
: ( ) Disable Interface.                                 :
: ( ) Obtain IP address automatically using DHCP.        :
: (*) Use the following IP address:                      :
:                                                        :
:     IP Address:  172.168.3.99                          :
:     Mask:        255.255.255.0                         :
:     Gateway:                                           :
:                                                        :
:                < OK >_    [ CANCEL ]                    :
:                                                        :
+--------------------------------------------------------+
```

8. Press ENTER at the warning about the restart of networking.

9. Use the Back options to return to the main login page, and then log out.

TIP *You might wish to update your DNS configuration to reflect these host names and IP addresses so you can use an FQDN in various management tools.*

Installing the VSA Management Console

You set up the VSA using the Management Console, which is in the CMC Windows (.exe) file you downloaded from the HP LeftHand Web site. You should install this application using a typical installation, which is sufficient for the examples in this chapter.

Your PC must have a valid or routable IP address to communicate with your VSA. Before you begin, you might as well check that your management station can actually ping the VSA. You're not going to get very far in the next step if you can't.

Load the CMC, and the Welcome to Find Modules Wizard will start. Choose to search by IP address or host name.

Click the Add button and type in the IP address or host name of the VSA. This dialog box may report the status as Unknown until you click Finish, when it will change to Newly Found. You can then click Close to close the dialog box.

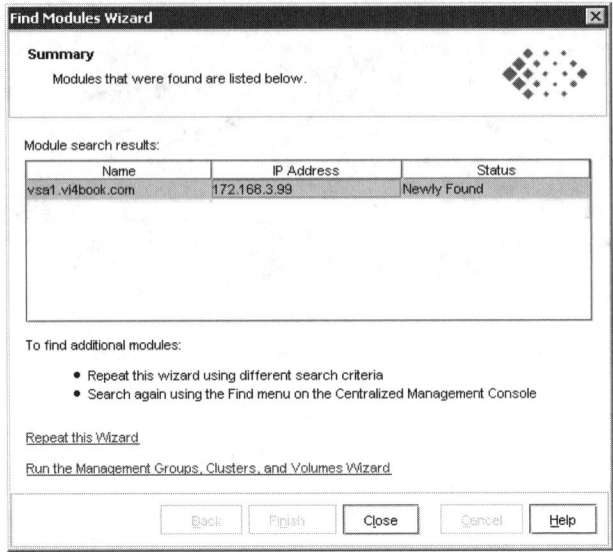

Configuring VSA Management Groups, Clusters, and Volumes

The VSA setup is broken down into three stages: creating a management group, creating a cluster, and creating a volume.

NOTE *My instructions assume that your VSA was not found during the discovery process and that it needs to be added manually through the Management Console.*

A VSA must be in its own management group. During this process, you will be able to set friendly names for the groups and volume names. It makes sense to use names that reflect the purpose of the unit in question such as SanFran_Management_Group; SanFran_ Cluster; and AD, Citrix, File, SQL, Web, and so on for volume names. Of course, it is entirely up to you what naming convention you adopt. The only restriction is that these names cannot contain spaces. You can use camel case or the underscore character to improve readability.

Volume is another word for a LUN. When you create a volume, you are creating a block of storage that is unformatted and that can be addressed by another system (in our case ESX) once formatted files are created on it.

NOTE *Some storage vendors refer to this process as creating a file system. This can be a little confusing, as many people associate this with using ext3, VMFS, or NTFS. A volume or file system is another layer of abstraction between the physical storage and its access by server. It allows for advanced features such as thin provisioning and virtual storage.*

A volume can either be fully or thinly provisioned. With thinly provisioned volumes, the disk space presented to a server or operating system can be greater than the actual physical storage available. So a volume can be 1TB in size, even though you have only 512GB of actual disk space. You might know this concept as virtual storage, where you procure disk space as you need it, rather than up front. The downside is you really must track and trace your actual storage utilization very carefully. You cannot save files in thin air.

Here is the procedure for running the Management Groups, Clusters, and Volumes Wizard from the Management Console:

1. In the Getting Started node, click Management Groups, Clusters and Volumes, and then click Next.

2. Choose New Management Group. For the management group name, type something meaningful (SanFran_Management_Group in this example) and select the VSA you wish to add (vsa1.vi4book.com in this example).

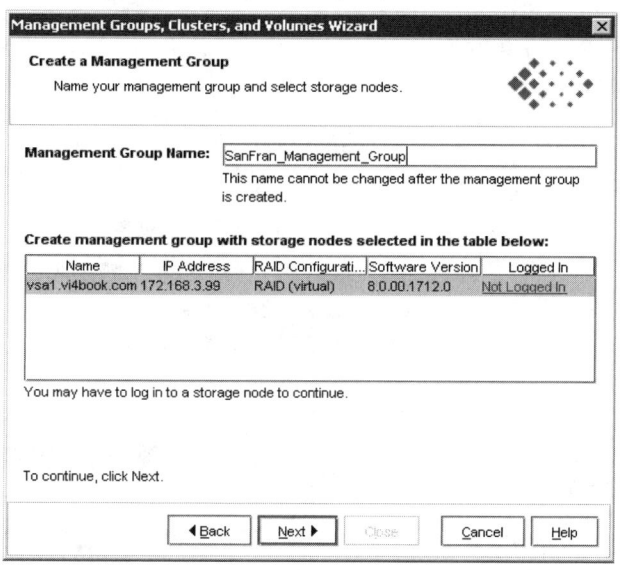

3. Set a username and password. This username and password are stored in a separate database internal to the VSA. The database is in a proprietary binary format and is copied to all VSAs in the same management group. It is in no way connected to the

logins to your vCenter or Active Directory environment. If you are the forgetful kind, you might want to make some record of these values.

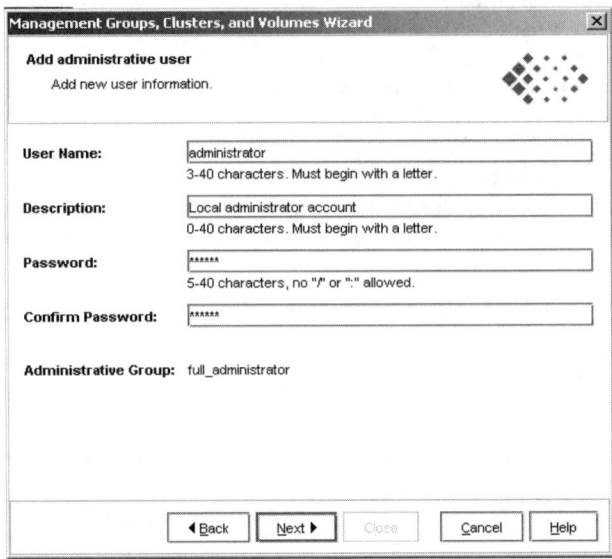

4. Choose Manually Set Time.

NOTE   *As the VSA is a virtual appliance, it should receive time updates from the ESX host, which is in turn configured for NTP. To enable this, I edited the VMX file of my VSA and set the* `tools.syncTime = "TRUE"` *option.*

5. Choose Standard Cluster. Type in a cluster name (SanFran_Cluster in this example).

6. Set a virtual IP (VIP). This is mainly used by a cluster when you have two VSAs within the same management group. Strictly speaking, it isn't required for this demonstration, but it's best practice to set this now for possible future use. For this example, I used my next available IP of 172.168.3.97.

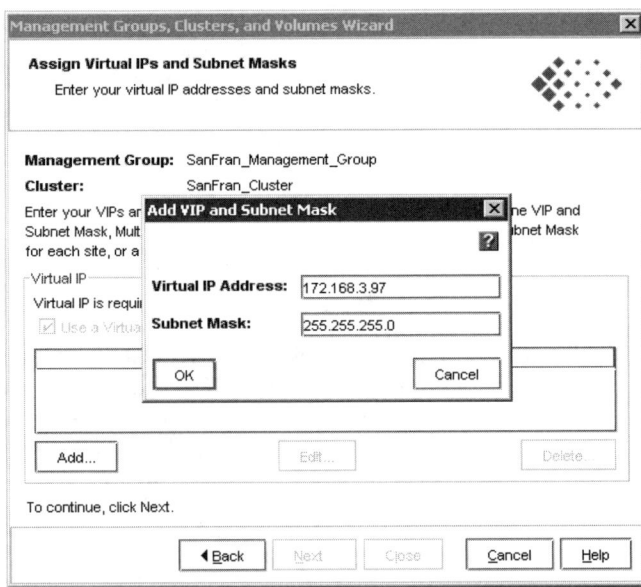

7. Type in a volume name (citrix in this example, to store Citrix-based virtual machines), set the volume size (such as 1TB), and choose Thin for Provisioning. In this example, the size of the "physical" disk is 48GB, but with thin provisioning, I am going to present this storage as if it were a 1TB volume/LUN. A replication level option would be used if I was replicating within a management group.

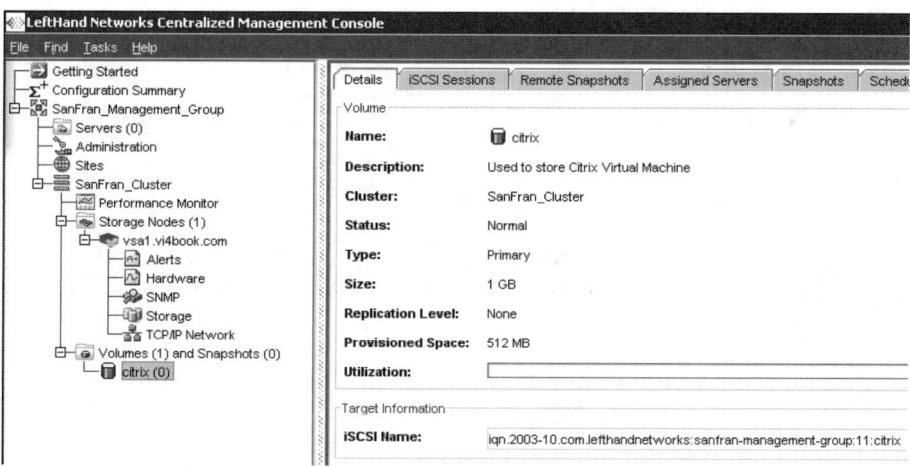

NOTE *You can switch between thin and full provisioning for volumes at any time you wish.*

At the end of the setup process (which can be quite lengthy), the management group, cluster and volume will be created.

Creating More Volumes

Creating additional volumes is very easy in the VSA Management Console. Simply right-click the Volumes node and choose New Volume.

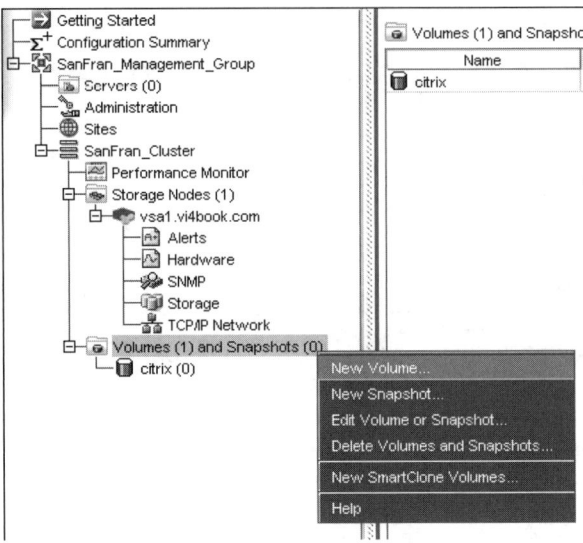

In the New Volume dialog box, enter a volume name and size.

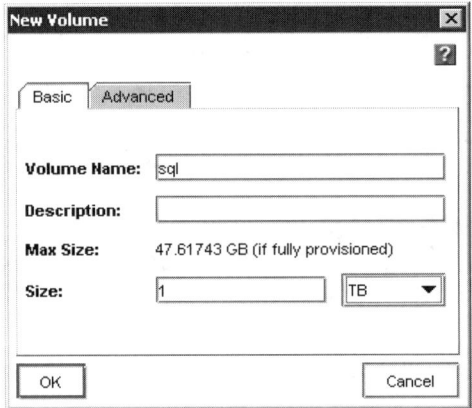

If you are prepared to use thin provisioning, click the Advanced tab and select the Thin radio button. Alternatively, your volume must fit within the size available on the disk (in my case, 47.61GB).

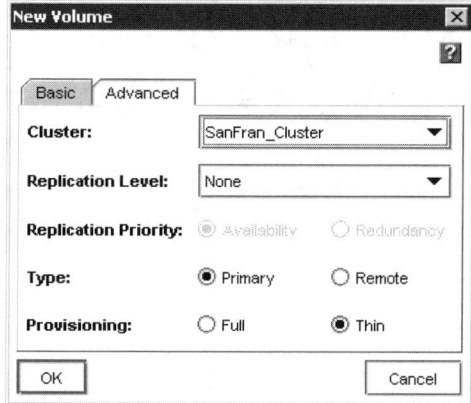

For demonstration purposes, I created a number of volumes. Notice how each has been thinly provisioned with 1TB. Also notice that the VSA automatically generates an IQN for the target.

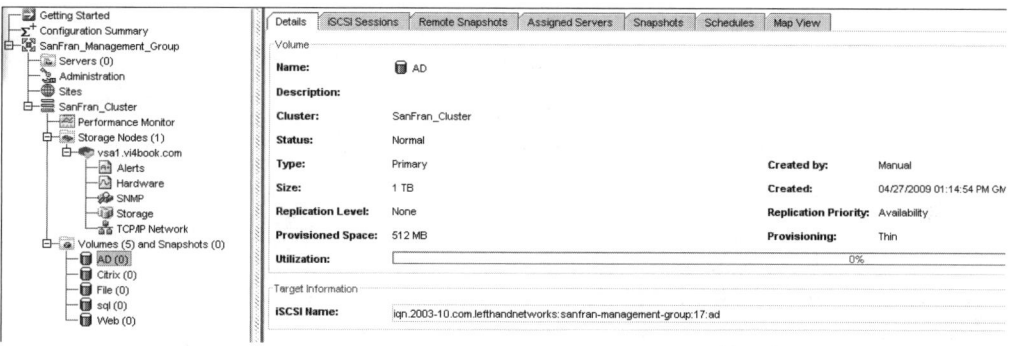

Adding Servers

In the new version of the HP LeftHand VSA, the old method of allocating volumes to servers, which used volume lists and authentication groups, has been changed. Version 8 introduces the ability to add servers to the VSA in a registration process, which in turn allows you to select which servers can access which volumes. Here are the steps:

1. Right-click the Server(s) node in the Management Console and select New Server.

2. In the Name field, type a friendly name. For this example, I used the FQDN for the server.

3. Enable the CHAP required option.

4. In the CHAP Name field, enter the IQN of the ESX host.

5. In the Target Secret and Initiator Secret fields, type a password.

CHAP is optional. It possible to require that CHAP authentication is bidirectional, in that both the server and storage must authenticate to each other. This is the most rigorous security you can currently configure. Target and initiator secrets (passwords) must be at least 12 characters long. Additionally, the target secret and initiator secret cannot be the same.

Repeat this process for all your other ESX hosts that will require access.

Assigning Servers to Volumes

Once you had added your ESX hosts, you can allocate each of them the correct volumes. This is a very easy process and can be carried out in a number of ways: select a host and assign a volume to it, select a volume and assign a host to it, or assign hosts when you create a new volume.

To select the host, right-click a server in the Managment Console and choose Assign and Unassign Volumes and Snapshots.

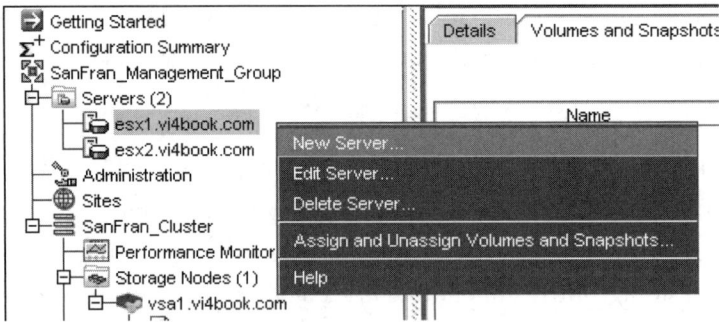

In the dialog box, select the assigned volumes and permissions. For this example, I selected every volume and accepted the default permission of Read/Write.

Assign and Unassign Volumes and Snapshots		☒
Choose volumes and snapshots to assign to server 'esx1.vi4book.com'.		?

Volume or Snapshot Name	Assigned	Permission
📦 AD	✔	Read/Write ▼
📦 Citrix	✔	Read/Write ▼
📦 File	✔	Read/Write ▼
📦 sql	✔	Read/Write ▼
📦 Web	✔	Read/Write ▼

Repeat this process for all other servers that will require access. When you perform this task a second time, you will receive a warning that more than one server can see the same volumes. Remember that this is safe because VMFS is a clustered file system.

Configuring ESX for iSCSI

Configuring ESX for using iSCSI with a software initiator requires setting up a VMkernel port group for IP storage and connecting ESX to the iSCSI software adapter. Optionally, you can enable CHAP authentication.

If you are using a hardware initiator, you do not need to set up a VMkernel port group. For example, with QLogic iSCSI adapters, the IP address, subnet mask, and default gateway values are set in the adapter BIOS (press ALT+Q to access it). If you are using ordinary NICs, as I am, you will need to create a VMkernel port group to set these values.

NOTE *In ESX 3.x, in the vSwitch for an iSCSI software initiator, you needed to configure two port groups: a VMkernel storage port group and Service Console port group on the same network as the iSCSI target. This was required because, although the I/O or read/writes of iSCSI went via the VMkernel's IP stack, the discovery and authentication process was driven by the Service Console. In ESX 4.x the requirement for a second Service Console connection has been removed. Of course, this was never required for ESXi product, which does not have Service Console networking.*

Setting Up a VMkernel Port Group for IP Storage

In Chapter 5, I showed you how to set up a VMkernel port group for VMotion as an example. Here, I'll demonstrate setting up a vSwitch with a VMkernel port group for IP storage, which you can use to communicate with your iSCSI systems.

For clarity, I have set up the HP LeftHand using 172.168.3.99 addresses. I will allocate 172.168.3.101/24 to my VMkernel storage port group for my server called esx1.vi4book.com.

1. In the vSphere Client, select your ESX host.

2. Click the Configuration tab. In the Hardware pane, select Networking.

3. Click the Add Networking link.

4. Choose VMkernel and click Next.

5. Click Next in the next dialog box.

6. In the Port Groups Properties dialog box, type a friendly name for this connection, such as **ipstorage**. Then click Next.

7. Type a valid IP address and subnet mask for the VMkernel port group.

8. Optionally, set a default gateway. If your iSCSI systems are behind a router, you will need to set a default gateway entry for the VMkernel port group. To do this, from the Configuration tab, select DNS and Routing, click Properties and set the default gateway on the Routing tab of the DNS Routing and Configuration dialog box.

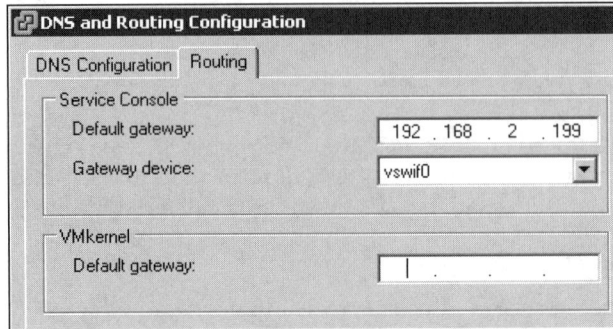

In the absence of a router, I often set the default gateway to be one of the iSCSI or NAS nodes on my network, as I can use this address to test my VMkernel IP configuration using the VMware ESX command `vmkping -D`. This will create a vSwitch configured as shown in the following example, which shows the vSwitch with two NICs.

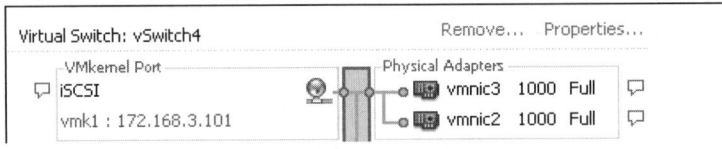

NOTE *In reality, my four servers are rapidly running out of NICs. This underscores an important point: The more NICs you have, the easier life is, and the more redundancy and separation of network traffic you can achieve.*

Connecting ESX to an iSCSI Software Adapter

Apart from the networking differences, the iSCSI software adapter is configured in the same way on ESXi 4 as it is in the Classic edition of ESX. Before proceeding, you might wish to manually open the iSCSI client ports from the security profile. Currently, ESX 4.*x* will do this automatically.

1. In the vSphere Client, choose the ESX host from the list.

2. Click the Configuration tab. In the Hardware pane, choose Storage Adapters.

3. Select iSCSI Software Adapter and Properties.

4. In the General tab, click the Configure button.

5. Select Enable, and then click OK. Note that it can take some time for these dialog boxes to refresh. The following example shows how the IQN data will be updated to show that the initiator is enabled. This procedure will automatically generate a unique iSCSI initiator (iqn.1998.01-com.vmware:esx1-69cb2357 in this example) and alias (esx1.vi4book.com in this example). If desired, you can click the Configure button again and set your own IQN values.

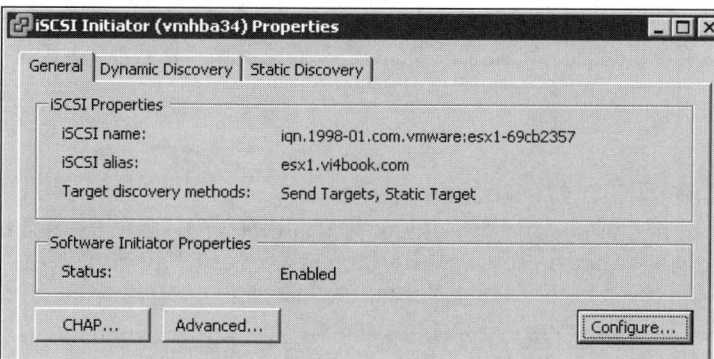

CAUTION *If you wish to disable the iSCSI software stack using the GUI this will force a message to reboot the ESX host.*

6. Select the Dynamic Discovery tab and click the Add button.

7. Type in the IP address of your iSCSI target. After clicking OK, you will be prompted to issue a rescan.

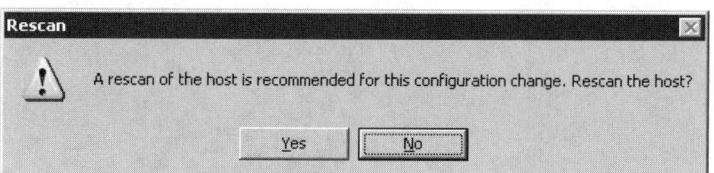

TIP *If you choose to not run the rescan at the time, or need to correct an error, you can always force a rescan by clicking the Rescan link in the top-right corner of the window and choosing OK to the Rescan dialog box.*

The following example shows the LUNs presented to ESX1 after the rescan has completed. If you select the vmhba34 software device, you should see the LUNs you presented from the HP LeftHand VSA. The vmhba32 device isn't a real physical device; it is more like a virtual HBA or alias device, because it's actually the ESX server network cards—the vmnic devices that allow the access to the iSCSI appliance. Clicking the Path button will allow you to see the friendly IQNs of the iSCSI target, rather than just disk names.

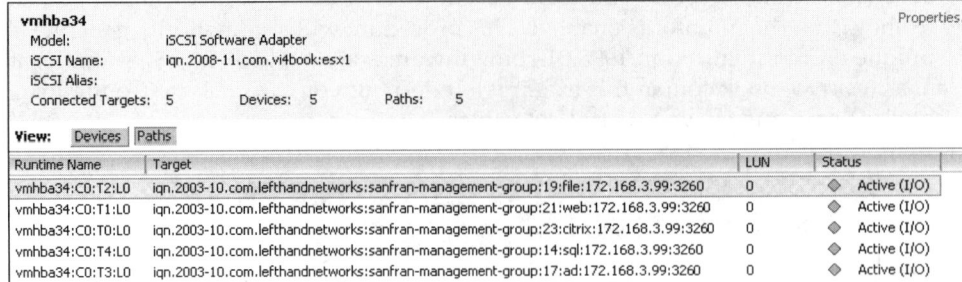

Setting Up iSCSI with CHAP Authentication

Optionally, you can tighten security by with CHAP authentication. In this scenario, in addition to the IQN, you can specify CHAP secrets (passwords). In ESX 4, it is possible to set the requirement for a password on both the target and the initiator.

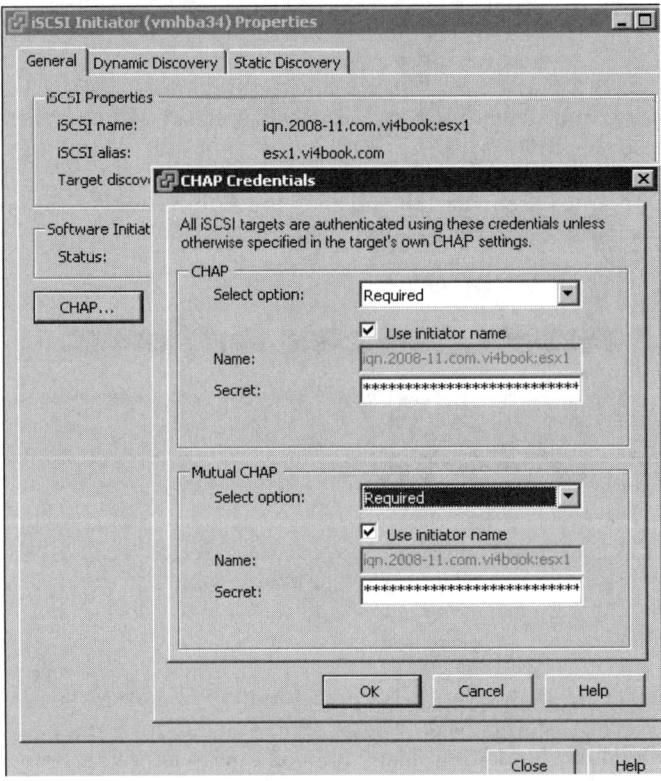

It is possible for each target to have a different CHAP secret assigned to it. The preceding example assumes you are using the same password across all targets. If this is not the case, on the Dynamic Discovery tab, you can add the target more than once, each time supplying a different CHAP secret.

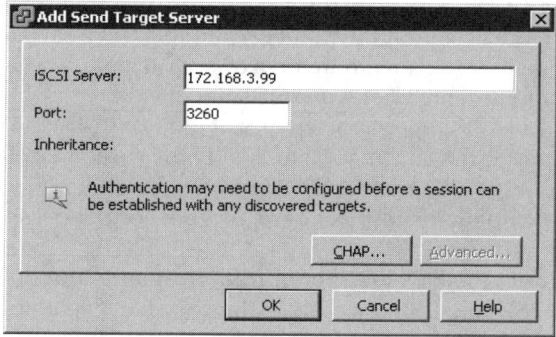

NOTE *In ESX 3, CHAP authentication was unidirectional only. The target (the storage location) would be set with a password, and the ESX host would need to be configured with the correct password to see the LUNs/volumes.*

Managing VMFS Volumes

VMFS is VMware's own proprietary file system. It now supports directories and a maximum of 30,720 files in a VMFS volume, with up to 256 VM in a volume. These numbers merely represent a soft limit, rather than a hard limit.

A VMFS volume can be used in virtual machines, templates, and ISO files. VMFS has been designed to be safe with very large files such as virtual disks. Another key property is that VMFS supports multiple access—more than one ESX host can present the same LUNs formatted with VMFS without fear of corruption. This is achieved by using a sophisticated file and LUN locking system to prevent corruption of data, referred to as SCSI reservations. To enhance performance and reliability, VMware improved VMFS in version 3 to significantly reduce the number and frequency of these reservations. It's important to know that these locks are dynamic, not static or fixed.

Whenever an ESX host powers on a virtual machine, a file-level lock is placed on its files. However, periodically, the ESX host must go back to confirm it is still functioning—still running that virtual machine and still locking those files. VMware refers to this as an ESX host updating its *heartbeat* information. If an ESX host fails to update these dynamic locks or heartbeat region of the VMFS file system, then the virtual machines files are forcibly unlocked. This is pretty critical in features like VMware HA. If locking were not dynamic, the locks would remain in place when an ESX host failed, and no other host would be able to power on that virtual machine, which would be locked, so HA would not work.

VMware does give guidelines for the number of ESX hosts that should be allowed access to a single VMFS volume. In ESX 2.*x*, the maximum was 10 ESX hosts with access to a VMFS volume. In ESX 3.*x*, this was increased to 32 ESX hosts. This value has been increased in ESX 4.0 Update 1 to allow for upto 64 ESX hosts in the same DRS/HA Cluster.

VMFS uses a distributed journal. If a crash does occur, ESX does not carry out a full file system check (fsck) on VMFS volumes, but merely checks the journal. This is decidedly quicker; however, existing ext3 partitions are still checked by the fsck method from Linux.

Formatting Volumes with VMFS

Whenever possible, you should format VMFS volumes from the vSphere Client. One well-known way to optimize disk I/O is to keep the system from crossing track boundaries, known as *disk alignment*. MBRs frequently limit the number of hidden sectors to 63, which causes the default starting sector of disks that show more than 63 sectors per track to be sector 64. This can cause track misalignment, which defeats efforts to not cross track boundaries. The problem is further complicated by the characteristics of today's disks and controllers. Some disks don't accurately report track information to avoid other problems. Disks can also have a different number of sectors on the inner and outer tracks. Disk alignment is an effort to improve performance by keeping the number of sectors per second passing under the heads more or less constant.

If you format volumes in the ESX installer or from the command line using fdisk, the start sectors will not be 128K-aligned. In contrast, the vSphere Client automatically ensures that disk alignment takes place when you format a VMFS volume in the GUI.

CAUTION *If you are using RDM files to access raw or native LUNs, disk alignment should be done within the guest operating system. This is because, fundamentally, Windows or Linux is in charge of the file system. Tools like Microsoft DiskPart should be used if you think your virtual machines would benefit from disk alignment.*

As with any format procedure, there is a huge potential for losing data. When using the interface, take notice of any warnings that the vSphere Client produces, as in the following example. There is no "undo format" facility in ESX 4.*x*, so if you wipe out terabytes of data during the process, you will need to resort to your backup solution.

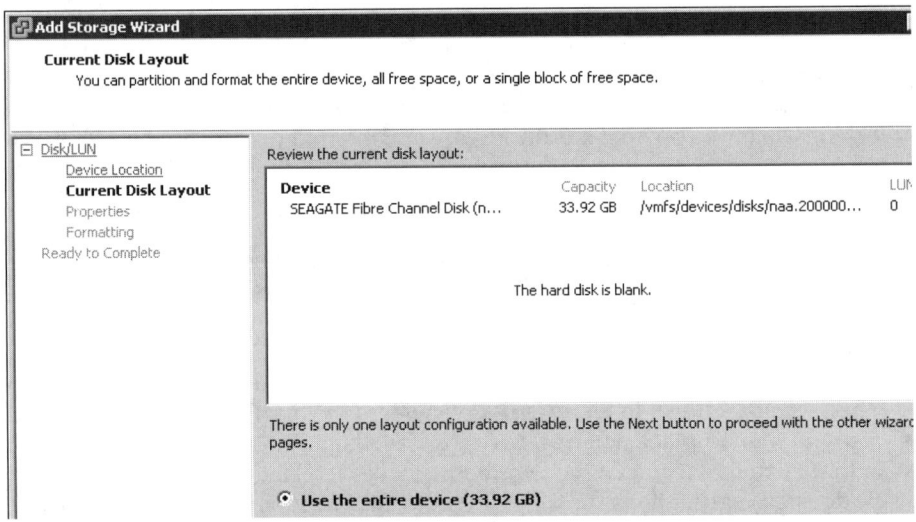

During the format process, you will be asked to set a block size (1MB, 2MB, 4MB, or 8MB). This controls the maximum file size that can be held in a given VMFS volume (256GB, 512GB, 1024GB, or 2048GB). Block sizes do not greatly affect performance in VMFS, but they do affect maximum virtual disk (VMDK) file size. Sometimes this can be largely a theoretical issue, especially if your LUN size is less than the smallest file size of 256GB. Generally, I recommend using an 8MB block size, as this allows you to have large VMDK files.

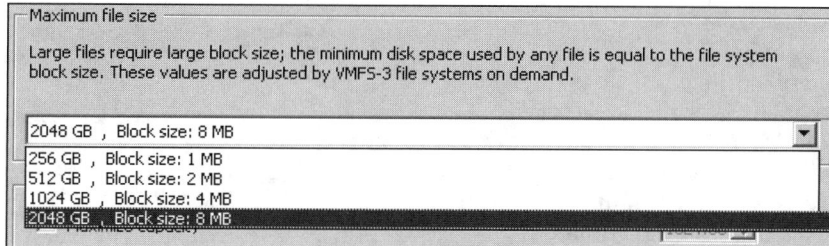

You will also have an option to maximize capacity, which sounds more complicated than it actually is, especially if you have accepted the default of "Use the entire device" in a previous dialog box. It merely means to use all of the LUN space for the VMFS volume.

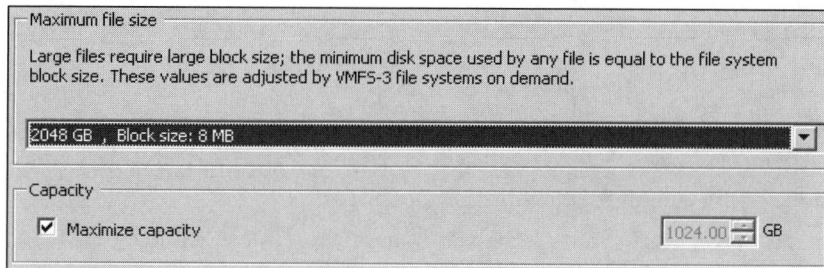

You can adjust this to make the VMFS volume smaller than the LUN size. There isn't any advantage to this, and the free space left over is not easily accessible to the vSphere Client. While it is possible to create multiple VMFS volumes on a single LUN, this can affect performance. Although multiple ESX hosts can still access the VMFS volumes, doing so can impose a LUN-wide SCSI reservation, which temporarily blocks access on multiple VMFS volumes where only one VMFS volume might need locking. For these reasons, I recommend creating one VMFS per LUN. (In fact, I wish VMware would remove this option altogether from the vSphere Client.)

You will also need to set a datastore name during the format process. VMFS volumes are known by four values: volume label, datastore label, vmhba syntax, and UUID. Volume labels need to be unique to ESX hosts, whereas datastore labels need to be unique to vCenter. If you had four ESX hosts, each with a local VMFS volume called storage1 or datastore1, you would find that as you added them to vCenter, the datastore label would be relabeled automatically, like so:

Volume Label	Datastore Label	Volume Label	Datastore Label
storage1	storage1	datastore1	datastore1
storage1	storage1(1)	datastore1	datastore1(1)
storage1	storage1(2)	datastore1	datastore1(2)
storage1	storage1(3)	datastore1	datastore1(3)

As you can see, it's possible to end up with two different labels for the same VMFS volume—a volume label that is different from the datastore label. For this reason, I recommend adopting a naming convention that ensures a level of uniqueness is maintained, especially for local ESX host storage—something along the lines of esx1_local will suffice.

If you do have differing labels, the easiest solution is to relabel the VMFS volume to make both values the same. To change the volume label, right-click the VMFS volume, choose Properties, and click the Rename button. This can be done even when you have running virtual machines stored on the VMFS volume.

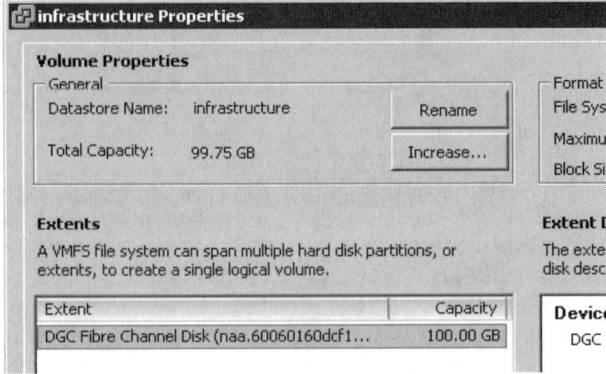

NOTE *Unfortunately, the friendly IQN names of the iSCSI target are not displayed in the wizard. You may wish to make a note of the vmhba syntax for them before beginning the formatting process.*

To format a VMFS volume, follow these steps:

1. In the vSphere Client, select your ESX host.

2. Click the Configuration tab. In the Hardware pane, choose Storage (SCSI, SAN, NFS).

3. Click the Add Storage link.

4. Choose Disk/LUN.

5. Select the LUN you wish to format. The following example shows the iSCSI LUNs presented by the HP LeftHand VSA setup and two Seagate Fibre Channel disks. I have a USB stick plugged into the ESX host as well. Notice how each "disk" is being enumerated as a separate SCSI target, rather than by its LUN number.

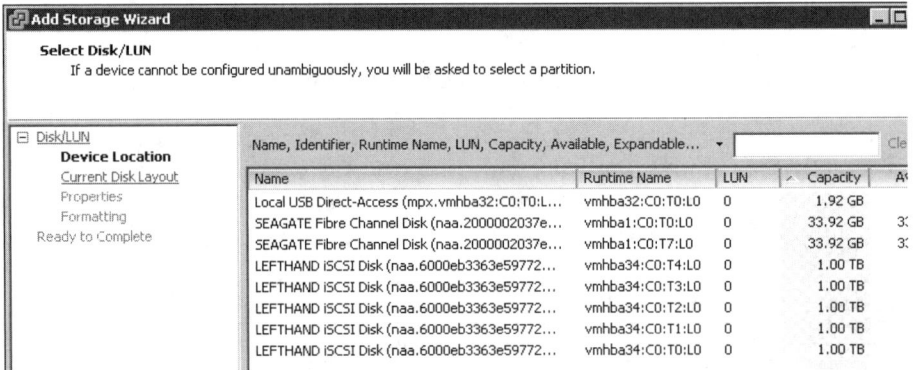

6. Set a datastore name, such as **SQL** or **san_disk1**.

7. Set your maximum file size parameters.

8. Click Finish to begin the formatting process.

One common question is why, after formatting a 100GB LUN, you don't receive 100GB of VMFS storage. Like any file system, this storage system needs to have storage to function. In NTFS, this would be something like the Master File Table (MFT). In VMFS, we refer to this as *metadata*. The VMFS metadata is stored in files with the .sf extension in the root of the VMFS volume, which consumes space on the disk. With a LUN or disk that is only 1.2GB in size, approximately 44% is taken up by metadata information. If you have a LUN of 10GB, about 4.8% is used for metadata information. If a LUN is 50GB, approximately 0.98% is used for metadata. So, the moral of the story is that the bigger the LUN, the smaller the percentage of metadata overhead.

Increasing the Size of VMFS Volumes

The ability to increase the size of the VMFS volume dynamically is a new feature in ESX 4.*x*. In previous releases, although it was possible to increase the size of LUN on the storage array, the VMFS partition would stubbornly remain the same size and not automatically grow. Even if you had a SAN or iSCSI system that could dynamically make a LUN increase from, say, 500GB to 1024GB, the original VMFS partition remained the original format size of 500GB. I suspect you have probably come across this in other operating systems and file systems, such as Windows and Linux, and in some cases had to resort to using tools like Partition Magic or Microsoft DiskPart to resolve this issue. But VMware did not offer this type of tool for VMFS. The only solutions were to create an extent, do a backup and restore, or carry out a rather intrusive storage VMotion to relocate your files to a new LUN of the right size. To do this, you would need to have the free space, create a LUN that is 1512GB in size, and copy the data in the 512GB LUN to the 1512GB. Afterward, what you did with the empty VMFS and LUN was up to you. Most people would delete the smaller LUN so this capacity could be used elsewhere.

Fortunately, now ESX has a utility for increasing the size of a volume built into the vSphere Client. This will increase the size of a VMFS volume to take up free space within the same LUN. If you have previously used VMFS volume extents to resolve this issue, I recommend using the built-in Increase option instead. However, both methods allow you to increase the capacity of a VMFS volume without affecting powered-on and in-use virtual machines.

NOTE *Even though you can adjust the size of existing volume, I still recommend that in your design, you carefully plan the LUN sizes. Another approach would be to use virtual storage, if that feature is available to you, and allocate more space to the ESX host than is physically available. This approach effectively solves the problem of how big to make your LUNs. VMware do recommend rescan and quiesce of IO prior to a grow for "maximum safety." So in my own mind I'm think the less I have to carry out this task the better. I would recommend carrying out any grow task on VMFS volume to be after snapshot of a volume or backup—and planned for window when users are not present. This isn't to say I've had bad experiences, far from it—but more that I would cautious about using any re-partition tool on live volumes holding live data.*

Using the Increase Datastore Capacity Wizard

In the following example, I have VMFS volume that was originally made as 25GB, but the LUN on which it is stored actually has 34GB of capacity. This can be a little bit tricky to see in the vSphere Client. However, if you open the properties of a VMFS volume, this information appears on the right side of the dialog box.

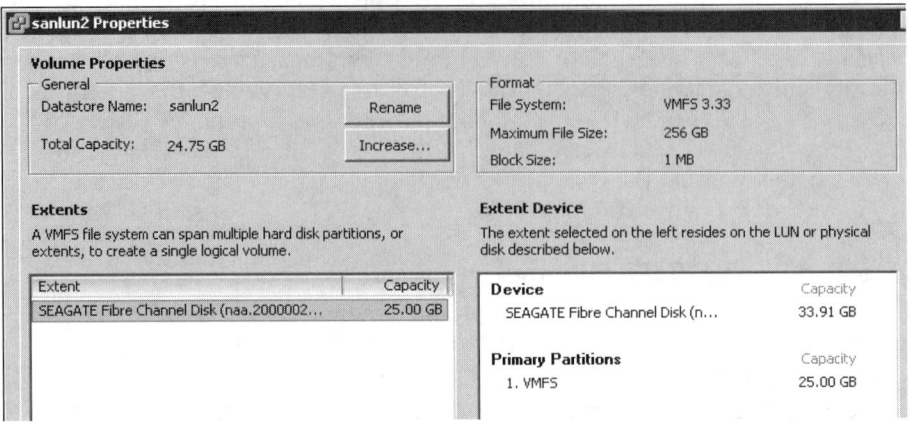

Before you increase the size of a volume, you might want to make a note of the Network Address Authority (NAA) value or the vmhba syntax. In the wizard, you will need to select the *same* volume to indicate you want to increase the size of the VMFS volume into an area of free space on the *same* LUN. Once you are in the wizard, you will not be able to see the VMFS volume by its friendly datastore name.

To increase the volume's size, right-click the VMFS volume, choose Properties, and click the Increase button. Then select the disk on which you wish to increase the VMFS volume size. In this example, selecting the right volume is easy—it's the only one with Yes in the Expandable column.

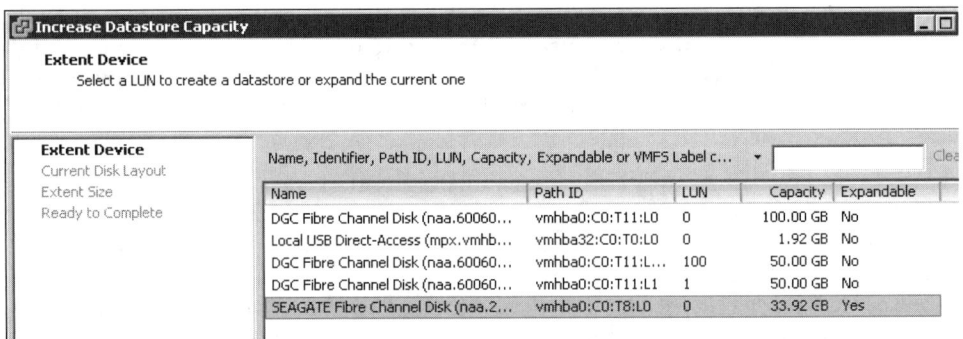

In the Current Disk Layout section of the wizard, you will see that the system intends to expand the VMFS into areas of free space.

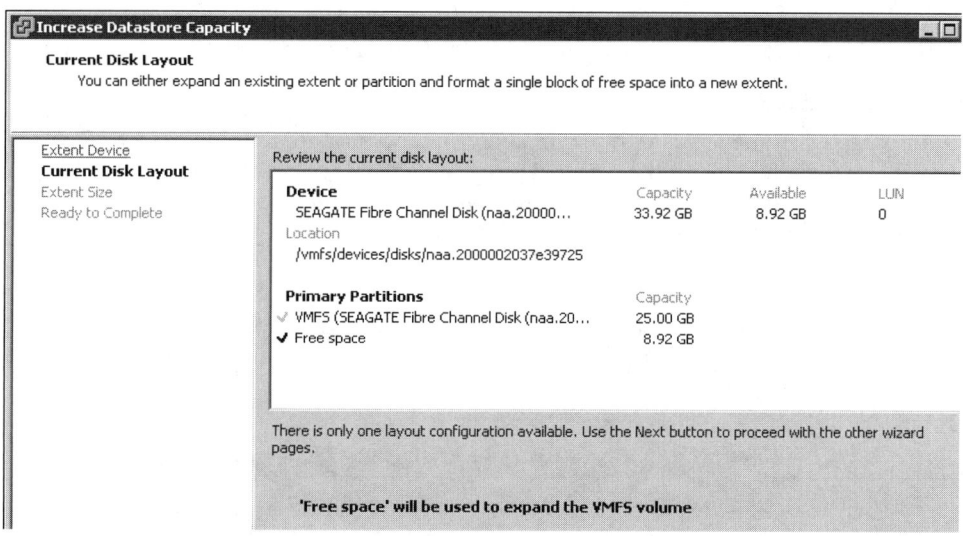

Increasing the Size of VMFS Volumes with Extents

Generally, we create one VMFS partition per LUN, with the maximum size of a single VMFS volume being 2TB. The only way to exceed this limitation is by creating what VMware calls *extents*. Another reason to create an extent is if you are running out of space in a given VMFS volume.

CAUTION *VMFS extents are not looked upon favorably by the VMware community. There are concerns about predicting and guaranteeing performance. There are data-integrity worries about the possible loss of the "master" VMFS volume, say through a firmware upgrade to an array that goes wrong. Lastly, VMFS volumes have no reverse gear. Once they are in place, they are quite tricky to remove without extensive relocation of your virtual machine files.*

The widespread use of SCSI-2 hardware causes this 2TB limitation, and it is one that ESX shares with a number of x86 operating systems. SCSI-2 hardware uses a 16-byte address, which limits the maximum single LUN size. SCSI-3 equipment does not have this limitation, but we have not yet reached the tipping point for most operating system vendors to move to it completely. Fortunately, SCSI-3 equipment is backward compatible with SCSI-2.

If you primarily use Windows, you will probably recognize extents. They function very similarly to Microsoft's volume sets or spanned volumes. Most people in the VMware community recommend that you steer clear of this feature. I would agree with this assessment, and suggest that you use extents only as a temporary work-around.

In extents, one LUN is stuck to another LUN to make the original VMFS larger. This could introduce performance headaches if the first LUN had a different RAID level or a different number of disk spindles. Any extents feature is only as good as the operating system that underpins it, and most people would prefer a permanent hardware solution to this issue, rather than a software work-around.

To extend an existing VMFS, you need a free, empty LUN. The vSphere Client does a good job of hiding existing VMFS volumes to inhibit you from accidentally deleting valuable data.

However, it does not hide any other LUNs, as do other operating system's file systems, so be very careful—there is no "undo extents" feature. To remove an extent, you remove the file system, along with any data.

The only real "gotcha" with extents is a scenario like this one: Let's say you later choose to extend a VMFS volume to make it bigger, and you add storage that makes the VMFS 2TB. It would still be formatted with the original block size. If this were 1MB, you would still be limited to the maximum file size of 256GB used by your original format.

With these caveats in mind, creating an extent is actually an easy process:

1. In the vSphere Client, select your ESX host.

2. Click the Configuration tab. In the Hardware pane, choose Storage (SCSI, SAN, NFS).

3. Right-click the VMFS volume you wish to make larger and choose Properties.

4. Click the Increase button.

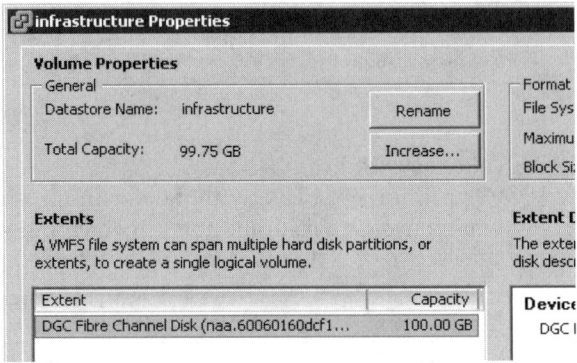

5. Select a LUN from the list. Before proceeding, confirm that the LUN is blank.

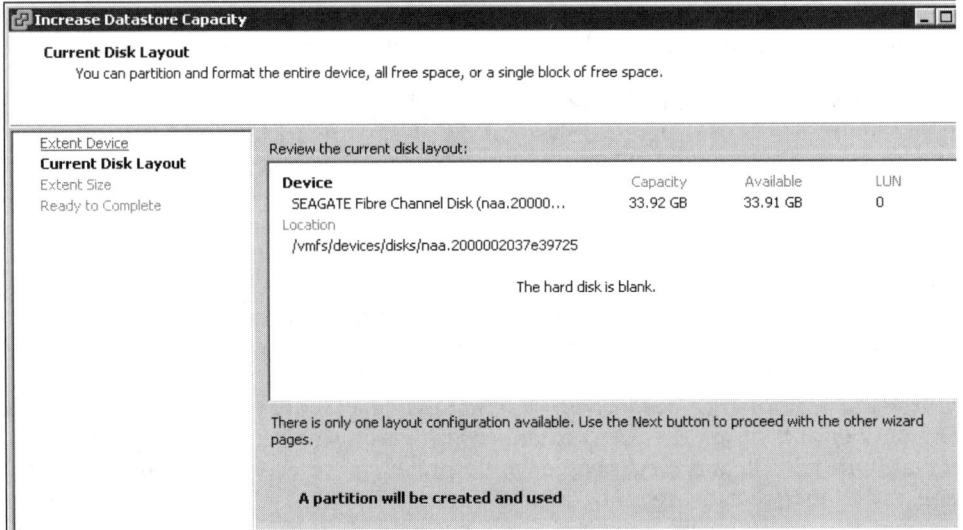

6. Click Finish.

At the end of the process, you should be able to see that VMFS volume's capacity has been increased by the aggregation of two or more LUNs into a single addressable VMFS volume.

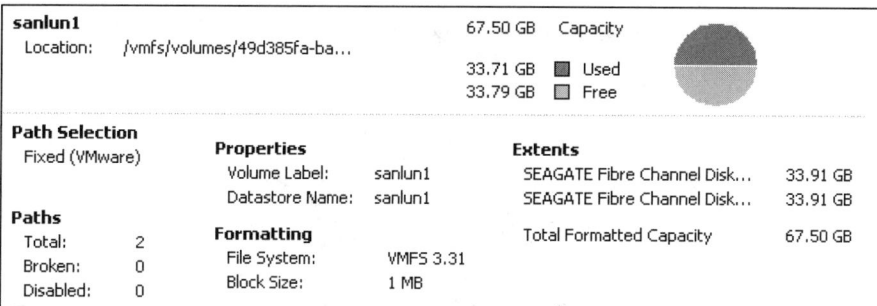

Viewing Free Space and Disk Alarms

One enhancement in vSphere 4 is that VMware have judiciously decided to turn on disk alarms by default. Although disk alarms have always been available, you needed to enable them, and there wasn't much in the way of an on-screen notification of this in the vSphere Client. These deficiencies in the previous version have now been addressed.

In the Summary tab or the Configuration/Storage window of the vSphere Client, you will see these types of alarms:

Datastore	Status	Capacity	
isos	⚠ Warning	67.50 GB	15.4
templates	⚠ Warning	135.00 GB	22.9
infrastructure	✓ Normal	33.75 GB	10.
esx2:local	◆ Alert	67.75 GB	9.5
file	◆ Alert	1,023.75 G	23.2
web	✓ Normal	1,023.75 G	1,023

You will also see them at the top of Hosts and Clusters view, on the Alarms tab, where they are defined.

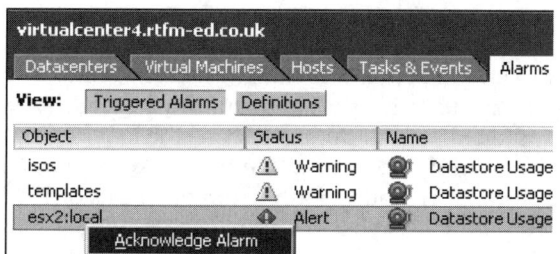

These alarms are triggered when you have less than 25% free space (Warning) and less than 15% free space (Alert). In the preceding example, I filled the practically empty "file" VMFS volumes with a virtual machine with a 1024GB virtual disk, which triggered an alarm.

Another great storage view is in vCenter. If you Click the Home icon, then the Inventory icon, then Datastores. Here you can see all the datastores of all your datacenters and the alarms.

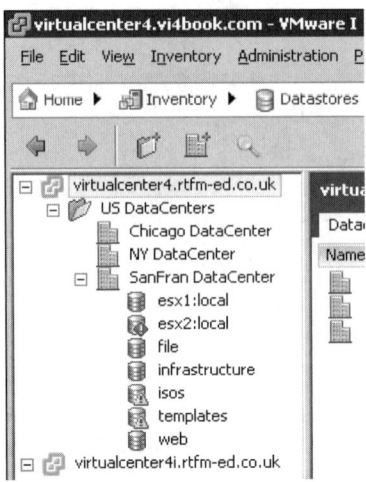

Configuring Multipathing with Fibre Channel and iSCSI SAN

By virtue of having many HBAs in the ESX hosts and many storage processors (SPs) on the SAN array, it is possible to have many paths from one ESX host to a given LUN. In the past, VMware did not use the multiple HBAs for load balancing, but merely for fault tolerance. This situation changed with VI3.5, which introduced a round-robin method. It is very likely that vendors will offer more sophisticated methods of load balancing HBAs, such as EMC's PowerPath product. To do this, the VMkernel would need to be able to find out if a given SP was active or passive. An active SP can take a continual disk I/O load, whereas a passive SP functions only if the active one fails. In this respect, an active/passive SAN would be unsuitable for load balancing, whereas an active/active SAN would be a good candidate.

This aside, ESX does allow us to control the preferred path to a LUN on the SAN using the vmhbaN:C:T:L:V syntax. The first policy, which is the default, is called Most Recently Used (MRU) and is used with active/passive SPs on a SAN. The second policy, called Fixed and Preferred, is used with active/active SPs on a SAN. This second policy allows for manual disk I/O optimization. The third and final policy is called "Round Robin," which allows the VMKernel to cycle through the HBAs in effort to distribute the load.

With the MRU policy, the ESX install program scans the PCI bus, looking for storage adapters. The first Fibre Channel device found that the VMkernel has a driver for is set as the preferred path to the storage. The other paths from other SPs or HBAs are not used, except when this preferred path fails. When a failure occurs, a HBA connected to the passive SP takes over the disk I/0. The time taken to detect a failure and to use this redundant link is usually configured in the firmware of the HBA. It must be quick enough not to cause the VMkernel to think it has lost all connection to the storage. When the link on the active HBA returns (perhaps it was a failed Fibre Channel cable or switch), MRU does not return to the original HBA on the ESX host. In other words, MRU does failover, but not failback. If you wish to return to the original path, you must use the vSphere Client or command-line tools.

In contrast, the Fixed and Preferred policy allows you to hard-code HBAs to service a given LUN. This enables you to configure, for example, that vmhba1 is the preferred path for LUN20 using SP0, whereas the preferred path for LUN21 is vmhba2 using SP1. This way, you can distribute the disk I/O across multiple HBAs and SPs. However, your SAN must support active/active on the SPs for this to work. When a failure occurs, the VMkernel is able to use any available path to the LUN, and when the link is restored it returns (fixed) to its original path. In other words, Fixed and Preferred does failover and failback. This can give you problems when you have a path that is intermittently available. If this happens, you can temporarily disable a path in the vSphere Client while you resolve the source of the problem, such as a faulty HBA.

Managing Multiple Fibre Channel Paths

You can view your multiple paths (if you have multiple HBAs) to a LUN within the vSphere Client. Simply select your ESX host, click the Configuration tab, right-click a VMFS volume, and choose Properties. In the dialog box, click the Manage Paths button.

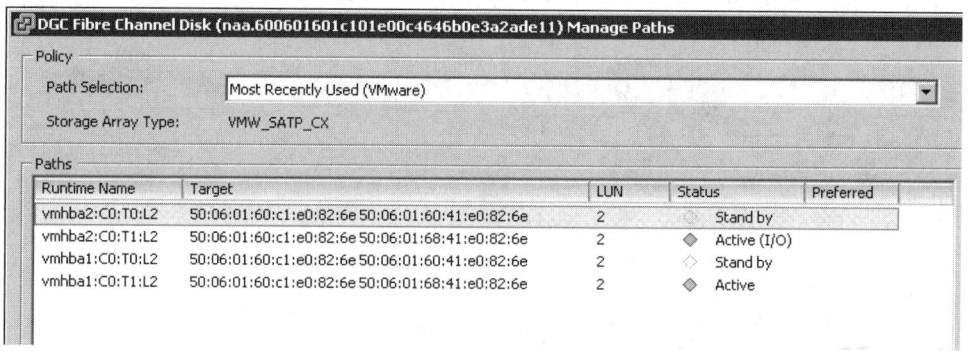

This example show the four paths available from two HBAs, each plugged into a different switch which is in turn plugged into two separate paths (vmhba1:0, 1:1, 2:0, and 2:1). You can see the vmhba2:1 is the active path (indicated in green with I/0 at the end), and the other paths are merely waiting for a failure to occur. Incidentally, VMware supports up to a maximum of 32 paths. VMware using the vStorage APIs tries to identify your storage array and apply the correct policy. So in the dialog box above the ESX host has correctly determined that my array is an EMC Clarrion CX3. This type of array is a the pseudo-active/passive type—and so the MRU policy has been assigned to it by default.

NOTE *Some storage people might disagree with this representation of the paths to the LUN. They may argue that if an ESX host has two adapters, it has two paths to a given LUN. Whatever your position is in this argument of four paths versus two paths, only one path is used at any one time using the standard plug-ins.*

In the dialog box, you can see that storage array type is set to be VMW_SATP_CX, using the MRU path selection policy. SATP stands for Storage Array Type Plug-ins, which are plug-ins that handle path failover, monitor path health, and report changes to the Native Multipathing Plug-in (NMP). From the NMP, a path selection policy is chosen, using the the Path Selection Plug-ins (PSP). VMware has three types of path selection policies (MRU, Fixed, and Round Robin). Storage array vendors may provide their own PSP, which could expose a vendor-specific multipath option. Many vendors are now offering their own dynamic load-balancing multipath software in this plug-in format to provide fault tolerance and performance improvements from the ESX host to the array.

TIP *If a LUN is unformatted, you can still see the paths by selecting the Storage Adapters link from the Hardware pane. Select your Fibre Channel device and then right-click a path to a LUN (for example, vmhba1:0:10) and choose the option Manage Paths on the context menu.*

To enable the Fixed and Preferred policy for a path from the Manage Paths dialog box, choose Fixed from the Path Selection drop-down list.

CAUTION *Switch to the Fixed and Preferred policy only if you know you have a SAN that supports active/active storage controllers/processors.*

To change the Fibre Channel path used, right-click the path you wish to use and select Preferred. The Disable option allows you to prevent a particular path from being used at all.

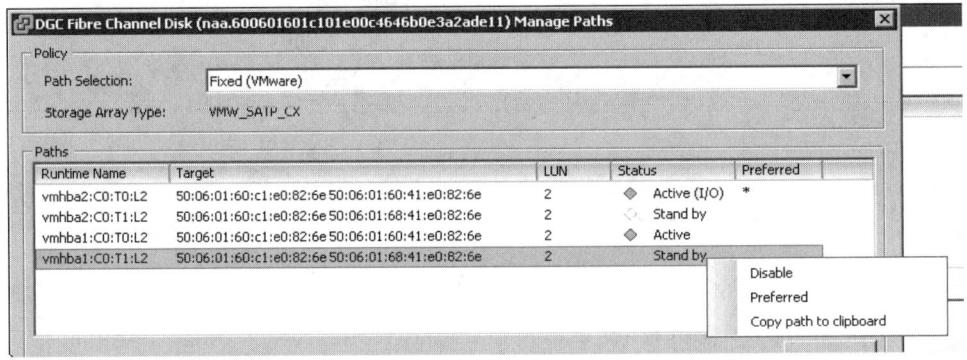

The following example show the paths after changing the policy. The asterisk (*) indicates which is the preferred path, and the status has changed to active for vmhba1:0:1.2

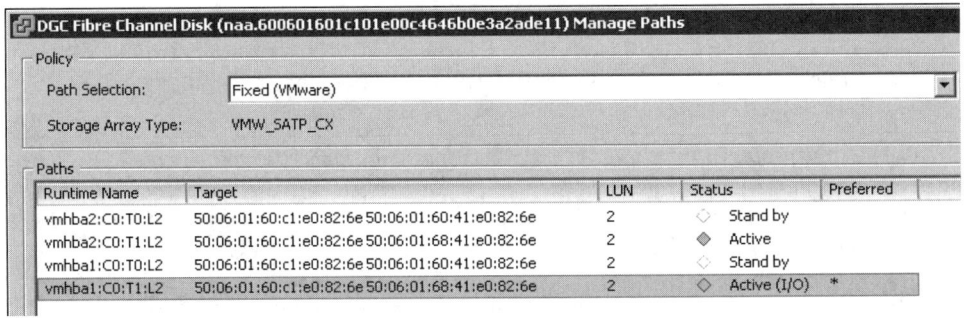

TIP *You can also manage paths using the esxcfg-mpath command-line tool. If you run esxcfg-mpath as root, it will show you how to list paths and enable/disable paths.*

Install, License, and Configure Third-Party Path Selection Policies

In addition to VMware's own path selection policies, many third-party storage vendors have responded favorably to VMware opening up their APIs to external companies. These take the form of third-party "Path Selection Plug-ins." These PSPs can be downloaded from the storage vendors Web site, and extend the capabilities of your ESX host to include advanced multipathing and load-balancing feature. Generally, these PSP are not for free and will require a license to function correctly. As an example EMC has allowed their PowerPath technology to be available to VMware ESX. It's perhaps not relevant in this book to delve too deeply at this third-party software but if you're interested I've written a very short guide to getting started with EMC's PowerPath for VMware located here:

> http://www.rtfm-ed.co.uk/docs/vmwdocs/whitepaper-emc-powerpath.pdf

Viewing Broken Paths

Paths can and do fail, and the vSphere Client will alert you to this fact by using red mark next to path marked with the words "dead."

If you are at the command line of an ESX Classic host and you have lost access to SAN altogether, you will see the lost VMFS volumes flagged in red and white text.

```
47878034-85f68aff-4754-001560ace43f   infrastructure
493db934-9fbf83c4-18ff-001560ace440   isos
49d385fa-ba8db4e9-38d5-001560aa6f7c   local_esx2
49da273c-733e4a90-d2ec-001560aa6f7b   sanlun1
49e6ac2c-ddb7b87e-ed22-0015600ea5bc   templates
```

Configuring NAS Storage

With the improvements and extension of the VMkernel's IP stack, VMware has introduced NAS support. More specifically, VMware supports the Linux Network File System (NFS) for file servers, in which a file server shares, or exports, folders.

Linux is supported natively by VMware using NFS and ext3 as the file system. If you prefer to use Windows, you will need to set up something like Microsoft Windows Services for UNIX (SFU) using NTFS partitions. SFU emulates NFS support for a Windows server. Fortunately, SFU is free, as long as you have paid for a valid Windows license. Alternatively, you could use free virtual appliances, such as Openfiler and FreeNAS, instead. Whatever you decide to use as the platform for NFS, it's important to know that VMware ESX Server supports only version 3 for NFS using TCP as the transport protocol.

The following are some common uses for NAS:

- You might use NAS to store ISO files of guest operating systems (Windows, Linux, Solaris, and Novell), rather than locating these on SAN- or iSCSI-based storage, which is expensive. If you have a lot of ISO files, they can take up a lot of space, and you may prefer to put them on cheaper NAS storage.

- If you have a large amount of zoning and masking in a Fibre Channel array, NAS can be easier to implement for ancillary storage requirements. So it would be possible to have 10 or 20 clusters of ESX hosts each in separate Fibre Channel zones, while they shared a common NAS share for ISO files.

- You could use NAS-based storage to hold your templates. The downside is that every time you created a new virtual machine from a template, this would generate a significant amount of network activity.
- NAS can hold running virtual machines.

The cool thing about the NAS support is that you don't need to spend your hard-earned dollars on a SAN or iSCSI just for test and development environments. NAS would be sufficient. Perhaps you're one of those guys with a truckload of hardware in your basement or garage and you want to set up your own VI3 environment, but your budget won't stretch to even an MSA1000 (the HP StorageWorks Modular Smart Array). In this case, NAS could be viable. (Personally, I would prefer to use an iSCSI emulator because it would allow me to use VMFS.)

NAS does have its limitations, and there is a great deal you cannot do with NAS-based storage. With VMware, with NAS on its own (not in a nonmultifunctional configuration) by definition, VMFS is unavailable. This can be problem when new features or functionality are developed. Occasionally, VMware may support a new feature or product only with its file system. For example, when VMware Site Recovery Manager was first released, NFS was not supported. As for Site Recovery Manager 4.0, NFS is supported. Additionally, ESX server booting, RDM files, and clustering inside a virtual machine are not supported. There is limited support for VMware Consolidated Backup, which can be run inside a virtual machine for testing purposes, with backup occurring across the network.

NOTE *I want to make it clear that I don't regard NAS as a substandard technology. In fact, there are aspects of some NAS technologies that make them superior to their SAN and iSCSI cousins. Many high-end NAS appliances from companies like NetApp offer features that are not present in other storage offerings, for the same level of performance (or better). So if you have an idea that a Fibre Channel SAN represents the racehorse of storage and NAS the donkey, dismiss that notion right away. A good NAS appliance will normally support other storage protocols: Fibre Channel SAN, iSCSI SAN, or NAS. In many ways, these appliances represent a multifunctional option. The future is storage arrays that allow you to plug into them in any way you like.*

Setting Up NFS on Red Hat Linux

In the sample setup, I used Red Hat Enterprise Linux AS release 3 (Taroon Update 2) as my NFS/NAS server. I configured the Red Hat Linux machine with a 10GB boot disk and 50MB data disk with a folder I created called /iso.

To set up NFS on Red Hat Linux, log on to your NFS file server and edit the /etc/ exports file like so:

```
/iso     172.168.3.0/24 (rw,no_root_squash,sync)
```

This allows the server—any ESX server with a VMkernel storage port group in the range of 172.168.0.0—to access the mounting point called /iso. The `rw` gives this server read and write access. The default is that the root user does not get full access to the volume. The command `no_root_squash` allows applications like vCenter read/write access to the volume. Normally, root access to NFS volumes is squashed (denied). You can specify additional security settings using /etc/hosts.allow and /etc/host.deny files associated with the portmap service/daemon. The `sync` command controls how data will be written back to the disks when services disconnect from the export or when the NAS is shut down.

Start your nfs service/daemon with this command:

```
service nfs start
```

To make these NFS services start automatically at bootup, use the chkconfig utility, which allows you to make safe changes to run-levels in Red Hat Linux.

```
chkconfig nfs on
```

Setting Up NFS on Windows with SFU

The instructions in this section are based on Windows 2003 with Service Pack 1. I have also made SFU run successfully on Windows 2000 with Service Pack 4.

Windows does not allow unchallenged access to shares without authentication. As Windows and the ESX host do not share a common end-user database, we need some method of mapping the users on the ESX host to Windows. The method I have chosen is a simple mapping of the accounts using the files present on the ESX host.

Installing SFU

Follow these steps to install SFU:

1. Copy the password and group files from any one of your ESX servers. These files are held in /etc. You can use the free WinSCP tool to copy the files from the ESX host to your Windows server.

2. Extract the SFU package, and run the MSI package called SfuSetup.msi.

3. Choose Custom Installation.

4. Expand Authentication tools for NFS, and select the User Mapping Service.

5. Select Next to the next dialog box without making any changes.

6. Under Local User Name Mapping Service, select Password and Group files.

7. Type the name and path for the passwd and group files, such as **c:\etc\passwd** and **c:\etc\group**.

8. Select the Windows domain. Select Next.

9. Accept the location for the installation.

10. Watch the status bar, check your email, make a cup of coffee, wonder how long you spend watching status bars … oh, and at the end of this, reboot your Windows/NFS server.

Creating a User Mapping Between Administrator and Root

Follow these steps to create a user mapping between the Windows Administrator account and the UNIX root account:

1. From the Start menu, select Windows Services for UNIX.

2. Run the MMC, Services for UNIX Administration.

3. Select the User Name Mapping node.

4. Choose the Maps option, and under Advanced Maps, click Show User Maps.

5. Click the List Windows Users button and select Administrator.

6. Click the List UNIX Users button and select root.

7. Click the Add button.

8. In the warning box, click OK.

9. At the top of the console, click the Apply button.

Sharing a Folder

Follow these steps to share a folder:

1. In Windows Explorer, right-click a folder and choose Share and Security.

2. Select the NFS Sharing tab.

3. Choose Share this folder.

4. Click the Permissions button, and then select Allow root access.

5. Change the type of access to Read-Write. (If you're just using this share for ISO files, you could leave this as Read-Only.)

6. Click OK to exit the sharing dialog boxes.

CAUTION *Watch out for case-sensitivity of your share names. Although Windows is not case-sensitive, it perfectly emulates NFS, which is case-sensitive. If you want to remain sane, make the names all lowercase without any spaces.*

Confirming the Windows/NFS Server Is Functioning

On the Windows/NFS server, check that things are working before you add in the NFS share as IP storage through the vSphere Client.

The `rpcinfo -p` command lists listening ports on the server (notice TCP, NFS v3, port 2049):

```
rpcinfo -p
program      version protocol  port
-------------------------------------------------
   100000      2      udp      111     portmapper
   100000      2      tcp      111     portmapper
   351455      1      tcp      904     mapsVC
   100005      1      udp     1048     mountd
   100005      3      tcp     1048     mountd
   100021      1      udp     1047     nlockmgr
   100021      4      tcp     1047     nlockmgr
```

```
100024        1        udp      1039     status
100024        1        tcp      1039     status
100003        2        udp      2049     nfs
100003        3        udp      2049     nfs
100003        2        tcp      2049     nfs
100003        3        tcp      2049     nfs
```

The `showmount  -e` command exports a list on the NFS server:

```
showmount -e
/iso                                    All Machines
ls -l
D:\sources\vmware\os-ISO's>ls -ls
total 11322628
1392128 -rwxrwxrwx+ 1 +Administrators   513     712769536 Feb  1  2005 wxp.iso
1251856 -rwxrwxrwx+ 1 +Administrators   513     640950272 Aug 25  2004 nt4.iso
```

Adding an NFS Mount Point

The process for adding an NFS mount point to an ESX host is the same whether you are using Linux NFS or Microsoft Windows SFU.

As an ESX administrator, you have an override option with permissions. Even if an NFS export has been set up as read/write, you can mount it into ESX as read-only. This allows you to offer NAS as storage for ISO files but disallow it for other processes. Effectively, this would prevent users from accidentally creating a virtual machine on NAS storage, when SAN or iSCSI is preferred.

For this example, I used an FQDN name when specifying the NFS server. The Service Console is configured to resolve DNS names like this. If you have any doubts about name resolution, try using `nslookup` at the Service Console on the name, and validate the results.

1. In the vSphere Client, select your ESX host.

2. Click the Configuration tab. In the Hardware pane, select Storage (SCSI, SAN, NFS).

3. Click Add Storage on the right side of the vSphere Client window.

4. In the wizard, choose Network File System.

5. In the Locate Network File System dialog box, enter the name of your NFS server (in this example, nfs1.vi4book.com).

6. In the Folder field, enter the name of the mount/volume you wish to access (/iso in this example).

7. Optionally, choose the "Mount NFS read-only" option. This option is useful if you don't have management rights over the NAS, and do not wish your virtual machine users to be able to create virtual machines on this type of storage.

8. For the datastore name, enter a name for NFS mount point (nfs1-iso in this example). Remember that NFS comes from Linux. Even if you're using SFU, export/share names are case-sensitive!

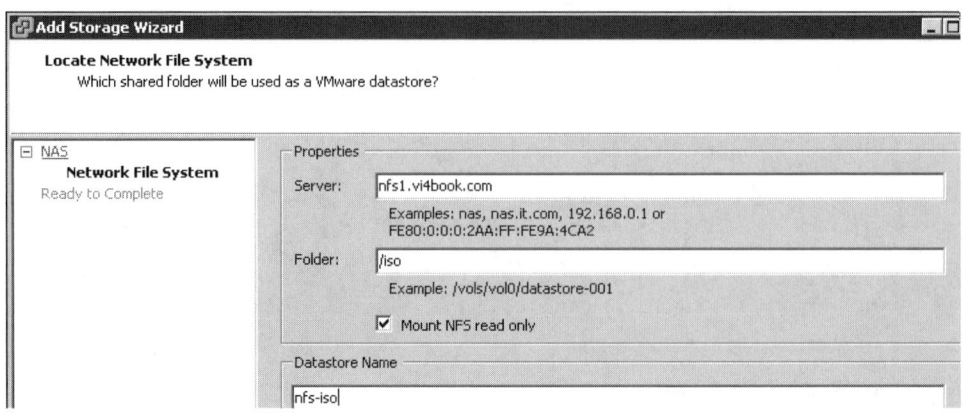

TIP *Occasionally, the NAS may be unavailable. If you want to force a reconnection to a NFS export, you can do this through the Service Console with the* `esxcfg-nas  -r` *command.*

NAS mount points appear in the storage views just like any VMFS datastores, and are mounted in the same path, despite the fact they are not VMFS volumes under /vmfs/volumes.

Removing an NFS Mount Point

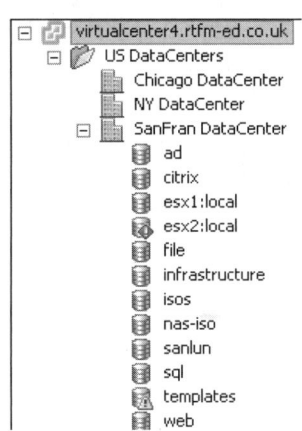

Removing a NAS NAS mount is very simple—merely by right-clicking a NFS mount point you will see an umount option in the context menu. Unlike the delete option with VMFS volume, this does not delete files in the volume. It merely removes the "mount" or mapping—see it a bit like doing in Windows the command "net use x: /delete." This only removes the drive mapping to X: but doesn't destroy the files in share. If you are unmounting a NFS volume I would recommend powering off all the VMs in held on the NFS, and removing them from the inventory. If you don't each and every VM stored on the NFS will be flagged as "inaccessible." Failure to do this will usually result in a "Mount is in use" error message.

Storage Views and Maps

New to VMware vSphere are storage views and improved mapping features. You will find the Storage Views tab on every node in vCenter. You can choose to see reports or maps. The Show All Virtual Machines report view shows every virtual machine and its storage usage.

SanFran DataCenter					

Summary Virtual Machines Hosts Performance Tasks & Events Alarms Permissions Maps **Storage Views**

View: Reports Maps

Show all Virtual Machines ▾   VM c

VM	Multipathing Status	Space Used	Snapshot Space Used	Disks
fs01	Degraded	4.00 GB	0.00 B	1
dc02	Degraded	4.00 GB	0.00 B	1
ctx02	Degraded	4.00 GB	436.00 B	1
ctx01	Degraded	4.00 GB	436.00 B	1
sql02	Degraded	4.00 GB	0.00 B	1
dc01	Degraded	8.00 GB	0.00 B	2
fs02	Degraded	4.00 GB	0.00 B	1
web01	Degraded	4.00 GB	0.00 B	1
sql01	Degraded	4.00 GB	0.00 B	1
web02	Degraded	10.00 GB	889.00 B	1

In this example, the Degraded entries in the Multipathing Status column indicate that my ESX hosts do not have fault tolerance to my storage array. Probably the most useful aspect of this storage view is the Snapshot Space Used column, which shows you how large your snapshots are. Another useful view is Show All Datastores (no prizes for guessing what that displays!).

The storage view maps give you a much more visual idea of the relationships between your ESX hosts, virtual machines, virtual machine HBAs, SCSI devices, and datastores. In the following example, I removed some options to simplify the view.

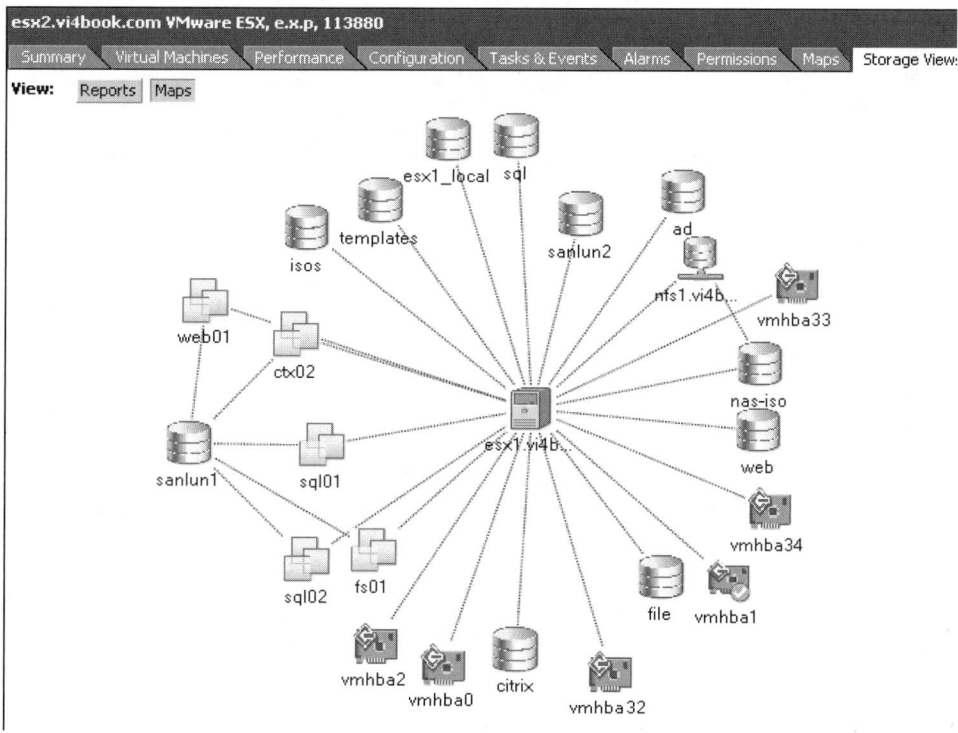

As you can see, the virtual machines held on ESX2 are stored mainly on a VMFS volume called sanlun1. You can drag the individual icons around to tidy up the view (similar to working with a Visio diagram). You can also right-click any object and use the Hide Node option to suppress the display of an individual object and its relationships on the chart.

Summary

In this chapter, we examined the three main storage platforms available to ESX server. We also addressed how to format SAN and iSCSI LUNs with VMFS. The material about networking and storage in this and the previous chapter is pretty critical. Get your networking and storage sorted out before you even begin creating virtual machines, and your life will be that much more trouble-free. They are the absolute bedrock of the platform.

With the ESX host server correctly configured, you are ready to set up virtual machines, as described in the next chapter.

CHAPTER 7 | Creating and Modifying Virtual Machines

This chapter covers how to create a virtual machine (VM) for the first time. Once you have created your first VM, you can duplicate it to quickly create other VMs, as described in the next chapter.

We will first look at the virtual hardware available within a VM. Then we will examine what it is like to set up Windows and Linux within a VM, and how to install VMware Tools to your guest operating system. I will also address how to add hardware to the virtual machine, and show how it is possible to enable direct access to a SAN or iSCSI system within a VM.

Next, I will cover how to use the snapshot facility, originally introduced in ESX 3.*x*. This facility allows you to undo operations within a VM and is used in the process of backing up a VM while the VM is powered on. Then you will learn how to unregister, remove, and delete a VM.

The final sections give you a quick jumpstart on how to create a VM from an existing physical server using VMware vCenter Converter and some tips on setting up a VMware ESX testing environment.

Before you jump right in and start installing a VM, you should check out the list of supported guest operating systems (OSs) at http://www.vmware.com/pdf/GuestOS_guide.pdf, especially if your guest is not Microsoft Windows. With OSs like Solaris, Novell, Linux, and FreeBSD, there can often be quite a surprising gap between what is officially supported by VMware and the current distribution.

What's New with Virtual Machines?

- Support for VMs with eight vCPUs and up to 255GB of RAM

- New power-on defaults (a "soft" power off rather than a hard power-off)

- Hot add of memory and CPUs to guest OSs that support it

- Thinly-provisioned virtual disks, so virtual disks only take up the blocks they consume and do not waste free space—ideal for virtual desktop environments

- Broader range of guest OS support, including legacy systems such as Windows 3 and Windows 9*x*, including support for IDE-based virtual disks

- Support for Windows 2008 (32- and 64-bit), Ubuntu Linux, Debian Linux, FreeBSD, OS/2, SCO, and older versions of Solaris

- Virtual Machine Communication Interface (VMCI), an experimental and revolutionary method of communication between two VMs on the same ESX host that does away with using network protocols, NICs, and network card drivers

---

What Defines a Virtual Machine?

As you might know already, a VM is defined by a collection of files, as listed in Table 7-1.

When you create a VM, what you're actually doing is creating a text file with the .vmx extension, which defines the following VM properties:

- VM's name
- Storage location

File	Description
.vmx	Configuration file in text format
.nvram	VM's virtual BIOS file
.vmdk	VM's metadata/descriptor virtual disk file
.flat-vmdk	VM's data virtual disk file (OS/applications, data)
.vswp	VM's swap file
00001.vmdk	Snapshot file
.vmsn	Snapshot memory file
.vmsd	Snapshot manager file
.log	Log file
.vmxf	Internal metadata file
.rdm	RDM file with virtual compatibility
.rdmp	RDM file with physical compatibility

TABLE 7-1   Files That Make Up a VM

- Guest OS type
- Number of virtual CPUs (vCPUs)
- Number of virtual NICs and their associated port groups
- Type of virtual SCSI adapter used
- Size and location of virtual disk

Virtual Motherboard

The VM itself presents the appearance of real hardware, even though we know it is actually software. When the guest OS makes a hardware request, it believes the VM is a physical machine with a physical motherboard.

An ESX VM actually uses an Intel 440BX-based virtual motherboard with an NS338 chip. VMware selected this motherboard because it has good compatibility and reliability with the entire guest OSs supported by ESX; it can even cope with older OSs like Windows NT 4.x. This selection of the motherboard defines the virtual hardware that can be used within the VM. So what are the options allowed by this virtual motherboard? Here's a quick list of what is supported:

- One or two virtual floppy drives
- One or two virtual CD/DVD drives
- PS/2 interfaces for keyboard and mouse
- Many PCI slots—enough for up to four virtual SCSI controllers and/or ten virtual NICs (by default, the video controller consumes one PCI slot, as does enabling the paravirtualization feature, discussed later in this chapter)
- One to eight vCPUs

- Up to 255GB of RAM
- One parallel port
- One or two serial ports
- One USB controller

NOTE *Notice that there is no support for a sound card. For the most part, this is not a problem. If you use Terminal Services to connect to a Windows guest running inside a VM, you can have sound redirected to the client device.*

USB, Parallel, and Serial Devices

The lack of native USB support (which is available in VMware server and VMware Workstation VMs) has been addressed in vSphere 4. However, it is not currently possible to add a USB device to the ESX host and present that to the VM. One can only assume that VMware introduced the VM USB controller support to address compatibility issues that have occurred with some USB redirection services commonly used in virtual desktops.

In the past, the lack of USB support could cause a problem if you were running software that required a dongle for licensing purposes. The most common solution was to purchase an IP-enabled USB hub, such as the Digi AnywhereUSB Network-Enabled USB Hubs, and redirect the USB calls to the network. Despite the native support for a USB controller, this redirection is likely to continue to be the preferred method.

Parallel and serial devices are not fully virtualized, and their functionality is provided by the Service Console, not the VMkernel. There is a huge drawback to configuring parallel and serial devices in this way. You will be limited by the number of physical parallel and serial ports at the back of the ESX host, and modern servers generally do not have any parallel ports. You will be in trouble if you have more VMs that require this kind of hardware than you have physical ports available.

Also, if you did configure parallel or serial devices in this way, you would be unable to use VMotion with that VM. Recall that VMotion is the process of moving a powered-on VM from one ESX host to another. A VMware ESX server is very clever, but not clever enough to unplug a licensing dongle from the back of one ESX host and plug it in the back of another during a VMotion operation. Similar to the solution to the USB problem, to address the need for parallel or serial ports, many people purchase an IP-enabled parallel or serial hub and redirect the hardware calls through the network instead.

When dealing with USB, parallel, or serial dongles for software licensing purposes, it may be well worth approaching the ISV to see if an alternative licensing model is possible.

Virtual CDs and Floppies

Physical CD/DVDs and floppies are rarely used in a VM. Generally, you convert them into ISO or FLP files. After a CD or floppy disk has been "ripped" to an ISO file, you then upload this to NAS, SAN, or iSCSI storage, depending on your preference.

To create ISO files, you can use CD-burning software like Nero, WinISO, MagicISO, PowerISO, or WinImage. Also, Linux tools such as the `dd` command and the `mkisofs` command will create ISO images for you, but you should be aware that the dd command does not intrinsically verify that the ISO is a perfect image of your physical CD.

To copy these files to a storage address with ESX, you can use the Datastore Browser.

Keyboard and Mouse Interface

Of course, VMware has yet to produce the VMware keyboard and mouse like Microsoft. If you ever see a VMware keyboard and mouse, check the date on your calendar, as it might be April 1. After all, these PS-2 connections don't physically exist; therefore, you cannot plug in a physical keyboard and mouse.

To interact with a VM, you open a Remote Console session. This is similar in functionality to an ILO/RAC card or IP KVM switch on a physical machine. It allows you to watch a VM boot up just like a physical machine. It also allows you to send keyboard and mouse movements from your management PC to the VM.

During the installation of your guest OS, the graphics will be quite poor and you might also experience poor mouse performance. While installing a guest OS, a standard VGA driver is used. After the guest OS is installed, you can install VMware Tools. Among many other things, VMware Tools adds a VMware virtual video adapter driver and VMware virtual mouse driver. These significantly improve graphics and mouse operations.

> **How Much Virtual Hardware Should You Give a VM?**
>
> One of the most common mistakes made by people new to virtualization is to create VMs with the same amount of virtual hardware as the real hardware used for physical machines. In this case, every VM created ends up being defined with four vCPUs, 4GB RAM, and a 72GB virtual disk, even if the VM uses only 10% of these resources.
>
> A better practice is to define the VM with the minimums that you feel your applications or services need to run. Resources can always be increased later if you set them too low. The golden rule is that it is always easier to give away resources on a need-to-use basis than it is to take back needlessly allocated resources. A good analogy for this is permissions. We only give the users the permissions they need, as it is always easier to grant more privileges than it is to take privileges away. In this respect, this issue is also about setting reasonable expectations. Allocating too many resources to the VMs your operators manage will then set the expectation that all VMs should be configured in this way.
>
> Ironically, I've noticed the pendulum has started to swing in the opposite direction to this recommendation, with people occasionally giving the VM far too few resources, and then getting complaints from end users about poor performance. Generally, this happens when companies outsource the build of their virtual infrastructure to a third-party consultancy firm, and then never review the default settings for their templates.

Setting Up Your First VM

Using the Create New Virtual Machine wizard, you can complete the steps for creating a VM. Then you can boot up your new VM and install the guest OS.

Creating a VM

In this section, I will guide you through the creation of your first VM, stopping along the way to point out some handy tips and tricks, and explain some of the less obvious options in the wizard.

To begin, from the Host and Clusters view, select your ESX host and click the New Virtual Machine icon. Choose Custom (so you can see all of the options).

Specifying a VM Name and Location

Type in a friendly name for your VM. I recommend avoiding spaces and special characters, and restricting the name to alphanumeric characters. I also advise using just lowercase letters. If you work from the command line, you may need to type the name of the VM. Life is much harder if you have used a mix of cases, special characters, and spaces. The vSphere Client is quite happy with special characters, but you will find other utilities, such as the Web Access service, do not like special characters.

In this dialog box, you should also see the datacenter name within which your ESX host is located. If you have created folders for VMs in the VMs and Templates view, you will be able to put the VM into the correct folder, as illustrated in the following example:

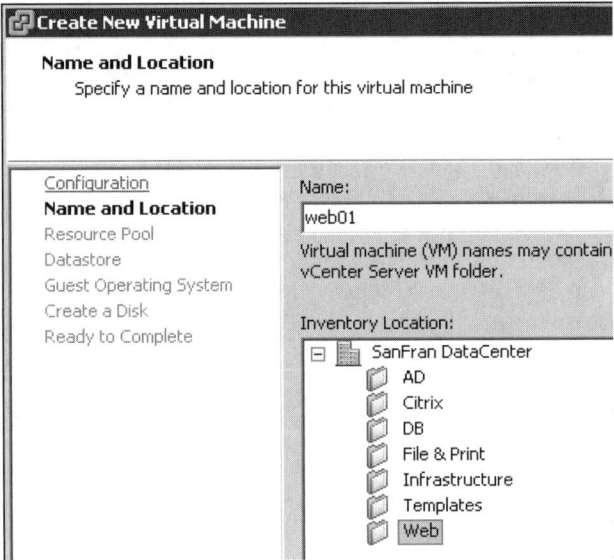

Choosing a Datastore

Next, choose a datastore for the VM's files. This dialog box tells you two very useful things:

- How much free space you have on a datastore. Virtual disks can be quite large files, so you will want to select a datastore that has enough free space for your VM.

- Whether the datastore is available to more than one ESX host or on a shared storage (indicated in the Access column). Shared storage is a requirement for VMotion and VMware clustering technologies such as DRS, DPM, HA, and FT.

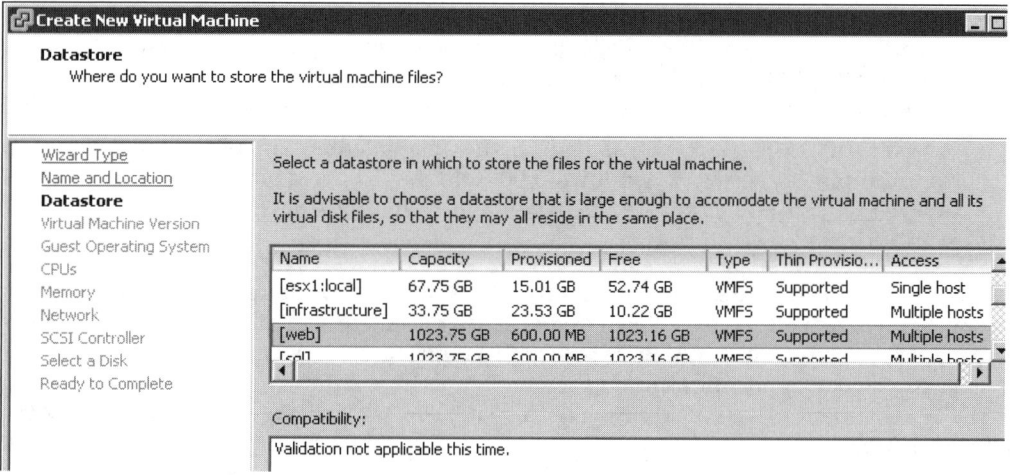

Choosing the VM Version

Your next choice is which VM version you want to use. This is a new feature in VMware vSphere and allows for backward compatibility with previous versions of ESX.

You might ask how we got from VM 4 to VM 7. Well, VMware has its own version number for the virtual machine monitor (VMM), which increments whenever changes are made across the range of VMware virtualization platforms (including VMware Workstation, Server, and ESX). As you might expect, you won't get access to all of the new features of the new VMM if you chose to run it in a legacy-style mode.

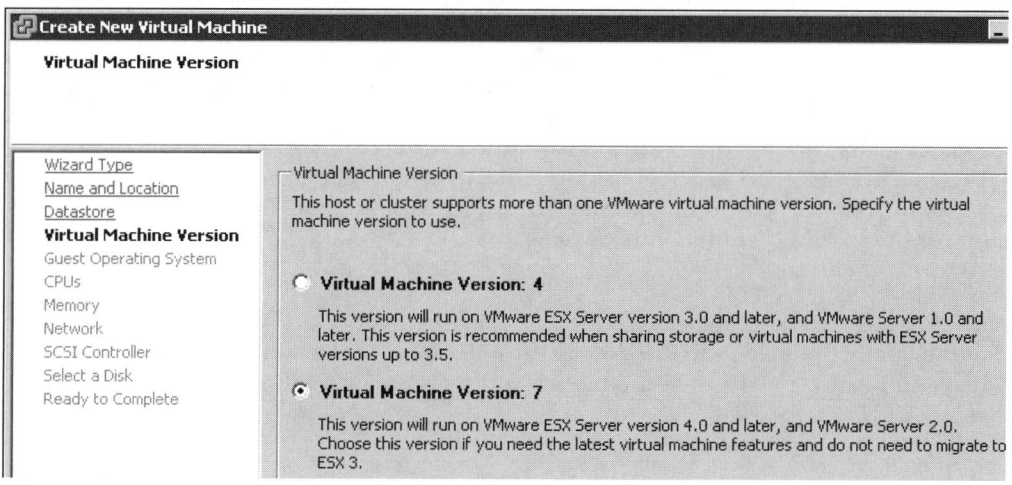

Selecting the Guest OS

From the pull-down list, choose the guest OS that will be run inside the VM. This is important for two reasons:

- It will assist the system when you install VMware Tools. VMware Tools ships as a Microsoft Installer (MSI) package for Windows guests, and as a Red Hat Package Manager (RPM) file and as a .gz zip file for Linux guests. By selecting the correct OS in the list, you will find the right version of VMware Tools is installed to the guest OS.

- Selection of the guest OS will sometimes dictate the remaining defaults in the wizard. For example, if you select Windows 2000 from the list, the default for the virtual SCSI adapter will be a BusLogic device; if you select Windows 2003, the default is an LSI Logic device.

New in vSphere 4 is extended support for old Windows-based systems such as Windows 3.1, 95, and 98. This has been done to bring ESX and vCenter more in line with the other VMware virtualization platforms such as VMware Workstation, and to allow people to run legacy applications in legacy OSs. So perhaps Windows 98 could be included in a VDI environment using something like Virtual Network Computing (VNC) to facilitate remote connectivity for the end user.

NOTE *You might wonder why VMware has chosen to support older OSs on what is meant to be an up-to-the-minute, enterprise-class virtualization platform. Well, believe it or not, some corporations still use these OSs and have legacy applications that are too costly to be ported to a new Windows platform. They may need to retain access to these systems only for legacy data or compliance reasons.*

Another anomaly is support for Microsoft Windows Small Business Server (SBS). You might think it surprising to find SBS here, but this does allow large corporations to buy out smaller startups and convert there existing infrastructure into a virtual infrastructure quickly. It also allows those small businesses to grow by adding additional VMs to their ESX environments should they later need a dedicated terminal server or SharePoint server to complement their initial investment in VMware and Microsoft. I'm not saying this is the best way, but it certainly allows the possibility of starting off with a big server and ESXi 4 for free, which then grows into a multi-ESX host environment with features like DRS/HA being added at a later stage.

In the Linux pull-down list, VMware has added support for Debian, Ubuntu (since ESX 3.5), and Asianux. On the Solaris pull-down list, there is experimental support for older distributions of Sun's OS, including version 9 and 8. Finally, under Other, VMware has added support for DOS, OS/2, FreeBSD, and SCO.

Configuring CPUs and Memory

The next steps are to configure the VM's vCPUs and memory.

For the number of vCPUs in the VM for the guest OS, I recommend starting with one, and then adding more if later if desired. Microsoft does not officially support switching from many CPUs to a single CPU.

NOTE *There are ways of forcing a downgrade of CPUs, such as using the DevCon utility from the Windows Driver Kit (available from the Microsoft Developer Network Web site). These methods are not officially supported, but they frequently do work.*

Adding an extra vCPU does not necessarily improve performance, especially if your applications or services are not multithreaded. In order to leverage the real benefit of multiple vCPUs, the physical hosts may need physical sockets or cores. This is because of the way the VMkernel schedules the processes that are to be executed. I will elaborate more on this subject in Chapters 10 and 11, which cover resource monitoring and management.

The amount you set for the VM's memory through the wizard will act as a limit or maximum to be allocated to the VM. Even if you have free memory available, the VM will never exceed this amount.

Creating Network Connections

Next, select which port group will be used in the VM and how many NICs it needs. The guest OS you chose dramatically affects the contents of Adapter pull-down list in this dialog box. Since ESX 3.5, VMware has written different drivers for different guest OSs. These drivers generally improve performance or compatibility.

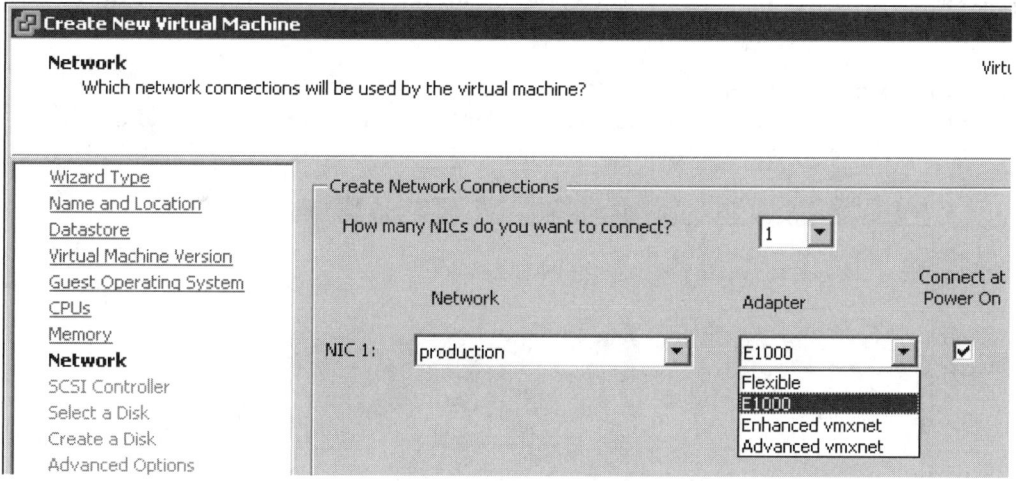

NOTE *Whether VMware chooses to write a network driver for a given OS depends largely on its popularity on the ESX platform. Increasingly, this will driven by changes made by the OS vendors. For example, Microsoft no longer intends to create 32-bit versions of Windows. As 64-bit OSs have become more widely adopted, VMware has started writing network drivers for them.*

The following adapters are available in the example (with Windows Server 2008 64-bit chosen as the guest OS):

- **E1000**   This adapter is for compatibility. For example, you might choose it to virtualize firewalls or other appliances that normally run on physical systems and have yet to be updated by the vendor or to run OSs not normally supported by VMware.

- **Flexible**   This adapter is so named because it will work with or without VMware Tools being installed, say with a boot CD such as WinPE or BartPE.

- **Enhanced vmxnet**   This adapter allows for jumbo frame support with large MTU values and/or TSO engines on physical NICs.

- **Advanced vmxnet**   This builds on the Enhanced vmxnet feature set that has been available since VI3.5 and adds multiqueue support (also known as Receive-Side Scaling in Windows), IPv6 offloads, and MSI/MSI-X interrupt delivery. Advanced vmxnet is available only on VMs with hardware level 7 and a limited set of OSs.

Guest OS support for Enhanced and Advanced vmxnet changes from release to release. When creating a new VM, the wizard allows you to click a hyperlink to the Knowledge Base article 1001805 on VMware's web site to find out the latest support information:

http://kb.vmware.com/selfservice/viewContent.do?externalId=1001805

Additionally, it is possible to configure a VM without a NIC at all. The usefulness of such a VM would be pretty limited, but it is an option that is available. Lastly, disabling the Connect at Power On option has the same effect as pulling out a network cable from a physical server.

Selecting the Storage I/O Adapter

As with the network connection, the choices available for controller type depend on which guest OS you chose. In this example, I opted to install Windows Server 2008 64-bit.

Four types of virtual SCSI adapters are available for this VM. In previous releases, there were only two options. What's new here is the addition of LSI Logic SAS and VMware Paravirtual.

Most guest OSs now defaults to LSI Logic SAS. As SAS drives become increasing popular, the controllers required for them are more commonly included on OS CDs.

Additionally, as with the vmxnet driver for networking, VMware has written a driver for storage as well: VMware Paravirtual. If you select this prior to installing Windows, you will receive an error saying that Windows cannot find any hard disks. This is because the Windows CD-ROM does not contain a driver for the device.

The other two choices in this example are LSI Logic Parallel and BusLogic Parallel. If you are installing Windows Server 2003 Enterprise Edition, I recommend using the LSI Logic Parallel controller. Because I opted to install Windows Server 2008 64-bit, use of a BusLogic driver is not recommended, as there isn't a BusLogic Driver for that controller on the Windows Server 2008 CD.

Of course, it is possible for a VM to have more than type of disk controller. You could have the boot disk use LSI Logic SAS, and use VMware's Paravirtual controller for the other drives.

Selecting and Creating a Disk

Next, in the Select a Disk dialog box, choose to create a new virtual disk. You would choose to use an existing virtual disk if you had copied a virtual disk from some other source, such as Openfiler or the HP LeftHand VSA. The Raw Device Mapping option is used to give a VM direct access to a SAN or iSCSI LUN. I will cover this option in the "Adding Virtual Hardware" section later in this chapter.

Next, specify disk capacity, provisioning, and location. Before discussing the disk size, we need to consider the provisioning options.

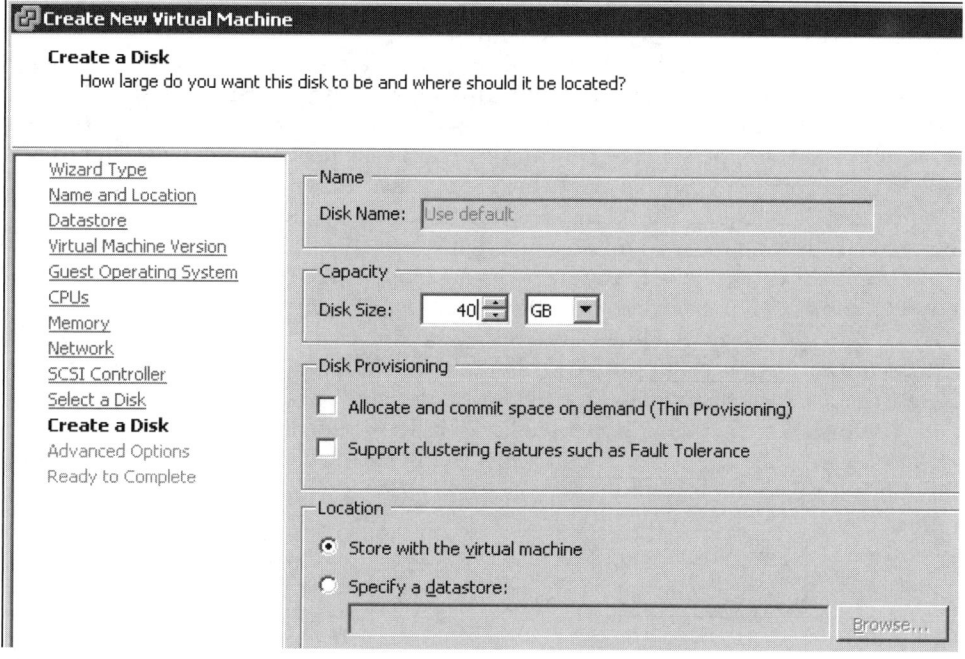

In vSphere 4, three types of disks (thick/zeroedthick, thin, and eagerzeroedthick) are natively supported in vCenter. We have always had the ability to create a "thick," or monolithic, virtual disk. When this type of virtual disk is created, it takes up *all* the space you allocate here. ESX virtual disks do not grow as more data is created inside them. This format offers the best performance. As a flat file, the virtual disk will be created in contiguous blocks within the VMFS volume.

What's new is the support for thin provisioning. You may be familiar with this format from VMware Workstation. With a thin virtual disk, although you may ask for a 40GB disk, it actually grows in size as you add data. This would be a good space-saving format for test VMs or perhaps VDI environments where you are trying to reduce the storage costs for many VMs. As I don't have a vast amount of storage space in my lab environment, I use thin provisioning frequently. You might question the logic of using thinly provisioned virtual disks on thinly provisioned LUN/volumes from your storage vendor's array, but many storage vendors now recommend this. Think of it as a "double-whammy," where you are being ultra efficient at the VMware and storage array level.

CAUTION *The thin provisioned format is incompatible with the new VMware FT feature.*

If you have any intention of using the VMware FT feature with your VM, it is best to enabled FT support here. If you do not, VMware FT will convert the virtual disk to the correct format, but this is quite intrusive to the system.

If you don't enable FT support on the virtual disk, it will be created as a "zeroedthick" disk, whereas if you do, it will be created as "eagerzeroedthick" disk. What is the difference between these two types of thick disk? On the surface they look the same, so whatever you do, if you ask for a 40GB disk, it will be 40GB on the VMFS volume. The difference is in how they are created. In a zeroedthick disk, the file is created very quickly, and any existing data on the physical disk is overwritten as data is written to the virtual disk as needed. In an eagerzeroedthick disk, the process takes much longer, as the blocks inside the virtual disk are zeroed out. Although the eagerzeroedthick format is slower to create, it is faster to read and write to because the free blocks inside the virtual disk are guaranteed to be blank and available for use. This major performance improvement is needed for VMware FT to function correctly. It's interesting and no coincidence that the eagerzeroedthick disk is also required in some third-party clustering software such as MSCS.

Now, let's consider the disk size. How big should a virtual disk be? It's precisely this question that thin virtual disks address, but remember the caveat that thinly provisioned virtual disks are *not* currently supported with VMware FT. Despite this, I think this question is unlikely to go away, as historically the disk space demands of OSs are on the rise. For example, Windows Server 2008 Enterprise with 2GB RAM, cleanly installed, consumed nearly 8GB of disk space on my 40GB thinly provisioned virtual disk, as you can see from the following excerpt from the Summary page of this VM.

Resources	
Consumed Host CPU:	66 MHz
Consumed Host Memory:	961.00 MB
Active Guest Memory:	102.00 MB
Provisioned Storage:	42.00 GB
Unshared Storage:	7.59 GB
Committed Storage:	7.59 GB

Much of your decision about the disk size will depend on the size and quantity of data your applications consume. One "gotcha" is giving a VM a large amount of memory, but a very small virtual disk when using the monolithic format for the operating system. You might find you lack space for the swap space for your given guest OS. Now that the amount of memory can be changed so easily, this needs some consideration. What free space would there be for a swap file or partition if you started with 250MB of RAM and then later changed to 2GB RAM? Virtual disks can be made larger, and there are methods for making them smaller, as discussed in the "Managing Virtual Disks" section later in this chapter.

Finally, the option to "Specify a datastore" allows you to store the VM's virtual disks at an alternative location. Perhaps you have two virtual disks: one for the boot disk and the other for data. Many people like to put their boot disks and data disks on different LUNs, which have different numbers of spindles, RAID, or replication frequencies.

Specifying Advanced Options

In SCSI systems, adapter 0 and ID 0 are used to indicate the location of the boot disk (SCSI 0:0). A VM conforms to all the SCSI conventions, with the SCSI adapter using ID7. Remember that the VM presents to the guest OS the appearance of real hardware. You can have up to four virtual SCSI adapters if you wish, with up to 15 virtual disks attached to each adapter. Although the range is from 0:0 to 0:15 (which is actually 16 SCSI IDs), ID 0:7 is used by the controller itself. In this example, I choose SCSI 0:0.

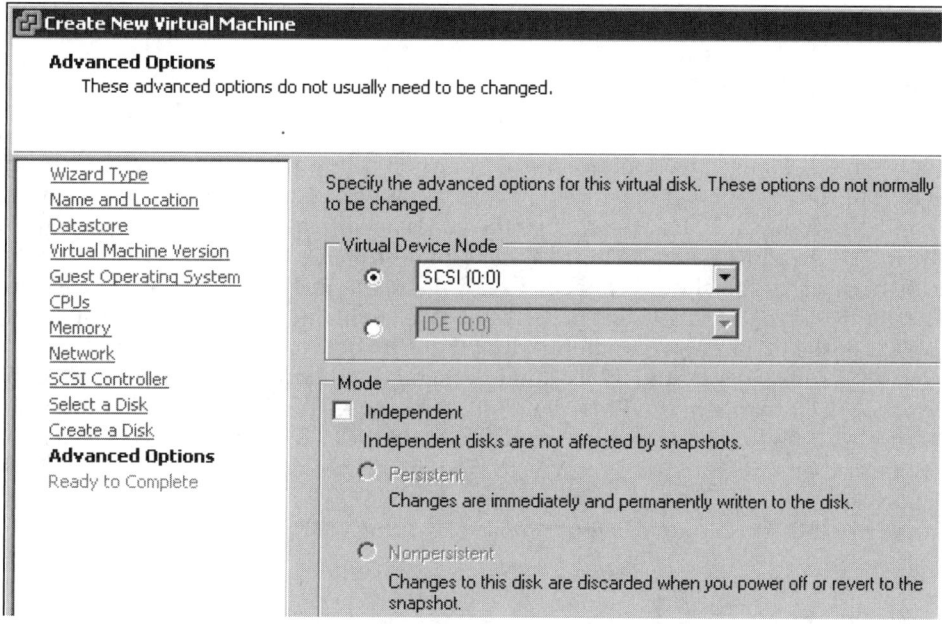

In the vSphere Client 4 release, VMware has extended the support for IDE controllers for virtual disks as well. This allows for much older legacy OSs to function (such as Windows 3, 95, and 98), where SCSI support was limited to say the least. Additionally, it should make the importing of VMware Workstation VMs easier, where IDE was once the default option for all virtual disks. In the past, we had to go through quite a lengthy and tedious conversion process for this to work. In vSphere 4, a newly created Windows XP VM now defaults to using an IDE drive.

I will cover the mode options offered here when I delve into the snapshot feature later in this chapter.

Finishing the VM Creation

Lastly, check your selections in the Summary page, click "Edit the virtual machine settings before completion," and then click Finish. You will see another dialog box that contains advanced configuration settings.

Installing the Guest Operating System

When you first power on a VM, its boot order is as follows:

- Floppy
- CD
- Hard disk
- PXE

The second time you power on a VM, the boot order is changed to this:

- Floppy
- Hard disk
- CD
- PXE

As you can see, on the first boot up, the assumption is that you will probably be booting to a CD-ROM ISO file to install the guest OS. The second time, it is assumed that the VM is going to boot from the hard disk. This stops the annoyance created by some vendors' OSs where their CDs do allow the operator to skip booting from the CD. It also means that if you want an easy life, you should connect an ISO file to the VM before the first power on to avoid having to use the VM's BIOS F2 or ESC keystroke to change the boot order. If you fail to connect a CD at the first boot, you will find that the VM boots to PXE and searches for a DHCP server. If subsequently the CD is connected and then the VM rebooted, because the boot order has been changed, the VM would still not boot to the CD! In fact, this problem so bedevils most people's first use of the product that in ESX 3.5, VMware introduced a boot delay option and an option to force the VM to load the BIOS on power on (discussed in the next section).

To attach an ISO file to the VM, you can use one of the following:

- The ESX server's physical CD
- The CD-ROM drive or ISO file on your management PC
- An ISO file on a centralized datastore

The last option is the best in terms of performance, flexibility, and low administration cost. As discussed in Chapter 6, the ISO file could be copied to an SAN, iSCSI, or NAS storage.

To use an ISO file on a centralized datastore, follow these steps:

1. In the list of devices, choose CD/DVD Drive 1, in the Edit Settings dialog box

2. Choose the option Datastore ISO file

3. Select a datastore where you have copied the ISOs of your guest OS and select the ISO file.

4. Before leaving the Virtual Machine Properties dialog box, ensure the "Connect at power on" option is enabled.

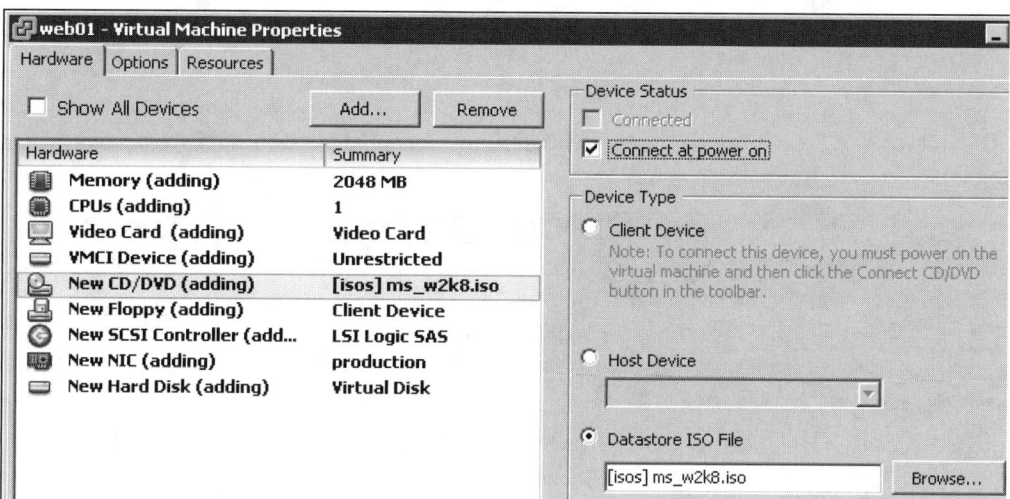

5. To open a window on the VM, right-click your VM and choose Open Console. Alternatively, you can click the Launch Virtual Machine Console icon.

In the Remote Console window, you can use the keystroke CTRL+ALT to release your mouse and keyboard focus.

Powering On and Off VMs

You have several options for powering off and on your VM, including a soft shutdown, which is the new default of the Power Off button. You can also set a boot delay upon startup, and automatically start and stop VMs.

Powering Off Your VM

In all previous versions of VMware's VI, the Power Off and Reset buttons carried out a hard, nongraceful power off or reboot of the VM.

This would be akin to pulling out the power cord on a physical machine, or flipping the power switch on a physical server. These buttons' defaults have now changed to soft and graceful shutdown of the guest OS or a soft boot. The change has probably been introduced to prevent accidental hard-power events generating unwanted results, not least questions from the shutdown tracker service in various versions of Windows.

If you do want to do a quick-and-dirty hard power off of a VM, you need to use the right-click menu options instead:

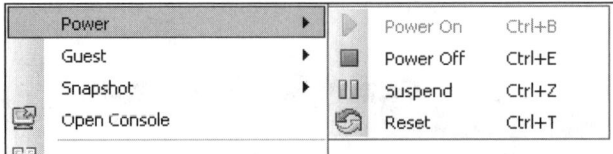

The defaults of these buttons can be adjusted on a per-VM basis in the Edit Settings dialog box. On the Options tab, select VMware Tools.

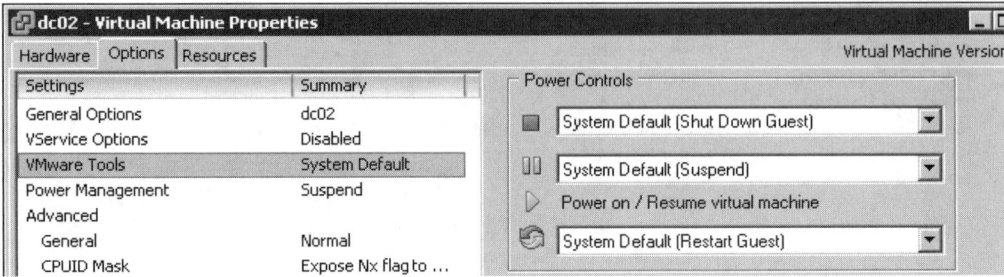

Setting a Boot Delay

Sometimes you will find that a VM boots up so quickly that you cannot send the ESC or F2 keystroke fast enough to interact with the VM at a BIOS-settings level. If this is the case (say you want to temporarily boot to a CD or an ISO image with the VM), it is easily fixed by setting a BIOS boot delay. This feature was introduced in VI3.5.

To set the boot delay, right-click the VM and choose Edit Settings. On the Options tab of the Virtual Machine Properties dialog box, choose Boot Options. Set a boot delay in milliseconds, such as 10,000 for 10-second delay. (Personally, I find it odd that VMware choose to use such a small integer for this value. I will leave you to debate the merits of a 10,000 ms delay over a 10, 0001 ms delay in the boot process!)

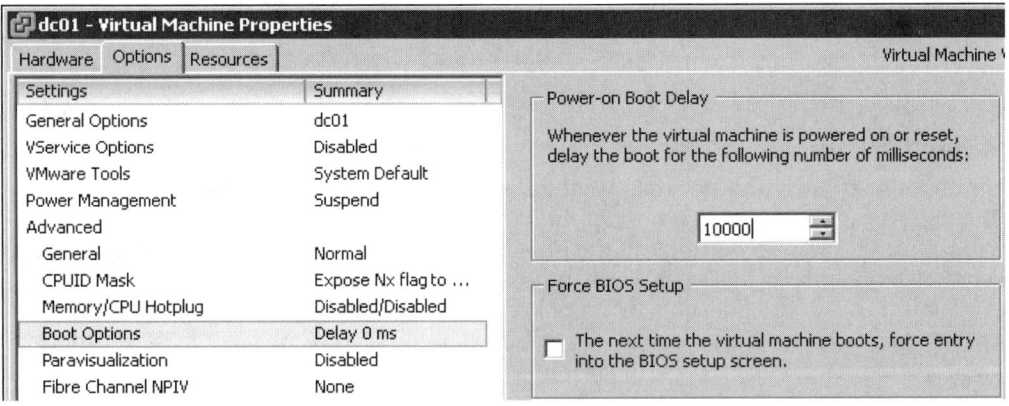

This dialog box also contains the Force BIOS Setup option. I don't use this option, because I'm worried I might enable it, get distracted, and find that the next time I boot up a VM from vCenter, it goes into the BIOS screen rather than load my guest OS.

Automatically Starting and Stopping of VMs

ESX has the ability to gracefully power off and on your VMs if you choose to shut down or reboot an ESX host. This Guest Shutdown feature requires the use of VMware Tools, which you'll install in the next section. It sends a signal to the VM to begin its shutdown process.

Note that this option is useful for stand-alone ESX host environments. However, if you use features such as VMotion, DRS, and HA, the automatic start and stop feature will not do much for you. In fact, this feature breaks as soon as a VM is moved from one ESX host to another by VMotion, DRS, or HA. This is not a bug, but there by design. After all, as soon as you have VMotion, DRS, and HA, you start to care less about where your VM runs, as long as it does run. If you manually perform a VMotion operation to move a VM away from the ESX host that has this feature configured, and then return back to the ESX, it is dropped in the default location of manual startup. If you have VMotion, you are much better off simply moving the VMs to another ESX host before you reboot or shut down an ESX host.

If you want to configure automatic starting and stopping of VMs, follow these steps:

1. In the vSphere Client, select your ESX host.

2. Choose the Configuration tab. In the Software pane, select Virtual Machine Startup/ Shutdown.

3. In the top-right corner of the window, select Properties.

4. In the dialog box, under System Settings, enable "Allow virtual machines to start and stop automatically with the system."

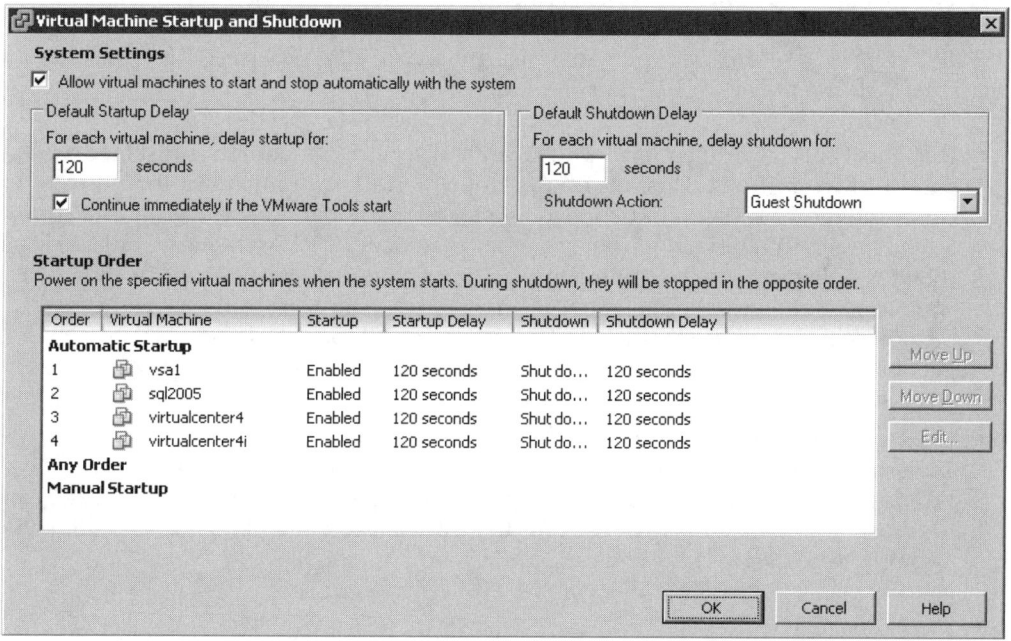

5. From the Shutdown Action drop-down list, choose Guest Shutdown.

6. Optionally, you can modify the startup and shutdown interval used between VMs to reflect the fact that some VM's services will take longer to start than others. As an option, you can ask the system to override the startup delay by first monitoring VMware Tools, which may begin sooner than the 120-second default value.

7. Optionally, use the Move Up and Move Down buttons to control the order of shutdown and startup for VMs that share service dependencies.

The Edit button in this dialog box allows you to set individual settings for each VMware override to the global system settings.

Setting up VMware Tools

After the guest OS is installed, you generally will want to install VMware Tools, which is a software package that is installed into the guest OS. It contains three components:

- **Drivers**   During the installation of VMware Tools, the installer copies across many drivers for the following devices: VMware SVGA II, VMware mouse, VMware SCSI driver (replaces Microsoft BusLogic driver if used in Windows NT and 2000), AMD Enhanced NIC driver (vmxnet.sys replaces pcntpci5.sys), a file system synchronization driver (used with VMware Consolidated Backup and the new VMware Data Recovery appliance), and a memory control driver (vmmemctl). These devices and the drivers that accompany them significantly improve performance, especially the vmxnet.sys network card driver.

NOTE *If you fail to install VMware Tools, the guest OS will use a vlance.sys driver, which virtualizes as a standard AMD PCnet family NIC. The vlance.sys driver significantly increases the CPU overhead on a VM, and as consequence, reduces overall performance. Therefore, installing VMware Tools is highly recommended.*

- **Heartbeat service or daemon**   The Heartbeat service or daemon is installed as part of VMware Tools. This service is used to alert the administrator that the guest OS inside the VM has malfunctioned. Under normal operation, a VM should have a small green icon next to it in the vCenter Inventory. If a VM "hangs," blue-screens (BSOD), or experiences a kernel panic in Linux, you should see this icon change to a red exclamation mark. The guest OS error stops the VMware Tools Heartbeat service, which then triggers an alert or an alarm. Although this is useful, you may get false-positive alerts occurring when you first power on a VM, because the guest OS is still loading and the Heartbeat service has yet to start.

- **Configuration applet or script**   An applet or script is used to configure VMware Tools after the installation process has completed. If you install VMware Tools to Windows, an icon for the configuration applet will appear in the taskbar tray near the clock. If you install VMware Tools to Linux without a GUI, then you will have a configuration script that you can run instead.

Installing VMware Tools for Windows

To install VMware Tools on a Windows guest OS, right-click your Windows VM, select Guest, select Upgrade/Install VMware Tools, and then click OK. Next, choose the type of installation you want to run. A typical installation configures only features that are required with VMware ESX. A complete installation configures features for all VMware platforms: ESX, Server, and Workstation. A custom installation allows you to select which components you require. Interestingly, there are some "hidden" driver options in the custom installation. For example, you will see the Wyse Multimedia Support driver for use in VDI environments using Wyse terminals.

In the background, the system connects to an ISO file called window.iso held on the ESX host. Windows should autorun this CD and execute the VMware Tools.msi file. If you attempt to open the VM's settings while a VMware Tools installation is in progress, you will receive a warning message.

Installing VMware Tools for Linux

For Linux systems, there are two VMware Tools packages: an RPM format package and a package in zipped format of tar.gz. After extracting the tar.gz file to a temporary location, a script is used to install and configure VMware Tools. If you are running a graphical front end to Linux, you can use a utility called VMware Toolbox for further configuration. Lastly, ensure your Linux installation includes the tools required to use a C compiler (such as gcc), as VMware Tools will need to compile the VMware drivers for your kernel.

Installing VMware Tools with the RPM File

Follow these steps to install VMWare Tools using the RPM file:

1. Log on as root to the Linux VM.

2. Right-click your Windows VM, select Guest, and then select Upgrade/Install VMware Tools. Click OK. This switches on the CD-ROM and points to the appropriate ISO file that contains VMware Tools, located at /usr /lib /vmware / isoimages /linux.iso.

3. Mount this ISO file as if it were a physical CD-ROM with the following command:

```
mount -t iso9660 /dev/cdrom /mnt/cdrom
```

4. Execute the RPM file with the following command:

```
rpm -Uvh --nodeps VMwareTools-4.x.X-XXXXX.i386.rpm
```

The RPM switches are the following:

- U stands for upgrade. Although this is a clean install, the same command could be used to upgrade VMware Tools to a newer version.

- V shows verbose information during the installation.

- h shows "hash marks," or status information, to inform you of the progress of the installation.
- --nodeps forces an install, regardless of software dependency errors.

Here, I have used a mixture of short switches that need only one - sign and longer, friendlier switches that need two - - signs.

After the install process has completed, you can use the script /usr/lib/vmware-config-tools.pl inside the Linux VM to configure the VMware Tools package.

Installing VMware Tools with a Script

Follow these steps to install VMware Tools with a script:

1. Log on as root to the Linux VM.
2. Right-click your Windows VM, select Guest, and select Upgrade/Install VMware Tools. Click OK. This switches on the CD-ROM and points to the appropriate ISO file that contains VMware Tools, located at /usr /lib /vmware /isoimages /linux.iso.
3. Mount this ISO file as if it were a CD-ROM:

   ```
   mount /dev/cdrom /mnt/cdrom
   ```
4. Copy the .gz version of the VMware Tools to the /tmp directory:

   ```
   cp /mnt/cdrom/*.qz /tmp
   ```
5. Unzip this .gz file:

   ```
   tar -zxvf /tmp/vmware-linuz-tools.tar.gz
   ```

   The z switch indicates that the tar command should uncompress the files. The x switch indicates that files should be extracted. The -v switch gives you a list of files being extracted.
6. Change into the vmware-linux-tools directory created by the unzip process, and run the installation script:

   ```
   cd /tmp/vmware-tools-distrib
   ./vmware-install.pl
   ```
7. Accept the default locations for the file copy. The script will create directories for locations that do not exist currently.
8. Choose Yes to allow the system to run the script /usr/bin/vmware-config-tools.pl.

Configuring VMware Tools

VMware Tools has a number of configurable options, especially in Windows. Most of these options are self-explanatory, but I will discuss some of the most important ones: time synchronization, scripts triggered by power events, and shrinking of virtual disks.

Enabling Time Synchronization

The most common configuration is for time synchronization to enable the NTP service on the ESX host. The NTP service that provides accurate time to ESX is either on your own network or on the Internet. Then, using VMware Tools, the VM synchronizes its time with the ESX host, which results in both ESX and the VM having the correct time.

In VMware Tools for Windows and for other guest OSs, time synchonization with NTP is not enabled by default. This is because many guests OSs have their own time synchronization feature. In the case of Windows, this is the Windows Time service. You cannot have two time synchronization services within the same machine—the services would conflict with each other, and the VM would not be a trusted source for time. To use the time synchronization feature from VMware Tools. You must first disable the guest OS's method.

The VMware Tools version of time synchronization happens once every minute and is not currently configurable. For this reason, some time-sensitive VMs might still need their time set from systems that update their time at a more frequent interval.

Of course, there is no requirement to make a VM machine receive its time from ESX. It is entirely possible to still receive time updates from Active Directory's PDC emulator, which is the default. However, if you have virtualized your Active Directory environment or intend to do so, using the VMware Tool's time synchronization feature is not a wise idea.

TIP   *If you wish to learn about other methods of timekeeping in a VM, consult the VMware Information Guide, which is available from http://www.vmware.com/pdf/vmware_timekeeping.pdf.*

Enabling VMware Tools Time Synchronization in Windows   Before you enable VMware Tools time synchronization, disable the Windows Time service. To do this, in Administrative Tools and Services, double-click the Windows Time service and choose Stop. From the Start-up Type pull-down list, choose Disabled. Then log off and close the Remote Console window.

To enable a Windows VM to use VMware Tools time synchronization, double-click the VMware Tools icon in the taskbar tray, and enable "Time synchronization between the virtual machine and the ESX Server."

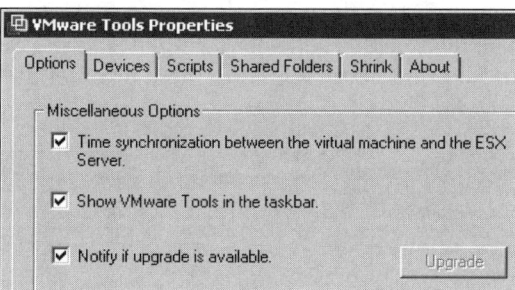

Special considerations must be followed if your VM is running an Active Directory and is a domain controller. VMware Knowledge Base article 1318 (http://kb.vmware.com/ selfservice/microsites/search.do?cmd=displayKC&externalId=1318/) outlines this:

> "If you use a virtual machine as a primary domain controller for a Windows network, the primary domain controller must run the Windows Time service as a time server, to provide time to secondary domain controllers and other hosts on the network. However, that primary domain controller does not need to use the Windows Time service as a client to receive time synchronization input for its own clock. You can still use VMware Tools to synchronize the virtual machine's clock while running the Windows Time service in a server-only mode."

This is done by engaging the Windows Registry option called "NoSync."

Enabling VMware Tools Time Synchronization in Other Guest OSs   In other guest OSs, you enable time synchronization by editing the .vmx file of the VM, as follows:

1. Shut down your VM.

2. Open a SSH session on your ESX host, and elevate your rights to root using the `su -` command.

3. Use nano or your preferred text editor to open the VM's .vmx file. Here is the nano command:

   ```
   nano -w /vmfs/volumes/web/web01/web02.vmx
   ```

4. Scroll to the end of the file and change the `tools.syncTime` option from `"FALSE"` to `"TRUE"`:

   ```
   tools.syncTime = "TRUE"
   ```

5. Save the file, and exit your text editor.

6. Power on your VM.

Using Configuration Scripts

As I mentioned earlier, you can have scripts executed when a VM's power status changes. This can be useful to handle reboots and shutdowns. For example, it is sometimes quicker to reboot OSs like Windows by stopping services before the call to reboot the VM. If you were running Windows inside the VM, you could use a .bat file with the Microsoft `net stop` command to stop services.

Occasionally, there are annoyances like dialog boxes that stop successful reboots or shutdowns. Rather than having to log on to the VM and deal with these prompts, you could script them away.

In my work, I deal extensively with Microsoft Terminal Services and Citrix XenApp. When I use the Restart Guest option in the vSphere Client, I sometimes see the the following dialog box:

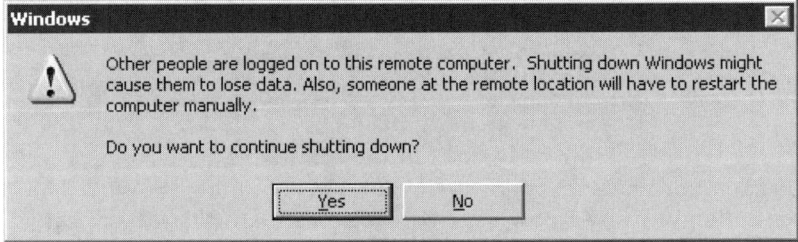

Such a request merely times out if there is no one to respond to these dialog boxes.

To fix this problem, I used the Microsoft `tsshutdn` command with the power-down script, as follows:

1. Log in to the VM.

2. Browse to C:\Program Files\VMware\VMware Tools\.

3. Right-click the poweroff-vm-default.bat file, choose Properties, and remove the read-only attributes.

4. Right-click and choose to edit the file.

5. Add the following to the .bat file:

```
tsshutdn 0 /reboot /delay:300
```

tsshutdn has many options. The two 0 values stop any warnings or delays and start the shutdown immediately. The following command gives the users 120 seconds to log off, and then shutdown would begin 30 seconds after all logoffs had completed:

```
tshutdn 120 /powerdown /delay:30
```

The messages go to all users, whether you are using the Microsoft RDP or Citrix ICA protocol.

CAUTION   *Shutdown and reboot guests use the same script in VMware Tools. This means that if you used the work-around described here and signaled the VM to shut down, it would in fact reboot. The only way to shut down the guest would be to log in and do a manual shutdown within Windows.*

Using the Shrink Feature

In ESX 3.*x*, the shrink feature was being deprecated; in other words, it was removed. In fact, when VI3 first came out, this feature was no longer supported by VMware in an ESX 3.*x* VM. This was a shame, because it is actually a useful feature. Fortunately, VMware reconsidered and reintroduced the shrink feature in VI3.5!

The shrink feature optimizes a disk before exporting (copying) it to another storage system by removing deleted files. As you might know, most guest OSs do not actually remove files physically from either a physical disk or a virtual disk. Files are marked for deletion in the file system database, and then are overwritten by new files. The downside for us is that when we copy a virtual disk elsewhere—say, prior to converting a VM to a template—we get both our real data and our deleted data. The shrink feature used to write out the deleted files with zero values, thus reducing the overall size of the disk. It is not recommended to use this feature with thin virtual disks as this will cause the disk to be inflated.

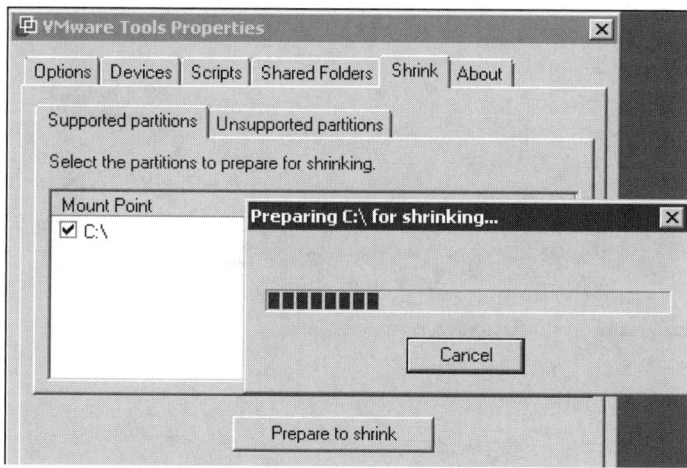

Other Shrinking and Secure Deletion Tools

The downside of the shrink feature is that it is a GUI tool only, which means if you wish to automate the shrinking process with a script, your options are limited. However, all is not lost. Many community forum members still prefer a tool called SDelete, which has been updated to shrink as well as carry out secure deletions, which was its initial goal.

You can download SDelete from what used to be the Sysinternals Web site. Microsoft purchased the web site and its tools in July 2006. You will now find the site, renamed as Windows Sysinternals, at http://www.microsoft.com/technet/sysinternals/default.mspx. SDelete is listed under File and Disk utilities.

Plenty of secure delete tools are available for other other guest OSs, such as Linux, Solaris, and Novell NetWare.

Checking If VMware Tools Is Up to Date

VMware Tools is normally updated when a new version of ESX is released. There are two main ways you can see if your VMware Tools version is out of date:

- Inside the VM, the VMware Tools icon will change to have a yellow exclamation mark next to it.

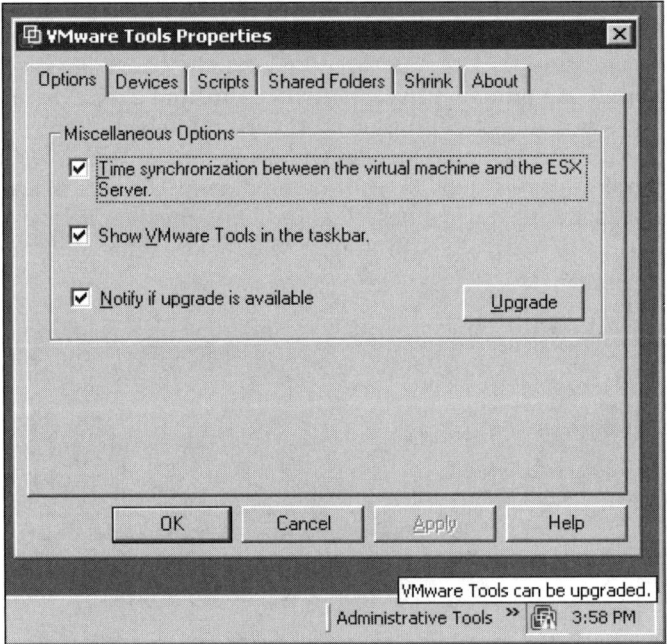

- From vCenter, select anywhere in the Virtual Machines tab, right-click the column headings, and add the column called VMware Tools Status.

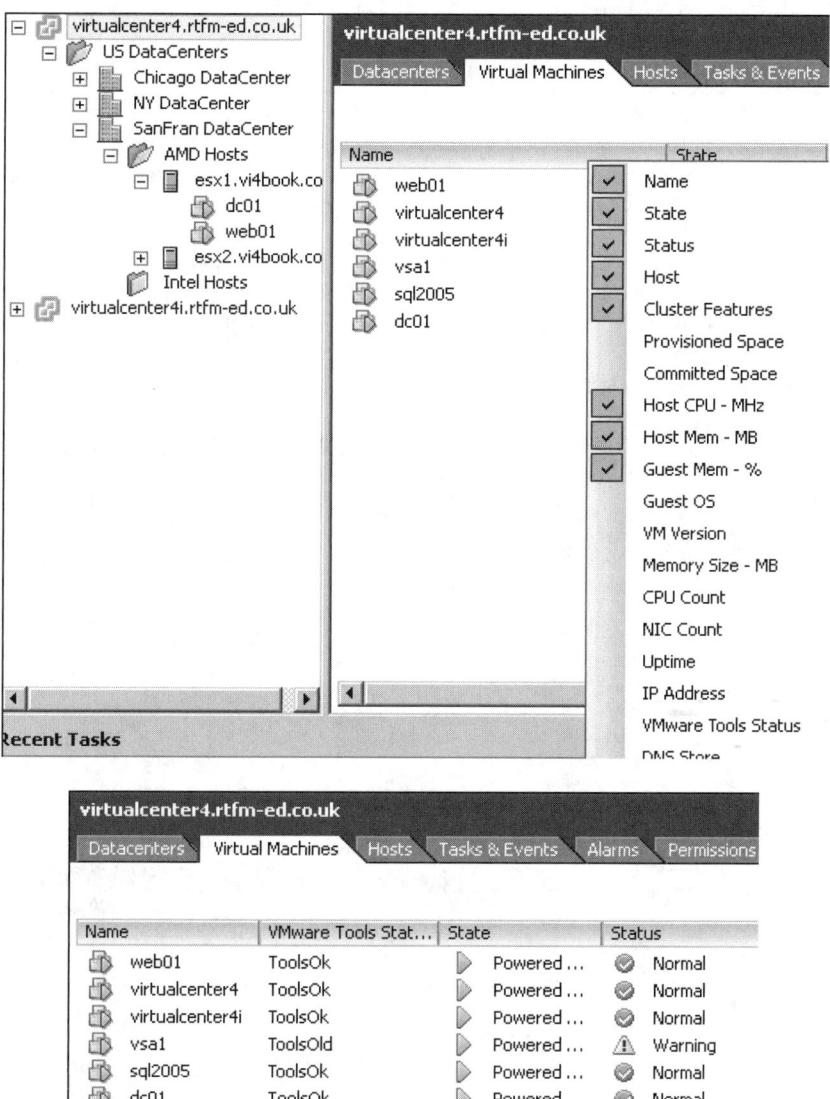

Upgrading Virtual Hardware and VMware Tools

If you are running an old VM created on ESX 2 or 3, or some other VMware platform, you probably need to upgrade its virtual hardware level and its version of VMware Tools.

> **TIP**   *The order in which you carry out these tasks is significant. You might experience fewer hardware-detection problems if you first upgrade VMware Tools, and then upgrade the VM's virtual hardware. Additionally, some users experience odd problems with static IP address details being "lost" if they upgrade virtual hardware before upgrading VMware Tools.*

If you do not upgrade the VM's hardware, some of the options in the Virtual Machines Properties dialog box discussed in the following sections will simply not be there. The definitive way to tell which version of VM you are working with is in the Virtual Machine Properties dialog box. The following examples show a brand-new VM created on vSphere 4 and a VM created with VI3, respectively.

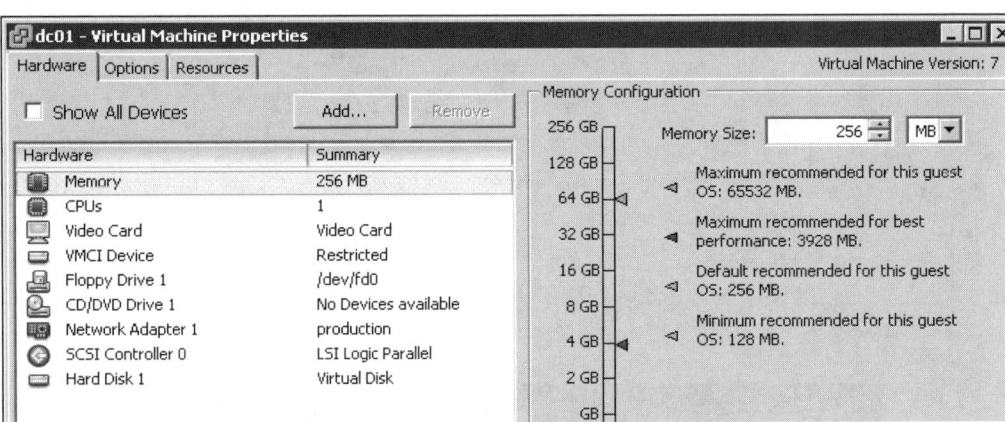

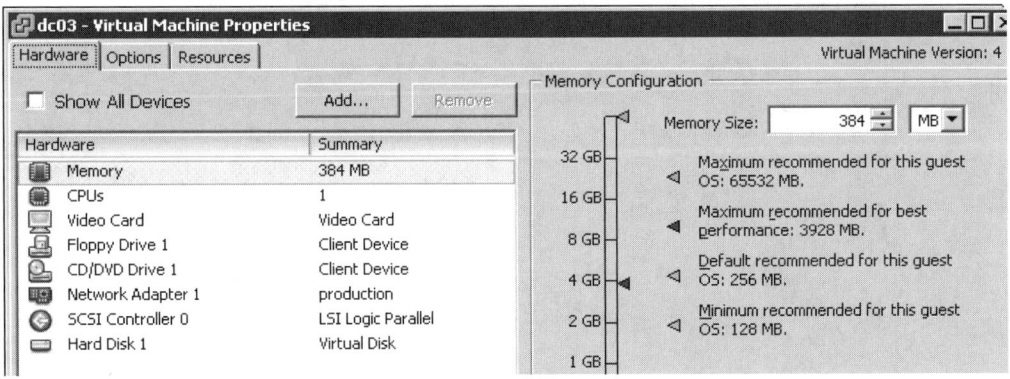

As you can see, the VM called dc03 does not have a reference to the VMCI device. If you wish to see a list of your VMs and sort them by VM version, a column option to show this is available on the Virtual Machines tab in the vCenter Inventory.

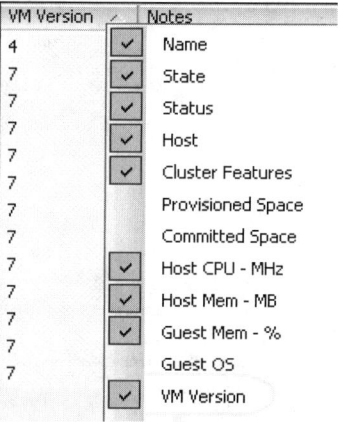

Version 4 VMs and older will have the Upgrade Virtual Hardware option, to upgrade them to version 7. Right-click your Windows VM and select Guest to access this option.

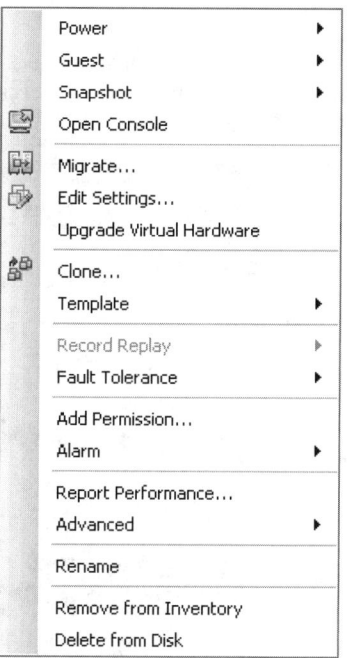

The Upgrade Virtual Hardware option appears only when the VM is powered off. After powering on the VM, the OS will try to plug-and-play new devices such as the VMware

VMCI device. This will fail, as Windows will not be able to locate a driver for the device, and it remains marked as an unknown device in Windows Device Manager.

Although the upgrade does not directly affect your applications, it is recommended that you back up your VM before carrying out this upgrade process. When you select the option, you will see a warning message with this recommendation.

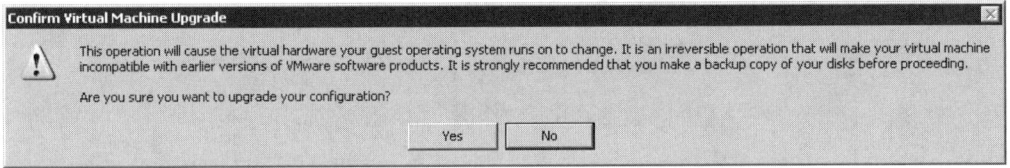

The Guest menu also includes an option to Install/Upgrade VMware Tools. When you select this option, you will be asked if you wish to carry out an interactive or automatic upgrade of VMware Tools. An interactive upgrade allows you to control the installation process, critically deferring the reboot until a time that suits your maintenance times. An automatic upgrade occurs silently and will automatically reboot the Windows guest OS. Despite the use of the term "upgrade," it essentially uninstalls the old version of VMware Tools and then installs a brand-new copy.

Adding Virtual Hardware

If you wish to change the virtual hardware configuration (increasing CPUs, RAM, or NICs) of your VM, in most cases, you will need to power it down. However, in some guest OSs, you can "hot add" a virtual disk. This includes Windows XP Professional with Service Pack 2, Windows 2003, and many distributions of Linux.

Additionally, you may wish to allow your VM direct access to a SAN or iSCSI LUN, achieved by a special mapping file called an RDM. This metadata text file essentially "tells" the VM which LUN to access. Of course, the VM doesn't actually connect directly to the SAN or iSCSI system. Instead, the VMkernel intercedes (using a process called binary translation) on its behalf using VMkernel drivers to access the SAN or iSCSI via the ESX host's physical HBA.

Giving a VM Direct Access to a SAN or iSCSI LUN

There are several reasons to use RDM files in preference to virtual disks:

- While some companies are happy to store their data within the virtual disk format, more conservative companies might prefer their data to be stored in the OS's native file system.

- You may have existing data held within NTFS, ext3, or another proprietary file system to which you merely wish the VM to have access. This will also allow you to leverage natively the file systems support.

- RDM files are required for some clustering scenarios, such as running a clustering service between two VMs on separate ESX hosts (referred to as a "cluster-across-boxes").

- You may wish to leverage your guest OS's native disk and file system tools to carry out certain tasks. For example, the Microsoft's DiskPart tool allows you to "stretch" an NTFS partition to fill free space. This can be an advantageous feature if your SAN supports expanding a LUN to increase its size.

- Some third-party applications from a storage vendor, such as EMC's "Replication Manager" software, may require RDM-style access to the array to function.

However, note that RDMs, like virtual disks, are limited to a maximum LUN size of 2TB. At the moment, a VM sees the size of the VMDK/RDM by using a calculation based on the number of cylinders, heads, and sectors, rather than the modern GUID Partition Tables (GPT) approach adopted by the recent Microsoft OSs, which allows much large LUN sizes.

There are two compatibility modes when you create an RDM file: physical and virtual compatibility. Physical compatibility allows the VM to treat the raw LUN as if it were a physical machine. There are no special features or options with physical compatibility. Virtual compatibility, on the other hand, allows the VM to treat a raw LUN as if it were a virtual disk. It allows for advanced features such as different disk modes and VMware snapshot files. Physical compatibility is used only in scenarios where you are installing clustering software such as MSCS into the VM. VMware use RDM files to allow the VM cluster pair access to the quorum and shared volumes that make up a Node A/Node B clustering system. I recommend using virtual compatibility in all other cases.

RDM files have the extension .vmdk, just like virtual disks, and they can be stored alongside the VM's other files or in a different datastore if you wish. If you wish at a later stage to convert an RDM file into a virtual disk, this can be done with either Storage

VMotion (SVMotion) or via a cold migration (moving the VM while it is powered off). This conversion process is covered in Chapter 12.

To add in a RDM file on a running VM, follow these steps:

1. Right-click the VM and choose Edit Settings.

2. Click the Add button.

3. Choose Hard Disk from the list of devices.

4. Choose Raw Device Mappings as the type of disk.

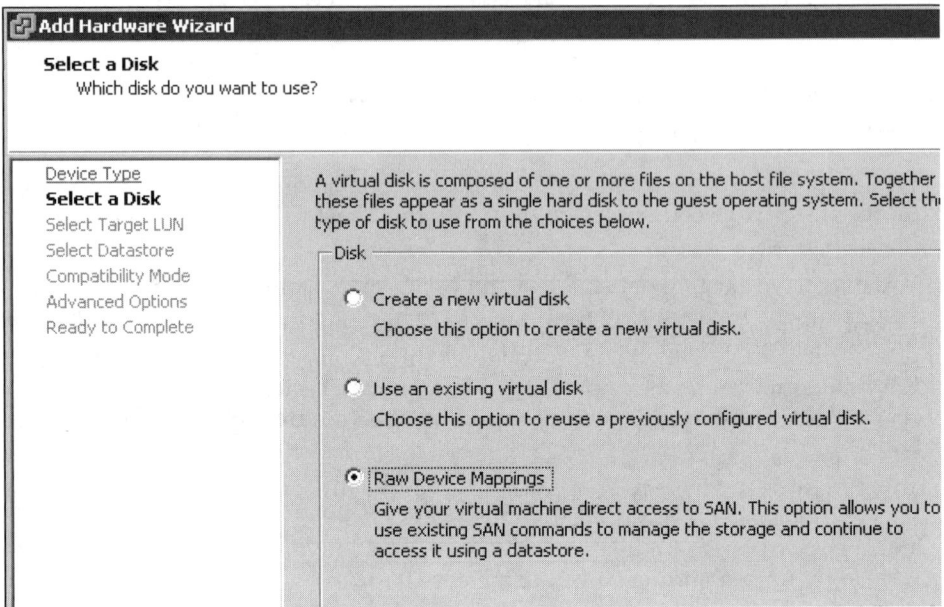

5. Select the LUN you wish to present to the VM.

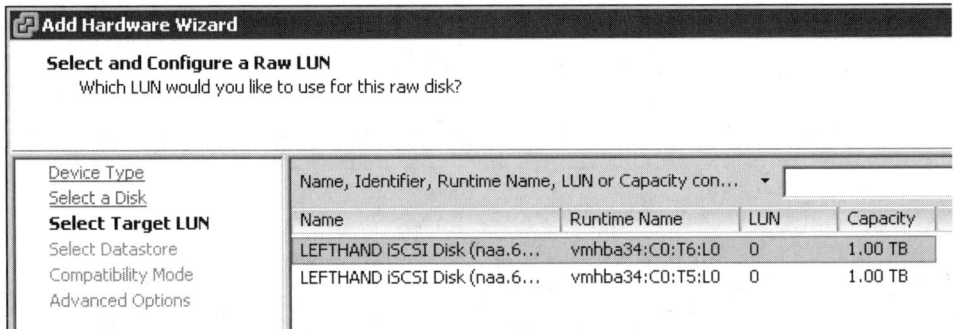

6. Choose to store the RDM file with a VM. Because RDM files are just small text files (albeit with a .vmdk extension), it is safe to store them alongside the VM's other smaller files such as the .vmx, .nvram, and .log files.

NOTE *In the case of VMware snapshots, the files that make up the snapshot would not be held on the RDM LUN, but on an ESX datastore—the most likely candidate being where the VMX file was being stored.*

7. Choose Virtual Compatibility.

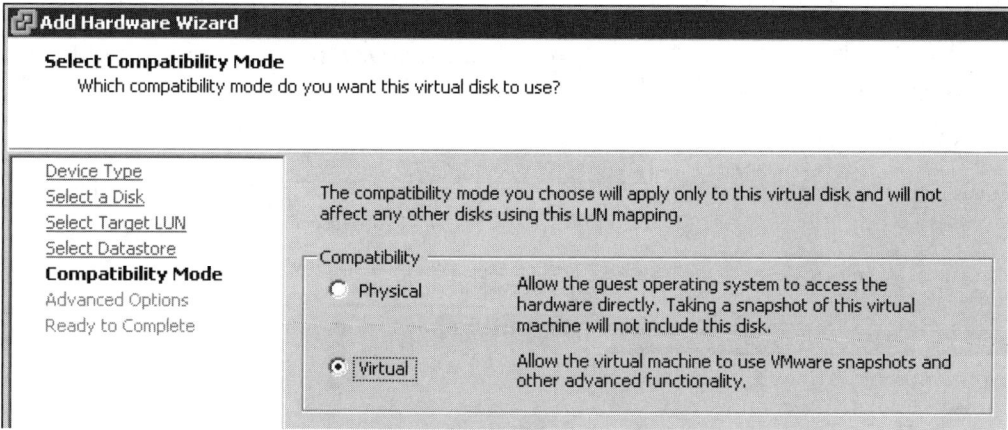

8. Choose a SCSI node, for example SCSI 0:1.

9. Click Finish, and then close the Virtual Machine Properties dialog box.

10. If you are running Windows, rescan your disks. To do so, from Computer Management, choose Storage, right-click Disk Management, and choose Rescan Disks.

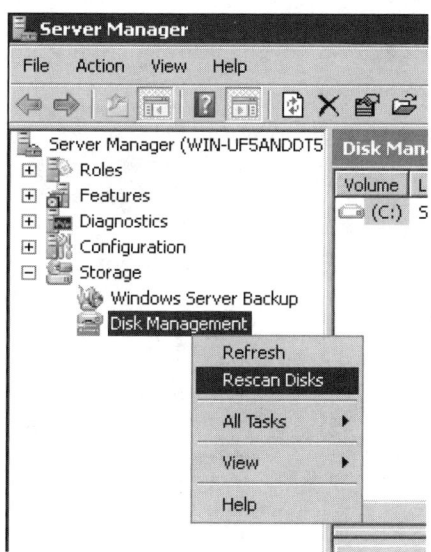

Hot Adding Virtual Disks to Linux

Adding hard disks to a Linux VM while it is powered is possible. However, the process of rescanning the virtual SCSI bus is not particularly easy. Fortunately, you can use a script that is freely available to rescan for new storage devices after adding a virtual disk. The tool is a bash shell script called scsi-rescan.sh and was originally written by Kurt Garloff of Germany. You can obtain Kurt's script from his Web site, under "Rescan SCSI Bus," at http://www.garloff.de/kurt/linux/.

After adding the virtual disks to the Linux VM, download the scsi-rescan.tar.gz file, and extract it with the `tar` command:

```
tar -xvf scsi-rescan.tar.gz
```

Once the file has been extracted, execute the scsi-rescan.sh script. If the script fails to execute, try using the `sh` command instead:

```
sh scsi-rescsn.sh
```

This should run the script, producing output similar to the following:

```
Host adapter 0 (mptspi) found.
Scanning hosts  0 channels 0 for
SCSI target IDs  0 1 2 3 4 5 6 7 , LUN's  0
Scanning for device 0 0 0 0 ...
OLD: Host: scsi0 Channel: 00 Id: 00 Lun: 00
     Vendor: VMware   Model: Virtual disk      Rev: 1.0
     Type:   Direct-Access                     ANSI SCSI revision: 02
Scanning for device 0 0 1 0 ...
NEW: Host: scsi0 Channel: 00 Id: 01 Lun: 00
     Vendor: VMware   Model: Virtual disk      Rev: 1.0
     Type:   Direct-Access                     ANSI SCSI revision: 02
1 new device(s) found.
0 device(s) removed.
```

Using the command `fdisk - l` will give you a list of all mounted, unmounted, and unpartitioned drives, as in the following example:

```
Disk /dev/sda: 2147 MB, 2147483648 bytes
255 heads, 63 sectors/track, 261 cylinders
Units = cylinders of 16065 * 512 = 8225280 bytes
   Device Boot      Start         End      Blocks   Id  System
/dev/sda1   *          1          13      104391   83  Linux
/dev/sda2             14         196     1469947+  83  Linux
/dev/sda3            197         261      522112+  82  Linux swap /
Solaris
Disk /dev/sdb: 2147 MB, 2147483648 bytes
255 heads, 63 sectors/track, 261 cylinders
Units = cylinders of 16065 * 512 = 8225280 bytes
Disk /dev/sdb doesn't contain a valid partition table
```

This means `fdisk /dev/sdb` could be used to partition and format the new virtual disk.

Hot Adding NICs

In vSphere 4, it's now possible to add a NIC to a virtual machine. This is because a great many of the newer OSs support a hot-pluggable PCI bus. This feature is likely to be limited by the guest OS type. I've tested the following procedure with Windows Server 2008 Enterprise, and it worked like a charm.

1. Right-click the VM and choose Edit Settings.
2. Click the Add button.
3. Choose Ethernet Adapter.
4. In the Network Type dialog box, select the adapter type, port group, and power state of the new NIC.

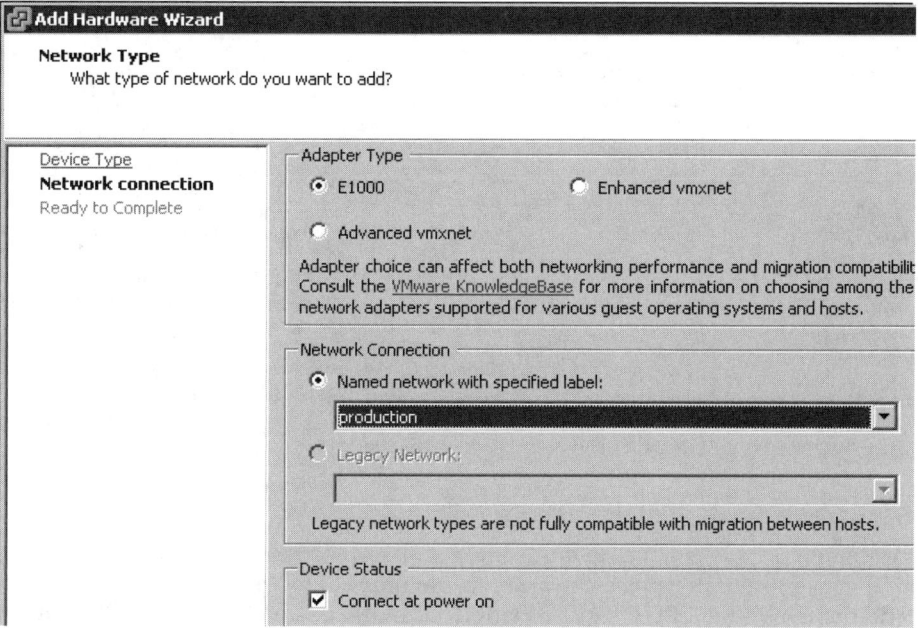

The new NIC will appear in the Network Connections window.

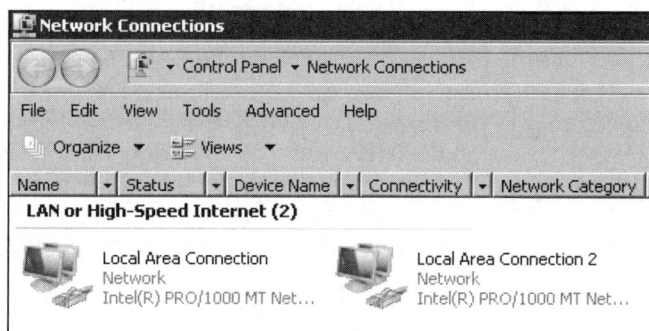

Hot Adding Memory and CPUs

In addition to being able to hot add disks and NICs, some new guest OSs support hot adding of memory and CPU. The option to do this is disabled by default, but can be enabled through the Options tab of the Virtual Machine Properties dialog box. Under Advanced, you'll find the Memory/CPU Hotplug option.

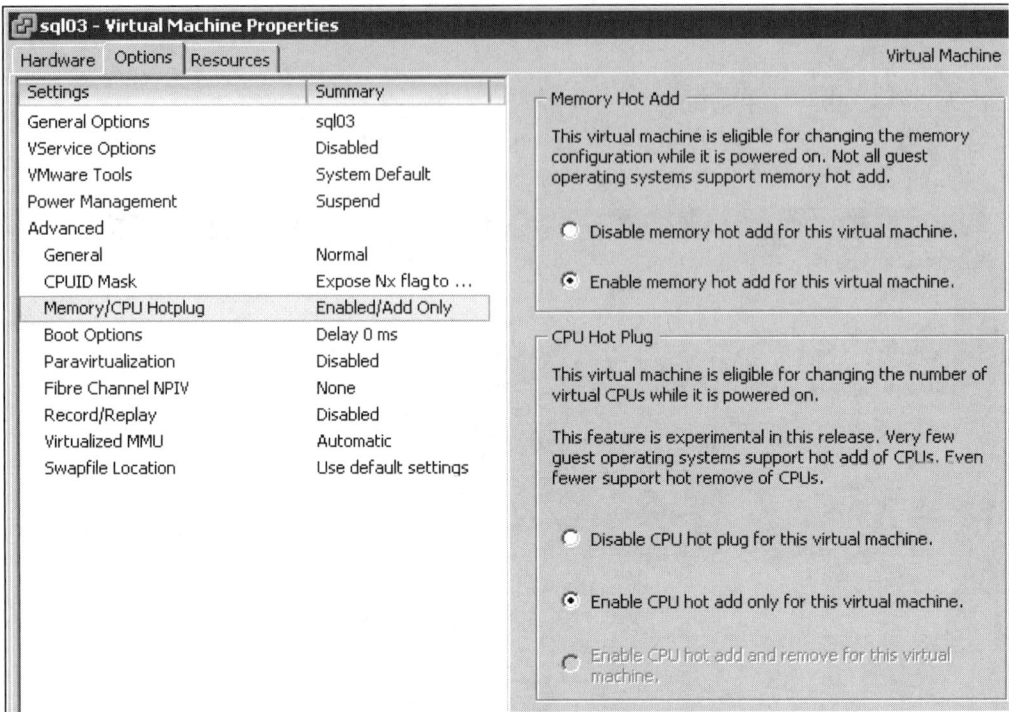

Unfortunately, as this is not a default setting, you do need to power off the VM to enable the feature, which rather negates the point! It is not enabled by default because, currently, the hot add of memory or CPUs is incompatible with the new VMware FT feature. In fact, VMware FT only supports VMs with one vCPU anyway. If you think this feature is going to be very important to you, I recommend that you make it a default within your templates. But beware of this incompatibility prior to enabling VMware FT on your VM.

As the Virtual Machine Properties dialog box indicates, hot adding a CPU is an experimental feature not yet fully supported by VMware, and very few guest OSs currently support the hot removal of CPUs. The only Windows-based guest that currently supports hot adding both CPU and memory is Windows Server 2008 Datacenter and Itanium. Other flavors of Windows, such as Windows Server 2008 Enterprise and Windows Server 2003 Enterprise, support only hot adding memory. This restriction is caused by how Microsoft compiles ntoskernel to support different features based on the version type. This demonstrates how sometimes VMware is limited by the support of the guest OS in terms of what bleeding-edge features it can actually deliver.

After enabling these options and powering on the VM, you will find that that the memory and CPU parts of the Hardware tab of the Virtual Machine Properties dialog box are available, as shown in the following examples.

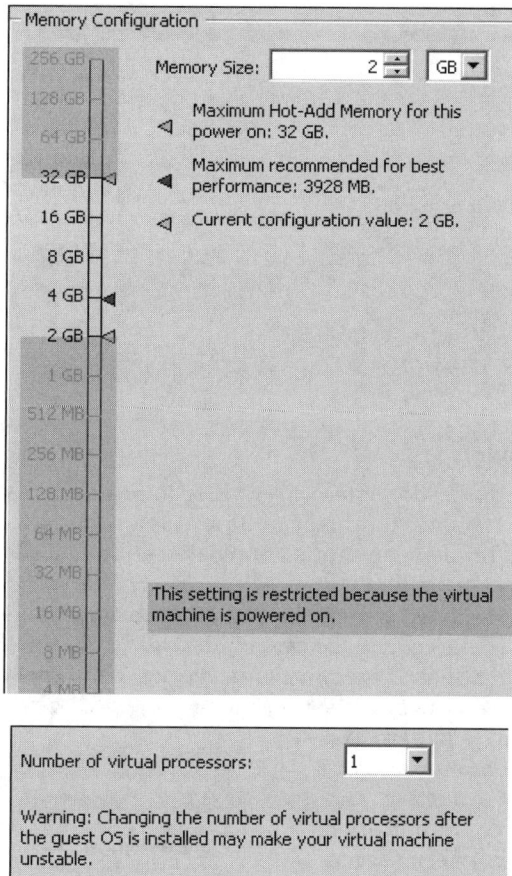

Notice how you cannot reduce the overall amount of RAM allocation (2GB in this example) because this is in use. In other words, you can only hot add memory; you cannot hot remove it.

Adding IDE Drives to Windows

In this release, VMware has added IDE hard disk support to ESX. Previously, the IDE channels on an ESX VM were used only to offer a virtual floppy disk and virtual CD-ROM to the VM. This introduction to IDE support will please many VMware Workstation users who in the past struggled to get their VMs from Workstation into the VI2/VI3 environment. The main reason for its introduction is that VMware is supporting a much richer legacy guest OS list than in any previous release.

If you are creating a VM to run an older OS, make sure you use the Custom option when you define the VM. This will expose in the UI the ability to use an IDE virtual disk, rather than a SCSI drive.

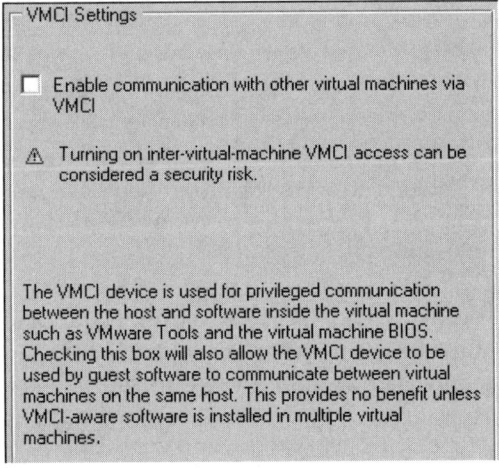

Create New Virtual Machine

Advanced Options   Virtual
These advanced options do not usually need to be changed.

Wizard Type
Name and Location
Resource Pool
Datastore
Virtual Machine Version
Guest Operating System
Memory
Network

Specify the advanced options for this virtual disk. These options do not normally need to be changed.

Virtual Device Node
○ SCSI (0:0)
◉ IDE (0:0)

Enabling the VMCI Device

The Virtual Machine Communication Interface (VMCI), introduced in VMware Workstation 6, is now available in ESX 4. It allows for direct communication from one VM to another on the same ESX host and for limited communication between the ESX hosts, the VMs' BIOS, and VMware Tools.

VMware Workstation 6 shipped with two sample applications called sharedMemApp and datagramApp, intended to demonstrate the capabilities of VMCI. The sharedMemApp writes the VM's current time into a shared memory area every second; the client VM can attach to this application to see the time of the server using the VMCI device. Such direct communication bypasses the standard TCP/IP communications commonly required for a client/server application to function, and could massively improve communications between server VMs and between server VMs and to VDI VMs.

At the time of writing, there are no commercial applications that are VMCI-aware. Clearly, VMware hopes such applications will be developed.

You can enable ESX VMCI support through the Options tab of the Virtual Machine Properties dialog box.

Once enabled, the VMware VMCI bus device appears in Device Manager in Windows under System Devices.

VMCI Settings

☐ Enable communication with other virtual machines via VMCI

⚠ Turning on inter-virtual-machine VMCI access can be considered a security risk.

The VMCI device is used for privileged communication between the host and software inside the virtual machine such as VMware Tools and the virtual machine BIOS. Checking this box will also allow the VMCI device to be used by guest software to communicate between virtual machines on the same host. This provides no benefit unless VMCI-aware software is installed in multiple virtual machines.

Using VMDirectPath I/O

VMDirectPath I/O is a brand-new feature exclusive to vSphere 4, which allows the VM to connect directly to PCI devices of the ESX host. Each VM can have a maximum of devices assigned to it, and the number of VMDirectPath devices cannot exceed eight per ESX host.

VMDirectPath will be attractive to administrators who have exceptionally high network or disk I/O within the VM, which might under normal operations preclude the OS from being virtualized. Currently, the ESX host that runs VMDirectPath I/O must utilize the Intel Nehalem generation of CPUs, and the list of supported devices is quite small:

- Intel 82598 10 Gigabit Ethernet adapter
- Broadcom 57710 10 Gigabit Ethernet adapter
- QLogic QLA25xx 8Gb Fibre Channel (Experimental)
- LSI 3442e-R and 3801e (1068 chip–based) 3Gb SAS adapters (experimental)

In the future, VMDirectPath I/O may widen to support other propriety devices that have historically made physical servers difficult to virtualize.

If your hardware supports VMDirectPath I/O, you will see the devices listed under Advanced Settings on the ESX host's Configuration tab. VMDirectPath I/O devices are allocated with the Add Virtual Machine Hardware wizard, using the PCI/PCIe device option.

Note that VMDirectPath I/O is incompatiable with VMotion. If you use this feature, some of the automation discussed later in this book, such as VMotion, DRS, FT, and maintenance mode, will be unavailable to the VM.

Configuring VM Features

For your VMs, you can configure video settings, a static MAC address, and the memory management unit (MMU). You can also enable N-Port ID Virtualization or paravirtualization.

Configuring a Static MAC Address

ESX automatically generates a dynamic MAC address using an algorithm that uses the path to the VMs .vmx file (/vmfs/volumes/*volname/vmname/vmname*.vmx) and the Universal Unique ID (UUID) of the physical server. Despite such fancy features as VMotion, the VM's auto-generated MAC address is very unlikely to change.

There may be some cases where you would prefer to set a static MAC address that can never change (unless an administrator makes the change), such as for DHCP client reservations or licensing based on MAC addresses (almost as annoying as licensing dongles, in my experience).

In the physical world, each network adapter manufacturer gets a unique three-byte prefix called an Organizationally Unique Identifier (OUI), which it can use to generate unique MAC addresses. Within the vSphere Client 4 product, two OUIs are automatically generated:

- One if you create VMs on ESX without vCenter; begins with: 00:0C:29
- One if you create VMs with vCenter; begins with: 00:50:56

Within the vCenter range, VMware has carved out a range of MAC addresses within the 00:56:56 OUI range for manual assignment. The valid range is from 00:50:56:00:00:00 to 00:50:56:3F:FF:FF. It's important not to go beyond 3F; otherwise, conflicts with other VMware platforms such as VMware Workstation and VMware Server can occur.

In the past, we had to manually edit the MAC address by using text editors like nano or vi at the Service Console to modify settings in the .vmx file. Since VI3.5, we have been able to set a MAC address in the Virtual Machine Properties dialog box of VM, under the properties of the virtual Ethernet adapter.

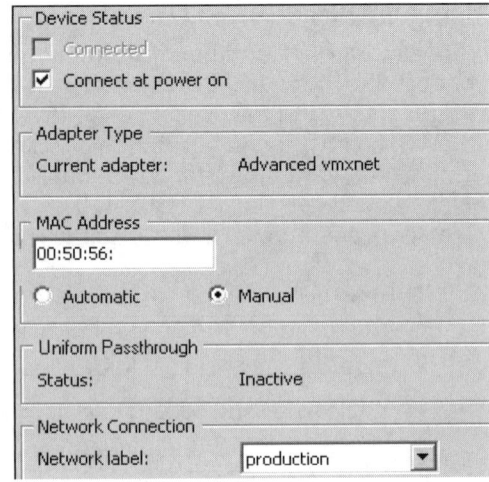

Changing a MAC address is not a casual event. You should at the very least document your changes and make a database or spreadsheet that records the MAC addresses and IP addresses used, together with the name of the VM that "owns" those MAC address details.

Some guest OSs, such as Linux, store their MAC address details in text files such as ifcfg-eth0, and boot processes will complain about the MAC address being different in these text files compared to your static MAC address in the .vmx file. Under the default security settings of a vSwitch or port group, communication would be allowed, but it's perhaps best avoided in the first place. To avoid problems, I recommend setting the static MAC address (if you think you need one) before installing the guest OS.

Enabling N-Port Virtualization

N-Port ID Virtualization (NPIV) is a feature of the new Fibre Channel cards from QLogic and Emulex. Support for NPIV was introduced in VI3.5. Up until then, only the physical ESX hosts could see the WWN of a Fibre Channel device. With the introduction of NPIV, it is now possible to present LUNs directly to the VM. In many respects, this represents an advancement of security in the arena of storage.

Up until VI3.5, LUNs were presented to ESX hosts (this is still the case, by the way), but it was up to the VMware administrator to use the RDM feature to allocate the right LUNs to the right VMs. Clearly, it was possible for the *same* LUN to be allocated to VMs. While VMware would, in most cases, ensure that only one VM would be able to be powered on and have access to the storage, NPIV provides more safeguards. With NPIV, five conditions must be met for the VM to see the LUN on the storage array:

- The LUNs must be allocated to the ESX host(s) WWN.
- The VM must have an RDM file.
- The VM must have a valid WWN.
- The Physical Fibre Channel Switch must support and enabled for NPIV
- The HBA must support NPIV

It's as if the VM had a virtual Fibre Channel card, when in fact, all it has is a RAID controller card driver.

The NPIV feature does have a number of requirements before it will function properly:

- NPIV must be enabled on the SAN switch.

- NPIV is supported only for VMs with RDM disks. VMs with regular virtual disks continue to use the WWNs of the host's physical HBAs.

- The physical HBAs on the ESX/ESXi host must have access to a LUN using its WWNs in order for any VMs on that host to have access to that LUN using their NPIV WWNs.

- The physical HBAs on the ESX/ESXi host must support NPIV. If the physical HBAs do not support NPIV, the VMs running on that host will fall back to using the WWNs of the host's physical HBAs for LUN access.

- Each VM can have up to four virtual ports. NPIV-enabled VMs are assigned exactly four NPIV-related WWNs, which are used to communicate with physical HBAs through virtual ports. Therefore, VMs can utilize up to four physical HBAs for NPIV purposes.

- As you can see with this last requirement, there may be a performance advantage to NPIV. It is possible with some arrays to set a priority option based on the WWN.

You can enable NPIV on the VM and allow VMware to generate the WWN values through the Virtual Machine Properties dialog box, on the Options tab, under Fibre Channel NPIV.

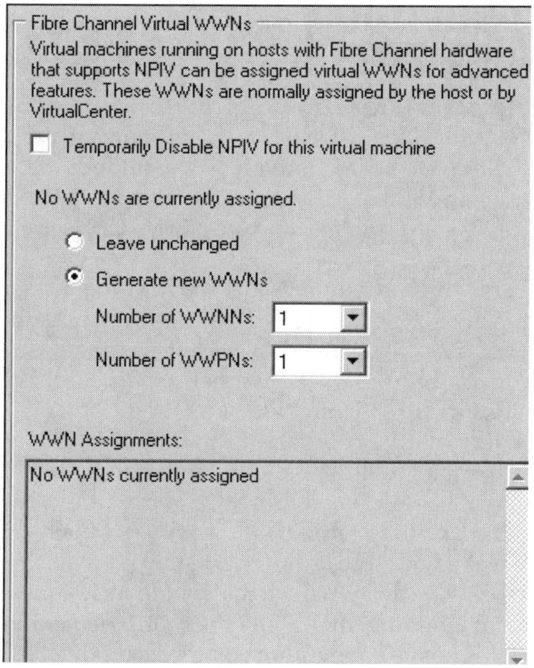

Fibre Channel Virtual WWNs

Virtual machines running on hosts with Fibre Channel hardware that supports NPIV can be assigned virtual WWNs for advanced features. These WWNs are normally assigned by the host or by VirtualCenter.

☐ Temporarily Disable NPIV for this virtual machine

No WWNs are currently assigned.

○ Leave unchanged

◉ Generate new WWNs

Number of WWNNs: [1 ▼]

Number of WWPNs: [1 ▼]

WWN Assignments:

No WWNs currently assigned

After enabling this setting, when you return to it, you will find VMware has generated WWN and WWPN values. The dialog box also offers the option to remove the WWN value.

Fibre Channel Virtual WWNs

Virtual machines running on hosts with Fibre Channel hardware that supports NPIV can be assigned virtual WWNs for advanced features. These WWNs are normally assigned by the host or by VirtualCenter.

☐ Temporarily Disable NPIV for this virtual machine

The current WWN assignments were created by VirtualCenter.

◉ Leave unchanged

○ Generate new WWNs

    Number of WWNNs: `1`

    Number of WWPNs: `1`

○ Remove WWN assignment

WWN Assignments:

Node WWN:
28:2e:00:0c:29:00:00:01

Port WWN:
28:2e:00:0c:29:00:00:02

Enabling Paravirtualization

In the world of virtualization, there are many different flavors. Generally, VMware has three types of execution: direct execute, binary translation, and paravirtualization.

Direct execute allows the VM to speak natively to the underlying physical CPU to make direct calls to the instruction set of the CPU. This is the preferred form of execution, as it offers the best performance. It is also the reason compatible CPUs are required for features like VMotion and VMware FT.

Binary translation occurs whenever there is an interrupt request generated inside the VM by the guest OS. As the guest OSs generally have no awareness they are running inside a VM, the interrupts generated by the virtual NIC and the virtual SCSI device must be intercepted or translated down through the VMkernel (the hypervisor) to a real, physical device using a device driver for a Broadcom NIC or a QLogic HBA.

Binary translation is a very mature software technology, and many organizations (including VMware) have spent a lot of time and money in making it as efficient as possible. However, no matter what virtualization vendors do, direct execute always outperforms binary translation, and so the search to reduce the penalty of binary translation continues.

Up until recently, there was a widespread conviction that paravirtualization would offer this improvement. However, recent hardware I/O virtualization techniques such as NPIV and MMU (Memory Management Unit) together with other enhancement in the CPUs, have cast doubt over paravirtualization's possible long-term significance. Nonetheless, paravirtualization remains an important development that virtualization vendors do not want to ignore.

In essence, paravirtualization describes a situation where the guest OS is given some VM awareness to a layer just above the hypervisor to which the VM hooks into. In VMware, this is called VMI Paravirtualization. This can reduce the downside of binary translation.

Before you consider enabling paravirtualization, you should be aware of its requirements and limitations:

- Enabling VMI Paravirtualization uses a PCI slot inside the VM, which reduces the total of virtual PCI slots from six to five.

- Generally, only Linux OSs have fully embraced paravirtualization.

- It can introduce a VMotion problem if not all of your ESX hosts support paravirtualization.

- It is possible to cold migrate a paravirtualized-enabled VM, but powering on to an ESX host that lacks the paravirtualization attribute could reduce its performance.

- Currently, paravirtualization is incompatible with VMware FT.

You can enable paravirtualization through the Options tab of the Virtual Machine Properties dialog box. There are no configuration tasks required, apart from meeting the requirements in the preceding list.

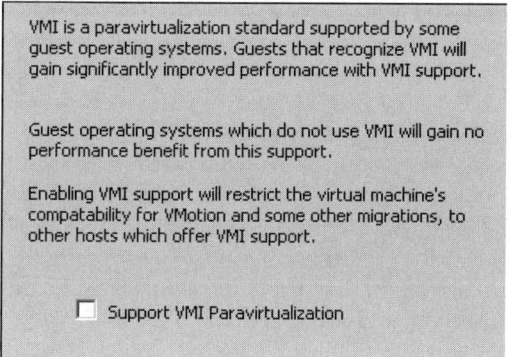

Configuring the Memory Management Unit

The option to virtualize the MMU, called Hardware Page Table Virtualization, was introduced in VI3.5. It's a hardware enhancement option that may or may not improve performance, depending on whether your CPUs support the feature and if your workloads are memory-intensive. Prior to the introduction of this feature, memory management was purely the responsibility of the VMkernel.

Within the VMkernel, there are two page tables: one for VM memory and one for physical machine memory. The VMkernel maps the hexadecimal memory ranges from one to the other, allowing for some fancy memory management features that, at the moment, are unique to VMware. As the VMkernel is fundamentally the attributor of access to hardware, this allows for avoiding the duplication of memory contents within and between VMs, commonly referred to as Transparent Page Sharing (TPS). It also allows VMware to deallocate memory from one VM to anther using a memory driver installed to the guest OS along with VMware Tools.

While the page tables do allow for advanced memory features, their use does incur a CPU penalty, especially for guest OSs that make regular changes to their memory contents. Both Intel and AMD have recognized this CPU hit, and in their more modern CPUs offer a hardware-based page table system, commonly referred to as Nested Page Table (NPT), to improve overall CPU utilization. The good news is that this feature is enabled by default, and it does *not* generate a CPU incompatibility issue that might upset features like VMotion.

The VMkernel can interrogate the CPU and allow the VM to use the MMU if it is available; if it is not available, the VMkernel simply ignores it. Using the MMU will nearly always improve performance, but the scale of improvement is very much dependent on your OS and the application workload generated within it.

If you wish to change this default behavior (which I do not recommend), you will find the option on the Options tab of the Virtual Machine Properties dialog box, under Virtualized MMU. You can switch off this option on a per-VM basis.

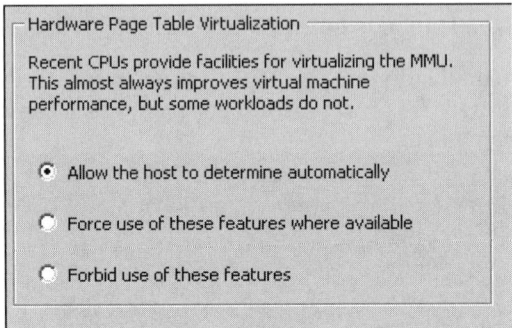

Managing Virtual Disks

You can resize your virtual disks using a variety of methods. You can also convert a thin virtual disk to a thick virtual disk, and vice versa.

Resizing Virtual Disks

Increasing the size of virtual disks has always been relatively easy process, and with VI3.5, you could do this directly from the GUI of the Virtual Infrastructure Client. The thorny issue has been not so much increasing the size of the virtual disk, but how to handle the fact that the partition tables of the affected guest OS do not magically grow to fill the new free space. The problem has been exacerbated by the fact the boot OS disk of Windows, the C: drive is still excluded from being resized using Microsoft tools. While this will undoubtedly improve with Windows 2008 and Windows 7, it's still handy to know of methods that are independent of the guest OS tools.

The following are the methods you can use to resize your virtual disks:

- Use the Dell ExtPart utility. This is by far the fastest, cheapest, and most flexible approach. It can be carried out while the VM is powered on, and it can be used against the C: drive.

- Increase the size of the virtual disk, and use QTParted from the Knoppix Live CD to increase the size of the partition. This utility is free.

- Increase the size of the virtual disk, and use Partition/Volume Magic/Manager to increase the size of the partition. This is a commercially supported repartitioning tool.

- Increase the size of the virtual disk, and use Microsoft DiskPart to increase the size of the partition. This method is fine if all you wish to resize is a Microsoft disk that is not the OS disk.

- Add a second virtual disk of the right size, and use Symantec's Norton Ghost on the disk. This is the slowest method, but it has one critical advantage: it allows you to make a virtual disk smaller.

NOTE *If you have created a virtual disk that is far too large, you may want to convert it to the thin virtual disk format, rather than trying to make it smaller. The procedure for converting a thick virtual disk to a thin virtual disk is covered in the next section.*

Here, I will demonstrate the first two methods, since they are quick and free.

Using Dell's ExtPart Utility

The ExtPart utility is freely available from Dell's web site for the moment. Critically, it will work only on Windows VMs. The URL for this is much too long to reproduce; needless to say, an Internet search on extpart.exe took me directly to the place I needed to be.

Here's the procedure for using this utility to resize a virtual disk:

1. From the inside the Windows VM, download the Dell extpart.exe utility. Extract the zip file to the C: drive.

2. Open the Virtual Machine Properties dialog box, and increase the size of the virtual disk.

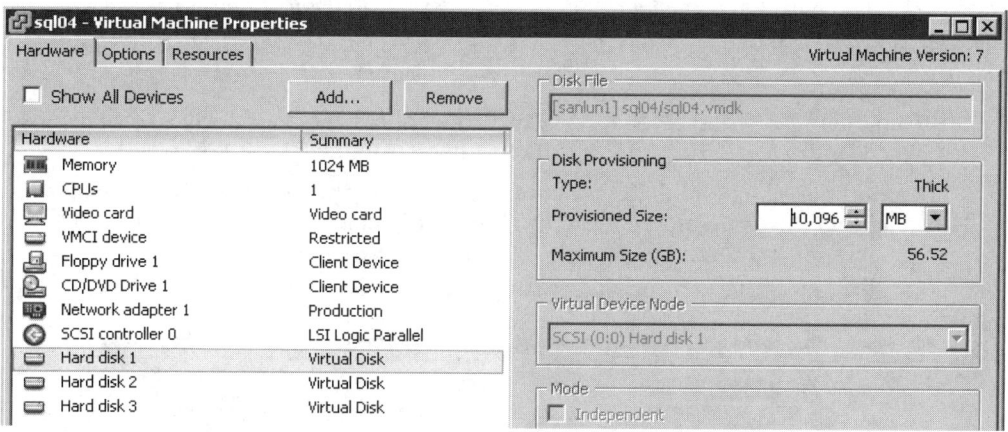

3. Open a Windows command prompt and navigate to the directory where you extracted the Dell ExtPart utility.

4. Issue the command `extpart`.

5. Type in the drive letter that represents the partition you wish to increase in size (C: in this example).

6. Type in how much you want the drive to grow. My old size was 4GB (4,096), and I increased my virtual disk to 10GB (10,096). To use all of the partition, I entered 6000 (10,096–4,096).

```
Command Prompt

C:\dell\ExtPart>extpart.exe

ExtPart - Utility to extend basic disks (Build 1.0.4)
(c) Dell Computer Corporation 2003

Volume to extend (drive letter or mount point): c:

Current volume size     : 4102 MB (4301788672 bytes)
Current partition size  : 4102 MB (4301789184 bytes)

Size to expand the volume (MB): 6000

New volume size         : 10095 MB (10585902592 bytes)

C:\dell\ExtPart>
```

Using the Knoppix Live CD and QTParted

The next best method is using a repartition tool such as QTParted, which is a free and available on the Knoppix Live CD, which you can download from http://www.knopper .net/knoppix/index-en.html. The nice thing about QTParted is, unlike Dell's ExtPart utility, it works with almost any OS and file system.

Follow these steps to use these tools to resize a virtual disk:

1. Download the Knoppix Live CD and upload the ISO file to a datastore accessible by the VM.

NOTE *During the download, you might want to make a backup of the VM. I've never had a problem with the Knoppix Live CD, but it's perhaps best to have a plan B, in case plan A doesn't work out as expected.*

2. Attach the ISO file to the VM. You may also want to set a boot delay so you can use the ESC key during startup to force the VM to boot to the CD-ROM.

3. Power off the VM. Note that it is actually possible to increase the size of a virtual disk *without* powering down the VM. However, you may still be limited by the guest OS's repartitioning tools.

4. In the Virtual Machine Properties dialog box, increase the disk size.

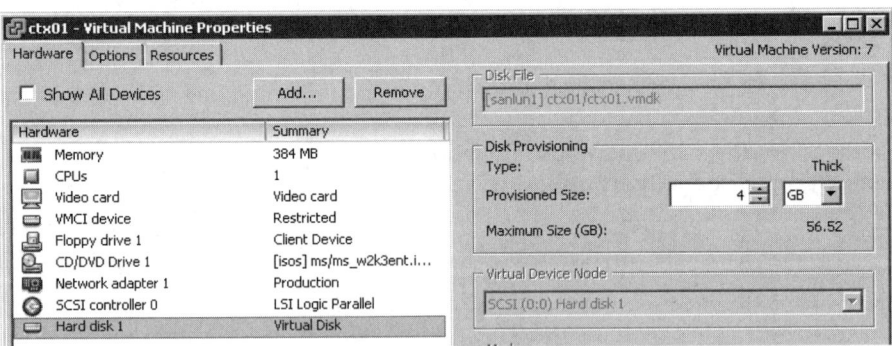

5. Power on the VM. Press ESC at the VMware BIOS message to force the VM to boot the Knoppix Live CD.

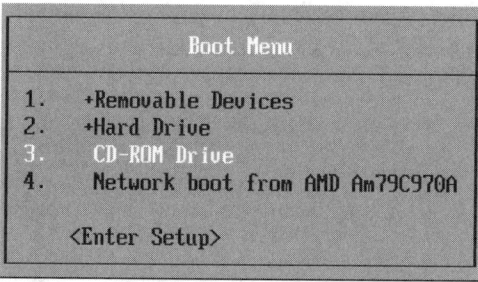

6. After the CD-ROM has finished booting, select the Knoppix Start (K) button, choose System, and then choose QTParted.

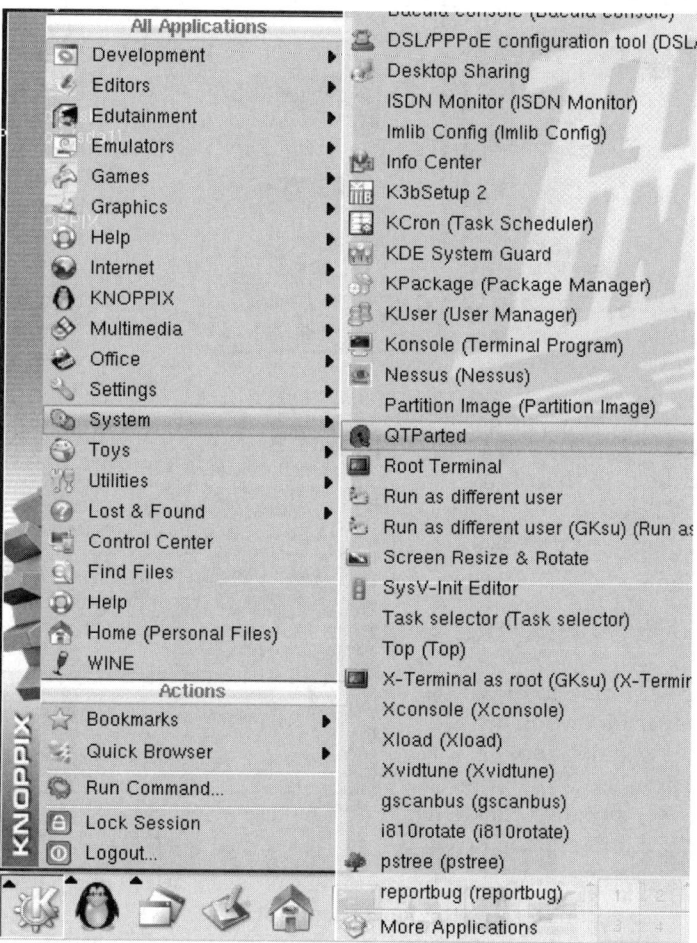

7. Select the disk you wish to manage (/dev/sda in this example).

8. Select the partition in the disk that you wish to resize.

9. Right-click and choose Resize. In the following example, you can see I have a small 2GB partition using NTFS, with a virtual disk that is actually 10GB in size, with 8GB of it unpartitioned.

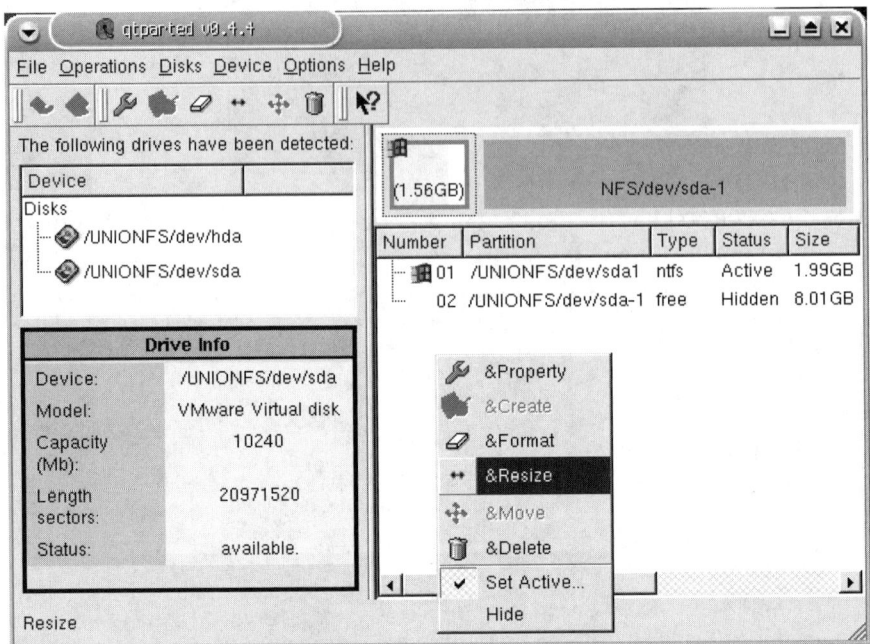

10. Adjust the size of the partition using click-and-drag or by inputting the new size of the partition. Click OK.

11. From the QTParted File menu, select &Commit.

12. Read the warning, and then select Yes.

13. As you have booted to the CD-ROM, the partitions you are manipulating should not be mounted or in use. When the process has completed, click OK in the confirmation dialog box.

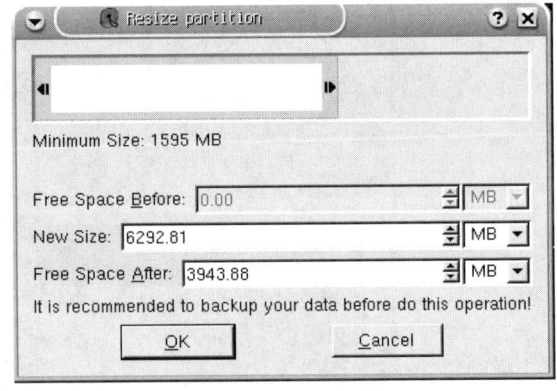

14. Exit the Knoppix environment by pressing CTRL+ALT+DELETE and selecting the option to restart your computer. On the very first boot, Windows 2003 will carry out a full file system check on the virtual disk you modified with QTParted.

Converting a Thin Virtual Disk to a Thick Virtual Disk

In previous versions of ESX, changing virtual disk types was quite a painful process that required quite good knowledge of command-line tools, in particular the `vmkfstools` command. That command still exists, and much of its functionality remains the same. In Chapter 17, I will explain how to use it to identify disk types. However, in this section I will show you how easy it is to use vCenter to convert a virtual disk from one format to another using just the mouse.

As discussed earlier, it is now possible to create a thin virtual disk. So although the guest OS sees the virtual disk as, say, 50GB in size, in fact its true on-disk size may be much smaller. In principle, this is much like virtual storage in physical arrays.

Apart from editing the settings of a VM to find out the disk type used, often you can tell by merely examining the storage usage information on the summary page of a VM. As you can see in the following example, I have a VM that has an 11GB virtual disk, but currently is storing only 2.29KB of data. In fact, I haven't even formatted or partitioned this virtual disk yet. With the thick virtual disk, the values for provisioned storage and used storage are the same. You should know that these statistics are not especially dynamic—they do not refresh very frequently.

Resources	
Consumed Host CPU:	0 MHz
Consumed Host Memory:	0.00 MB
Active Guest Memory:	0.00 MB
	Refresh Storage Usage
Provisioned Storage:	11.00 GB
Not-shared Storage:	2.29 KB
Used Storage:	2.29 KB

However, these numbers do not tell you definitely which disks are thick or thin; they merely give you a guide for how much disk space the VM occupies. It's possible for a VM to have a mix of both thick and thin virtual disks.

You can easily convert a virtual disk from thin to thick format using the Datastore Browser. The VM must first be powered off. Locate the virtual disk you wish to convert, right-click, and choose the Inflate option.

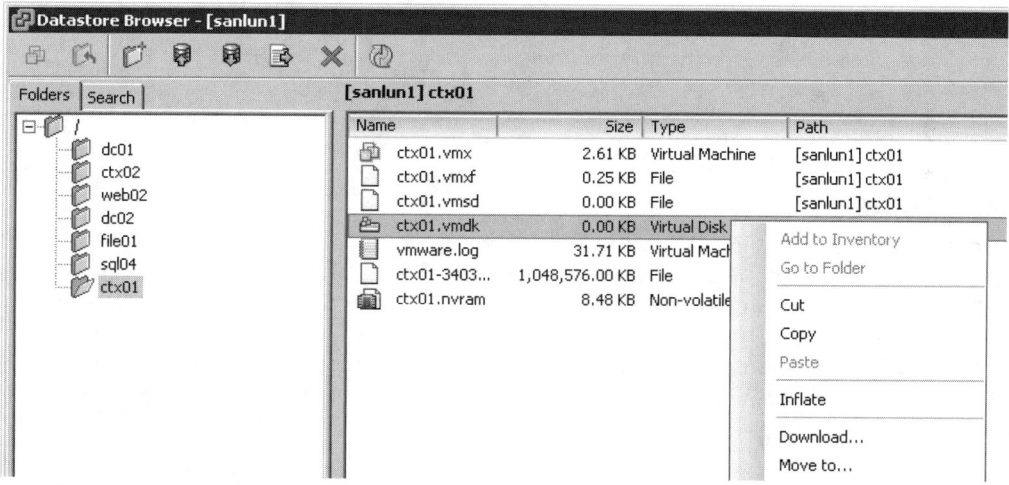

The time the inflate process takes depends greatly on the size of the virtual disk. For example, my 11GB virtual disk took just under 40 minutes to complete. This is because it is converting the disk in a format valid for VMware FT referred to as eagerzeroedthick disk. As noted earlier, vCenter defaults to a zeroedthick disk format. The eagerzeroedthick disk type takes longer to create and convert. I will provide more details about these disk types in Chapter 16.

Converting a Thick Virtual Disk into Thin Virtual Disk

Another method of converting a virtual disk is through migration—either a cold migration (moving a VM when it is powered off) or with SVMotion (relocating the VM's files while the VM is powered off).

Before you start the migration process, make a note of the datastore location of the VM's virtual disk. In this example, I will be keeping the virtual disk on the *different* datastore and using the migration process just to convert the virtual disk type.

1. Right-click the VM and select Migrate.

2. Select Change datastore.

3. Select the *different* datastore from the one on which the virtual disk is currently located.

4. Choose the desired format, which is the "Thin provisioned format" option in this example:

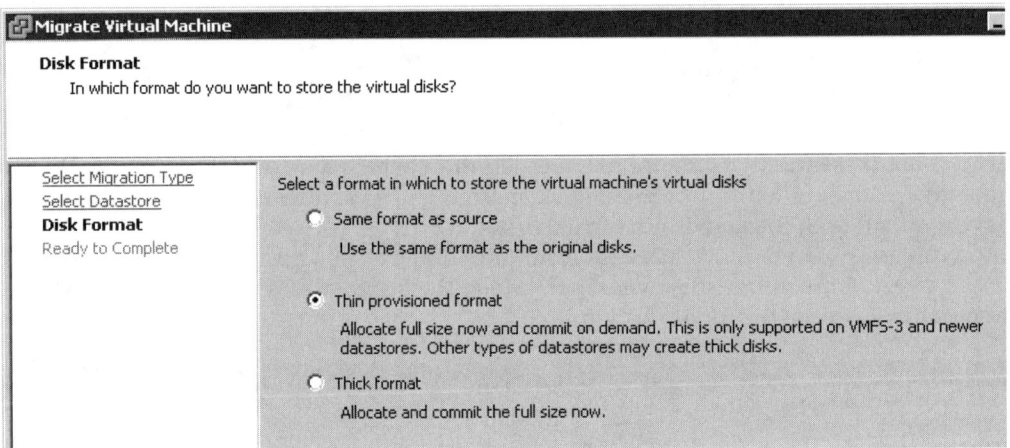

Using Snapshots

The snapshot feature was introduced in VI3 and replaced the old redo files of ESX 2.*x*. Snapshots have much of the same functionality as redo files, plus some extra features. Snapshots allow you to capture the state of a VM at a point in time (which includes both disk and memory states), and then to go back to that state (revert to snapshot) if necessary. Snapshots can be created and deleted even when the VM is powered on. This is another improvement on ESX 2.*x*, which forced us to power off the VM and then change the disk mode of a VM.

When you create a snapshot, all the new changes in the disk and memory are actually going to a differences, or *delta*, file. In this respect, when you capture the state of a VM at a point in time, you are actually creating something more like a bookmark that you can use to return to a set point.

A good example of using snapshots might be when you are making a fundamental change to a VM and are unsure of the consequences of your actions, such as when you are applying a new service pack. In this way, the snapshot delivers a type of undo functionality. This has been available in ESX since version 2.*x*, but now you can have up to 32 levels of undo within a given VM, whereas in the previous release you were restricted to just one level. So in ESX 4.*x*, you can make a change, create a snapshot, make another change, create another snapshot, and so on. In this respect, working with a VM is a bit like working with a file, saving as you go along, so you can go back to the last-known good state of the file if something goes wrong.

Using snapshots during backup is also popular. When a VM has a snapshot applied, all the read and write events that would normally be sent to the virtual disk are actually sent to a delta file. Under normal operations (without a snapshot), the virtual disk is locked by the file system and cannot be manipulated. However, when a snapshot is applied to a VM, the virtual disk is unlocked and can be copied to another location for backup purposes.

Despite these really useful features, snapshots are not without their "gotchas" and best practices. Currently, snapshots are applied to *all* virtual disks and RDM files in a VM. This includes system drives that contain OSs and application information, and also drives that store end-user data. The action of reverting a snapshot, which takes a VM "back in time," therefore has the potential to result in a loss of data. Additionally, time-sensitive operations could be disrupted by reverting to a snapshot. Let's take an extreme example, such as taking a snapshot of a VM while it is copying a file to another system through the network. Some hours or days later, when you choose to revert to the snapshot, this VM would think it was still copying a file. However, the destination system would still be in your time, and the network file copy would fail. There are many systems that are time-sensitive, especially authentication services like Microsoft Active Directory, so this is one to watch carefully.

TIP *If you power down a VM first, it is much faster to take a snapshot because no memory contents need to be saved. When you revert to the snapshot, your VM is returned to its powered-off state.*

Some users have reported severe problems with committing snapshots above the 2GB size. Additionally, some VMware Communities forums members have criticized the poor management of the snapshot management file. This normally happens because of a failure to commit a snapshot file above the 2GB range.

The general opinion in the VMware community is that while the snapshot feature can be useful, it should be used sparingly and is perhaps best restricted to test and development VMs.

Another concern is that snapshots grow incrementally over time in blocks of 16MB. If you allow a VM to run on the delta file for a long period of time, it could become quite large. Also, depending on how much disk I/O your VM generates, you may need to watch the amount of free space required to continue running on the delta file. VMware recommends not allowing any snapshot to grow beyond 2GB in size for performance reasons.

In the past, people ran scripts daily to monitor snapshot usage, but with vSphere 4's new alarms and alerts, these may be needed less frequently. Some administrators still prefer to run scripts to generate their own customer alarms and reports. Rather than reinventing the wheel, I recommend using the following scripts that various bloggers have made publically available:

http://www.virtualvcp.com/content/view/85/30/

http://sourceforge.net/projects/esxhealthscript/

Creating a Snapshot

To create a snapshot, log in to the VM, right-click it, choose Snapshot, and then select Take snapshot, or click the Snapshot icon.

New to vSphere 4 is the ability to quiesce the file system of the guest OS. This provides a more consistent snapshot state, and is frequently used in the backup of a VM.

In the dialog box, type in a name and description for the snapshot. In this example, I am going to use this snapshot to demonstrate making a mistake and going back to a good state.

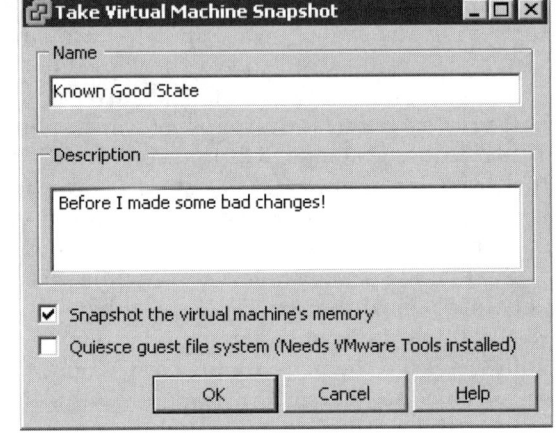

After taking the snapshot, I make some changes I do not want to keep. When I demonstrate this to customers in a Windows VM, I tend to copy Program Files repeatedly. After doing this, I then demonstrate the revert to snapshot feature, discussed in the next section.

You might like to be able to see the delta file growing. To do this, open an SSH window on the ESX host in /vmfs/ volumes or in the vSphere Client using the Browse Datastore feature (as shown in the following example) by selecting your ESX host, clicking the Summary tab, right-clicking the VM's datastore in the Resource pane, and choosing Browse Datastore.

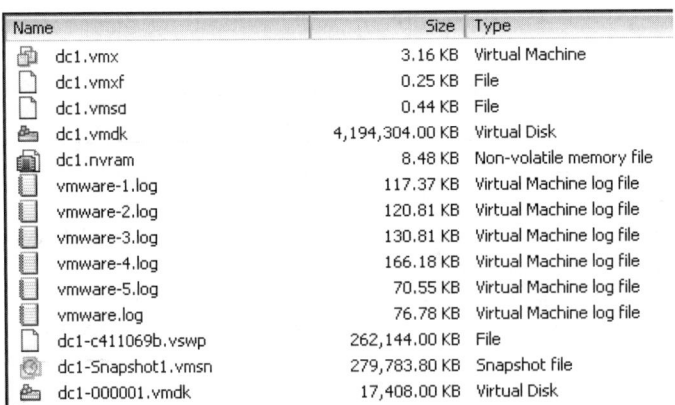

Name	Size	Type
dc1.vmx	3.16 KB	Virtual Machine
dc1.vmxf	0.25 KB	File
dc1.vmsd	0.44 KB	File
dc1.vmdk	4,194,304.00 KB	Virtual Disk
dc1.nvram	8.48 KB	Non-volatile memory file
vmware-1.log	117.37 KB	Virtual Machine log file
vmware-2.log	120.81 KB	Virtual Machine log file
vmware-3.log	130.81 KB	Virtual Machine log file
vmware-4.log	166.18 KB	Virtual Machine log file
vmware-5.log	70.55 KB	Virtual Machine log file
vmware.log	76.78 KB	Virtual Machine log file
dc1-c411069b.vswp	262,144.00 KB	File
dc1-Snapshot1.vmsn	279,783.80 KB	Snapshot file
dc1-000001.vmdk	17,408.00 KB	Virtual Disk

The .vmsd file is the main "manager" file. The .vmsn file is the memory contents of the VM. The dc-00001.vmdk file is the delta, or differences, file.

Reverting to a Snapshot

There are two ways to control reverting to a snapshot: a quick method, which just reverts to the very last snapshot, or using the snapshot manager, which assists in dealing with multiple snapshots.

Reverting to the Last Snapshot

To use the quick method to go back just one level of your snapshot, right-click the VM in the menu, select Snapshot, and then select Revert to Snapshot, or click the Revert to Snapshot icon.

Click Yes to confirm that you want to continue with the process.

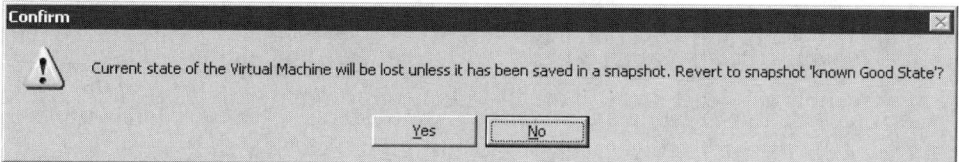

Using the Snapshot Manager

To use the snapshot manager to revert to a snapshot, right-click the VM, select Snapshot, and choose Snapshot Manager, or click the Snapshot Manager icon. The following example shows my VM. Notice how the snapshot name and description assist me in remembering the state that the VM will be in before the revert process. You can change this name and description by clicking the Edit button in the Snapshots window.

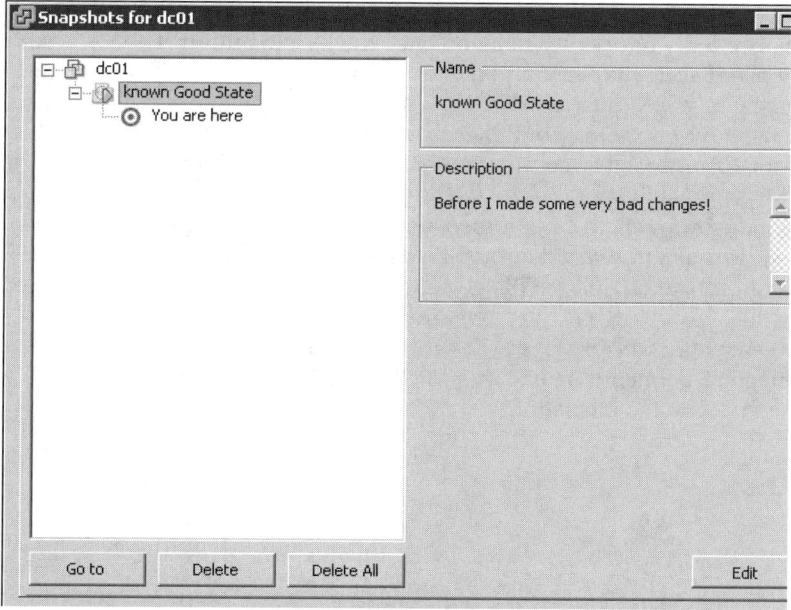

Select the snapshot you want to revert to, and then click the Go to button. You will be warned that your current state (with all my bad copies of Program Files in this example) will be lost. Choose Yes to continue with the reversion. Close the Snapshots window, and in a short while, your VM will be returned to its original state.

CAUTION Although you have gone back in time, or reverted to your snapshot, the snapshot feature is still engaged. If you reenter the Snapshots window, you will still see the name of the snapshot. This can be very useful for repeated attempts at configuration processes where you have five or six steps, and you are not sure of the correct procedure because of poor documentation from a software vendor. It also means that it is very easy to unknowingly leave a snapshot engaged. You can tell if you have a snapshot enabled from the vSphere Client. If the Revert to Snapshot icon is dimmed, you are not using a snapshot; if it is available, then you are using it.

Deleting a Snapshot

As you might have noticed in the previous example, the Snapshots window also contains a Delete button. I've found that some of my customers struggle with this particular feature of snapshots, not least because we all feel uncomfortable with Delete buttons; we fear we might lose the stuff we want to keep. It's worth saying very clearly that when you delete a snapshot using the Snapshot Manager, you are not going to lose your changes in the delta file.

Here's an analogy I use with my customers to help them understand the process. When you click to create a snapshot, it's like you have used a camera and taken a photograph of your VM at that time. A half hour later, you think you might make another change, so you take another photograph of the VM. When you choose to revert to a snapshot, you are going back in time that half hour; it's a bit like time-travel. When you choose to delete a snapshot, you are going back through those old photographs and deciding you no longer need them because they are so old and out of date. Just because you delete an old photograph of a VM doesn't mean you will lose the current image you are using.

Here's what actually happens when you click the Delete button: The VMware ESX server takes the contents of your snapshot and copies the data in the delta file into your virtual disk. Once the delta file has been merged with the virtual disk, the delta file is then deleted. Some people prefer the old terminology of ESX 2.*x*, which was to "commit" to merge the file into the virtual disk, and "discard" to remove the file and revert back to the last-known good state of the VM.

When I demonstrate this to customers, I usually make a change I would normally wish to keep, such as a local password reset. I then delete the snapshot and prove that my password change has taken effect. This helps to reenforce the idea that the Delete button doesn't mean "lose my changes" but "keep my changes."

To delete a snapshot, simply right-click the VM, select Snapshot, and then choose Snapshot Manager. Select your snapshot and click the Delete button. Choose Yes to confirm you are happy to delete the snapshot.

The Delete All button rolls up all your snapshots and commits all the changes accrued in the delta files. If you do use the Delete All button, the confirmation dialog box states this very clearly.

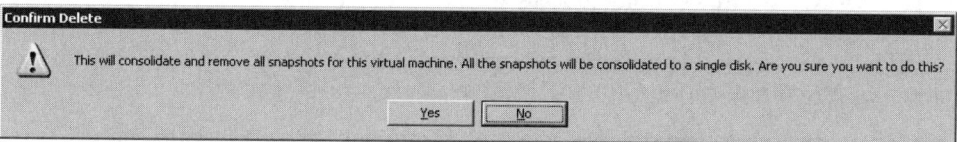

Changing Disk Modes

It's perhaps worth saying that it seems likely that VMware will be removing this disk mode feature in later releases of vSphere. When you define a virtual disk, you are asked to set its disk mode. There are effectively three different modes:

- **Nonindependent mode**   This is the default mode, and the only one that allows the snapshot feature.

- **Independent Persistent mode**   This mode treats the virtual disk as a normal disk—any I/O is committed to the disk immediately, and snapshots are not allowed. Of course, you must still shut down the guest OS properly to flush the contents of memory to the disk. This is due to file-system caching, present in many modern OSs. You can use this mode to disable snapshots on a VM. Of course, a much better way to disable access to the snapshot feature is with permissions.

- **Independent Nonpersistent mode**   This mode marks the virtual disk as volatile. Any changes made after this switch stop any I/O events from entering the disk. Every time you power the VM off and on, your changes are lost. Some customers use this with test and development VMs or with training VMs that always need to be reset to a given state. What actually happens is changes accrue in a delta file, but at power off, they are never merged into the virtual disks. Taken to the logical conclusion, this could be very useful in a VDI environment or kiosk VM. Imagine a situation where you have one only VMDK file of Windows XP wasting valuable space on the SAN, and each user receives a delta version. At the end of the working day, these VMs are powered off and reset to the golden state before the users made changes.

Changing disk modes requires the VM to be powered off.

You can enable the Independent Persistent or Nonpersistent disk mode from the Virtual Machine Properties dialog box. Select Hard Disk in the list of devices. You can then choose your desired mode.

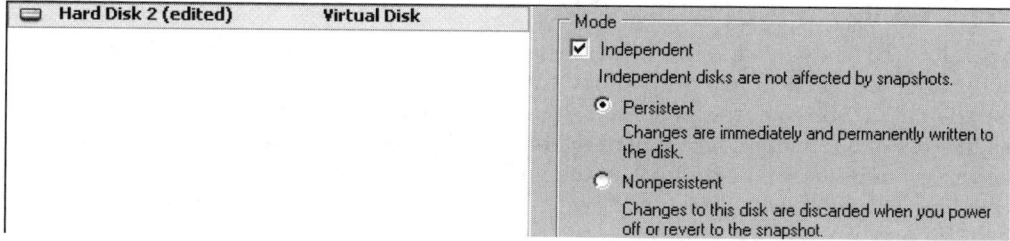

Be aware that disabling snapshots by enabling Independent Persistent mode in this way can have undesired consequences. It means the end of hot backups of the VM, where the files of the VM are backed up despite the fact that the VM is powered on. This is because the snapshot feature is used in technologies like VCB to "unlock" the files of the VM prior to the start of the backup. Despite the mode being enabled on just one virtual disk as the example shows, it does disable the use of snapshots for the *entire* VM. If you try to create a snapshot of a VM in this mode, you will receive an error message.

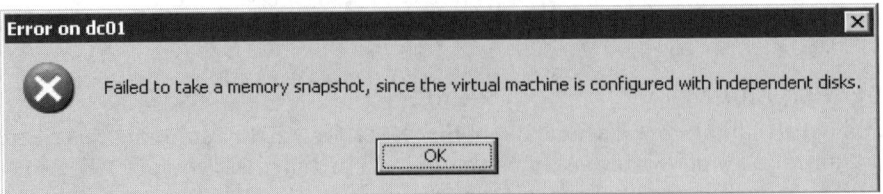

If you enable Nonpersistent mode, you could then make all manner of crazy changes to the VM. If you shut down the VM and then power it back on, it will be reset to its original state. In this case, all the changes accrue in a snapshot file called delta_REDO, and these changes are always discarded.

dc1.vmx	3.40 KB	Virtual Machine
dc1.vmdk	4,194,304.00 KB	Virtual Disk
dc1.nvram	8.48 KB	Non-volatile me
vmware-13.log	75.23 KB	Virtual Machine
vmware-8.log	75.40 KB	Virtual Machine
vmware-9.log	77.67 KB	Virtual Machine
vmware-10.log	76.83 KB	Virtual Machine
vmware-11.log	76.78 KB	Virtual Machine
vmware-12.log	62.22 KB	Virtual Machine
vmware.log	68.32 KB	Virtual Machine
dc1.vmxf	0.25 KB	File
dc1.vmsd	0.49 KB	File
dc1-c411069b.vswp	262,144.00 KB	File
dc1.vmdk-delta.REDO_qu3qN3	16,394.00 KB	File
dc1.vmdk.REDO_qu3qN3	0.23 KB	File

Note that you must do a complete shut down of the VM—such as by using the Guest Shutdown option or Power Off option—and then do a power on for this to work. A soft reboot of the VM is not enough.

Removing, Adding, and Deleting VMs

It is possible to remove a VM currently registered on an ESX host and listed in vCenter and add it to another ESX host in a different vCenter environment. The important thing to note is that the only requirement is for shared storage. Effectively, this achieves a manual move of a VM from one vCenter environment to another. If you have reinstalled an ESX host or vCenter, you might need to add VMs to the host in order to power them on.

Adding and removing VM is a relatively simple task, but beware of doing this to move a VM from one ESX host to another; in other words, unregistering a VM from one ESX host and registering it to a different ESX host. When the VM is powered on, a prompt will appear, asking what you would like to do with a change in the VM's UUID.

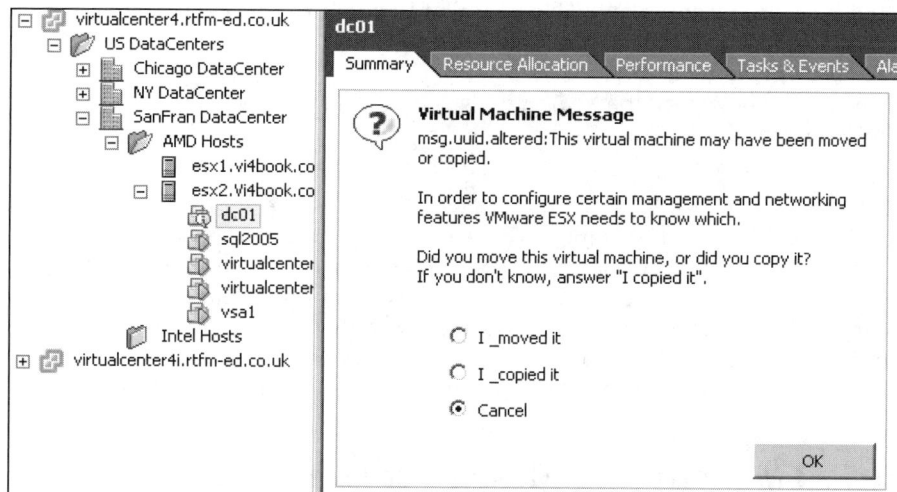

The UUID is often used by management systems to track pieces of hardware separately from the OS it runs. Physical servers have a UUID, and this allows us to wipe Windows from a physical server and install Linux, but still have the management system recognize it as the original piece of hardware. In simple terms, the UUID is a hardware identifier that has no dependencies on the operating system installed. VMs also have a UUID value, which is held in the .vmx file and generated from the real UUID of the ESX host.

In most cases, it is best to choose "I moved it" to retain the VM's identity in management systems of this type. If you were *moving* a VM, you should *not* create a new UUID. This means a VM manual move retains its original identity, or UUID. If you were manually *copying* a VM using command-line tools (which is not recommended—you should use templates or the clone feature), you *should* create a new UUID. What you need to avoid is two VMs with the same UUID, as this would cause problems in management systems that use the UUID or introduce the possibility of duplicate MAC addresses.

If you move a VM using vCenter either powered on (VMotion/hot migration) or powered off (cold migration), the UUID is unaffected.

Adding a VM

To add a VM, follow these steps:

1. Select an ESX host.

2. From the Summary page, right-click the datastore where the VM resides and choose Browse Datastore.

3. Locate the VM's .vmx file, which is held within its directory.

4. Right-click the .vmx file and choose Add to Inventory.

5. In the wizard, choose a folder location for your VM. Click Next to move through the remaining dialog boxes.

Removing a VM

Removing a VM does not delete the files that make up a VM; it merely removes the VM from the ESX host and vCenter lists. This is similar to when you remove virtual disks inside a VM by choosing Remove from Virtual Machine, as opposed to when you select "Remove and delete files from virtual disk."

To remove a VM, power off the VM, right-click a VM, and choose Remove from Inventory. Choose Yes to confirm the removal.

Deleting a VM

Deleting a VM is a permanent operation. There is no undo button or recycle bin in ESX. If you accidentally delete a VM, it is gone for good. Your only resort would be restoring it using your backup strategy. Similarly, there are no triple "Are you sure?" dialog boxes or "Please confirm with a four-digit PIN" messages. You are asked only once to confirm the deletion.

To delete a VM, right-click it and choose Delete from Disk. Read the message in the dialog box, and choose No if you are at all unsure!

P2V of a Physical Machine with vCenter Converter

In fairness, physical to virtual conversion (P2V) should be covered in a book devoted to it. However, a book that extols the virtues of virtualizing existing physical environments should include at least a brief overview of converting physical machines to VMs.

In the real world, many large companies still opt for what is termed a "P2V jumpstart." This is where experienced consultants from your P2V vendor visit your organization for about a week. During that week, they introduce and set up the software required and assist you in your first few P2V events. This workshop approach works better than, say, conventional classroom training, which tends to be rather unrealistic. You really need to know about your specific hardware, OS, application software, and environment before embarking on the P2V process.

In my experience, people get very fixated on the copying of P2V. This is actually quite a small part of the process and the least interesting. The interesting part of virtualization and P2V is the preanalysis of the existing physical environment and the postconversion cleanup phase; in other words, before you actually switch over to the VM and after you decommission the physical machine.

VMware offers VMware vCenter Converter (formerly VMware P2V 2.*x*), but you're not restricted to using VMware's software in this process. For example, you might use PlateSpin PowerConvert or Leostream P2V. Additionally, some hardware vendors like Dell, IBM, and HP have gotten in on the act, offering their own tools for converting physical systems into VMware VMs. Another alternative is to check out free P2V solutions, such as Ultimate-P2V (http://www.rtfm-ed.co.uk) and MOA Project (http://www.sanbarrow.com). But be aware that these free solutions do not ship with any warranty or commercial support. Additionally, they are unlikely to have fancy postconfiguration P2V features.

You might wish to investigate how these various tools actually achieve the cloning process. Some vendors install an agent into the existing physical machine, which then allows it to be visible to the management console used for cloning. The advantage is that you can remotely convert the physical machine while it is powered on, which can be important because of uptime challenges that P2V inherently introduces. From a hardware perspective, it might be a good solution for very old server hardware. As there already is an existing OS with the right drivers for networking and storage, there is a greater chance of actually being able to get the configuration out of the physical box and into the VM. The disadvantage of this hot cloning method is that you have altered the original physical host. Many organizations have an ideological problem with this approach. They argue that this could affect failback procedures, and so they prefer the physical machine to be "closed" during the conversion process.

Other P2V solutions make the physical server boot from a CD and duplicate the server. This is advantageous because you can be sure that every file will be copied, as there are no open files, and no changes are made to the original server. The disadvantages are server downtime and the possibility that the vendor's boot CD will not recognize the hardware (critically, the NIC and storage controller). The best P2V solutions will offer a combination of both, which is the case with vCenter Converter.

Many of these tools are geared up for Windows P2V events, although some of them also offer Linux-based conversions. So if you're working in a heterogeneous OS environment, you might want to research the guest OSs supported. vCenter Converter is a Windows application that is installed to your management PC. When it was first released, it was limited to experimental support for Linux, but now Linux is fully supported.

Here, we will look at a very small part of the P2V process—the conversion software—and also some very simple clean-up routines. The examples use vCenter Converter. vCenter Converter ships in two formats: Starter and Enterprise. The Starter Edition is agent-based and is free. The Enterprise Edition can use an agent or boot CD. Both the agent and boot CD possess the same user interface, so if you have access to both, there isn't any learning curve involved. (What surprises me, and something I have never understood, is why only Enterprise customers gain access to the coldclonecd.iso file, especially given that it essentially duplicates the same functionality as the online agent method.)

Lastly, although I am emphasizing the P2V functionality of vCenter Converter, you should know that it has a lot of other cool features, such as the following:

- It can convert VMware VMs across multiple VMware platforms, and therefore is compatible with ESX 4.*x*, 2.*x*, VMware Workstation 4 and higher, VMware Player, and VMware Server. It is also backward compatible with GSX versions (since rebranded as VMware Server).

- It can convert third-party formats like Symantec Backup Exec System Recovery, Norton Ghost, Microsoft Virtual Server, and Microsoft Virtual PC.

- It can also be used to restore backups of VMs using the VMware Consolidated Backup system.

It integrates with other VMware management tools. In the future, vCenter Converter is likely to integrate with VMware Site Recovery Manager, which will allow Site Recovery Manager to virtualize your distaster recovery plans easily, even for physical systems.

CAUTION   *After a P2V process has completed, some editions of Windows will need to be reactivated. Windows will see the new virtual disk as a brand-new hard drive, and the GUID associations with the old hard drive will be reset.*

Before You Begin: Engage Brain

Before you jump in to P2V with both feet, perhaps you want to step back and think about other ways of proceeding. P2V is often sold as a silver-bullet way of getting from the physical world to the virtual world. However, P2V software is just that—software—and comes with its own issues, challenges, and bugs. Additionally, there many ways of migrating one physical system to another physical system, and these migration methods will usually work in a VM as well. Consider that if you have ever moved a database from one version to another—say from SQL Server 2000 to SQL Server 2005—there's no reason why such similar processes won't work for a VM.

If your physical machine exhibits problems in Windows already, guess what happens when you apply P2V software? That's right—the same problems get ported over to the VM.

Also, some systems are resistant to P2V software. For example, I would not consider a P2V of Microsoft Active Directory environment a good choice, especially when I can cleanly install Windows to a VM and use Microsoft's Dcpromo and the replication engine of Active Directory to gradually decommission my physical Active Directory environment, again using Dcpromo to remove physical domain controllers. Remember also that Active Directory has its own unique time needs to be addressed.

Where P2V is an absolute godsend—and an absolute requirement—is in a situation such as when you have some aging Windows NT 4 member server with software from a vendor who went into voluntary liquidation some 18 months ago. The guy who built this box left the company two years ago. And yes—you've guessed it—he didn't document one darn thing about how this system is configured.

Installing vCenter Converter

In its agent format, VMware vCenter Converter is both a service and a vSphere Client plug-in. The plug-in adds a right-click Import Machine option on to a cluster or an ESX host. This option starts a wizard to carry out the conversion itself.

Installing the Converter software is very easy. It doesn't need a database back end. All it needs is a valid vCenter username and password to gain access to vCenter to add itself to the list of available plug-ins. Converter will install in vCenter or a stand-alone system.

Follow these steps to install vCenter Converter:

1. Execute autorun from the vCenter CD.

2. From the list, select vCenter Converter.

3. Accept the usual suspects of the Welcome, EULA, and path for Converter's files.

4. Select Typical. The Typical option installs the core features that make up the Converter package and an optional CLI tool as well. The agent, which is normally installed to a physical machine, can be installed manually to the physical machine if the automatic method fails.

5. Supply the username and password required for the Converter service to communicate with vCenter.

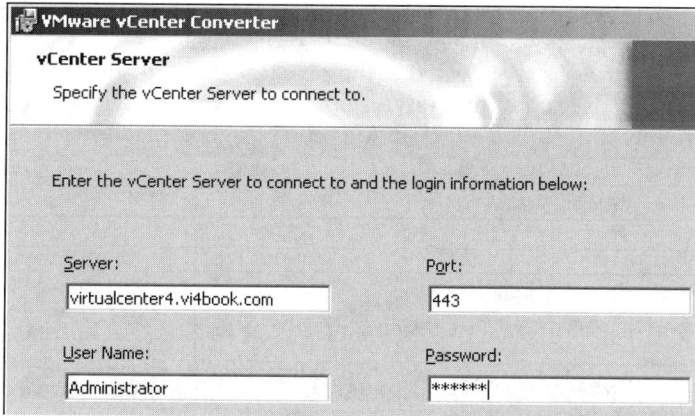

6. Click Next if you have not altered the default ports on which the vCenter web service listens.

7. Click Next, and accept the use of an FQDN as the method of identifying the vCenter server on the network.

8. Click the Install button.

Once the installation has completed, you should find within the vSphere Client the option to download and install the vCenter Converter plug-in in the Plug-in Manager window.

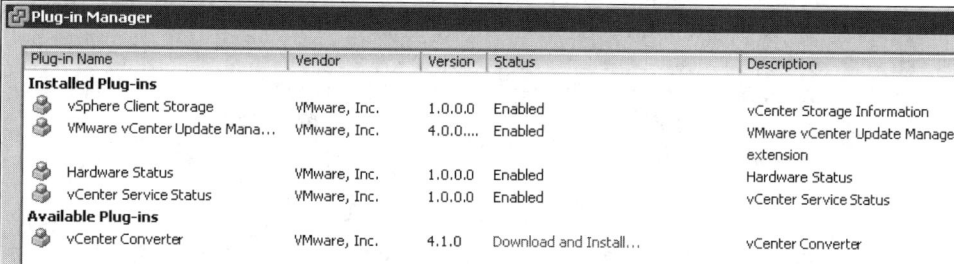

Then you can use the Converter with the agent or with the coldclonecd.iso file.

NOTE   *The success or failure of either of the vCenter Converter methods is dependent on a large number of different factors, but personally I have found the cold clone CD method to be more dependable and reliable than the online agent method. I've seen the cold clone CD method succeed on the same physical system where the agent has failed.*

Using vCenter Converter with the Agent (Enterprise Mode)

Before you begin the P2V process, verify that you can log in to the physical server with administrator credentials and ensure you have no mapped drives or other network connections to the physical server on your management PC.

Note that if you cannot get communication or authentication working, you can always resort to using the vCenter Converter boot CD at the physical server. One of the biggest challenges of using the agent method is communication, especially if your vCenter Converter is separated from the physical machine by firewalls and NATs.

Once vCenter Converter has connected to the physical machine, it will install an agent to the physical machine. At the end of the conversion process, the agent can be automatically uninstalled or manually uninstalled—it is up to you. The agent installs itself as a service called VMware Converter Service in Windows.

Follow these steps to perform the P2V with the agent:

1. Click the Import Machine button.

2. Click Next to move to Step 1: Source.

3. For Source Type, select the Physical Computer option.

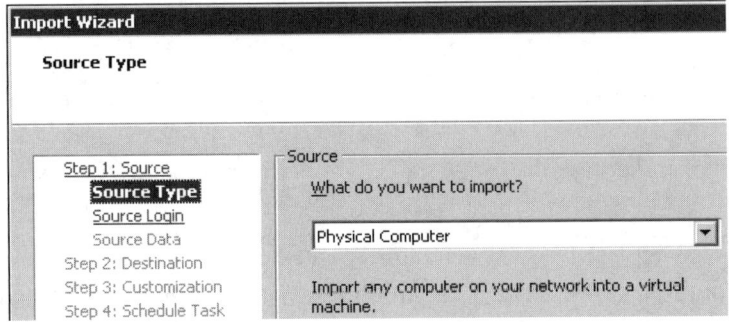

4. Provide source login details by entering the name/IP address of the physical system and a valid username and password. In the dialog box, type in the name or IP address of the physical server, and then enter the administrative credentials for the physical machine. These must be expressed in the format of *DOMAIN\Username* if you do not know the local administrator account or password.

5. Select the "Automatically uninstall the files when import succeeds" option. Notice how the dialog box warns you that if you are converting Windows NT 4/2000 systems, you may need to reboot the physical machine to allow the agent to run. A common cause of the agent not installing is the Windows Firewall, which blocks the communications required for the vCenter Converter to speak to the physical machine.

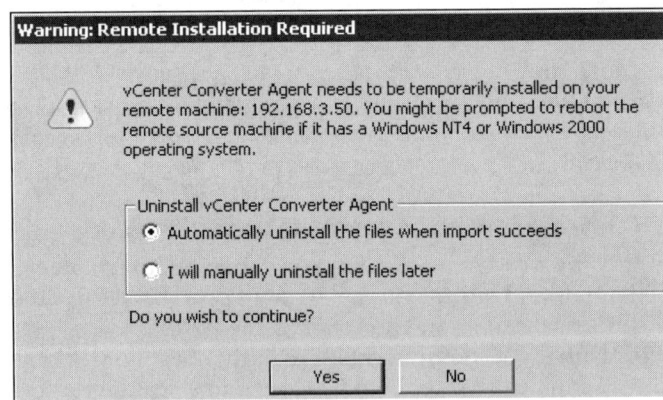

6. Select the source data. You need not necessarily copy your data; you can just select your OS partition. You might decide that the data can be moved to the virtual world in a more efficient and less intrusive way. Consider that the main thing P2V is trying to capture is the configuration of the physical machine, rather than its data contents. Additionally, you can choose to resize disks. Physical systems may have large mirrored disks to protect the OS partition, and frequently these disks waste space. The following example is a little distorted, as the system I've connected to is just another VM, which I am pretending is a physical machine!

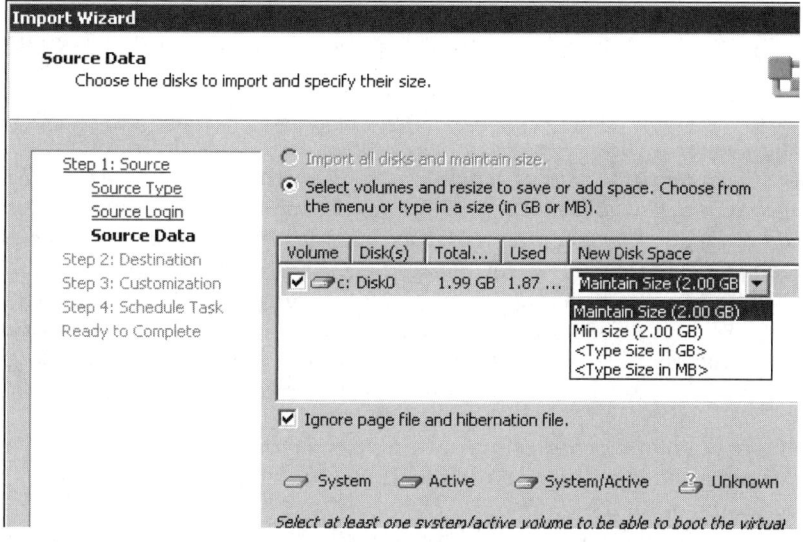

NOTE *Due to vCenter Converter's ability to resize disks, I've heard of people using this (or Norton Ghost) as a way of resizing the partition scheme inside a VM once a virtual disk has been made larger. Personally, I don't prefer this method. Instead, I use something like the Knoppix Live CD's QTParted utility to resize the partition tables, as described earlier in the chapter.*

7. Choose Next to move to Step 2: Choose a Destination. If you right-click an ESX host at the start of the wizard, it will use that ESX host as the destination.

   Type in the name of the new VM, and select the folder in vCenter to hold the VM.

   Select a VMFS or NAS datastore. The Advanced button allows you to locate the VM's files on different datastores.

   Select which network port group you wish to use. I recommend initially using an internal switch or having the virtual NIC disconnected to avoid any potential IP or NETBIOS name conflicts.

   Enable Install VMware Tools.

TIP *New to Converter in vSphere 4 is the ability to remove Windows System Restore checkpoints. These can waste space, and won't be particulary useful in this new virtual world.*

Click Next, and then click Finish.

You can watch the status of your conversion from the Converter windows. Additionally, the Task Progress tab will give you an overview of the steps the Converter is completing.

I recommend choosing No to the option of powering on the P2V'd VM at the end. There are some cleanup and postconfiguration tasks you can do from the vSphere Client before you power on the new VM.

Using vCenter Converter with the Cold-Clone Boot CD (Enterprise Mode)

The Enterprise Edition of vCenter Converter also comes with the option to download a boot CD. This allows you to reboot a physical server and clone the disk while the system is offline. The boot CD is actually a modified version of Microsoft WinPE environment.

NOTE *Previous editions have used a Debian CD and then later the Knoppix Live CD. I don't know what prompted VMware to move in this direction, but I think the reason was threefold. One is that it is substantially easier to add drivers for networking and storage. Another is that WinPE's competitor is the highly popular BartPE; however, according to Microsoft, to run BartPE, you should really purchase a license for Windows XP or Windows 2003. Many people don't, which is very naughty of them as it upsets Microsoft a great deal. WinPE has the advantage that VMware can distribute it under a legally watertight license agreement to customers who perhaps don't even use Windows. Finally, it allowed VMware developers to write a very easy and intuitive user interface, consistent both in agent and cold-clone modes. You'll notice how the look and feel of the cold clone CD is practically identical to the agent method.*

VMware vCenter Converter supports all the flavors of Windows and is happy if the disk is basic or dynamic. It will not convert volumes configured with Microsoft's software implementation of RAID.

You need at least 264MB of RAM for cold cloning to work. If the memory size on the physical system is more than 364MB, the boot CD will create a RAM drive, which improves the performance of the CD.

During the boot-from-CD process, your physical machine will need an IP address. Clearly, the easiest way to do this is to have temporary DHCP services during the time of the P2V conversion. This will avoid the additional steps for having to set static IP addresses for each conversion.

Follow these steps to use the cold clone boot CD to perform the P2V:

1. Download the ISO file from VMware's web site.

2. Burn the ISO file to a CD using your burner software. (If your server supports ILO or RAC boards with virtual media, you could just use the ISO file as it is.)

3. At the prompt, press any key to boot from the CD.

4. In the dialog box, choose Yes to answer "Would you like to update network parameters at this time?"

5. Confirm your DHCP server has leased the boot CD and IP address. If you don't have access to a DHCP server, input your static configuration.

6. Click the Import Machine button.

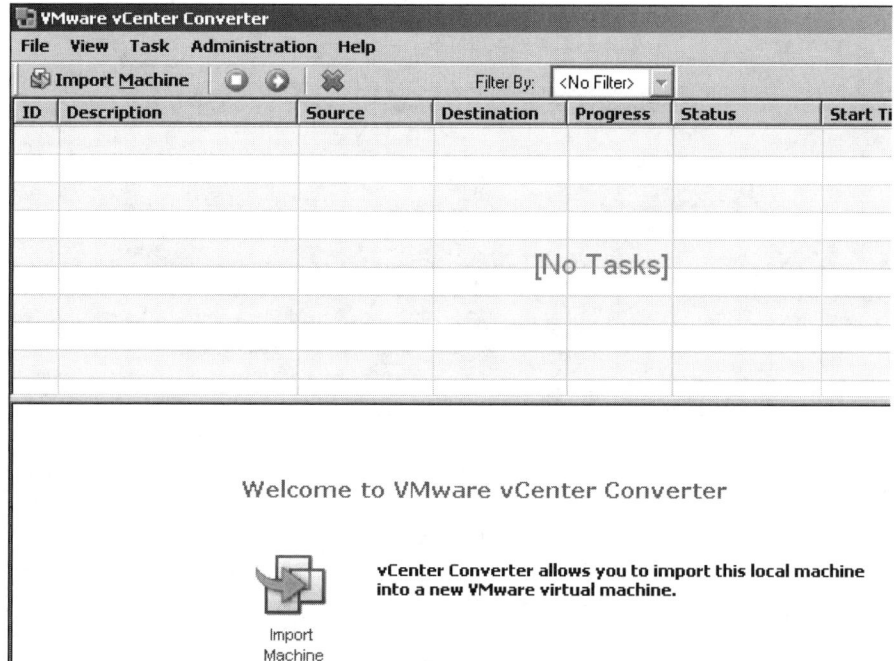

7. Click Next to move to Step 1: Source.

8. In the Source Data dialog box, choose "Select volumes and resize to save or add space."

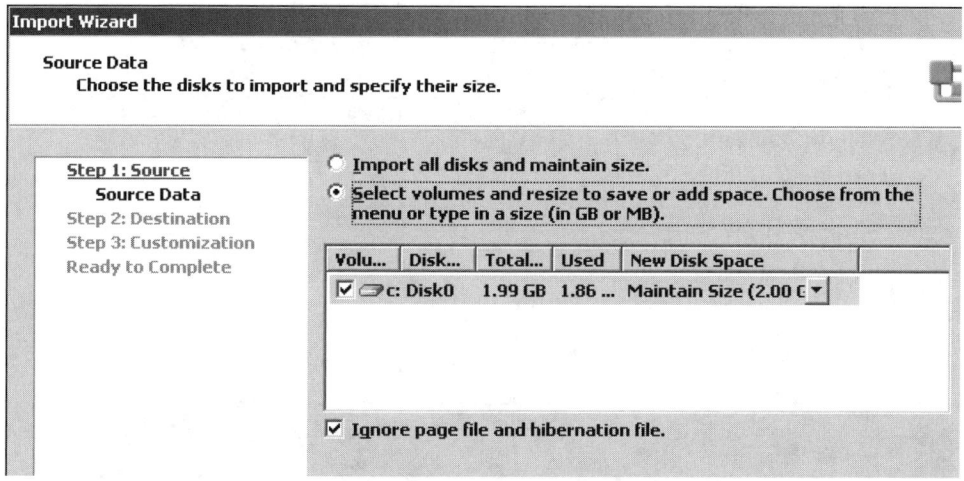

9. Choose Next to move to Step 2: Destination.

10. Choose vSphere Virtual Machine.

11. Provide the FQDN, login name, and credentials to access your ESX host or vCenter server.

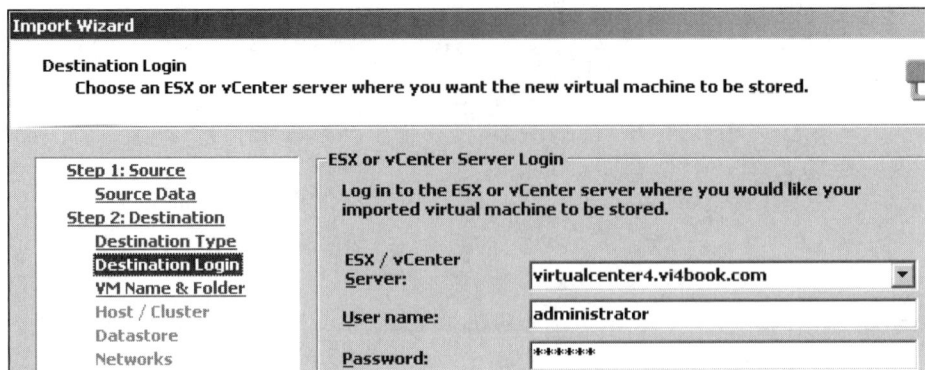

12. Type in a name for your new VM.

13. Select an ESX host or cluster to run the VM.

14. Select a VMFS or NFS datastore location for the new VM.

15. Choose a network port group for the VM.

16. Allow the system to install VMware Tools.

17. When the conversion is complete, select File and Exit in Converter.

During the process of conversion, the utility provides details about the status of the process.

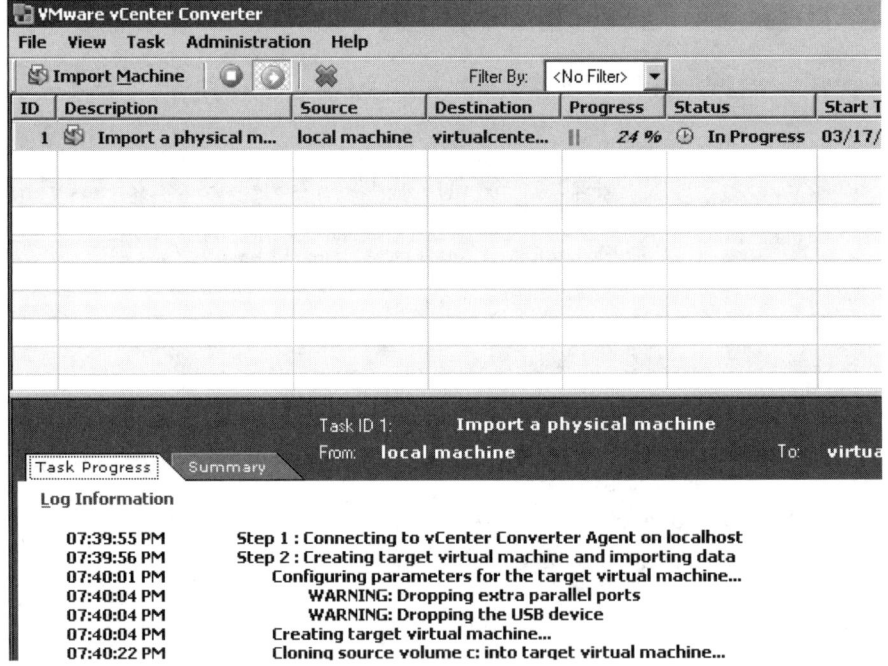

Cleaning Up After P2V Conversion

After any P2V conversion, there is a significant amount of cleanup work that needs to be completed. Here's a brief checklist of the kind of tasks you may need to consider:

- Shut down the VM.
- Edit the settings of the VM. Remove legacy devices like serial ports and parallel ports.
- Remove stale software. Doing this reduces the time spent on removing stale hardware, as deinstalling drivers sometimes removes the references in hardware management tools. Such software may include the following:
  - Hardware drivers (graphics, sound, NICs, RAID controller)
  - Remote access software such as VNC
  - Hardware agents such as HP Insight Manager, IBM Director, and Dell OpenManage
- Remove stale hardware with Device Manager. In Device Manager, change the view to show hidden devices (Windows 2000's Add Hardware Devices has a similar option). This clearly shows you the old hardware, which you can right-click and choose Uninstall. Run Device Manager with this batch file:

```
@echo off
cls
set devmgr_show_nonpresent_devices=1
start devmgmt.msc
```

The following example shows the stale hardware of a P2V VM. You can see the old hard drives (a Western Digital and a Maxtor) and various USB sticks that have been inserted into the physical server. You can also see an old Sony CD-RW drive, and lastly, the old 3COM network card.

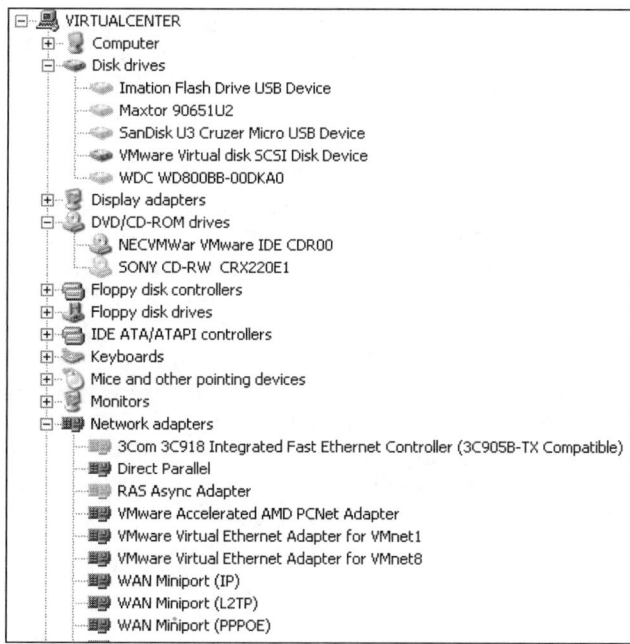

Reconfigure networking. After the P2V conversion, your old NIC will be gone, and your new NIC from VMware will have lost its original TPC/IP settings.

As you can tell, the postconfiguration process is not insignificant. Much of this process could actually be scripted. RTFM Education's Web site (http://www.rtfm-ed.co.uk/?page_id=8) has a white paper and some sample scripts that have been developed to address this issue. An interesting one uses Microsoft's DevCon utility to compare the VM to the physical machine and automatically remove the stale hardware that appears in Device Manager. Older research using the ESX 2.x platform showed the script could remove about 60 to 80 unwanted devices in most Windows environments. That said, VMware's stated advice now is to remove only stale hardware you can be 100% sure will not affect Windows. The removal of a NIC can cause annoying pop-up dialog boxes because the IP addresses are still referencing a device that is no longer present.

Using Guided Consolidation for P2V Conversion

Essentially, Guided Consolidation combines a largely slimmed down version of the VMware Capacity Planner tool with VMware vCenter Converter. Guided Consolidation is not intended to replace VMware Capacity Planner.

The Guided Consolidation wizards lead you through the process of analyzing existing physical hosts to assess the virtual hardware required to make them run efficiently. Currently, Guided Consolidation allows only the conversion of Windows physical machines, and is dependent on a browsing feature to locate them on the network. This can be somewhat slow, and there is currently no method to manually add a physical machine by NETBIOS name or IP address with the Guided Consolidation wizard. However, it is still possible to trigger the use of vCenter Converter from the right-click menus of vCenter, thus bypassing the "discovery and analysis" phase of Guided Consolidation.

In my tests, I found the system preferred to use shared storage VMFS volumes over my local VMFS volumes, which had more free space in them. For this reason, you might still prefer to use the vCenter Converter tool without the Guided Consolidation wizard.

In my training courses, I tell my students that I regard Guided Consolidation as the "mini-me" (that's an Austin Powers reference there) version of VMware's Capacity Planner product, by which I mean that the Guided Consolidation feature has a similar agenda, but much reduced functionality.

Guided Consolidation vs. VMware Capacity Planner

Guided Consolidation may address the needs of much smaller VMware shops that have a relatively small number of physical machines and/or regard a VMware Capacity Planner exercise as too expensive. VMware Capacity Planner is not a shrink-wrapped software product that can be bought off the shelf. It is sold directly by VMware Professional Services Organization (PSO) and VMware Authorized Consultants (VACs) with a combination of the software plus consultancy services. However, I've heard of both VMware and VACs "rolling-up" the cost of a Capacity Planner project as part of presales activity or an overall virtualization project. As ever, the bigger you are, the more freebies and sweeteners you can try to squeeze these folks for!

Given the choice between Guided Consolidation and Capacity Planner, I would choose the latter every time. Although Guided Consolidation is good, it is somewhat limited. The quality of the performance data is not especially detailed, and although it will produce reports on CPU and memory, it doesn't offer any advice about minimum disk space needed per VM when converting a physical machine to a VM.

Installing Guided Consolidation

In order for Guided Consolidation to work, the correct user account(s) and user rights must first be configured. The account must have the following privileges to work successfully:

- A member of the local administrators group on vCenter
- A domain account with read rights to the domain
- Administrative rights over the physical machines to gather performance data (this user can be different from the accounts)

In the simplest configuration, you can create one user account that carries out all of these tasks; however, you will probably face security restrictions that prevent this. Security and correct authentication are probably the biggest issues in using the Guided Consolidation feature. vCenter does not set these additional privileges for you, so you should be sure to set them before using this feature.

Follow these steps to install Guided Consolidation:

1. Execute autorun from the vCenter CD.

2. From the list, select vCenter Guided Consolidation Service.

3. Accept the usual suspects of the Welcome, EULA, and path for services files.

4. Set the credentials for the vCenter Collector Service. This service gathers information from your physical world as part of the consolidation process.

5. Select the default port numbers used by the vCenter Consolidation Service.

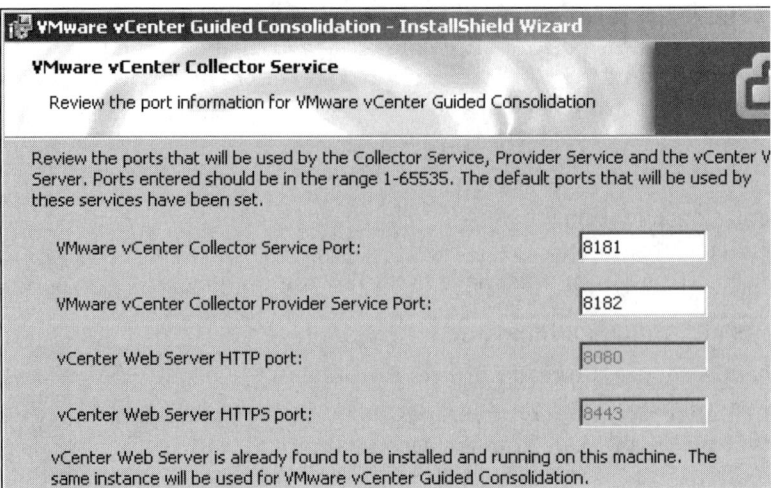

6. Set the name of your vCenter and username/password. This allows the Guided Consolidation Service to add a plug-in to the vSphere Client.

7. Set the FQDN to identify the Guided Consolidation server on the network.

8. Click the Install button.

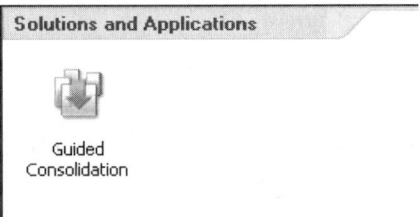

Unlike some other plug-ins, the Guided Consolidation plug-in is enabled automatically. It can be located under Home in the Solutions and Applications tab.

Performing a Discover, Analyze, and Conversion Operation

The Guided Consolidation process has three phases:

- **Discover**   The discover phase is where it finds physical machines on your network and domain, and begins collecting performance data.

- **Analyze**   Next, the analyze process normalizes that data and presents it to the administrator in a format that facilitates identifying good candidates and systems that, due to their poor configuration, might not work efficiently in a VM.

- **Conversion**   Finally, Guided Consolidation makes calls to the Converter APIs to create the impression of a seamless workflow from "physicalization" (if you will) to virtualization.

Here are the steps for running Guided Consolidation:

1. Navigate to Home, Solutions and Applications, then Guided Consolidation.

2. Click the Configuration tab. Under Active Domains, click the Add button.

3. Select the domains you wish to analyze.

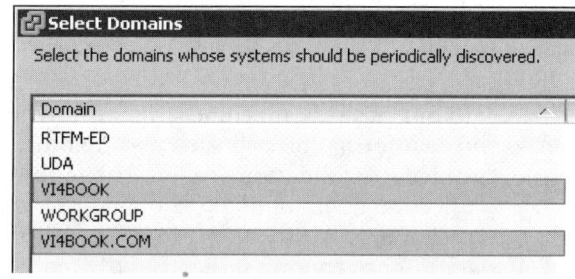

NOTE *I've often found that setting the active domain first speeds up the discovery of computers within that domain. Generally, the Configuration tab is used to check the service status of Guided Consolidation and to change the credentials used to authenticate and collect information from the physical machines.*

4. To set the default system credentials, click the Change button. Enter the domainname\username and password. The dialog box clearly states you must use the "old-style" NETBIOS *domainname\username* format for the credentials.

5. Click the Analysis tab, and then click the Start Analysis button.

6. Choose "Select the computers by domains," and select your domain from the list. This should produce a list of found computers.

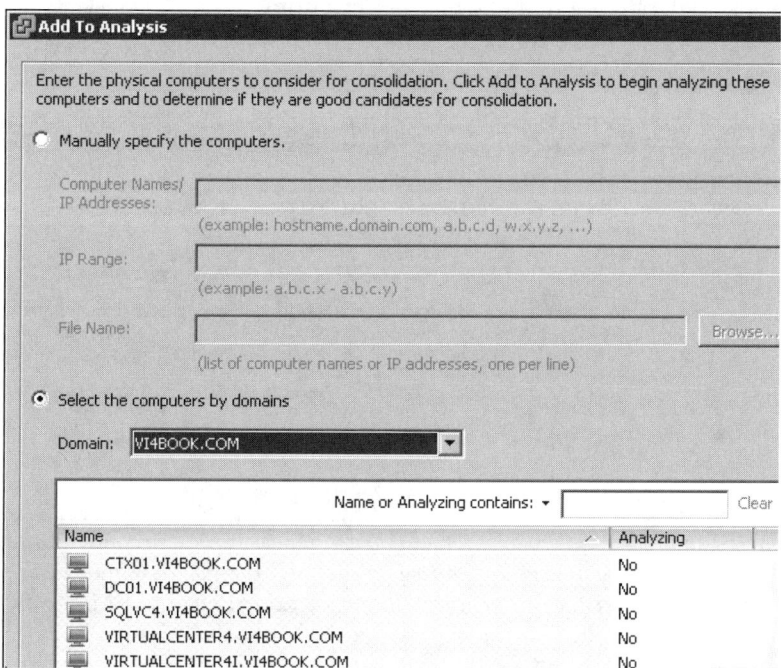

7. Select the computers you wish to analyze from the list, and then click the Add to Analysis button.

8. In the Set Authentication dialog box, select "Use the Configured default credentials."

9. The Guided Consolidation system will collect information about the performance of your physical machines. It is well worth leaving this to run some time. The more information collected about your physical machines, the more accurate the guided consolidation will be. The following example resulted from running the collection over about 4 to 5 hours. The columns highlighted in red are meant to be charts; in reality, they are so limited that they defy proper analysis. The Confidence column indicates Low mainly because not enough time has been allocated to the process.

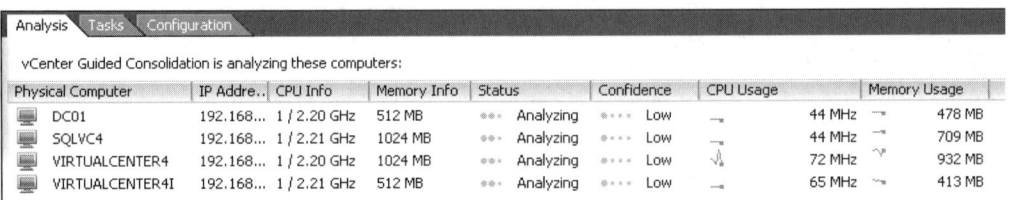

10. Select a physical machine from the analysis list, and click the Plan Consolidation button. This will produce recommendations about converting a physical machine to a VM and also trigger the conversion process if you so wish.

11. In the Specify Destination dialog box, select a number an ESX hosts.

12. Click Next, and the Guided Consolidation wizard will recommend an ESX host for the soon-to-be-converted physical machine.

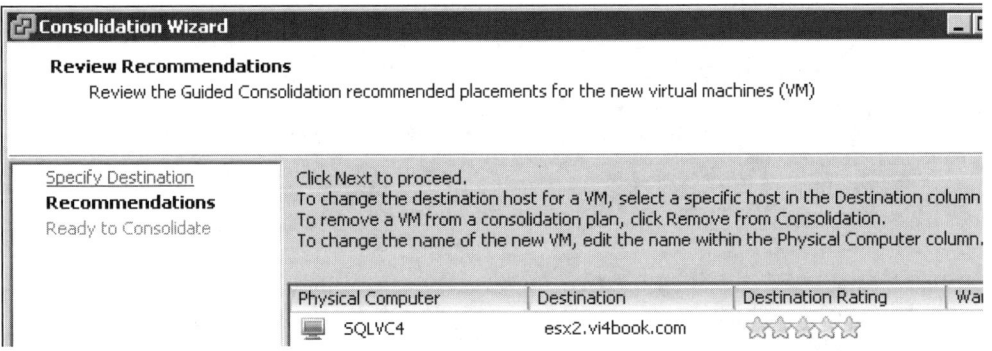

NOTE *This conversion process is very silent, and you are not asked for any configuration parameters. This can lead to unexpected consequences. For example, the datastore selected is the volume with the most free space—in my case, this happened to be a local VMFS volume.*

13. To trigger a manual conversion to a VM, right-click the physical machine in the Analysis list, select Convert to Virtual Machine, and choose Manually.

The Guided Consolidation wizard will run the Converter wizard described earlier in this chapter.

Setting Up a VMware ESX Testing Environment

Nearly every week, my students ask me about the cheapest method of setting up a lab environment for ESX and vCenter. This subject is off the beaten track for us really, because I am assuming you have access to reliable and supported hardware. However, here I will outline some of the options, based on my own experience of trying to do a lot with a little.

As an independent, freelance instructor, finding the resources to do development work has been one of my major challenges. Over time, I've made a significant investment in hardware to enable me to learn new products, features, and configurations. Along the way, certain companies and individuals have helped me out. In fact, their input has been invaluable. So when in 2008, I wrote my book on VMware Site Recovery Manager, Adam Carter of LeftHand Networks very generously offered me NFR licenses for its virtual SAN appliance (the VSA). Then in 2009, Chad Sakac of EMC arranged the long-term loan of 14U with Celerra and Clariion hardware. In the same year, Vaughn Stewart of NetApp arranged for me to have two NetApp FSA2020 systems as well. In fact, much of this book has been written with this storage at the back end. But I do remember when I had fewer resources, and my lab environment consisted of two Dell 1650 PowerEdge servers with Pentium III processors. It's surprising how you can build an environment reliable enough to learn vSphere 4 with comparatively low-spec hardware.

Option A: Two ESX Servers and a NAS, Please!

Two ESX servers and a NAS are my preferred setup, and more or less what I started with back in the old days (2003). I used the VMware Hardware Compatibility List (HCL) to identify cheap 1U equipment that I was able to source on eBay—the great OEM supplier of all home network hobbyists.

There are some distinct advantages to this approach. The main one is that if it's on the VMware HCL, it will work. Back in the ESX 2.*x* days, if it wasn't on the HCL, you had a slim chance of even getting through an installation routine. These days, I would look for an ILO/RAC board and much more memory than the 2GB of RAM I started with. That said, you don't need a truckload of memory to get a usable environment. Believe it or not, my old servers are still in my rack, acting as my remote access to the rest of my environment. Despite being Dell PowerEdge 1650 servers with Pentium III processors, they still run ESX 3.5 without any problems. (Although they will probably wind up in the skip once I've removed the additional Intel PRO Gigabit Adapters I bought for them.)

The big limitation of this hardware was that I lacked a SAN. In the early days, I experimented with and got working a shared SCSI bus system using a very old JBOD I owned. I was really pleased when VI3 was released that it had NAS support. It meant I could cobble together a two-node cluster and practice with DRS and HA. I acquired a SAN together with disks and cables from a former colleague of mine for around $450. As you might expect, at that price, it wasn't a fantastic piece of equipment, but it has served me well (and continues to serve me well with vSphere 4).

Keeping the SAN going has required some investment. For example, I replaced the QLA2200 cards with some eBay-sourced QLA2340 cards and some new SC-LC cables. Despite the official I/O and SAN guide stating what's supported and tested, VMware ESX is pretty much clueless about what exists as an array at the other end of the Fibre Channel cable. My SAN is actually a Sun StorEdge A5000 array. I have no idea how old this kit is— probably the Jurassic Era (the documentation about the array was last released in 1999). For vSphere 4, I invested in a Fibre Channel switch, because ESX 4 did not allow me to connect directly to the array.

There are some downsides to this approach, including noise and power. Much depends on whether you have a spare room, basement, or garage and an understanding partner who is prepared to put up with both!

Any hardware from eBay is unlikely to have the newest CPU attributes required for features like VMware FT, and the moment you buy it, it will become superseded. The trick with this approach is to accept that this is the reality of IT and try to squeeze as much usage from the device as possible. For example, the processors in my HP ProLiant DL385 G1 do not support VMware FT. I have four of them. I'm thinking of decommissioning my old Dells, and making two HP ProLiant Servers (which have redundant SAN connectivity and more memory) their replacements. They have ILO/RAC functionality; the Dells do not. The other two remaining HP ProLiant Servers I will sell on eBay, and use that income to offset the purchase of something that does VMware FT.

Option B: Run on PCs

Since ESX 3.5, I've noticed more and more people on the VMware Communities forums talking about running ESX on white-box servers that they have assembled themselves. In fact, this has became so popular that, for a while, VMware had an advertisement on its welcome page asking people to share those configurations. Many a blogger has typed away into the wee small hours about their white-box setup.

The main advantage of this approach is that you will get a lot more bang for your buck with your white-box ESX host. Also, this setup is generally much quieter and consumes less power. I admit that I've been sorely tempted to bring my kit back in-house as I've watched my colocation charges grow and I've acquired more hardware. However, for the moment, I'm sticking with option A because of this donation of storage from EMC and NetApp. Additionally, I want my work to reflect the use of real-world equipment as much as possible.

The downside of the white-box approach is that you're on your own if it doesn't work. So, for example, if you had an unexpected error, you might not know whether it was you, the VMware software, or the white box that was the cause of the problem.

Option C: Virtualize ESX

Ever since the xtravirt.com web site published a PDF on how to get ESX 3 running inside VMware Workstation, VM people have been abuzz about virtualizing ESX. The guys at xtravirt.com have retested their original VM to show you can run ESX 4 inside a VM running on VMware Workstation. You can find the information at http://xtravirt.com/xd10089. Do note that this area is largely undocumented and unsupported by VMware.

The concept is a simple one: Build one super über-ESX host—perhaps a white box with a large amount of memory—which then runs many smaller ESX hosts inside it, essentially virtualizing the virtualization layer. The advantage of this is the same as with virtualization in general. You need less hardware, and the virtual ESX host is very flexible; for example, you can give it as many NICs as the VM allows.

I've done some very low-level experimentation with virtualized ESX and have been *mildly* successful in the approach. I was able to install and boot an ESX host running inside a VM on ESX 4. I was able, using advanced and undocumented settings in the .vmx file, to power on a VM running inside the virtual ESX host. Others have experimented using VMware Server and VMware Workstation with more success. All of these people report poor performance.

Personally, I wasn't enamored with this approach. For me, the big disadvantages for the ESX-in-a-box approach is the poor performance and the fact that the virtualized VM is limited to IP storage such as iSCSI/NAS—as currently, the VM doesn't have a virtual QLogic card! Additionally, in order to get this virtual ESX configuration to work, you will need to use undocumented values in the .vmx file (leaked out of VMware and onto the forums). Also, you will probably need to have modern CPUs that have a hardware-assist attribute, such as AMD-V or Intel VT. (I gained access to some HP ProLiant DL380 G5 machines, which had the Intel E5430 processor with Intel VT enabled in the BIOS.)

However, you might be interested in trying out this setup. Occasionally, a virtualized ESX host may be useful for destructive tests or for product demonstrations.

When creating the VM which will contain the ESX host software, use following options:

- VM Version 7
- Other (64-bit) option
- Two vCPUs
- 2x NICs using e1000 as the type
- 20GB virtual disk

Connect the ESX VM to a VM port group or vSwitch with promiscuous mode enabled from the Security tab. If you fail to do this, you will not be able to ping or communicate with the ESX host.

Before powering on and installing the ESX server software, you will need to modify the .vmx file to allow a VM to execute on the virtualized ESX host. This is sometime referred to as the "nested" VM. If you don't make this change to the virtualized ESX host, when you try to power on the nested VM, you will receive an error message.

To circumvent this restriction, an edit the .vmx file as follows:

1. Right-click the virtualized ESX VM.

2. Select Edit Settings.

3. Choose the Options tab and click the Configuration Parameters button.

4. Click the Add Row button.

5. In the Name column, add the `monitor_control.restrict_backdoor` entry.

6. In the Value column, set the new parameter to `true`.

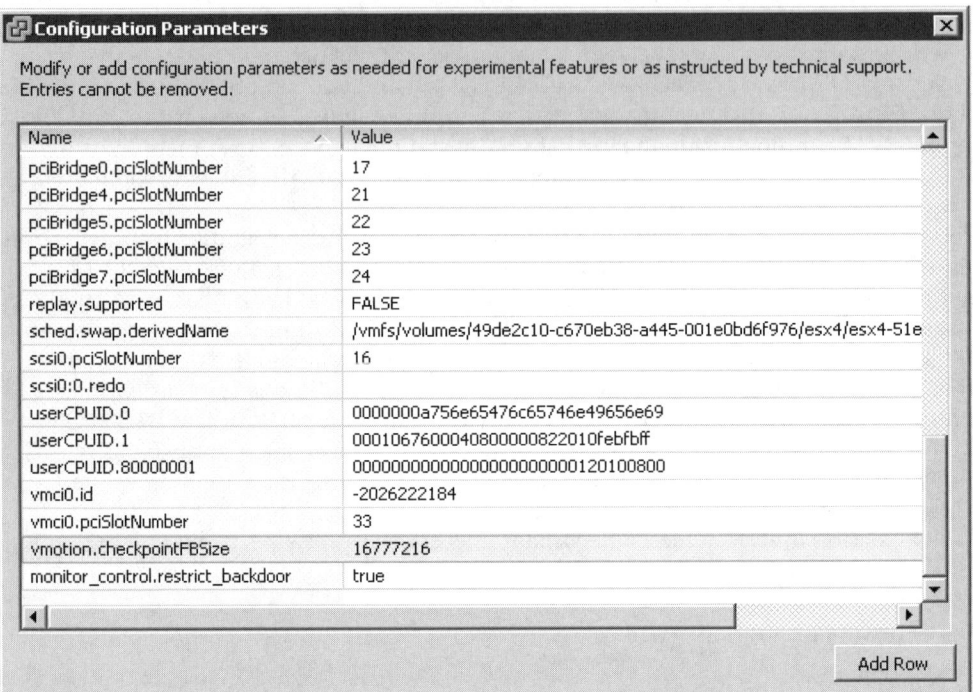

Summary

In this chapter, I've tried to show you the options that you have for provisioning new copies of Windows or Linux. This is a major feature of VMware vCenter. Research has shown that the provisioning process (the process of deploying a new server) can take weeks. With VMware templates, described in the next section, you can have a new server online in a matter of hours.

In fact, what might need reviewing are the other procedures that create bottlenecks in the process. Frequently, these are not technical issues but IT management processes, such as the time it takes to request and process things like DNS registrations, change management requests, approvals, and security audits. Alongside I/O virtualization and VDI, some people think the "next big thing" to hit IT will be management applications that automate the whole workflow process.

CHAPTER 8 | Rapid VM Deployment

Y ou can create quickly create a new VM in VMware vCenter merely by duplicating an existing VM, a process that uses clones and/or templates. Some more experienced users of VMware refer to this as using a "golden master," but whatever term you choose to use—template, clone, image, or golden master—they all mean the same thing: you've taken an existing VM and copied it.

Templates are not a new feature, but VMware has not stood still and rested on its laurels. The developers have introduced new features that accelerate and improve an aspect of the product that is very solid, so we are now free to move our VMs around with the new OVF format, and even duplicate a VM while it is running. This chapter describes the various methods available for duplicating VMs.

Some companies persist in using PXE booting within the VM to leverage their existing deployment tools such as Microsoft Remote Installation Services (RIS), Symantec's Altiris, or HP's Insight Rapid Deployment Pack. Quite often, this is done to save time by removing the need for validating existing build processes. Another reason may be merely political— making it easier to implement VMs by changing as little as possible about existing business practices or procedures. Even if you persist in using these methods, you can still use templates merely to predefine your VM configuration settings, such as how much RAM, how many CPUs, and on which network the VM will reside.

What's New in VM Duplication?

- Hot cloning (copying) a VM
- Open Virtual Machine Format (OVF)

Duplicating VMs

There are three main ways to duplicate VMs:

- **Clone to Template**   This copies the VM and converts it to the template format. If you have used previous versions of vCenter, you will find it is just like a conventional template in vCenter 1.*x*. During the creation of the template, you have the ability to compact the files, which significantly reduces the size of the disk, but both compacting and creating a VM from this format is slower than if it were in its original format. Of course, a good reason to compact a template is to save on disk space. If you use the compact format, it is recommended that you use a VMFS volume as the storage location.

- **Convert to Template**   This simply marks a VM as a template. It is much quicker than using Clone to Template, as no copy process is generated. It takes seconds to mark a VM as a template and seconds to convert it back to being a VM. First, build the VM and convert it to a template. When the software inside the template becomes out of date, you can quickly make it a VM again. Power on the VM and run your software update. Then you can convert the VM back to the template format. Another way to consider this template format is merely as a VM that you can't power on, or a VM that is used only as the source for creating new VMs.

- **Clone Virtual Machine**   There is nothing particularly special about the Clone option; it merely copies the VM. You do lose out on the features of the two preceding options, such as being able to copy and compress the source, and being able to quickly update the base VM.

To clone a VM, you need rights to the VM, as you do with the other two options. But as templates can be stored and moved into other locations where different permissions reside, templates are often easier to work with than VM clones from a delegation and permissions perspective, too.

Preparing for Templates

Before you create a template, you need to ask yourself a couple of questions:

- How big should the guest OS boot partition to be? When you create a new VM from a template, there is no easy way to adjust on the fly the size of the VM's boot disk.
- How much software will you include in your base OS, beyond installing the OS and VMware Tools? For example, you might wish to consider including a service pack, hot fixes, antivirus software, and possibly a backup agent.

NOTE   *Most people balk at the idea of including products such as Active Directory, Citrix XenApp Server, or Microsoft SQL Server in a template, because experience has shown these create more problems than they solve. Sometimes vendors do not support it, and if they do, their products often need extensive preparation both before and after the VM template is created. These steps often take a long time, and their outcome is may be unpredictable. Such products are often best installed by secondary scripts after the VM has been created. This can sometimes rule out the template process being "blamed" by application owners as being the source of their problems.*

Creating a template of a VM doesn't just duplicate the VM's virtual disks. Additionally, the VM's .vmx configuration file is duplicated and renamed with the .vmtx extension. This means that all the settings behind your VM are being duplicated, too. This saves time by reducing the number of wizards and dialog boxes you need to complete. However, this can also result in the inclusion of undesirable settings, like connections to removable devices such as CD-ROMs, floppy disks, or internal switches. These settings can cause problems with VMotion, DRS, DPM, and FT, so I recommend disabling these devices before creating your template.

In the past, one of the challenges of templates was keeping their software up to date. This is a similar to what PC deployment people face when using disk-cloning software to build new PCs. It is relatively easy to build a PC and duplicate it with PowerQuest Drive Image Pro or Norton Ghost. The tricky thing is keeping the library of images current. The same problem bedevils templates in VMware, not least because whenever a new build of ESX is released, VMware Tools also requires a software upgrade. The Convert to Template option, introduced in VI3, significantly eases the management of templates and makes it incredibly simple to keep the software inside a template current with regular updates, such as the following:

- Service packs
- Windows updates

- YUM updates
- Antivirus definitions
- Backup agents

In VI3 to create a template or clone, the VM had to be powered off first. This changed in VI3.5 and onwards, so you are now able to hot clone a VM. This can be useful if you have a production VM that you wish to duplicate and reconfigure, without worrying about breaking the original VM.

However, be aware that you cannot create a template while a snapshot is engaged on the source VM. You will find the Clone, Clone to Template, and Convert to Template options are dimmed in this case.

Storing Templates

Unlike with vCenter 1.*x*, there is no specific location for templates in the vSphere Client interface. Most users create a folder to hold them in the VMs and Templates view. To create such a folder, click Home and switch to this view.

Right-click your datacenter and choose New Folder. Then type in a folder name. I use _Templates, which makes sure it is always at the top of the list in the view.

Where templates are physically stored—iSCSI, SAN, or NAS—depends on your resources. Generally, the template LUN is presented to all ESX hosts in a given vCenter datacenter to allow centralized management and access to the templates themselves. Since VI3.5, template deployment has been possible across datacenter objects, but care must be taken if you do this, as it can create unwanted network utilization.

Cloning to a Template

Follow these steps to use the Clone to Template option. Before you begin this process it's a good idea to confirm that virtual device such as the CD-ROM or Floppy drive is disconnected. This can cause problems with the VMware VMotion feature and also decrease performance. If they are not disconnected then every VM created from the template will inherent these settings. Remember that the template also holds which virtual switch port group the new VMs will be use by default. You should avoid internal virtual switches as they are incompatible with the VMware VMotion feature.

1. Select a VM you have powered off as your source for the template.

2. Right-click the VM, select Template, and then select Clone to Template.

3. Enter a friendly name, such as **base-w2k3-sp2-build**, and select the folder as the location in the Inventory (_Templates in this example).

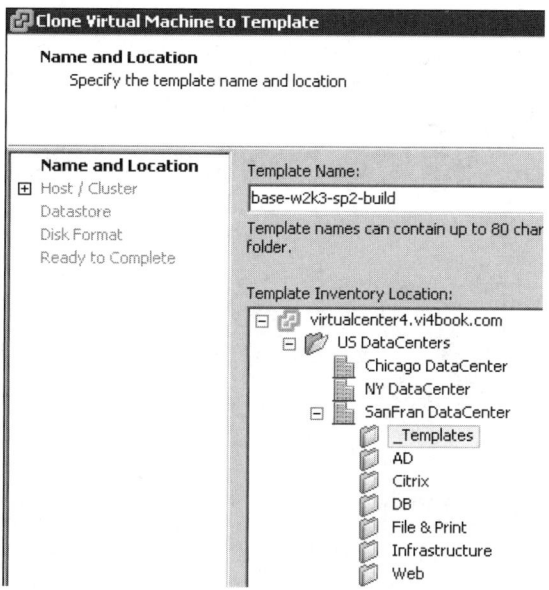

NOTE *I chose esx1.vi4book.com as the location for this template. As with a VM, although a template is "registered" with a particular ESX host, this is not a problem, as long as the template is stored on shared storage visible to the ESX hosts that will use that template. Even if that ESX host is lost and reinstalled, you can still browse the datastore where the template was stored and register the .vmtx file with another ESX host.*

4. Select the physical location for storing the template files. The Choose a Datastore for the Template dialog box will assist you in selecting a good storage location for the template. It will show you the amount of free space, file system format (such as VMFS), and, critically, if that volume is available for single host or many hosts. I recommend a LUN or NAS export presented to all your ESX hosts.

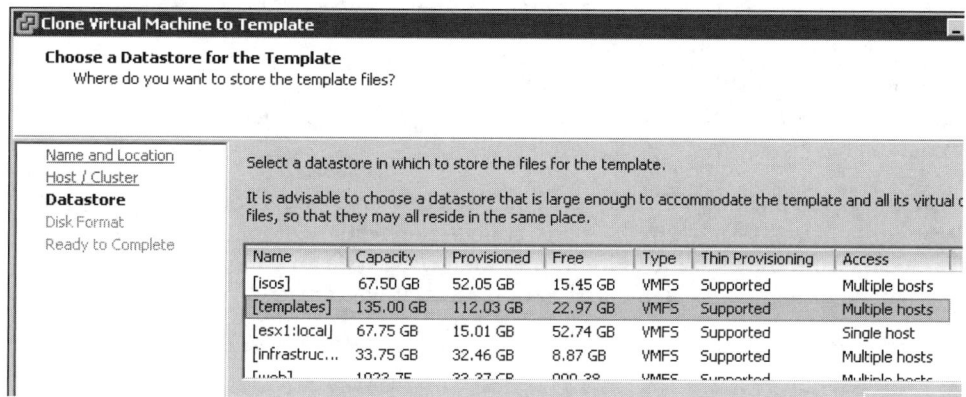

5. Choose a disk format. Your choices are Same as Source, Thin Provisioned, or Thick. This example use the thin provisioned format. This format makes it slower to create and deploy a template, but does save a large amount of precious space. I tend to use it for the VMs I use infrequently, such as Novell NetWare and Solaris.

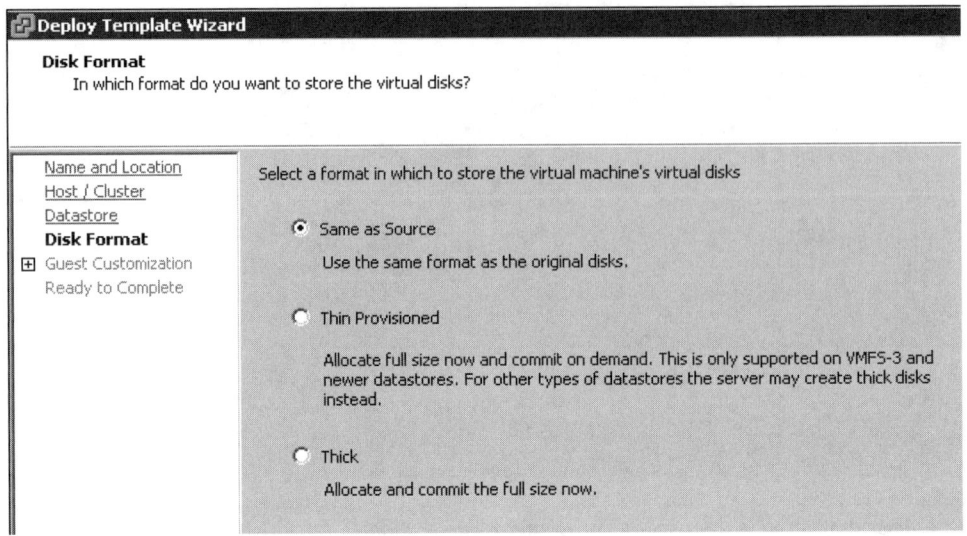

NOTE   *When you create a new VM from a thin provisioned template, you must use the Thick option to return it to being a fully allocated, monolithic thick disk.*

6. Click Finish to create the template.

Converting a VM to a Template

As mentioned earlier, the Convert to Template method offers a quick way of making a template, as well as converting it back to a VM so you can update it for software changes.

NOTE   *If you convert a VM into a template in the Host and Clusters view, the VM seems to disappear from the list. This isn't a bug, but by design. You will find your VM in the VMs and Templates view.*

To use this option, simply select a VM you have powered off as your source for the template, right-click it, select Template, and choose Convert to Template. You'll see that the VM disappears from the list. Click Home, and then click VMs and Templates. Your new template will be located in the same VM folder where it was created.

Right-click your new VM template, and you see a Convert to Virtual Machine menu option. This allows you to quickly return the template to a VM, so you can easily keep the software within the VM up to date.

Using VM Templates

Before you rush ahead and clone or create a new VM from a template, you need to make a one time change to vCenter, especially if you're creating a Windows VM. Once this is done, it's quite easy to use a template to create a VM.

Adding Sysprep Support to vCenter

Windows cannot be duplicated without resetting a number of attributes such as the following:

- NetBIOS name
- Domain membership
- IP settings
- Security identifier (SID)

If you are creating new Linux VMs from a template, you will have fewer attributes to reset, such as the host name and IP settings.

Fortunately, vCenter supports Microsoft's System Preparation (Sysprep) tool. VMware also has some open-source scripts that help change some attributes inside Linux.

Unfortunately, Microsoft does not allow third parties like VMware to distribute Sysprep as part of their product code. Instead, you must manually copy Sysprep to vCenter.

The important point is that you do *not* need to manually run Sysprep inside the VM before making it into a template. VMware handles that for you during the deployment phase of using templates.

After you've copied Sysprep to vCenter, VMware's Guest Customization wizard will appear during the process of creating a new VM. It allows you to reset Windows attributes prior to the first proper boot of Windows. VMware uses the information gathered in this wizard to create an answer file for the mini-installation wizard that normally runs after running Sysprep manually. VMware uses a disk mount service in the vCenter to access the virtual disk of the VM to inject Sysprep and the answer file.

There is one "feature" of Sysprep of which you need to be aware. If you wish your Sysprep VM to join a Windows domain, you must run a DHCP server with a scope for a subnet where the VM resides. When the Sysprep mini-installation process is running, it is set to be a DHCP client (even if you specify a static IP configuration in the Guest Customization wizard), and static IP configurations are not applied until the first full boot of Windows. Therefore, without a valid IP configuration from a DHCP server during the Sysprep process, the VM would not successfully join a domain. This is an attribute of Sysprep and not a bug in the VMware template process.

Lastly, at various times in vCenter history, VMware has seen fit to move the storage location of Sysprep in the file system of the vCenter server. In a clean installation of vCenter

4.*x*, the current location should be C:\Documents and Settings\All Users\Application Data\VMware\VMware VirtualCenter\Sysprep.

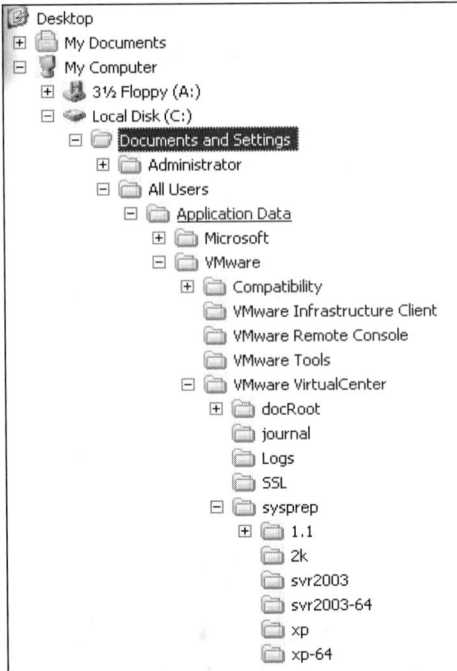

You can find Sysprep within the support\tools\deploy.cab file on most Windows versions (such as Windows 2000, Window XP, and Windows 2003). If you are running Windows Vista, you will find Sysprep in the \Windows\System32\ directory. You can also find copies of Sysprep on the Microsoft Download Center Web site, as follows:

- Sysprep 1.1: http://www.microsoft.com/downloads/details .aspx?familyid=0C4BFB06-2824-4D2B-ABC1-0E2223133AFB&displaylang=en
- Windows XP Service Pack 3: http://www.microsoft.com/downloads/details .aspx?FamilyID=673a1019-8e3e-4be0-ac31-70dd21b5afa7&displaylang=en
- Windows 2003 Service Pack 2: http://www.microsoft.com/downloads/details .aspx?FamilyID=A34EDCF2-EBFD-4F99-BBC4-E93154C332D6&displaylang=en

Creating a New VM from a Template

Follow these steps to create a VM from your template.

1. In the VM and Templates view, right-click the template and choose "Deploy this virtual machine from template."
2. Type in a name for the new VM, and then select a folder location.
3. Select an ESX host on which the VM will run.
4. Select a datastore where the VM will be stored.

5. Select a disk format for the VM. If when you created the template, you selected Thin Provisioned and you choose Same as Source here, you will create a thinly provisioned disk. If you want to return the virtual disk to its original thick, or monolithic format, select the Thick option here.

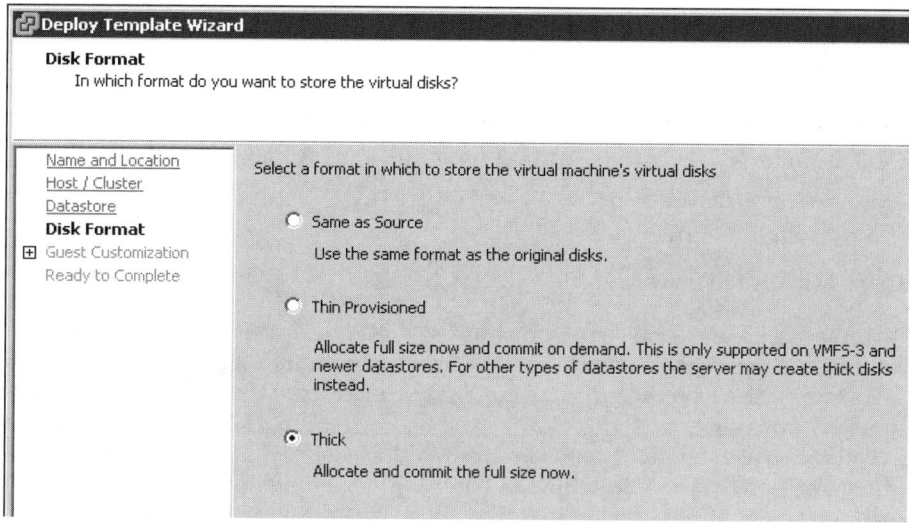

6. Choose Customize using the Guest Customization wizard. Note that this option will be unavailable if Sysprep has not been copied to vCenter and your VM is running a Windows guest OS.

NOTE *The dialog boxes differ when creating a template from a Linux guest OS. VMware has a built-in script that executes inside the Linux guest to reset its IP and host name settings.*

7. Continue through the wizard. The remainder of the dialog boxes should be fairly self-explanatory to anyone who is familiar with Windows. If you have a copy of Windows that requires an OEM number (such as Windows 2003), it is a good idea to input this now; otherwise, the Sysprep mini-installation wizard stalls waiting for user input.

8. At the end of the Guest Customization wizard, you will have the option to save your inputs for further use. This saves you from needing to fill in the Guest Customization wizard every time you use it. To do this, use the third option, "Customize using an existing customization specification," and enable the option "Use the Customization Wizard to temporarily adjust the specification before deployment" at the bottom of the dialog box.

Remember that you can confirm the disk format of a VM by editing its settings and selecting its virtual disk(s).

Using the Customization Specification Manager

Occasionally, you will accidentally save a custom configuration that you would rather delete. Also, you may want to modify an existing custom configuration. The Customization Specification Manager allows you to manage these from a single GUI. With the Customization Specification Manager, you can do the following:

- Copy an existing custom configuration
- Edit an existing custom configuration
- Rename an existing custom configuration (using the Properties option)
- Export to an XML file
- Import from an XML file
- Use a Microsoft Sysprep.inf file

This import feature is useful to previous users of vCenter 1.*x* and 2.*x*, which used an XML format for storing custom configurations. You will find it in the vSphere Client under Edit and Customization Specifications. Although the VMware way of running sysprep is very automated, you might prefer to use the Microsoft Sysprep .INF file because it has some advanced settings which are not exposed to the VMware wizard. A good example of this is, is where the Microsoft Sysprep .INF file can control in which organizational unit the Window computer account is created in Active Directory, the VMware wizards do not.

To access this application, in the vSphere Client, click Home. On the Management tab, click the Custom Specifications Manager icon.

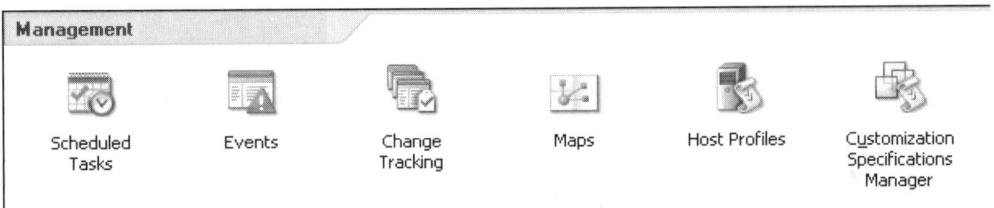

Select the configuration you wish to manage and right-click to access the options.

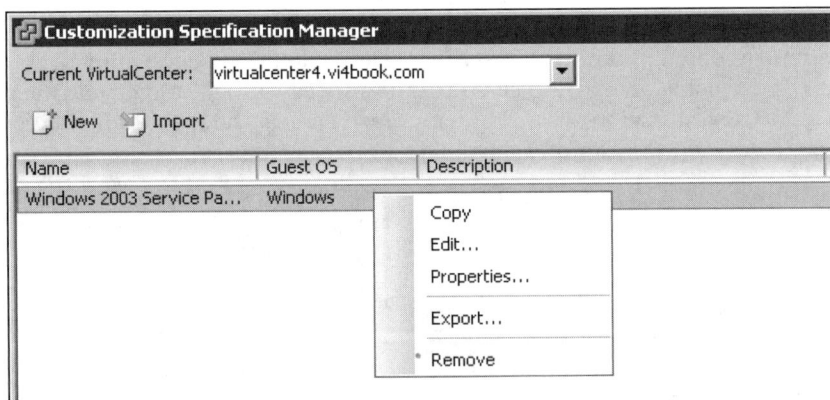

Using the VMware Open Virtual Machine Format (OVF)

The OVF format is designed to make VMs more portable. The use of OVF files is currently very closely allied to the growing virtual appliance space, allowing virtual appliance vendors to introduce additional parameters to the configuration of appliances. This reaches beyond the usual suspects of the ESX host, network, and datastore for the appliance.

NOTE *If the virtual appliance vendor does not introduce additional parameters in the import wizard, then generally the virtual appliance will have some kind of "run once" shell that walks you through the configuration of the appliance to set such items as IP settings and host names.*

You can import virtual appliances from many locations, such as the VMware Virtual Appliance Marketplace, a hard drive or DVD, or a Web site. You can export (create) OVF files from existing VMs, but care must be taken with respect to licensing, both of the guest OS and applications within it. Additionally, if the source VM is one that you have created, you may wish to reset values that are specific to your environment and clean up components that are not needed by the recipient.

Importing a Virtual Appliance

Previous chapters have included examples of downloading and installing virtual appliances. Here, I will review importing a virtual appliance that is in OVF format, and also one that is in a zip file.

Importing a Virtual Appliance in OVF Format

As an example, I will walk you through importing a virtual appliance that runs old DOS-style games, available from the VMware Virtual Appliance Marketplace. I've selected it because it take just a short time to download.

1. In the vCenter File menu, choose Browse VA Marketplace.
2. Select Nostalgia.

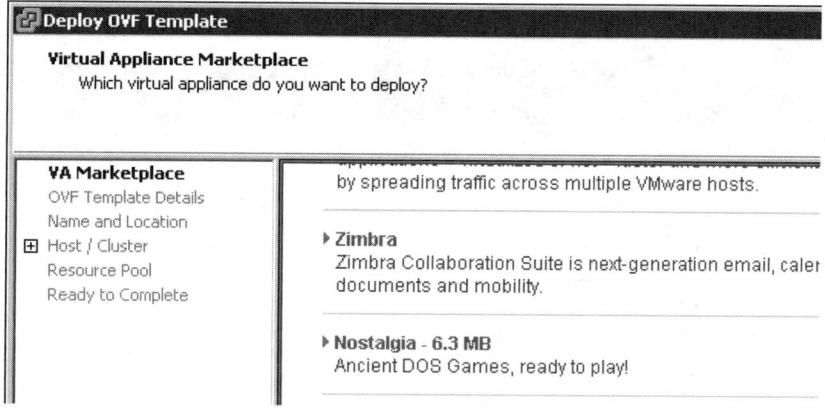

3. Read the summary, and then click Next.
4. Select a location in the vCenter Inventory for the appliance.

5. Select an ESX host or cluster on which to run the virtual appliance.

6. Select a datastore to hold the virtual appliance.

7. Select a port group on a vSwitch for the virtual appliance

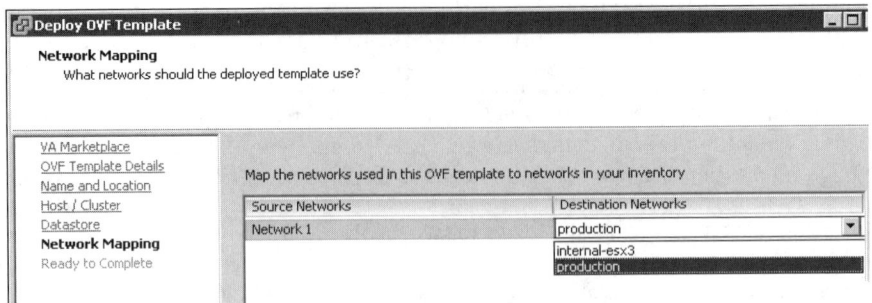

8. Click Finish. You will see a download progress bar.

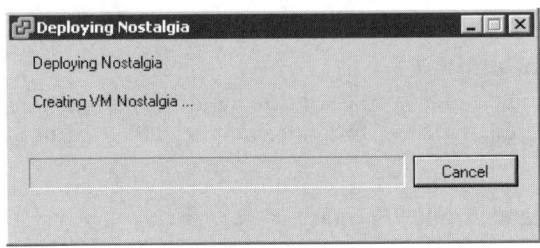

NOTE *VMware Tools has not been installed to Nostalgia, and please do not contact me for instructions on the keystrokes or the best strategy to win the flight simulator game!*

Currently, the Nostalgia virtual appliance exhibits an EMM386.EXE error message. Now that, my friend, *is* nostalgia. As Peter De Vries said, "Nostalgia isn't what it used to be."

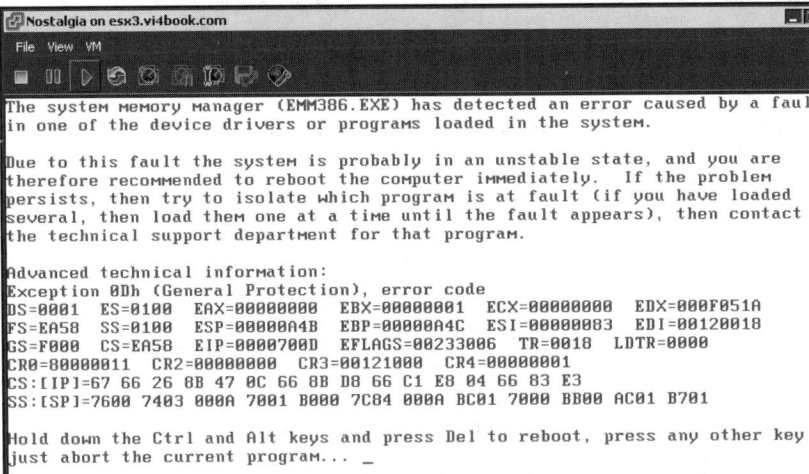

Importing a Virtual Appliance in Zip Format

You might virtual appliances available to download from a vendor's Web site. If you're lucky, simply knowing the URL of an OVF file should be enough for you to import it. However, you might find that this doesn't work because of firewall restrictions. For this reason, many vendors bundle the OVF files into zip file, which you extract and import locally. Here's an example of importing the Ultimate Deployment Appliance (UDA), which you will learn more about it in Chapter 15.

1. Download the ESX version of the UDA from http://www.rtfm-ed.co.uk/downloads/uda20-beta-ovf.zip to you management PC.

2. Right-click and extract the uda20-beta-ovf.zip file.

3. In the vCenter File menu, select Deploy OVF Template.

4. Select Deploy from File and use the Browse button to locate the OVF file.

5. Click Next to accept the description.

6. Set the UDA VM name and location in the Inventory.

7. Select a datastore location.

8. Select a network port group.

Exporting a VM in OVF Format

It is also possible to power off one of your VMs in the vCenter Inventory and export it to an external source. This can be to the local disk of the vCenter server or network resource. The file is exported in the 2gbsparse format (which means just the data is exported, not the free space in the disk) together with an OVF file. Therefore, it can be used to reimport a VM from one vCenter to another or the original vCenter.

Here's the procedure for exporting a VM in OVF format:

1. In the vCenter Inventory, select the VM you wish to export.

2. In the File menu, choose Export, and then choose Export OVF Template.

3. In the Export OVF Template dialog box, type in a friendly name. Use the Browse button to select your destination. Select your optimization method. Enable the option to create a folder for the OVF template. In this example, the virtual appliance will reside on a Web site, so I chose to optimize it for Web delivery.

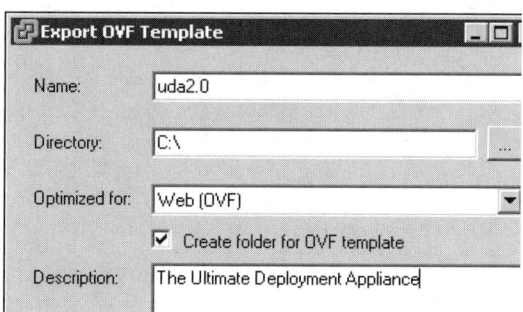

4. Click OK. You will see the progress of the export process.

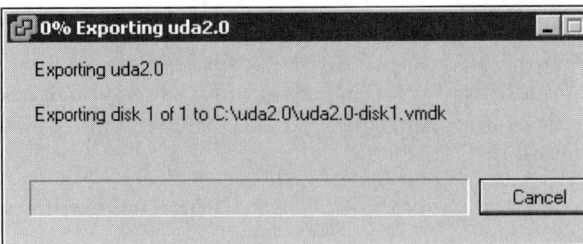

Summary

The ability to duplicate a VM has been around in VMware's technologies for some time and still remains a major time-saving feature. Leveraging the fact that the VM is actually just a file allows this duplication to take place. Using the approach, many businesses have seen their deployment times slashed from weeks to days or from days to hours. However, this ability has introduced a new term to IT: *VM sprawl*. The ease of creating a VM has led to their rapid spread. Currently, there are only two ways to stop VM sprawl: introduce paper-based change-management procedures or adopt a workflow technology like VMware vCenter Orchestrator and Lifecycle Manager to properly track, trace, and automate the whole process.

CHAPTER 9 | Access Control

You're probably quite familiar with the principles of allowing privileges from other systems you manage. If you are preparing for the vSphere 4 exam, you might want to spend some time making sure you completely understand the different roles used to assign privileges. (I remember being tripped up by some very specific questions about what these roles could and could not do when I took the VI3 exam back in 2006.)

This chapter discusses the configuration of ESX and vCenter for user rights. It is not unusual in large datacenters to have tiers of responsibility. Just as with ordinary users, we cannot depend on the good will of members of the IT department to stick within their job function. The only way to enforce change control is with tools that allow delegation.

Whether you use ESX in a stand-alone mode or with vCenter, the model for security is the same, with the only difference being where the users and groups come from. With ESX in a stand-alone mode, users and groups are created locally to the ESX host. If you use vCenter, your users and groups can be located in Active Directory or Windows NT 4 domains, or users can be local to the vCenter server.

What's New with VMware Access Control?

- Additional roles of Datastore Consumer and Network Consumer

- The ability to set rights to folders of datastores (perhaps useful for limiting users to datastores that are shared and replicated elsewhere, preventing ordinary users from accessing storage that does not belong to them or that is local to the ESX host)

The VMware Security Model

The VMware model of security involves three components. If you are a fan of the AGLP acronym (Accounts are put into Global groups that are allocated to Local groups to which you assign Permissions), you can think of VMware's model as GRP: users or Groups are added to Roles, which are assigned Privileges. In fact, it's not possible in the GUI to assign privileges to users or groups without first assigning a role.

NOTE *In the past, there were some issues in vCenter with using Microsoft groups. In early versions of vCenter, the administrator had to stick rigidly to the AGLP model, and other group strategies did not work. This issue has been addressed in recent vCenter versions, and you can use any model for group membership supported by Microsoft.*

As vCenter has an organization of system of folders, datacenter objects, and subfolders, a system of inheritance does exist—if you set a role on a folder, it will pass your privileges down the folder hierarchy. It is possible to stop this inheritance further down the hierarchy if you wish. Of course, this system is not intended to be as sophisticated as a file system's permissions system, but it is generally fit for its purpose. As with other permissions systems, a user's position in the IT management hierarchy has nothing to do with the access-control hierarchy. So you might give a nontechnical senior manager read-only rights at the top of the tree, and give a server engineer administrator rights in a datacenter.

The vSphere Client does a very good job of hiding and disabling features for which the user has no privileges. In the Inventory, depending on your privileges, objects may be hidden, ESX host names may not be displayed, right-click menu options may be dimmed, and buttons on toolbars may be disabled.

Assigning and Using Roles

In total, there are 11 predefined roles. Three of these are available to a stand-alone ESX host and vCenter; the remaining eight roles are available only to vCenter. You are not required to use these predefined roles. You can create your own custom roles with the privileges you specify.

The following are the predefined roles. The first three (No Access, Read-only, and Administrator) are common to both ESX and vCenter.

- **No Access**   This role is usually used for exceptions to the rule. For example, say you have a group called SanFran, which contains 100 users, but 3 of those users should not have access to the resource in question. Rather than creating another group with 97 users, you add in the group, and then add in the users who should not have access, choosing the No Access role for them. The effective permission for those three users, despite their group membership, would be No Access.

- **Read-Only**   As you would expect, this role provides only the ability to view items; no changes may be made.

- **Administrator**   This account has the highest privilege of all users. By default, the built-in local group of Administrators is used with this role. This may not always be desirable, as a full administrator in Windows may not necessarily be a full administrator in VMware vCenter. However, there must be a default to allow access. It is not possible to remove the last full administrator.

- **Virtual Machine User**   This role assigns a privilege only to VMs. Used on a datacenter with inheritance, it allows the user to power on and off, reset, and suspend a VM. It also allows the user to open a Remote Console window on a VM. Frequently, Windows or Linux operators are given this role, unless a more appropriate method can be used to deliver them to their environment. For example, it may be more viable to allow telnet SSH access to Linux operators and RDP access to Windows operators.

- **Virtual Machine Power User**   This type of user has the ability to change some (but not all) of a VM's settings. The role allows access to some advanced VM options, such as creating and reverting to snapshots.

- **Resource Pool Administrator**   We have yet to cover resource pools (they are discussed in Chapter 11). Put simply, it is possible to create pools of CPU and RAM and allocate groups of VMs to the pools. This offers a quick and easy way to assign resources at a group level, rather than modifying the settings of each and every VM. The Resource Pool Administrator role allows you to delegate management responsibility for the pool. Given the highly specific nature of this role, it is usually assigned to the resource pool object itself, rather than elsewhere in the Inventory.

- **Datacenter Administrator**   This role allows the user to create new datacenter objects. However, the user has very limited rights to interact with the VM. Specifically, the datacenter role has no privileges to create Remote Console sessions. So, the main teaching point here is that just because a built-in role has a fancy name, that does not mean the users with this role have rights to anything they wish.

TIP   See the roles as being a bit like job titles in organizations. A big, fancy job title doesn't always mean the actual position has a lot of authority or privileges.

- **Virtual Machine Administrator**   This role allows full control over a VM's properties, right down to the permission to delete VMs from the ESX host and vCenter. Depending on where in the hierarchy this role is set, it is possible for this role to add and remove ESX hosts from vCenter. So, this demonstrates how the label on a role may not actually reflect the role's privileges. Although the label would suggest that this role allows only administrative rights over VMs, it actually does include a whole series of other privileges.
- **VMware Consolidated Backup User**   This role was added to VI3.5 to facilitate the setting of permissions for VMware Consolidated Backup users. The rights granted to this role are just enough to allow Consolidated Backup to function. When you use Consolidated Backup, it needs user rights in vCenter to locate the VM to be backed up, make a snapshot of it, and then handle some small file functions that are required to export the VMs files to another destination.
- **Datastore Consumer**   This is a brand-new sample role in vCenter. It has only one privilege: the ability to allocate space to a datastore.
- **Network Consumer**   Another brand-new sample role, this also has only one privilege: "Assign network to a Virtual Machine, Host Service Console, VMkernel Virtual NIC or Physical," under the network privilege.

For details on the privileges that make up a specific role, consult the VMware technical documentation.

Now that you know which roles are provided, it is time to see how to configure them. Of course, the possible permutations of privileges are infinite, so I cannot show all of them, but I will give you a feel for assigning and using roles within vCenter and ESX.

To carry out the next series of tasks, you will need a collection of test users and some groups. For these examples, I created a Windows global group called Active Directory VM Users and added four user accounts: Mike, Carmel, Nathan, and Meg.

Assigning a Predefined Role

In this demonstration, I decide to allow AD VM Users access to the AD folder of the SanFran datacenter.

1. Right-click a VM folder in vCenter where you wish to apply permissions and choose Add Permission.

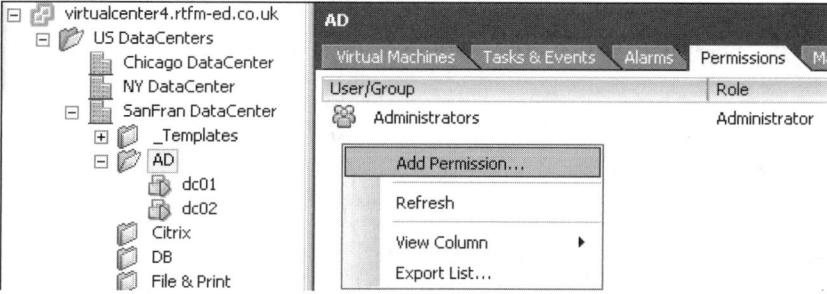

2. Under Users and Groups, click the Add button.

3. Browse your system for your user group and click OK.

4. Under Assigned Role, select the role (Virtual Machine User in this example). Optionally, you can disable the Propagate to Child Objects option, and the privileges will be applied to this folder only, and not to subfolders.

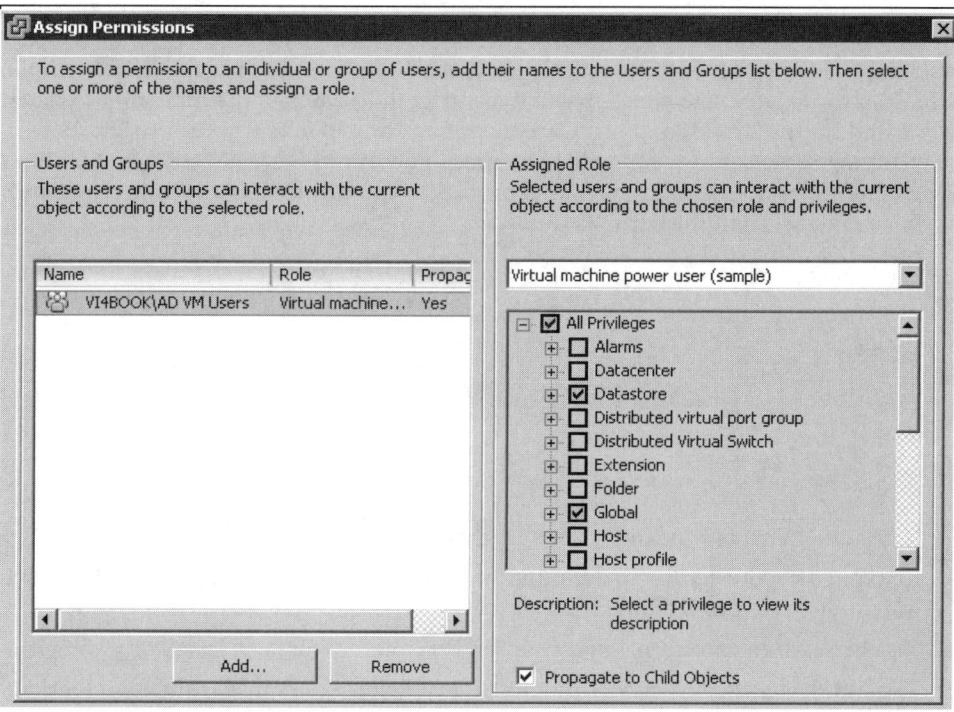

After you've assigned permissions, aside from clicking each and every folder to see if there are permissions set on them, you can also see the permissions from the Roles view in the Administration tab.

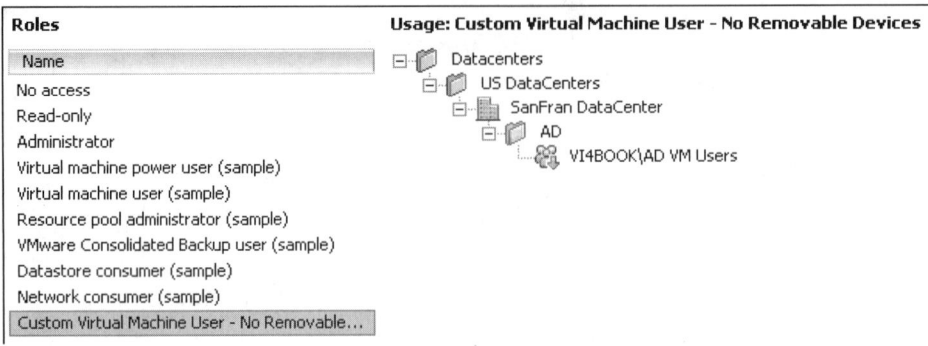

Creating Custom Roles

The built-in roles are samples that you can easily modify to suit your needs. For example, the Virtual Machine User role allows users to connect the VMs to removable devices such as CD-ROMs and floppy drives, and modify connections to vSwitch port groups. In some cases, modifying these settings can cause warnings and errors with VMotion and DRS, so it would be better if the role did not have this privilege. You can easily duplicate a role and remove this privilege from the copy, as follows:

1. Click the Home icon. On the Administration tab, select the Roles icon.

2. Right-click Virtual Machine User and choose Clone.

3. Rename the clone to give it a unique and meaningful name, such as **Custom Virtual Machine User - No Removable Devices**.

4. Right-click the custom role and choose Edit Role.

5. Expand the categories, navigating to All Privileges, Virtual Machine, Interaction.

6. Remove the check next to Device Connection. This disallows access to CD-ROM, floppy, and network device reconfiguration. If you merely wished to disallow CD-ROM and floppy reconfiguration, there are separate options for those privileges.

7. Return to your original folder where the built-in role was set, and select the Permissions tab.

8. Double-click the group you assigned the original role, and select custom role (Custom Virtual Machine User - No Removable Devices in this example).

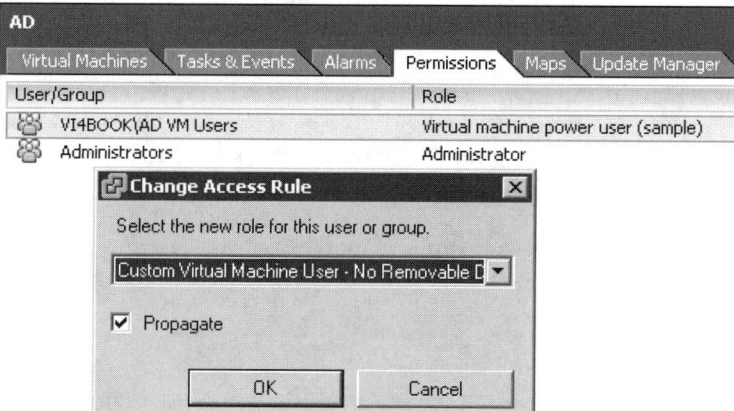

Changes in privileges like this take effect immediately, without the user being required to log out and log in again.

Removing Custom Roles

Removing a custom role is very easy. If you do it without first assigning a replacement role to a user or group, vCenter will ask you to allocate another role first. This happens only if the role you are removing is currently in use in the vCenter Inventory. This is done to ensure that you don't deny your users their rights altogether, effectively crashing them out of the vSphere Client.

To remove a custom role, follow these steps:

1. Click the Home icon. On the Administration tab, click the Roles icon.

2. Right-click custom role from the list and choose Remove.

3. Click OK to confirm you wish to delete the role.

4. In the Delete Role dialog box, select "Reassign affected users to" and choose an appropriate role.

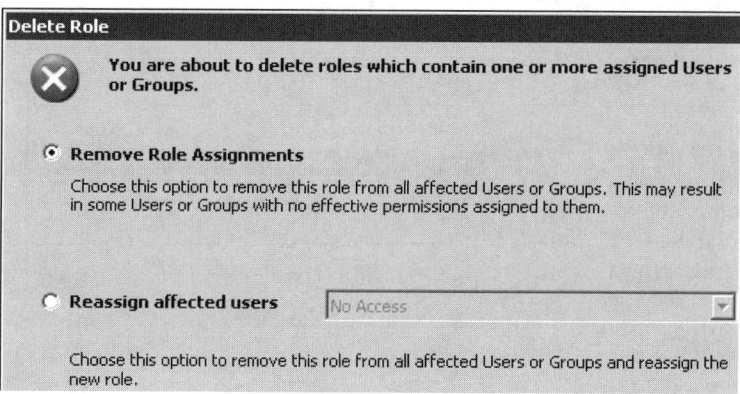

Permission Anomalies

There are two main permission behaviors you could regard as unexpected in the vCenter product. Firstly, as an administrator it is possible to deny yourself rights to an object such as a folder. If you do this the folder disappears immediately, and since you cannot select the object there is no method available to add yourself back into the access control list. The only resolution to this error is to log in as a user with privileges to the object, and reassign the rights. To some degree this entirely logical, but on a practical level it feels wrong. Secondly, is the way privileges accrue using groups. You would think that if you were member of two groups—one with read-only and the other with administrative rights on an object—that you would be the administrator of the folder. Wrong! In the world of VMware when your privileges are assigned by multiple group membership, then you get the most restrictive privilege. In the case above you would get read-only rights.

Managing User Access

When users log in with the vSphere Client, their view is restricted to the permissions you have assigned to them. In the previous example, the AD VM Users were restricted to accessing only the VMs in the AD folder in the SanFran datacenter. Also, because the privilege of Device Connection was removed, the networking options are dimmed.

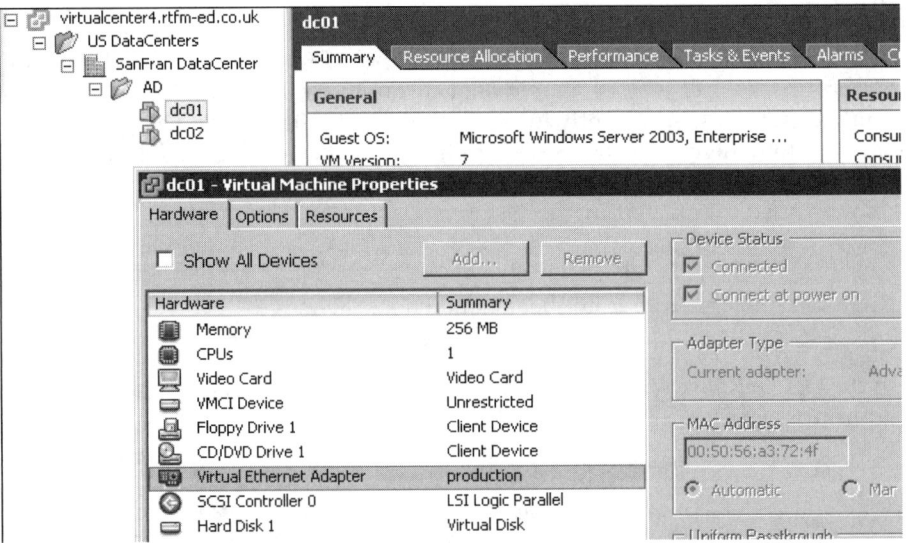

If a user has previously logged in to a vCenter environment that is set up for linked mode, the client may return the following error, which occurs because the client lacks privileges in the other vCenter environment.

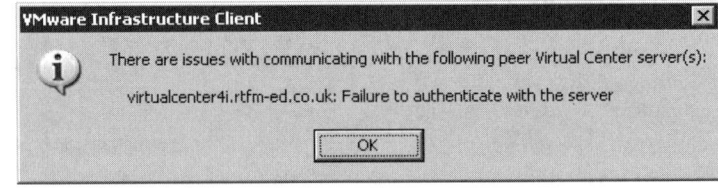

Sending Messages to Users and Disconnecting Users

You can send a "Message of the day" to users, and also disconnect users if you wish. These options are available in the Roles view (click the Roles icon on the Administration tab).

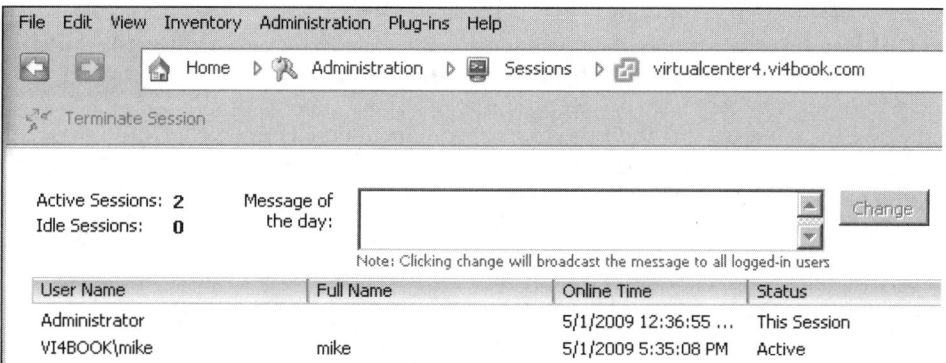

This view shows the existing sessions. To disconnect a user, select that user's session and click Terminate Session. To send a message to currently connected users, enter it in the message text box, and then click the Change button.

Using the Web Access Service

Given the restrictive nature of permissions, is there any point in giving VM users access to the full vSphere Client? It's true that this can become just another piece of client-side software to be maintained. And as long as users can use Microsoft RDP or SSH to access their VM, do they even need privileges inside vCenter? Maybe not, but do keep in mind that some organizations forbid the use of Microsoft RDP in their environments, as they consider it a security risk. One way round this impasse is to use vCenter permissions together with a Web Access service that facilitates VM management.

The Web Access service runs on the ESX host and the vCenter server. This is used to present an operator-style user interface that allows operators to manage their VMs. The beauty of this service is that operators can manage only VMs and nothing else, and it avoids the need to install the vCenter Client on every operator's PC. Web Access requires no setup routine at all. All that is needed is a web browser and the URL of the vCenter or ESX hosts. If you point your web browser at the vCenter system, you will need to supply a Windows user account to log in. If you point your web browser at the ESX host, it will need local users created on it for the service to work.

The Web Access service has a number of neat features. One is that it gives the operator a console view of the VM and also provides a full-screen view. Also, the operator can copy a URL that points directly to the VM and paste this into an email message or a shortcut.

To use this web service, open a Web browser to your vCenter server (in my case, the address is https://vCenter.vi4book.com/ui). Both the ESX and vCenter Web Access services generate a certificate using OpenSSL during the installation. The performance of the Web service can be improved by either installing the built-in certificate to your Web browser or creating a trusted certificate using your own Certificate Authority.

With Internet Explorer 7, you will need to allow pop-ups to this Web site. Additionally, if you want to see a console window on a VM, the VMware Remote Console plug-in needs to be installed.

Log in with your vCenter username. I recommend testing this with a user account you have set up with limited permissions, as it is more realistic.

The standard layout of the Web Access service interface when managing a VM includes toolbar options to power on, power off, suspend, and restart a VM. In many ways, it has the look and feel of the vSphere Client, except in a web page.

Additionally, you have the ability to manage devices such as the NIC, CD-ROM, and floppy drive. The Console tab gives you a view of your VM. This requires the installation of an ActiveX control in Internet Explorer to work. Enabling the console view also enables the dimmed icon between the Restart button and the NIC icon. This icon allows you to take the console view into a full-screen view (press CTRL+ALT to return to a normal view).

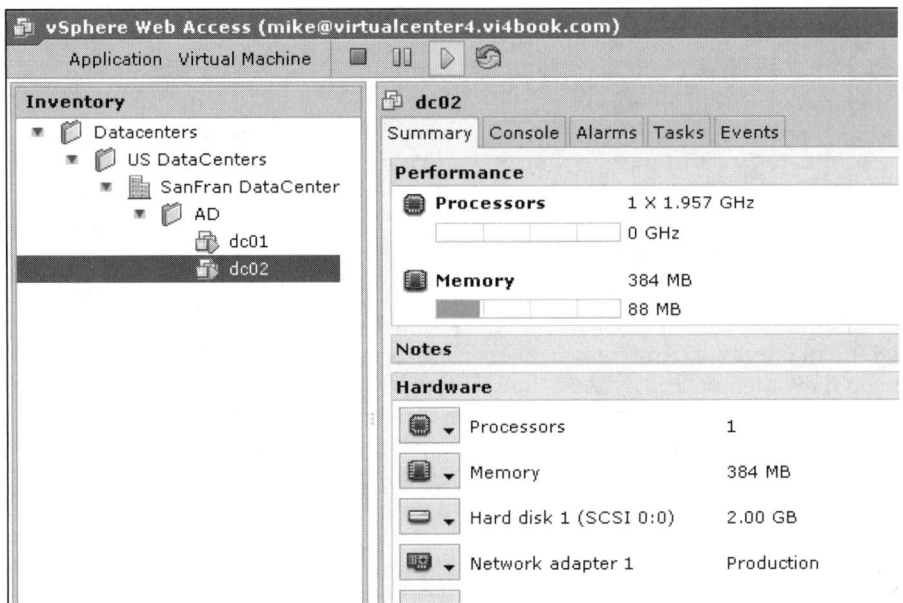

To generate a URL for a particular VM to be sent to a user by email, in the Commands pane, select Generate Virtual Machine Shortcut.

Highlight the text in the dialog box (as in the following example) and paste it into an email message.

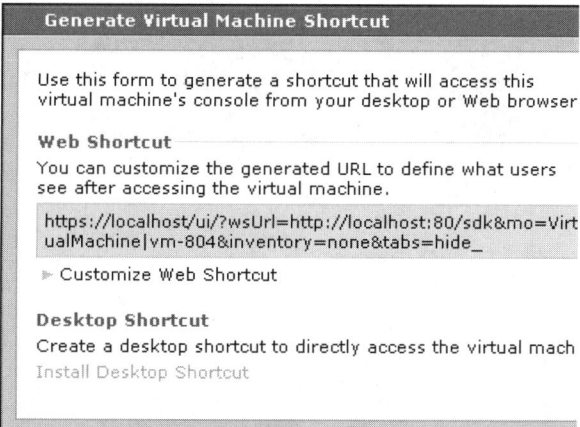

An Access Control Example: Create VMs and Restrict Storage Access

As a more interesting assignment of permissions, I will demonstrate how I allow my users to create VMs. I let these users create new VMs, but not have access to local storage. The main reason for this is that local storage is not a valid format for VMotion or any of the VMware clustering features. Additionally, if you are using array-based replication, these local storage locations are not part of any replication strategy.

Assigning a Custom Read-Only Rights Role to vCenter

To create a VM, you need to be able to do the following:

- Assign the VM a name.
- Allocate it to a datacenter and folder.
- Allocate it to an ESX host or cluster.
- Select a storage location.

At the very least, you need read-only rights to browse the environment. I generally set this privilege at the "root" of the vCenter environment. If you wish your VM Administrator to have access to the Guest Customization wizard (described in Chapter 8), then you may need to assign higher privileges or create a custom role to enable this option.

Here is the procedure for creating the custom read-only role:

1. From the Roles view, select the Read-Only role, and then click the Clone Role button.
2. Rename the new role to something meaningful, such as **Read-Only – With Guest Customization**.
3. Right-click and choose Edit Role.

4. In the Edit Role dialog box, expand Virtual Machine and Provisioning.

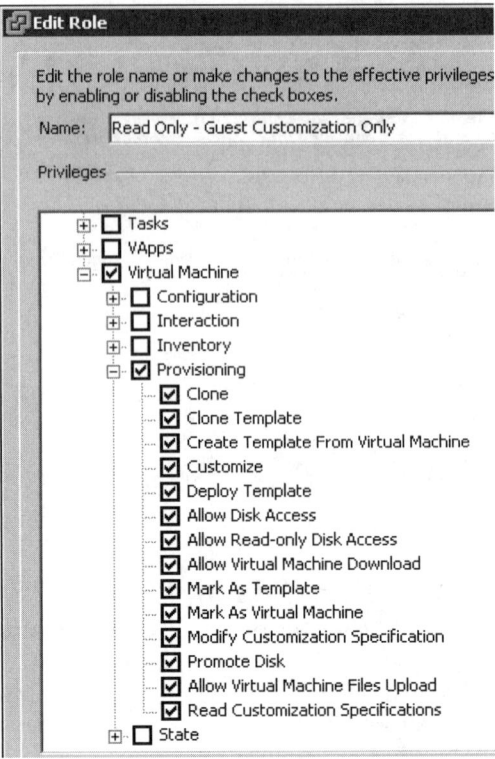

5. Select the name of your vCenter (virtualcenter4.vi4book.com in this example).

6. Select the Permission tab.

7. Right-click and choose Add Permission.

8. Click the Add button to add your user group.

9. Assign the custom role you created (Read-Only – Guest Customization Only in this example).

Assigning the Virtual Machine Administrator Role to the Datacenter

Follow these steps to assign the Virtual Machine Administrator role to the datacenter:

1. Select the name of your datacenter (SanFran Datacenter in this example).

2. Select the Permission tab. You should see that the Read-Only – Guest Customization Only role has been inherited.

3. Double-click this role and change it to Virtual Machine Administrator.

4. Click OK to confirm that you want to change the permission at this location.

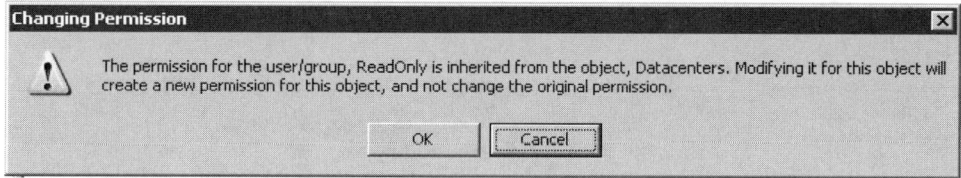

Reorganizing Datastores in Folders

In order to effectively set permissions in vCenter, its best to create folders and then drop the right datastore in the right folder.

To create folders, click the Home button, and on the Inventory tab, choose the Datastores icon.

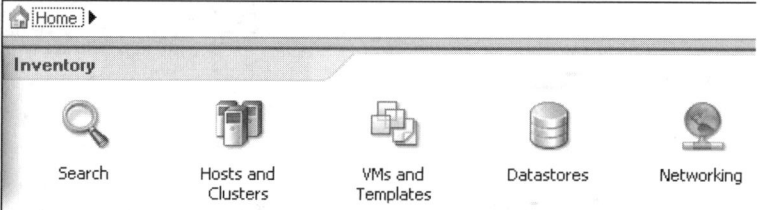

Right-click the datacenter, create a new folder, and then drag-and-drop datastores to the folder. In this example, I created Local Storage and Shared Storage folders.

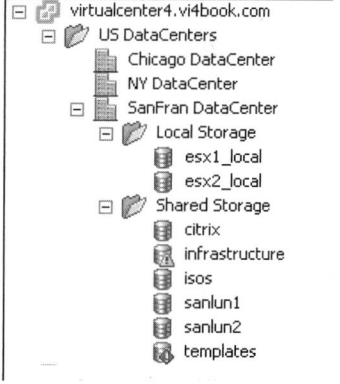

Denying Rights to the Folder Containing Local VMFS Volumes

By default, because you have set Virtual Machine Administrator on the properties of the datacenter, this privilege is also inherited down through the hierarchical structure of vCenter. In order to block access to the Local Storage folder, you need to use the No Access role.

To make the new assignment, select the Local Storage folder. Then double-click the inherited permission and select No Access. Finally, click OK to confirm the change.

Although this hides the local storage in the main datastore view, it doesn't suppress it in the process of creating a VM. However, if the VM administrators tried to select it, they would receive an access denied message.

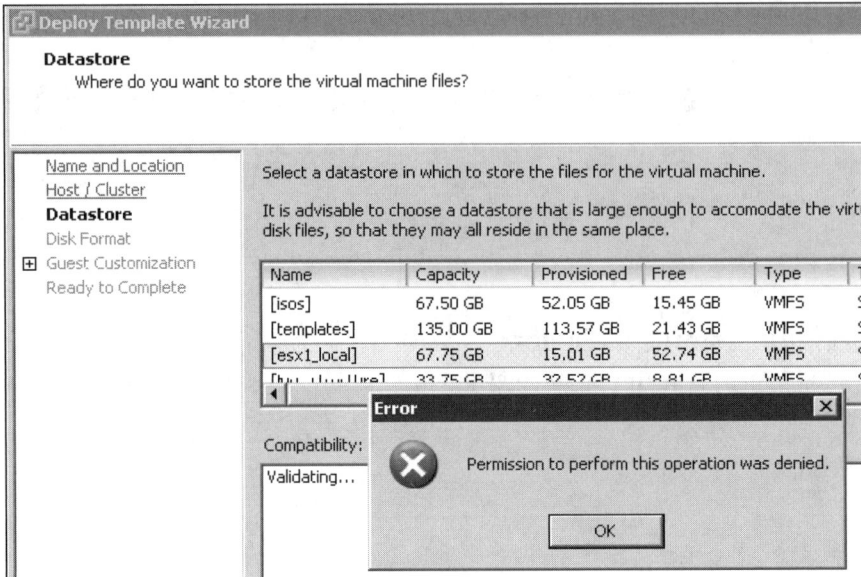

Summary

This chapter showed how it easy it is to delegate responsibility to others within your group or team. Also, you saw that the Web Access service is useful if your team needs only operator-style access to VMs. It also lets you avoid needing to install the vSphere Client on a lot of PCs.

CHAPTER 10 | Resource Monitoring

Identifying performance bottlenecks can be tricky in a virtualization environment. After all, we have many VMs, all executing on the same underlying hardware. How do you identify which VMs are the cause of poor performance and which are not? Some people choose to move VMs to an isolated ESX host and do their performance analysis there. This way, you can see if that particular VM is the source of the problem or the problem is its relationship to others. If a VM is still performing badly when it has access to all the resources of an ESX host, this might indicate the problem is within the guest OS layer, rather than at the virtualization layer.

The key to fixing performance problems in any environment is appreciating what tools are available to collect performance information. The only reliable, guaranteed method of monitoring performance is using VMware or third-party tools that collect performance information outside the VM. This will allow you to identify the constraining resource. Invariably, this will be one of the four core resources: CPU, memory, network, or disk.

It's important to be familiar with how to monitor the resources of VMs before embarking on making changes. If you don't know the source of your performance problems, how do you know what to change? And, critically, how can you verify that your changes have resolved your problem?

What's New in Resource Monitoring?

- VMware performance counters added to Performance Monitor
- Massive increase in the number of alarms
- Better condition statements for alarms, such as being able to state how long a condition must be true before the alarm is triggered, together with the ability to specify multiple conditions in single alarm, and set whether these form an AND or OR statement
- A frequency option for alarm actions to control, for example, whether you receive email only once or repeatedly
- An acknowledgment option for alarms to confirm they have been seen or dealt with
- The return of a vmkusage-style performance charts (last seen in ESX 2.x)
- Coming soon, VMware vCenter AppSpeed, a virtual appliance that assists in monitoring performance

---

Introduction to VM Resource Monitoring

Many administrators make two common mistakes when evaluating performance in VMware: using the guest OS's performance analysis tools and assuming that poor performance is caused by the VM itself.

Administrators tend to use performance analysis tools such as Microsoft's Task Manager or Linux commands like `vmstat` and `top`. Unfortunately, these tools have been designed for the guest OS when it runs directly on physical hardware, not on virtual hardware. In the world of virtualization, these tools may have limited usage. I still use Task Manager to identify crashed applications and use the End Task button to kill processes, but I don't use Task Manager's graphic chart to see the percentage utilization for the virtual CPU, because this is not a true reflection of the resources granted to it. After all, Microsoft does not allocate these resources—that's the job of the VMware ESX kernel.

Additionally, all performance analysis is time-critical, including statistics such as page swaps per second and CPU cycles per second. The problem is that the VM does not see the CPU's physical clock, so averages and such can be skewed.

It is possible to run performance tools inside the VM if they have been written with the VMware vSphere Guest SDK. Two examples are Richard Garsthagen's VM PerfMon and VM Time utilities, available for free from http://www.run-virtual.com/.

New to vSphere 4 is the introduction of VMware VM performance counters in Microsoft's Performance Monitor utility. Two performance objects are added to a VM after installing VMware Tools: VM Memory and VM Process. Within each object type, you can add a number of counters to the Performance Monitor chart.

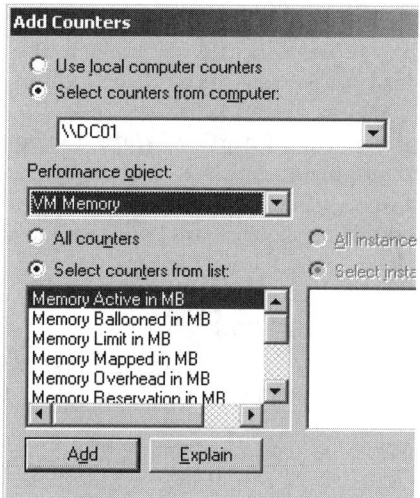

The other typical mistake made by many administrators is to assume that poor performance is caused by the VM itself. However, a slow network response, for example, could be caused by configuration settings in the guest OS, perhaps bad DNS server search orders, or poor settings in application software. All the tips and tricks you have learned to improve performance in the guest OS, such as disabling unneeded services, still apply inside a VM.

On its own, virtualization does not inherently improve performance or the reliability of your guest OS, unless your VM is running on significantly better hardware than the previous existing physical systems. In fact, contrary to popular opinion, VMs quite frequently outperform physical machines for this very reason.

User Experience as a Measure of Performance

There is another way of measuring performance, and it's called "user experience." How fast or slow does a given system "feel," and can you judge that against an agreed sense of acceptable usage? For example, what is an acceptable login time for a desktop PC connecting to a domain controller running in a VM? Is it 10 seconds, 30 seconds, 1 minute, or 1 hour? Appealing as this approach might be to a modern IT department wedded to the concept of being user-focused, it has some big problems. As the login example demonstrates, it is a highly qualitative approach and extremely subjective. Also, user expectations are constantly rising—what is fast today is regarded as slow three months later.

There is also the element of human perception to take into account. A student once told me how his company upgraded all the end users' monitors in the building over a weekend. When the users came back on the Monday, they were absolutely adamant that the overall system was faster, despite the fact that the only thing that had changed was screens.

If you accept user experience as the only measure of performance, you are wasting your money on memory, CPU, and upgrades of the network. You might as well go out and buy some pretty new monitors instead!

VM Resource Allocation

Before we look at the tools for monitoring performance, you need to understand how the VMkernel allocates resources to the VMs. We're concerned with the four core resources: CPUs, memory, network, and disk.

Network and disk resources were covered earlier in this book. In Chapter 4, I discussed the merits of traffic shaping for networking. In Chapter 6, I showed how correctly configuring the SAN or iSCSI for multipathing and selecting the correct RAID level can greatly affect performance. Here, I will focus on CPU and memory resources, but I will cover the metrics and counters that can be used to diagnose bottlenecks in networking and disks later in this chapter.

CPU Allocation

Some issues involved in CPU resource allocation are VMkernel load balancing and scheduling, the number of virtual CPUs in VMs, hyperthreading, and the use of Virtual SMP.

VMkernel Load Balancing and Scheduling

When VMs run, they execute their instructions on the physical CPUs of the ESX host. Within the ESX server, the VMkernel is configured to monitor the load on the CPUs, looking for a CPU that is doing less work than others. If the VMkernel spots a significant disparity in the load on one physical CPU compared to another, it will schedule that VM's threads to execute on a less busy CPU. This monitoring is configured at intervals of every 20 milliseconds and places a burden on the VMkernel. However, the performance gained by carrying out this analysis more than offsets the burden. The value of 20 milliseconds is configurable, and you may decide to make it less frequent if you feel your CPU load across an ESX host is relatively uniform. So if you don't experience large fluctuations in CPU activity, you can change the frequency.

The scheduler is designed to distribute CPU requests intelligently within the ESX host and reduce contention as much as possible. *Contention* is the term we use to describe a scenario where resources are scarce and two or more VMs "fight over" the resource, such as a CPU.

Single vCPUs vs. Multiple vCPUs

A single-vCPU VM executes its threads on a single physical socket or core at any one time. In contrast, a dual- or quad-vCPU VM executes its instructions on more than one physical socket or core.

Many OS vendors are geared up for CPU upgrades, but often have limited support for CPU downgrades. It's perhaps best to begin with one vCPU inside a VM and upgrade as needed, rather than making every VM have multiple CPUs when it might not benefit from them. Remember that for Virtual SMP to really pay dividends, you need the underlying physical hardware resources (as discussed shortly). You should also have in the back of your mind that VMware FT currently supports only VMs with just one vCPU. The decision to give every VM multiple vCPUs would block any opportunity to leverage VMware FT.

Also, the more CPUs you allocate to the VM, the harder it is for DRS to find an opportunity to perform a VMotion migration to move the VM to a better ESX host. The term that is sometimes used is having plenty of "hardware execution contexts," or put another way, plenty of sockets or cores to run a dual or quad vCPU. Sometimes VMware use the term *slots* to describe this. The fewer slots an ESX host or DRS cluster has, the fewer VMotion events can take place.

Hyperthreading

If you are using hyperthreading on Intel Xeon processors, the VMkernel treats each logical CPU in the Xeon chipset as if it were a physical processor. So a two-socket processor with hyperthreading enabled would actually appear as if it had four physical processors. When it comes to dual-vCPU or quad-vCPU VMs, the VMkernel scheduler always makes sure it runs the VM on two different logical processors in two different sockets.

There are some cases where hyperthreading actually degrades CPU performance, especially when CPU utilization is high. You might have already experienced this with resource-intensive products such as Oracle, Microsoft SQL Server, and Microsoft Exchange. I have seen this personally in the terminal service environments with Citrix Presentation Servers.

For the most part, hyperthreading is a good feature to enable, but watch out for some high-end and processor-intensive threads that would prefer to use the whole physical socket, rather than just a logical processor within it.

The new Intel processors have been overhauled with new version of hyperthreading on version 3, and there are intriguing reports of improvements in performance of anywhere from 5% to 30%. However, as ever, the improvements depend on the workloads on the ESX hosts.

As general rule of thumb, very CPU-intensive VMs will not like hyperthreading, but non-CPU-intensive VMs might receive a performance boost.

Here's a good analogy for hyperthreading. Imagine you have a narrow country lane that you would like to enable for two-way traffic. Rather than widening the road, you draw a line down the center of the road. This is what happens with hyperthreading. The CPU package is able to take bidirectional communications. However, the actual width of the communication channel has not widened. So although you might get two small cars (small CPU transactions) up and down this road, if a large vehicle (a single large CPU transaction) comes along, it will need to use both lanes anyway.

It is possible to have some per-VM controls on how a VM executes on a processor with hyperthreading available. These settings are available on the Resources tab of the Virtual Machine Properties dialog box (right-click a VM and choose Edit Settings to open this dialog box). Under Advanced CPU, three Mode options are available:

- **Any**   More than one VM can execute on the logical CPU.

- **None**   VM receives all of the CPU not shared with other VMs.

- **Internal**   VMs with two vCPUs gets exclusive access to a CPU and its logical CPUs. This setting does not affect VMs with four vCPUs.

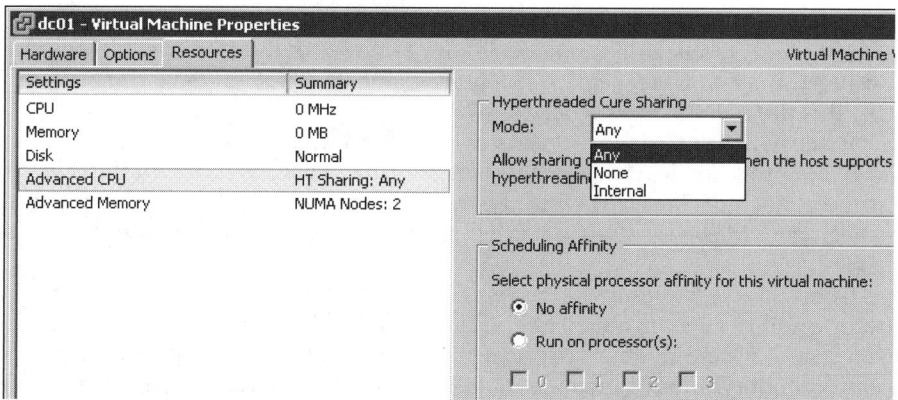

Virtual SMP

To get the benefit of Virtual SMP, you need plenty of cores or sockets. There is little point in creating a dual-vCPU VM if you have only two sockets or two cores. All this will do is give the VMkernel's scheduler more work to do and increase the chances of two VMs competing for a resource.

Very simply, the more sockets or cores you have, the more opportunities the VMkernel scheduler has of finding a CPU not in use or not used heavily, which will then make the VM perform better. To really leverage the value of vSMP, you need four sockets/cores for dual VMs and eight sockets/cores for quad-based VMs.

Remember that Microsoft does not officially support downgrading an instance of Windows from dual or quad to a single CPU VM. Additionally, not all applications and services are multiprocessor-aware (or multithreaded), so sometimes adding an additional vCPU could make no difference to performance at all.

Due to these issues, the decision to use vSMP should be made with care, on a case-by-case basis. One way of finding out the impact of such a change could be to clone an existing uniprocessor VM and upgrade the duplicate to be a dual or quad VM. You could then decide to delete or roll back to the old VM if your test showed the upgrade did not improve the situation (or even made it worse).

NOTE *In the future, the concern about vCPUs might become less significant. Intel has already created a multicore processor that has up to 100 cores in a single socket under its Tera-scale Computing Research Program. This CPU was created for experimental purposes only and will probably never see the production market. However, it might not be too long until each VM executes on a dedicated core of its own. Of course, by then we might want to run 50, 60, or even 100 VMs on a single ESX host.*

CPU, Guest OS Kernel Updates, and Idling

Excessive CPU activity can be caused within a VM after the P2V process. When you P2V a multiprocessor physical machine, it is possible to downgrade to a uniprocessor VM, or conversely, to upgrade a single CPU physical machine to be a multiple vCPU VM. For this to work properly, you need to carry out a kernel update.

In the world of Microsoft Windows, a kernel update means changing the ACPI Function from an ACPU Multiprocessor to an ACPI Uniprocessor within the Device Manager. Nowadays, OSs like Windows 2003, Vista, and 2008 will carry out this upgrade automatically. For older OSs from Microsoft, this is a manual process.

While upgrading is well supported, Microsoft has never really supported downgrading the Hardware Abstraction Layer (HAL). The process, whether automated or manual, replaces the HAL file (hal.dll) and the ntoskernel.exe file.

The incorrect HAL or ACPI functionality can cause a VM to make CPU demands, even when it is not handling any legitimate CPU requests. This is because without the correct HAL, the VMkernel cannot "idle" the VM correctly. In other words, the VMkernel doesn't know how to manage the VM correctly when it is in an idle or inactive state, because Windows has the wrong HAL.

Microsoft has made moves in recent releases of Windows to inhibit even the administrator's ability to change the HAL. Ostensibly, this has been done to protect novice administrators from changing the HAL, as it can cause a BSOD, which puts the OS in a state from which it cannot (without a great deal of effort and skill) be recovered. Fortunately, you can sidestep such "protection" using CLI tools freely available from Microsoft. One such excellent hardware management CLI is DevCon. You will find it as part of the Windows Driver Kit, available from the Microsoft Developer Network web site.

For example, the following DevCon script would forcibly downgrade a multiprocessor HAL Windows 2003 or Windows XP VM to use just a uniprocessor HAL. The part that does the work is `devcon update %windir%\inf\hal.inf ACPIPIC_UP`, which instructs the Windows kernel which HAL to use.

```
@echo off
cls
rem Author:    Mike Laverick
rem URL:       http://www.rtfm-ed.co.uk
echo =================================================
echo ==Downgrading ACPI to Uni-Processor==============
echo =================================================
echo.
echo Please Wait
devcon sethwid @ROOT\PCI_HAL\0000 := !E_ISA_UP !ACPIPIC_UP !ACPIAPIC_UP
!ACPIAPIC_MP !MPS_UP !MPS_MP !SGI_MPS_MP !SYSPRO_MP !SGI_MPS_MP > nul
devcon sethwid @ROOT\ACPI_HAL\0000 := !E_ISA_UP !ACPIPIC_UP !ACPIAPIC_UP
!ACPIAPIC_MP !MPS_UP !MPS_MP !SGI_MPS_MP !SYSPRO_MP !SGI_MPS_MP
devcon sethwid @ROOT\PCI_HAL\0000 := +ACPIPIC_UP
devcon sethwid @ROOT\ACPI_HAL\0000 := +ACPIPIC_UP
devcon update %windir%\inf\hal.inf ACPIPIC_UP
echo Done!
echo.
echo ===========================================
echo ==Script Completed=================================
echo ===========================================
echo.
echo ===========================================
echo ==Press any key to reboot the Virtual Machine================
echo ===========================================
pause > nul
devcon reboot
```

In the case of Windows 2000, the HAL references in the INF file are slightly different, so to downgrade the HAL would require a slightly different script, such as the following.

```
@echo off
cls
rem Author:    Mike Laverick
rem URL:       http://www.rtfm-ed.co.uk
echo =============================================
echo ==Downgrading ACPI to Uni-Processor====================
echo =============================================
echo.
echo Please Wait
devcon sethwid @ROOT\PCI_HAL\0000 := !E_ISA_UP !ACPIPIC_UP !ACPIAPIC_UP
!ACPIAPIC_MP !MPS_UP !MPS_MP !SGI_MPS_MP !SYSPRO_MP !SGI_MPS_MP
devcon sethwid @ROOT\ACPI_HAL\0000 := !E_ISA_UP !ACPIPIC_UP !ACPIAPIC_UP
!ACPIAPIC_MP !MPS_UP !MPS_MP !SGI_MPS_MP !SYSPRO_MP !SGI_MPS_MP
devcon sethwid @ROOT\PCI_HAL\0000 := +ACPIAPIC_UP
```

```
devcon sethwid @ROOT\ACPI_HAL\0000 := +ACPIAPIC_UP
devcon update %windir%\inf\hal.inf ACPIAPIC_UP
echo Done!
echo.
echo =============================================
echo ==Script Completed===========================
echo =============================================
echo.
echo =============================================
echo ==Press any key to reboot the Virtual Machine================
echo =============================================
pause > nul
devcon reboot
```

You can find copies of these scripts on my web site (http://www.rtfm-ed.co.uk/?page_id=8), under the section labeled "Sample P2V Post-Configuration Scripts for P2V and Sample ISO File."

CAUTION *Be sure you back up or take a snapshot of your VMs before running the DevCon scripts.*

Memory Allocation

Transparent page sharing, the balloon driver, and the VMkernel VM swap file affect the allocation of memory to your VMs.

Transparent Page Sharing

ESX server deploys a number of memory management techniques to boost the amount of available RAM and to dynamically manage the system should physical memory become scarce. The first and most important of these is Transparent Page Sharing (TPS), introduced in Chapter 7.

If you run more than one copy of Windows or Linux on an ESX host, the VMkernel can identify that very similar information is likely to be duplicated in memory. So in the case of two instances of Windows, there is likely to be more than one copy of files such as explorer. exe, svchost.exe, lsass.exe, spools.exe, and so on. The same scenario exists for every guest OS supported by ESX in a VM. The VMkernel spots these duplicates and produces a single read-only copy. The read-only attribute is important from a security perspective, as it prevents the possibility of one VM modifying the memory contents of another VM.

If a VM needs to modify the contents of its memory, the VMkernel seamlessly generates a read-write copy of the file and instructs the VM where to find the file in memory. This is all done without the guest OS or the VM realizing it is taking place. In other words, the sharing of pages of memory is invisible (or transparent) to the guest OS. It can be achieved because it is the VMkernel that is really in charge of the hardware, not Windows or Linux.

VMware's own research has shown that around 30% of Windows guest OS memory is duplicated between VMs when they are running on ESX. The values for the other guest OS are somewhat lower (because of Windows systemic memory hungriness), but all VMs benefit from TPS to a greater or lesser degree.

You can see how much memory is being saved through TPS on the Resource Allocation tab of a VM, which shows the amount of memory that is shared with other VMs. In the following example, you can see that 105MB has been identified as shared with other ESX hosts on the same ESX host. The longer a VM is powered on, the more pages of memory TPS will find are overlapping between the VMs.

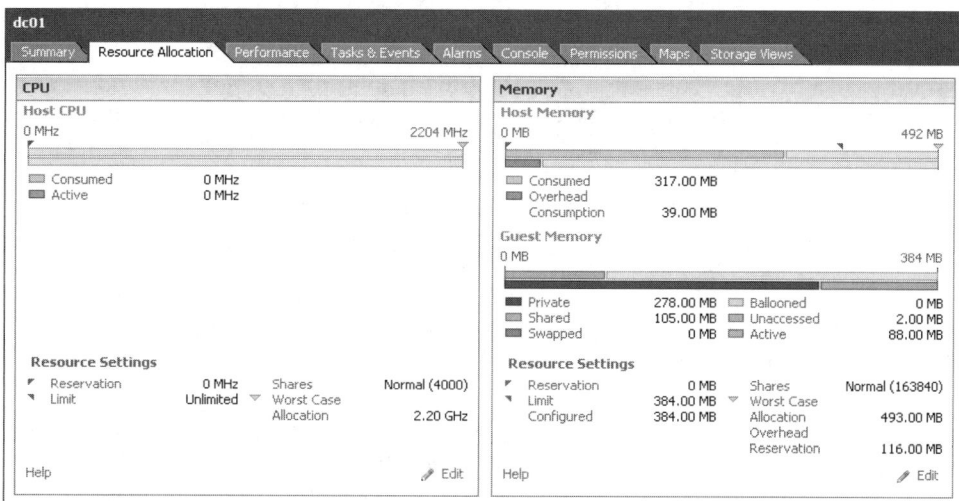

A more interesting representation of the total amount of memory saved via TPS can be viewed with the command-line utility esxtop. When you first run esxtop on the ESX host, it defaults to showing CPU statistics. However, if you type m, it will show memory statistics. In the following example, you can see there has been a 522MB saving on memory from running four VMs on the ESX host.

```
 9:34:57pm up 16 days 22:20, 127 worlds; MEM overcommit avg: 0.00, 0.00, 0.00
PMEM  /MB:  3927   total:    300    cos,    446 vmk,    1154 other,    2027 free
VMKMEM/MB:  3537 managed:    212 minfree,   657 rsvd,   2518 ursvd,   high state
COSMEM/MB:    10    free:   1600  swap_t,  1599 swap_f:   0.00 r/s,    0.00 w/s
NUMA  /MB:  1669 (  944),  1872 ( 1082)
PSHARE/MB:   535  shared,    13 common:    522 saving
SWAP  /MB:     0    curr:     0 target:                  0.00 r/s,    0.00 w/s
MEMCTL/MB:     0    curr:     0 target,    996 max
```

GID	NAME	MEMSZ	GRANT	SZTGT	TCHD	%ACTV	%ACTVS	%ACTVF	%
18	vobd.4220	19.63	1.43	19.63	1.43	0	0	0	
19	vmkiscsid.4228	7.21	1.85	7.21	1.85	0	0	0	
20	vmware-vmkauthd	5.93	2.12	5.93	2.12	0	0	0	
50	dc01	384.00	383.71	314.86	57.60	5	7	4	
51	ctx02	384.00	383.70	340.66	96.00	8	13	7	
52	file01	384.00	383.70	345.70	99.84	6	12	5	
53	web01	384.00	383.75	283.73	92.16	5	11	5	

The net result of TPS is a massive savings in the amount of RAM required to run a VM. I personally have seen savings of 1GB to 1.5GB on a server with as little as 2GB of physical RAM.

The TPS feature also helps to offset the memory wasted by actually having a virtualization layer in the first place. After all, 300MB of RAM is "lost" when the Service Console loads.

The VMkernel take up around 25MB in memory. Running one VM with one vCPU consumes 54MB of memory, with 64MB of memory consumed for a dual-vCPU VM. TPS helps offset this virtualization overhead, sometimes even canceling it out altogether.

The vmmemctl Driver

When you install VMware Tools into a VM, along with an improved network and mouse driver, a memory control driver is installed as well. Its file name is vmmemctl, but it is normally referred to by VMware as the "balloon driver," because it uses the analogy of a balloon to explain how this driver works.

The most important thing to know about vmmemctl is that it is engaged only when memory is scarce and VMs are fighting over that resource—in other words, when contention is occurring. By itself, vmmemctl doesn't fix the problem of a lack of resources or unexpected peak demands for memory. In fact, its biggest use is as an indicator that there is a memory problem, so it is useful as a counter that draws the administrator's attention to potential problems.

NOTE   *Of course, one way of reducing the chance of running out of memory is to buy more physical resources. But remember this important fact: ESX delivers the memory to the VM only as it needs it, on an on-demand basis. The whole point of virtualization is to use resources efficiently and effectively, and escape the whole "let's just throw more resources (money) at the problem" approach that got us in such a mess in the first place.*

How does the vmmemctl driver work? Well, during normal operation where memory is plentiful and VMs are not in contention, the driver does nothing. It sits there inside the VM, deflated like a saggy balloon at the end of the party. However, when memory is scarce and the VMs are fighting over the resource, the vmmemctl driver begins to inflate. In other words, it begins to make demands for pages of memory. This generally occurs in a VM that you have marked as having a low priority on the system. The guest OS obeys its internal memory management techniques, freeing up RAM by flushing old data to its virtual memory (page file or swap partition) to give the vmmemctl driver ranges of memory. Next comes the clever bit—rather than hanging on to this newly allocated memory, the vmmemctl driver hands over its memory to the VMkernel. The VMkernel in turn hands over this memory to the other VMs that really need it. When memory demands return to normal and are no longer scarce, the balloon driver deflates and gracefully hands back the memory it claimed to the guest OS.

Again, on its own, the vmmemctl driver doesn't fix the problem, which is a lack of memory. It does, on the other hand, give us a clear indicator of a potential problem. As with TPS, the Resource Allocation tab of a VM and the `esxtop` utility (set to show memory statistics) will show ballooning activity if it is occurring.

Additionally, vmmemctl allows us to configure (along with other tools covered in the next chapter) the system for worst-case scenarios by offering guaranteed levels of service to VMs that need it if memory becomes low.

The VMkernel VM Swap File

As you'll learn in the next chapter, you have several ways to handle the allocation of memory to a VM. It is possible to configure a VM to guarantee that a VM always runs in memory and never uses virtual memory. To do this, you would need quite a large amount of memory, depending on how much you allocate to a VM when you create it.

It is also possible to configure a VM for what is referred to as *memory overcommitment*. This is where you allocate more memory to VMs than is actually physically present on an ESX host. This allows for very high VM-to-ESX ratios without the need to buy more memory. The difference between what you allocate and how much physical memory you have is made up by the VMkernel VM swap file. Naturally, some anxieties surround this idea, not least the issue of performance. We all know that despite caching on SAN controllers and the increases in disk spindle speeds, memory is faster because there are no moving parts.

In the world of ESX, the VMkernel VM swap file is used only as a last resort. In other words, in order to get repeated read-write activity on the swap file, all memory must have been used on the ESX host. This is significantly different from the way guest OSs use their swap files and partitions. In Windows, it is not unusual to see page faults and swaps, even on a server with a lot of physical RAM. This is because Windows has always seen physical RAM and swap space as if they were one single block of memory. In the case of ESX, we would expect to see swap activity only in the extreme case where all RAM had been depleted.

As with the balloon driver, swap activity is a symptom rather than the cause. It is an indication that an ESX is low on memory or VMs have been poorly configured with more memory reservations than they actually need.

Identifying Resource Constraints

Now that you know how resource are allocated to VMs, let's look at how to monitor those resources. Here, I'll point out which measures are the most important to watch.

CPU Monitoring

Along with the overall amount of CPU used and the amount each VM is using, a much more revealing measure of actual VM performance is available: the ready value. The ready value means the VM is ready to execute processes and is waiting for the CPU to allocate a slice of CPU time.

It is perfectly fine for a VM to be using 99% of the CPU, as long as its ready value remains low. A high CPU usage value merely indicates a VM is processing; it doesn't necessarily mean that the VM is performing badly. It could reflect benign CPU cycles caused by an application that is inherently CPU-intensive. However, if the ready value grows, this usually indicates the VM is ready to run, but the CPU is not ready to supply the CPU time it demands.

Does VMware give any guidelines on what appropriate CPU ready values should be? Yes, it says that anything constantly over 5% should be looked at as a potential bottleneck.

Often, there is a close relationship (an inverse proportion in some case) between the percent of CPU used by a VM and the ready value. As a VM is allocated more CPU time, its ready value should go down, and as the percent of CPU time allocated value goes down, the ready value should grow. For this reason, many people say that the ready value should instead be called the wait value, as it indicates how long a VM is waiting for the CPU to respond.

If you wish to see very high CPU ready values, take two VMs doing a very CPU-intensive task and, using the processor affinity options for a VM, peg them to the same physical CPU. The Scheduling Affinity settings are available on the Resources tab of the Virtual Machine Properties dialog box, under Advanced CPU. The net effect of this would cause contention as the two VMs fought over the same resource.

CAUTION *The processor affinity settings could have a catastrophic impact on performance if configured incorrectly. CPU affinities also introduce a VMotion incompatibility, stopping the use of VMotion in its tracks. As a consequence, this means advanced clustering features such as DRS and DPM cease to function as expected, and features like VMware Update Manager that depend on DRS automation for their smooth function also cease to work as well as expected. As you will see in later chapters, reliable and effective VMotion is essential for many high-level datacenter automation tasks.*

Memory Monitoring

Memory problems in a VM could be caused by an application or guest OS mishandling its memory allocation. It's not uncommon for malign applications or services to demand an allocation of memory and not gracefully hand it back. We label such applications or services as having a *memory leak*. The source and cause of these memory problems lies not with the VM but with poorly written OSs, and more frequently, even more poorly written application code. Despite the existence of TPS and the balloon driver, it is beyond the scope of any virtualization platform to make bad code good.

As stated earlier, the ESX VMkernel prefers to use physical RAM in all cases. Only when physical RAM is scarce and VMs are fighting over access to RAM do the per-VM swap file and the balloon driver become engaged. Once you know this, you can use the vCenter performance charts or `esxtop` command-line tool to look for any persistent swap I/O and ballooning. Any swap or balloon driver activity indicates a memory problem.

Network Monitoring

Before you blame a VM or an ESX host for slow network response, it's worth asking yourself this question: Would this system be as slow if it were running on a physical host?

Frequently, the source of network bottlenecks exists in your physical network or at the slowest node of, for instance, a branch office. Additionally, networking problems could easily be the result of poor configuration of network settings within the VM. Perhaps your VM has the wrong default gateway or DNS settings, causing long round-trips or long DNS queries.

Occasionally, when I teach a course, I watch people troubleshoot networking problems. They check all the settings of the VM, but sometimes fail to use the tools they are very familiar with, such as ipconfig, ping, and so on. Network troubleshooting should begin with the basics, before we overcomplicate the process by checking the VM's settings.

It is legitimate to capture, analyze, and measure the amount of packets sent or received to a VM. A network packet sent from a VM or received from a VM is unchanged (unless traffic shaping is engaged).

There is a close relationship between network activity and physical CPU usage. This is because the load-balancing mechanism of the IP hash (covered in Chapter 4) in itself causes the VMkernel to use the physical CPU. Additionally, a lot of small TCP transactions inside a VM can cause the physical CPU to be busy, as the VMkernel works harder to move packets from the physical NICs to the virtual NICs via the vSwitch. As a consequence, increasing physical CPU availability will help increase network performance.

If network performance is poor in the VM, check the following configuration settings:

- Confirm that VMware Tools has been installed. VMware Tools replaces the driver for the virtual NIC with one that is idealized for virtual networking.

- Check that the physical NICs selected for that VM's vSwitch are 1000Mbps interfaces.
- If you are using 100Mbps, ensure that you have set the correct speed and duplex.
- Ensure that no operator has incorrectly engaged the traffic shaper module. The traffic shaper module is designed to throttle a VM that malignly wishes to hog the network pipe at the expense of other VMs.

Disk Monitoring

Generally, we use disk reads and writes to check what volume of disk activity is occurring, and disk queue lengths as an indication that storage is a bottleneck. In this case, it is reasonable to use guest OS tools to monitor disk activity—a megabyte written to a virtual disk is no different than a megabyte written to a physical disk. VMFS is such a lightweight file system that it can be disregarded as the source of a bottleneck.

Before you consider any changes to the VM's settings, confirm that you have correctly configured and optimized your storage. In Chapter 6, I discussed the importance of correctly setting multipathing. You may also wish to experiment with different RAID levels, as these can have an impact on storage performance.

Additionally, you may wish to double-check that the guest OS has been correctly configured. Perhaps the VM is running out of disk space and is thrashing the disk looking for free space. Alternatively, a lack of memory inside the VM will force it to engage its swap file, which increases disk activity.

There are two good counters to check. Firstly, "Kernel disk command latency" indicates the time on average that the VMKernel spent on each SCSI command. VMware have stated that values great than 2-3ms indicated an array or ESX host, which is saturated with excessive IOPS. Secondly, "Physical device command latency" measures the average time a physical device took to complete a SCSI command. Values in excess of 15-20ms again indicate an array which has become saturated.

Accessing Performance Data

I've mentioned various counters that can expose a bottleneck in the system. Now let's look at where you can view these values and parameters. The best way of assessing performance data generally is to use the Performance tab in the vCenter Inventory. However, there are other places where you will see more high-level information. For instance, if you select your datacenter, and select either the Virtual Machine tab or the Host tab, you will get a view of information like CPU, host memory usage, VM memory usage, and information about your ESX host's resources (such as amount of memory, number of NICs, and uptimes), as in the following examples:

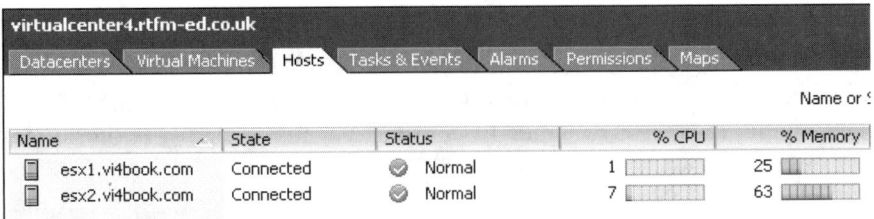

But if you really want to drill down and see performance statistics in detail, you will go to the Performance tab, as described in the next section.

Using vCenter Performance Charts

The vCenter Performance tab appears for the following object types in the Inventory:

- **DRS and HA clusters**   The default counter shows CPU usage in megahertz. DRS and HA are covered in Chapter 13 and Chapter 15, respectively.
- **ESX hosts**   The default view shows CPU statistics using four counters.
- **Resource pools**   This uses the same counter as for DRS and HA clusters. Resource pools are covered Chapter 11.
- **Individual VMs**   The fault view shows CPU statistics using three counters.

The default counters used can be customized.

All of these counters collect information every 20 seconds. This is the fastest refresh that charts can offer and is referred to, slightly confusingly, as *realtime*. This currently cannot be made any faster (and I think collecting performance stats any quicker than this rate would constitute a performance hit in its own right!).

Information can be collected over longer periods for the purpose of tracking endemic trends. The defaults allow you to view information over a day, week, month, and a year. Additionally, the custom option allows you to set your own time frame; for instance, you could use it if you collect and view performance trends on a quarterly basis.

CAUTION *All performance data is time-critical. It's absolutely imperative that time is correctly set on both the ESX host and the vCenter server. Failure to do so can result in the Performance tab not returning any information at all. The message you receive is "Performance data is currently not available for this entity."*

In Chapter 1, I showed you how to set up an NTP server to be the source of time, configured to communicate with a publicly available NTP server, and then how to configure an ESX host to be a client of your internal NTP server. If you need to correct a time-latency issue, do remember to wait to allow time for statistics to be collected.

Here, I will demonstrate how to use the vSphere charting features to monitor CPUs. You can apply the same approach to monitoring other resources, such as memory, network, and disk.

NOTE *Those of you who have been using VMware's ESX and vCenter products for some time will notice that the charts are now very much like the old vmkusage utility we used to have in ESX 2.x days.*

Viewing CPU Utilization

The best view to see overall CPU utilization is on the properties of an ESX host. The View option at the top of the Performance tab allows you to switch the view to see a summary of VMs.

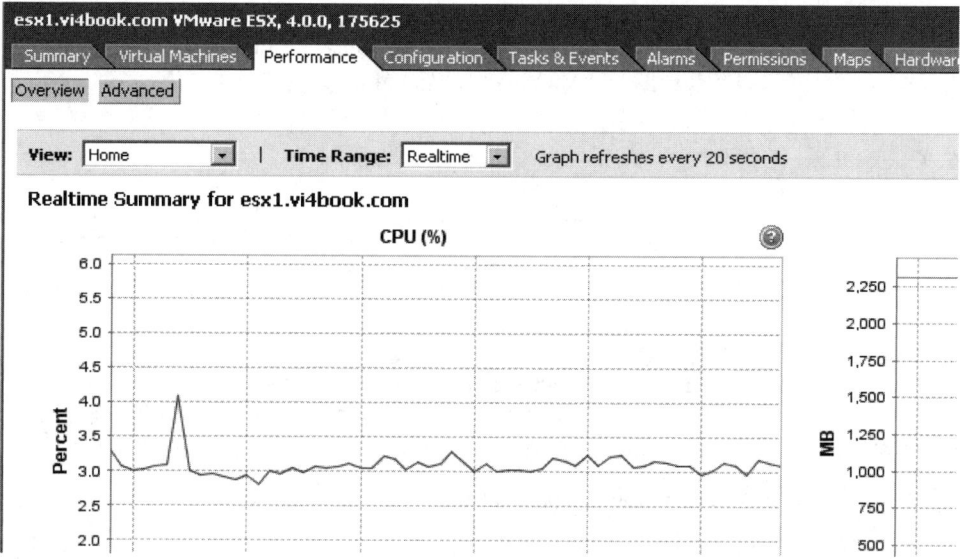

You can also change the Time Range option from Realtime, Past Year, or Custom, which allows you specify your own time frame.

As discussed earlier in the chapter, the CPU ready value is a good indicator of VM performance. To see the ready value for a VM, follow these steps:

1. Select a VM in the list.
2. Choose the Performance tab.
3. Click the Advanced button.

4. Click Chart Options.

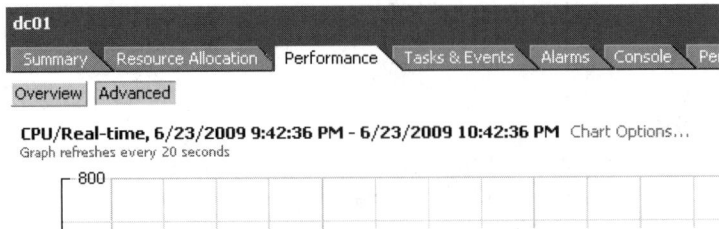

5. On the right side of the dialog box, under Description in the Object section, deselect the check box next to the VM's name, and select the vCPU underneath.

6. Under Description in the Counters section, scroll down the list of counters, and select CPU Ready.

7. Click OK.

NOTE *The* esxtop *command-line tool also allows you to see the ready value on VMs and compare and contrast them. Chapter 11 provides more details about using this tool.*

Generating CPU Activity

If you want to generate a lot of CPU activity for testing purposes, you can do this by using Microsoft Calculator. Yes, Microsoft Calculator can be a very CPU-intensive application, depending on what you're calculating. Here's a calculation that will do this:

1. Open Microsoft Calculator in the VM.

2. Change to the scientific view.

3. Type **9999999**.

4. Click the n! button.

Every so often, Windows complains that this calculation will take a long time, and asks if you would you like to stop the process or continue the calculation. The calculation continues until you stop it or it is completed.

The n! button calculates factorials. A *factorial* is the product of a positive integer and all positive integers less than itself. For example, the factorial of 4, written as 4!, is 4 × 3 × 2 × 1 = 24. So calculating the factorial of 999,999 results in a lot of calculations!

I picked up on this method of quickly generating CPU activity from Brian Madden's article "Citrix buys Application Performance Management vendor Reflectent. Is this a YAM?" which you can read online at http://www.brianmadden.com/content/content .asp?ID=589.

Setting Chart Options

In the previous section, you saw how to use the Customize Performance Chart dialog box to add the CPU ready value for the VM to the chart. This is quite a busy dialog box, with many options.

On the left side of the dialog box, under Chart Options, the core resources of CPU, Disk, Memory, and Network are listed. Expand one of these, and then select an interval: Real-time, Past day, Past week, Past month, Past year, or Custom. Selecting the Custom interval activates the Last and From options in the dialog box.

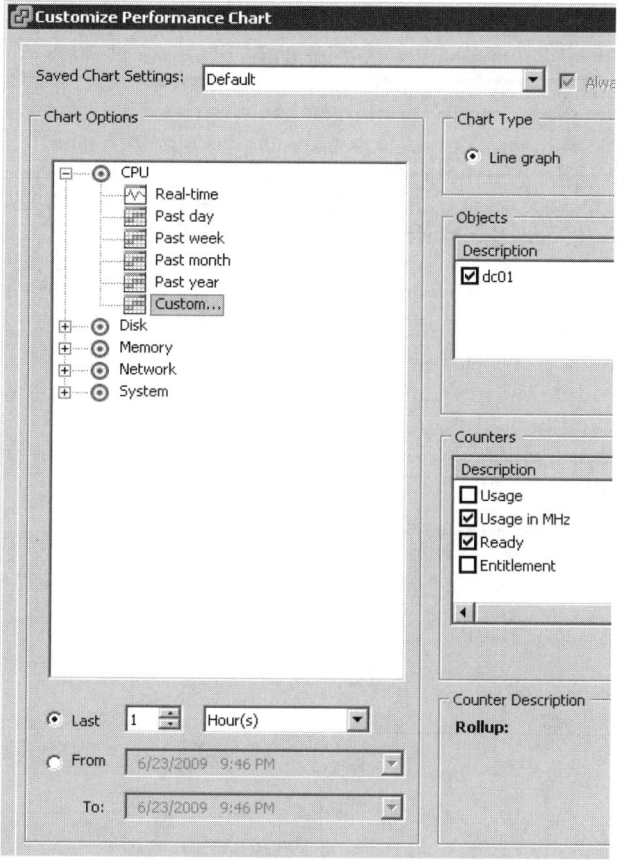

NOTE *Unfortunately, it's not currently possible to show CPU, Disk, Memory, and Network together in four little charts for comparison purposes. This would be useful for working out something like whether disk activity was actually a symptom of excessive swap activity within the guest, and caused by a lack of memory.*

The Chart Options list on the properties of a VM also includes System. In the context of a VM, this allows you to see its average uptimes and the regularity of its heartbeat. These can be taken as a very general measure of the availability of a given VM. Clearly, long uptimes with regular heartbeats mean your VM is alive and healthy. Poor uptimes and an irregular heartbeat, or no heartbeat at all, are generally signs that your VM is not doing well, and is need of intensive care or resuscitation. One reason for not receiving a heartbeat at all from a VM is because the VMware Tools service has failed to start or not been installed.

On the right side of the dialog box, the Chart Type section offers options for the chart's appearance. On an individual VM, you get only two options: Line Graph and Stacked Graph. For an the ESX host, three types are available: Line Graph, Stacked Graph, and Stacked Graph (Per VM). (Personally, I find line graphs are clearer and easier to interpret.)

Under Objects, the Description section shows the resource's objects. Every resource CPU has objects, usually either the entire VM or its individual vCPUs. In turn, every object has attributes, or counters, which shows the available performance statistics.

In the Counters section, you can select additional metrics to gather more data about performance. There are many, many counters on every single resource. You can see a very brief counter description here, but this is not always very helpful. For example, the description for the CPU Ready counter is "CPU Time spent in Ready State." I recommend consulting the VMware documentation and learning about the counters available on a case-by-case basis, depending on your performance issues.

Configuring Alarms and Alerts

Alarms and alerts are built into vCenter. Fortunately, VMware has massively increased their number, because quite frankly, in vCenter 1.x and 2.x, they were very modest in scope. In the past, we were limited to alarms just on ESX hosts and VMs. In vSphere 4, we now have alarms on datacenters and clusters. Additionally, VMware has taken the precaution of turning on some of the most important alarms; in the past, this was left to the end user.

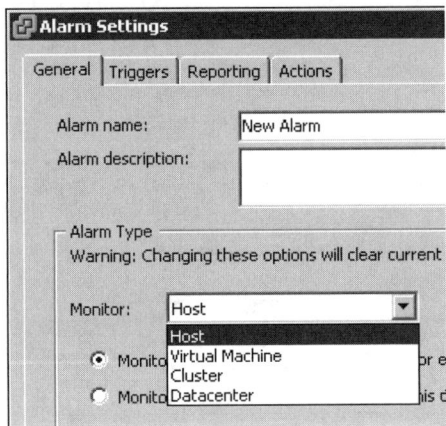

NOTE *Often VMware's other management products, such as Site Recovery Manager, boost the number of alarm conditions. So it is with pleasure that I can now say I will no longer be explaining each and every alarm condition, because there are just too many!*

The built-in alarms and alerts, defined at the top of the Inventory in Hosts and Clusters view, are inherited down the Inventory and applied to all ESX hosts and VMs. If you wish to change these, you must modify them at the point at which they were inherited. If you wish to create new alarms and alerts with different settings, you must delete the built-in ones and create ones of your own on the relevant folder.

Modifying Alarms

A good example of modifying an existing alarm is the built-in alarm on ESX hosts called Host Connection and Power State. Currently, when an ESX host becomes unavailable, it will enter a not responding state first, and after some time, it will become disconnected. These messages can occur when rebooting an ESX host or if you have a network failure. Currently, the alarm issues an alert only when disconnected.

NOTE *You can force an ESX host to enter the disconnected state forcibly by right-clicking the ESX host and choosing Disconnect.*

Here are the steps for modifying the Host Connection and Power State alarm:

1. In the Inventory, select Hosts and Clusters.

2. Select the Alarm tab.

3. Click the Definitions button.

4. Double-click the Host Connection and Power State alarm.

5. Select the Triggers tab.

6. Change the existing Host Connection State settings to Warning: Not responding, and Alert: None.

7. Click Add.

8. Change Host CPU Usage (%) to Host Connection State.

9. Change Warning to None. Leave the Alert set to Disconnected.

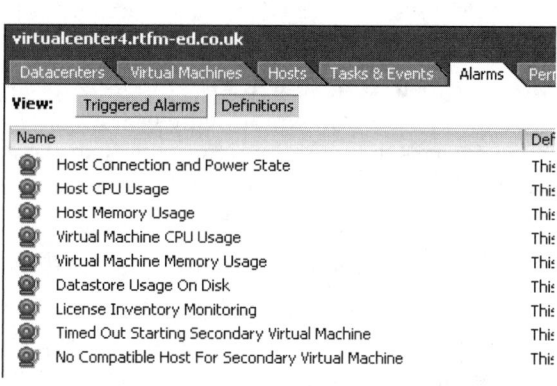

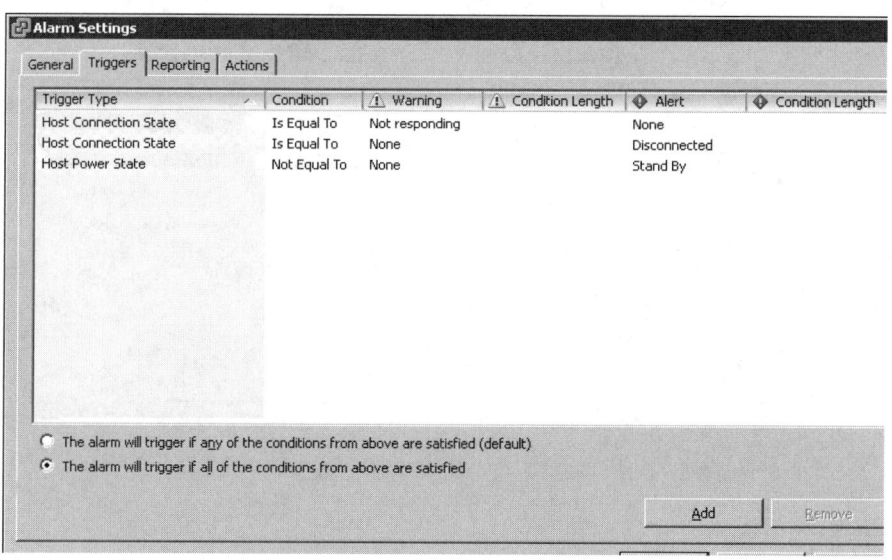

After following these steps, you would receive a yellow warning if an ESX host failed to respond, followed by an alarm if it became disconnected.

In vSphere 4, using the Triggers tab, you can now specify that *all* of these conditions must be true or *just one* must be true before triggering an alarm.

The Host Power State Stand By alert option is for the DPM feature. In VI3.5, VMware added this feature to a DRS cluster. DPM allows VMware to power down ESX hosts into a standby mode, and power them back on when resource demands require it using the Wake-on-LAN (WoL) support of most modern NICs. In vSphere 4, this method has been vastly improved by using the server's ILO/RAC card interface to send power instructions directly to the server.

NOTE *The intention of DPM is to massively reduce power consumption by having only the ESX host that you need powered on. It's a really useful feature in test and development, DR environments, and VDI, and it has a role to play in production datacenters running server-based VMs, especially if you don't have true 24/7/365 operations. Chapter 14 covers DPM.*

Creating Custom Alarms

An alarm I have wanted for many years is one on VM snapshots. As discussed in Chapter 6, VMware says that you should not allow the snapshot delta file size to grow beyond 2GB. Fortunately, we now have the ability to receive an alarm on that very event! Here are the steps for creating a custom alarm for a VM:

1. In the Inventory, choose Hosts and Clusters.

2. Select the Alarm tab.

3. Click the Definitions button.

4. Right-click and choose New Alarm.

5. For the alarm name, type in a friendly name, such as **Virtual Machine Snapshot Size**.

6. Under Alarm Type, choose Virtual Machine.

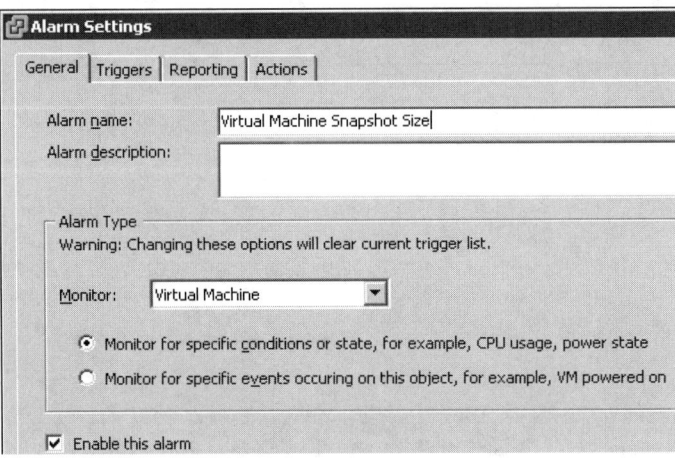

7. Click the Triggers tab.

8. Select Add.

9. Select VM Snapshot Size (GB) from the pull-down list.

10. Adjust the initial Warning and Alert settings to be the appropriate values (1GB and 2GB, respectively, in this example).

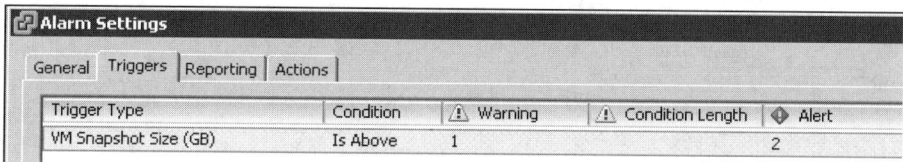

To test the alarm, I filled a VM with dummy files to make the snapshot delta files grow. This did result in the first warning being triggered.

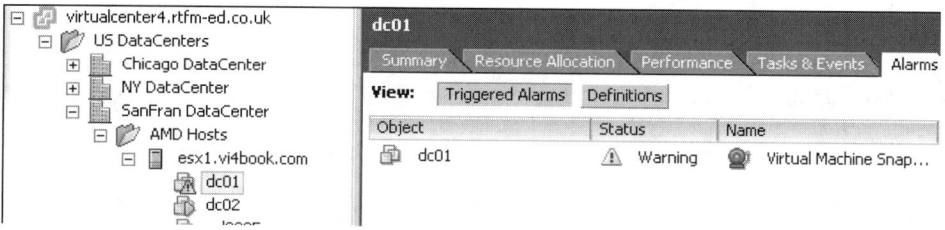

CAUTION *Be careful when using VM state alarms that monitor the power state of the VM, such as whether it is powered on or powered off. If you do this, you can create alerts on the VMs that are not a problem. The system is doing its job giving you an alarm even when a condition is met. As most VMs are powered on in a production environment, it's not a terribly useful alarm condition. The same can happen if you set an alarm on VMs that are powered off. This generates an alarm on a VM that isn't even powered on. This could be an irritation in test and development environments, where many VMs are powered on only when needed.*

Configuring Alarm Tolerance and Frequency

The Tolerance and Frequency settings on the Reporting tab of the Alarm Settings dialog box allow you to control how "chatty" an alarm can be. This can be useful to stop unwanted SMTP/SNMP alerts.

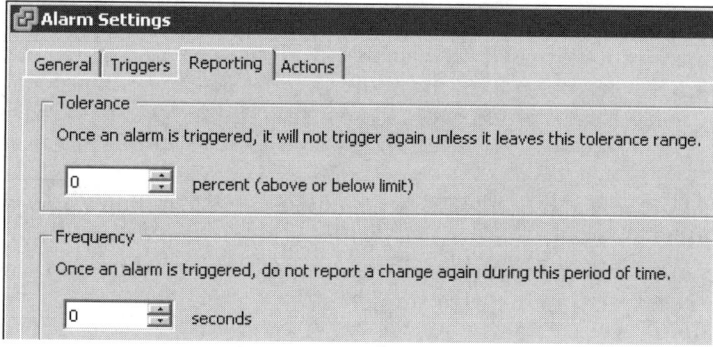

The Tolerance setting affects alarm conditions that are set by a percentage (as opposed to Boolean conditions, which are logical, such as VM or host state conditions). So, it is possible to send an alert when a warning reaches 75%, but not send another warning until it changes by another 5% below or above 75%.

The Frequency setting allows you to modify how often vCenter checks on an alarm that has already been triggered. So you can ignore an alarm for, say, 60 minutes before it sends out another.

Configuring Email Alerts

Configuring vCenter to issue email messages generated by alarms requires vCenter to know the Simple Mail Transfer Protocol (SMTP) details, server name, and both the sender's (From:) and recipient's (To:) email addresses. These settings are configured in the vCenter Management dialog box.

CAUTION *Due to the absence of a password field, the email alerts feature requires authentication switched off. In fact, for this to function correctly, your SMTP server must be configured as an open relay. If this SMTP server is Internet-facing, it will be a magnet for spammers. Therefore, you should make sure that whatever you set here is an internal-only email system.*

Follow these steps to configure email alerts:

1. In the menu, choose Administration and vCenter Management Server Configuration.

2. Select the Mail section of the dialog box.

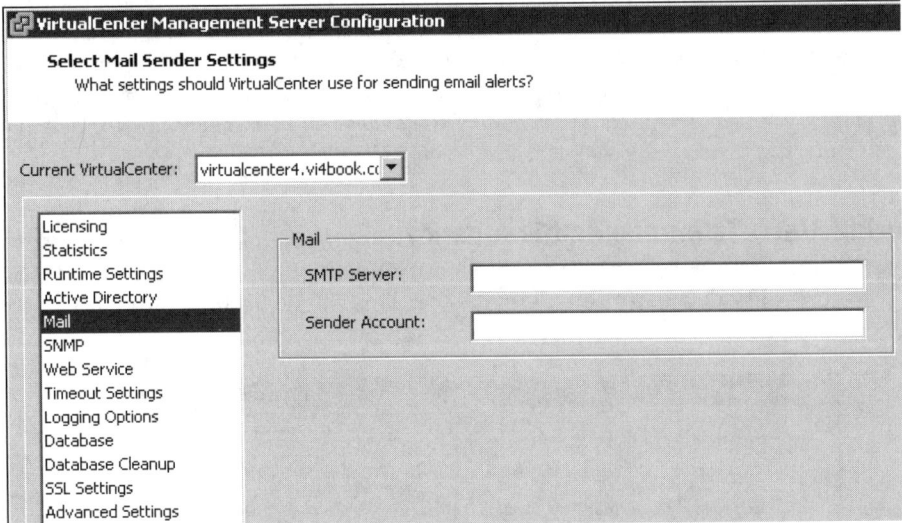

3. In the SMTP Server field, type the name of your mail server (smtp1.vi4book.com in this example).

4. In the Sender Account field, type the name of account used to send email (vCenter@vi4book.com in this example).

5. Open an alarm, such as the Virtual Machine Snapshot Size alarm you created earlier.

6. Choose the Actions tab.

7. Click the Add button. Choose "Send a notification email."

8. Click in the Value column, and type the To: recipient email address.

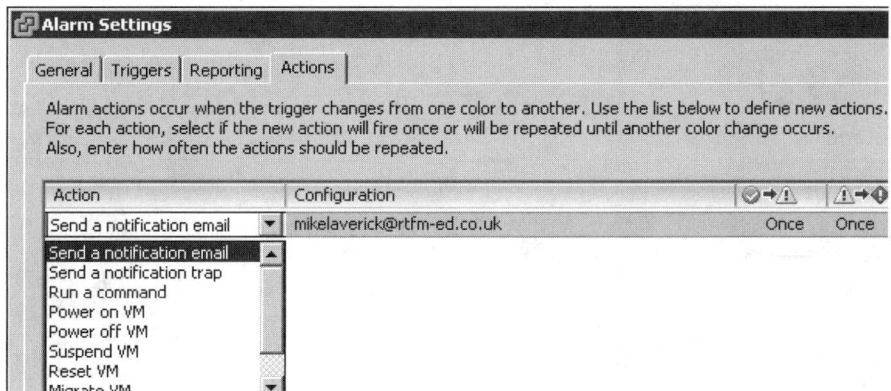

9. Change the first column from a green check to a yellow exclamation mark. In this example, you will receive a warning if the snapshot reaches 1GB, and another warning if it reaches 2GB.

Configuring SNMP Alerts

You can also configure vCenter to issue Simple Network Management Protocol (SNMP) alerts. Generally, large corporations invest in commercially available SNMP products, such as HP OpenView Operations Manager (OVO). Additionally many free SNMP management tools are available, which are useful if you merely wish to test that SNMP is correctly configured.

NOTE *In practice, it is unusual to run an SNMP management tool on the vCenter server itself. If you wish to do this, you need to modify vCenter's default SNMP management settings, found in the vCenter Management Server Configuration dialog box (accessible from the Administration menu).*

This example shows you how to use a free tool called Trap Receiver from Network Computing Technologies, available from http://www.ncomtech.com/, to test the SNMP configuration.

1. Download and install Trap Receiver to the vCenter Server.

2. Run the Trap Receiver application from the Start menu by choosing the Start the Service button.

3. Open an Alarm definition. In this example, I chose the Virtual Machine Snapshot Size alarm.

4. Select the Action tab.

5. Click the Add button.

6. Choose "Send a notification trap," and then click OK.

Notice that you can set more actions for VMs than you can for an ESX host, including responses such as the following:

- Run a command
- Power on or off a VM, suspend a VM, and reset a VM
- Migrate (VMotion) a VM
- Reboot or shut down the guest OS

The following example shows the SNMP trap caused by the VM snapshot alarm in Trap Receiver.

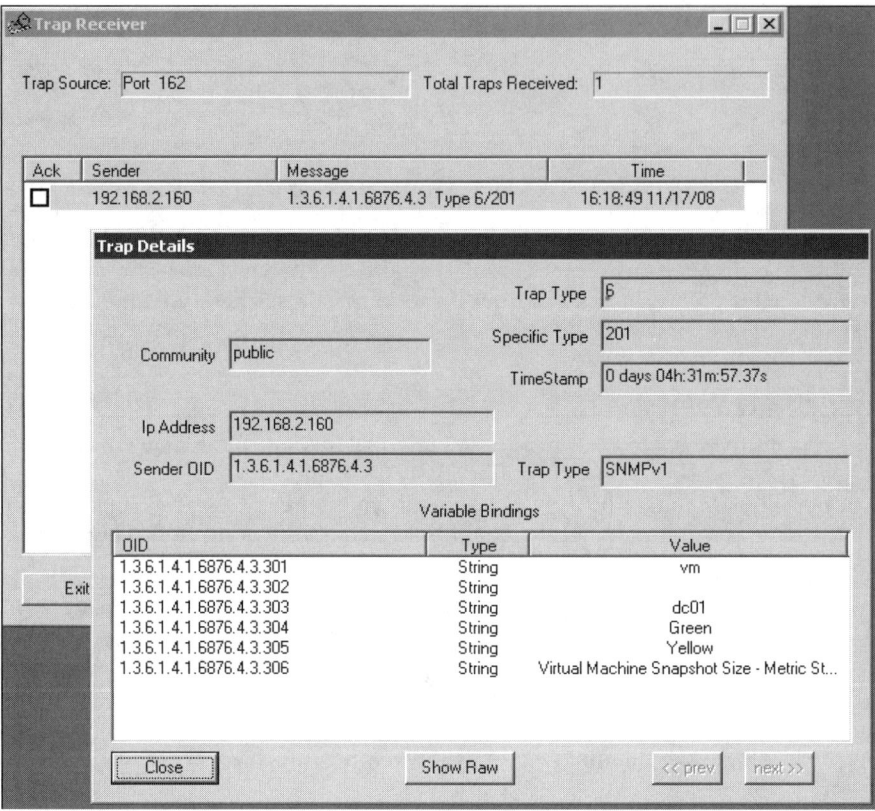

Acknowledging Alarms

In previous releases, there was no easy way to temporarily turn off an alarm for an individual VM. The most we could do was to temporarily disable an alarm if we felt that it was incorrectly generating unwarranted alerts. Also, it was impossible to acknowledge an alarm and mark it as addressed, so that other team members would not elevate the problem based on the same vCenter alarm.

This limitation has now been removed, and we have the ability to acknowledge alarms. To do this, simply right-click the clarm, and choose Acknowledge Alarm.

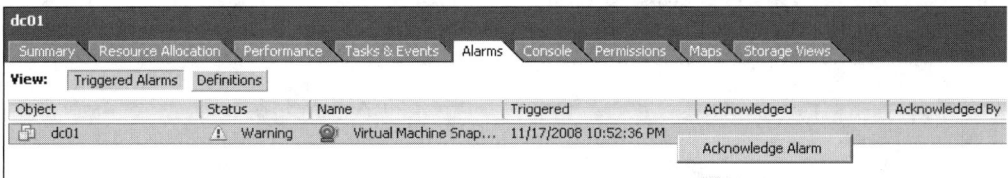

Viewing Events and Tasks

As you have probably noticed, vSphere's Recent Task pane shows ongoing processes. In a multiple-administrator environment, it allows you to see tasks triggered by other vCenter administrators.

A record of all tasks and events is kept in vCenter, and the Tasks & Events tab appears at every point in the Inventory. As you navigate down the Inventory, you gradually see less and less focused information on a particular VM. The following example shows a type event view on a VM. You can toggle between tasks and events by clicking the corresponding button at the top of the Tasks & Events tab.

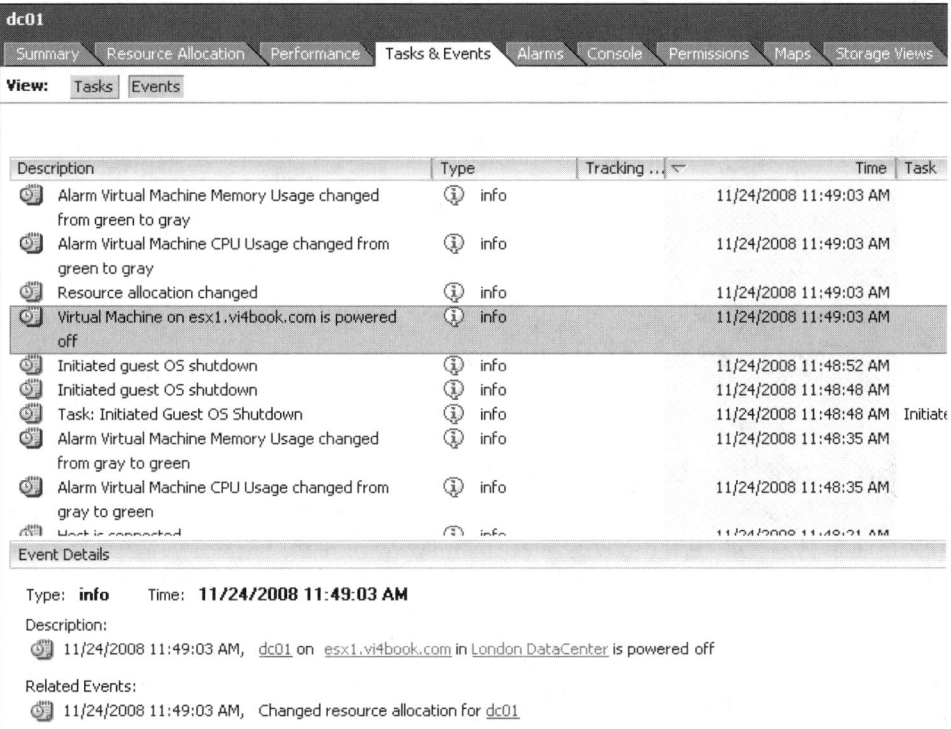

If you fail to make a note of a warning message that appeared on the vSphere Client, you will generally find it in the Tasks & Events tab.

Configuring Scheduled Tasks

vCenter does have the ability to automate some repetitive tasks without requiring you to know a scripting language. Scheduled tasks are configured with a point-and-click interface and allow you to automate tasks such as the following:

- Change the power state of a VM (power on, power off, and resume)
- Clone a VM
- Deploy a VM from a template
- Create a new VM (not from a template)
- Migrate a VM (VMotion)
- Take a snapshot of a VM
- Add an ESX host
- Change resource settings of a resource pool or VM (new)

NOTE *A slight limitation is that although you can schedule adding an ESX host into vCenter as a task, you can add an ESX host only to a datacenter object, not a folder within a datacenter.*

To create and modify scheduled tasks, under Home, choose the Management tab and click the Scheduled Tasks icon.

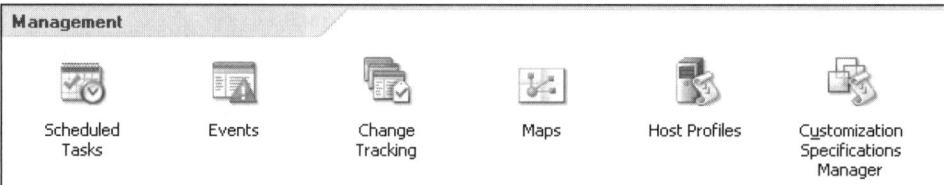

The only configuration for scheduled tasks that may not be straightforward is how to express the time for an event to happen. Most users would expect the system to use a 24-hour format. Instead you type in a time, say 10:00, followed by a.m. or p.m.

Accessing and Exporting Log Files and Support Data

vCenter and ESX both have logging information, which could be useful in troubleshooting scenarios and for liaising with VMware Support. Additionally, this can become a management issue—how long will logging data be retained and how frequently will the logs be rotated?

Accessing and Exporting vCenter Logs

To access your vCenter and ESX logs, in the vSphere Client, under Home, choose the Administration tab and click the System Logs icon.

You can export your logs for both vCenter and ESX hosts (to be submitted to VMware Support, for example) by clicking the Export Diagnostic Data button.

This starts a task called Generate Diagnostic Bundles in the Recent Tasks view.

Additionally, you can create VMware Support log bundles directly at the vCenter server itself. To do this, choose Start, then Programs, then VMware from the menus, and select "Generate vCenter Server log bundle."

This method generates a vcsupport-*M-DD-YYY-HH-MM*.zip file on the vCenter desktop.

Generating ESX Host Log Files

The main location for ESX logs is in /var/log. This location is used to store log files for the Service Console and the VMkernel. Files that begin with the characters *VMK* are VMkernel logs; all other files are Service Console log files.

Individual log bundles and VMware Support files can be generated at the Service Console using a script. To do this, log on to the Service Console as root. Then type **cd** to make sure you are located at /root. Next, type **vm-support**.

This tool gathers all your logs and configuration information and zips it into a handy .tgz file. These files are then uploaded to VMware's FTP site (rather than being sent in with email), which is accessible to you when you open a service request (SR) with VMware Support.

TIP *Log rotation is handled at the command line on a per ESX host basis using the* logrotate *utility.*

Summary

As you can see, once again vCenter has reached another level of maturity as a management platform with extended alarms on new objects such as datacenters and clusters, together with new conditions on which to trap events. Additionally, old users will welcome the return of vmkusage-style performance charts, which were removed from ESX 2 when ESX 3 was released.

CHAPTER 11 | Resource Management

Thisᴵchapter discusses the tools available to you for managing the performance of VMs. You can adjust resource parameters for CPU, memory, and disk on a per-VM basis or you can drop groups of VMs into resource pools to manage their CPU or memory. Resource pools allow you to treat VMs as groups, rather than individuals, and quickly apply resource settings to them, thus reducing your administrative burden.

It is possible to cap, or *limit*, and also guarantee a minimum, or *reservation*, of either CPU or memory to a VM or a resource pool. Additionally, VMware's proportional share system provides more dynamic control over a VM's resource usage, as it responds to changes in resource demand relative to each VM and ESX host. At an extreme level, it is possible to peg a resource to a VM with features such as CPU affinities—hard-coding a VM to have exclusive access to a CPU.

In this chapter, I use an airline analogy to explain how resources are managed in ESX. Each plane will represent an ESX host, and a fleet of airplanes will represent a VMware DRS cluster. (VMware's DRS is an invaluable resource management tool, which integrates very closely with VMware's HA; it is discussed in Chapter 13.) Every plane has a fixed capacity in terms of the number of passengers it can comfortably accommodate. Each of the seats will represent a VM. If the airline has 200 seats per plane and 10 planes, that is a total of 2000 seats. But the 200 seats per plane represent a fixed limit on capacity. Fundamentally, these 2000 seats exist as a logical capacity; a passenger can board only one plane, just as a VM can currently execute on only one ESX host, not a cluster. Access to the plane is controlled by a unique system of reservations, which is intended to guarantee not that you fly, but that a certain quality of travel, like business class, will be provided. In contrast, economy passengers do not make reservations. They merely turn up and hope there will be access.

What's New in Resource Management?

- Improved charts on all datacenter objects, including the cluster, the ESX host, and the VM

- vApp, which allows grouping VMs by function with startup and shutdown orders, as well as resource management via a user interface that is similar to resource pools

---

Setting Limits

You can impose limits on a VM or resource pool for CPU resources (by megahertz) and for memory (by megabytes). In fact, limits are imposed on a VM from the perspective of memory when you first define a VM.

When you create a VM, you set the maximum amount of memory. A VM cannot exceed the amount allocated to it, even if free physical memory exists. At first glance, this seems quite restrictive; however, from an architecture point of view, it has to happen. If we have poorly written applications and OSs, we need to avoid the situation where a VM is able to drain a physical host of its entire available RAM, thus causing a reboot of the physical server. Using the airplane analogy introduced at the beginning of this chapter, it's not possible for a single passenger on the plane to take up all the space at the expense of the other passengers.

Additionally, there are some fixed limits we cannot exceed. If there are only 200 seats on the plane, we cannot allow 201 passengers to board. Similarly, if the ESX host or pool resources are totally consumed, a limit has been reached. We cannot magically find additional resources, with one exception. When all memory has been depleted, it is possible for a VM to use its VMkernel swap file.

In contrast, there are no default limits on CPU usage. If a VM demands CPU time, and that CPU time is available, then this is allocated to a VM. One possible reason to cap, or limit, a VM's usage of CPU is when you know you have a poorly written application that regularly crashes, and perhaps when it crashes it hogs the CPU of the ESX host. Using CPU limits is one method (among many) to control these kinds of VMs.

Some Terminology Notes

In the ESX 2.*x* product, the word *maximum* was used, but in VI3 and vSphere 4, VMware changed the term to *limits*, as this more clearly describes the feature.

Additionally, some time ago, VMware moved away from allocating limits on CPUs by a percentage value and now prefers to use megahertz, which is a more accurate measure of CPU usage. In the context of CPUs, 10% of a 1.44 MHz processor is decidedly different from 10% of a 2.6 MHz processor.

Similarly, with CPUs in ESX 2.*x*, VMware used to set a value called a *minimum*. This term was changed to *reservations*. Again, the label change was introduced to be more meaningful.

Setting Reservations

In addition to limits, we can also use CPU or memory reservations. One analogy that can help when thinking of reservations is to compare them to the flight reservations. These reservations are supposed to guarantee a resource in the form of a seat. Similarly, a CPU or memory reservation in megahertz or megabytes is intended to guarantee the resource to the VM or resource pool. In this case, there are no default reservations for CPU or memory, unlike the default limit on memory set when creating the VM. You can regard these reservations, or guarantees, as offering a way of ensuring that you meet certain performance levels. Perhaps you could even regard them as a way of meeting service level agreements (SLAs).

For a flight, the airline must have the resources to meet your reservation in order to allow you to board or check in. Similarly, if the memory reservation on a VM is 256MB of RAM, and that amount of RAM is physically not available, you will be unable to power on the VM. VMware refers to this as *admission control*. If you configured a situation where a VM must get 1000 MHz of CPU time, but the physical host can offer only 500 MHz of CPU time, the VM would not power on. It would be a bit like having a 200-seat airplane and saying you could guarantee reservations to 201 passengers. There are physical limits that cannot be exceeded, and the same goes for an ESX host.

If a passenger makes a reservation for ten seats in business class, those seats must be there. Our airline imposes a very special definition of customer care that states if a business class reservation cannot be met, rather than pushing our customer into economy class, we refuse admission to the flight. (I admit that at this point, the airline analogy doesn't work perfectly, but it is helpful in most cases.)

There is a very interesting and useful relationship between memory limits and reservations and the VMkernel swap file. The difference between the reservations subtracted from the limit determines the size of the VMkernel swap file. I mentioned using the VMkernel swap file as an indicator of potential performance problems in the previous chapter. Here, I will delve a little deeper into different ways of using it. Explaining how to use the VMkernel swap file is perhaps best done with a couple of examples:

- **Difference between limit and reservation** You have a VM with a 512MB limit and 256MB reservation. Powering on the VM would create a 256MB VMkernel swap file (512 – 256) and guarantee that the VM would receive 256MB of RAM. The VM would not power on if there was insufficient space for the swap file.

- **No difference between limit and reservation** If you set the limit to 512MB and the reservation also as 512MB, and powered on the VM, ESX would not create a VMkernel swap file at all. It would run the VM entirely in a memory reservation of 512MB.

- **Big difference between limit and reservation** If, on the other hand, the VM was given a 16GB limit, and the default of 0MB was used for the reservation, a 16GB VMkernel swap file would be created. This VMkernel swap file is created in the same location as the .vmx file, which could be on extremely expensive shared storage such as a SAN. Since VI3.5, we have been able to store this swap file in a different location to save space. This is especially relevant if you are encoding very large differences between the limit and reservation values for memory on a VM. Relocating the swap file is discussed in Chapter 13.

With the first example, if you had an ESX host with 2GB of physical RAM, you could run at least eight VMs before running out of memory (2048MB / 256MB). You would not be able to power on a ninth VM, because there would be insufficient memory to meet the reservation guarantee. If all the VMs simultaneously wished to use memory up to the limits (512MB × 8), you would get swap activity. You hope that this would be such an unlikely event that it would be safe to configure the system this way.

Perhaps you find this memory overcommitment a bit scary. You are concerned about the negative aspects of swap activity, and you wish to have a cast-iron guarantee that your VMs will always run in memory. If this is the case, you could use the second example. When you set the VM's limit and reservation to be the same value, no swap file is created, and the VM is guaranteed to always run in memory. However, on a 2GB system, the effect of this policy would be very significant. You would be able to run only four VMs, not eight (2048MB / 512MB). If you tried to create a fifth VM and power it on, that wouldn't work, as all the memory would have been reserved for use by your other VMs.

So, the first example might be configured by someone who is optimistic and is looking for very high VM-to-ESX host ratios, or someone trying to run as many VMs with as few resources as possible. The second example might be employed by someone who is pessimistic or conservative, or who has so many resources there is no need to use the VMkernel swap file.

You might want to know which camp I am in—optimistic or pessimistic. I'm optimistic, and that puts me in line with more than 80% of VMware customers, who leverage the VMkernel swap file and use memory overcommitment. As a result, they get incredibly high consolidation ratios and excellent utilization of their hardware. It may be a gut instinct in our industry to err on the side of caution, but this will leave you vulnerable to becoming far too cautious, and as a consequence, failing to get the most out of your virtualization project.

The last example is a warning. If you set extremely high values on memory, with no reservations, the ESX host will generate an extremely large swap file. Just as with memory reservations, you need the physical megabytes of disk space to create the VMkernel swap file. In the third example, if you didn't have 16GB of free disk space in the LUN where the VM is stored, it would not power on, as there would be insufficient resources to guarantee the difference between the limit and reservation.

The Share System

Another system is at play in the gap between limits and reservations—the *proportional share system*. Shares allow you to indicate that, when a resource is scarce, one VM or resource pool is more important than another. To use our analogy, it's like the airline treating a Hollywood star as more important than the average guy on the street.

Share values can be applied on a per-VM basis or on resource pools. Unlike limits or reservations, which are fixed and unchanging, shares react dynamically to resource demands. The share value can be specified by a number (usually in multiples of 1000) or by user-friendly text values of Normal, High, and Low. The important thing to remember about the share value is that it is only relevant when the resource is scarce and contention is occurring. If the resource is plentiful or VMs do not need to compete over resources, the share value does nothing at all.

In my discussions with VMware, I've been told that many customers do not use the proportional share system as much as VMware might like. Why might this be? First, customers frequently don't understand how shares work. Also, shares take effect only when things are performing badly, and many people try to configure their ESX hosts and VMs so this never happens. Personally, I am a big fan of the share system. What especially appeals to me are its dynamic nature and its ability to react to changes.

If you or your customers are still struggling with the concept of shares, you might like to consider a couple of other analogies. You could see the share values like shares in a company that are quoted on global stock exchanges. The amount of shares a company chooses to issue is up to that company; what matters is the number or portion of your shares. The greater amount of shares you hold in a company, the more of a stake in the business you own. Therefore, a big share owner of 5000 shares has much more influence than a share holder with just 1000 shares.

Here's another analogy I use regularly in courses. Imagine you have three children: a baby, a five-year-old, and a teenager. When you come home after a hard day's work, they all demand your time. Here, your time is like the CPU, and each of your children is a pesky VM making demands on your tired brain. Being a particularly cruel parent, you decide to take a permanent marker and write 3000 on the baby's forehead, 2000 on the toddler's forehead, and 1000 on the teenager's forehead. You decide you're like one of the ESX hosts you manage at work, and this is your parental strategy from now on!

In this analogy, when you are faced with contention (when you come home from work), you give the baby one-half (3000 / 6000), the toddler one-third (2000 / 6000), and your teenager one-sixth (1000 / 6000) of your valuable time. Now when it's mid-evening, you decide that the baby is tired enough to go to sleep. You're in luck tonight, as he is out for the count in seconds. You now can give two-thirds of your time to the toddler (2000 / 3000) and one-third (1000 / 3000) of your time to the teenager.

When the toddler goes to bed (after much crying and wailing), you are facing no contention at all. Just as you're settling down to watch your favorite sitcom, the teenager comes down from her bedroom (perhaps the Internet connection has failed or her games console has broken). She now decides this will be an opportune time to discuss why college is a waste of time and how she should really follow her favorite drug-taking band around the country. Now you can give all of your time to teenager (1000 / 1000) in persuading her that while a life of drunken debauchery might have its appeal, it won't lead her to a prosperous career in IT like yours.

Finally, everyone goes to bed. Contention is over, and you get the opportunity to get some well-earned Z's. But then, at 3:00 AM, you hear crying from the baby's room. You're out of luck, as it is your turn to feed the baby. However, rest assured that as long as you get to the baby quickly, he will not wake the others, and you are able to give 100% of your time to getting back in bed as quickly as possible!

All joking aside, the analogy does illustrate some points. First, share values adjust depending on the level of contention. Second, when there is no contention, the share value does nothing at all. Third, when you become a parent, you will have no time to yourself whatsoever!

As mentioned earlier, you can set the share value by using friendly labels of High, Normal, and Low, offering a more intuitive way of dividing up resources. You see these whenever you create a new VM. You can use these text labels on a VM and also in resource pools. Here are the actual settings these labels apply:

- **High**   Allocates 2000 shares per vCPU; 20 shares for every 1MB allocated to the VM.
- **Normal**   Allocates 1000 shares per vCPU; 10 shares for every 1MB allocated to the VM.
- **Low**   Allocates 500 shares per vCPU; 5 shares for 1MB allocated to the VM.

As you can see, High is twice as much as Normal and four times as much as Low. There is also another assumption at play here. VMware assumes that the more memory you assign to a VM, the more sensitive it is to a lack of memory. So when contention takes place, the VM wins a greater slice of memory resources. This assumption might not always be the case (although it frequently is). You could have a memory-intensive application that is not business-critical. Whether you like it or not, even if you use the text labels, you are effectively assigning a value. If there is a 4:2:1 ratio between High, Normal, and Low, that's just like setting 4000, 2000, and 1000 or 2000, 1000, and 500.

Processor Affinities

One extreme method of controlling the VM's access to CPU resources is to peg it to a specified CPU by setting processor affinities. As explained in the previous chapter, internal to the physical server, the VMkernel dynamically moves the VM to work on the best CPU inside the ESX host. You can switch off this feature from the properties of a VM (on the Resources tab, under Advanced CPU).

I regard this configuration as a last resort, for the following reasons:

- Configuring it is very administration-intensive. Not only do you need to configure the VM in question to use only CPU3, for example, but you also must configure every other VM not to use CPU3, to truly dedicate a VM to given CPU.

- CPU affinities are incompatible with VMotion.

- As DRS is effectively an automated VMotion for performance, CPU affinities also break DRS. Removing CPU affinities on a VM running on a ESX host that is already a member of a DRS cluster is possible, but very convoluted.

Virtualization Overhead and Sizing the VM

An important factor to remember is that virtualization is not "free" from a resource allocation perspective. Adding a virtualization layer, regardless of the virtualization vendor, involves some overhead.

As a general rule, the greater the size of the resources allocated to the VM, the more that this overhead grows. So, the more RAM or CPUs you assign to the VM, the more resources need to be allocated by the VMkernel to support that VM—and that's overhead that begins when you power on a VM, before the guest OS has even loaded.

Some examples of this exist within the VMware documentation. For example, a two-way vCPU VM with 1GB memory creates an overhead of 176MB. An eight-way vCPU with 32GB memory generates 1647MB of overhead. Additionally, 64-bit based guest OSs generally add to this overhead.

The moral of the story is that you should allocate the amount resources that the VM needs, and don't "overspec" the VM. Where possible, use a 32-bit OS (bearing in mind that some services, such as Microsoft Exchange 2007, actually require a 64-bit edition of Windows to function).

Resource Pools

Resource pools are optional. It is possible to have stand-alone ESX hosts and DRS clusters without resource pools. If you did this, you would merely be accepting the defaults that VMware places on VMs. These defaults are good ones—they prevent a VM from hogging the CPU and memory leaks from getting out of control. The intention of the defaults is to prevent the ESX host from becoming unstable and to make sure one VM does not affect another VM.

Resource pools affect only CPU and memory resources. So if your goal is to control disk and network activity, this must be done using the properties of the VM or a vSwitch, respectively.

For CPU and memory resources, which are very critical, resource pools offer an effective way of applying limits, reservations, and share values. The task of right-clicking each VM and setting these values is very administration-intensive, whereas dragging and dropping a VM to the correct resource pool is an easy task. If you are trying to calculate the total share value, it is easier to compare a small number of resource pools than to compare a large number of VMs.

Resource pools can be be created in two main places:

- On a stand-alone ESX server, which divides the resources of a single host into smaller units, or pools

- On a VMware cluster, which divides the total resources of many servers into pools

Resource pools function the same if they are on a stand-alone host or a cluster, but they really come into play in clusters, where the need to divide up resources logically is usually more pressing.

You could create resource pools based on department (sales, accounts, or distribution), function (web servers, database, or file servers), or IT infrastructure (test, development, and production).

Some people find resource pools a tricky concept, despite the fact they use this feature in a very similar way for storage. A storage array is full of physical disks that are all of a fixed size. Using the array's management tool, we can carve these disks up into LUNs. The LUNs are presented to the physical server as if they were physical disks. The advantage of doing this is we are freed from the constraints of the geometries of the disk. We use resource pools in precisely the same way. The pool represents a logical allocation of memory and CPU, which free us from the physical constraints of the ESX host. However, these units of the LUN and resource pool are very much intermediary management layers. Fundamentally, the buck stops with the hardware. We must at some stage write data to the surface of a metal disk, and we must at some stage find CPU cycles and blocks of memory on a physical server in the cluster.

Applying the airline analogy, each of the airplanes represents an ESX host. A DRS cluster represents the collective capacity of all the airplanes, but fundamentally a passenger can fly on only one airplane, not on two simultaneously. The air traffic controllers are very clever guys who can detect some airplanes stretched to capacity and move passengers from one plane to another while they are flying. This is called VMotion in ESX.

A Resource Pool Example

Let's work through an example that shows how resource pools work. First, we will run two VMs with a CPU-intensive process. Initially, there will be no contention. We will introduce contention by forcing them to run on the same physical CPU. Then we will create resource pools with different share values to show how resource pools help you control resources and demonstrate that the shares feature works dynamically.

Creating CPU-Intensive Events

To create CPU activity in a VM for testing purposes, you can use a freely available script written by VMware, which I've reproduced here. You can find it on the download page from the vmware-land.com website (it comes from the Performance Troubleshooting Lab that ran at in VMworld 2006):

http://vmware-land.com/downloads/vmworld.06.lab04-PERFORMANCE-MANUAL .pdf

Follow these steps to use the script on two VMs:

1. On the same ESX host, power on two Windows VMs.

2. On the root C:, create two files called **cpubusy.vbs**.

3. Cut and paste the following code to the cpubusy.vbs script:

```
Dim goal
Dim before
Dim x
Dim y
```

```
Dim i
goal = 2181818
Do While True
      before = Timer
      For i = 0 to goal
            x = 0.000001
            y = sin(x)
            y = y + 0.00001
      Next      y = y + 0.01
WScript.Echo "I did three million sines in " & Int(Timer - before +
0.5) & " seconds!"
Loop
```

4. Right-click the cpubusy.vbs file within each VM and choose the option called Open with Command Prompt.

CAUTION *Don't double-click the .vbs file, as this will produce dialog boxes from the* wscript
. echo *command. The idea of the script is that it shows very crudely how quickly the VM is
doing the calculation.*

At this point, you will find both VMs will generate alarms and alerts, and that both receive the same amount of CPU time. As you may recall from Chapter 10, the VMkernel does a great job of scheduling these VMs so they don't run on the same physical socket or core. The following example is from a command-line tool available in ESX Classic called esxtop, which shows how both VMs are running on separate physical sockets. This example was taken from a ProLiant DL385 Server, which has two AMD sockets with a dual-core processor.

```
root@esx1:~

 5:13:43pm up 3 days 21:21, 124 worlds; CPU load average: 0.47, 0.26, 0.12
PCPU(%):   23.82,   88.96,   99.45     9.26 ;    used total:    55.37
CCPU(%):    0 us,    4 sy,   96 id,    0 wa ;       cs/sec:       84

   ID     GID NAME               NWLD    %USED    %RUN    %SYS    %WAIT    %RDY
    1       1 idle                  4   177.46  193.87    0.00     0.00  204.83
    2       2 system                9     0.13    0.13    0.00   896.82    0.13
    6       6 helper               69     1.13    1.11    0.96  6875.73    0.65
    7       7 drivers              10     0.01    0.01    0.00   996.70    0.00
    8       8 vmotion               1     0.00    0.00    0.00    99.67    0.00
   10      10 console               2     2.04    2.08    0.14   196.84    0.42
   15      15 vmkapimod            13     0.00    0.00    0.00  1295.72    0.00
   20      20 vobd.4227             6     0.00    0.00    0.00   598.02    0.00
   21      21 vmkiscsid.4238        1     0.01    0.01    0.00    99.63    0.00
   27      27 vmware-vmkauthd       1     0.00    0.00    0.00    99.64    0.00
   34      34 dc01                  4   100.73  100.53    0.50   297.93    0.10
   35      35 dc02                  4    94.74  100.56    0.77   297.22    0.78
```

Notice that the ESX hosts see these as four separate physical CPUs (PCPU). You can see high utilization of 88.96% on core1 and 99.45% on core2. Additionally, you can see only two VMs are running, called dc01 and dc02, and they are responsible for most of the CPU activity.

Using the VMkernel's internal scheduler, both CPU-intensive processes have been scheduled to execute on separate cores in separate sockets. The result is quite low ready values (%RDY) of 0.10% and 0.78%, respectively.

Creating Contention

As explained earlier in this chapter, the share system operates only if contention is occurring and the resource in contention is scarce. You can easily generate CPU contention by forcing two VMs to run on the same CPU socket, core, or logical processor. This effectively stops the VMkernel scheduler from moving VMs from one CPU to another.

To make the two VMs use the same CPU, follow these steps:

1. Right-click your first VM and choose Edit Settings.

2. Click the Resources tab.

3. Choose Advanced CPU.

4. Choose under the "Schedule Affinity" category, and type in the number of just one CPU in the edit box. In this example, I am indicating I want the VM to execute on CPU core number 3. My ESX hosts are two-socket machines with dual-core processors, making the numbering 0, 1, 2, and 3. (In previous releases, radio buttons were used to indicate the core to use.)

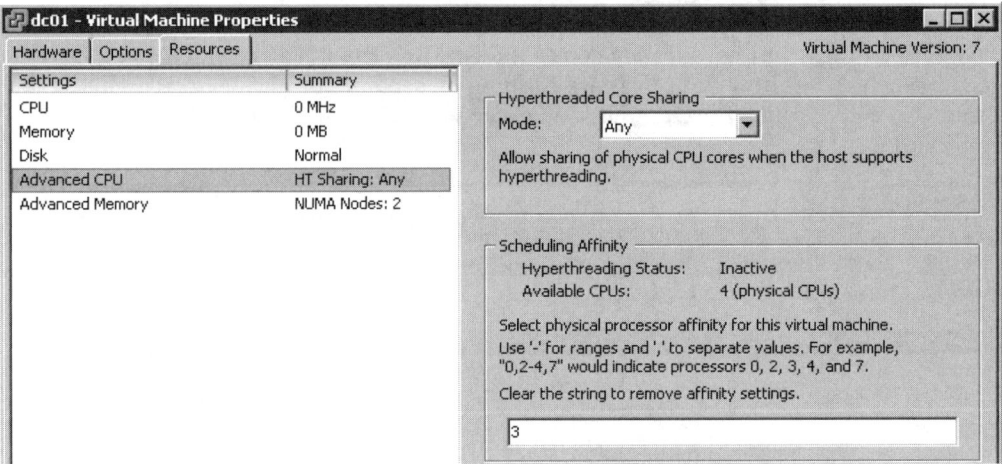

5. Repeat this process for the second VM running the cpubusy.vbs script.

This will create contention. You should see both VMs start to process fewer "sines" per second. In other words, they are running slower. The following example shows that only one physical CPU is now busy (all the cores are idle, whereas the fourth core is at 100%).

```
 root@esx1:~
 5:26:38pm up 3 days 21:34, 127 worlds: CPU load average: 0.52, 0.59, 0.55
 PCPU(%):    9.30,    1.05,    1.10, 100.00    used total:  27.86
 CCPU(%):    4 us,    5 sy,   91 id,    0 wa ;    cs/sec:    433

     ID    GID NAME              NWLD   %USED   %RUN    %SYS    %WAIT    %RDY
      1      1 idle                 4  289.44  292.54   0.00     0.00  108.85
      2      2 system               9    0.13    0.13   0.00   900.00    0.07
      6      6 helper              69    0.99    0.88   0.60  6900.00    0.28
      7      7 drivers             10    0.01    0.01   0.00  1000.00    0.00
      8      8 vmotion              1    0.00    0.00   0.00   100.00    0.00
     10     10 console              2    7.44    7.36   0.19   193.24    0.07
     15     15 vmkapimod           13    0.00    0.00   0.00  1300.00    0.00
     20     20 vobd.4227            6    0.00    0.00   0.00   600.00    0.00
     21     21 vmkiscsid.4238       1    0.02    0.01   0.00   100.00    0.00
     27     27 vmware-vmkauthd      1    0.00    0.00   0.00   100.00    0.00
     34     34 dc01                 4   49.81   50.21   0.11   299.44   51.66
     35     35 dc02                 5   49.92   50.09   0.19   399.78   51.78
     37     37 vm.4517              2    0.00    0.00   0.00   200.00    0.00
```

Additionally, you can see that each VM is getting roughly half of the CPU (49.81 and 49.92, respectively). This happens because, by default, every VM gets 1000 CPU shares each. Two VMs are running, for a total of 2000 shares, resulting in 1000 / 2000, or half, or 50%.

Also notice how the %RDY value has massively increased in size. Clearly, CPU affinities can be very dangerous (and there is no warning from the vSphere Client about creating this kind of configuration). In fact, this kind of CPU contention is precisely what we are trying to avoid.

Creating Resource Pools

Now we will create two resource pools, one called Production and the other called Test & Dev. We will give the Production resource pool 3000 CPU shares and the Test & Dev resource pool 1000 shares. This won't be enough to stop the contention created by the CPU affinity feature, but it will show that resource pools do offer an effective way of allocating more resources to one group of VMs than to another.

1. Right-click the ESX host.

2. Choose New Resource Pool.

3. Type a friendly name, such as **Production**.

4. Under CPU Resources and Shares, select Custom and type **3000**.

5. Choose New Resource Pool.

6. Type a friendly name, such as **Test & Dev**.

7. Under CPU Resources and Shares, select Custom and type **1000**.

8. Drag-and-drop one VM to Production and the other VM to Test & Dev.

If you look at the cpubusy.vbs script, you will see that one VM is running much faster than the other. Merely by calculating the CPU shares value, you can take a good guess at what the actual CPU utilization will be. You allocated a total of 4000 shares (Production's 3000 plus Test & Dev's 1000). This represents a production VM receiving 3000/4000 shares, or three-quarters, or 75%; and a testing and development VM receiving 1000/4000 or one-quarter, or 25%. The `esxtop` tool shows the current utilization.

```
root@esx1:~

 6:02:27pm up 3 days 22:10, 121 worlds; CPU load average: 0.51, 0.52, 0.25
PCPU(%):    3.28,    0.47,    0.72, 100.00 ;    used total:   26.12
CCPU(%):    0 us,    1 sy,   95 id,    4 wa ;       cs/sec:      306

   ID   GID NAME               NWLD    %USED     %RUN     %SYS     %WAIT     %RDY
    1     1 idle                  4   296.60   298.01     0.00      0.00   103.30
    2     2 system                9     0.10     0.10     0.00    900.00     0.06
    6     6 helper               66     0.15     0.14     0.00   6600.00     0.03
    7     7 drivers              10     0.01     0.01     0.00   1000.00     0.00
    8     8 vmotion               1     0.00     0.00     0.00    100.00     0.00
   10    10 console               2     2.56     2.66     0.11    197.98     0.02
   15    15 vmkapimod            13     0.00     0.00     0.00   1300.00     0.00
   20    20 vobd.4227             6     0.00     0.00     0.00    600.00     0.00
   21    21 vmkiscsid.4238        1     0.01     0.01     0.00    100.00     0.00
   27    27 vmware-vmkauthd       1     0 00     0.00     0.00    100.00     0.00
   34    34 dc01                  4    74.86    75.19     0.14    299.31    26.82
   35    35 dc02                  4    25.09    25.10     0.17    299.19    77.03
```

You can see that the physical CPU is still very busy. The dc01 VM is receiving 74.86% of CPU time, and its ready value has come down to 26.82%. The dc02 VM is receiving 25.09% of CPU time, and its ready value is at 77.03%. In a production environment, neither of these ready values would be regarded as remotely acceptable. Remember that this is an academic exercise where we are deliberately creating contention to show the effectiveness of resource pools.

You can also see the consequences of this contention simply by viewing how fast the cpubusy.vbs script is executing. The following example shows a significant difference in performance.

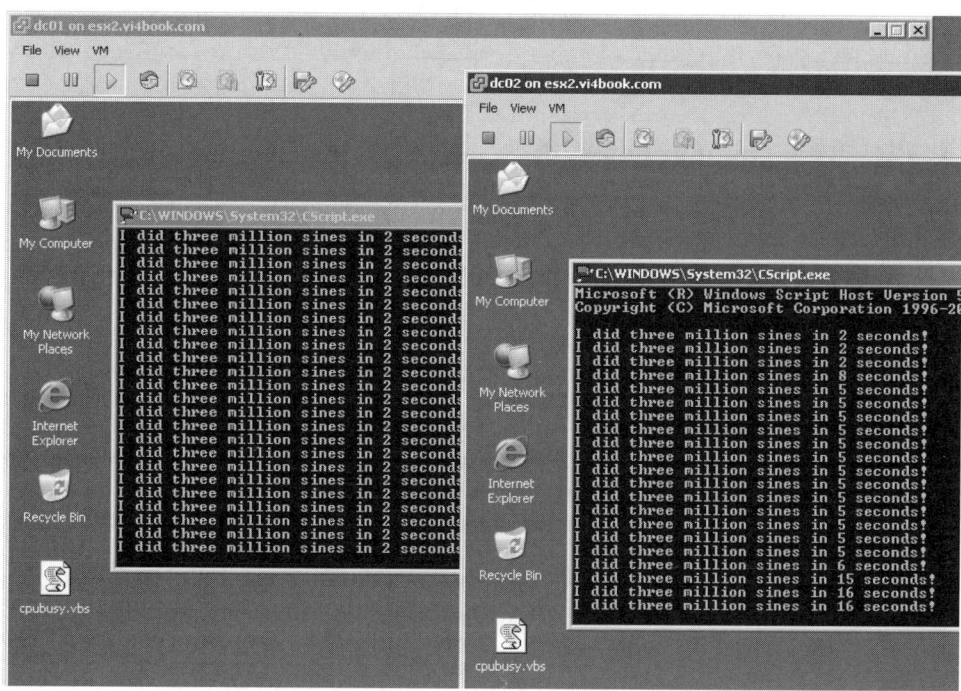

Finally, you can see both the CPU used and ready values in the VM's performance chart view. In the following example, you can see that dc02 is receiving a small amount of CPU, which is resulting in a high ready value.

As this example demonstrated, the VMkernel does a very good job of dealing with contention. In fact, everything that VMware does—whether it's CPU scheduling or DRS—is an attempt to avoid contention and poor performance.

CPU Ready Values and Multiple vCPUs

As I noted in the previous chapter, the CPU ready value can be a much better indicator of a CPU bottleneck than just overall CPU usage. As you saw in the previous example, the esxtop tool reports the actual CPU usage, whereas something like Microsoft Task Manager would just show these two VMs as receiving 100% of the CPU. In a way, that would be true—they would be receiving 100% of whatever the VMkernel allocates to them based on your resource pool share settings.

The CPU ready value can also be a very good indicator that you would benefit from Virtual SMP or multiple vCPUs. If you look back through the preceding esxtop examples, you will see that quite frequently, the CPU used plus the ready value added up to more than 100%. Even if you terminated one of the cpubusy.vbs scripts, you would probably still find the script would want to use 100% of the CPU.

With conventional performance analysis tools, it is impossible to see what a given process would "like" to have been, had it not been throttled by the physical limits of the CPU. In a VMware ESX server, the ready value can be a good indicator of the desired amount that is being denied. In the following esxtop example, I stopped the cpubusy script in dc02, and ran multiple copies of the script in just dc01. As you can see, the CPU is running at its maximum, and the ready value is consistently over 1.16%.

```
root@esx1:~

 6:18:43pm up 3 days 22:26, 121 worlds; CPU load average: 0.27, 0.28, 0.43
PCPU(%):    4.11,    2.37,    1.67,   99.70 ;   used total:    26.96
CCPU(%):    0 us,    2 sy,   97 id,    1 wa ;      cs/sec:       132

    ID   GID NAME              NWLD   %USED    %RUN    %SYS    %WAIT     %RDY
     1     1 idle                 4  290.90  293.53    0.00     0.00   105.13
     2     2 system               9    0.14    0.14    0.01   896.74     0.07
     6     6 helper              66    0.34    0.37    0.00  6576.88     0.04
     7     7 drivers             10    0.01    0.01    0.00   996.48     0.00
     8     8 vmotion              1    0.00    0.00    0.00    99.65     0.00
    10    10 console              2    2.29    2.23    0.11   196.92     0.15
    15    15 vmkapimod           13    0.00    0.00    0.00  1295.45     0.00
    20    20 vobd.4227            6    0.00    0.00    0.00   597.90     0.00
    21    21 vmkiscsid.4238       1    0.28    0.01    0.26    99.63     0.00
    27    27 vmware-vmkauthd      1    0.00    0.00    0.00    99.64     0.00
    34    34 dc01                 4   99.18   99.62    0.16   297.77     1.16
    35    35 dc02                 4    2.79    2.68    0.09   395.67     0.16
```

Now if you add 99.18 and 1.16 together, this comes to 100.34%. The argument follows that it is not possible for a single vCPU to offer more than 100% CPU. The only way to offer 200% or 400% is with two vCPUs or four vCPUs, respectively.

Share Values on VMs Within a Resource Pool

You might wonder if you can create resource pools within resource pools. The answer is that you certainly can. You might also wonder what happens to the share value set on VMs within a resource pool. The answer is that they are still effective, too. So it is possible to give one VM more shares of a resource pool than another VM.

For example, suppose we gave the Production resource pool 3000 shares and the Test & Dev resource pool 1000 shares. This would mean they would have a 75% and 25% split of the CPU time. If within the Test & Dev resource pool, one VM had 1000 CPU shares and another VM had 2000 shares, the 25% allocated to the Test & Dev resource pool would be divided accordingly. If contention occurred and CPU resources were scarce, this would mean that the first VM would receive about 8% of the CPU time and the second VM would receive 16%.

The moral of the story is that VMs get their resources not from the physical server directly, but circumscribed by the resource pool settings. As a consequence, share values are calculated within the boundaries of the resource pool.

Admission Control: Insufficient Resources to Power On?

"Insufficient resources"—it's not uncommon for people who are new to VMware ESX server to receive this message, indicating either insufficient memory or CPU required to power on a VM. It can happen with stand-alone ESX hosts and the VM's settings, ESX hosts with resource pools, and ESX clusters with resource pools. It can be extremely frustrating, because at first glance, it often looks like you have plenty of resources. For example, you know you have an ESX host with four quad-core CPUs (16 cores altogether) and 32GB or 64GB of RAM, and yet your VM still won't power on. The technical term that VMware uses to refer to this behavior is *admission control*, which refers to the resources required to power on your VM.

The source of these problems is always the same. It happens because a VM is given a reservation that is larger than the free resources currently available. Remember that reservations act as a guarantee to the VM or resource pool that a certain level of resources will always be available. In most cases, it's impossible to allocate a reservation that is greater than the resources that are free. This would be a bit like an airline selling more seats than it has physically available (a policy that is actually common practice in most airlines!). So the "Insufficient resources" message is like arriving too late at the airport and finding you have failed to make your reservation. Planes and hotels are not easy resources to expand. So, instead of adding more seats in the plane or building more rooms in the hotel, your admission is refused.

Admission Control Examples

This issue is best explained by a couple of examples. We will create this error message, and then look at ways of resolving it.

ESX Host Without Resource Pools

In this example, we will take an ESX host with a certain amount of free memory, try to allocate more RAM to the VM as a reservation, and see what happens.

First, let's see the amount of resources that are available. Select an ESX host and click the Summary tab. View the amount of memory resources available on the ESX host in the

Resources pane. The following example shows that this ESX host has 4GB of RAM, with 736.00MB currently in use. By my calculations, that's about 3369MB of free unreserved memory.

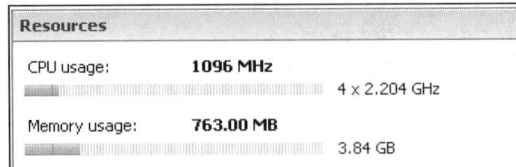

For a more detailed view of memory usage, run `esxtop` at the command line, and then type **m** on the keyboard to see memory statistics.

```
 6:37:44am up 4 days 10:45.  121 worlds; MEM overcommit avg: 0.00, 0.00, 0.00
PMEM   /MB:  3927   total:   300    cos,    406 vmk,      566 other,    2654 free
VMKMEM/MB:  3537 managed:   212 minfree,    552 rsvd,   2660 ursvd,   high state
COSMEM/MB:     5    free:  1600  swap_t,   1599 swap_f:   0.00 r/s,     0.00 w/s
NUMA   /MB:  1672 ( 1440),  1872 ( 1214)
PSHARE/MB:    73  shared      9  common:     64 saving
SWAP   /MB:     0    curr,     0 target:               0.00 r/s,     0.00 w/s
MEMCTL/MB:     0    curr,     0 target,    332 max

   GID NAME                MEMSZ    GRANT    SZTGT     TCHD %ACTV %ACTVS %ACTVF %AC
    20 vobd.4227           16.01     1.65    16.01     1.65     0      0      0
    21 vmkiscsid.4238       8.97     3.32     8.97     3.32     0      0      0
    27 vmware-vmkauthd      5.96     2.13     5.96     2.13     0      0      0
    42 dc02               256.00   255.99   380.19   192.00     7     37      8
    43 dc01               256.00   255.99   387.12   192.00     9     39     10
```

The `esxtop` utility shows there is 3927MB total physical memory, with 300MB allocated to the Service Console, 406MB in use by the VMK (the VMKernel), and 566MB allocated to "other," leaving 2654MB free. Here, you can also see that there is no swap file or memory control driver ballooning, indicated by the zero values.

Next, let's try to allocate more RAM than is available to a VM as a reservation. Power off a VM, and then right-click it and choose Edit Settings. On the Hardware tab, set the limit on the amount of RAM (6144MB in this example). Then click the Resources tab and set the memory reservation to be *less* than the amount of unreserved memory on the ESX host (2048MB in this example).

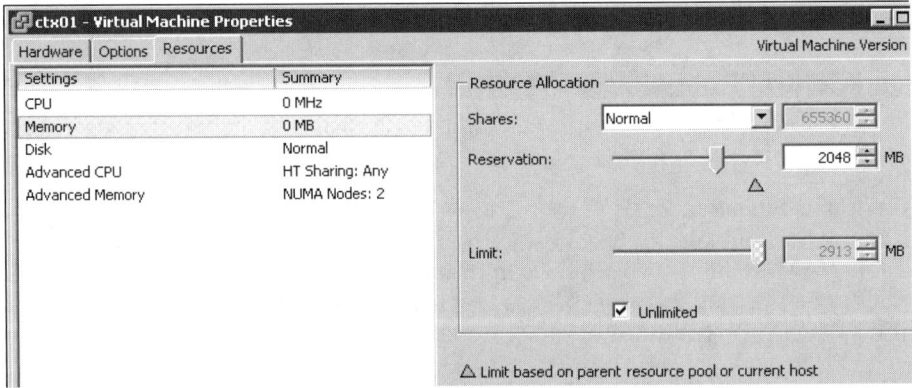

The orange triangle represents the point at which the VM reservation is getting close to the maximum amount of free unreserved memory on an ESX host or resource pool.

Now attempt to power on the VM. This will be successful, despite the limit being greater than the total amount of memory on the server. Remember that it is reservations that cause admission control warnings and the inability to power on a VM. This is the very essence of memory overcommitment—being able to allocate (or limit) more memory than is physically present on the ESX host. The problem will arise if you raise the reservation above the total amount of free, or unreserved, memory.

Modify another VM, and set the same limit and reservation values. Then attempt to power on the VM. This results in an "Insufficient memory resources" error message, as the reservation is larger than the amount of resources remaining on the ESX host.

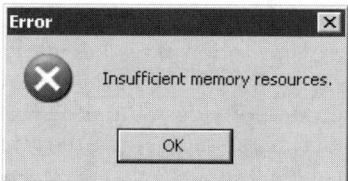

This was generated by creating a VM with 6GB limit and 2GB reservation, which was larger than the remaining amount of free, unreserved memory. It was easy to see from the memory statistics shown by the vSphere Client and `esxtop` that this would happen.

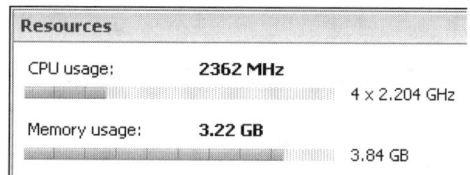

After allocating far more memory to my VM than I had available on my ESX host—by "over" overcommitting memory—I can see that the memory control driver was engaged.

ESX Host with Resource Pools and Nonexpandable Memory Reservations

One way of conceptualizing resource pools is to see them as taking a server and carving it up into slices of CPU or memory. In this respect, resource pools are logical divisions of resources, whereas servers represent a physical boundary. You might decide to take a physical server to create a resource pool with 25% of its resources and another resource pool that is 50% in size. This would leave 25% unallocated outside the resource pool.

You can get a very similar situation to that in the previous example, by powering off and resetting the same VMs. Reserve 2GB memory to the resource pool, but try to allocate more than what is free in the pool.

The critical point that will determine if a VM will power on is if the resource pool has an expandable reservation setting. If the resource pool is expandable, it can reach out and use the free 25% previously outlined. If the resource pool is not expandable, then it is locked within the confines of its own reservation. So, perhaps the Production resource pool would get 50% of the RAM in its reservation, with the resource pool set to be expandable, but the Test & Dev resource pool would get only 25% of RAM, set to nonexpandable. Once all the memory allocated to Test & Dev had been used from the reservation, a VM would not power on.

One selling point of expandable reservations is that if the resource is available, a VM can use it. The downside is that a rogue administrator could claim all the resources of the pool and its parents. In a way, the expandable option almost defeats the purpose of the resource pool, which is to control resources and prevent VMs from affecting the performance of others.

On its own, the expandable reservation doesn't make a VM perform faster as such; it just increases its likelihood of powering on and getting the resources allocated to it. In this respect, it's best to see the expandable option as a privilege—it's either on or off, or allowed or disallowed.

ESX Host with Resource Pools and Nonexpandable CPU Reservations

Now we will try some examples with nonexpandable reservations. To begin, right-click the Test & Dev resource pool and choose Edit Settings. Under Memory Resources, move the Reservation slider to 1024MB and remove the check next to the Expandable option

Next, we will modify a VM that tries to reserve more resources than is available in the resource pool. Power off a VM in the Test & Dev Resource pool. Right-click the VM and choose Edit Settings. On the Hardware tab, set the limit to 2048MB. Then, click the Resources tab and set the reservation to 1512MB. Attempt to power on the VM.

Again, you should receive an "Insufficient memory resources" error message. You can see why this happened from the vSphere Client's Resource Allocation tab for the resource pool (select the resource pool, click the Resource Allocation tab, and click the Memory button).

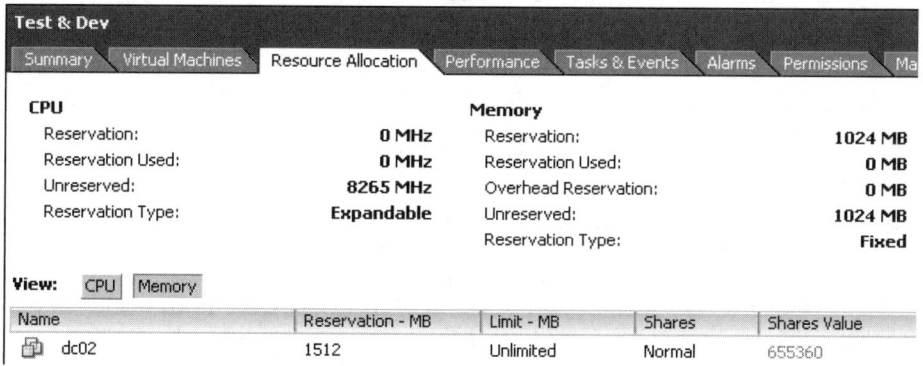

Test & Dev

Summary | Virtual Machines | Resource Allocation | Performance | Tasks & Events | Alarms | Permissions | Ma

CPU		Memory	
Reservation:	0 MHz	Reservation:	1024 MB
Reservation Used:	0 MHz	Reservation Used:	0 MB
Unreserved:	8265 MHz	Overhead Reservation:	0 MB
Reservation Type:	**Expandable**	Unreserved:	1024 MB
		Reservation Type:	**Fixed**

View: CPU   Memory

Name	Reservation - MB	Limit - MB	Shares	Shares Value
dc02	1512	Unlimited	Normal	655360

In this example, you can see that I've configured an inappropriate setting. I've given the dc02 VM a reservation of 1512MB, on a resource pool that has only 1024MB free unreserved memory. As the resource pool is fixed (the Expandable option was disabled), the VM cannot recursively work its way up the resource pools to find resources elsewhere, either in another resource pool (the parent) or a cluster.

Now let's see what happens with an unexpandable CPU reservation. Right-click the Test & Dev resource pool and choose Edit Settings. Under CPU Resources, move the Reservation slider to 1500 MHz and remove the check next to the Expandable option.

Next, we will modify three VMs that try progressively to reserve more resources than are available in the resource pool. Power off three VMs in the Test & Dev resource pool. Select the Test & Dev resource pool, click the Resource Allocation tab, and click the CPU button.

Edit Settings

Name: Test & Dev

CPU Resources

Shares: Custom   1000

Reservation: 1500   MHz

☐ Expandable

Limit: 8265   MHz

☑ Unlimited

Memory Resources

Shares: Normal   655360

Reservation: 1024   MB

△

☐ Expandable

Limit: 2915   MB

☑ Unlimited

△ Remaining resources available

Click into the Reservation – MHz column for the first VM and set the Reservation to 700 MHz. Repeat this for the other two VMs.

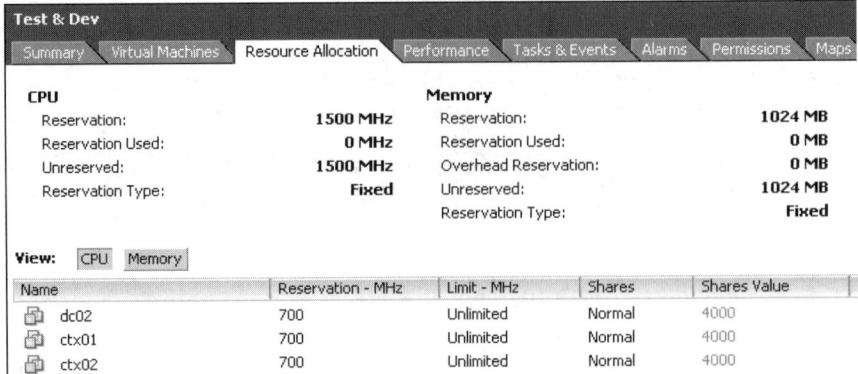

Here, we have a reservation on the resource pool that is fixed at 1500 MHz, and because all the VMs are powered off, 0 MHz of the reservation is used. As you power on the first VM, 700 MHz will be subtracted from the 1500 MHz, leaving 800 MHz.

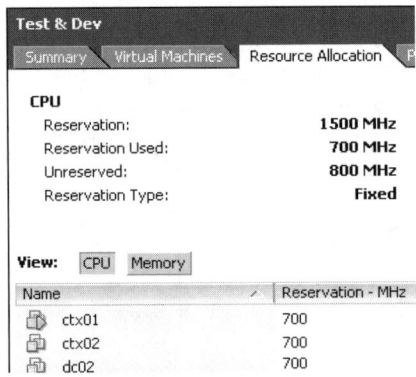

Powering on the next VM will reduce the amount of free unreserved CPU cycles for the resource pool to 100 MHz.

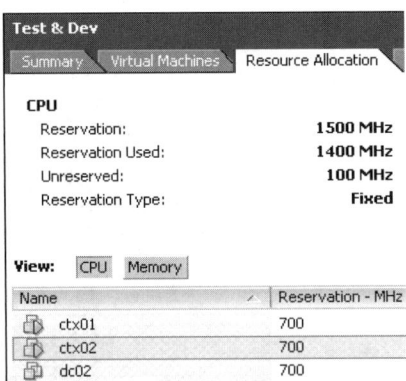

Attempting to power on the third VM will generate an admission control message, because the reservation (700 MHz) is bigger than the amount of free unreserved CPU cycle left on the nonexpandable (fixed) resource pool.

This is like you were taking a trip on a four-seat plane and you were the fifth person to arrive. There would be insufficient resources (seats) to make your reservation.

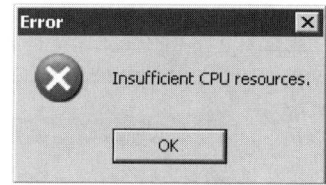

ESX Host with Insufficient Disk Space

Our final example of admission control comes from a lack of disk space. This is not to be confused with a lack of disk space to actually create a VM, say because its virtual disk size is bigger than the VMFS volume or you have failed to use thin provisioning. This disk-based admission control problem comes from having such a huge gap between your limit and reservation value that it results in a VMkernel swap file that is bigger than the amount of free space where the VM is located.

The easiest way to simulate this error is to find a VMFS volume with a limited amount of disk space, and set a very high limit value for memory. For example, my dc01 VM is held on a VMFS volume called sanlun, which has only 30GB of free disk space.

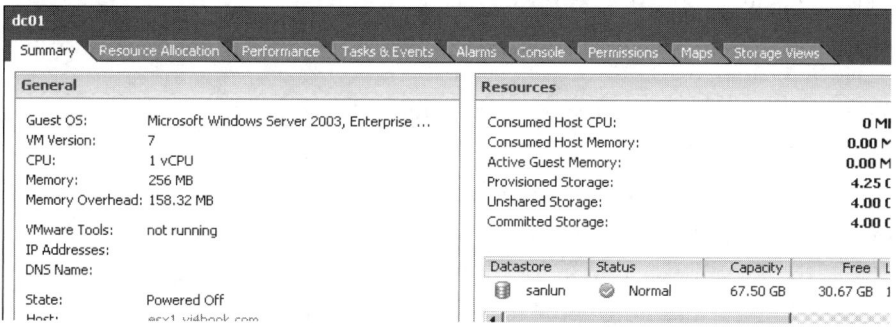

As you can see, the memory limit value is set to be very low at 256MB. Even if the reservation of memory were set to 0MB, this would result in a small VMkernel swap file of 256MB.

dc01.vmdk	4,194,304.00 KB	Virtual Disk
vmware-17.log	77.61 KB	Virtual Machine ...
dc01.nvram	8.48 KB	Non-volatile me...
vmware-12.log	62.22 KB	Virtual Machine ...
dc01.vmsd	0.00 KB	File
vmware-13.log	75.23 KB	Virtual Machine ...
vmware-14.log	76.41 KB	Virtual Machine ...
vmware-15.log	75.41 KB	Virtual Machine ...
vmware-16.log	274.11 KB	Virtual Machine ...
dc01.vmx	3.33 KB	Virtual Machine
dc01.vmxf	0.25 KB	File
vmware.log	56.86 KB	Virtual Machine ...
dc01-4631da0b.vswp	262,144.00 KB	File

After setting a limit value just above the amount of free space available in the VMFS datastore (33GB in this example), trying to power on the VM produced a "Failed to extend swap file" error message.

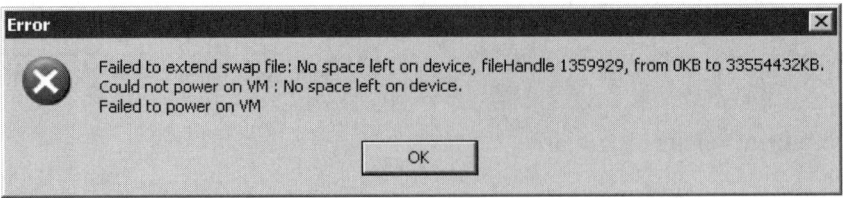

Resolving Admission Control Problems

If you are facing an admission control problem, there could be a number of solutions. The following solutions are listed in order of the change that would least impact the rest of the system to the one that would have the most impact.

- Decrease the amount of memory reserved for the VM, to allow its reservation to fit inside a resource pool or ESX host.
- Increase the amount of memory reserved for the VM, to allow a smaller swap file to be created.
- Increase the amount of free space in a VMFS volume for the swap file.
- Relocate the VM to a VMFS volume where there is more space.
- Increase the reservation of RAM to the resource pool.
- Decrease the amount of memory reserved for other VMs in the same resource pool.
- Enable the Expandable option for the reservation.
- Move the VM to a resource pool that has greater resources.
- Upgrade ESX hosts and add more memory.
- Add more ESX hosts.
- Change VMware HA settings.

VMware HA also imposes admission control on an HA-enabled cluster. If you think about it, HA is not just about restarting VMs when an ESX hosts fails at any cost. Even that is a resource management issue. After all, when an ESX host fails, you are losing capacity in the form of CPU and memory. VMware HA must make a judgment call on whether it is a good idea to power on a VM when you have lost an ESX host. HA is discussed in detail in Chapter 15.

Using vApps

A *vApp* allows you to collect together VMs that have shared dependencies and manage them as a group rather than as individual VMs. To some degree, the vApp environment can drift us into the area of developer tools. The intention of the vApp is to allow ISVs to package not just individual virtual appliances, but to deliver multiple-tier applications as single downloadable OVF package.

Here, I will give you a short introduction to vApps to get you up and running with its main features and concepts. Some features of vApps can be utilized immediately by the average administrator.

TIP   *If you wish to learn more about the development aspects of vApps, a good place to start would be the VMware vApp Developer blog at http://blogs.vmware.com/vapp/.*

For some time I toyed with leaving vApp in the "creating virtual machines" chapter, but in the end decided that actually vApp more logically slots in at the end of this resource management section—and in a moment you will see why. The concept of the vApp is actually quite a simple one—it's merely a grouping of VMs or virtual appliances that share a common relationship. In many respects, it's an extension of the virtual appliance concept, taking it beyond a single-task, stand-alone application to groups of services (appliances, if you will) that appear to the user as a single system. In the world of modern multitier applications, users are shielded from the complexity of all the different services required to provide their applications—all they normally see is a web browser and login page. The machinations and complexity of all these interlinked and integrated services which allow that to happen is something we all know they take for granted.

As with the resource pool feature, it is possible to assign resources to the vApp as well as the individual VM. That was my main reason in locating the section on vApps here. Just like resource pools, vApp has a resource management page that looks, feels, and behaves just like the resource pool dialog box. The vApp merely acts as container object for many VMs, so although the vApp icon appears once in the GUI, the VMs that make up the vApp can run on any ESX host within a given cluster.

vApp also integrates with the .OVF format we saw earlier in this book. The VMware vision is a grand and ambitious one—that multi-tier applications that require highly skilled people like you and me to configure and setup will eventually become downloadable and as easy to configure as virtual appliances. See, I told you it was a grand one. Personally, I'm a little skeptical of any vendor who tells me all I will have to do is click "next" and everything will be all right. But with that guarded skepticism in place, the principle and practice is a good one. Just as templates have reduced (but not eliminated) the deployment time, it is possible that vApp coupled with .OVF could deliver the same benefit. The operative word is "could" because it depends on the vendors of multi-tier applications adopting it as a standard or deployment option. Additionally, I still think that guys like you and me will still be needed to do high-level customization and maintenance—when these multi-tier applications fail. After all, they are software, and all those inter-connections introduce a complexity that simply clicking "next" might never really address!

vApp usage introduces TCP/IP configuration options. A substantial part of setting up a multitiered application in the first instance is sorting out which IP addresses to use and making sure they work correctly with DNS. You can use DHCP within the vApp to reduce these configuration roles.

NOTE *Personally, I prefer to have all my servers configured statically; in fact, many of the services and applications require it. In EMEA (and elsewhere), it's a well-established tradition and principle that DHCP and servers on the same network don't mix. However, I am beginning to detect rumbles of change in attitude toward DHCP, especially in the United States. I can only assume that people who opt for such an approach do so by using the client reservation feature of most DHCP servers. So, despite my personal skepticism toward dynamic IP settings for mission-critical services, I've chosen to document this in the book, in case the culture shifts in that direction.*

If none of these features really grabs you, here's one more that may be of interest: vApps allows you to group your VMs together into startup and shutdown orders, making it possible to bring up and down an entire multitier application, regardless of where the VMs are running. See it as a big power button on the vApp, rather than just for each and every VM. Although this is quite a modest feature compared with the rather loftier goals of vApps, many VMware users have hoped for and are glad that it has finally been delivered!

Creating a vApp

In this example, I'm using a Citrix Presentation Server environment as a multitier application. I have two Citrix Presentation Servers (ctx01/02). Before these servers boot up, a SQL Server instance (db01) must be started.

To allow remote access over the Internet, two components are needed: a Web server, which provides secure logon over HTTPS and presents the applications the users need, and Citrix Secure Gateway, which allows for firewall traversal and encryption of the users' keyboard and mouse movements. These components (wi01/wi02 and csg01/csg02) might as well start after the two Citrix Presentation Servers have started, as there is little point in having a Web service up if the associated encryption technology is not in place.

To create a new vApp, select the ESX hosts or cluster and click the vApp icon (or right-click and choose New vApp).

Type in the name for your vApp and a VM folder location (for example, I called mine Citrix-Portal). Accept the default settings in the Resource Allocation dialog box.

Adding VMs in a vApp

You can create new VMs within the vApp by right-clicking it and choosing New Virtual Machine. Additionally, if you create a new VM via a template, you are able to select a vApp as a destination through the wizard.

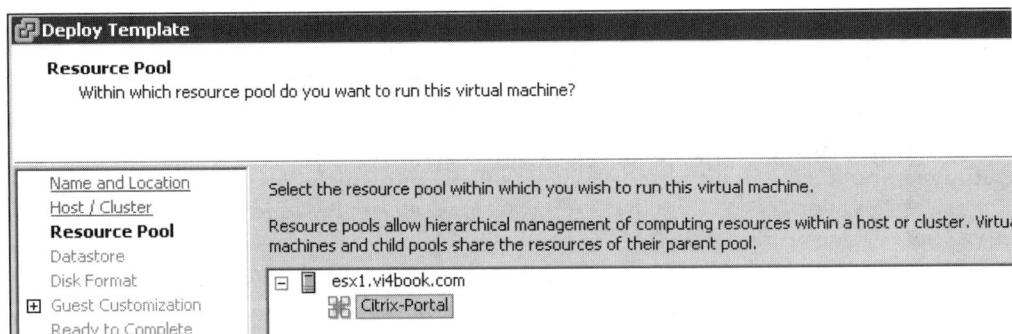

If you have existing VMs that you wish to add to a vApp, simply drag-and-drop them in the Inventory.

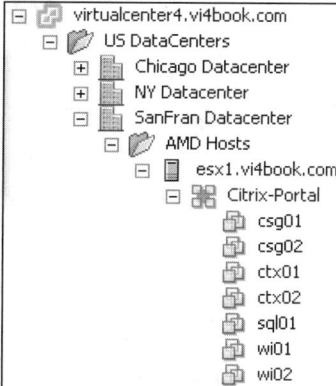

If at first you create your vApps on a stand-alone ESX host, and then later try to add it to a DRS-enabled cluster, you will receive a warning that vApps will be lost.

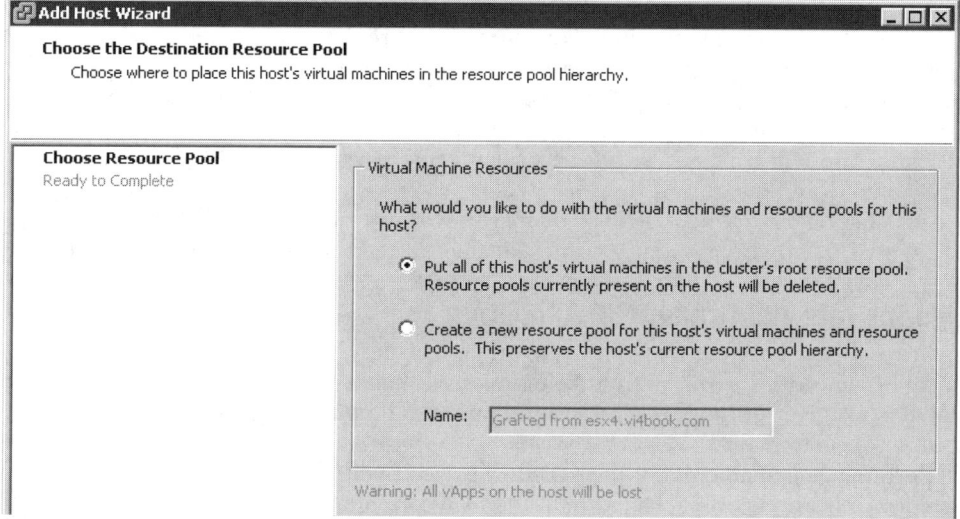

In other words, the vApp is deleted as an object in vCenter. The actually VMs do *not* get deleted. For this reason, I recommend creating a DRS/EVC-enabled cluster *before* creating or importing any vApps into your environment. (DRS and EVC are covered in Chapter 13).

Setting Startup and Shutdown Actions

To set the startup and shutdown actions for the vApp, right-click it, select Edit Settings, and click the Start Order tab. Use the up and down arrows to group your VMs together. For each VM, adjust the startup order with its group as you see appropriate, and enable the option to power on when VMware Tools is ready. For each VM, as the shutdown action operation, choose Guest Shutdown.

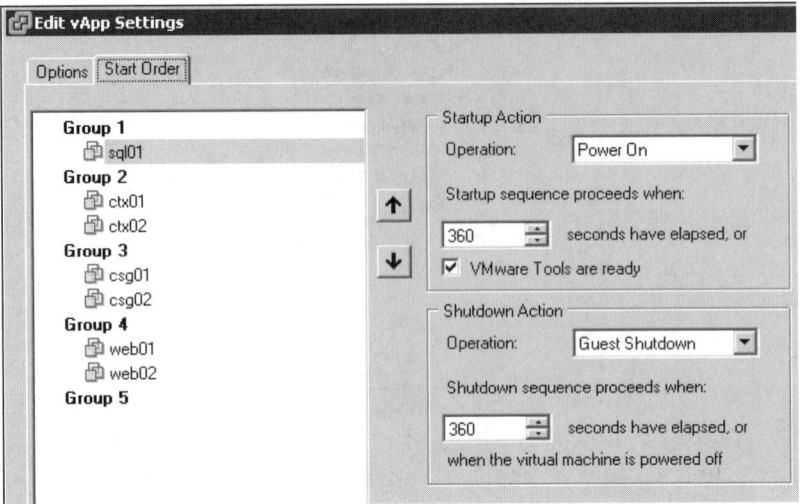

By setting the correct startup time, you can make sure that you give the services that start within the VM time to get up and running. The startup of the next VM will be triggered by the time value or when vCenter receives a signal from VMware Tools.

The most important setting here is changing the default options for shutdown. By default, the vApp will hard power off the VMs it contains, so you need to instruct it to gracefully shut down the guest OS.

The number of groups increases and decreases with the number of VMs you move up and down the list. This power-on order is automatically reversed when you shut down the vApp.

Configuring Internal Dynamic IP Allocation

So far, I have focused on features that the average administrator would use to make the managing of a multitier application easier. Now I will focus on how vApps could be used by ISVs to package multitier applications and automate their configuration; ready for distribution to customers.

It's perfectly reasonable that vApps could be used by large corporations to distribute those same applications prepackaged with their own company defaults. In this way, central IT becomes almost like an ISV operating within the business. One aspect of this, alongside dealing with the application settings, is handling the IP settings that each VM will have within the vApp.

IP address allocations come in three formats:

- **Fixed**   This is the default. Each VM or virtual appliance is statically configured for IP.
- **Transient**   This is very like DHCP. The VMs receive the internal IP address at bootup from a pool defined within the vApp itself.

- **DHCP**   This uses an existing DHCP server on your network to assign IP addresses. The IP address is retained by the VM after power down, based on the lease duration period set within the DHCP server service.

For demonstration purposes, in this example, I decided to support IP using the internal transient pool.

Creating a Pool and Associating It with a Network

Before you begin, you must create a pool of IP addresses to be used by the vApp. It's also highly desirable to place your vApp on a separate network or VLAN so you can more effectively control the leasing of IP addresses to the vApp. I created a vSwitch with a port group called citrix-net for this purpose, and made sure all my VMs within the vApp were configured for this port group. My internal transient range will not use IPv6 or have any references to external DHCP servers on my network.

VMware uses its own peculiar syntax for expressing IP address ranges; it doesn't correspond to the usual begin/end range that you see in most DHCP servers. In the example, I entered the following range:

192.168.3.30#5,192.168.3.80#5

The syntax is a starting IP (192.168.3.30) followed by the number (5) of contiguous IP addresses. Additional ranges (192.168.3.80) can be added by using a comma as a delimiter. The syntax in this example creates a pool of five IP addresses from 192.168.3.30 to 192.168.3.34 and another five IP addresses from 192.168.3.80 to 192.168.3.84. The two blocks of IP addresses put together constitute ten IP addresses allocated to this vApp.

When you enter an IP address range, validation is carried out within the dialog box to check your inputs. So if you had a range of 192.168.3.30#5 but set the subnet to be 192.168.2.0, this would produce an error in red in the dialog box. Additionally, ranges must be specified in numeric order, so 192.168.3.80#5,192.168.3.30#5 is not accepted and would produce an error message.

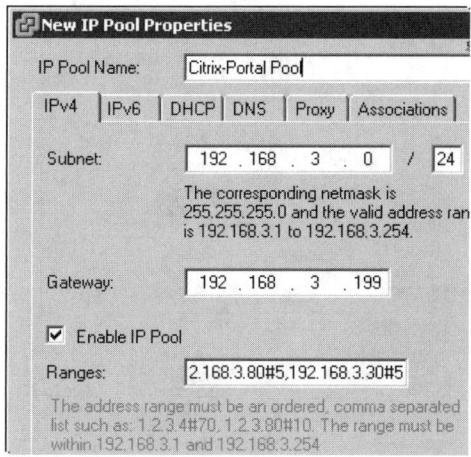

Follow these steps to create the pool and associate it with a network:

1. Click Home, click Networking, and then select a datacenter.

2. Select the IP Pools tab, and then click the Add button.

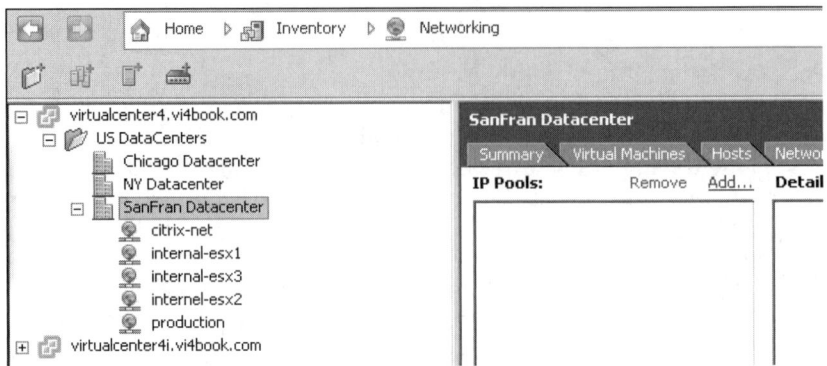

3. In the dialog box, type a friendly name for the pool (Citrix-Portal Pool in this example).

4. Enter the network ID using the CIDR notation. For example, 192.168.3.0 would be correct for a network using 24 bits or 255.255.255.0.

5. Enter the default gateway.

6. Select the Enable IP Pool option.

7. Type in a range of IP addresses to be used by the network. Click the View option to see the range.

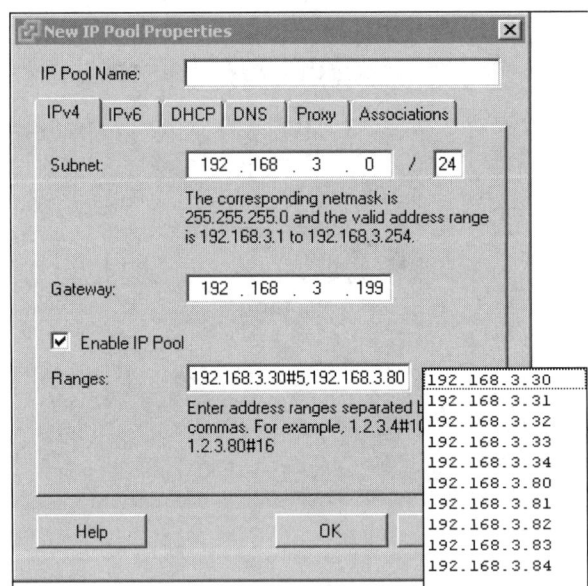

8. Select the DNS tab, and set your DNS domain name, search order, and IP addresses for the DNS servers.

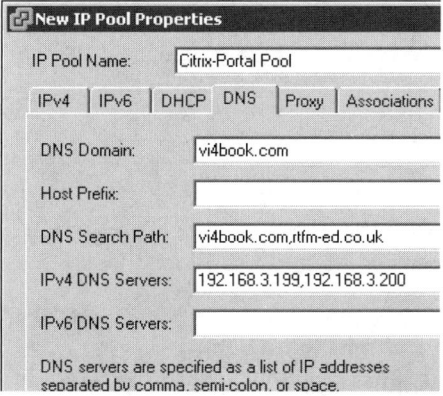

9. If necessary, set the name or IP addresses of the proxy servers that service this pool.

10. Click the Associations tab, and link this IP pool to the correct network (the citrix-net port group in this example).

After you've added the pool, its properties will be displayed in the IP Pool tab. Additionally, if you select the network associated with the pool, you will see which pool it is associated with (if any).

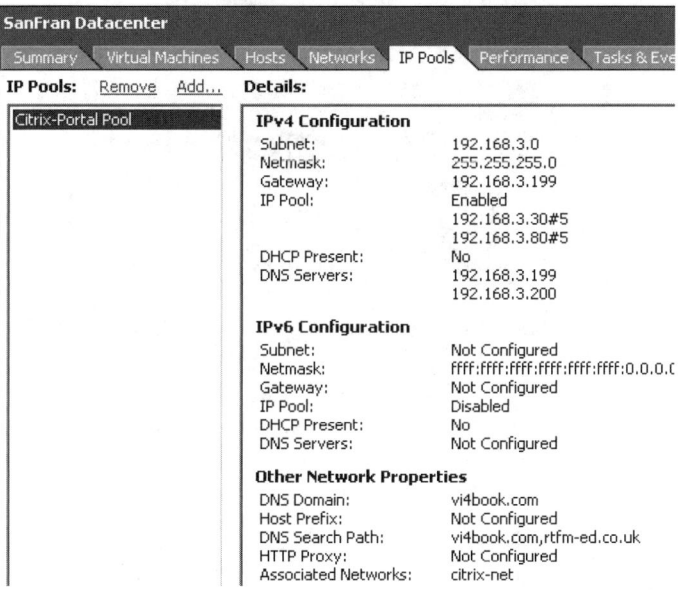

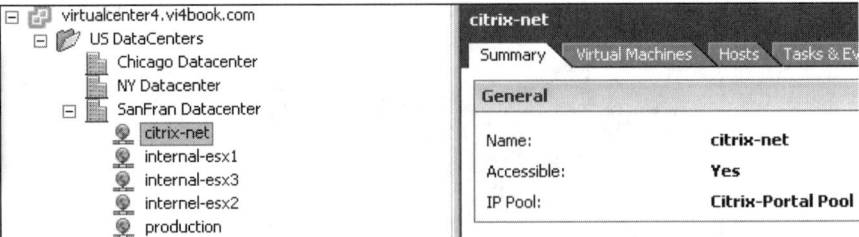

Enabling the IP Transient Pool on the vApp

As note earlier, we will use transient IP address allocations in this example. Follow these steps to enable it:

1. Right-click the vApp and select Edit Settings.

2. Select the Advanced option, and then click the IP Allocation button.

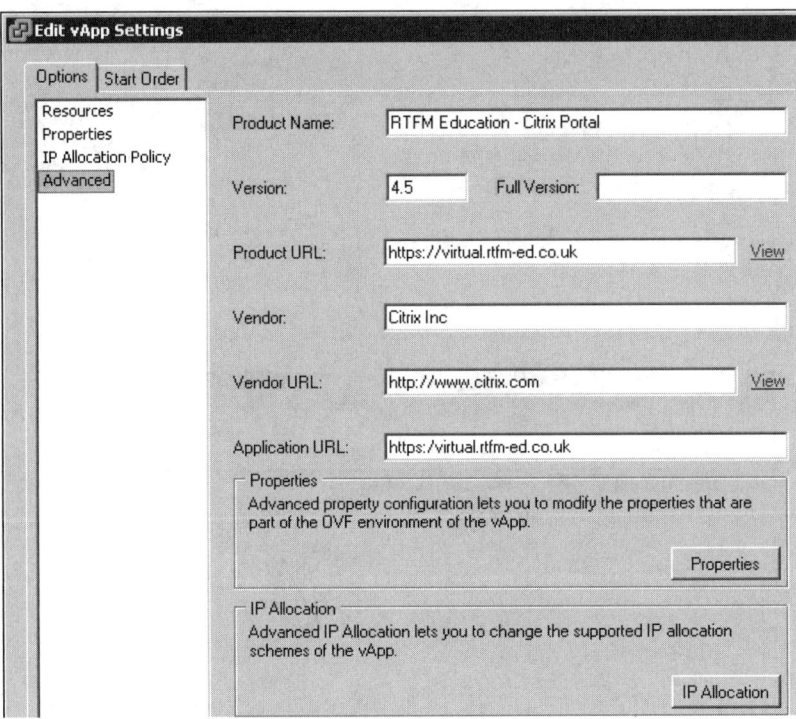

3. In the Advanced IP Allocation dialog box, select OVF as the format and IPv4 as the protocol.

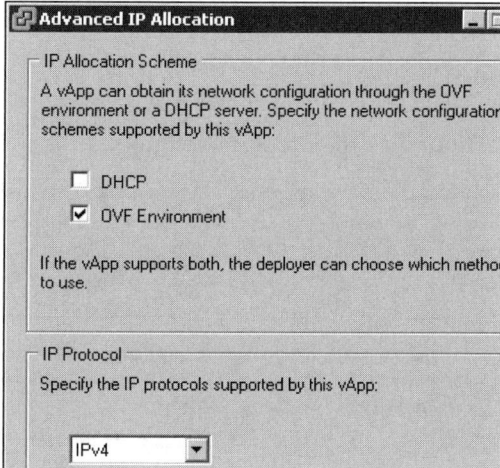

4. Click OK, and then select IP Allocation Policy. Choose the Transient option.

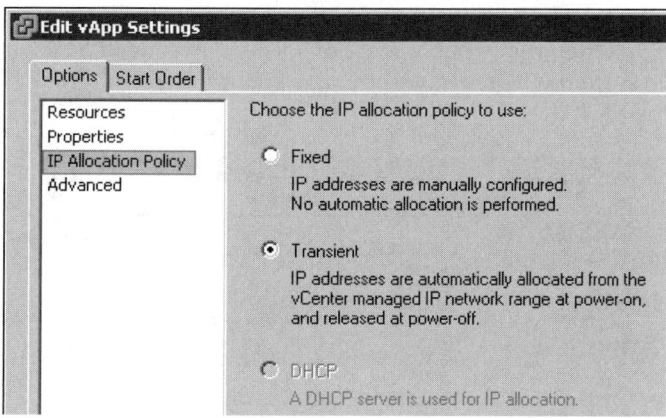

DHCP is disabled because you chose not to use an external DHCP server in the configuration. (Actually, I think that if you're going to head down the lonely route to using DHCP for servers, you would be more likely to use an external DHCP.)

Creating Variables for Each the VM in the vApp

The next stage is making sure that the VM in the vApp knows that the IP pool exists and will take an IP address from the pool. This is achieved by editing the advanced properties of the pool, and defining variables for allocating the IP address to the VM. Note that the Advanced Property Configuration dialog box is accessible only when the vApp is powered off.

When the vApp is powered on, this will configure each VM in the vApp with an XML file (accessible by CD-ROM or VMware Tools) from which an IP address can be assigned.

NOTE *There are a significant number of predefined variables, and it's possible for the developer of the vApp to add any number of user-defined variables to hold generic variables in the form of integer, string, or Boolean values, among others.*

Follow these steps to create the variables:

1. Right-click the vApp and select Edit Settings.
2. On the Options tab, select the Advanced category.
3. In the Properties section, click the Properties button.

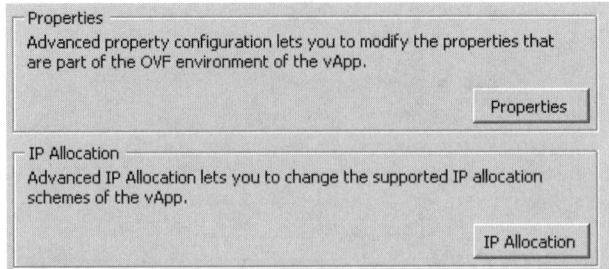

4. In the Advanced Property Configuration dialog box, click the New button.
5. In the Edit Property Settings dialog box, change the Label and ID values to **vmIPaddress**. These values can actually be anything you like; it is the next part that dictates the data that the variable will hold. There is no need to set a Category value, as the system will automatically place your variable in the Ethernet adapter section of the XML file.

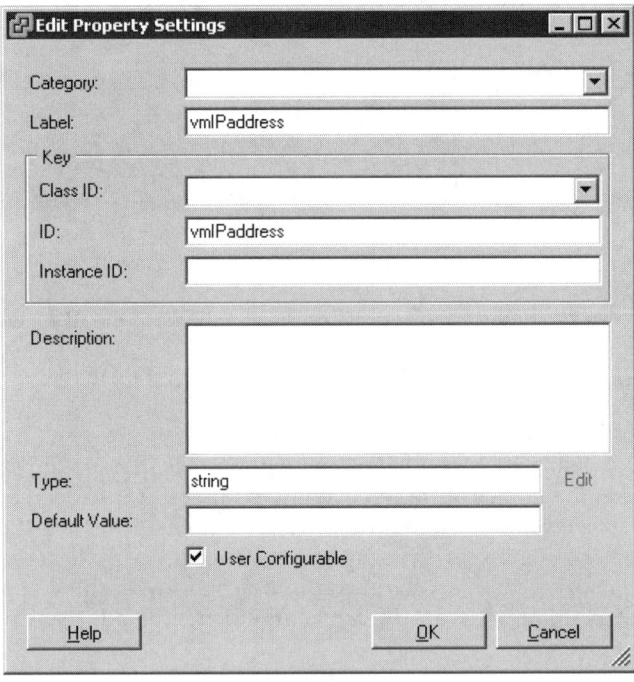

6. Currently, the variable type is string. Click the Edit link to modify it.

7. In the Edit Property Type dialog box, under the Static Property option, change the type to vApp IP Address. Select in which network this variable should find the IP pool you created earlier.

8. Click OK to close the dialog box. You should see this new variable in the Advanced Property Configuration dialog box.

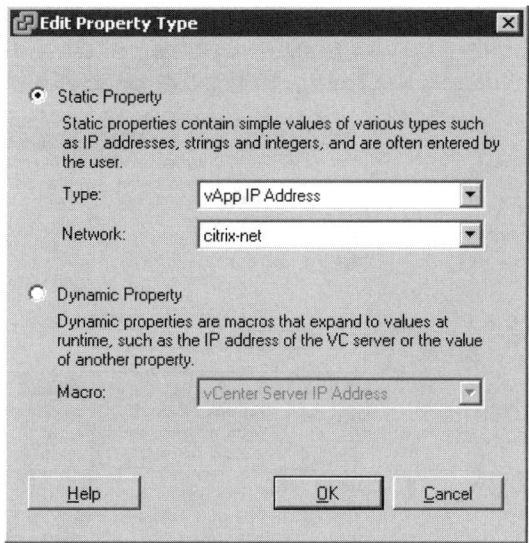

Enabling vApp Options on a VM in a vApp

The final part of the IP allocation process is making sure that each VM that makes up the vApp receives the right IP address from the pool. There are two main ways for vendors to do this, and both use an XML file to hold the parameters. It can be triggered by attaching an ISO image to the VM within the vApp and running a script from there or by calling the script from VMware Tools.

Here are the steps:

1. Right-click the VM in the vApp and select Edit Settings.

2. Click the Options tab. In the Settings column, select vApp Option.

3. In the right side of the dialog box, select the Enable radio button.

4. Select OVF Settings in the Settings column.

5. Select the option to provide the OVF environment transport by using an ISO image.

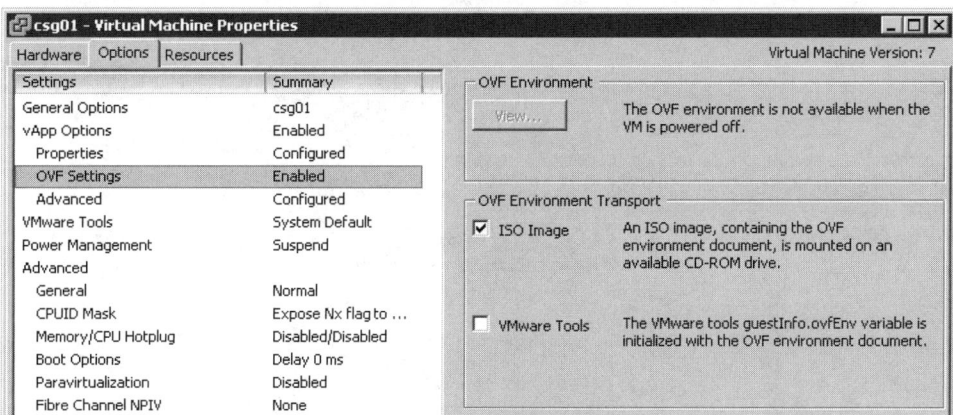

6. Repeat the preceding steps for each VM in the vApp.

7. Power on the vApp and wait for all the VMs to be available.

Click the View button to see the XML file associated with the VM (a read-only version). In the following example, you can see the XML file contains both a MAC address and an IP address taken from your IP pool, together with your own custom variable, or property.

```
-<Environment oe:id="csg01"
    xmlns:xml="http://www.w3.org/XML/1998/namespace"
    xmlns="http://schemas.dmtf.org/ovf/environment/1"
    xmlns:xsi="http://www.w3.org/2001/XMLSchema-
    instance"
    xmlns:oe="http://schemas.dmtf.org/ovf/environment/1"
    xmlns:ve="http://www.vmware.com/schema/ovfenv">
  -<PlatformSection>
    <Kind>VMware ESX</Kind>
    <Version>4.0.0</Version>
    <Vendor>VMware, Inc.</Vendor>
    <Locale>en</Locale>
  </PlatformSection>
  -<ve:EthernetAdapterSection>
    <ve:Adapter ve:mac="00:50:56:97:5f:ab"
      ve:network="citrix-net"/>
  </ve:EthernetAdapterSection>
  -<PropertySection>
    <Property oe:key="vmIPaddress"
      oe:value="192.168.3.83"/>
  </PropertySection>
```

The ISO image and VMware Tools options allow you to specify which method is used by the VM to grab an IP address from the vApp pool. With the ISO image method, an internally held ISO image is created on demand for each VM in the vApp attached to the VM at power on, in much the same way that an ISO image is used to install VMware Tools. The ISO image is stored in the same location at the VM's .vmx file and will inherit the naming of the VM; for example, a VM named CSG01 would have an ISO image called ovfenv-csg01.iso.

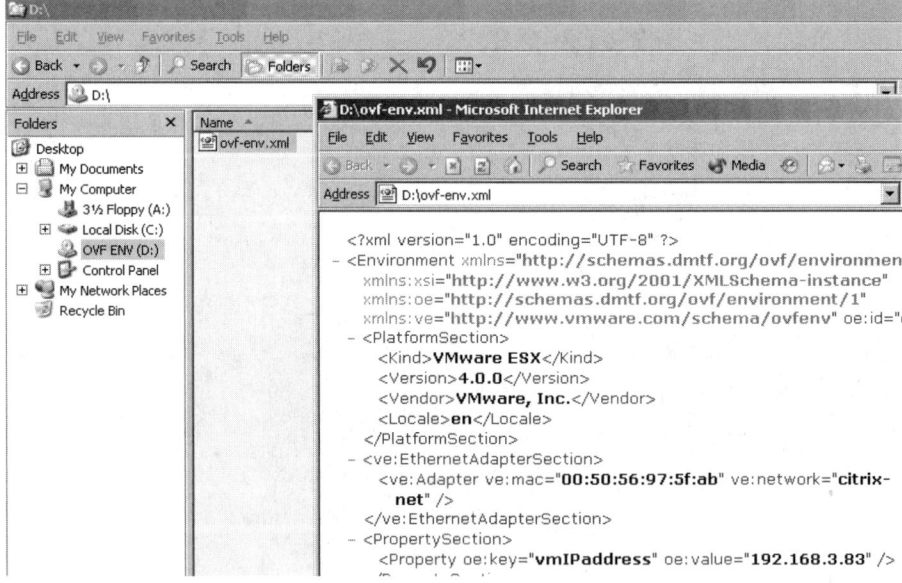

CAUTION *Vendor-specific OVF properties can be modified only when the vApp is powered down. These vendor-specific OVF properties allow for variables to be added to the OVF file import procedure, which means the vendor could prompt you to set a static IP and host name for each component of multitier applications.*

Merely having these IP settings either in the ISO image or the VMware Tools does *not* in itself allocate the IP address to the VM. To do that, the developer would write a script that would parse the XML data and, using OS-specific tools, modify the core IP settings and other files or registry locations where this information may be referenced. Currently, a few examples of how to write this "glue code" have begun to surface within VMware. A good place to look for such examples is on the VMware vApp Developer blog:

http://blogs.vmware.com/vapp/2009/07/selfconfiguration-and-the-ovf-environment
.html

Setting Descriptive (Advanced) Information

In the Advanced options of a vApp, you can set descriptive information about the application. This appears in the main Summary page of a vApp.

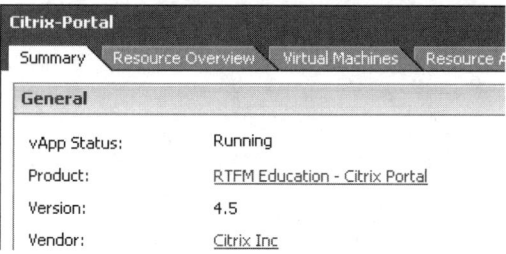

At this point, I've covered basically as much as can be done with vApps and OVF files merely using vCenter. If you want to investigate the true capabilities of vApps and OVF format, I recommend the VMware OVF Studio application, currently in beta, available from the VMware Studio site:

http://www.vmware.com/appliances/learn/studio/studio_beta.html

Summary

This chapter covered the available resource controls, including limits, reservations, shares, CPU affinity, and resource pools. I have outlined some of the advantages and disadvantages of each method, and given you a practical example of using resource pools and creating contention to demonstrate their effectiveness in conjunction with the proportional share system. I showed you how VM reservations of memory and CPU can cause a VM not to power on, referred to by VMware as admission control. Additionally, I gave some guidelines on how to resolve these power-on issues.

As you have seen, resource pools liberate you from the constraints of the physical world, similar to how LUNs liberate you from the limitations of disk geometries in the world of storage, and this is really great. But be aware that VMware has begun to really push the concept of the "software mainframe" and how VMs just run in pools of memory and CPU resources. Conceptually, I have no problem with this, but it does obscure the practical and physical limitations. Remember that whatever the size of the resource pool, fundamentally the buck stops with the physical hardware. A VM can see only the memory and CPU resources of an individual ESX host, whether it is a conventional rack-mounted server or a blade in an enclosure.

CHAPTER 12 | VMotion, Storage VMotion, and Cold Migration

T his chapter covers VMotion, Storage VMotion (SVMotion), and cold migration, which allow you to change hosts and datastores. SVMotion, introduced in VI3.5, is now much easier to work with from an updated user interface in vCenter. Additionally, SVMotion used to require VMotion to be configured first, but now it operates as entirely separate feature.

VMotion (Change Host)

To say we are moving a VM from one ESX host to another with VMotion is a bit of a lie. In fact, we very rarely move data around at all. If you cut and paste a file in a folder to another folder, what actually happens is the OS copies the file to the new location. Once this is completed, the original is deleted. Essentially, this is what happens with VMotion. The critical thing to stress is that the VM's files are not copied, but its memory contents are.

The VM on the first host (ESX1) is duplicated on the second host (ESX2), and the original is deleted. During VMotion, ESX creates an initial pre-copy of memory from the VM running on ESX1 into a VM on ESX2. During the copy process, a log file is generated to track any changes during the initial pre-copy process (it is referred to as a *memory bitmap*).

Once the VMs are practically at the same state, this memory bitmap is transferred to ESX2. Before the transfer of the bitmap file, the VM on ESX1 is put into a *quiesced* state. This quiesce process massively reduces the amount of activity occurring inside the VM that is being migrated. It allows the memory bitmap file to become so small that it can be transferred very quickly. This state also allows for rollback if a network failure occurs. In this respect, VMotion has a transactional quality—it is either successful or unsuccessful. What we don't get is two VMs on two different ESX hosts who believe they are the same. After the memory bitmap has been transferred, the end user is switched to using the VM on ESX2, and the original VM is removed from ESX1.

During this switch from one ESX host to another, there may be some dropped packets. Although the VM's physical MAC address does not change, the physical MAC address on the ESX host does. The VMotion process triggers a RARP packet to make sure all network devices on the same subnet as the VM are aware that packets destined for the VM IP address should be directed to a new MAC address.

> **NOTE** *In my experience, one or two lost packets are not enough to disconnect even a real-time networking system like Microsoft's RDP or Citrix's Independent Computing Architecture (ICA) protocol. In some cases, where I have been pinging a VM with* ping -t *(a constant ping), I've seen packets merely being delayed rather than dropped. Fundamentally, you will probably see more packets dropped daily on your WAN than you ever will with VMotion.*

For VMotion to function, both the ESX hosts and VMs must meet a number of requirements.

VMotion Requirements on the ESX Host

The following VMotion requirements apply to both the source and destination ESX hosts, and an inability to meet these requirements would be a good reason to resort to a cold migration instead.

- Shared storage/LUN visibility between the source and destination ESX hosts (SAN, iSCSI, or NFS). This includes the VMFS volume where the virtual disk(s) are and any RDM-mapped LUNs.

- A VMkernel port group on a vSwitch configured with 1000Mbps on the VMotion network. This VMkernel port group requires an IP address and a subnet mask.
- Access to the same "production" network.
- Consistently labeled vSwitch port groups (case-sensitive).
- Compatible CPUs.

If any one of these requirements cannot be met, VMotion will fail. Fortunately, most of the requirements can be purchased (shared storage and gigabit bandwidth) or reconfigured (same production network and consistently labeled switch port groups). The need for gigabit networking is to meet support and quality of service requirements, meaning that it is necessary to make sure that VMotion is dependable and reliable.

NOTE *I have successfully carried out VMotion with 100Mbps at full-duplex, but I have also seen it fail. Generally, these attempts have been in test and development environments, where full VMware support is not required. If you want full VMware support, you will need 1000Mbps networking. The cause of the failure with 100Mbps is a network timeout, merely because the amount of memory in the VM is large and frequently changing, and that 100Mbps pipe cannot bring the state of the two VMs close enough to trigger the VMotion.*

There is one showstopper: incompatible CPUs. Remember that although 99% of a VM is isolated from physical hardware, the one exception is that vCPUs do see specific attributes of the CPU. This is because, as discussed in the "Enabling Paravirtualization" section in Chapter 7, there are generally three types of execution in virtualization: direct execture, binary translation, and paravirtualization. Because CPU incompatibilities are a common problem, I will provide some details about how to discover them.

CPU Incompatibilities

One reason to do a cold migration is because your servers do not share CPU compatibility. Of course, many people attempt to purchase the same make and model of server, and indeed I've heard stories that some hardware vendors will keep CPUs in stock that match your server's specification. However, I think that in the short-term, it's likely that you will face CPU incompatibilities at some point, as you purchase new hardware and as VMware exposes more of these features to a VM to improve performance, stability, and security. For example, vSphere 4 introduces yet another CPU compatibility requirement for the new VMware FT feature. Here's a list of current attributes that would cause VMotion to fail due to CPU incompatibilities:

- **Processor vendor and CPU family** VMware does not allow the administrator to carry out VMotion events from Intel processors to AMD processors. Within a given vendor's line of products, there are "family" differences that would prevent VMotion from one generation of a vendor's processor to another.
- **Multimedia Instructions (SSE)** SSE stands for Streaming SIMD Extensions, and SIMD stands for Single Instruction, Multiple Data. These allow for improvements in processing for multimedia applications and have their roots in the Multimedia Extensions (MMX) feature found in some early Intel Pentium II processors. SSE incompatibilities are especially difficult to fix, as the instructions execute deep in the heart of the user mode space of most OSs.

- **Hardware assist features** In Intel VT and AMD-V processors, these are relatively recent enhancements that allegedly improve performance specifically for virtualization activity. They represent the first stages by Intel and AMD to create processors designed for virtualization. Right now, the jury is out on whether these features make a big impact on OSs like ESX, but they are a step in the right direction and do represent a VMotion barrier.

- **Execute Disable attribute** In Intel XD and AMD NX processors, this attribute is designed to secure processors from attacks and exploits used by hackers.

Of course, there are other processor differences—such as the number of cores, sockets, clock speed, and amount of onboard cache. However, these attributes are ignored in VMotion, so they are not a concern.

You will soon know you have some kind of CPU incompatibility if you attempt a VMotion where one exists. Before the VMotion, ESX validates the source and destination ESX hosts, and it will stop the wizard with a warning if a CPU incompatibility exists. If this validation check were not done before the VMotion, then a VM would probably crash when it arrived at the destination, because the VM would try to execute instructions that used a feature of the CPU that suddenly had been removed.

However, the vSphere Client sometimes does not give you meaningful information about these CPU incompatibilities. All the vSphere Client will tell you in the Summary tab of an ESX host are things like the number of CPUs, their clock speed, vendor, and family. Critically, it doesn't tell you anything about the incompatibilities that exist within the physical CPU, such as SSE3, NX/XD, Intel VT, or AMD-V.

Although other vendors (such as Citrix and Xen) have been able to demonstrate apples (Intel) to oranges (AMD) live migration, VMware's current position is that this is fraught with dangers for the stability of the VM, and it currently has no intention of relaxing the conditions placed on CPU compatibility. With that said, there are ways to weaken this check by creating CPU identification masks or editing the vCenter vpxd.cfg file, as discussed shortly.

Perhaps the long-term fix for this issue is projects inside Intel and AMD that seek to remove this problem altogether for their chipsets. These projects, such as Intel's FlexMigration and AMD model-specific registers (MSRs), are already bearing fruit, as you will see later when we look at DRS in Chapter 13. Working with the CPU vendors, since VI3.5 Update 2, VMware has introduced a new feature called Enhanced VMotion Compatibility (EVC), which leverages these innovations from the CPU vendors. EVC is covered in Chapter 13.

NOTE *It won't come as a surprise to you that Intel and AMD do not intend to enable interoperability between their CPUs. Here's a recent quote from Jake Smith, a member of Intel's Advanced Server Technologies team: "Our goal is to create flexibility, based on what [the customers] purchase today, for future generations of Intel processors . . . We do not do cross-company enablement." (from http://searchservervirtualization.techtarget.com/news/article/ 0,289142,sid94_gci1267906,00.html)*

Let's look at some ways to avoid CPU incompatibilities.

Buy for Compatibility

Of course, one of the easiest ways to avoid CPU incompatibilities is to buy for compatibility. Simply put, this means being careful in your purchases to ensure that each ESX host has identical CPUs. This is attractive to organizations that have the purchasing power to buy blocks of servers. It's inevitable that over time, you will not be able to buy the same hardware as two years ago. If this happens, you can see these new servers as representing a new "cluster" of ESX hosts that share common attributes. However, this approach will not help a company that buys hardware on an as-needed basis.

Read the Fine Manual

There are a number of ways of finding out the attributes of your CPUs and whether your server hardware possesses compatibility issues. In recent months, both Dell and HP have released compatibility documents that will allow you to compare your hardware. I've yet to see an IBM document on this topic, but I dare say there will be a Redbook on the subject shortly. I was able to find a document on the vmetc.com Web site that does a good job of listing IBM-compatible servers; unfortunately, it's a little out of date.

The following compatibility documents are available:

- Dell: http://www.dell.com/downloads/global/solutions/vmotion_compatiblity_matix.pdf

- HP: ftp://ftp.compaq.com/pub/products/servers/vmware/vmmotion-compatibility-matrix.pdf

- IBM: http://vmetc.com/2007/11/04/vmware-vmotion-compatibility-guide-for-ibm-system-x-and-bladecenter-servers/

While these documents are useful, they don't really help if you already have a mix of hardware vendors who use the same CPUs. Perhaps your organization deliberately does not buy from the same server vendor for strategic reasons. Perhaps there was a recent shift from one vendor to another, such as from HP to Dell.

NOTE *It's entirely possible for there to be compatibility between hardware from different vendors if the chipsets are the same.*

Use CPU Vendor Tools

Both AMD and Intel have their own tools for reporting the CPU types present in a system. The downside of these tools is that they may flag attributes that are not a problem with VMotion. You can download the relevant tool from the Intel or AMD Web site:

- Intel: http://www.intel.com/support/processors/tools/piu/

- AMD: http://www.amd.com/us-en/Processors/TechnicalResources/0,,30_182_871_9706,00.html

Use VMware CPU Identification Utility (cpuid.iso)

Located on the ESX CD in the /images directory is a file called cpuid.iso. This can be attached using an ILO or RAC board via virtual media, or burned to a physical CD. The cpuid.iso file is bootable and will show you the characteristics of your processor. The ISO file is also freely available on VMware's download Web site (http://www.vmware.com/download/shared_utilities.html) if you do not have access to the ESX media. You will find it under CPU Compatibility Tools.

The following example is an ILO capture of the information from a HP ProLiant DL385 Server with two AMD dual-core processors.

```
Reporting CPUID for 4 logical CPUs...

All CPUs are identical

     Family: 0f Model: 21 Stepping: 2

     ID1ECX      ID1EDX      ID81ECX     ID81EDX
     0x00000001 0x178bfbff 0x00000002 0xe3d3fbff

Vendor                        : AMD
Processor Cores               : 2
Brand String                  : "AMD Opteron(tm) Processor 275"
SSE Support                   : SSE1, SSE2, SSE3
Supports NX / XD              : Yes
Supports CMPXCHG16B           : No
Supports RDTSCP               : No
Supports 3DNow! Prefetch      : Yes
Supports FFXSR                : Yes
Supports Extended Migration   : Yes
Supports 64-bit Longmode      : Yes
Supports 64-bit VMware        : Yes
Supported EVC modes           : Opteron Gen 1/2
```

This shows that "All CPUs are identical" within the ESX host. There are some rare cases, such as after a reseller CPU upgrade, when one physical server may have different CPU types.

Additionally, you can see the vendor is AMD, and my sockets contain two processor cores. There is full support for NX/XS and full support for 64-bit guest OSs. Longmode is an Intel mode. Only Intel 64-bit (EM64T) chips with VT are supported for 64-bit guest OSs. Intel uses the term *Longmode* to describe this type of CPU. It's also worth noting that Intel CPUs may be VT-capable but have that functionality disabled by the BIOS.

The RDTSCP and CMPXCH16B attributes belong to the Intel processors, and so the results show that they are not supported by my AMD processors.

For detailed descriptions of the attributes identified by cpuid.iso, see the *VMotion Information Guide* (http://www.vmware.com/files/pdf/vmotion_info_guide.pdf).

Use Third-Party Tools

Richard Garsthagen is currently a Senior Evangelist for VMware in EMEA. He was formerly a VMware Certified Instructor (VCI); in fact, he was the first instructor in EMEA for VMware. In his spare time, Richard is an enthusiastic blogger (http://www.run-virtual.com) and evangelist for the vCenter SDK.

The vCenter SDK allows people to develop their own tools for vCenter in practically any programming language. Richard wrote an application called VMotion Info for VI3, which uses the SDK to unveil the CPU attributes of your server hardware. When the beta program started for vSphere 4, I contacted Richard to see if he would update the utility to include attributes such as checking for Intel VT and VMware FT support. Richard has very kindly updated this tool utility to make it compatible with vSphere 4 and check for the new CPU attributes you really care about. The really cool aspect of Richard's application is that it can be run against existing ESX hosts, without having to reboot them, as is necessary with the cpuid.iso method.

The following screenshot shows Richard's application taken from his Web site.

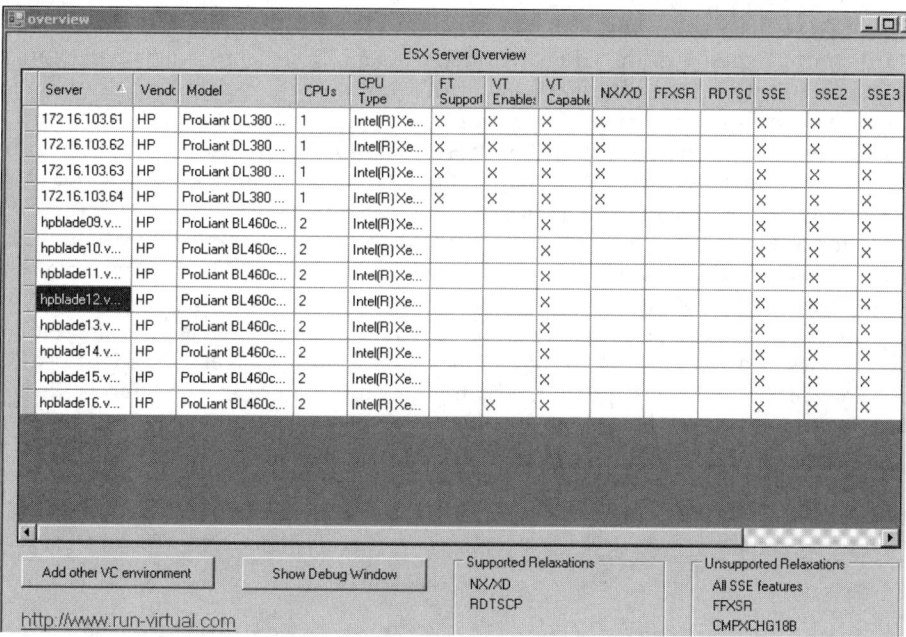

And the next screenshot shows the results for my servers.

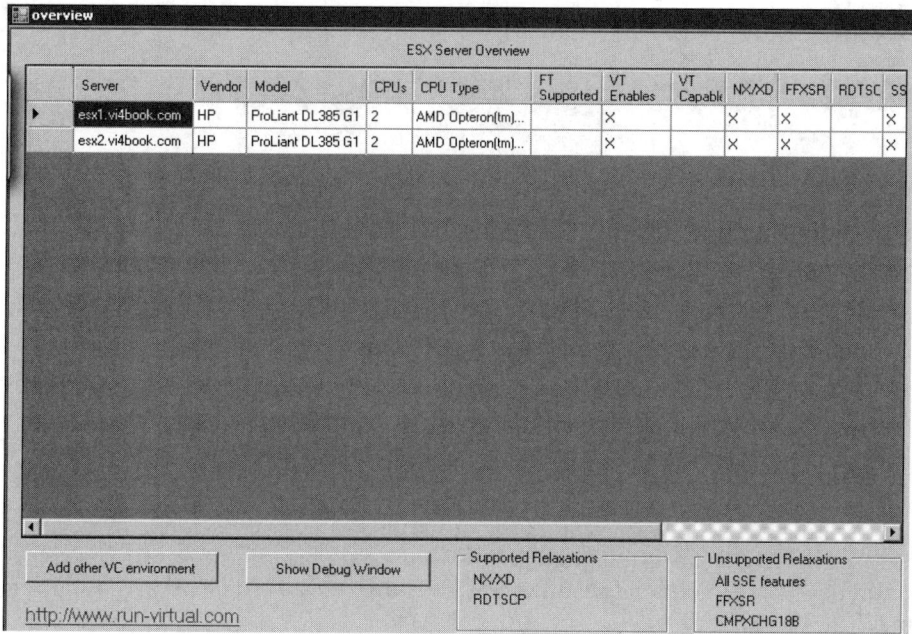

Manage CPU Incompatibilities with CPU Identification Masks

There are some CPU incompatibilities that you can do nothing about, such as the difference between an AMD CPU and an Intel CPU. However, VMware offers a way to enforce compatibility at the expense of the CPU attribute. Using a *CPU identification mask*, you can hide, or mask, attributes of the physical CPU from the VM— like putting a pair of blinkers on the VM, as you would on a horse. For example, you might mask the AMD NX attribute to allow VMotion to occur between two ESX hosts that don't share the same CPU attributes. If the VM cannot see the NX attribute, it will not use it. The VM can then be moved to an ESX host running on CPUs that do not support that feature.

CPU identification masks are a property of a VM and can be accessed by clicking the Options tab and selecting Advanced. As the following example shows, it is possible to hide (and expose) the NX/XD flag from the guest. The Advanced button allows you to create custom CPU identification masks (say to hide the SSE3 attribute) for the VM, specified by a long series of ones and zeros. (Personally, as I mentioned earlier, I feel CPU identification mask usage has probably been superseded by the development of EVC, which is discussed in the next chapter.)

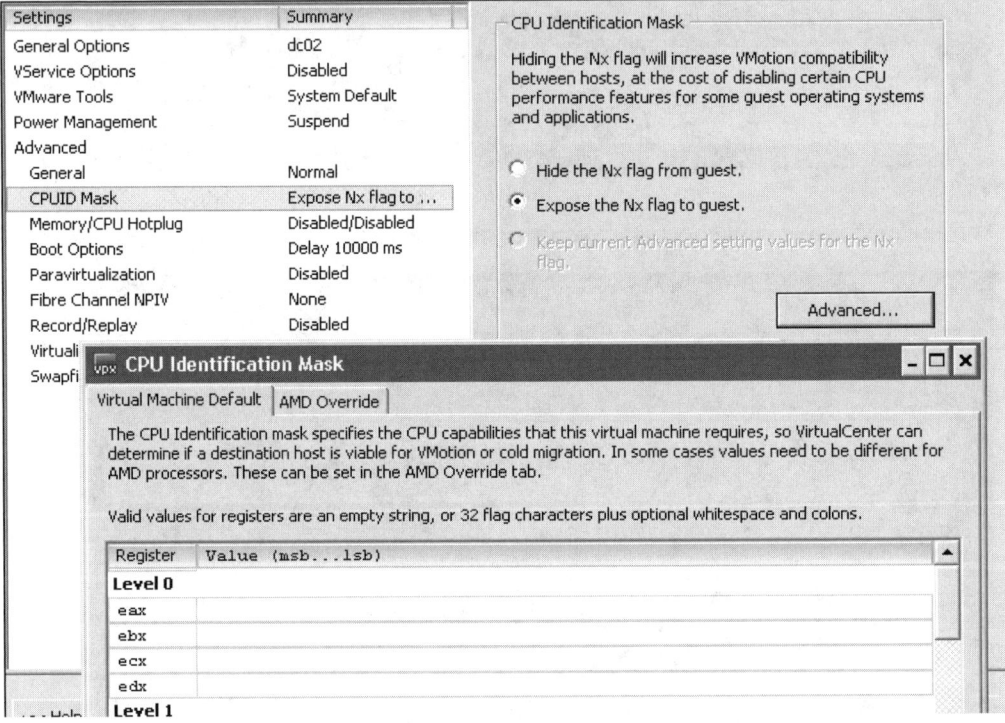

At VMworld 2006, there was a useful presentation delivered by Matthias Hausner entitled "Migrating between Apples and Oranges with VMware VMotion in VMware Infrastructure 3." It contained some material about the Advanced button and emerging CPU incompatibilities. You can obtain this presentation from http://download3.vmware.com/vmworld/2006/tac1356.pdf.

A general VMware Knowledge Base (KB) article covers this long-running issue of CPU attributes and offers information about custom CPU identification masks. The KB article also outlines ways you can set a "global" mask that affects all VMs by modifying the vCenter vpxd.cfg file. Knowledge Base articles specific to Intel and AMD processors are also exist. The following articles are available:

- General information: http://kb.vmware.com/kb/1993
- Intel-specific information: http://kb.vmware.com/kb/1991
- AMD-specific information: http://kb.vmware.com/kb/1992

Also, there is a thread where forum members discuss their relative successes and failures at creating their own custom CPU identification masks:

http://www.vmware.com/community/thread.jspa?threadID=50828

VMotion Requirements on the VM

VMotion also has some requirements for VMs. Fortunately, these are configurable and unlikely to cause you many headaches once you have resolved them. When you initiate a VMotion, you may see two types of messages: warnings and errors. Warnings can be bypassed; they are merely cautions that a problem could occur. Errors must be resolved before continuing.

VMotion Errors

Here is a list of the VMotion errors:

- **Inconsistently named port group**   VMotion expects the port group names for both the VMotion vSwitch and the VM port group to be spelled the same, and in the same case. For example, *vmotion* and *VMotion* would cause a warning, as would *Production* and *production*.

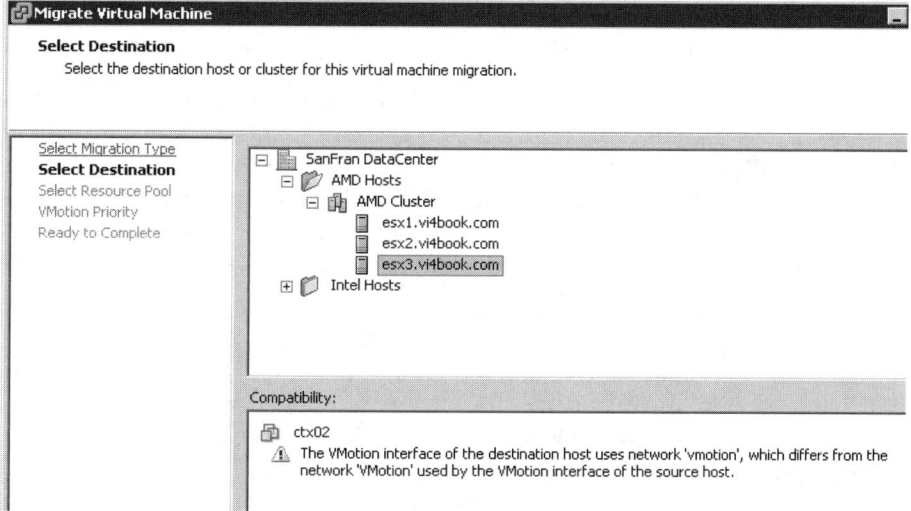

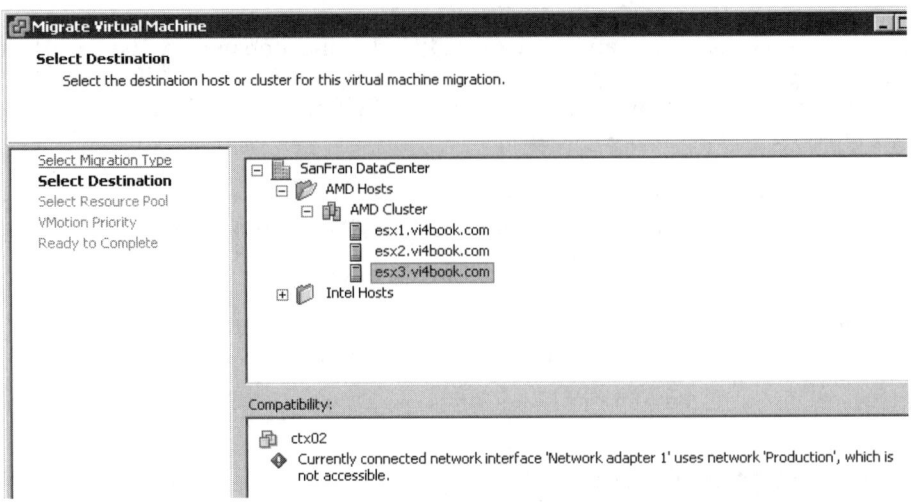

- **Active connections to use an internal switch** By *active*, VMware means that the VM is configured and connected to the internal switch. VMotion cannot guarantee that the same internal switch exists on the destination host and would offer the same uninterrupted connectivity to the VM.

- **Active connection to use a CD-ROM or floppy that is not on shared storage** Here, *active* means that the VM is configured and connected to the CD or floppy device. VMotion cannot guarantee that the CD or floppy will still be accessible on the destination host.

- **CPU affinities** VMotion cannot guarantee that the VM will be able to continue to run on the specific CPU number on the destination.

Caution *CPU affinities can also cause problems with DRS (and are disabled with DRS). If you set up CPU affinities on a VM on a stand-alone ESX host and later join it to a DRS cluster, you will find it cannot be moved with VMotion. There is a work-around to losing your control over CPU affinities in DRS without necessarily powering off the VM, entering maintenance mode, and removing the ESX host from the DRS cluster. The loss of configuration options over CPU affinities applies only in the fully automated mode. It is possible to temporarily switch the cluster to partially automated or manual. This will reenable the CPU affinity feature on the VM, which will then allow you to remove the CPU affinity problem. This is very irritating, and so I would recommend avoiding CPU affinities unless you have a totally compelling reason to use them.*

- **VMs in a cluster relationship** In the past, the virtual disks and RDM files used in VM clustering (such as MSCS) had to be held be on local storage for VMware Support; shared storage is a requirement for VMotion. This local storage requirement, which blocked the use of MSCS with VMotion, has now been removed. However, there are still other requirements that block the VMotion of cluster pairs:

  - The uptime is delivered by the VM cluster. If you wanted to move a VM cluster, you could power off one node and cold migrate it, and then power it back on.

If you repeated this process with the second node, effectively you would have moved the cluster without downtime (of course, the reliability of this approach is only as good as your clustering software).

- Because there is a potential loss of packets on the heartbeat network during VMotion, there could be unwanted cluster failover.

- Clustering software is highly dependent on SCSI reservations to lock storage to decide which node is active and which node is passive. If you attempted a VMotion event in active node, the SAN array would have received a SCSI reservation on the quorum disk from the WWN of the source host. Once the VMotion had been successful, the array would receive a renewal for that lock from the WWN of the destination host. It would reject that reservation because the destination node didn't have the reservation in the first place.

- **No visibility to LUN**   This is where the destination host does not have visibility to the RDM LUN. RDM files are not incompatible per se with VMotion. In fact, one of the major reasons they were introduced in ESX 2.5.0 was to allow VMotion of VMs that were natively accessing storage, as previously the mechanism that was used to allow native access broke VMotion. The issue here is of LUN visibility and VMotion's requirement of shared storage. That means visibility of VMFS and RDM LUNs to both ESX hosts.

- **Inconsistent security settings on a vSwitch/port group**   I'm happy to admit I only discovered this incompatibility in 2008. I found it largely by accident, because I rarely tamper with the default settings of the Security tab on the vSwitch or port group, and if I do, I'm generally very consistent. However, if you have two ESX hosts' vSwitches or port groups with mismatched security settings, this will result in a VMotion error message. VMware does not allow a VM's security status to change merely because it is moved from one ESX host to another. After all, that wouldn't be very secure!

The following screenshot shows all the VMotion errors.

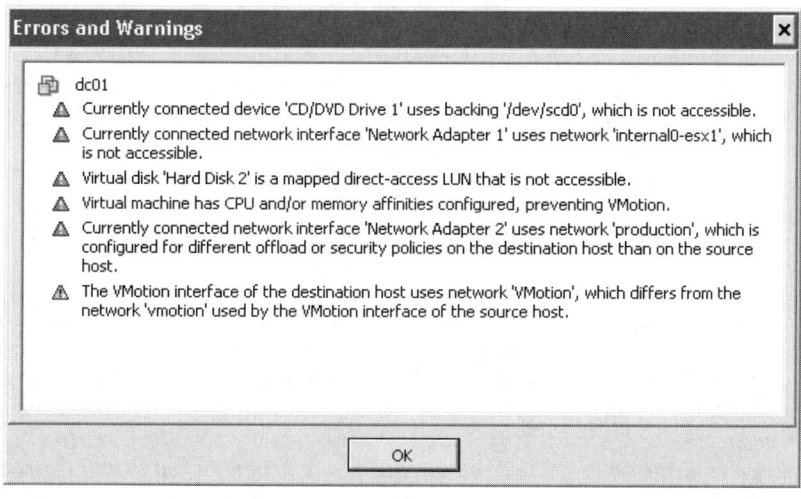

NOTE *If you are using DRS in any mode (manual, partial, or fully automated), it will attempt to correct VM errors to allow the VM to be moved. For example, if you have a CD-ROM or floppy drive actively connected to a local device and attempt a manual VMotion, VMware will automatically disconnect these devices prior to the VMotion.*

VMotion Warnings

The following is a list of VMotion warnings:

- **Configured to an internal switch**   By *configured*, VMware means that the VM is set to use the internal switch. However, on the VM, under Network Adapter and Device Status, Connected and Connected at Power On are not enabled.

- **Snapshots**   There could be warnings when deleting or reverting to snapshots when the VM is moved. Personally, I have carried out VMotion events with snapshots engaged and never had a problem. After all, the files that make up a snapshot would be on shared storage. Nonetheless, the vSphere Client warns you about having snapshots applied.

- **Misuse of 100Mbps network card for VMotion**   If you do configure the VMotion switch with a 100Mbps NIC, you will receive a warning about this configuration. You will still be allowed to carry out a VMotion event; however, its reliability will not be guaranteed or supported.

The following screenshot shows all the warnings.

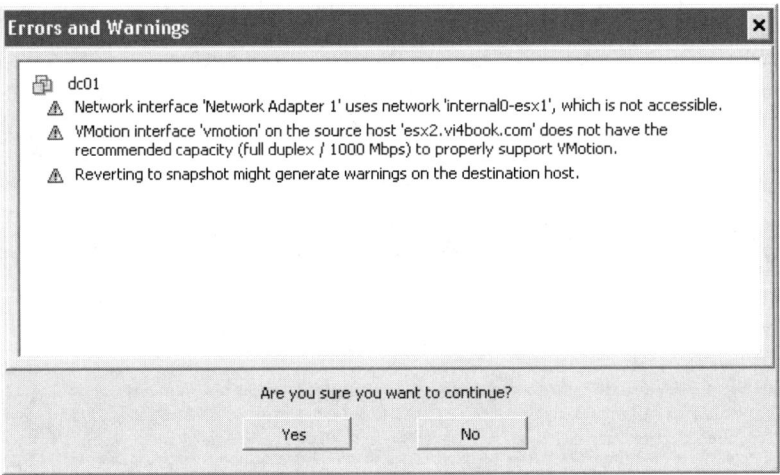

CAUTION *Just as these errors, warnings, and requirements can stop a manual VMotion, they can also stop automatic VMotion generated by VMware DRS, so it's important to resolve them whenever possible. It's worth saying that many newer features, such as DPM and the VMware Update Manager, assume VMotion will occur without errors. Personally, because VM users and operators have a tendency to forget to disconnect CDs and floppies when they finish using them, I frequently disable access to these devices using permissions, as discussed in Chapter 9.*

Resolving VMotion Errors and Warnings

Now that you are familiar with the typical VMotion errors and warnings you may receive, let's look at the most efficient ways of resolving them.

Removing CD-ROM and Floppy Errors and Warnings

The most common errors are ones concerning active connections to removable devices. So the simplest way to turn these errors (which cannot be bypassed) into warnings (which can be bypassed) is to disconnect those devices. However, you will most likely want to remove all warnings as well.

The best way to remove all CD-ROM floppy errors and warnings is to disconnect the devices within the VM, and then set them to use a client device. This removes any path statements to either local resources, such as /dev/fd0 or /dev/cdrom, and also any path statements to ISO or FLP files held on a local datastore, such as /vmfs/volumes/storage1. Here's how to configure this:

1. Right-click the VM and choose Edit Settings.
2. Select Floppy Device 1.
3. Remove any checks next to Connected and Connected at Power On.
4. Select Client Device.
5. Select CD/DVD Drive 1.
6. Remove any checks next to Connected and Connected at Power On.
7. Select Client Device.
8. Click OK in Virtual Machine Properties dialog box.

One way of resolving this for many VMs is to use a scripting engine such as VMware's PowerCLI, which adds cmdlets to the Microsoft PowerShell environment. For example, the following piece of PowerShell would cause every VM to have its CD-ROM drive disconnected:

```
get-vm | get-cddrive | Set-CDDrive -Connected $false
```

Removing CPU Affinities

You should remove any CPU affinities you have on a VM prior to joining the ESX host it resides on to a DRS cluster. CPU affinities and DRS clusters are incompatible with each other, and the configuration options for CPU affinities are removed from the interface in a fully automated mode. If you join your ESX host to the DRS cluster, and then build your VMs, you will discover that you cannot configure the CPU affinity feature at all. The root of this incompatibility with DRS stems from the incompatibility with VMotion.

To disable CPU affinities and return your VM to being able to execute on any CPU, change the configuration as follows:

1. Right-click the VM and choose Edit Settings.
2. Select the Resources tab and choose Advanced CPU.
3. Select the No Affinity option.
4. Click OK in the Virtual Machine Properties dialog box.

If you switch your DRS cluster back to manual or partial automation, the CPU affinities settings will be available again.

Removing Internal Switch Errors and Warnings

If you have configured VMs to use virtual switches that are internal, there will be errors and warnings with these VMs. Remember that the goal of VMotion is to move a VM while powered on and while users are connected. One of the requirements of VMotion is for the VM to remain on the same VLAN during the move, and for the VMotion network to be in the same VLAN with dedicated gigabit NICs.

There are two work-arounds to this internal vSwitch issue:

- Temporarily configure the VM to a "production" port group where communication would be enabled.

- Temporarily disconnect the VM from the internal switch, carry out the VMotion event, and then reconnect it to a port group at the destination. This temporary disconnection produces a warning, rather than a hard error, and so you will be able to continue with the VMotion. To temporarily disconnect a VM from an internal switch, select the network adapter in the Virtual Machine Properties dialog box, and remove the checks for the Connected and Connected at Power On options.

Both of these work-arounds are more than likely to disconnect users and, therefore, do not strictly meet the requirements for a true VMotion. That said, you might prefer these solutions compared to the alternative, which is to shut down the VM (which most definitely disconnects users!), and then cold migrate the VM to the new ESX host.

Whatever approach you take, you are likely to need to reconfigure the VM's networking and confirm that users can still connect as normal after the move has been completed. Where possible, I suggest avoiding internal switches if VMotion and DRS are important to you, as they create more problems than they resolve in this aspect of the product.

Enabling VMotion on Standard vSwitch

VMotion requires a VMkernel port group with a valid IP address and subnet mask for the VMotion network. A default gateway entry is not required, as VMware does not support VMotion across routers or WANs. If you are running out of NICs on your servers, you could just create an additional VMkernel port group on an existing vSwitch.

Chapter 4 detailed how to configure a standard vSwitch for VMotion. Here's a quick recap:

1. In the vSphere Client, select your ESX host.

2. Click the Configuration tab.

3. In the Hardware pane, select Networking.

4. Click the Add Networking link.

5. Choose VMkernel, and then click Next.

6. In the Port Groups Properties dialog box, type a friendly name for this connection, such as **vmotion**.

7. Select the "Use this port group for VMotion" option.

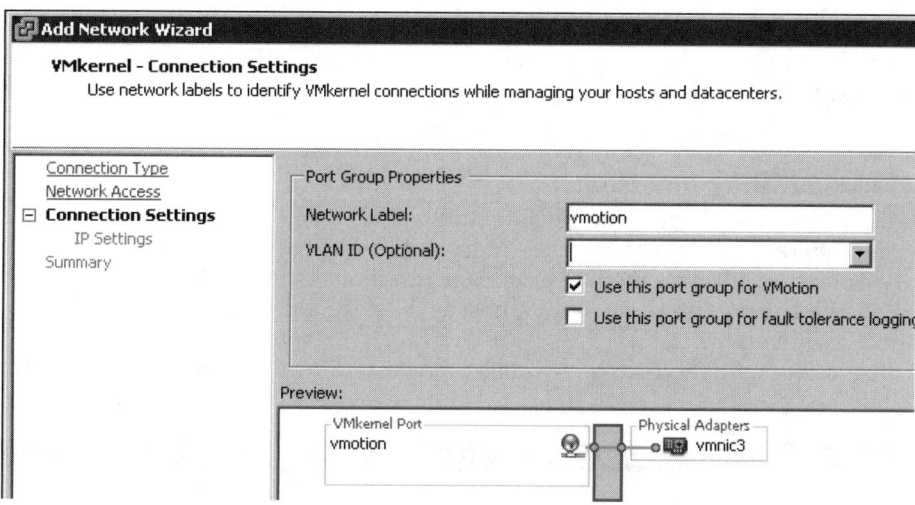

8. Set an IP address and subnet mask for VMotion.

Initiating VMotion

To initiate VMotion, you can use drag-and-drop or a menu option. Personally, I prefer to use the drag-and-drop method, as you are asked fewer questions in the migration wizard.

VMotion by Drag-and-Drop

The drag-and-drop method even allows you to drop your VM into the correct resource pools if you have them on a stand-alone ESX host. You can also drag-and-drop multiple VMs by SHIFT-clicking to select them. The VMotion will occur for each VM in turn (one after another), to preserve bandwidth on the VMotion network and prevent network timeouts.

To use this method, simply select your VM and drag-and-drop it to the ESX host/resource pool. Then select either "Reserve CPU for optional VMotion performance (Recommended)" or "Perform with available CPU resources." The first option allows the VMotion event to occur only if there is no chance of degrading performance. The second option allows the VMotion to go ahead, even if performance could be degraded. These settings do not control how quick the VMotion event is, but rather set controls for the VM's availability.

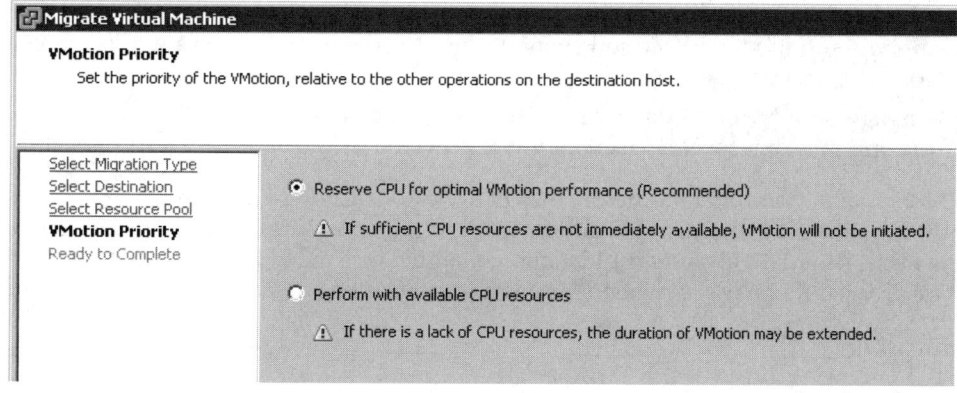

NOTE In previous releases of VMware's vCenter and ESX, the Migrate Virtual Machine wizard choices were referred to as high and low priority, but essentially, they are the same in vSphere 4 and function in the same way.

VMotion Without Drag-and-Drop

You can start a VMotion event without using drag-and drop, either by right-clicking a VM and choosing Migration or by selecting the Migrate to New Host option in the Command pane of the Summary tab. This method asks more questions than the drag-and-drop method. You will be asked to select an ESX host as the destination and also where you wish to add it to a resource pool.

This wizard-based method has a new dialog box that allows you to select the migration type.

You have three choices:

- **Change host** This means to carry out VMotion if the VM is powered on, and cold migration (without changing the location of the VMs file) if the VM is powered off.
- **Change datastore** This means to move the VMS files. If the VM is powered on, this will result in an SVMotion event. If the VM is powered off, this will result in a cold migration of the VM's files.
- **Change both host and datastore** This means cold migration. In the example here, the option is dimmed because the VM is powered on.

SVMotion allows you to relocate the files of a VM to a different datastore, but we are currently not allowed to perform SVMotion and VMotion as a single task, but only as two separate tasks. Alternatively, you could claim a maintenance mode and carry out a cold migration. This could be useful when you want to move a VM to a different ESX host where no common shared storage is available. Another use of cold migration is to get round the restrictions of VMotion, such as moving a VM between an Intel and AMD host.

Storage VMotion (Change Datastore)

One format of moving a VM was first introduced between ESX 2.*x* and 3.*x*, and it was sometimes referred to at the time as Data Motion or DMotion, among the VMware Communities forum members. DMotion is not an official VMware term; the official term is Storage VMotion or SVMotion.

SVMotion was initially introduced for seamlessly migrating VMs from an old file system on ESX 2 to a new file system on ESX 3. One method of upgrading from ESX 2/ vCenter 1 to ESX 3/VirtualCenter2 was by moving a VM from ESX 2 VMFS 2 storage to ESX 3 with VMFS 3 storage. SVMotion allows this to be done without shutting down the VM. Prior to its introduction, upgrading from ESX 2 to ESX 3 required powering off the VM and carrying out a cold migration. The process moved the VM from one ESX host (version 2) to another (version 3), as well as moving the VM's files. This was achieved by engaging an ESX 3.*x* snapshot on the VMFS 3 volume, which then unlocked the disks stored in the VMFS 2 file system so they could be copied to the new storage. Even though DMotion was not an official term, its origins came from the names given to snapshot delta files created during this migration: DMotion-scsi0:00_vm2-delta.vmdk and DMotion-scsi0:00_vm2.vmdk.

The technology has certainly moved on from this early inception to aid in upgrades from VI2 to VI3. There are many reasons to use SVMotion, such as the following:

- Decommission an old array whose lease or maintenance warranty is expiring.
- Switch from one storage type to another, say from a Fibre Channel SAN to an iSCSI SAN.
- Move VMs or virtual disks out of a LUN that is running out of space or is saturated from a performance perspective.
- Ease future upgrades from one version of VMFS to another.
- Convert RDM files into virtual disks.

SVMotion was introduced in VI3.5. At that time, it was Perl script contained within the vSphere CLI tools. In vSphere 4, VMware have integrated SVMotion into the graphical client. Functionally, SVMotion is similar to VMotion, but its goal is not to move the VM from one ESX host to another, but to move the VM files from one VMFS volume to another, without needing to power down the VM.

Requirements for Storage VMotion

The requirements for SVMotion are the same as those for VMotion, covered earlier in the chapter, with some additions. SVMotion used to require that VMotion was configured first. Technically, it is possible to carry out SVMotion without VMotion being enabled. If you do so, you will find your migration type choices are limited if you attempt a move while the VM is powered on.

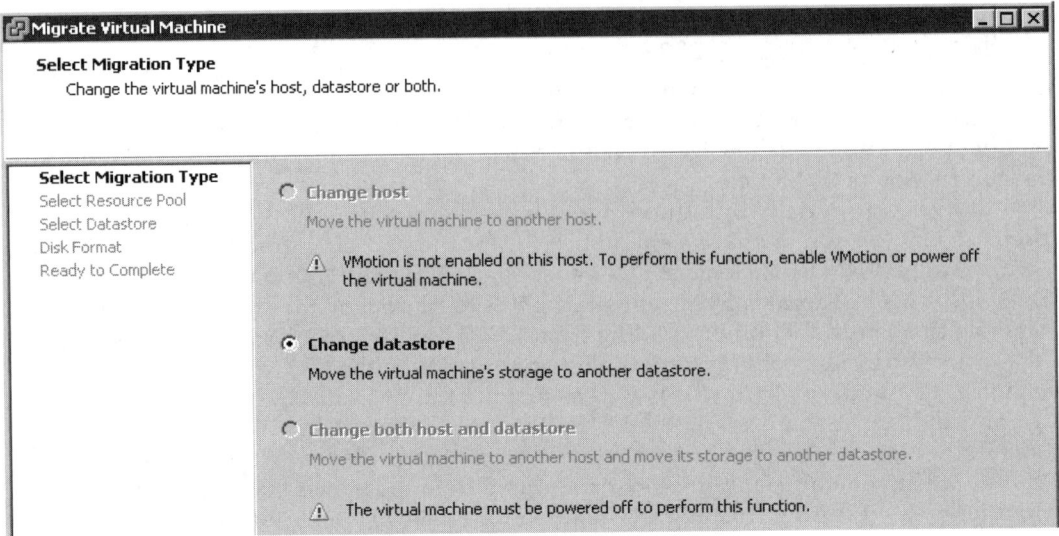

The following are the additional requirements for SVMotion:

- **Spare memory and CPU cycle**   In VI3.5, the SVMotion process created a special helper VM. This helper VM was not shown in the user interface, but ran in the background. The helper VM's memory allocation settings were exactly the same as those for the source VM. As a consequence, there was temporary memory doubling during the SVMotion process. In vSphere 4, the memory required to carry out SVMotion has been massively reduced, and the entire process is much more efficient than before. In vSphere4 SVMotion no longer needs a helper VM during the move of the files.

- **Free space for snapshots**   I won't patronize you by stating the obvious (that you need free space at the destination VMFS volume for SVMotion). What's more important is that you will need free space for the snapshot that is created during the SVMotion process. This snapshot is used to unlock the files in the file system so that they can be copied to the new location. At the end of the SVMotion process, the delta files that make up the snapshot are merged into these new .vmdk files. As with VMotion, SVMotion is more of file copy/file delete process than a file move operation.

- **Time**   You will need some time. Despite the process taking place while the VM is running, SVMotion is significantly more I/O-intensive than VMotion. SVMotion is not quicker than a cold migration.

- **Concurrency**   VMware recommends that you carry out a maximum of four SVMotion events at any one time.

Performing SVMotion from the GUI

A classic example of performing SVMotion is to fix a VM user or operator error, such as storing a VM on local storage. As I have frequently stated, shared storage is a major prerequisite for VMotion, DRS, HA, and FT. A VM located on local storage is excluded from all these wonderful features and risks being ignored in your DR plan because it is held on nonreplicated storage. The following example uses my test configuration, with the dc02 VM having two virtual disks on local storage on the esx2.vi4book.com host.

Here are the steps for using the migration wizard to initiate SVMotion:

1. Right-click the VM and select Migrate.

2. Choose the Change Datastore option.

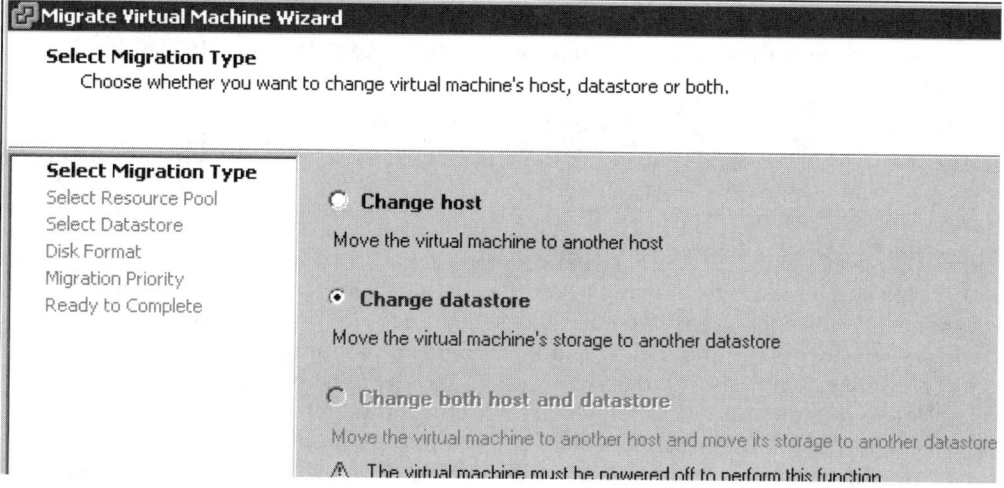

3. Select the ESX resource pool, if available.

4. Select the new datastore location.

5. Select the Same as Source option to maintain the VM's virtual disk format.

CAUTION *If you are using an RDM file and wish to avoid it being converted to a virtual disk, the Same as Source option makes sure it remains an RDM file. To convert an RDM file, choose either the thin or thick formats. You should be careful with RDM files, as currently no warning or message appears to inform you that the conversion is taking place. You could find yourself converting a 1TB LUN into a virtual disk by accident.*

6. Select High Priority.

7. If you want to place individual virtual disks on different datastores, click the Advanced button.

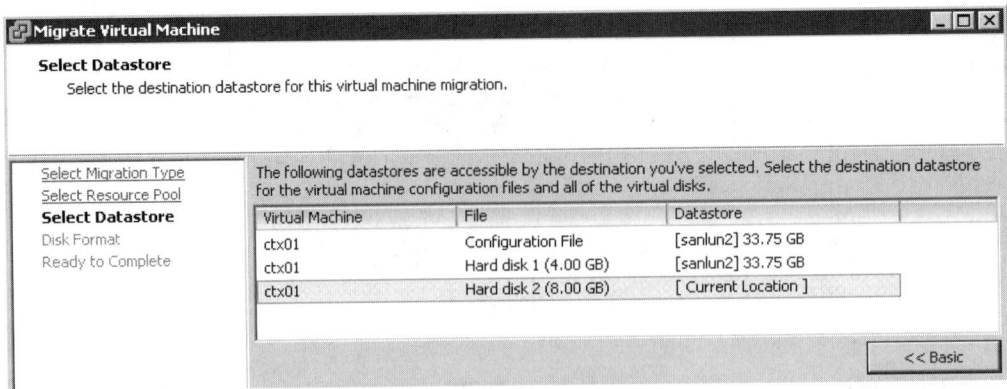

After you complete the wizard, you will see that the Recent Tasks bar lists Relocate Virtual Machine storage.

Performing SVMotion from the vSphere CLI

SVMotion can still be carried out using a script available from VMware. Personally, I prefer this approach, because it can easily be tied to a schedule to run bulk SVMotion tasks at a time when users are not around. Additionally, it offers more granular control, with the ability to go right down to individual virtual disks and the files that make up a VM, allowing you to relocate the VM to any datastore type you see fit.

The vSphere CLI (vCLI) is a collection of commands commonly found on the ESX Classic host, which can be used remotely against an ESX host or vCenter. It is just one of many such CLIs and toolkits. It ships in three formats: a Windows version, a Linux version, and a downloadable VM. I prefer the Windows version, which I install on my Windows PC. You can download vCLI from the VMware Web site. Unfortunately, it's kind of tucked away in the Communities part of the Web site (http://communities.vmware.com/community/developer/vsphere_cli), rather than on the standard download page where you first downloaded ESX and vCenter.

The vCLI utility svmotion.pl can be used interactively (prompting you for the required options) or noninteractively. I recommend using the utility interactively once to become familiar with the required variables, before using the noninteractive tool at the command line with switches.

Before you begin the SVMotion, you will need to know the path to the .vmx file. The path is not specified in the same way as it is at the Service Console (for example, /vmfs/volumes/virtualmachines/vm1/vm1.vmx) but in syntax you see only in vCenter, which looks like this:

```
[virtual machines] vm1/vm1.vmx
```

You will find this syntax in the Virtual Machine Properties dialog box, on the Options tab under General Options.

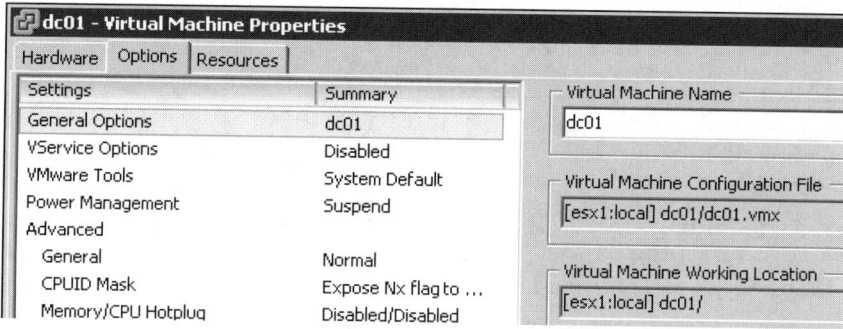

CAUTION *svmotion.pl, like other command-line tools, is case-sensitive. This includes passwords, datacenter names, the path to the .vmx file, and the path to the destination datastore.*

Moving the Entire VM Interactively

In the interactive mode, the svmotion.pl script asks you all the questions that need to be answered to relocate the VM. In many ways, it's like a wizard, but without being graphical. Here's the procedure, showing the prompts and sample responses:

1. Open a command prompt on the system on which you have installed vCLI.

2. Type the following command:

   ```
   svmotion.pl --interactive
   ```

   The CLI will print the response Entering interactive mode. All other options and environment variables will be ignored.

3. Provide the name or IP address of the vCenter server.

   ```
   Enter the vCenter service url you wish to connect to
   ```

   (e.g. https://myvc.mycorp.com/sdk, or just myvc.mycorp.com):

   ```
   virtualcenter4.vi4book.com
   ```

4. Provide your username and password to connect to vCenter.

   ```
   Enter your username: administrator
   Enter your password: vmware
   ```

   vCLI will then respond with the message Attempting to connect to https://virtualcenter4.vi4book.com/sdk.

5. Type the name of the datacenter that holds the VM.

   ```
   Enter the name of the datacenter: SanFran Datacenter
   ```

   You do not need to provide quotation marks to represent spaces in the name, but vCLI is case-sensitive, hence the capital *S, F,* and *D* in the example.

6. Using the syntax found on the settings of the VM, provide the path to the .vmx file.

   ```
   Enter the datastore path of the virtual machine (e.g. [datastore1]
   myvm/myvm.vmx): [esx1_local] dc01/dc01.vmx
   ```

7. Supply the name of the destination datastore.

   ```
   Enter the name of the destination datastore: sanlun
   ```

   You do not need to type in square brackets ([]) to specify the datastore name. Remember that spaces in a VMFS volume name are *not* supported and not recommended.

8. To move the entire VM to a different location, answer no to the question about moving just the virtual disk. You can also move disks independently of the VM by choosing yes, as described in the next section.

   ```
   Would you like to individually place the disks (yes/no)? no
   ```

The following screenshot shows this interactive vCLI session.

```
C:\Program Files\VMware\VMware vSphere CLI\bin>svmotion.pl --interactive

Entering interactive mode.  All other options and environment variables will be i
gnored.

Enter the VirtualCenter service url you wish to connect to (e.g. https://myvc.myc
orp.com/sdk, or just myvc.mycorp.com): virtualcenter4.vi4book.com
Enter your username: administrator
Enter your password:

Attempting to connect to https://virtualcenter4.vi4book.com/sdk.
Connected to server.

Enter the name of the datacenter: SanFran DataCenter
Enter the datastore path of the virtual machine (e.g. [datastore1] myvm/myvm.vmx)
: [esx1_local] dc01/dc01.vmx
Enter the name of the destination datastore: sanlun

You can also move disks independently of the virtual machine.  If you want the di
sks to stay with the virtual machine, then skip this step..
Would you like to individually place the disks (yes/no)? no

Performing Storage VMotion.
0% !----------------------------------------------------------------------------
-----------------------! 100%
    ###################_
```

After answering the last question, you will see progress bars as the VM is moved from one VMFS volume to another. You will also see the standard Relocate Virtual Machine storage task in the Recent Tasks bar.

Recent Tasks		
Name	Target	Status
⬛ Relocate Virtual Machine storage	🗗 dc01	30% ▭

Moving Individual Virtual Disks Interactively

In this example, I have a VM with two virtual disks (one for the guest OS and one for data). However, it's been decided to place the data VMDK file on a different SAN LUN, which presents a different RAID level and number of spindles, in the hopes this will improve the disk I/O for data. The source VM is currently stored on a VMFS volume called sanlun1, and I wish to move this data VMDK file to a VMFS volume called sanlun2.

1. Open a CMD prompt on the system where you have installed the vSphere CLI

2. Type the command:

   ```
   svmotion.pl --interactive
   ```

   The CLI will then print the response `Entering interactive` mode. All other options and environment variables will be ignored.

3. Next, provide the name or IP address of the vCenter server.

   ```
   Enter the vCenter service url you wish to connect to
   ```

   (e.g. https://myvc.mycorp.com/sdk, or just myvc.mycorp.com):

   ```
   virtualcenter4.vi4book.com
   ```

4. Next, provide your username and password to connect to vCenter.

   ```
   Enter your username: administrator
   Enter your password: vmware
   ```

   SVMotion will then respond with the message `Attempting to connect to https://virtualcenter4.vi4book.com/sdk`.

5. Next, type the name of the datacenter which holds the VM.

   ```
   Enter the name of the datacenter: SanFran DataCenter
   ```

   You do not need to provide speech marks to represent spaces in the name, but SVMotion is case-sensitive hence the capital *S*, *F*, *D*, and *C* in SanFran DataCenter in my example.

6. Next, using the syntax found on the settings of the VM, provide the path to the .vmx file.

   ```
   Enter the datastore path of the virtual machine (e.g. [datastore1]
   myvm/myvm.vmx): [sanlun1] dc01/dc01.vmx
   ```

7. Supply the name of the destination datastore:

   ```
   Enter the name of the destination datastore: sanlun1
   ```

8. Respond yes to move disks independently of the VM:

   ```
   Would you like to individually place the disks (yes/no)? Yes
   ```

8. Type the path to the virtual disk you wish to move.

   ```
   [sanlun1] dc01/dc01_1.vmdk
   ```

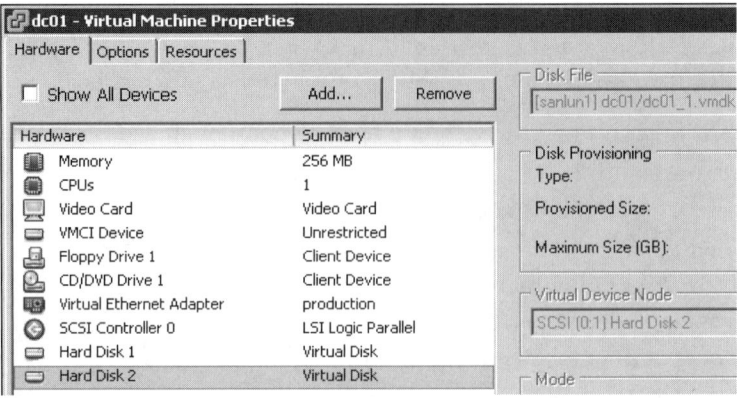

9. Type the name of the datastore to which you wish to move the VM.

   ```
   sanlun2
   ```

After answering this last question, you will be asked if you wish to move another virtual disk. If you choose No, you will see progress bars as the VMDK file is moved from one VMFS volume to another.

The following screenshot shows this interactive vCLI session.

Notice how `sanlun1` is referenced twice: once for the location of the .vmx file and again to indicate the .vmx file is not being moved. When I first attempted the move of the VMDK file, I mistyped its name, and I left this error in place to show how easy it is to make a slight mistake! After I correctly specified the path to the VMDK file, vCLI asked for the new location, and I specified `sunlun2`.

Moving the Entire VM Noninteractively

It is possible to supply all this command-line information as a single string. It's tricky to get every aspect of the syntax correct, so I recommend patience and persistence. One reason to do this is so you can schedule a SVMotion to occur at night when users are not around, or because you have a bulk SVMotion task that needs to be scheduled and staged in order not to saturate the I/O to the storage array.

The following is an example of a SVMotion with all the parameters provided for moving an entire VM to a new location. Here, I've split the command over a few lines for readability. In this example, the VM is stored on the SAN, but currently both virtual disks (dc01.vmdk and dc01_1.vmdk) are stored on the same VMFS volume called sanlun1. I want to move the second virtual disk (dc01_1.vmdk) to a VMFS volume called sanlun2. This will split the VM into two different datastores. This is a common configuration for improving disk performance by reducing I/O contention on the LUNs or volumes themselves.

```
svmotion.pl --server=virtualcenter4.vi4book.com --username=administrator --
password=vmware
--datacenter="SanFran DataCenter"
--vm="[esx1_local] dc01/dc01.vmx: sanlun"
```

All vCLI commands require the HUP—host, username, and password—to authenticate to vCenter. Next, I specify the datacenter that contains the VM; notice in this case, I must use quotation marks to indicate the space between *SanFran* and *DataCenter*. Last, I specify the path to the .vmx file and use a colon (`:`) is used indicate the new destination for the VM's files. One of the "features" of this is that if a VMFS volume contains a colon, then `svmotion.pl` gets very confused because this is used as an escape character to tell the Perl script that the next variable is the datastore destination. (I hope this "feature" will be corrected by VMware with future updates, as it has been around since VI3.5.)

When the SVMotion is done this way, the CLI does not report any progress (you won't see any progress bars). You do, however, see the Relocate Virtual Machine task in the vSphere Client.

The following screenshot shows the syntax of this basic full relocation of the VM.

```
C:\>svmotion.pl --server=virtualcenter4.vi4book.com --username=administrator --pa
ssword=vmware --datacenter="SanFran DataCenter" --vm="[esx1_local] dc01/dc01.vmx:
 sanlun"_
```

Moving Individual Virtual Disks Noninteractively

It is also possible to move individual virtual disks from one location to another noninteractively. The syntax of this command is a little tricky. It requires the location of the disk followed by the new location.

For the next example, suppose that someone has added a second virtual disk to dc01, but has located that virtual disk on local storage, which is preventing it from working with VMotion and DRS. So, I want to move a virtual disk from local storage (esx1storage1) to SAN-based storage (sanlun2).

The first part of the syntax is pretty straightforward, as it is merely the credentials of the vCenter server.

```
svmotion.pl --server=virtualcenter4.vi4book.com --username=administrator --
password=vmware
 --datacenter="SanFran DataCenter"
```

The next part of the syntax indicates the current location of the VM's .vmx file, followed by the destination I would like it to have.

```
--vm="[sanlun1] dc01/dc01.vmx: sanlun1"
```

The "[sanlun1] dc01/dc01.vmx indicates the source; the : sanlun1" specifies the destination. By making the source and destination the *same* datastore, I'm effectively indicating the smaller files that make up the VM.

This next line indicates that I would like to leave the dc01.vmdk file in its current location, sanlun1. The second part indicates that the virtual disk called dc01_1.vmdk on sanlun1 is to be moved to the VMFS volume called sanlun2.

```
--disks="[sanlun1] dc01/dc01.vmdk:sanlun1, [sanlun1] dc01/dc01_1
.vmdk:sanlun2"
```

The net effect of this command is that the first disk (dc01.vmdk on sanlun1) would stay in its current location, and dc01_1.vmdk on sanlun1 would be relocated to sanlun2. Notice the comma after --disks="[sanlun1] dc01/dc01.vmdk:sanlun1,. This allows you to specify the location of multiple disks.

The following screenshots show what I typed in the CLI, and then the VM with two virtual disks stored on two different datastores, one imaginatively labeled sanlun1 and the other called sanlun2.

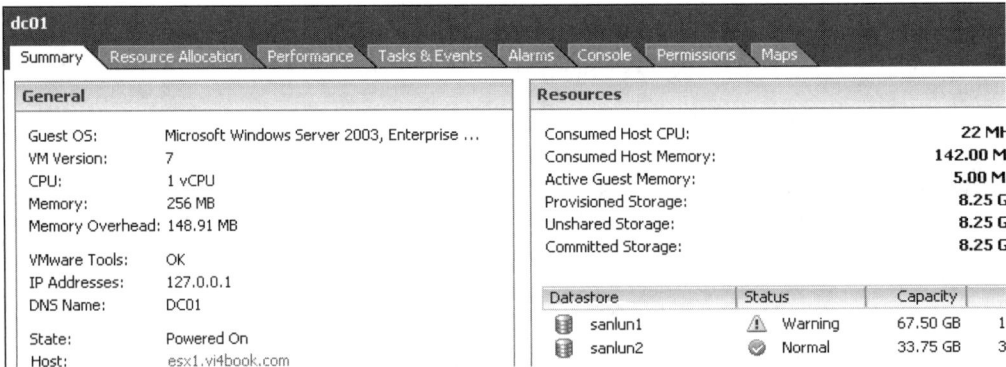

Cold Migration (Change Host and/or Datastore)

When all hope is lost, and you simply cannot work around the VMotion or SVMotion requirements, there is always cold migration. Cold migration has none of the stringent requirements of VMotion. The only requirements are that both ESX hosts reside in the same datacenter and that the VM is powered off.

If both ESX hosts have visibility to the same storage, then cold migration can be incredibly quick, and the VM downtime kept to the minimum. If the two ESX hosts do not share storage, then a cold migration can take much longer. In the worst-case scenario, where only local storage is available, it would generate network traffic on vSwitch0, as a cold migration would use the Service Console network interface to move the VM's file from one host to another. In the best scenario, your cold migration might be throttled by only the speed of your SAN as it moves the VM's file from one SAN LUN to another in the same disk array.

Another compelling reason to use cold migration would be if you have a VM restriction that is not reconfigurable. For example, you might wish to move a VM cluster using MSCS or Veritas Cluster Server. As a VM cluster still requires that VMDK and RDM files are stored locally for full VMware support, VMotion is impossible. In this case, you would follow this procedure:

- Shut down the secondary node in the cluster.

- Temporarily remove (but not delete) the quorum and shared RDM files. This is necessary; otherwise, the cold migration would attempt to move them also, and they would be locked by other VMs in the cluster group.

- Cold migrate the VM.

- Add the quorum and shared RDM files you removed earlier.

- Power on the VM cluster.

As long as there is at least one cluster node up at any one time, you could still achieve the VM uptime you require. To do this successfully, the quorum and shared disks must be on shared storage. So a "cluster-in-a-box" scenario, where all the quorum and shared virtual disks are possibly held on local storage, would need to be completely powered off and cold migrated.

One scenario for cold migration might be that while the ESX hosts share common storage, they do not share common CPUs. In this case, VMotion or SVMotion is not an option. You could perform a cold migration as follows:

1. Shut down the guest OS on the VM.

2. Make a note of the VM's current datastore, as you will need it in step 4.

3. Drag-and-drop the VM to the destination ESX host/resource pool.

4. Choose to keep VM configuration files and virtual disks in their current location, by selecting the same datastore location you noted in step 2.

5. Choose for the VM's files to remain the same as the source.

6. Once the move is complete, power on the VM.

Although the task is flagged as a Relocate Virtual Machine storage, if the two ESX hosts share access to the same datastore, then it should be blisteringly quick. In fact, it is simply an automated register and unregister of the VM's files from one ESX host to another.

Summary

As you can see, a VM is probably the most portable container for storing applications. You can move a VM from server to server, and from blade to blade, whether it's powered on or off. Not only that, but you can also move the files that make up a VM from one storage type to another.

This all has its roots in the early concept of *encapsulation*, in which everything about your guest OS configuration and the data itself are wrapped up in a discrete set of files. Increasingly, the VM is just a container that we use to hold the applications with which end users interact. It's this portability that VMware hopes will make its technologies the basis of the so-called cloud computing model. Without this encapsulation, the idea of moving applications in and out of a private/internal cloud to an external/public cloud would be just a pipe dream.

CHAPTER 13 | VMware Distributed Resource Scheduler

This chapter covers VMware's Distributed Resource Scheduler (DRS). In the simplest case, DRS is just an automated VMotion. When DRS recognizes an imbalance in the resources used on each ESX host in a cluster, it rebalances the VMs among those hosts. Another major feature of DRS is initial placement. This allows DRS to decide where to place or power on a VM for the first time.

These two features of DRS closely integrate with VMware's HA software. So if an ESX host crashes, say because of hardware failure, HA is in charge of detecting the crash and making sure VMs are started on other nodes in the cluster, generally on the ESX host that has the smallest load. Once HA has finished its work, DRS will eventually rebalance the cluster. If the failed server comes back online again and rejoins the DRS cluster, its free capacity will be recognized, and VMotion will be triggered to utilize the ESX host.

In this chapter, you'll learn how DRS works and how to set it up. We'll also look at how to enable Enhanced VMotion Compatibility and relocate the VMkernel swap file.

What's New with DRS?

- Improved error reporting to help troubleshoot errors

- Enhanced VMotion Compatibility, forcing your new servers to have backward compatibility with old servers (the beginning of the end of VMotion CPU compatibility requirements, with VMware leveraging Intel FlexMigration and similar features from AMD)

- Ability to relocate large swap files from shared and expensive storage to cheaper alternatives (have your cake and eat it with memory overcommitment, without the storage penalty)

DRS Overview

A lot of people mistakenly believe that when they use DRS, they should see an even number of VMs on each ESX host. This is not the intention of DRS. After all, different VMs create different amounts of resource demands.

While we are hoping for a relatively even load on ESX hosts, the primary goal of DRS is to improve the VM's performance. So load balancing is not a goal in its own right. Fundamentally, if DRS judges that VMotion of a VM will not improve the VM's performance, it will not move it to achieve some ideal of a perfectly balanced cluster. For this reason, it is not unusual to see DRS put a large number of VMs on one ESX host and a small number of VMs on another. DRS must make judgment calls about whether the penalty of VMotion is worth the performance gain. Generally speaking, smaller VMs with 32-bit OSs and just one vCPU are more likely to be moved to another ESX host, because they are easier to migrate than a large VM with 64-bit OS and four vCPUs.

Although VMware has tested up to 32 ESX hosts in a single DRS cluster, which demonstrates excellent scalability, the actual DRS algorithms are quite conservative and currently will not allow more than 60 VMotion events per hour. DRS checks for an imbalance in the cluster once every five minutes.

Some people worry that they may get a "DRS storm" when an ESX host fails. They think that if an ESX host fails, it triggers VMware HA, which then causes VMs to power on the remaining ESX hosts. This creates an imbalance in the cluster, which then triggers a mass number of VMotion events, or a DRS storm. This simply does not happen, because DRS would wait at least five minutes before checking the cluster, and it would offer only recommendations based on your migration threshold. This allows the administrator to control how aggressively DRS tries to rebalance the cluster.

When you implement DRS, you can choose from three different levels of automation and also set a migration threshold. The automation levels allow you to impose some rules and regulations. Additionally, DRS clusters can have resource pools.

DRS Levels of Automation

DRS offers three different levels of automation:

- **Manual**   The administrator is offered recommendations of where to place a VM and whether to VMotion a VM.

- **Partially automated**   DRS decides where a VM will execute. The administrator is offered recommendations of whether to VMotion a VM.

- **Fully automated (default)**   DRS decides where a VM will execute and whether to VMotion, based on a threshold parameter, obeying any rules or exclusions created by the administrator.

NOTE *Setting DRS to manual or partial automation does not break VMware HA. If an ESX host fails, the VM gets powered on without asking where to power it on. If an ESX host failure occurs, the VM is powered on, and only later do you get recommendations to rebalance the cluster.*

At first glance, many administrators would choose manual, as they prefer to be in control of their systems. However, this might not necessarily be a good decision, for several reasons:

- If you want to power on, say, 10 or 20 VMs simultaneously, dealing with 10 or 20 initial placement dialog boxes can become irritating.

- Will you always have the vSphere Client open to see recommendations and then act on them?

- If VMotion events are included as part of change management requests, then you will waste time waiting for such requests to be processed. By the time you get approval for the VMotion, the performance will have changed, rendering the request invalid. If VMotion is included in change management, then you will need to be able to call a DEFCON 1 approval process to handle VMotion requests efficiently.

So, perhaps it's time to learn to give up some control and have VMware move VMs for you. If you have particularly politically sensitive VMs that shouldn't be moved without prior approval, you can exclude them from the DRS process.

Application Owner Concerns

Some application owners take the position that if the VM is working, and no users are complaining about performance, then why bother with a VMotion? Personally, I see the merits in this attitude—after all performance is just one measure of an application; stability and predictability are others.

If you come across people with this perspective, the best way to approach them is to acknowledge their perspective and remind them that there are tools we can use to guarantee performance does not fluctuate greatly from one day to the next. For example, we can impose limits and reservations on a VM, and also isolate a VM from the global rules of DRS, making that VM behave manually or partially automated. Such a VM would move from one ESX host to another only with the express permission of the vCenter administrator. If you wish, you could even include this in your change management process.

When most application owners voice a concern about the automated nature of DRS, their main worries are that VMotion cannot be relied on and that it could affect the user's access to the application. Such opposition to VMotion and DRS is generally centered on a lack of knowledge and experience with VMotion.

Migration Thresholds

In addition to the three different levels of automation, you can set a migration threshold for DRS. This allows you to specify how aggressive DRS should be in balancing the cluster of ESX hosts. You can choose from five threshold levels, beginning with conservative and ending with aggressive, with the default set in the middle of these two extremes.

When a VM is selected as a candidate for VMotion by DRS, it will be given a priority rating of from one to five, and the threshold level ties in directly with this, as follows:

- **Level 1–conservative**   Triggers a VMotion if the VM has a level five priority rating. Level five priority recommendations are rare. You may receive this recommendation when one of your affinity rules is breached or when putting an ESX host into maintenance mode.

- **Level 2–moderately conservative**   Triggers a VMotion if the VM has four or more priority.

- **Level 3–default**   Triggers a VMotion if the VM has three or more priority.

- **Level 4–moderately aggressive**   Triggers a VMotion if the VM has two or more priority rating.

- **Level 5–aggressive**   Triggers a VMotion if the VM has one or more priority rating.

DRS Rules and Regulations

DRS automation levels allow you to specify a global rule for the cluster, and it is possible to have per-VM exceptions to this rule. This allows you to flag sensitive VMs as requiring administrator intervention. It is also possible to completely exclude VMs from DRS because of incompatibility reasons. A classic example of this is excluding a MSCS pair, as it lacks compatibility with VMotion and therefore with DRS.

You can also impose *affinity* and *anti-affinity* rules. This allows you to specify that two or more VMs must be kept together (affinity) or kept separate (anti-affinity).

For example, if you have two VMs that are very network-intensive, they should be kept together (have affinity) so they remain on the same vSwitch in the same ESX host. Why? Because when two VMs communicate on the same vSwitch, the physical data layer is not touched, and networking is as fast as the CPU and memory can manage.

As another example, you might decide to keep two CPU or memory-intensive VMs separate from each other (set an anti-affinity rule), so that they do not compete for those resources. Another reason to keep VMs apart is that they share the same role. It doesn't make much sense to have two identical VMs on the same ESX host that could fail; you want to distribute them across many ESX hosts. Using anti-affinity rules, you could avoid an all-your-eggs-in-one-basket situation, where all your domain controllers, Web servers, or Citrix servers end up on the same ESX host.

Most application vendors scale their systems for redundancy and performance. These systems have enough resiliency that VMware HA is good enough protection for them, as long as you make sure that DRS never puts two VMs with the same role on the same ESX host. You can reserve the use of VMware's FT for VMs that really require it, such as stand-alone VMs that cannot be clustered with conventional methods.

CAUTION *It is possible to configure affinity rule conflicts. The vSphere Client will allow you to configure a rule where VM1 loves VM2, and VM2 loves VM3, but that VM3 hates VM1. This becomes like a plotline in a soap opera. Fortunately, the vSphere Client will warn you that you are creating a logical impossibility.*

Resource Pools and DRS Clustering

Just as stand-alone ESX hosts can have resource pools, so can DRS clusters. In fact, it probably makes it more compelling to use resource pools in a VMware cluster, as you are more likely to want to carve up the aggregate of many ESX hosts in a cluster into small pools of resources.

When you add an existing stand-alone ESX host with resource pools into a DRS cluster, you will be asked what you would like to do with them. You have two options: to remove the stand-alone resource pools and start again, or to graft them to the DRS cluster. If you choose the latter option, you will see in the DRS cluster the name of the resource pool followed by "Grafted from . . .," indicating where the resource pool was originally created. If a resource pool on a stand-alone ESX host does not contain any VMs, it is not grafted to the DRS cluster; it is simply removed.

NOTE *Personally, I like to remove existing resource pools and define new ones. I don't bother with stand-alone resource pools at all. I use them only with DRS clusters. All the limits, reservations, and share values imposed on a stand-alone ESX host are unlikely to be relevant to a cluster of ESX hosts that provide six times the resources.*

Preparing for DRS

Make sure you have VMotion configured correctly before you begin setting up DRS. A good test is to check that you can VMotion every single VM in your system. DRS currently makes no checks for VMotion whatsoever when it is enabled. In fact, you can even set up DRS without VMotion being enabled on a VMkernel port group! If you ever have problems with DRS or even HA, a manual VMotion will at least check that you have fulfilled the requirements of all three features.

The most common mistake I have seen is the simplest: forgetting to put a check in the Enable VMotion box when you create a VMkernel port group. You can confirm VMotion is enabled by looking at the Summary tab of each of your ESX hosts.

A good way to check if you have the basic relationships in place—shared networking and shared storage—is by using the map feature. Maps allow you to see a graphical representation of your system. The following example shows my two ESX hosts, which both have access to the same storage and networking.

esx1.vi4book.com VMware ESX, e.x.p, 113880	
Summary / Virtual Machines / Resource Allocation / Performance	
General	
Manufacturer:	HP
Model:	ProLiant DL385 G1
Processors:	4 CPU x 2.204 GHz
Processor Type:	AMD Opteron(tm) Processor 275
Hyperthreading:	Inactive
Number of NICs:	4
State:	connected
Virtual Machines:	6
VMotion Enabled:	yes
FaultTolerance Enabled:	no
Active Tasks:	

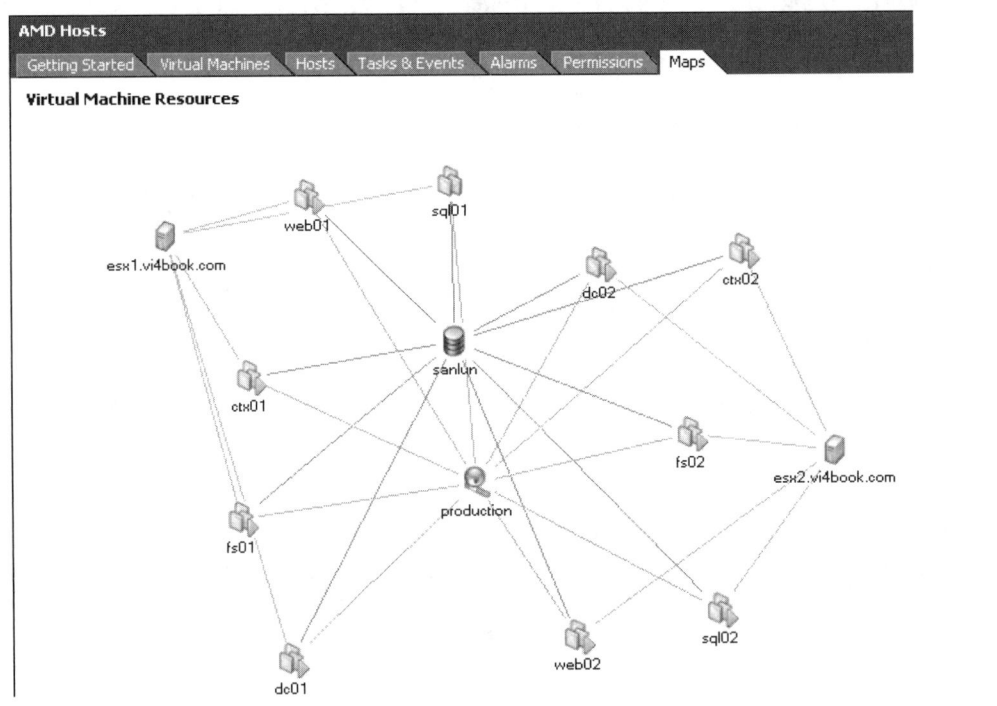

In contrast, the next example shows a situation where a VM is not on shared storage in the DRS cluster. Notice the red X next to the ESX host.

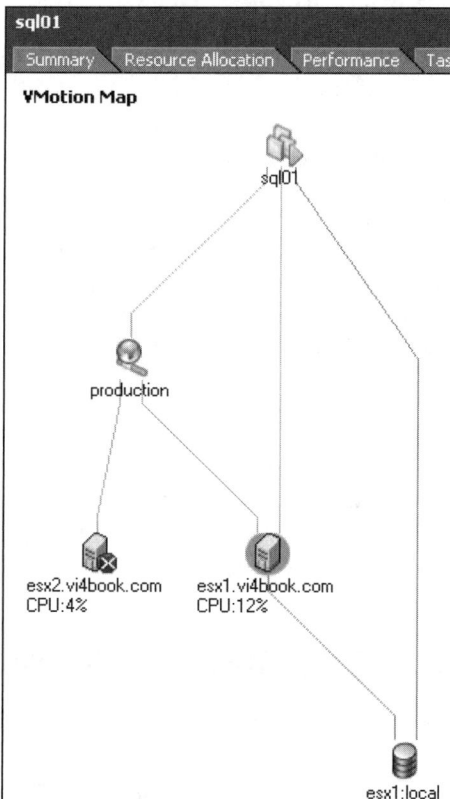

Maps can be saved in a JPEG, BMP, or EMF format for documentation purposes. To save a map, in the vSphere Client's File menu, select Export, and then Export Maps.

TIP   *Currently, VMware does not offer a method to convert maps into a Microsoft Visio format. However, other companies offer software that can do this. One example is Veeam Software's Veeam Reporter Enterprise (http://www.veeam.com/veeam_reporter.asp). Additionally, the Virtualization EcoShell Initiative (thevesi.org) allows you to export the result of PowerCLI queries to charts and Visio diagrams, and currently it is free to download and use.*

If DRS cannot move a VM, the vCenter system gives you a good indication of why.

Recent Tasks			
Name	Target	Status	Initiated by
Migrate Virtual Machine	sql02	Virtual machine has CPU and/or memory affinities configured, preventing VMotion.	System

Unfortunately, when you are using DRS with the maintenance mode feature, the quality of the messaging is not up to the same quality.

Configuring DRS

I will first show you how to set up a DRS cluster in manual mode. This is so you can get some experience with the recommendation system and have full control before switching to fully automated mode. I won't demonstrate the partially automated mode in this chapter, as it is merely a hybrid of manual and fully automated.

Setting Up a DRS Cluster in Manual Mode

For this manual mode cluster example, we'll use the aggressive option to increase the likelihood of seeing DRS recommendations. If your VMs have modest performance demands, are few in number, and are on ESX hosts with plenty of CPU and memory resources, you might rarely, if ever, see a recommendation. In practice, I recommend the default setting, or even making DRS more conservative than it already is.

Follow these steps to create the cluster and add ESX hosts:

1. In vCenter, in the Hosts and Clusters view, right-click and choose New Cluster, or click the New Cluster icon.

2. Type in a friendly name for your cluster, and select Turn on VMware DRS. I named my cluster AMD Cluster, since I am creating it within the AMD host folder (only my AMD servers have the CPU compatibility required for VMotion and DRS).

3. Change the automation level to Manual.

4. Move the slider bar to Aggressive and click Next.

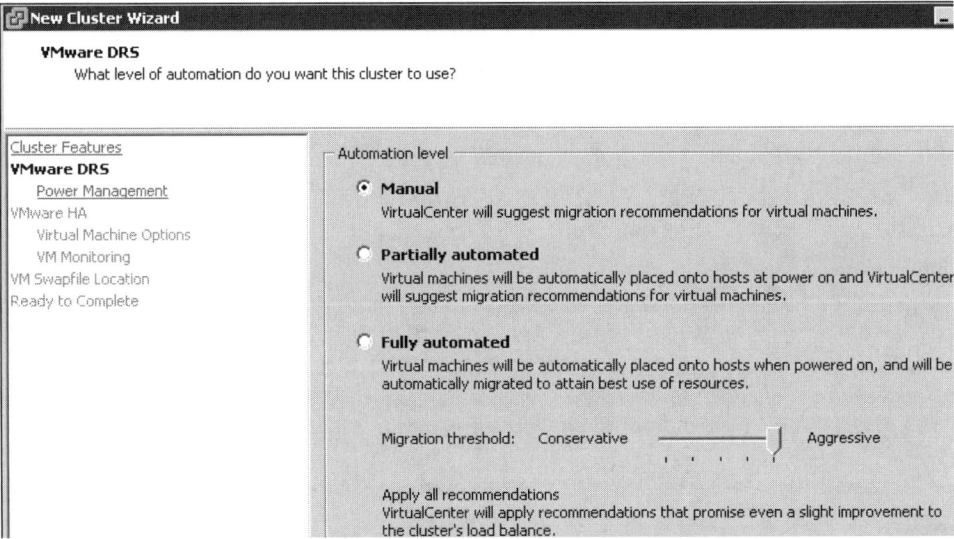

5. For this example, do not enable DPM (it's covered in Chapter 14).

6. Accept the default settings for the VMkernel swap file location.

7. Click Next and Finish.

8. Drag-and-drop your first ESX host into the cluster.

9. Accept the default, which removes any existing ESX host-based resource pools.

10. Repeat this operation for the remaining hosts that you want to add to the cluster (of course, these hosts must meet the VMotion requirements).

The following example shows the main Summary tab for my AMD Cluster. Here, you can see that DRS is enabled and my two ESX hosts are offering eight cores with a collective amount of 17GHz of CPU time and 8GB of RAM. In the VMware DRS pane, you can see that currently no recommendations have been generated by DRS.

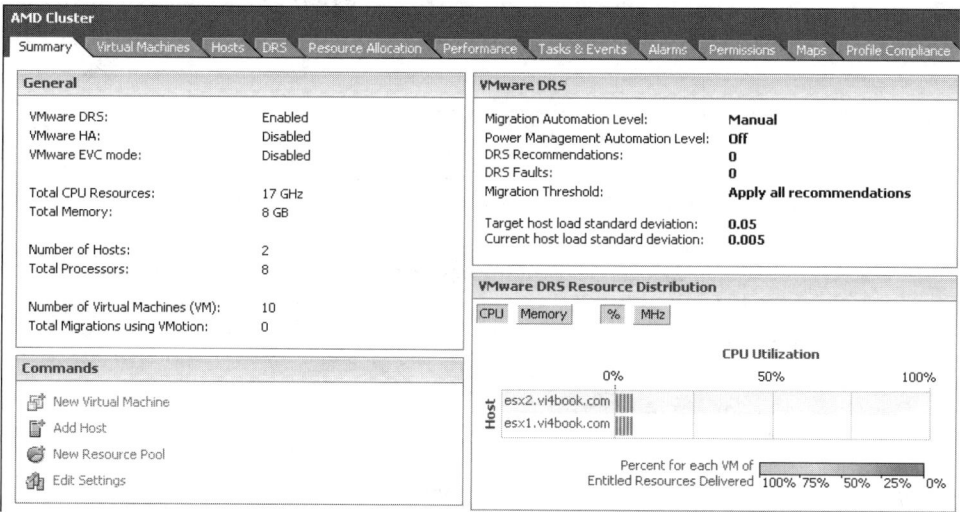

In the DRS Resource Distribution pane, the first chart shows how balanced my hosts are. As you can see, the two ESX hosts are very well balanced. Neither is using much CPU or memory. My VMs are mainly idle, and therefore 90% of the cluster resources are not in use. You can adjust the chart to see either CPU or memory, and represent these resources either as a percentage or as a physical resource in megahertz or megabytes.

The VMware DRS pane also includes two deviation values:

- **Target host load standard deviation**   This value represents a goal—a level of load imbalance that is tolerated.

- **Current host load deviation**   This value indicates the current load imbalance within the cluster. If this value grows and imbalance is allowed to grow and grow, it will eventually trigger an alarm, as in the following example.

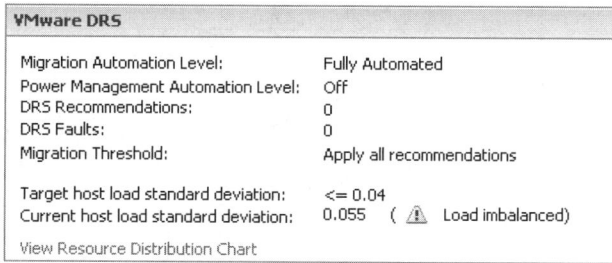

The cause of this imbalance usually is that DRS has recommendations pending that have been accepted by the administrator, or that rules that have been set up to prevent DRS from reaching an ideally balanced cluster. It doesn't in itself mean that you have a performance problem.

Viewing and Applying Recommendations

One way to create a recommendation is to deliberately unbalance a cluster. I did this by moving all the VMs on esx2 to esx1 with a manual VMotion. In the following example, you can see I have three DRS recommendations. This means that DRS has identified three VMs whose performance would be improved if they were moved to another ESX host.

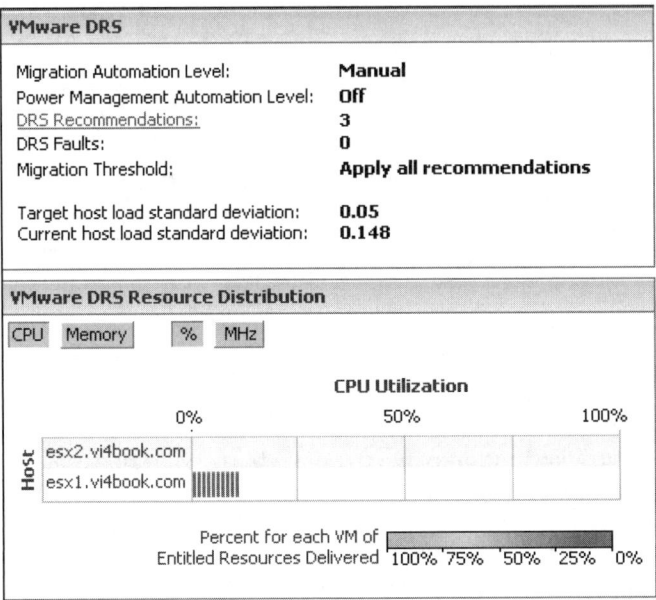

As you can see, there is no VM load on esx2 whatsoever. If you hover the mouse pointer over the % bars on an ESX host, you will also see a pop-up window that indicates each VM's allocation in the cluster. In this example, the VM called web01 is demanding 44MHz of CPU and receiving 44MHz. In this case, the cluster is delivering 100% of the VM's demands.

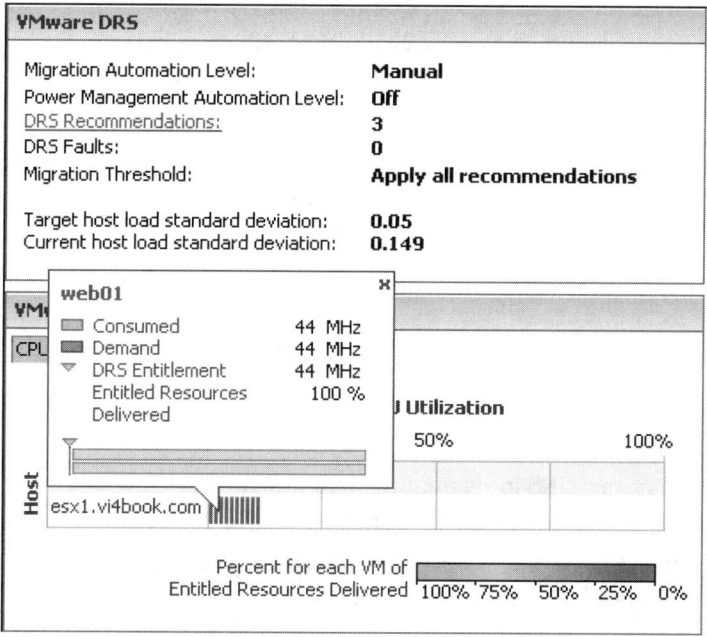

This DRS tab shows the priority ratings, recommendations, and reasons. In this example, the reasons for the recommendations are "Balance average memory loads." My VMs are not especially resource-intensive, but they do use memory, and my ESX hosts have only 4GB memory, which is quite a low amount compared to real-world values.

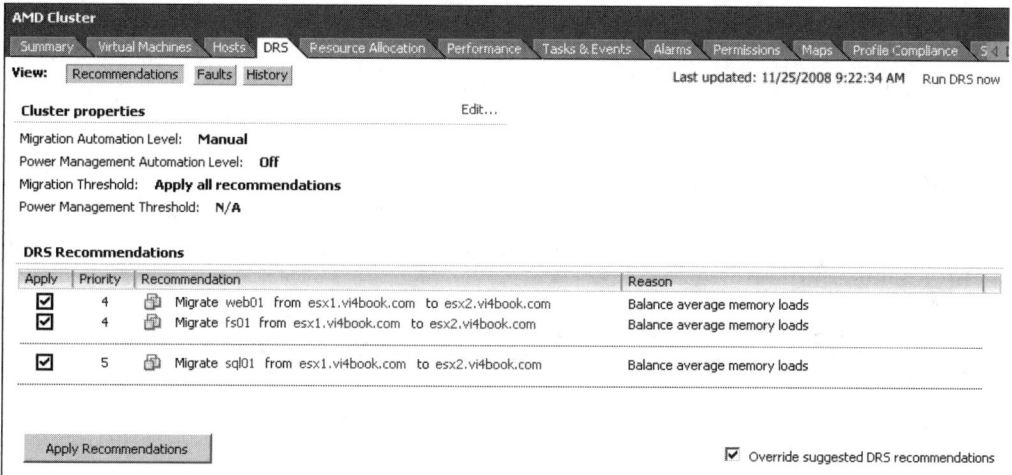

If you click the Apply Recommendation button, DRS with VMotion would move all three VMs. If you select the "Override suggested DRS recommendations" option, you will be able to manually decide which VMs should be moved.

The Run DRS now link in the top-right corner of the tab forces DRS to recalculate the cluster (it replaces the Generate Recommendations button, which was introduced in VI3.5). Clicking the Faults button on the left will tell you if you have had any VMotion errors, as discussed in the "Viewing DRS Fault Reports" section later in this chapter. Clicking the History button records the DRS events that have taken place.

TIP   *If you do not see the DRS recommendation, you can sometimes trigger it by adjusting your DRS threshold to be more aggressive. Alternatively, you could try running the cpubusy.vbs file in one of the VMs.*

Choosing Initial Placement

When you have configured DRS in manual mode, you will be asked to choose the VM's placement when you power it off and then power it on again.

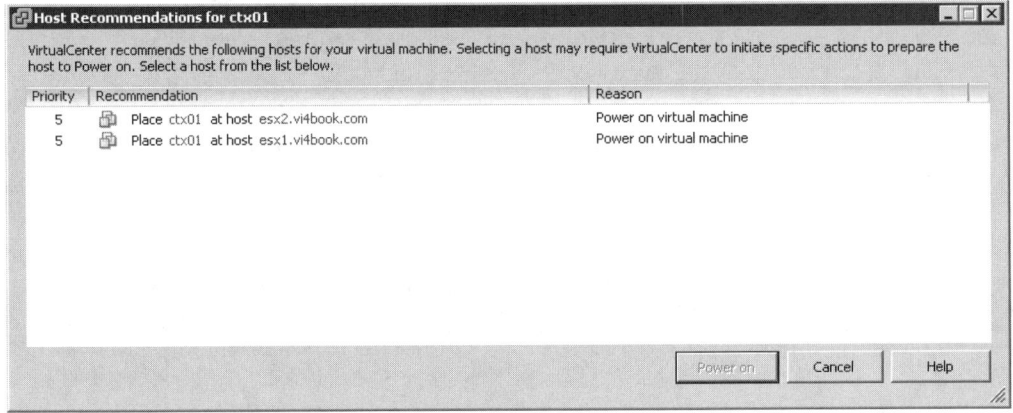

The dialog box is sorted in order of recommendation, with the ESX host at the top of the list as the most appropriate one for the VM. Select the ESX host you prefer the VM to run on, and then click the Power On button. These initial placements are recorded in the History log alongside the VMotions triggered by DRS.

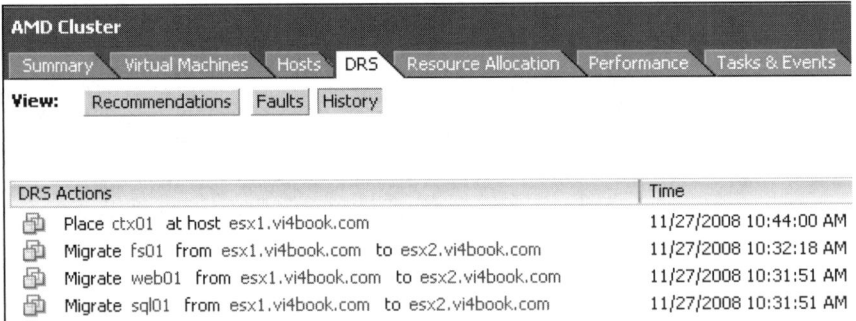

NOTE *Previously, the initial placement dialog box gave basic information about the amount of free unreserved CPU and memory resources that were available. This is no longer shown in the dialog box.*

You will be asked to choose initial VM placement only with the DRS manual mode. With the partial and fully automated modes, the VM will be powered on the most appropriate ESX host without asking you to confirm it.

Configuring DRS Cluster Affinity/Anti-Affinity Rules

As stated earlier, two types of controls are available for individual VMs: affinity (keep VMs together) and anti-affinity (separate VMs) rules.

Here is the procedure for setting an anti-affinity rule:

1. Right-click the cluster and choose Edit Settings.
2. Select Rules.
3. Click the Add button.
4. Type in a friendly name for the rule, such as **AD Domain Controllers**.
5. Under the Type option, choose Separate Virtual Machines.

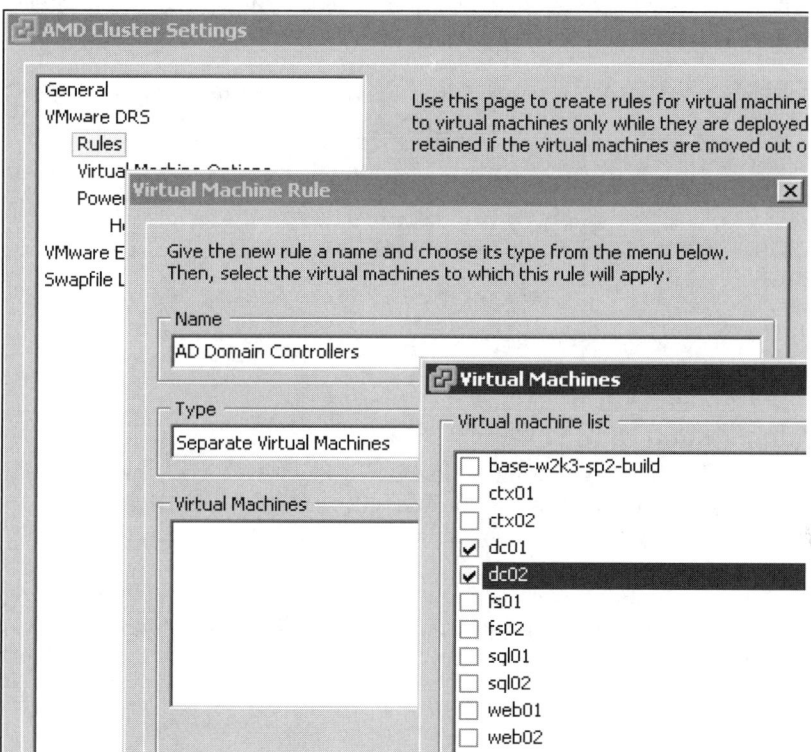

6. Select the VMs to which you want to apply the rule (dc01 and dc02 in this example), and then click OK.

7. Click OK to create your rule.

The following example shows a situation where dc01 and dc02 are residing on the same ESX host, which is a breach of my anti-affinity rule that they should be kept apart, so the reason for the migration is to "Satisfy anti-affinity rule." You will receive a similar recommendation if you have created an affinity rule, and the two VMs are not on the same ESX host.

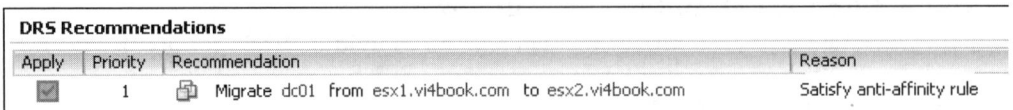

CAUTION   *vCenter does check your affinity rules when you first power on a VM. However, it does not check your affinity rules to warn administrators when they try to carry out manual VMotion events that breach affinity rules. If an administrator carries out a manual VMotion, it is entirely possible to accidentally trigger a five-star recommendation by manually putting two VMs together that should be kept separate, or separating two that should be kept together. Interestingly, if you use fully automated mode, this still happens, but DRS automatically performs another VMotion to undo this administrative error.*

As stated earlier, rule conflicts are possible. The following example shows this occurrence.

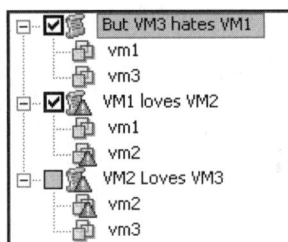

Setting Custom Automation Levels

If desired, you can set a custom automation level on a sensitive VM. As you might remember, VM clustering in any of its forms is incompatible with VMotion and DRS. A good example of custom automation levels is completely disabling DRS on VMs that run some kind of clustering software.

To set a custom automation level, right-click the cluster and choose Edit Settings. In the dialog box, select Virtual Machine Options. Select each VM you want to have a custom setting, and choose the automation type from the drop-down list. The following example shows disabling nodeA and nodeB.

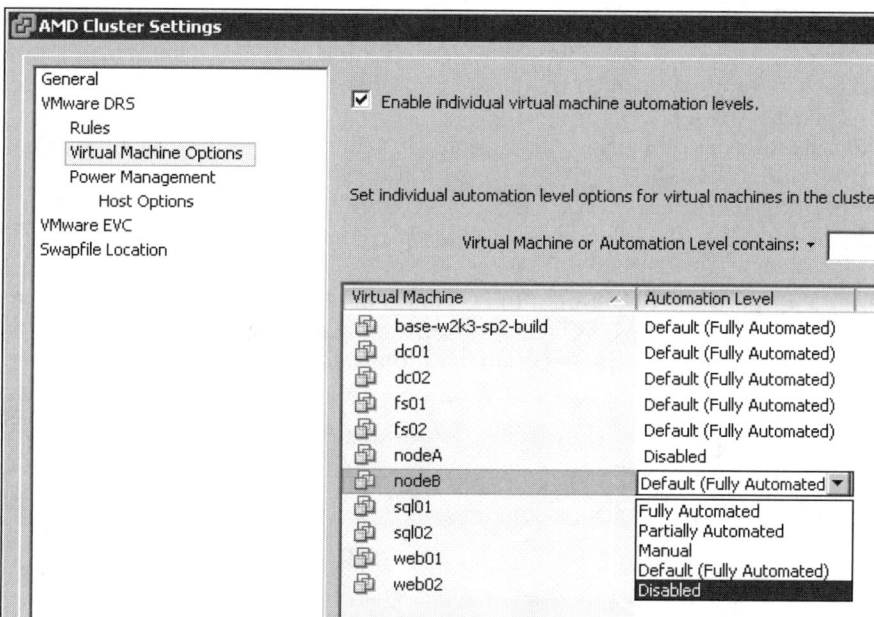

NOTE *In previous versions, even with this option to exclude the VM clusters from DRS, in a manual or partial automation mode, you were still asked which ESX host to power on (nodeA or nodeB, in this example). This annoyance has now been removed, and if a VM is stored locally it just powers up on the server where the VM is located locally.*

Configuring Fully Automated DRS Using Maintenance Mode

Maintenance mode is an option available next to shutdown and reboot on an ESX host. You have probably shut down and rebooted your ESX host a couple of times since you started reading this book, so you might ask, "Why leave this topic until now?" Well, the main reason is that maintenance mode becomes really interesting and cool when combined with DRS.

Stated very simply, maintenance mode is an isolation state used whenever you need to carry out critical ESX host tasks such as upgrading firmware, ESX hosts, memory, or CPUs, or patching the ESX software. This isolation state will prevent other vCenter users from creating new VMs and powering them on your ESX host. It will also prevent any manual VMotion events created by an administrator or automatic VMotion events generated by DRS. Maintenance mode does survive reboots, which allows administrators time to confirm that their changes have been effective (like adding a new hardware device such as a NIC or a HBA) before VMs can be executed on the ESX host.

When maintenance mode is triggered in the context of DRS, you should find at the very least it will generate five-star recommendations to move the VMs from the ESX host. With fully automated DRS, the VMs are just moved without any recommendations.

From VI3.5 onward, maintenance mode will not just move powered-on VMs, but also powered-off and suspended VMs. The main reason for this extended functionality is for VDI environments. In VDI environments, either the users or their "broker" can manually or automatically cause a VM to be powered off or suspended when users log out of their session.

The intention is to save valuable CPU and memory resources when the user's desktop is not in use. As you could never know when the user would log in again, it's important their virtual desktops are moved from an ESX host in maintenance mode to an ESX host that is available in the DRS cluster.

How maintenance mode works will depends on your configuration, as follows:

- **Stand-alone ESX host without DRS**   The administrator must VMotion all VMs to another ESX host manually. If VMotion is not available, the administrator must power off all VMs before maintenance mode is triggered.

- **Manual or partial DRS automation**   This generates recommendations that must be applied to evacuate the ESX host of all currently running VMs. The following example shows a migration recommendation triggered by maintenance mode.

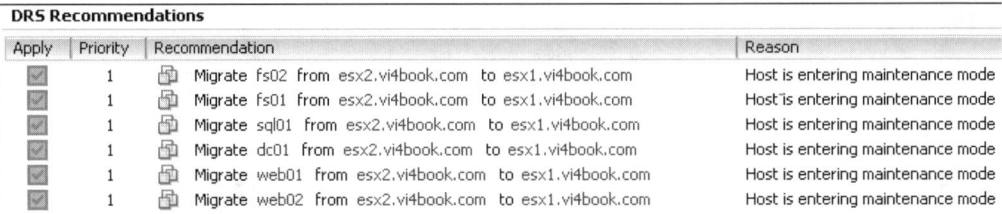

- **Fully Automated DRS**   DRS automatically moves the VMs of the ESX host to other nodes in the cluster, obeying your rules and regulations where possible.

Follow these steps to change the DRS cluster in the previous example from manual to fully automated, and enable maintenance mode:

1. Right-click your cluster and choose Edit Settings.

2. Change the automation level to fully automated. Then click OK.

3. Select one of your ESX hosts in the cluster.

4. On the Summary tab, in the Commands pane, select Enter Maintenance Mode.

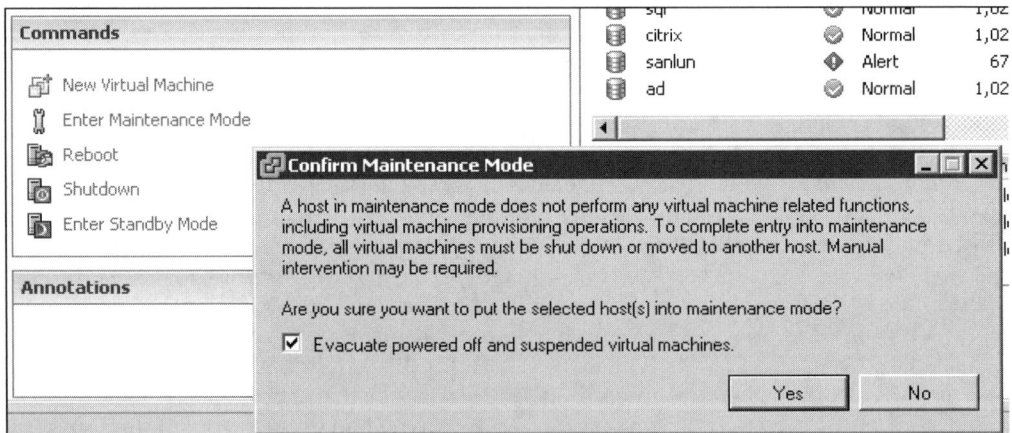

This should trigger an automatic VMotion of all your VMs from that host onto other ESX servers. The vSphere Client will warn you that for maintenance mode to complete, manual intervention may be required by the administrator to resolve why a VM is not moving.

At the end of this bulk VMotion event, no VMs will remain on the ESX host, and the icon for the ESX host will change to indicate it is in maintenance mode.

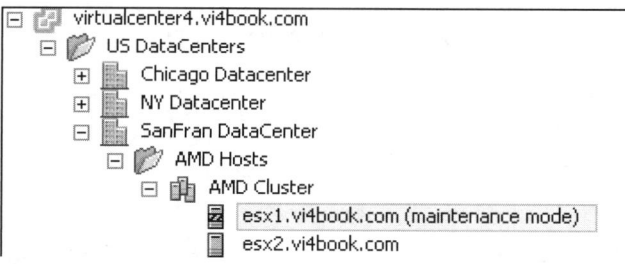

Where Are My VMs Running?

We don't know. Once you have engaged fully automated mode, you will not really know (depending on how conservative or aggressive you have configured DRS in the settings) from one hour to the next where your VM will be running. For some people, this is a difficult concept, as they are so tied to the physical world. Remember that fundamentally, a VM executes on only one ESX host at one time. If you want to know on which ESX host a VM is currently running, there are two ways to check:

- On any object that contains your VM (root container, datacenter, folder, or cluster), select the Virtual Machines tab, right-click the descriptive names of one of the columns (such as name), and enable the option "host."

- Find your VM in the Inventory. In the General pane of the Summary tab, you should see a field that specifies its state and on which ESX host it is currently executing.

Resolving Maintenance Mode Problems

One of the most common problems people experience in maintenance mode is that it hangs and does not complete. When using maintenance mode, either when an ESX host is in stand-alone mode or in a DRS/HA cluster mode, the VMs currently residing on the host must either be moved (via VMotion) or powered off. If a VM cannot be moved or powered off, the maintenance mode waits for you to resolve the problem. Unfortunately, the vSphere Client currently doesn't prompt you that maintenance mode is waiting, nor tell you in a big, friendly pop-up box why maintenance mode is hanging. However, if you carefully read the maintenance mode dialog box, you'll see that the vSphere Client does warn you about the requirements for maintenance mode to complete.

Maintenance mode problems usually arise when DRS is in a fully automated mode, but is unable to move all the VMs to other ESX hosts in the cluster. When this happens, maintenance mode just sits there—no warnings or pop-up windows appear. If you try powering on a VM, you will receive the message "The operation is not allowed in the current state."

I must admit that the first time I saw this message, it had me stumped. It turned out that one of the students had attempted to enter maintenance mode earlier, and then carried on with other tasks. This meant that, at first glance, the Recent Task pane view at the bottom of the vSphere Client did not show the message "Entering maintenance mode. . . ."

While in the process of entering maintenance mode, you will find you cannot carry out many tasks except for ones that would resolve the problem, such as the following:

- Performing a manual VMotion
- Powering off a VM
- Canceling maintenance mode (by right-clicking the task in the task pane and choosing Cancel)

Nine times out of ten, you will find that there is a property of the VM that is causing the problem. One tip is to try a manual VMotion, as this should create a meaningful pop-up message that will help you resolve the problem so the host can complete entry into maintenance mode. Typically, DRS's inability to move a VM is caused by the following VM errors:

- Connected removable devices that are configured for local storage or local devices
- Connected internal switches
- RDM files to LUN not presented to other ESX hosts
- VM clustering
- CPU affinities

Viewing DRS Fault Reports

As noted earlier, clicking the Faults button on the DRS tab in vSphere 4 shows you any errors that occurred during a DRS procedure. A number of circumstances will trigger an entry in the fault report view, including the following:

- **Virtual machine is disabled for DRS**   VM is disabled for DRS, as in the case of nodeA/nodeB in a MSCS scenario.
- **Virtual machine not compatible with any host**   An ESX host with CPU incompatibility issues has been added to the DRS cluster.

- **Affinity rule violated when moving to another host**   An affinity rule that has been defined for a VM has be broken to meet the requirements of DRS.

- **Host incompatible with virtual machine**   DRS considers migrating a VM to a host, but finds that the host is incompatible with the given VM. Among other incompatibilities, setting CPU affinities will generate this error message.

- **Host has virtual machine that violates anti-affinity rules**   You have a two-node DRS cluster and two VMs with anti-affinity rules, and one of the ESX hosts is unavailable. The automatic power-on of partial or fully automated DRS fails, and you are confronted with the manual placement dialog box.

- **Host has insufficient capacity for virtual machine**   There is a lack of CPU or memory resources to successfully move a VM.

- **Host in incorrect state**   ESX host is powered off or in standby mode, or it is in a disconnected mode or not responding.

- **Host has insufficient number of physical CPUs for virtual machine**   DRS tried to VMotion a VM with multiple vCPUs (Virtual SMP), but there are not enough physical CPUs at the destination ESX host.

- **Host has insufficient per-CPU capacity for virtual machine**   The ESX host does not have enough CPU or memory capacity for running the VM.

- **The virtual machine is in VMotion**   The VM is already in a state of being in VMotion, so DRS cannot move it.

- **No active host in cluster**   There is no host in a valid state within the resource in which to move the VM, so an affinity rule may be fixed. This can occur, for example, if all the hosts are disconnected or in maintenance mode.

- **Insufficient resources**   This is an admission control fault, caused by a requirement in a resource policy that cannot be met. For example, this can occur if a power-on event is attempted and there are insufficient CPU, memory, or disk resources.

In the following example, I created a deliberate error (CPU affinities), and then triggered maintenance mode. All my VMs moved, except one—the one with CPU affinities!

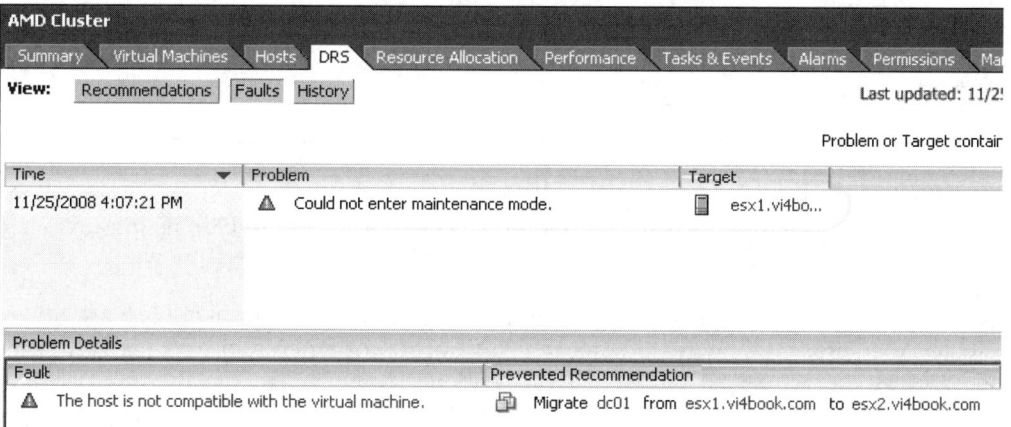

Unfortunately, the quality of these fault reports is not always fantastic, and may not help you identify the source of the problem you already know you have.

In other situations, the fault report does a good job of explaining the source of the problem. For example, when you have a two-node ESX cluster with two VMs that have the anti-affinity rule set, and you try to enter maintenance mode, it will hang at 2% and leave you with a clear message in the fault report.

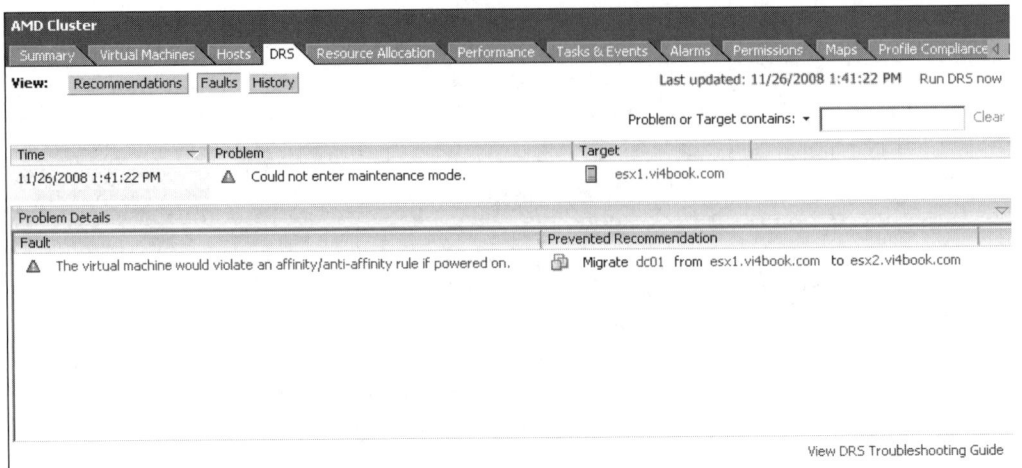

Clicking the View DRS Troubleshooting Guide link here opens an HTML-based help file that outlines a wide range of possible problems with DRS. In this example, to resolve this problem, I merely temporarily disabled my anti-affinity rule, and then clicked the Run DRS now link.

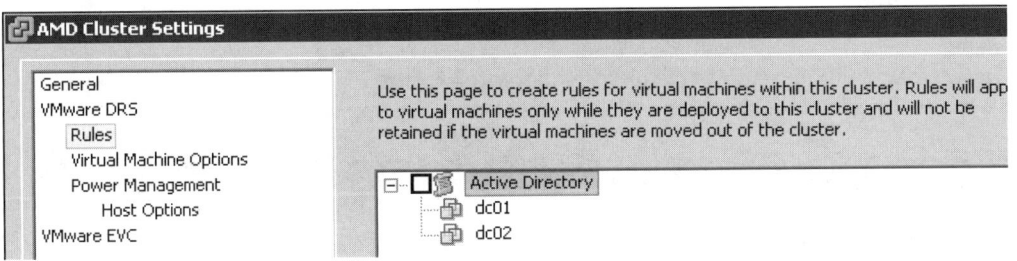

Creating Resource Pools on a DRS Cluster

As noted earlier, you can create resource pools on a DRS cluster to carve up its resources into smaller pools. Resource pools on a DRS cluster work in exactly the same way as an individual host.

Although the vSphere Client gives the impression that the resource pools hang off the cluster, they are actually created on each ESX host. Fundamentally, a VM is executed on an ESX host, not across ESX hosts. This would require some type of grid-computing hardware, which currently is cost-prohibitive for most organizations. Therefore, when a VM demands its reservation for memory, for example, that reservation must be found physically on an ESX host. Remember that resource pools and DRS clusters represent a logical grouping of resources—we are still constrained by the physical limits of each of our ESX hosts.

When a VM is moved from one ESX host to another in DRS, its resource pool membership remains the same. Again, many people think that the resource pool represents a physical location, but it is merely a software concept that allows allocating resources and controlling performance of VMs.

The following example shows the resource pools I've created on my DRS cluster. (This is not intended to be a recommendation on how you should set up resource pools, but merely an example of one method).

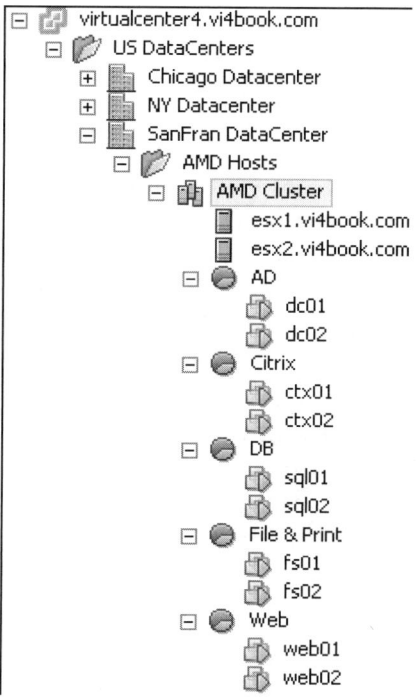

System Resource Pools

Resource pools are used to manage internal ESX processes as well. On every ESX host there is a system root resource pool. Contained within this resource pool are child resource pools used to manage the VMkernel tasks. There is no practical usage of this within the ESX host for a production environment, but I thought you might like to know about these resource pools.

You can see the ESX host root resource pool by selecting its Configuration tab, choosing System Resource Allocation, and clicking Advanced, as shown in the following illustration.

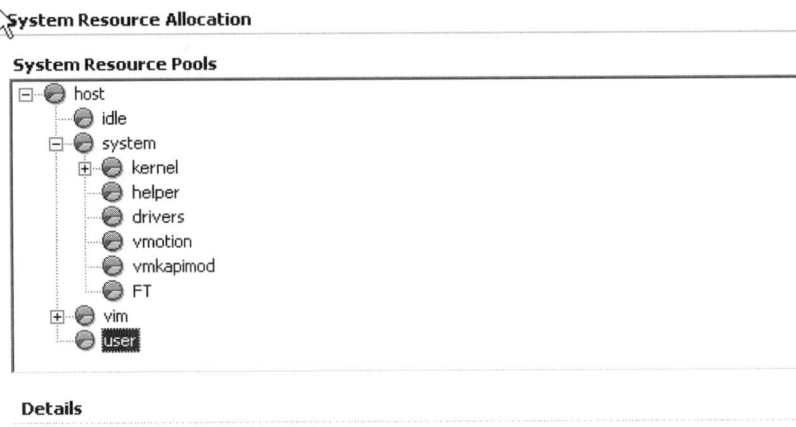

Enabling Enhanced VMotion Compatibility

In the ideal world, all the CPUs you cluster will be exactly the same, but as discussed in Chapter 12, CPU incompatibilities are likely to occur in the real world. The Enhanced VMotion Compatibility (EVC) support feature was introduced in VI3.5 Update 2 to help address this problem.

As also discussed in Chapter 12, the newer CPUs that are being created by Intel and AMD have the ability to mask attributes of the processor. EVC allows them to use this feature to make them compatible with *older* ESX hosts running on *older* CPUs. Processors that support features like Intel's FlexMigration or AMD-V Extended Migration will be able to negotiate a common set of features to ensure compatibility is achieved. Conceptually, EVC creates a common baseline of CPU attributes to *engineer* compatibility.

Currently, the list of CPU types supported by EVC is short, but it will only grow over time:

- Intel Core 2 (Merom)
- Intel 45nm Core 2 (Penryn)
- AMD Second Generation Opteron (Rev-E/F)
- AMD Third Generation Opteron (Barcelona)

Unfortunately, to enable EVC, you must first power off all your VMs. The VMs need to be powered off because EVC generates CPU identity masks to engineer compatibility between hosts. As VMs see and use these attributes at power on, they can't be removed while they are in use.

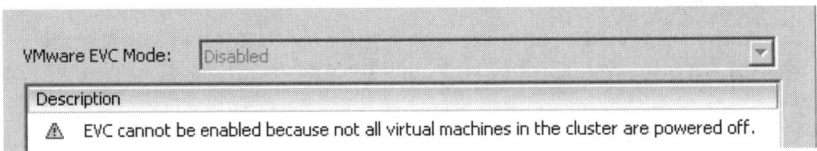

For this reason, you may wish to enable this feature when you first create a DRS cluster. You may want to follow this build order:

1. Install vCenter.

2. Create cluster.

3. Enable DRS/EVC.

4. Add ESX hosts with lowest capabilities first before powering on VMs.

5. Configure networking and storage.

6. Create VMs.

To enable EVC, first ensure all VMs are powered off. Then right-click the cluster and select VMware EVC. In the Cluster Settings dialog box, enable EVC for your CPU vendor type.

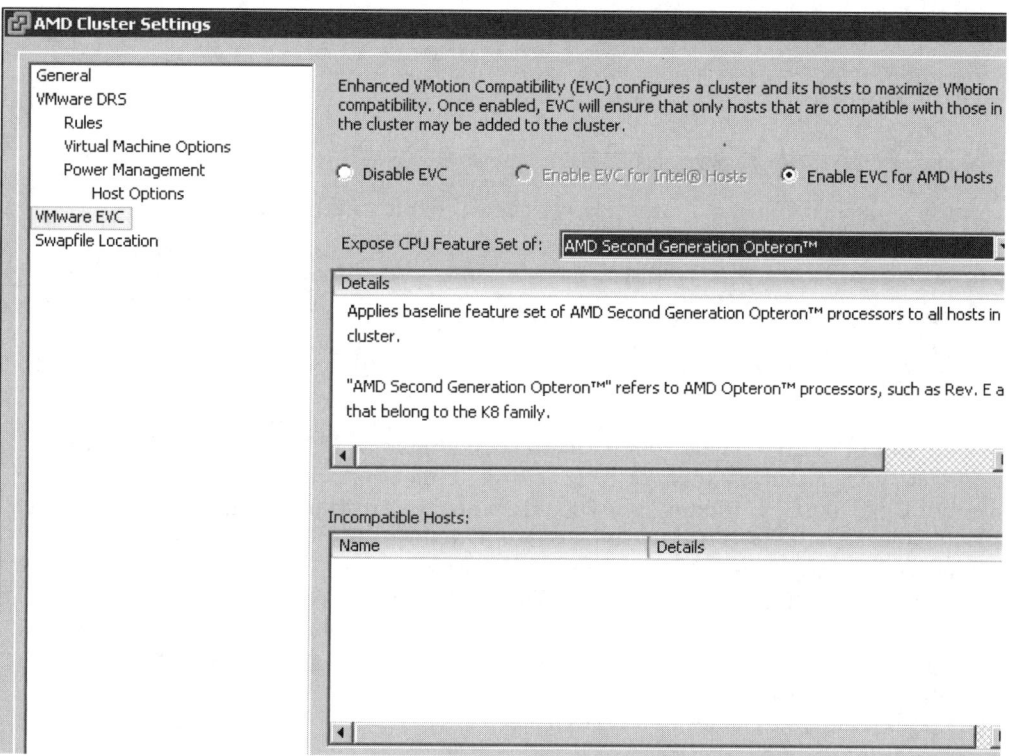

After enabling EVC for the first time, the Current CPUID Details button will become available. Clicking this shows you the current CPU identity mask imposed on the cluster.

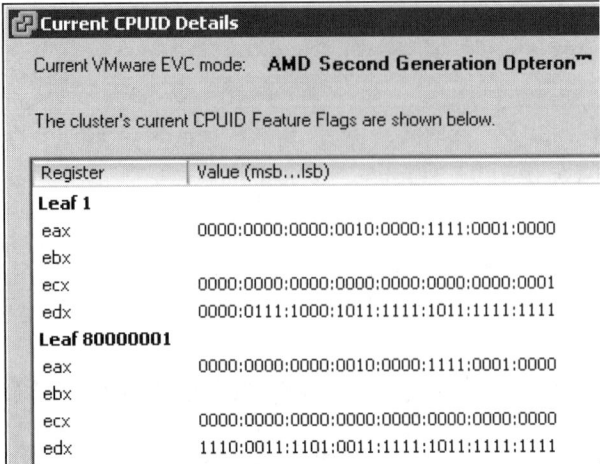

Once EVC has been enabled, it will check if a new ESX host matches the common baseline of CPU attributes established when it was first enabled. EVC will produce an error or warning if various CPU attributes have not been enabled in the server BIOS.

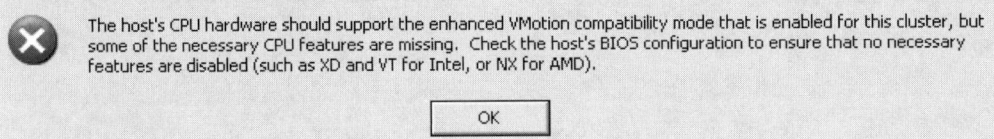

It's important to understand that while the developments of Intel and AMD are to be commended, you cannot see them or EVC as silver bullet that will fix all problems. Remember EVC, like CPU identity masks, only hides the attributes to the VM that could cause CPU incompatibility. For certain user mode requests like SSE we are very much dependent on developers writing well-behaved code that makes the requests in an appropriate manner. (I don't wish to make disparaging and sweeping statements about programmers here, but I'm sure you have all come across developers who don't appreciate the difference between HKEY_LOCAL_MACHINE and HKEY_CURRENT_USER.)

The *VMotion Information Guide* from VMware (http://www.vmware.com/files/pdf/vmotion_info_guide.pdf) states this very clearly:

"EVC utilizes hardware support to modify the semantics of the CPUID instruction only. It does not disable the feature itself. For example, if an attempt to disable SSE4.1 is made by applying the appropriate masks to a CPU that has these features, this feature bit indicates SSE4.1 is not available to the guest or the application, but the feature and the

SSE4.1 instructions themselves (such as PTESE and PMULLD) are still available for use. This implies applications that do not use the CPUID instruction to determine the list of supported features, but use try-catch undefined instructions (#UD) instead, can still detect the existence of this feature."

As this is very much a bleeding-edge feature that is likely to evolve rapidly alongside other processor developments, I refer you to the latest information in VMware's *VMotion Information Guide* for the current support requirements.

Relocating the VMkernel Swap File

Since VI3.5, we have had the ability to change the location of the swap file. This might be necessary to save space on expensive storage. This will be of special interest to people who set very large limits and very small reservations, as that results in a very large swap file.

The relocation of the swap file can be done with or without the clustering features being enabled. I chose to cover this feature here, as the change does have an impact on VMotion and DRS. For this reason, I do *not* recommend relocating the swap file, unless you have a very compelling reason to do so.

To relocate the VMkernal swap file, first, configure the cluster. Right-click the cluster and select Swapfile Location. Select the "Store the swapfile in the datastore specified by the host" option.

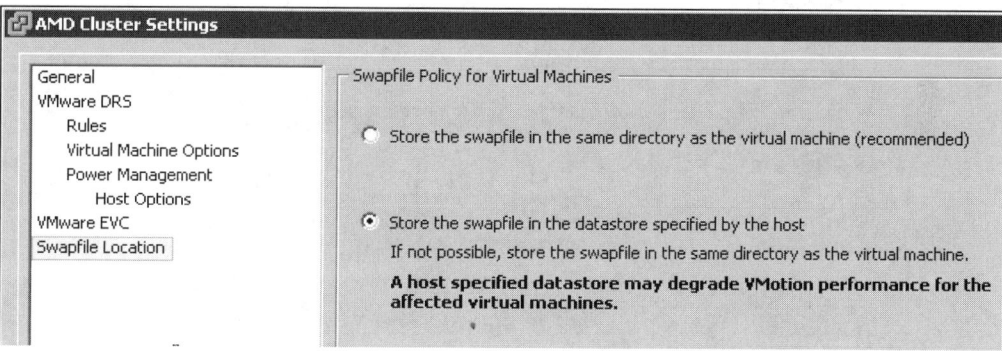

Notice the operative word in the warning beneath this option—it *may* degrade performance, not that it *will*. Much will depend on whether reads and writes are happening to the swap file (in the best of all possible worlds, this should not be happening), and where you relocate it. Do keep in mind that all the ESX hosts need visibility to this share for VMotion to function.

Next, configure the new location for the swap file by selecting each ESX host and clicking the Configuration tab. In the Software pane, select Virtual Machine Swap File location, and then click the Edit button.

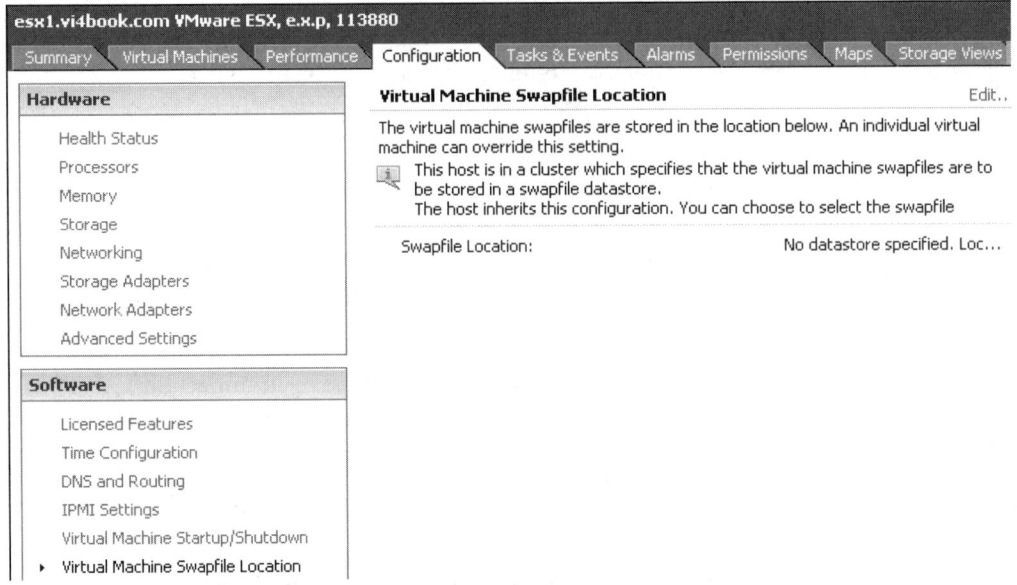

In the Virtual Machine Swapfile Location dialog box, select your new storage location.

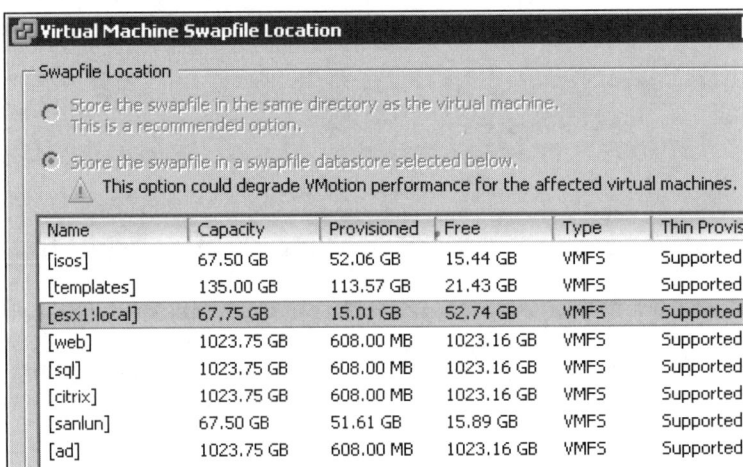

As you power on VMs, their swap file will be relocated. I chose to locate my swap files on local storage, as shown in the following screenshot. As you would expect with local storage, the VMotion process creates a new swap file at the destination ESX host, and removes the original swap file from the source ESX host.

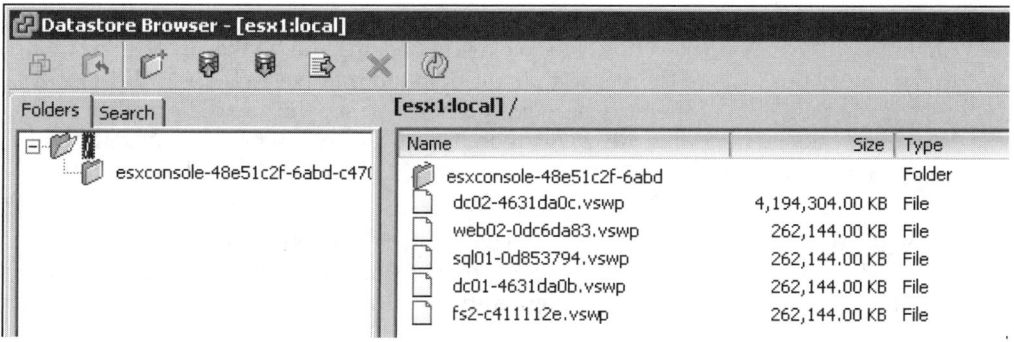

Summary

As you saw in this chapter, once you have VMotion configured, all manner of possibilities become available, such as allowing DRS to decide where your VMs execute and to move VMs around. Once you have a cluster, you will quickly become less attached to your individual ESX hosts and begin to regard them merely as a block of CPU and memory resources. This is not a bad place to be; it means you are gradually coming to the position where virtualization is second nature.

The only downside is that once you have clusters and resource pools, you begin to forget that the buck stops with the physical hardware. So in an effort to reinforce this point, I'm going to ask you some questions. Whether you get them right will be a good indicator of whether you have *really* understood performance management with VMware. This is an approach I use with my students in class. It allows me to confirm that I have been understood, to play with and undermine people's expectations, and to clarify misunderstandings. It's really my last chance to feel reassured that I haven't left my students more confused than they were when we started!

All three of these questions are examples of the admission control concept.

- **Question 1**   You have a DRS cluster constructed of 32 ESX hosts, each with 32GB of RAM. This amounts to a total of 1024GB of memory on the cluster. You then divide these resources into two resource pools called Prod and Test & Dev. You reserve 100GB RAM to the Test & Dev resource pool, and mark it as nonexpandable, and you reserve 800GB of RAM to the Prod resource pool, leaving it marked as expandable. You create a new VM with a reservation of 36GB, placing it in a Test & Dev resource pool. Would it power on?

  Answer   No, although the resource pool has a reservation of 100GB RAM, the ESX hosts can provide only a maximum of 32GB each. As such, the reservation on the VM exceeds the physical limit of the ESX host. This is an example of how the buck fundamentally stops with the limits of your ESX hardware.

- **Question 2**   On a stand-alone ESX host with 8GB of RAM, you create a VM with a limit of 10GB and reservation of 0MB. Would the VM power on?

Answer Yes, although the limit is much greater than the amount of physical memory of the ESX host, in this case, we are not asking the VMkernel to guarantee this memory but instead deliver it in an on-demand manner to the VM. If the VM used more than 8GB of memory, you would begin to see the swap file within the VMkernel take reads and writes. This is an example of memory overcommitment, where we can allocate to a VM or collection of VMs more memory than is physically present.

- **Question 3** You create a VM on a VMFS datastore with 40GB of free space. The virtual disk is fully provisioned using the thick format at 20GB. You give the VM a limit of 32GB and reservation 1GB. Would the VM power on?

Answer No, the size of the virtual disk would leave just 20GB of free space on the volume. The size of the VM swap file would be 31GB (32GB minus 1GB). If we add 20GB to 31GB, the total space required for the VM would be 51GB, which exceeds the free space on the volume. This is an example of a power-on failure created by a lack of free space for the swap file, rather than a lack of free memory or CPU.

CHAPTER 14 | VMware Distributed Power Management

In recent years, there has been much talk about creating a "green datacenter"—a drive to consume less power, intended to have both an economic and environmental impact. Distributed Power Management (DPM) addresses this concern and is integrated into DRS. Its job is to monitor the cluster's usage and move VMs during nonpeak usage to a fewer number of ESX hosts. The unneeded ESX hosts are put into a standby mode, so they consume less power in the server room.

In this chapter, you'll learn how DPM works and how to enable it.

What's New with DPM?

- Full support for DPM (it is no longer experimental)
- Replacement of the APCI/magic packets/WoL support with a much more reliable method integrated with ILO/RAC/DRAC boards

---

DPM Overview

The idea of VMware powering down and up physical servers in production environments will make some people nervous. Like many, I'm of the old school that believes once something is on, it should be left on—for fear it might not come on again! Perhaps we all need to reconsider our priorities. DPM is very reliable, and its effective deployment could save the business we work for a great deal of money.

DPM may come into its own in environments where the "always-on" approach is less significant. In test and development or DR environments, it's extremely wasteful to have servers powered on when they are not needed. Additionally, if you have substantial VDI implementation, you might like the idea of powering on ESX hosts only as and when the user LOAD changes.

According to most independent analysis, servers consume about one-third of the power in the datacenter, and network and storage devices consume similar amounts. So, the power savings that can be delivered by DPM must be seen in this overall context. Nonetheless, studies by VMware indicate that if enabled, DPM can result in 50% power savings, allowing servers to be turned on/off without affecting SLAs. At the launch of vSphere 4, it was claimed that just moving from VI3 to vSphere 4 could be expected to result in a 20% increase in power savings.

DPM maintains a lookup table for the amount of power consumption, and three main conditions are used to calculate the DPM process:

- Guest CPU and memory usage
- ESX host CPU and memory usage
- ESX host power consumption

Like DRS, the algorithm behind DPM is a conservative one. DPM takes into account a load history over a 20-minute period for power-off events. For power-on events, it checks every 5 minutes—after all, you do not want to wait too long for an ESX host to be powered on if more resources are needed.

Using DRS, VMs are grouped into either highly loaded VMs or lightly loaded VMs. If DRS detects that the highly loaded group is using more than 80% of the resources, this will trigger an ESX power-on event. If DRS detects that the lightly loaded group is using less than 45% of the resources, this will trigger power off of an ESX host.

Based on these two constraints, DPM runs a number of "what-if" simulations to determine the best VMs to move, to allow the power off of the best ESX hosts. DPM also interacts with VMware HA, so it does not power off so many ESX hosts that it breaks your rules for the number of ESX hosts you tolerate in a failed state; put another way, whether you have +1, +2, +3, or +4 redundancy.

NOTE *DPM is integrated into DRS so that other rules, such as reservations and affinity rules, are obeyed.*

The DPM feature is enabled on the properties of the DRS cluster. By default, it is switched off. As with DRS, it can be configured in a manual mode, where it offers recommendations that can be ignored or followed, or in an automatic mode, where DPM carries out a standby function automatically. Additionally, you can override the overall DPM settings for specific ESX hosts by selecting Host Options. You configure DPM through the Power Management dialog box on the properties of a DRS cluster.

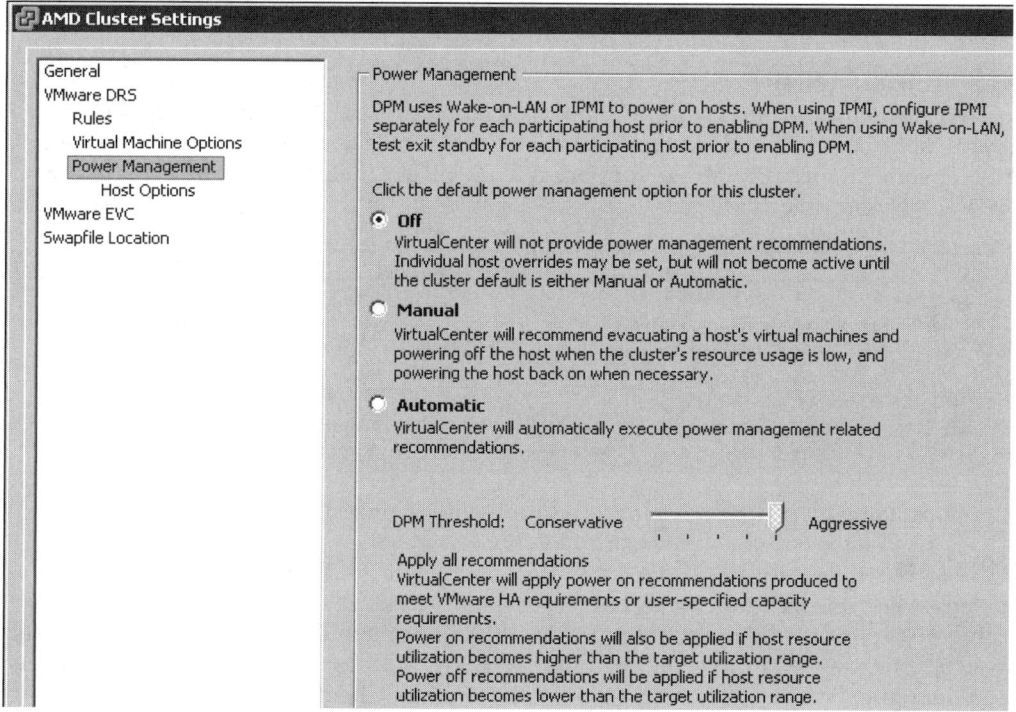

Preparing for DRS

Two methods can be used to enable DPM's soft power-on and power-off functionality: by using the Wake-on-LAN (WoL) feature of most modern NICs or by using the power management support delivered by most ILO/RAC/DRAC cards. You can check for WoL support before enabling DPM.

Also, when you choose to enable DPM, a dialog box appears, recommending that you test the standby option manually on each ESX host to confirm it supports soft power on.

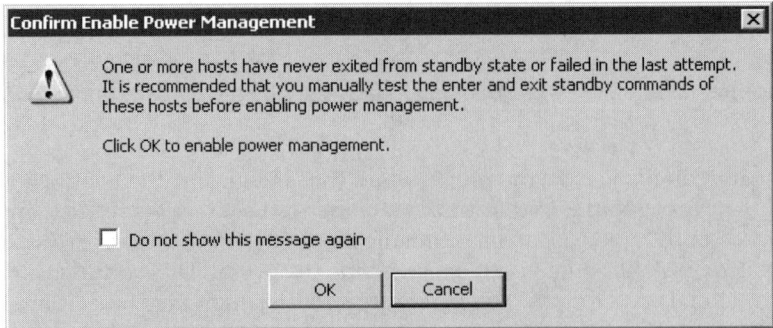

Therefore, you should perform this test before enabling DPM.

Checking WoL Support

You can confirm if your NICs support the WoL method on your ESX hosts using the vSphere Client. Select an ESX host and click the Configuration tab. In the Hardware pane, select Network Adapters. If WoL is supported, you will see that indicated by a Yes in the Wake on LAN Supported column.

Network Adapters

Device	Speed	Configured	Switch	Observed IP ranges	Wake on LAN Supported
NC7782 Gigabit Server Adapter (PCI-X, 10,100,1000-T)					
vmnic1	1000 Full	Negotiate	vSwitch2	194.00.00.00/254.00.00...	Yes
vmnic0	1000 Full	Negotiate	vSwitch0	194.00.00.00/254.00.00...	Yes
82546EB Gigabit Ethernet Controller (Copper)					
vmnic3	1000 Full	Negotiate	vSwitch4	194.00.00.00/254.00.00...	Yes
vmnic2	1000 Full	Negotiate	vSwitch3	194.00.00.00/254.00.00...	Yes

Manually Testing Standby Mode

As noted earlier, it is recommended that you test that each ESX host can enter and exit this standby mode correctly before enabling DPM. With or without DPM enabled, all ESX hosts have an additional power option called Enter Standby Mode available on the Summary tab and on the right-click menu of an ESX host in the vSphere Client.

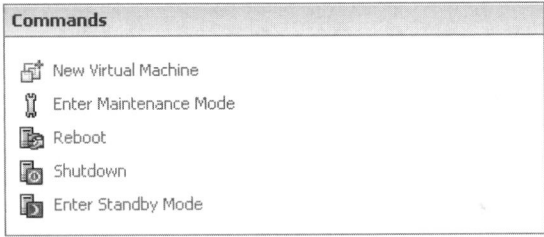

When you select this option, you will see the Confirm Standby dialog box.

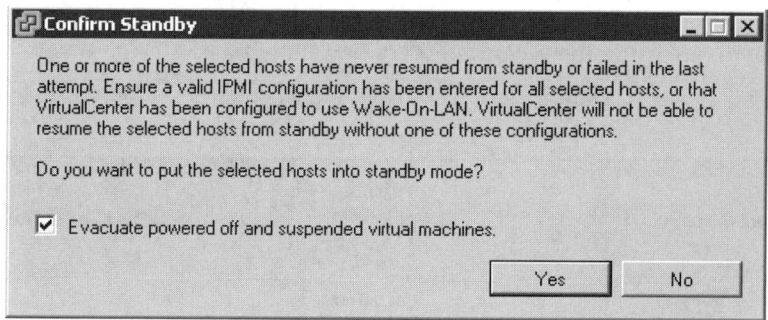

As with maintenance mode, this should trigger either level five priority recommendations or automatic VMotion events, depending on the level of automation you have selected for the DRS cluster. Also as with maintenance mode, standby mode can hang as it waits for the operator to confirm the VMotion of VMs, or when a VM cannot be moved because it does not meet VMotion requirements.

The following example shows the DRS recommendations waiting to be confirmed. Note that the Recent Tasks bar shows "Enter Standby Mode" at 2%, as it waits for the operator to act on the recommendations. If DRS is configured for fully automated mode, the VM would be moved without these prompts.

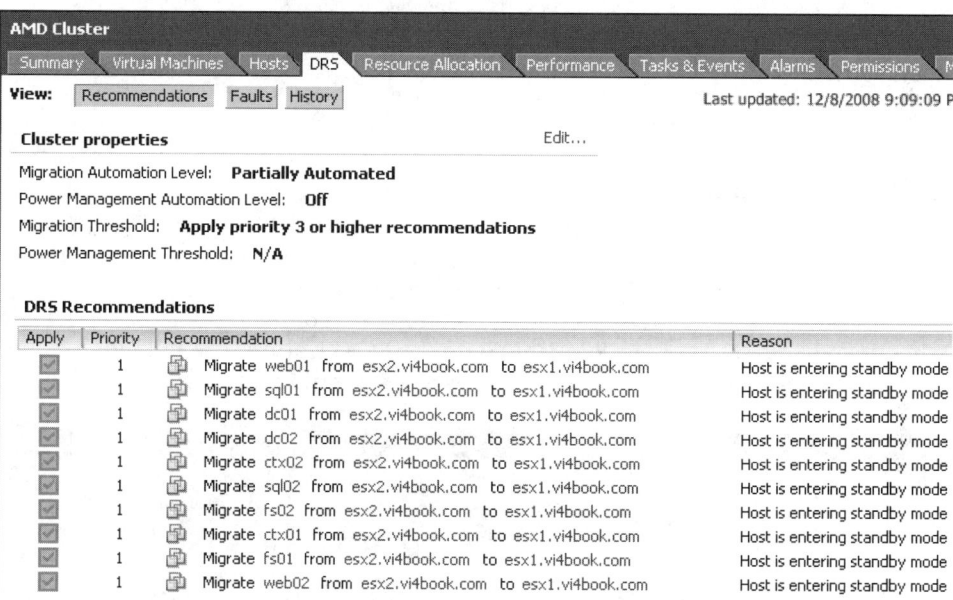

Once standby mode has completed, the ESX host will appear dimmed in vCenter with the label "Standby Mode" in brackets next to its name. This is very similar to status messages of "Not Responding" or "Disconnected" when a network or management agent error separates vCenter from an ESX host.

Additionally, the ESX host will have only one option available to it on its Summary tab, which is to power it back on. The following example shows this new status information and the new Power On button. This standby signal is sent from the vCenter server to the Service Console NIC if you are using the WoL method of handling the ESX host power state. If you using the ILO/RAC/ DRAC method, the signal is sent to the ILO/RAC/ DRAC/ card in the ESX host.

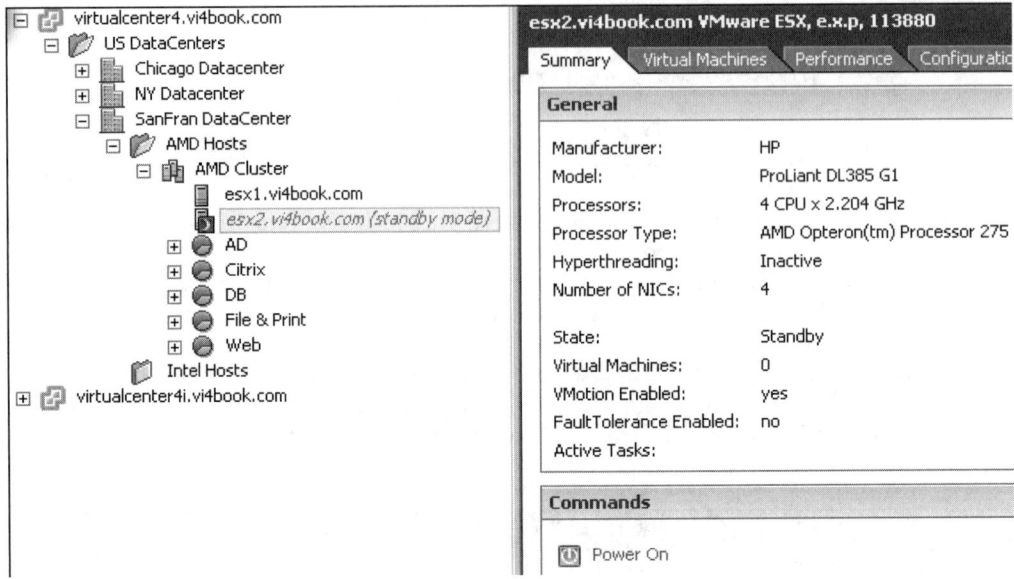

Enabling DPM on a Cluster

Once you are sure that entering and exiting standby mode is reliable, you can enable DPM on the cluster. Your options are to either enable it in manual mode or automatic mode. Using Host Options, you can configure DPM to suit the needs and policies of your organization. For example, you might exclude ESX hosts that don't support the WoL feature or that that you've found to not work reliably with the DPM feature. The following example shows a DPM cluster set to use automatic, with the choices for esx2.vi4book.com displayed.

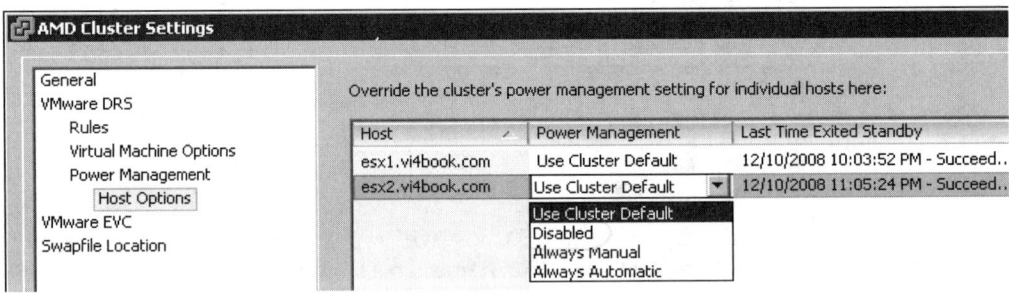

If you decide to use the manual mode, a new set of recommendations will appear when DRS and DPM decide that given the resource demands made by the VMs, it would be power-efficient to put some ESX hosts into standby mode. The following example shows the DRS tab with the recommendations generated under these circumstances.

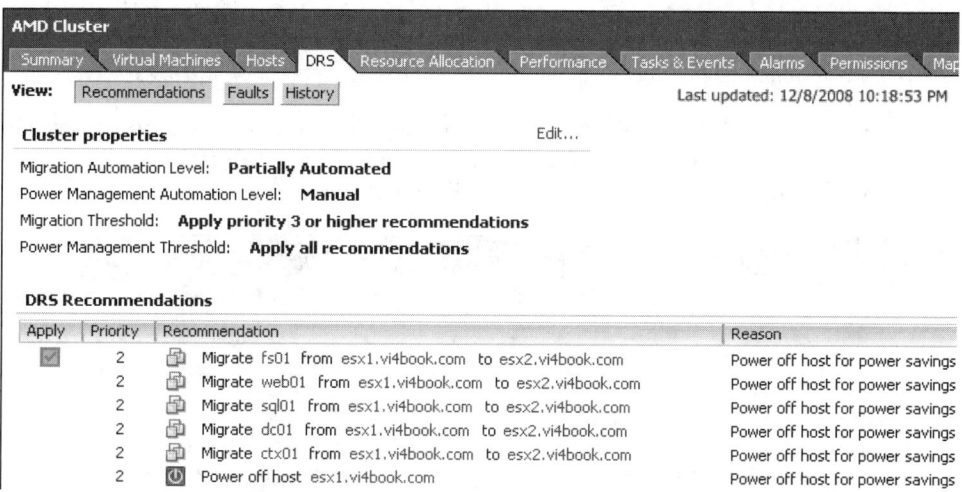

In this example, I am running very few VMs, which are doing very little in terms of workload. DRS and DPM have decided to migrate my VMs from esx1 to esx2, and put esx1 into standby mode to save on power. In this case, I would have only one ESX host running in the DRS cluster. These are the kinds of recommendations you would receive if you had not yet enabled VMware HA. With HA, at least two ESX hosts would be left powered on to maintain a minimum level of availability.

As you might expect, if your VMs subsequently begin to demand more physical hardware resources such as CPU and RAM, then DRS and DPM will together generate recommendations that the ESX host should exit the standby state and be powered on again. The following example was generated by running a CPU-intensive script inside one of the VMs, and by increasing the amount of memory allocated to two of the VMs.

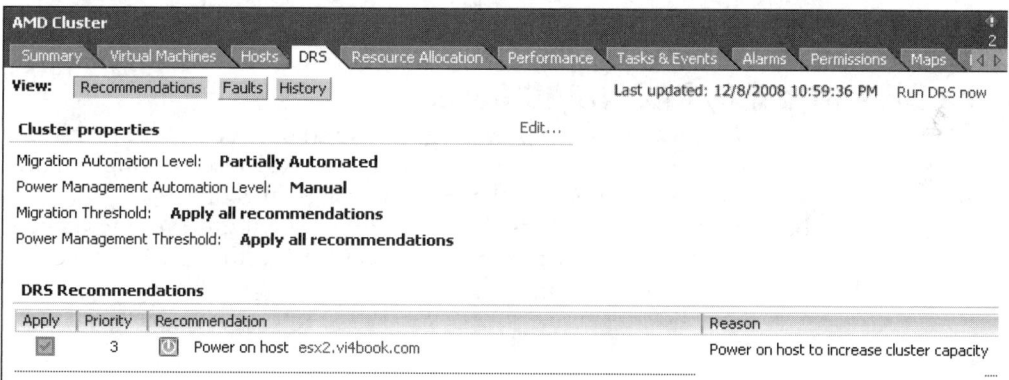

Again, these recommendations do not appear if DRS is in fully automated mode. In that case, ESX hosts are powered off and on as and when the VMs need the resources during off-peak and peak hours.

CAUTION *You'll need to conduct some capacity-planning exercises before implementing DPM in a production environment—unless you wish to explain to your boss why the thousands of dollars' worth of servers you have purchased spend most of their time powered off during the day!*

As shown in Chapter 13, the DRS Actions history log does a much better job of tracking and tracing both VMotion and DPM events than in the previous releases. The following example shows this log with both VMotion and DPM activity.

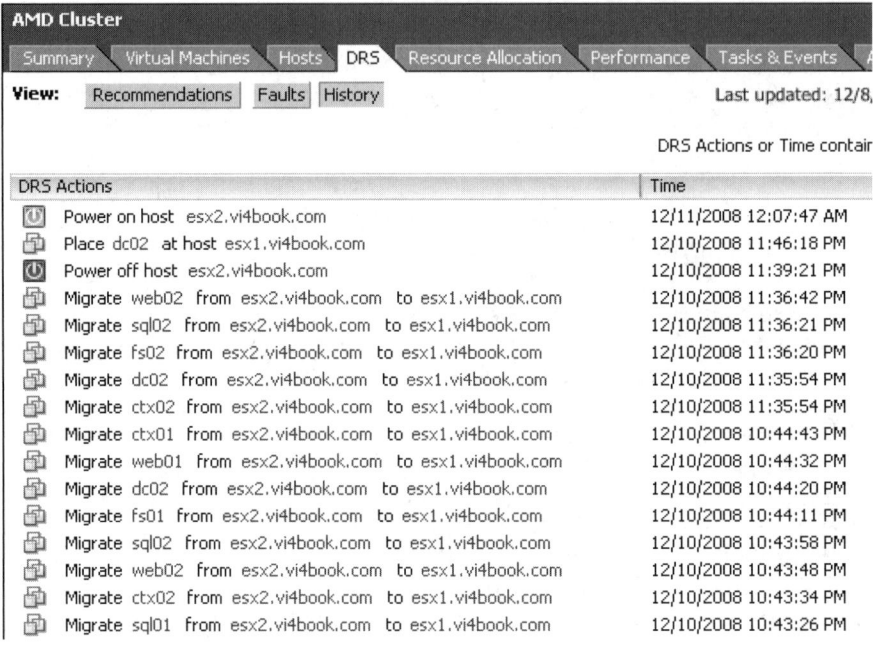

Configuring DPM with ILO/RAC/DRAC Cards

New to DPM is a much more efficient way of powering down and up an ESX host than using the WoL method. You can now configure your ESX host to use the Advanced Configuration and Power Interface (ACPI) features of your motherboard to trigger this process.

Although this process is more reliable, it is slightly harder to configure. You will need a user account with power management rights on each ESX host in the DPM cluster.

Additionally, you will need to know the MAC address of each ILO interface. I will take you through this process, but bear in mind that every ILO/RAC/DRAC board is different. In this example here, I am using ILO version 1, which shipped on many HP ProLiant systems in the current decade.

Preparing for Using ACPI Features for DPM

To find the MAC address of an ILO interface, log in to your ILO/RAC with administrative rights. On the System Status tab, click the Server Status link. Scroll down the window, and under Embedded NIC Assignment, you will see the MAC address of the ILO.

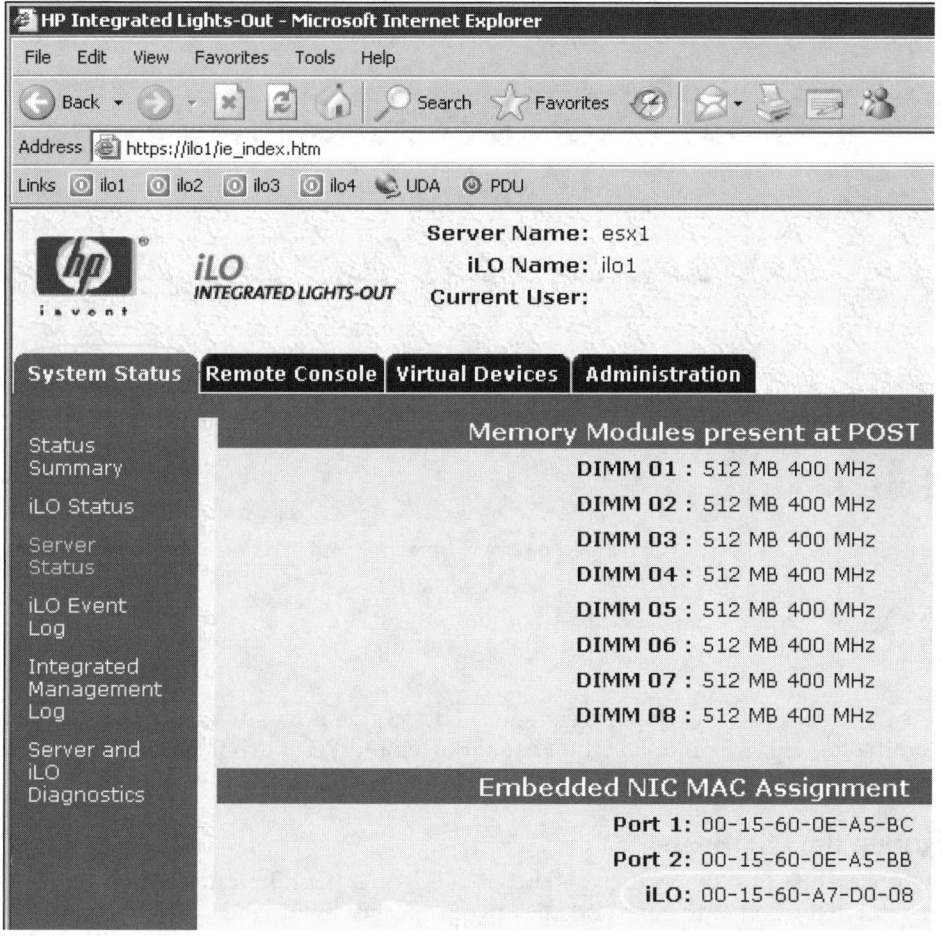

To create a DPM user account, select the Administration tab and click the Add button. Enter the account information, and then click the Save User Information button.

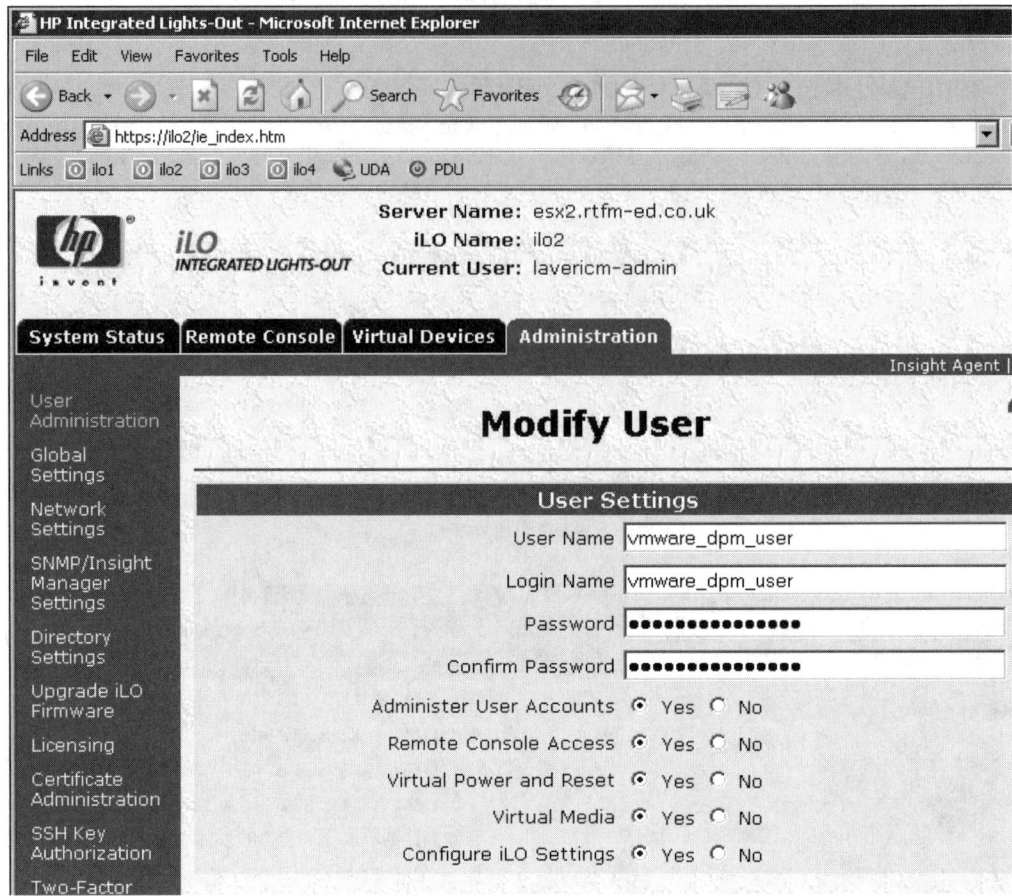

In my experiments with HP ILO version 1, I had to give my vmware_dpm_user full rights. I initially tried assigning just the Virtual Power and Reset privilege, but this generated a timeout error in vCenter.

Configuring the ESX Hosts

To configure an ESX host to use this method of DPM, on its Configuration tab, select Power Management in the Software pane and click the Properties link in the far-right corner.

In this dialog box, you'll see references to the BMC IP and MAC addresses. BMC stands for Baseboard Management Controller, a more industry-neutral term for this functionality.

The BMC is intelligence inside a standard called the Intelligent Platform Management Interface (IPMI) architecture, so you'll also see references to IPMI in various links and dialog boxes in the vSphere Client.

Complete the dialog box, perhaps cutting and pasting the MAC address of the ILO into the BMC MAC Address field. The MAC address must be entered using colons (:), rather than dashes, as are used in some ILO web pages.

Summary

As you are beginning to see, VMotion is the bedrock of many of the powerful datacenter management features, such as DRS, EVC, and DPM. An implementation of the product should put successful and reliable VMotion at the top of its list, because this integration does not stop here. When we look at the VMware Update Manager, the patch and upgrade management tool for vSphere 4, in Chapters 19 and 20, you will see that it also relies on VMotion to successfully patch or upgrade an ESX host.

DPM might be regarded by some as somewhat of a "toy," just as people regarded VMotion as such in the early days of virtualization. As with VMotion, I expect to see DPM become a mainstream feature very shortly. We live in economically constrained times, where the dependable flow of energy now seems doubtful. Whether you classify yourself as an environment skeptic or environmental evangelist, I think we can all agree that reducing or at least steadying our energy consumption can only be good for the organizations we work in and the planet as a whole.

By all means, tag DPM as part of your overall project to lower your carbon footprint. But like any technology, by itself, its effect is likely to be greatly diminished if it is not used as part of an overall strategy to reduce our crippling dependency on cheap energy from dirty sources. Additionally, our industry would have to look more closely at the way we consume and dispose of the materials we use, while at the same time adopting more energy-efficient devices that reduce the draw for power at the source. Remember that every day, 24 hours a day, the spindles in your storage arrays are spinning. So very soon we will see spindles spin down when they are not need, or even the moving of VMs from spindle based storage to solid state storage to improve performance.

CHAPTER 15 | VMware High Availability

This chapter covers VMware High Availability (HA). VMware HA has a very simple goal: when an ESX host crashes, so do the VMs on the failed host. However, within seconds, the other ESX hosts in the same HA cluster detect that the ESX host has failed, and they move the VMs that were once running on the failed ESX host onto the remaining functioning hosts and power them on. If DRS is enabled, it will then rebalance the cluster. DRS will also detect when the failed host is available again and rebalance the cluster.

In this chapter, you'll learn how HA works and how to set it up.

What's New with HA?

- Existing advanced options now available from the GUI
- New advanced options to control memory and CPU alerts
- Three different methods to indicate how to measure load on the cluster

---

HA Overview

VMware HA was not actually an original VMware product. Back in VI3, VMware procured a license for Legato's Automated Availability Manager (AAM) software and reengineered it to work with VMs. Legato is now owned by VMware's parent company, EMC, and has been rebranded as EMC AutoStart. However, the directories in /opt still retain the original Legato folder structure.

VMware's vCenter Agent interfaces with a VMware HA Agent, which acts as an intermediary layer to the AAM software. vCenter is required to configure HA, but it is not required for HA to function. Even if the vCenter server is down and unavailable, VMware HA will continue to function. This makes HA quite different from DRS and DPM, which do require vCenter for them to work.

The architecture of HA is peer-to-peer, with each ESX host in a mesh topology constantly checking each other for their availability. This check is done via the Service Console vSwitch.

When VI3.5 was released, VMware added experimental support for restarting failed VMs. In previous versions, when an ESX host failed, the selection process worked alphabetically through the remaining ESX hosts and powered on a VM on the first server that had sufficient resources to run that VM. This has been slightly refined so that VMware HA will power on your lost VMs on the best ESX host. This is intended to get the VM powered on and back online as quickly as possible, and reduce the amount of associated DRS VMotion events. As explained in Chapter 13, DRS is quite conservative in its checks, so if an ESX host crashes, you should not expect to suddenly get a lot of VMotion events or recommendations.

As with VMotion and DRS, HA also requires shared storage and shared networking. The only thing that HA does not require is CPU compatibility. After all, the VM is powered off when the ESX host fails and powered on a new ESX host when HA detects the failure.

In VI3, HA required DNS forward (name-to-IP address) name resolution. Back then, the VMware documentation stated that reverse DNS name resolution was also a requirement. This was true, but only if you added ESX hosts into vCenter by their IP addresses. If you added your ESX hosts to vCenter by FQDN, then all you needed to do was forward lookups. This was because the Legato AAM Agent has its own internal name resolution file called

FT_HOSTS, and if name resolution didn't happen or contained errors, the HA Agent would refuse to start. This became such a problem for VMware Support that the HA Agent has been reconfigured to remove this name resolution requirement.

That said, perhaps the best practice is to cover your bases and ensure that forward and reverse lookups are configured in DNS before configuring HA. After all, ESX and vCenter, as well as other products such as Microsoft Exchange, either recommend or require name resolution for other features. As with the license server, sort out your DNS issues before you even begin, and the HA setup and configuration should be relatively painless.

HA and Resource Management

HA introduces some careful reconsideration of resource management. Suppose you have seven ESX hosts in a cluster running seventy VMs and then you lose an ESX host. Will the remaining six ESX hosts be able to run the same number of VMs? One practical response is to design a system that has +1 redundancy, so instead of seven servers, you have eight. If one fails, you will still be able to achieve the same performance with fewer nodes. Additionally, if you need to take an ESX host down for a maintenance window, you will still have enough resources to accommodate this planned downtime.

Of course, the buck has to stop somewhere. Could you tolerate two, three, or four ESX host failures and still run the same number of VMs? The HA software allows you to configure such tolerances of ESX host failure, but the question is both an operational and design issue. This consideration will factor into how heavily you load your ESX hosts. You want to avoid ever loading an ESX host to 100%, because that could result in performance problems and insufficient resources for unexpected CPU or memory activity. For example, in a two-node cluster, you might not want to load an ESX host beyond 35%. If one of the ESX hosts failed, the total load would amount to a 70% load. So, the more ESX hosts you have in a HA cluster, the more they can be loaded, as the loss of one ESX host become less significant. Say you have a ten-node cluster, and you lose one ESX host—you have only lost 10%, or one-tenth of your resources, rather than the 50% of a two-node cluster.

Another way to handle resources is, on the remaining ESX hosts, power on only the necessary number of VMs needed to give acceptable usage. Perhaps you have 20 domain controller VMs running across 10 ESX hosts in a HA cluster. You know from testing and experience that for acceptable usage, you need only 15 VMs up and running at any one time. VMware HA allows you to disable VMs from HA altogether and also set priorities for which VMs are started first.

HA and the Split-Brain Phenomena

As mentioned earlier, the mesh topology that HA creates is driven by the Service Console vSwitch. If an ESX host in an HA cluster experiences a NIC failure or cable break, this can trigger the *split-brain* (a term those experienced in the world of conventional Windows or Linux clustering may recognize) scenario. This orphaned ESX host is sometimes referred to in VMware documentation as the *isolated host*. This isolated ESX host mistakenly believes that the other ESX hosts in the cluster have crashed, while all the other ESX hosts believe that the bad ESX host has crashed. In fact, the VMs are running perfectly fine on all the ESX hosts. This is like someone believing he is Napoleon and everyone else is crazy—the host believes it is fine and that the others are the problem.

ESX 4 and Split-Brain/Isolation

What is VMware HA's default behavior when split-brain occurs? The default is that the isolated host (the ESX host with the failed Service Console network) powers off all its VMs. This causes the VM's files to be unlocked in the shared storage, so the other ESX hosts can assume control and power on the VMs that were previously running on the isolated host. In other words, the default is to begin HA failover to the remaining ESX hosts. VMware HA does have an override option for this default, allowing the administrator to configure a VM to stay powered on when the split-brain event happens.

You might wonder how the split-brain condition gets triggered. If the ESX host is configured for a default gateway (router), it uses this IP address to determine if it is isolated. If an ESX host is isolated, it will use the lack of response from the default gateway to trigger the split-brain isolation response. If you don't have a default gateway (which would be very unusual!), then you can use the Advanced Settings button on an HA cluster to set an alternative IP device as the ping source.

Clearly, one easy way to protect your ESX environment from this very unpleasant split-brain phenomena (apart from regular trips to an expensive psychotherapist) is to make sure that the ESX hosts have redundancy on the Service Console networking. One method would be to use a second NIC behind vSwitch0 and patch it to a different physical switch. This would protect HA from NIC, cable, and switch failures. Alternatively, you could add a second Service Console port group to a switch used for another aspect of your virtual infrastructure such as VMotion.

Without redundancy of the Service Console or management network, you will definitely receive warning notifications on the HA cluster. In the beta and release candidates, the HA Agent would not even start without having this redundancy in place.

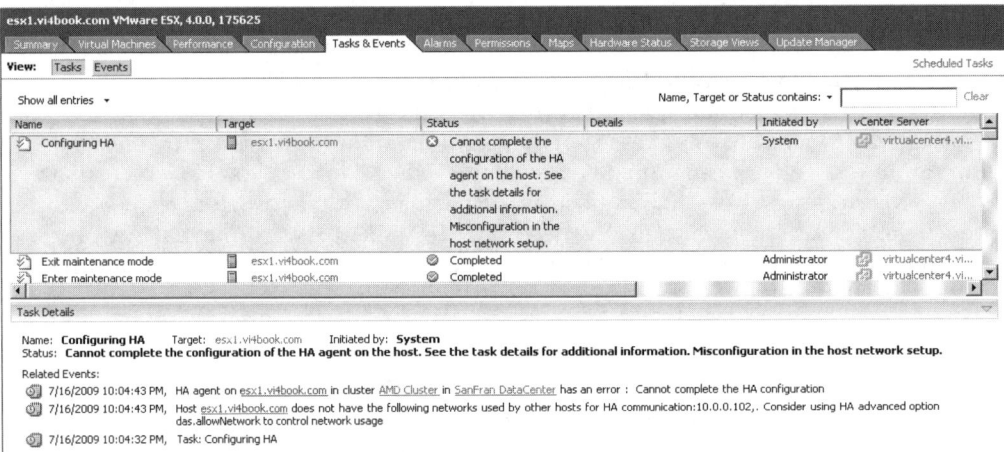

ESXi 4 and Split-Brain/Isolation

With ESXi 4, you must have at least one management port enabled for HA for the HA Agent to start and not produce an error message. Although it is somewhat annoying that VMware doesn't enable HA communication on your management networks, consider that you can have many VMkernel ports in ESXi 4 for management, VMotion, and IP-based storage, and it would be difficult for the product to decide which VMkernel interface should be enabled for HA.

You can enable HA on your management ports with ESXi 4 through the management network properties, as follows:

1. In the vSphere Client. select the ESXi host.
2. Click the Configuration tab, and select Networking in the Hardware pane.
3. Select Properties of vSwitch0. This is where you will find the first default VMkernel management network port group.
4. In the vSwitch0 dialog box, select the Management Network port group and click Edit.
5. Place a check in the Enabled box next to HA communication.

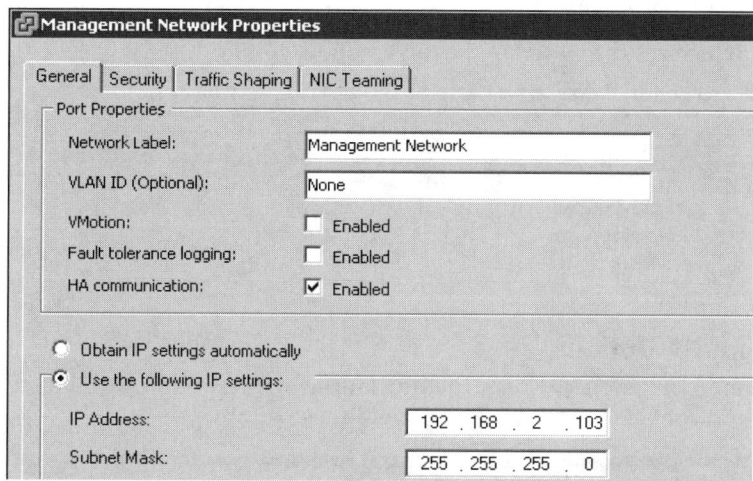

I'm not enabling VMotion in this example, as I have dedicated a gigabit adapter on vSwitch3. However, I do enable HA communication on the VMotion port group to allow for network management redundancy to prevent split-brain or ESX host isolation in ESXi 4.

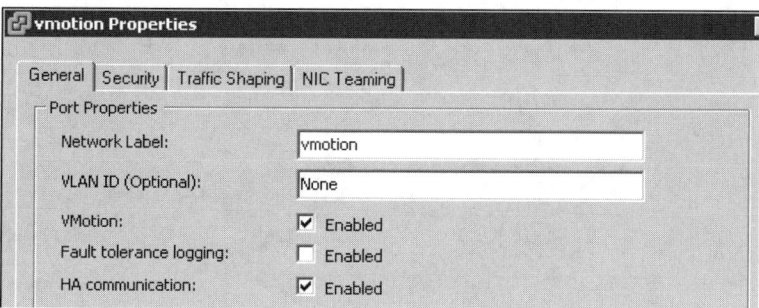

Enabling and Configuring VMware HA

I'll assume you already have a DRS cluster set up and, therefore, all that you need to do is enable HA on an existing cluster. If this is not the case, you will need to first create a cluster and drag-and-drop your ESX hosts into it, as described in Chapter 13.

Enabling HA on ESX Host Clusters

When you enable HA on an ESX host cluster, VMware will trigger the AAM software on each host, one at a time. Clearly, you cannot have an HA cluster with just one ESX host. Until another ESX host is configured, the cluster will have alerts and warnings on it. These will not disappear until you have at least two ESX hosts in the cluster enabled for HA.

Follow these steps to enable HA on a cluster:

1. Right-click the cluster and choose Edit Settings.

2. Click Turn on VMware HA. This will add a set of HA options in the left side of the dialog box.

3. Under General, select VMware HA. You will some settings associated with the cluster, which are discussed in the next section.

4. Click OK to enable VMware HA with the default settings.

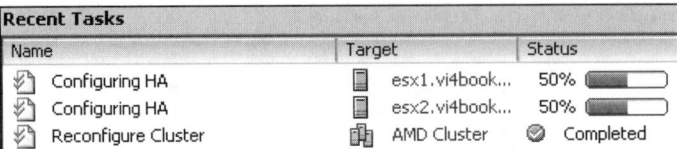

Setting VMware HA Options

The main VMware HA dialog box offers settings for host monitoring, admission control, and admission control policy. Let's look at each of these settings.

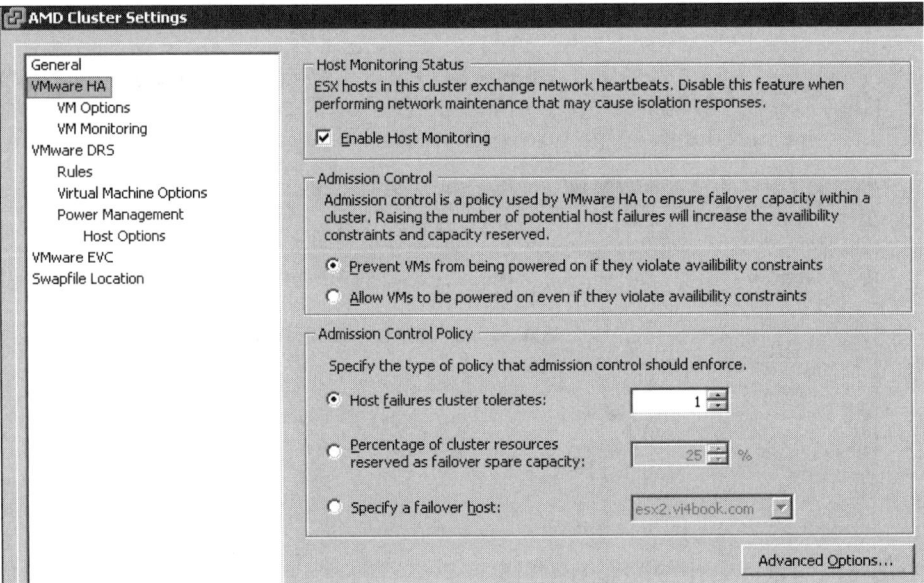

Enabling Host Monitoring

As the dialog box states, removing the check in the Enable Host Monitoring box allows you to switch off the network-based method of detecting ESX host failures if you intend to perform a major network function, such as updating the firmware on a router or repatching network cables. As the ESX host uses its default gateway value to check if it is isolated, this would include shutting down your default gateway for maintenance purposes.

This option differs from the Turn on VMware HA option in that the feature is not disabled—it's just temporarily suppressed to cover you maintenance of the network. If you removed the check next to Turn on VMware HA, the HA Agent would be stopped and disabled on each ESX host. With the Enable Host Monitoring option, the HA Agent process is still running, but it doesn't check for ESX host isolation response.

Configuring Admission Control Policy

You can control the number of ESX host failures you tolerate until the HA clustering stops powering on VMs on the remaining hosts. In the VMware HA dialog box, you can specify one of the following types of admission control policies:

- The number of ESX hosts you think could lose and still deliver acceptable performance
- A percentage of free resources
- A specific host

The third option is for a traditional active/passive clustering setup, where the passive node doesn't take a load until the active host fails. In contrast, the first two options allow for an active/active cluster, where all nodes take a VM load.

The controls for the number of hosts that can fail are not new to VMware HA. They have been around for some time since VI3 was released in the summer of 2006. Specifying a specific host for failover is also not a new feature, but previously was not available in the GUI of the HA cluster. In VI3, it was an option that you could specify as an advanced option. What is new in the vSphere 4 Client release is the ability to control this toleration of failure by the percentage of resources available in the cluster.

Maximum Host Failures   You can set up to a maximum of four host failures that can be tolerated. Remember that VMware recommends no more than 32 ESX hosts per HA cluster, so in reality, this means you could tolerate one-eighth of the ESX hosts failing. If a fifth ESX host failed, HA would not power up the lost VMs on the remaining 28 nodes in the cluster.

You might wonder why the maximum of four is used here. This limit stems from HA's roots in Legato's AAM, which is based on primary and backup AAM servers. The maximum number of primaries is five, and if one fails, secondaries do not automatically take over the role. The only time a primary relinquishes its role is if it is put into maintenance mode or removed from the cluster. At this point, an election process promotes a backup to be a primary. If all five primaries were lost simultaneously (although this is an extremely unlikely event—I can see it happening only if you had a blade-enclosure failure), then the AAM software would be broken. Personally, I would love to see this +4 redundancy barrier removed from VMware HA. The software restriction prevents us from tolerating a greater number of failures than perhaps is physically possible. If you wish to see which ESX hosts are currently holding the primary role you can use this command at the ESX Service Console:

cat /var/log/vmware/aam/aam_config_util_listnodes.log

Due to this architectural weakness in HA, many people recommend adding a maximum of only eight ESX hosts to a cluster, and if the hardware is available, four of the ESX hosts would be in one rack or enclosure and the other four would be taken from a different rack or enclosure. This "striping" across enclosures would protect you from a critical failure, and always guarantee there was at least one primary available at all times.

Of course, this assumes you don't have the failure of two racks or enclosures at the same time. It's at this point I think we veer off into "paranoid island," a special IT place where we consider all possibilities no matter how improbable. If we take this kind of thinking to its extreme, it will lead us into the arena of disaster recovery and business continuity planning. Remember that VMotion, DRS, HA, and FT were never intended to be used as disaster recovery/business continuity tools—they are *not* designed to cope with a complete site failure. If you're looking for VMware technology designed to do this, consider using the VMware Site Recovery Manager product.

As noted earlier, the more ESX hosts you have, the more you can load them and still tolerate an ESX host failure. Remember though, at the end of the day, a VM executes on a given ESX host. If that VM has a memory reservation, the memory must be found in physical memory. So although the DRS cluster might have 1GB of free memory left in the cluster and four ESX hosts, this 1GB of memory is actually not completely available. The spare capacity in a cluster is a logical representation of capacity, not a physical representation of where that memory actually resides.

Admission Control Choices   Above the "Host failures cluster tolerates" options are options associated with admission control. These are the rather confusingly labeled "Prevent VMs from being powered on even if they violate availability constraints" and "Allow VMs to be powered on even if they violate availability constraints." These are best explained with a scenario. If you had two ESX hosts with the "Host failures cluster tolerates" set to 1 and one of the ESX hosts failed, the default is set in such a way that you wouldn't be able to power on any new VMs. If the second option were enabled, then you would.

The default is preventing VMs from being powered on, since there is little point in powering on new VMs if you had host failures, as there would be fewer resources. If you had a ten-node HA cluster and you changed the "Host failures cluster tolerates" setting to 3, it would take three ESX host failures to occur before you could not power on a VM.

You can override the default behavior to allow VMs to be powered on. With this option, you could still power on VMs, even if three ESX hosts crashed. Sometimes in life what matters is not that a service performs well, but that it is available at all—for example, slow email servers might be better than no email servers.

However, without the default control in place, very undesirable situations could develop. For example, the last thing you would want is for VMware to tolerate the failure of 31 ESX hosts in a cluster, resulting in all the VMs running on a single ESX host! The chances are it would just fail because it was completely overloaded.

Percentage of Cluster Resources If you select the "Percentage of cluster resources reserved as failover spare capacity" option, the default is 25%. Once the resources of the cluster fall below 25%, then the HA restart process stops, with the assumption that there are insufficient resources left on the cluster to restart VMs.

As with the number of host failures option, you can use the "Allow VMs to be powered on even if they violate availability constraints" option to override this behavior. Alternatively, you can simply reduce the percentage value until your constraints are not being violated. There is clearly a danger in doing this, as it could result in accepting more failures than your memory and CPU resources can withstand. The following example shows how you can view your current cluster load and spare capacity on the Summary page of an HA cluster.

VMware HA	
Admission Control:	**Enabled**
Current CPU Failover Capacity:	**76 %**
Current Memory Failover Capacity:	**30 %**
Configured Failover Capacity:	**25 %**

Specific Failover Host It is possible to designate a preferred ESX host to failover to in the event of a failure. You can keep one ESX host in reserve just for HA events, in a kind of classic active/standby configuration. To achieve this, you would need to make sure DRS was enabled for manual automation. This would allow you to place all your VMs on the active ESX hosts, with no VMs on the passive ESX host.

I do not recommend this configuration, as I consider it a waste of good hardware. Also, it is much more efficient to load all the ESX hosts to the correct level. You can have your cake and eat it, too. In other words, you can have active/active VMware clusters, while at the same time making sure you don't overload any of ESX hosts with so many VMs that HA cannot find any more resources for failover. It just requires some up-front thinking and planning.

Configuring Advanced HA Settings

By clicking the Advanced Options button in the VMware HA dialog box, you can input additional parameters. These take the format of a text string together with a value.

Table 15-1 lists the settings available. (Taken from VMware's online help system. The URL for this page is quite lengthy so I created a blog post, available at http://www.rtfm-ed.co .uk/?p=490, to point to it back in the days of VI3.)

At the time of writing, some of these settings, such as das.defaultfailoverhost, are still valid, but values may be added and deprecated as the product evolves, so you should check VMware's online help for updates.

A useful parameter on this list is das.failuredetectiontime, which is the time it takes before an ESX host assumes it is isolated from the cluster. The default is 15 seconds, and this can be increased if you wish to protect your cluster from very temporary network outages.

Attribute	Description
`das.isolationaddress`	Sets the address to ping to determine if a host is isolated from the network. If this option is not specified, the default gateway of the console network is used. This default gateway must be some reliable address that is available, so that the host can determine if it is isolated from the network. Multiple isolation addresses (up to 10) can be specified for the cluster: `das.isolationaddressX, where X = 1-10.`
`das.usedefaultisolationaddress`	By default, HA uses the default gateway of the console network as an isolation address. This attribute specifies whether that should be used (`true|false`).
`das.defaultfailoverhost`	If this is set, HA tries to failover hosts to the host specified by this option. This attribute is useful to utilize one host as a spare failover host, but is not recommended, because HA tries to utilize all available spare capacity among all hosts in the cluster. If the specified host does not have enough spare capacity, HA tries to failover the VM to any other host in the cluster that has enough capacity.
`das.failuredetectiontime`	Changes the default failure detection time (with a default of 15,000 milliseconds). This is the time period during which a host has not received any heartbeats from another host before declaring the other host dead.
`das.failuredetectioninverval`	Changes the heartbeat interval among HA hosts. By default, this occurs every second.
`das.vmMemoryMinMB`	Specifies the minimum amount of memory (in megabytes) sufficient for any VM in the cluster to be usable. This value is used only if the memory reservation is not specified for the VM and is used for HA admission control and calculating the current failover level. If no value is specified, the default is 256MB.
`das.vmCpuMinMHz`	Specifies the minimum amount of CPU (in megahertz) sufficient for any VM in the cluster to be usable. This value is used only if the CPU reservation is not specified for the VM and is used for HA admission control and calculating the current failover level. If no value is specified, the default is 256 MHz.
`das.allowVmotionNetworks`	Allows a NIC that is used for VMotion networks to be considered for HA usage. This permits a host to have only one NIC configured for management and VMotion combined. By default, any VMotion network is ignored.

TABLE 15-1 Advanced HA Settings

Attribute	Description
`das.allowNetwork[...]`	Enables the use of port group names to control the networks used for HA. You can set the value to be `Service Console 2` or `Management Network` to use only the networks associated with those port group names in the networking configuration.
`das.isolationShutdownTimeout`	Sets the period of time the system waits for a VM to shut down.
`das.maxvmrestartcount`	Controls the amount retry attempts an ESX host will take to restart a VM before it gives up. This is used when use the "Leave Power On" option in the isolation settings
`das.slotMemInMB`	Defines the maximum bound on the memory slot size.
`das.slotCpuInMHz`	Defines the maximum bound on the CPU slot size.

TABLE 15-1   Advanced HA Settings *(continued)*

In the following example, I increased the `das.failuredetectiontime` option to be 1 minute (60,000 milliseconds).

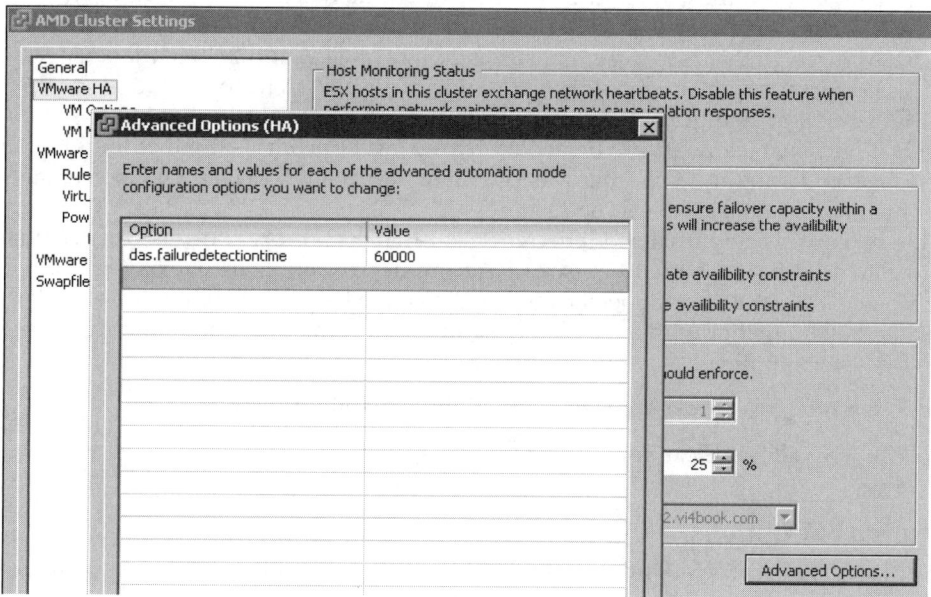

NOTE *Many of the advanced HA parameters begin with* das. *DAS was the development name of VMware HA back in the days of VI3, and it stood for Distributed Availability Service. This development name was dropped by VMware at the time of the General Availability (GA) of VI3 in 2006, as it was felt the name DAS was too widely in use elsewhere in IT. However, the name persisted in license files (back when VI3 used a Macrovision FlexNet license server) and in these advanced parameters.*

These last two values—das.slotMemInMB and das.slotCpuInMHz—are very important values, especially if using the "count the number of host available" method of controlling HA. Admission control uses the number of free "slots" to calculate the point at which HA has no more resources free to offer availability to VMs. The slot is representation of memory and CPU. Literally, the more "slots" you have free, the chances HA has of starting up a VM if an ESX host fails. VMware HA uses an algorithm to generate this slot value and it can be seen in the "Advanced RunTime Info" dialog box. Occasionally, this algorithm miscalculates the slot size, which can then result to being able to run far less VMs on a cluster than originally expected, especially if you use CPU or Memory reservations on a VM. By default, HA uses the *highest* CPU and the *highest* memory reservation. If one VM uses a CPU reservation of 2 GHz and memory reservation 512MB, and another VM uses a CPU reservation 1 GHz and memory reservation of 2GB—then HA will calculate a slot size of 2 GHz of CPU and 2GB of memory. In other words, it calculates a very conservative slot size. Further complexity is added if you understand that slots represents allocations of free CPU and memory—but these might be unevenly distributed across ESX hosts in a cluster. So on one ESX host there maybe 1GB of memory free, but another two ESX host there might only be 512MB free. In this case if the slot size is 2 GHz of CPU and 2GB of memory—there may be no host in the cluster capable of providing a slot for a VM to start in. It for this reason that new "slot" parameters were added to the Advanced Settings in HA in vSphere4. Personally, I find my customers are turned off by the level of complexity that thinking about slots imposes on them—and I see many are going to be attracted to using the percentage value as method of indicated reserved resources for HA.

As the book was being finalized it became clear that even more controls where being added to HA by VMware. I would personally recommend keeping an eye on Duncan Epping's blog "Yellow-Bricks." Specifically, his Web page lists more advanced settings that have been added, together with a detailed description of some of the anomalies generated by the older "slot" approach for counting free capacity.

http://www.yellow-bricks.com/vmware-high-availability-deepdiv/

http://www.yellow-bricks.com/ha-advanced-options/

Configuring VM Options

Under VMware HA, the VM Options choice allows you to set different startup priorities for VMs and also configure the isolation response should an ESX host suffer from the split-brain phenomena.

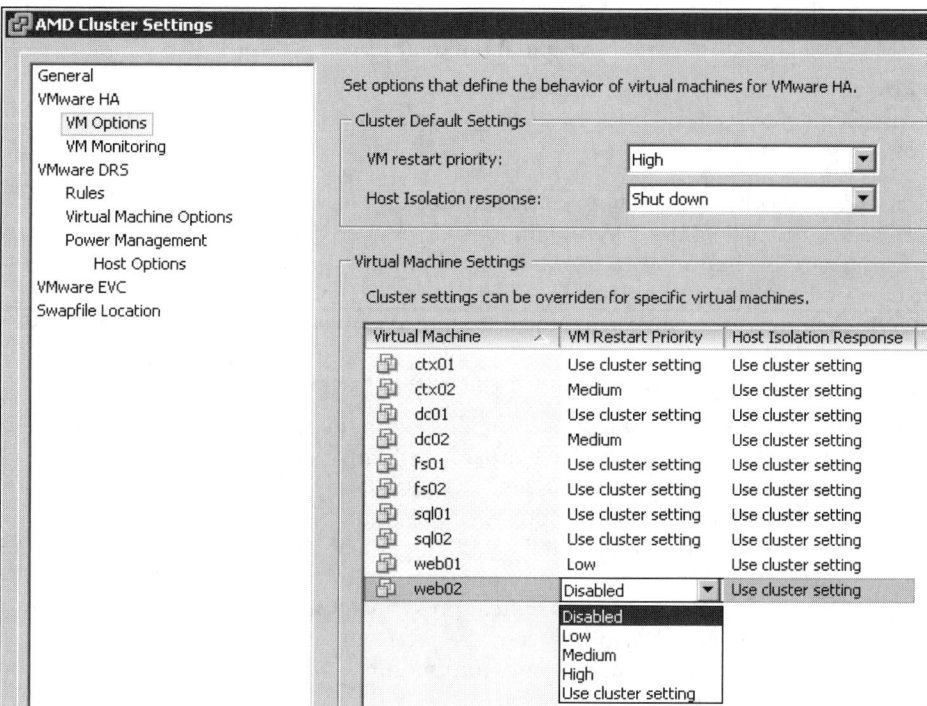

For the "VM restart priority" setting, the following choices are available:

- **Disabled**   This option can be used to exclude VMs from the HA restart process. It can be useful for testing and for noncritical VMs.

- **High**   VMs in this category are started before those set as Medium priority.

- **Medium**   VMs in this category are started before those set as Low priority.

- **Low**   VMs in this category are started last.

- **Use Cluster Setting**   This provides a way to set the default. So if 80% of VMs need to be started with high priority, you would use High, and then set your exceptions. Alternatively, if 60% of your VMs needed to be started with low priority, you would set Low, and specify your exceptions

The Host Isolation response setting allows you to control default behavior if an ESX host becomes isolated. In an ideal world, isolation should not happen because you have taken the appropriate steps to give the management network redundancy. However, if ESX host isolation, or split-brain, does happen, you have three choices to control it:

- **Shut down**   This option, which is new to vSphere 4, allows for a graceful shutdown of the guest OS if isolation is triggered. This is better than the power off option, which leaves the VM in a crash-consistent state.

- **Leave power on**   This option allows you to hedge your bets. You could mark some VMs to be shut down and others to have their power left on.

- **Power off**   This carries out a hard power-off of a VM, leaving it in a crash-consistent state. Guest shutdowns are not guaranteed to be successful, but power offs of VMs are.

These settings work because they control the locking on the files of a VM. So if "Leave power on" is set, the files of the VM remain locked because they are actively in use by the isolated ESX host. This is similar to trying to manipulate a file that is open in Microsoft Word or Excel. In contrast, if you choose "Shut down" or "Power off," the file-level lock is released, which allows other ESX hosts to access the VM files to trigger the HA process.

Configuring VM Monitoring

The VM Monitoring option was introduced in VI3.5 as an experimental feature. This allows for a restart of the VM should it fail. The feature is not only useful for VM failures, but also ESX host failures, because it ensures that even in a two-node HA cluster, if *both* hosts fail, when you restart them, the VMs will be powered on again.

The VM Monitoring feature is a little limited, given that it monitors only the VMware Tools service, and its response if this service fails is a restart of the entire VM. This limitation is actually deliberate. Monitoring your application services and taking remedial action if they fail are areas well covered by other technologies from other vendors, including Microsoft. Remember that VMware manages and monitors the virtualization layer of the VM, not the application layer of the VM.

If you don't like this VM Monitoring feature, it is possible to turn it off. (Toward the end of VI3.5, there were some cases where VM Monitoring was oversensitive and restarted VMs when they hadn't failed.) It is also possible to enable VM Monitoring for only specific VMs rather than enabling it for all VMs.

The restart of the VM is triggered by the ESX host not receiving a heartbeat signal from the VMware Tools service inside the VM. This can be configured by two variables—the duration of the lost heartbeat and the number of lost heartbeats in hours. This is intended to prevent false positives, resulting in the system unnecessarily restarting the VM.

You can set VM Monitoring sensitivity to Low, Medium, or High. Low is least sensitive to changes in the heartbeat, and High is the most sensitive. In other words, Low is less likely to restart the VM than High. You can also set a custom setting for the entire cluster, as well as set a per-VM sensitivity.

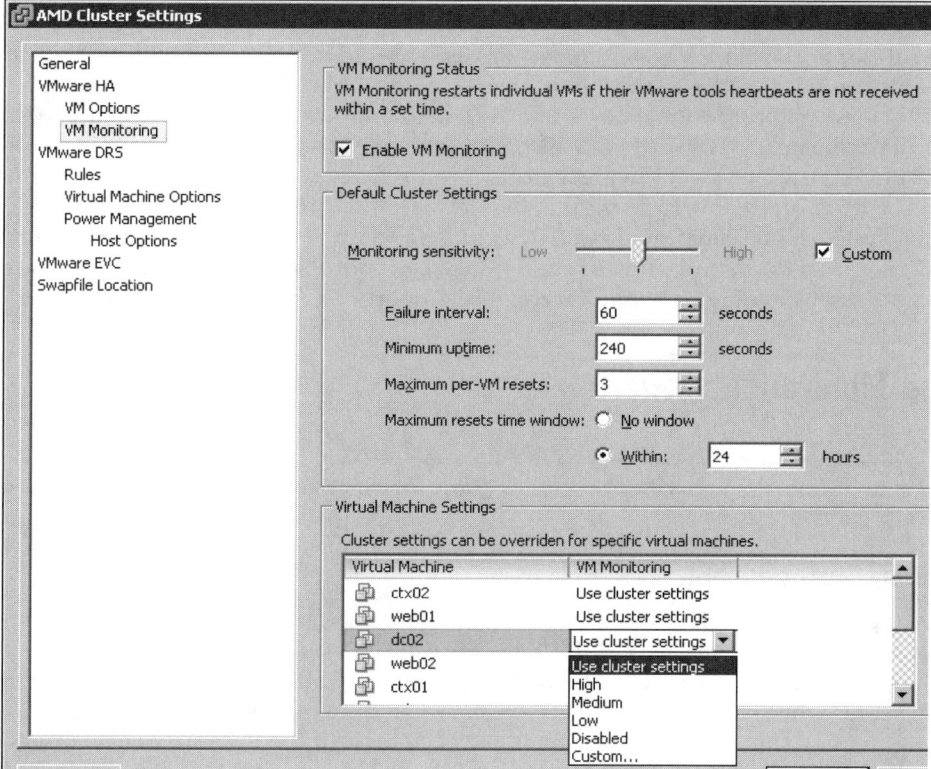

Low is so conservative that the chance of being triggered is so small you have to wonder if it's actually worth engaging. On the other hand, High is so aggressive that you might be anxious that it will mistakenly restart VMs unnecessarily. I recommend a compromise of the Medium setting.

The following is a summary of the default VM Monitoring settings:

- **High**   Restart VM if heartbeat has not been heard in 30 seconds, but ignore the first three of these events in one hour.

- **Medium**   Restart VM if heartbeat has not been heard in 60 seconds, but ignore the first three of these events in 24 hours.

- **Low**   Restart VM if heartbeat has not been heard in 120 seconds, but ignore the first three of these events in 7 days.

- **Custom**   Restart the VM if its heartbeat has not been heard in 60 seconds, with three of these events in a 24-hour period. The VM must be up and running 240 seconds before these settings apply. This is to ensure that VM Monitoring doesn't unnecessarily restart a VM simply because it is in the boot process and VMware Tools has not loaded yet.

Configuring VMware HA and VM Clustering

To gain full support from VMware, the virtual disks and RDM files used with VM clusters (using software such as MSCS) must be on local storage. This effectively excludes them from being used with VMotion, DRS, and HA. The software is so compatible that you do not need to dedicate hardware to your VM clusters. You can still run them; they just won't benefit from these advanced VMware features.

If you wish to learn how to configure VMs for use with MSCS and other guest OS's clustering systems, you can download a free guide from my Web site (http://www.rtfm-ed.co.uk/docs/vmdocs/virtualmscs.pdf). I don't see vendor-specific clustering software as core VMware technology, although using it is supported

Testing and Monitoring VMware HA

There are a couple of ways to test HA, but by far the most convincing is to remove the power from one of the ESX hosts. If you feel uncomfortable with a hard test, another method is to disable your vswif or Service Console interfaces until you find the ESX host becomes isolated.

Testing HA with ESX Classic

You might perform a test that disables Service Console interfaces not only to see if you were vulnerable to split-brain, but also to check if VMware HA was functioning correctly.

If I'm performing this kind of test, I like to do it from the ILO/RAC/DRAC card of the physical server while running an `esxtop` session. This allows me to monitor the status of the failed ESX host. So if I disable vswif0, I can check to see if the VMs survive an isolation event, and then if I disable vswif1, I can see if VMware HA is triggered. I also like to watch my other ESX hosts to see if the VMs arrive on them. Often, I will use `esxtop` in a PuTTY session, rather than using the vSphere Client. This is because it does appear to take time for the vSphere Client to refresh its views, which can lead to the impression that VMware HA hasn't worked, when actually it has.

If you wish to simulate the isolation response where an ESX host appears to have failed because of lost Service Console connectivity, you can use the following commands:

```
esxcfg-vswif -s vswif0
esxcfg-vswif -s vswif1
```

This disables the Service Console vswif interface. The command `esxcfg-vswif -e vswif0` will reenable it again.

CAUTION *The switch* −D *(in uppercase) disables all vswif/Service Console interfaces!*

VMware HA and VMotion

HA introduces a new VMotion error message. If the HA Agent fails to start, and then you subsequently try to carry out a VMotion to the ESX host in question, you will receive this error message.

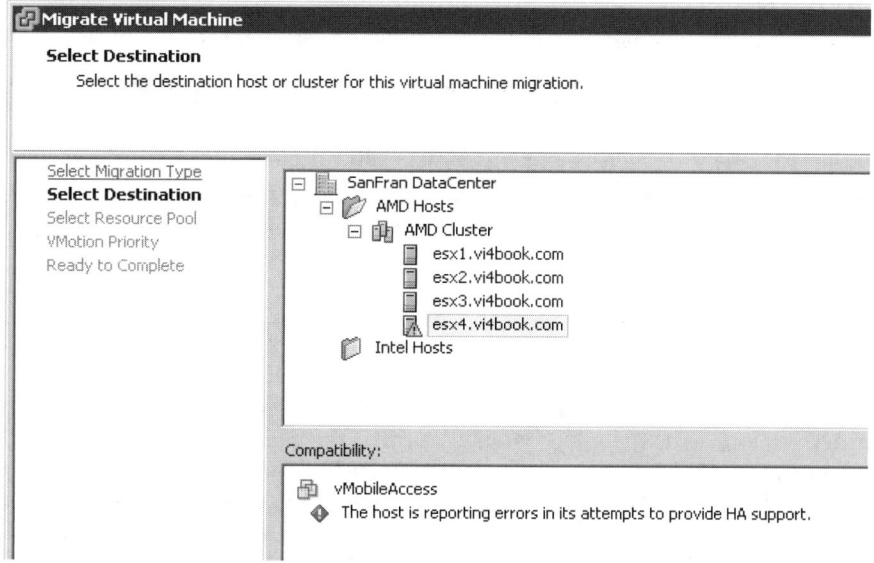

Clearly, the reason for this is to prevent the administrator from moving a VM to an ESX host that has HA error, with the resulting VM then having its protection removed by the move.

Monitoring a HA Cluster

Both DRS and HA will give you status information about the integrity of the cluster. In fact, you will likely see some of these notifications during the configuration of HA.

On the cluster icon itself, you will find different icons to represent the state of the cluster. The red exclamation point icon indicates a configuration problem, and the yellow exclamation point icon indicates the server with the DRS or HA issue. In HA, this happens nearly every time you set up the cluster, as it waits for at least two ESX hosts to fully start the HA Agent before clearing the alert. It takes some time for each ESX server to be enabled for HA, and when you have a HA cluster of just one server during the initial setup, HA reports this as a failure of the cluster.

The most common reason for the red icon on a DRS or HA cluster is administrators using the vSphere Client incorrectly. Once you have VMware clustering enabled, you should not "point" the vSphere Client directly to the ESX host, because this bypasses vCenter. The only reason to do this is if your vCenter environment has malfunctioned, and in that case, your time would be better spent resolving the problems with the vCenter server.

If the cluster icon has a yellow icon, this indicates that resources are scarce and reservations may not be met. In this case, you could experience admission control problems. The most common reason for this is that a number of ESX hosts have become unavailable and, as a result, the cluster has experienced a drop in total capacity.

In the following example, I generated a red exclamation mark on the cluster by raising my configured failover capacity to 50% on the cluster. On a two-node cluster, this is very likely to create a warning, especially if you have a number of VMs running. In my case, although I have 76% CPU capacity, I have only 30% memory capacity. If I reduced the value for configured failover capacity to be 30% or less, this warning would be removed.

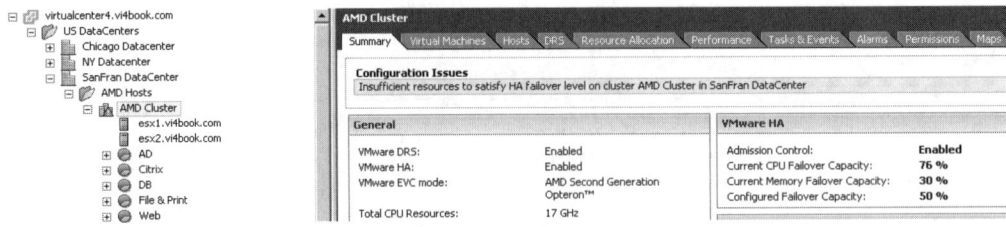

Summary

In this chapter, we looked at the many ways you can offer high availability to both the VM and the ESX host, by either VM clustering or HA clustering. You also saw how DRS and HA are so closely integrated with each other that you are unlikely to want to use them in isolation from each other.

Of course, you may desire a much higher level of availability than merely restarting your VMs. Perhaps you would like continuous high availability services, where one VM is mirrored on another ESX host, such that if an ESX host fails, the mirrored VM just picks up where the failed ESX host and VM left off. This technology is available. It's called VMware FT, and it's the subject of the next chapter.

CHAPTER 16 | VMware Fault Tolerance

By the time this book is on the shelves, you may know all about VMware Fault Tolerance (FT). However, right now this is bleeding-edge technology that very few people have actually configured and used. Although I say FT is "bleeding-edge," in fact, back at VMworld 2007, one of the founders of VMware, Mendel Rosenblum, demonstrated what then was called Continuous Availability. So, actually the feature has been in VMware labs for some years.

Like many others, I hope that FT will create a new surge of interest in VMware technologies, and at the same time lay to rest the ghost of MSCS and other availability technologies.

At the heart of FT is the record/replay feature, which first became available in VMware Workstation 6. Initially designed as a programmer's debugging tool, record/replay can capture all the virtual interrupts that take place inside a VM. It is likely that this feature will appear in future editions of vSphere 4. Once the hypervisor has a record/replay feature, the next logical part is redirecting this recording process to another VM on a *different* ESX host in real time. The assumption is that exactly the same events are replayed in a shadow, or secondary, VM, and they will be held in a synchronous state. Literally, as you click the Start menu in the primary VM, the same event occurs in the secondary VM. The process of keeping both VMs in sync is referred to as *lockstep* technology, and is an attribute of modern CPUs. VMware, working in conjunction with Intel and AMD, offers support for this CPU feature, which is often referred to as *vLockstep*.

In this chapter, you will learn how to enable and test FT. But first, let's talk about what really matters: the advantages and disadvantages of FT.

FT Advantages and Disadvantages

Here are some of the main advantages of FT:

- Offers real-time protection for VMs
- Avoids end users being affected by downtime or hardware failure
- Provides seamless failover without affecting the user's client application
- Works for all VMs, regardless of the software state (whether the application is stateful or stateless)
- Protects systems that cannot be given fault tolerance or high availability using other vendors' technologies

Here are some of the main disadvantages:

- FT requires modern CPUs that have the lockstep attribute. This means your existing hardware may be too old for use with FT.
- Currently, VMware recommend a maximum of 8 (4 primaries and 4 secondaries) VMs per ESX host.
- The secondary VM consumes CPU and memory resources, but is used only when a failure occurs. FT has a performance overhead on the protected VM. Tests internally have shown that while these overhead costs are not great, they are detectable. An overhead of around 5% to 10% has been demonstrated in testing environments.
- In addition to the CPU and memory hits, there is also a network overhead to maintain the FT logging network. VMware works on the basis of each FT protection consuming on average 50Kbps, plus the normal network traffic in maintaining the FT logging network.

- When using Windows 2000 32-bit and Solaris 32-bit systems, some known issues have surfaced on AMD processors. The guest OSs that have been most heavily tested are Windows 2003 Server, Red Hat Linux Enterprise 4, SUSE Linux 10, and Solaris 10 x86.

- Currently, VMware FT protects only VMs with one vCPU.

- Whereas, VMotion does not care about clock speed differences, VMware FT is sensitive to such differences. The CPUs of the ESX host holding the primary and second VM should not vary by any more than 400 MHz.

- It may be difficult to create a compelling usage case for FT if the application vendor already has some method of protecting the application services. You may wish to use VMware FT and HA together with whatever the application vendor offers to protect its services to obtain the highest level of protection possible for the VM.

- A great many features that are available to a VM protected by HA are lost when FT is enabled for a VM. These can either stop a VM from being protected by FT or simply be unavailable after a VM has been protected. These features include the following:
  - VMDirectPath I/O
  - VM clustering (MSCS)
  - Snapshots
  - SVMotion
  - Paravirtualization
  - NPIV
  - NPT
  - USB, sound, CD, and floppy
  - RDM files with physical compatibility (RDMs with virtual compatibility are supported)
  - Hot swap of CPU/RAM
  - DRS for the primary and secondary VM, and as a consequence, the automation that maintenance mode provides

---

NOTE *You can still use manual VMotion for both the primary and secondary VMs. In fact, there's special menu option for carrying out this task for the secondary VM.*

It is possible to work around some of these limitations by temporarily disabling FT for the primary VM, making the desired change, and then reenabling FT for the affected VM.

Once you are aware of the power and limitations of FT, you can construct usage cases and create your own policies about when its selective deployment is appropriate.

With a significant number of applications, the vendors offer a model of scaling their systems for both load management and fault tolerance. This practice extends to many different technologies and services, including Active Directory, web services, and Citrix/Terminal Services. As DRS allows you to create affinity rules to prevent these multinode systems from residing on the same ESX host, and when also using VMware HA, they are well protected from becoming single points of failure. In these cases, you could say we now have two classes of VMware availability to offer our systems: the gold class, "good enough" availability of vendor application scale-out and VMware HA, and the platinum class availability of VMware FT.

I can see that people will be very selective about which VMs will be granted VMware FT status. It's no surprise that when you activate VMware HA on a cluster, *every* VM is protected by default (as long as it meets HA's requirements), but VMware FT is enabled on a per-VM basis.

Hardware and Software Requirements for FT

As you would expect, the main requirements of VMware FT closely mirror the requirements for VMware HA and VMotion. Indeed, these features need to be enabled on the cluster beforehand. That means that FT has the standard requirements of shared storage, shared networking, compatible CPUs, and consistently labeled vSwitch port groups. VMware FT also adds the following additional requirements.

- **Compatible CPUs** CPUs must have a lockstep attribute. Intel CPUs must be enabled for Intel VT technology, or *hardware virtualization*, as some vendors put it.

- **HA clustering** You must ensure you have a working and functioning HA cluster. Once VMware FT is enabled, you will find that HA cannot be switched off.

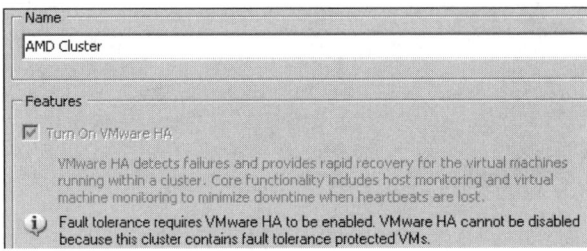

- **VMotion enabled** VMotion must work when you first enable VMware FT because it is used during the creation of the secondary VM. Both the primary and secondary VMs must be in the same memory state before the lockstep process can take over to keep the two VMs in sync.

- **FT logging enabled** FT logging should be enabled on a vSwitch to which you have dedicated NICs to the logging process. Ideally, the FT logging vSwitch should have two NICs assigned to it; otherwise, it will become a single point of failure. If at all possible, 10GB Ethernet is recommended, but not required, as gigabit connectivity should work as well. While it is possible to use your VMotion network as your FT logging network, the vSphere Client will warn you that this isn't good practice.

- **Correct type of virtual disks** VMs must have virtual disks set with the option Support Clustering Features such as Fault Tolerance enabled. FT requires the virtual disk to correspond to the eagerzeroedthick format; zeroedthick (the default format) and 2gbsparse (thinly provisioned) are not supported. FT will convert disks created in the other formats for you, but this requires the VM to be powered off, and the conversion does take time.

CAUTION Remember that it is currently not possible to convert the virtual disk to the eagerzeroedthick format using the right-click Inflate option on the properties of a thinly provisioned virtual disk in the Datastore Browser of the vSphere Client. Additionally, if you use the Thick option, cold migration and SVMotion do not convert the virtual disk to an eagerzeroedthick format. Instead these methods leave you with the standard zeroedthick disk format provided by default within vCenter.

Discovering CPU Types

As with VMotion, the CPU compatibility requirement may be the most challenging. As discussed in Chapter 12, the VMware CPU Host Info utility, available from http://www .run-virtual.com, reports on the CPU attributes of your server hardware. You can use it to check whether your existing CPUs support the lockstep attribute, if Intel VT is available, and whether it has been enabled in the BIOS of Intel-based ESX hosts. It also reports on VMware FT compatibility.

overview

	Server	Vendor	Model	CPUs	CPU Type		FT Support	VT Enables	VT Cap
▶	esx1.vi4book.com	HP	ProLiant DL380 G5	2	Intel(R) Xeon(R) CPU	E5430 @ 2.66G...	X	X	X
	esx3.vi4book.com	HP	ProLiant DL380 G5	2	Intel(R) Xeon(R) CPU	E5430 @ 2.66G...	X	X	X
	esx2.vi4book.com	HP	ProLiant DL380 G5	2	Intel(R) Xeon(R) CPU	E5430 @ 2.66G...	X	X	X

ESX Server Overview

In the official guides to FT, VMware lists the following as compatible CPUs (this is likely to change over time):

- Intel Core 2, also known as Merom
- Intel 45nm Core 2, also known as Penryn
- Intel Next-Generation, also known as Nehalem
- AMD Second Generation Opteron, also known as Rev E/F common feature set
- AMD Third Generation Opteron, also known as Greyhound

The following VMware Knowledge Base article (1008027) is well worth bookmarking for future reference on this issue:

http://kb.vmware.com/selfservice/microsites/search.do?language=en_US&cmd= displayKC&externalId=1008027

You can also use tools built into the ESX host to discover your CPU types. In ESXi, enter the following at the Tech Support Mode command prompt:

```
/sbin/vsish -e get /hardware/cpu/cpuList/0
```

```
Tech Support Mode successfully accessed.
The time and date of this access have been sent to the system logs.

WARNING - Tech Support Mode is not supported unless used in
consultation with VMware Tech Support.

~ # /sbin/vsish -e get /hardware/cpu/cpuList/0
CPU information {
    Family:15
    Model:33
    Type:0
    Stepping:2
    TSC Hz:2004545030
    Processor Hz:2004545030
    Bus Hz:200454503
    Name:AuthenticAMD
```

At the ESX Classic Service Console, enter this command:

```
cat /proc/cpuinfo
```

This will generate output similar to the following example:

```
[root@esx1 47878034-85f68aff-4754-001560ace43f]# cat /proc/cpuinfo
processor       : 0
vendor_id       : AuthenticAMD
cpu family      : 15
model           : 33
model name      : AMD Opteron(tm) Processor 275
stepping        : 2
cpu MHz         : 2205.080
cache size      : 1024 KB
fpu             : yes
fpu_exception   : yes
cpuid level     : 1
wp              : yes
flags           : fpu vme de pse tsc msr pae mce cx8 apic sep mtrr pge
xt 3dnow pni cmp_legacy
bogomips        : 4413.38
TLB size        : 1024 4K pages
clflush size    : 64
cache_alignment : 64
address sizes   : 40 bits physical, 48 bits virtual
power management: ts fid vid ttp
```

As you can see, my AMD CPUs are the wrong CPU family (15) and model (33) to be supported by VMware natively with VMware FT. But note that more than 50% of the servers on the VMware HCL do support VMware FT.

Using VMware SiteSurvey to Check FT Support

You can use the VMware SiteSurvey utility to determine if your hardware and software are suitable for VMware FT. After installing and loading the utility, you are able to select a cluster in vCenter, which will then report the status of each ESX host. The SiteSurvey tool will flag which processes are known to support FT and maintain compatibility for other features such as VMotion and DRS. At the time of writing, the supported Intel series are 3100, 3300, 5200, 5400, 5500, and 7400; the supported AMD series are 1300, 2300, and 8300.

NOTE *The Intel 5500 series is unusual as it does not share compatibility with any other processor.*

The SiteSurvey tool has a matrix that describes the compatible CPUs.

	Intel 3100	Intel 3300	Intel 5200	Intel 5400	Intel 5500	Intel 7400	AMD 1300	AMD 2300	AMD 8300
Intel 3100	O	O	O	O	X	O	X	X	X
Intel 3300	O	O	O	O	X	O	X	X	X
Intel 5200	O	O	O	O	X	O	X	X	X
Intel 5400	O	O	O	O	X	O	X	X	X
Intel 5500	X	X	X	X	O	X	X	X	X
Intel 7400	O	O	O	O	X	O	X	X	X
AMD 1300	X	X	X	X	X	X	O	O	O
AMD 2300	X	X	X	X	X	X	O	O	O
AMD 8300	X	X	X	X	X	X	O	O	O

Message	Meaning
incompatibleProduct	ESX host is not running ESX 4 or higher.
incompatibleCpu	The ESX server does not support hardware virtualization, such as Intel VT or AMD-V.
hvDisabled	The ESX server does support FT, but virtualization has been disabled in the BIOS, which prevents FT from running.
cpuidLimitSet	The ESX server has a BIOS option set that enforces a maximum limit on the CPU ID.
oldBIOS	The ESX server BIOS needs to be updated.
Unknown	An unknown BIOS configuration is preventing FT from working properly.

TABLE 16-1 SiteSurvey Messages

The SiteSurvey utility will also look at the CPU clock speeds and warn you if the clock speed of one host differs from another by a factor greater than 400 MHz. The SiteSurvey utility will examine the BIOS of the ESX host to check that certain attributes are available and issue warnings if various BIOS settings have not been engaged or are not present. Table 16-1 summarizes the SiteSurvey messages.

In addition to these checks, the SiteSurvey utility also checks the following:

- Whether the vSwitch assigned for FT logging is using at least 1GB Ethernet adapters on the same VLAN

- The existence of two VMKernel ports, one for VMotion and the other for FT logging

- Shared storage (also required for HA, DRS, and VMotion)

- License for FT

- Guest OS compatibility; for example, it will flag Windows XP (64/32 bit), Windows 2000, and Solaris 10 (32 bit) as being incompatible if you are using the AMD Barcelona chipset

For SiteSurvey to work, you must have at least one cluster defined.

To use SiteSurvey, first install the utility, and then load the application and log in to your vCenter. You can download SiteSurvey at this URL:

http://www.vmware.com/download/shared_utilities.html

If you have more than one cluster defined, select the cluster you want to check from the pull-down list. SiteSurvey will generate an HTML report that outlines each

ESX host. The following example shows that none of my AMD hosts are compatible with VMware FT.

VMware SiteSurvey Report

Version 1.0Beta

VirtualCenter Server: **virtualcenter4.vi4book.com**
Generated: **Mon Apr 06 18:45:58 2009**

Report for cluster **AMD Cluster**

To use FT, resolve the issues marked with X

The following ESX hosts are members of the cluster
but have **CPUs that do not support FT**:

esx1.vi4book.com   AMD Opteron(tm) Processor 270

esx3.vi4book.com   AMD Opteron(tm) Processor 275

esx2.vi4book.com   AMD Opteron(tm) Processor 270

During the writing of this chapter, VMware very kindly gave me remote access to servers in the UK that were Intel-based. These ESX hosts returned a positive message about supporting VMware FT as the following example shows. In this case, I deliberately did not enable FT logging to show how the SiteSurvey utility checks for FT requirements.

VMware SiteSurvey Report

Version 1.0Beta

VirtualCenter Server: 192.168.21.12
Generated: Mon Apr 27 16:30:38 2009

Report for cluster **Intel Cluster**

To use FT, resolve the issues marked with ✕

All ESX hosts in this cluster are capable
of running FT and can be clustered together.

Hosts which can work together as an FT cluster
CPU type and processor speed are compatible

esx1.vi4book.com (Intel CPU, 2670 MHz):

✓	ESX Build: **140815**		
✓	BIOS Compatibility		
✓	NIC faster than 1 Gb/S	✓	ESX licensed for FT
✓	ESX version: 4.0		
✓	VMotion NIC	✕	Logging NIC
✓	This host has shared storage:		

Volume: **49de2bf9-688f0dc0-4477-001e0bd6f976**

Enabling VMware FT

Enabling VMware FT is a six-step process:

1. Confirm certificate management.
2. Confirm that HA and VMotion function correctly.
3. Enable FT logging on a new port group.
4. Confirm the target VM has the correct disk type.
5. Check VM settings.
6. Enable VMware FT on a VM.

You should know that there exists a pop-up link which will briefly overview the requirements for FT in the vSphere Client. This pop-up appears on the "Summary" tab of each ESX hosts.

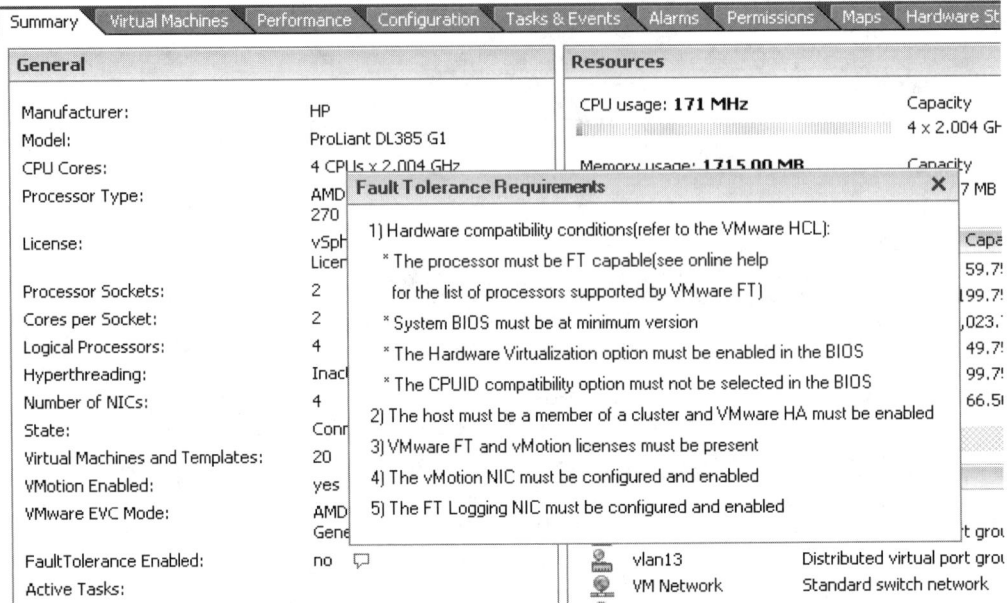

Confirming Certificate Management

VMware FT requires that ESX hosts are added to vCenter with checking of SSL Certificates enabled. Currently, when adding an ESX host to the cluster, you are challenged for the username and password of the root account. This validates your right to manage the ESX host with vCenter.

There is a small chance that the actual ESX host you are using could be spoofed. To prevent this, VMware has enabled, by default, a higher level of security, which uses an internally generated certificate to verify the identity of the ESX host. This is not dissimilar to the message you receive when you connect to an ESX host for the first time with PuTTY using the SSH protocol. It is worth confirming that this functionality has not been switched off by another administrator.

If ESX hosts are added to vCenter with just a username and password without this certificate check, VMware FT will not start correctly. You will be forced to reenable the checking of ESX hosts, and disconnect and reconnect the ESX hosts back into vCenter. To do this, in the Administration menu of vCenter, select VirtualCenter Management Server Configuration, select SSL Settings, and then enable the option to Check Host Certificates.

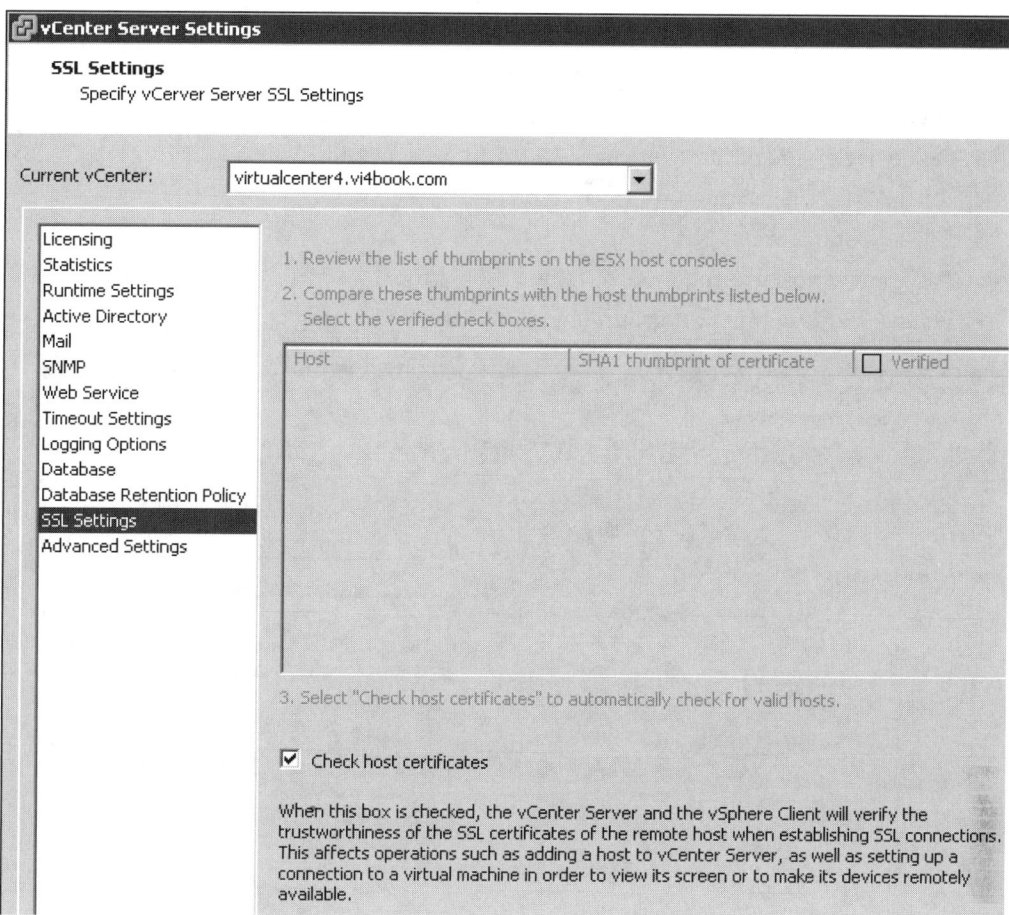

Confirming That HA and VMotion Function Correctly

You may want to confirm that HA and VMotion work before enabling FT, just to make sure nothing has changed. Also check that the HA Agent has successfully started on all your ESX hosts.

Enabling FT Logging on a New Port Group

VMware recommends creating a dedicated VMkernel port group purely for the FT logging track. Ideally, this should be teamed for network redundancy. There's little point in enabling VMware FT if its reliability is undermined by a failed NIC or an unreliable physical switch. This task needs to be carried out on all servers within the HA cluster.

Enable FT logging as follows:

1. In the vSphere Client, select the ESX host.
2. On the Configuration tab, select Networking in the Hardware pane.
3. On the right side of the window, select Add Networking.
4. Select VMkernel as the port group type.
5. Select at one or more NICs.
6. Type a new port group name, such as FT-Logging.
7. Enable the "Use this port group for fault tolerance logging" option.

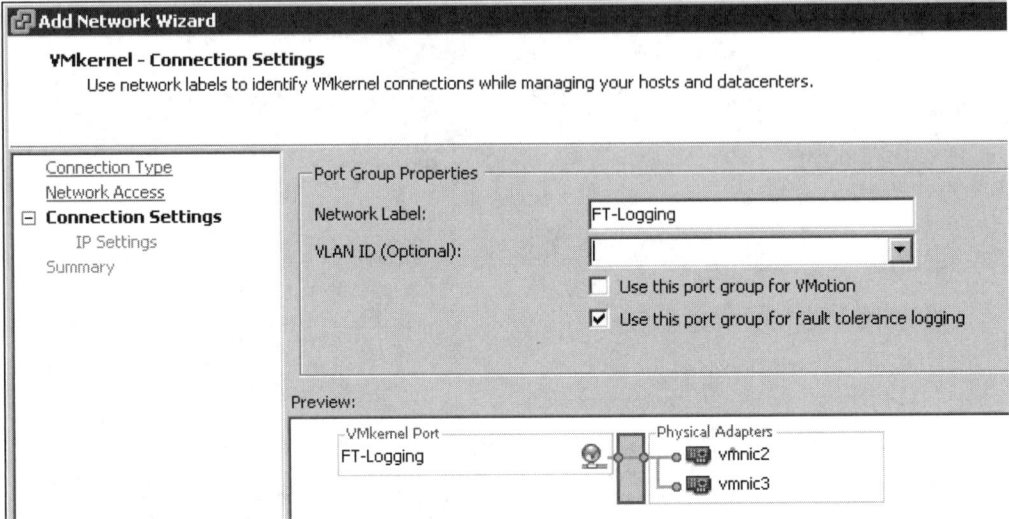

If you do reuse your VMotion port group, you will be warned about the potential performance hit this could generate. In an ideal world, your FT logging traffic would be on a different NIC from your VMotion traffic.

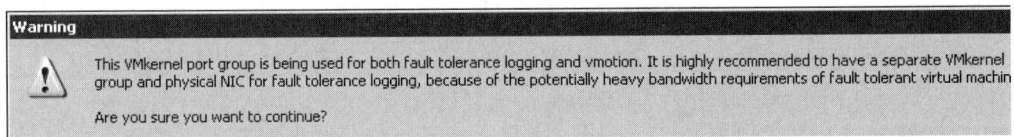

Of course it is indeed possible to enable FT Logging if you are using the new Distributed vSwitch. The option appears when you use the "Manage Virtual Adapter" wizard to create to set VMKernel port group settings as you would with VMotion.

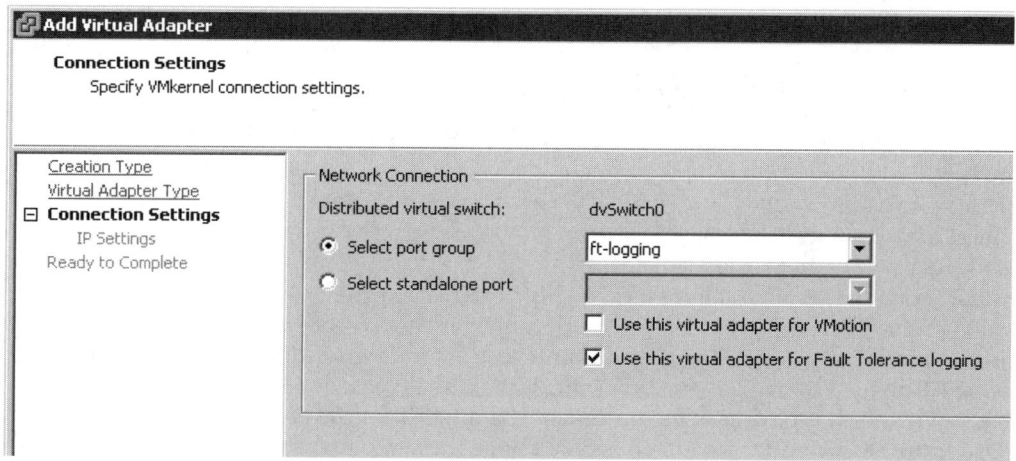

Confirming the Target VM's Disk Type

It is very easy to tell if a virtual disk is the thin type, which would be incompatible with VMware FT. Simply by editing the settings of the VM in question, and selecting its virtual disks in the Virtual Machine Properties dialog box, you can tell if it's a thick or thin disk. In the following example, you can see the virtual disk called sql04_1.vmdk is a thin virtual disk.

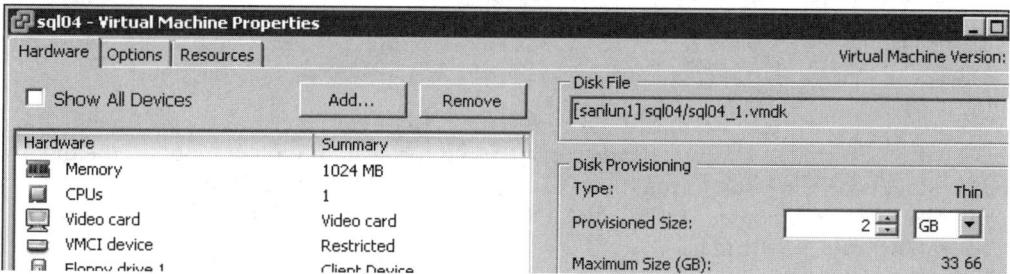

If you do have thin disks, and you still wish to protect the VM with VMware FT, the best strategy is to claim a maintenance window for the affected VM, and then power it down. Once it is powered down, enable VMware FT on the VM. This will trigger a conversion process that makes the thin disk an eagerzeroedthick disk.

Spotting a thin virtual disk from the command line is relatively easily if you understand that some command-line utilities will report the space as it is seen by the guest OS, say 20GB, whereas other tools show the actual disk space consumed. By comparing the outputs of the ls and du commands, you can see if there is a difference between the two numbers. If there is, the disk is thinly provisioned.

Using du -h against the virtual disk followed by ls -lh against the same file allows you to compare values. In the following example, the first virtual disk (ctx01.vmdk) is definitely not thinly provisioned, as both du and ls report the size of the file as 4GB.

For the second file (ctx01_1 .vmdk), du reports 0KB, whereas, `ls` reports 4GB. This indicates that the second disk is thinly provisioned.

In contrast, it is currently quite tricky to confirm either by graphical or command-line tools the real type of the virtual

```
[root@esx1 ctx01]# du -h  ctx01-flat.vmdk
4.0G    ctx01-flat.vmdk
[root@esx1 ctx01]# ls -lh  ctx01-flat.vmdk
-rw------- 1 root root  4.0G Feb  4 19:52 ctx01-flat.vmdk
[root@esx1 ctx01]#
[root@esx1 ctx01]# du -h  ctx01_1-flat.vmdk
0       ctx01_1-flat.vmdk
[root@esx1 ctx01]# ls -lh  ctx01_1-flat.vmdk
-rw------- 1 root root  4.0G Feb  4 19:42 ctx01_1-flat.vmdk
[root@esx1 ctx01]#
```

disk attached to the VM if you have used the thick format. Currently, vCenter shows all virtual disks as thick, whether they are zeroedthick or eagerzeroedthick. If you are at unsure, again I recommend claiming a maintenance window for the VM in question and enabling FT on the VM in a powered-off state. If the disk is zeroedthick, it will be converted to an eagerzeroedthick type during the process of enabling FT for the first time.

Using the Service Console, it is possible to use the vmkfstools utility against the -flat .vmdk files that make up a virtual disk to determine if the virtual disk is zeroedthick or eagerzeroedthick. Using the command `vmkfstools -D sql04-flat.vmdk` for the virtual disk in the previous example will send output to the VMkernel log file. You can view the last couple of lines of the VMkernel log file with the command `tail -n /var/log/vmkernel`. This is the important line in the output from the VMkernel log for a zeroedthick disk:

```
Apr 30 09:52:52 esx2 vmkernel: 15:21:54:07.962 cpu2:4180)len 2147483648, nb
2048 tbz 2048, cow 0, zla 3, bs 1048576
```

This is the important line in the output from the VMkernel log for a eagerzeroedthick disk:

```
Apr 30 09:53:02 esx2 vmkernel: 15:21:54:17.851 cpu3:4177)len 2147483648, nb
2048 tbz 0, cow 0, zla 3, bs 1048576
```

As you can see, the important difference is the `tbz` value. In an eagerzeroedthick disk, the `tbz` value is normally 0. If the flag is set to 0, then the system will zero out all the blocks in the virtual disk. This is the format that is acceptable to VMware FT. If the `tbz` value is any other number, it indicates that the disk has been created in the default format, which is not compatible with VMware FT.

The conversion of a thin or zeroedthick disk to an eagerzeroedthick disk requires exclusive access to the virtual disk in question, which can be achieved only in a powered-off state. If you try to enable FT on a VM with thin or zeroedthick disks, you will receive an "invalid device" error message.

Another method of checking if your virtual disks will need conversion is by looking at the last log file for your VM. If you use the `cat` command together with the `grep` command you can search the VM's log file disks that will not be compatible with FT.

For example:

```
cat vmware-14.log | grep 'FT enable'
VM has thin disk scsi0:0; FT enable will be disallowed
VM has zeroedthick disk scsi0:2; FT enable will be disallowed
```

This indicates that scsi0:1 is in the valid format but scsi0:0 and 0:2 are not, and would therefore need conversion to the eagerzeroedthick format.

Checking VM Settings

Confirm the following VM settings:

- Hot plug of memory/CPU not enabled
- No connected or configured CD-ROMs or floppy devices
- No snapshots
- Paravirtualization not enabled
- No RDM files with physical compatibility

Enabling VMware FT on a VM

To enable FT on a VM, right-click the VM, select Fault Tolerance, and then select Turn On Fault Tolerance. When you select this option, a dialog box will appear, warning you about the virtual disk type requirement. Notice how the status of the VM in the DRS cluster is changing. It will be set to be disabled for DRS using the per-VM option on the DRS cluster.

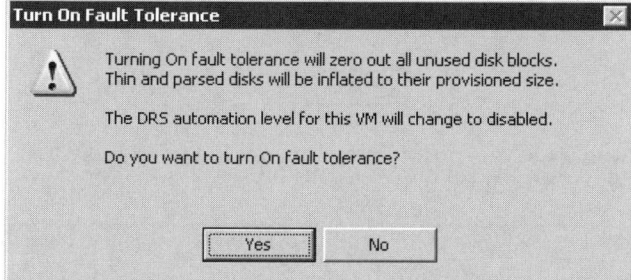

During the enabling of FT, a number of changes will take place. The first thing that happens is the secondary VM is created in the same location as the primary, and it does take some time for them to become synchronized. You can see this as being similar to the SVMotion process when a "helper" VM is created. So for a brief period, you will see what appears to be a duplicate VM in the same location in the vCenter Inventory.

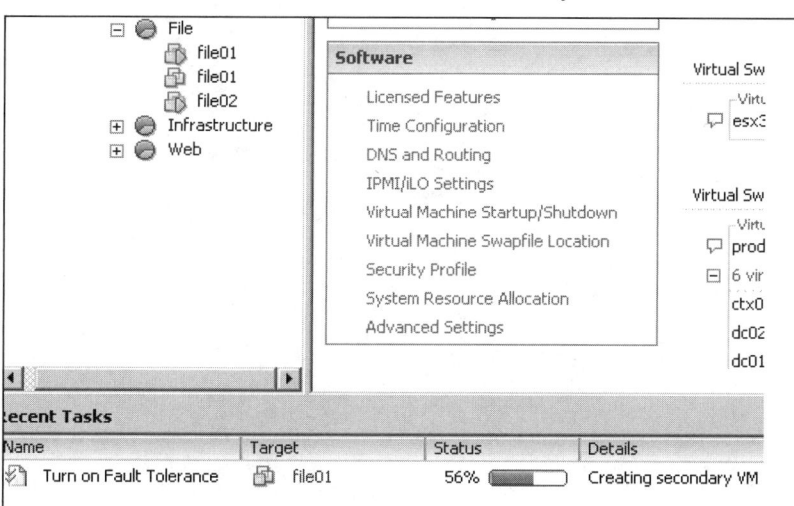

The difference here is that the creation of the helper system is critical. The secondary VM is always created on a different ESX host to the primary.

The second visual change is in the icon of the primary VM. At the end of the process, the icon for the primary VM will have changed to show the famous boxes-within-boxes VMware logo filled in dark blue.

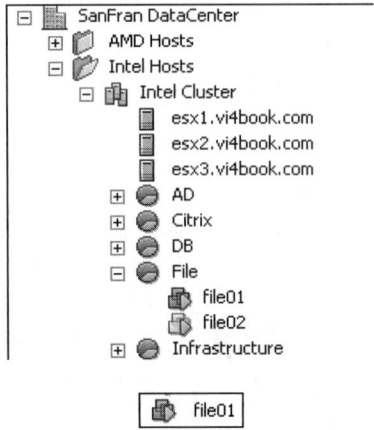

Although the secondary VM is not visible in the main Hosts and Clusters view, it does appear in the main Virtual Machines tab.

| file01 | Powered On | Normal | esx1.vi4book.com |
| file01 (secondary) | Powered On | Normal | esx2.vi4book.com |

Once the protection is established and working, you should see a new pane in the Summary tab of the primary VM. Additionally, if the primary VM is not protected, you should see a red exclamation mark icon on the VM. The following examples show a protected VM and an unprotected VM, respectively:

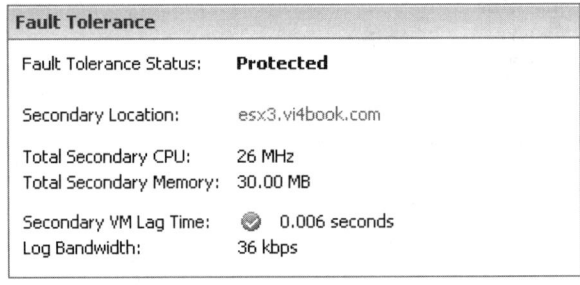

Fault Tolerance

Fault Tolerance Status:	**Protected**
Secondary Location:	esx3.vi4book.com
Total Secondary CPU:	26 MHz
Total Secondary Memory:	30.00 MB
Secondary VM Lag Time:	0.006 seconds
Log Bandwidth:	36 kbps

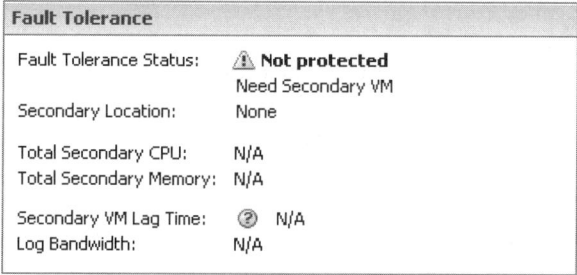

As you can see in the protected VM example, the Fault Tolerance pane shows where the secondary is located, and how much CPU and memory are being used. The lag time value shows how in sync the secondary is with the primary, and the log bandwidth value shows how much bandwidth is being consumed on the FT logging network.

Once both the primary VM and secondary VM have been started, it is possible to open Remote Console windows on both. However, you will not be able to interact with the secondary VM's Remote Console window, and it will be marked as read-only in the status bar beneath the standard icons. You can interact with the primary VM, and should see that whatever actions are carried out in the primary Remote Console window appear in the secondary Remote Console window. By opening a Remote Console window on both primary and secondary VMs, you can see in a real-time view that VMware FT is working.

In the following example, the primary VM appears on the right, and the secondary VM on the left. I opened the Clock application in the primary window so I could monitor how in sync they were from a time perspective. Notice that the toolbar prompt indicates you cannot interact with the secondary VM, and that the Remote Console session is marked as read-only.

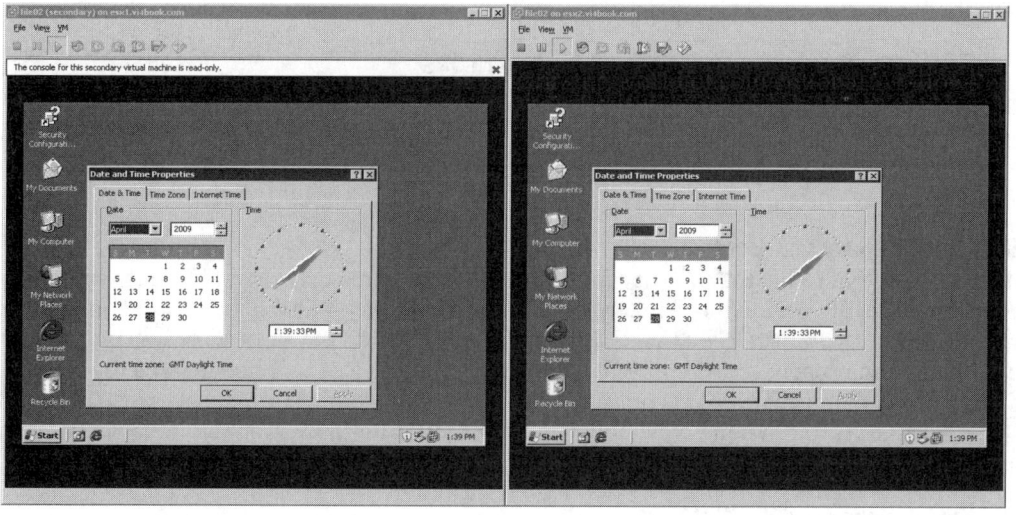

Testing VMware FT

It is possible to test VMware FT without actually attempting a hard crash of an ESX host, although I certainly recommend hard tests, as I'm a firm believer in rigorously verifying that technology delivers in the real world.

Soft Testing VMware FT

Two types of soft tests can be carried out: a test failover on the primary and a restart on the secondary. The test failover halts the primary VM, and forces the secondary VM to take over the role at the same time it changes the ownership of the VMs to different ESX hosts, thus simulating a situation where the primary ESX host failed.

Before you begin testing, you may wish to make a note of the current location of the primary and secondary VMs. Additionally, you might like to open a Microsoft RDP or ping -t session on the primary to confirm that packets are not lost during the test, as you might do with VMotion.

In this example, the primary VM is called sql03. The primary is located on esx2.vi4book .com, and the secondary is located on esx3.vi4book.com.

🖥️	sql02	192.168.21.45	esx2.vi4book.com
🖥️	sql02 (secondary)		esx3.vi4book.com

To perform the test, right-click the primary VM, select Fault Tolerance, and then choose Test Failover. During this process, you should see that if you have three or more ESX hosts in the cluster, the current secondary is restarted on a different ESX host, and then brought into sync with the primary. Then the primary is restarted on another ESX host.

🖥️	sql02	esx3.vi4book.com	Powered On
🖥️	sql02 (secondary)	esx2.vi4book.com	Powered On

Hard Testing—Real-World FT What-if Scenarios

For the tests in this section, I deliberately went with three ESX hosts in the clusters, as this allows me to explain and demonstrate all the possible scenarios associated with VMware FT. Essentially, these correspond to a series of "what-if" questions based on different types of actions.

Failure of a Primary ESX Host

If the ESX host that holds the primary fails and you have three or more ESX hosts, the secondary VM will become the primary, and a new secondary VM will be created on the third ESX host. If you have only two ESX hosts in a FT cluster, the secondary will become the primary, and no new secondary will be created until the lost ESX host rejoins the cluster. Until this time, the primary VM is not protected.

In my tests, I found when I crashed an ESX host, all stateful memory contents were maintained, and only one ping packet was lost when the crash occurred.

Failure of a Secondary ESX Host

If the ESX host that holds the secondary VM fails and you have three or more ESX hosts, a new secondary is created on the third ESX host. During this period, the VM is unprotected until a new secondary VM is created.

Simultaneous Failure of Primary and Secondary ESX Hosts

If both the ESX hosts that hold the primary and secondary fail at the same time, the VM is restarted using HA on any remaining ESX host. If you have more than three ESX hosts, once the VM has restarted, if there are enough ESX hosts, then FT is reenabled on the primary and a new secondary VM is started.

In some cases, I had to wait a long time for VMware FT to reprotect the VM after this unusual and unlikely situation. I found disabling and reenabling FT on the primary was enough to make it work again.

Failure of the FT Logging Network

If you fail to protect the FT logging network, you could end up with a split-brain situation, where the primary ESX believes the secondary ESX host has failed, and vice versa. If the primary ESX host becomes orphaned from the network, the primary VM ceases to be the primary, and the secondary takes over. The original primary VM is removed, and the secondary assumes the role of the primary. If enough ESX hosts exist, a new secondary is created on a ESX host where the network has not failed. In summary, if split-brain does occur, a failure is assumed, and FT behaves in the same way as in the first scenario (failure of a primary ESX host).

Alternatively, if the secondary ESX host has become orphaned from the network, then the second scenario (failure of a secondary ESX host) applies. If enough ESX hosts exist, a new secondary is created on a third ESX host. During this period, the VM is unsupported until the secondary is started. In this case, FT behaves in the same way as in the second scenario.

Maintenance Mode and Migration with VMware FT

As you might recall, even if you have DRS set to be fully automated, all FT-enabled VMs are currently disabled from DRS functionality. In the following example, you can see the VMs called file01 and file02, which both have the FT-style icon and are set to be disabled from DRS functionality.

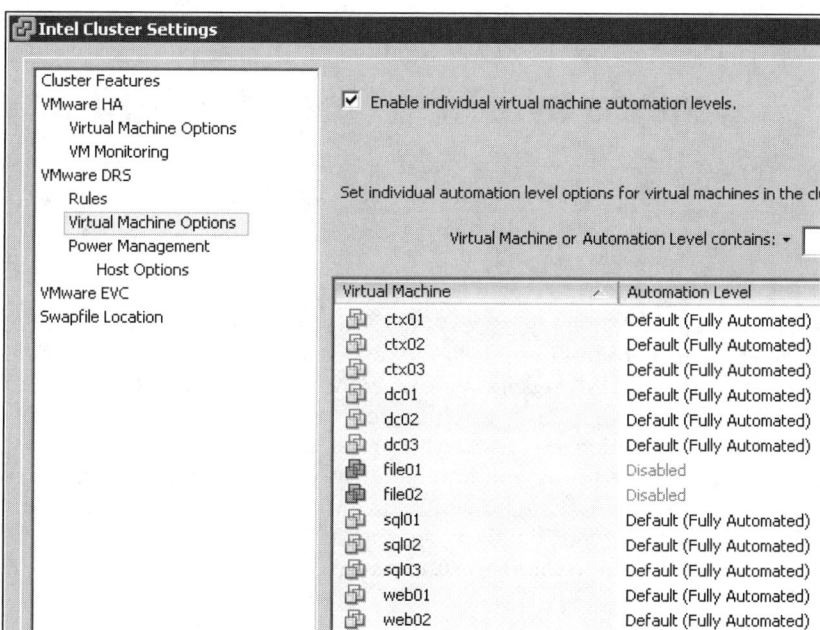

The consequence of this is that if you enter into maintenance mode, the FT primary VM does not automatically get moved to another ESX host. Therefore, the FT primary VM would need to be moved with VMotion manually.

FT does introduce new VMotion errors to prevent you carrying out illogical tasks, such as trying to place the primary and secondary VMs on the same ESX host.

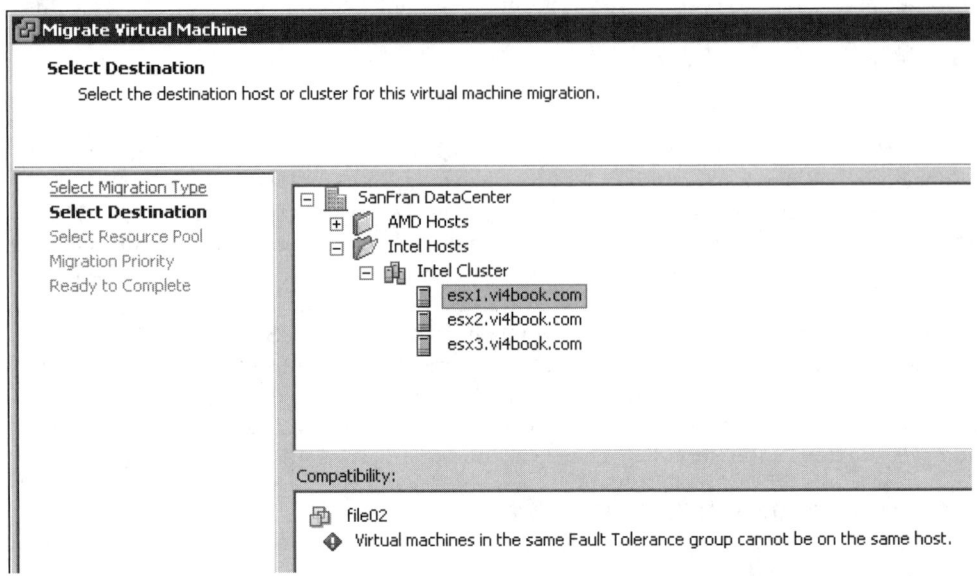

Additionally, even if you do select the correct ESX host, you may see a warning message if you select a resource pool location when completing the VMotion wizard. This warning is a benign one that merely reminds you that changing the primary VM's resource pool location will also change the secondary VM's location.

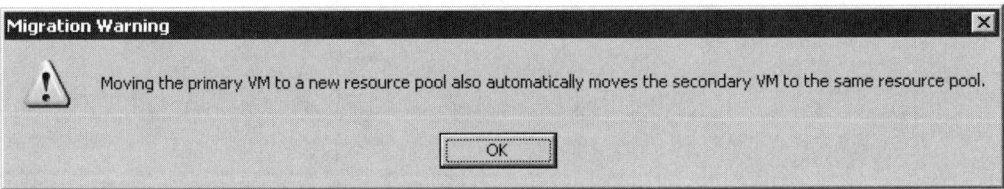

VMware FT's current lack of integration with DRS has undesirable consequences elsewhere in the vSphere 4 environment for other aspects of automation—specifically, the VMware Update Manager (VUM) service. One of VUM's main goals is to patch ESX hosts automatically without affecting VMs. A patch process invariably means a reboot of the ESX host. VUM utilizes both VMotion and DRS to automate the process of evacuating VMs from the affected host prior to scheduling a maintenance mode and reboot. Of course, this automation stops if any VM cannot be moved with VMotion or is disabled to DRS, leaving the status bar of maintenance mode stuck stubbornly at 2%. If you are using VUM and FT is enabled, the operator will need to intervene and manually move the FT-enabled VM.

It is also possible to move the secondary VM to a different ESX host. In fact, there's a special option to do that without needing to first relocate the secondary. To access this option, right-click the primary VM, select Fault Tolerance, and then choose Migrate Secondary.

In my test, when I put an ESX host in maintenance mode, which "owns" the secondary VM while the other VMs move off the ESX host, the secondary VM did not get moved and needed to be moved manually.

Turning Off or Disabling FT

There are two options that allow you to stop FT on a VM:

- **Turn Off Fault Tolerance**   This option turns off FT and completely undoes the process outlined in this chapter. The primary VM returns to the status of an ordinary unprotected VM, and the secondary is destroyed.

- **Disable Fault Tolerance**   This option stops the FT process temporarily, but does not destroy the secondary. This can be used to carry out tasks on the primary VM that cannot be done once it is protected by FT. For example, you may wish to move the VM to another storage location with SVMotion.

Turning Off FT

To turn off FT, right-click the VM, select Fault Tolerance, and then select Turn Off Fault Tolerance. You will see a warning dialog box.

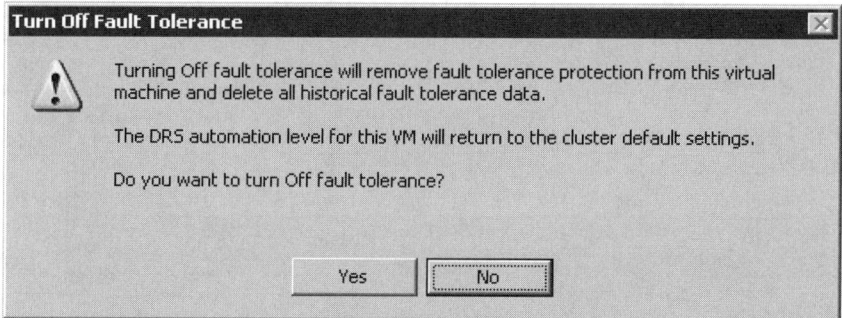

This will cause the secondary VM to be powered off, unregistered from the ESX hosts, and then deleted. The icon of the primary VM will change back to the standard VM icon.

I have occasionally seen the option to turn off FT fail. As you know, when VMware FT is enabled, a secondary VM is created on a different ESX host. Just like a real VM, this secondary VM has a .vmx file, which is registered on the secondary ESX host. Occasionally, this secondary VM does not get deregistered from the ESX host. Indeed, when VMware FT is reenabled, I've sometimes seen two secondary VMs appear in the list: an orphaned secondary and the partner to the primary. If this happens, a restart of the management service on the ESX host, where the orphaned secondary exists will be enough to unlock it in vCenter so that it can be manually removed from the Inventory.

Disabling FT

To disable FT, right-click the VM, select Fault Tolerance, and then select Disable Fault Tolerance. You will see a warning dialog box.

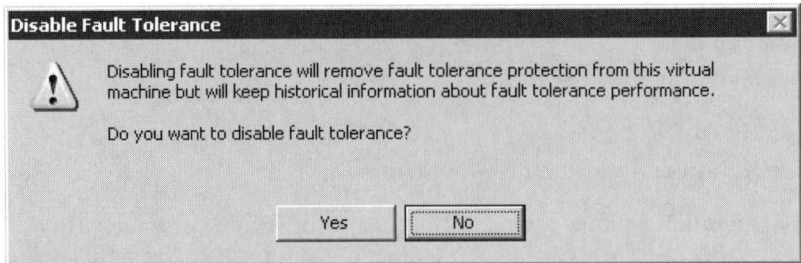

This will cause the secondary VM to be powered off, but it will remain registered on the ESX host but not started. The icon of the secondary VM will be dimmed and be lableled "(secondary) (disabled)." Additionally, the now unprotected primary VM will have a yellow exclamation mark icon in the Inventory, indicating that FT has been disabled for the VM, and therefore it is not protected.

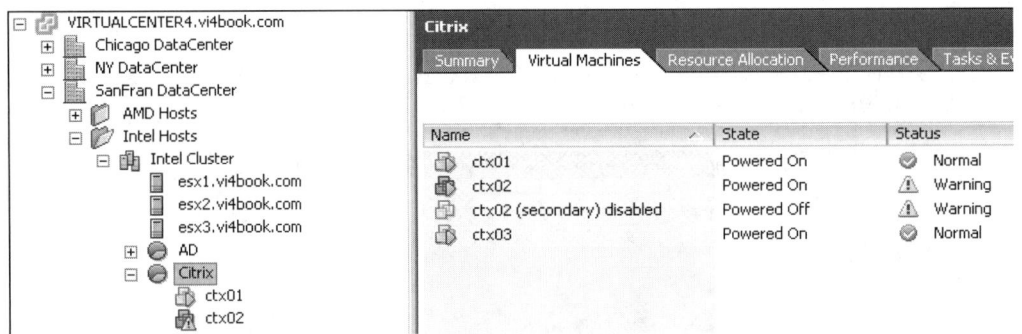

Summary

As you have learned in this chapter, FT is an amazingly powerful technology. I have a feeling it will have the same "wow" factor that VMotion had in the early days of VMware virtualization. It has the potential to sweep away complicated software solutions and, at the same time, really challenge expensive and proprietary hardware solutions.

However, FT is not without its limitations. Its lack of integration with DRS will have effects on other aspects of the vSphere, notably maintenance mode and VUM. Additionally, in this first release, it is limited to protecting single vCPU VMs, which account for only a certain portion of the VMs that organizations possess.

Nonetheless, FM is an exciting and interesting technology because it offers the tantalizing prospect of extremely high availability for systems and services, without the need for expensive proprietary hardware; instead, we can use standard commodity x86 hardware.

CHAPTER 17 | vSphere Advanced Configuration Tools

One of my favorite quotes is from a student of mine some years ago, who said, "If I've done it more than twice, I've scripted it." Once you get over the initial thrill of configuring something for the first time and making it work, the task will soon become a chore to you, full of possibilities for human error. Automation and scripting are most useful when tasks are repetitive, frequent, and tedious. If a task is inconsistent, infrequent, and interesting, the benefits of scripted automation diminish. Before I automate any task, I ask myself, "Given the time it takes to write, test, and verify an automated process, will the result yield long-term benefits beyond reducing human error? After all, scripts are written by humans, and are as likely to create errors as any manual process, depending on how well they have been written."

The command-line environment of VMware has improved in leaps and bounds in recent years since VI3 was first released. We now have many possibilities for scripting common tasks, and each of these possibilities come with advantages and disadvantages. In addition, the new host profiles feature allows us to copy the entire configuration of an ESX host and apply it to other hosts in the cluster. While host profiles offer a fantastic way of automating the configuration of an ESX host, the new scripting APIs allow for other tasks to be automated as well.

For those who are more experienced with VMware, you may now feel very comfortable and confident with the ESX Service Console; many of the commands you may be familiar with from ESX 3 are pretty much the same. However, it's important to understand that the ESX Classic Service Console will not be around forever. Therefore, it may be wise to familiarize yourself with one or more of the newer command-line interfaces—you might actually be surprised to find they are better.

What's New with VMware Configuration Tools?

- Host profiles, which almost eliminate the need for complex scripted installations
- The next generation of command-line tools, which allow everyone—from novices to experienced ESX administrators—to script configurations of not just ESX hosts, but also the vCenter environment

---

Configuration Tool Overview

The following configuration tools are available for working with VMware:

- **Local CLI at the ESX host**   The local CLI allows you to leverage your knowledge and familiarity with ESX 2 and 3. It appeals to administrators who find command-line utilities with switches and options easier to learn. Unfortunately, this requires root-level access (either with su or sudo) and a remote SSH connection using say the PuTTy application. You will find it difficult to write scripts that manipulate VMs in this interface, as the ESX host does not know the location of *all* VMs in a given datacenter—only vCenter knows this. As you have seen in previous chapters, VMs are highly mobile creatures that can be moved from one ESX host to another for many reasons. Additionally, commands executed at the local CLI don't always update in the vSphere Client until a refresh, or in some cases, a complete restart of the ESX host management service.

- **vSphere CLI**   The vCLI allows you to execute many of the commands of an ESX host from your Windows/Linux workstation remotely without an SSH session. This might be your only option if you are using ESXi 4, where an interactive CLI prompt at the physical server is not fully supported. Unfortunately, not all the commands available at the local CLI are available in the vSphere CLI. You might find it lacking certain utilities you have grown used to, such as `vdf` and `esxcfg-vswif`. As you can tell by the lack of support for `esxcfg-vswif`, the vCLI is really geared for the ESXi 4 product, because without the ability to add a second Service Console connection, you cannot properly configure a ESX Classic system for the VMware iSCSI software initiator or configure a second heartbeat connection for VMware HA.

NOTE *Recently, VMware made the vCLI in the free version of ESXi read-only. As such, it can be used only to retrieve settings from the ESX host; it cannot be used as a configuration tool. It's my sincere hope that VMware will reverse this decision in future versions of the vCLI.*

- **vSphere PowerCLI (Toolkit for Windows/PowerShell Toolkit)**   This is part of the incredibly powerful next generation of CLI tools. It plugs into vCenter remotely and carries out many functions that aren't even exposed in the GUI. Unfortunately, if you don't have good object-oriented knowledge (of objects, properties, attributes, and so on), it can be tricky to master. However, it is more functional than either the local or remote CLIs. Additionally, if you master PowerShell with VMware, you will be able to reuse your skills in other vendors' tools that plug into PowerShell.

- **vSphere Perl (Perl vSphere PowerCLI)**   For all intents and purposes, the Perl Toolkit exposes the same functionality as the PowerShell Toolkit. The only differences are their different syntax and conventions.

- **vSphere Management Assistant**   The vSphere Management Assistant aggregates much of the functionality seen in the vCLI and the Perl Toolkit. It allows for an interactive CLI to ESX Classic and ESXi. It also automates much of the authentication issues, meaning you have no real need to disclose the root account of an ESX Classic host to give administrators access to the Service Console.

- **Host profiles**   Host profiles are not a scripting engine or CLI tool, but they can carry out many of the postconfiguration tasks of an ESX host normally undertaken with scripting. If the whole concept of scripting fills you with terror, host profiles are a very powerful way of achieving a similar result—automation and consistency. They may be especially attractive to ESXi users, because unlike ESX Classic, there is no "install" aspect to host profile to automate, say the installation of management agent or backup agent—is this limitation which might make other scripting APIs more attractive. You can see host profiles as an extension of the server profiles you sometimes find on a blade system—the server profile on a blade system configures the hardware, and the ESX host profile configures software. Host profiles are covered in the next section, so if you're interested, read on.

All the different command-line based tools I will be covering in this chapter can be found on the main VMware Developer Community forum page:

http://communities.vmware.com/community/developer#sysadmintools

---

NOTE *I suspect there will be some people who will be very disappointed with the decline of the Service Console, but given that so much of our work now centers around vCenter and its features (VMotion, SVMotion, DRS, DPM, HA, VM-HA, and FT), you have to wonder how useful the Service Console actually is apart from for interactive troubleshooting! For this reason, I will be covering the vCLI and PowerShell tools in this chapter, as I personally believe that the more skills and tools you have at your beck and call, the better. A little knowledge is a dangerous thing, as the famous poet Alexander Pope once said. However, I have not completely abandoned my old friend the COS! I offer a vSphere 4 version of my Service Console guide on my Web site. You will find all my free guides are located at http://www.rtfm-ed.co.uk/?page_id=7.*

Implementing Host Profiles

When I was teaching the VI3 product, practically every week, a student would ask if there was a way of capturing the configuration of an ESX host and applying it to another, either to force it to have the same configuration or confirm it was configured correctly. In a nutshell, this is precisely what host profiles do for vSphere 4.

Essentially, a host profile acts like a policy object that can be applied to either an ESX host or cluster in the vCenter Inventory. While host profiles are a GUI feature available in vCenter, rather than a command-line tool, they have the potential to significantly reduce the need to develop scripted solutions to automate common tasks.

Back in the VI2 and VI3 days, the only way to achieve consistency in ESX host configuration was with scripted installations. Now you have the choice between scripted installations and host profiles, so you can choose the method that best suits you and your organization. If you want maximum control over any of the settings that make up your ESX Classic host, then a scripted installation is the way to go. On the other hand, if you're using ESXi 4, host profiles might be the better route, because they are relatively easy to use and require no scripting knowledge whatsoever. In fact, some settings that are very straightforward to achieve with host profiles can be quite tricky with scripts. Whatever your preference, you can still use host profiles as a way of confirming your ESX hosts have matching settings.

NOTE *The host profile feature is available only to Enterprise Plus customers, so you may have no choice but to use scripts to automate the postconfiguration of an ESX host.*

Host profiles have five main functions:

- Capture the configuration profile of an existing host.
- Apply the configuration profile to a new host.
- Confirm that an ESX host is correctly configured.
- Prompt the administrator for per ESX host settings such as VMkernel network configuration for IP data for iSCSI, VMotion, HA, and FT. You could have one profile per ESX host, but it makes more sense to have a few host profiles applied to many ESX hosts.
- Apply the profile as an ESX host is added into vCenter cluster—a mere drag-and-drop event configures the ESX host!

Host profiles do have several limitations. You have little control over the storage stack, except for NFS mount points, and you cannot install additional software to the ESX host. Additionally, host profile configuration does not complete before the HA Agent starts, thus creating HA Agent errors, which require a restart of the HA Agent. This last limitation might discourage some ESX Classic users from adopting host profiles, as administrators quite frequently want to script the installation of various software required for backup, UPS, hardware, or other vendor-specific management agents. It's for this reason that host profiles might appeal more to ESXi 4 users. By definition, ESXi is a sealed build that cannot be customized beyond the soft postconfiguration stages, and this postconfiguration is a sizable part of the work of rolling out ESXi *en masse*.

With this said, I don't want to box myself or you into a corner. You could use a combination of strategies, such as scripted installations to get the ESX Classic product on to the physical server, with the postconfiguration handled by host profiles.

CAUTION *Keep your host profiles for ESXi and ESX Classic separate from each other. Horrible things will happen to you if you get them mixed up, including the destruction of an ESXi management network. Does that sound like I'm speaking from bitter experience?*

Creating a Host Profile from an Existing ESX Server

Host profiles are associated with the vCenter you logged in to when you created them—this is even the case if you are using the new "linked mode" feature; they are not available *across* multiple vCenter instances even in linked mode. If you are not careful, it is possible to log in to one vCenter instance, and then create a host profile that cannot apply, because it was taken from an ESX host it does not manage. If you are unsure which vCenter instance is your target, check the title bar of the vSphere Client. If you wish to switch your vCenter target without closing and reopening the client, navigate to Home, then Management, click the Host Profiles icon, and then select the vCenter server from the pull-down list.

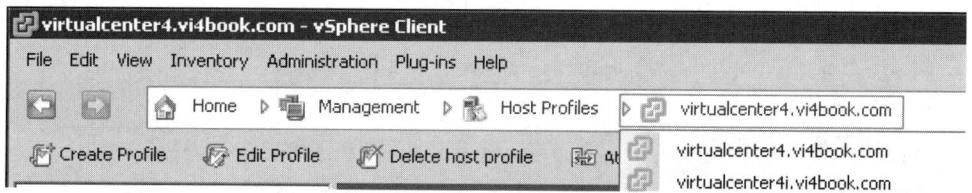

For the examples in this section, I reset my environment. I began with a clean installation, and applied a modest vSwitch, NTP, and firewall configuration to esx1.vi4book.com. The network configuration consisted of the following:

- vSwitch0 for management
- vSwitch1 with multiple VM port groups for VLANs 10, 11, and 12
- vSwitch2 with a VMkernel port group for VMotion and a second Service Console connection for HA heartbeats

- vSwitch3 for dedicated VMware FT logging

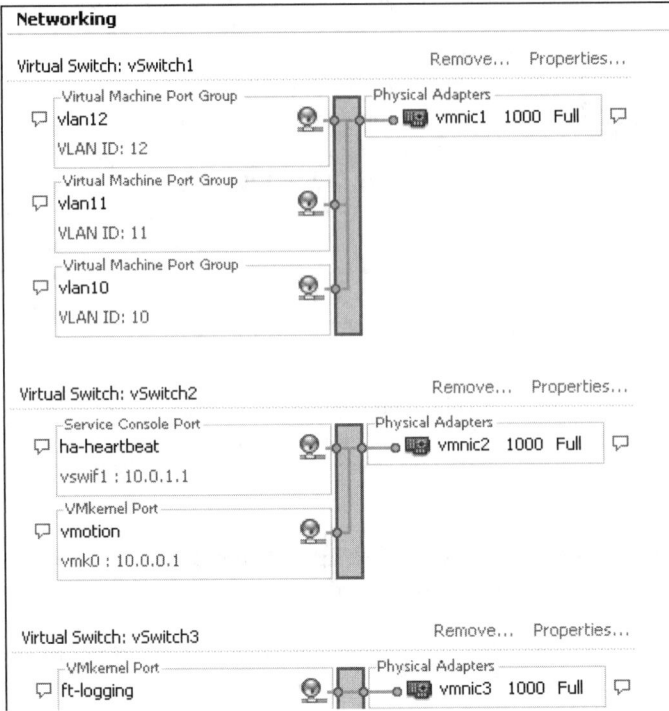

Host profiles have a dizzying number of settings. So, the best way to create a profile is to take one based on an existing ESX host, as this reduces the time wasted navigating the profile interface looking for settings.

Here are the steps for creating a new host profile from an ESX host:

1. Right-click the source ESX host and choose Host Profile.

2. Select Create Profile from Host.

3. Type in a friendly name and description in the Profile Details dialog box.

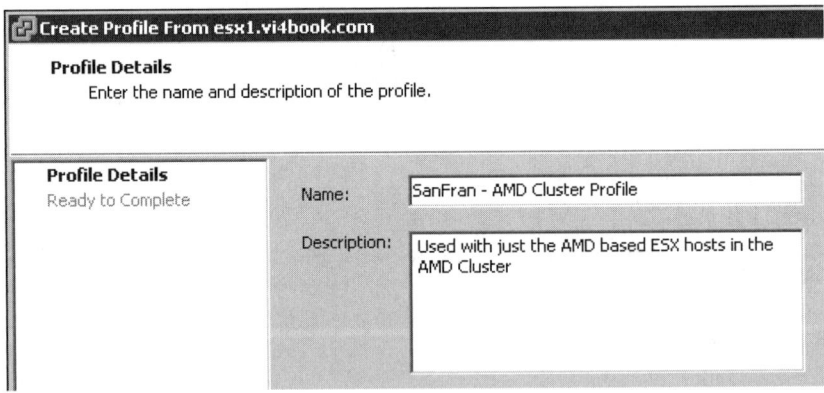

4. Click Next, and then click Finish. This will create a host profile under Host Profiles.

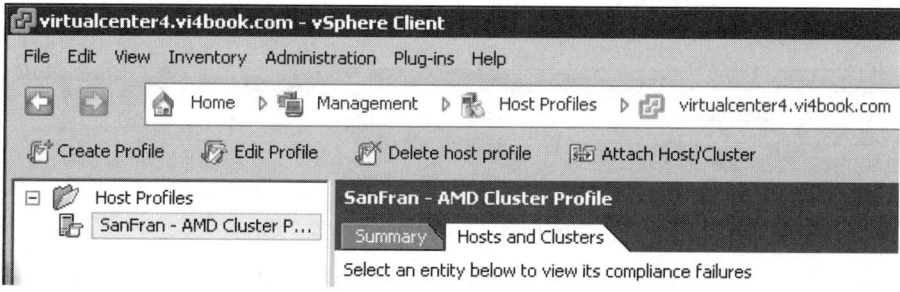

Editing a Host Profile

One major reason to edit a host profile is to deal with the settings that cannot be applied to every ESX host because they are unique, such as the VMotion, HA heartbeat, and FT logging IP addresses. Additionally, you might wish to completely reconfigure a group of ESX hosts, such as by adding a new VLAN to a vSwitch. This could be more easily accomplished with host profiles than manually.

NOTE   *There are a great deal of settings in a host profile—far too many for me to explain each and every one. That would be like me writing a Microsoft Active Directory book, and then describing each and every setting in a Group Policy Object. For the most part, the settings should make sense to anyone who has read this book cover to cover. If you have skipped parts, that might not be the case!*

Follow these steps to edit a host profile:

1. Navigate to Home, then Management, and click the Host Profiles icon.

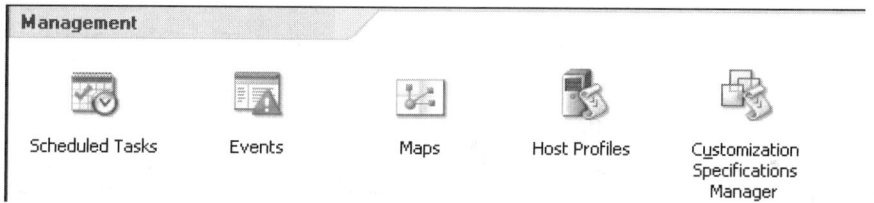

2. Select the host profile you wish to edit, and then click the Edit Profile button.

3. Navigate to Network Configuration, Host Port Group, vmotion, IP Address Settings.

4. Select IP Address, and in the right pane, select the "User specified IP address to be used while applying the configuration" option. This option will prompt the user who adds the ESX host to the cluster to specify an IP address.

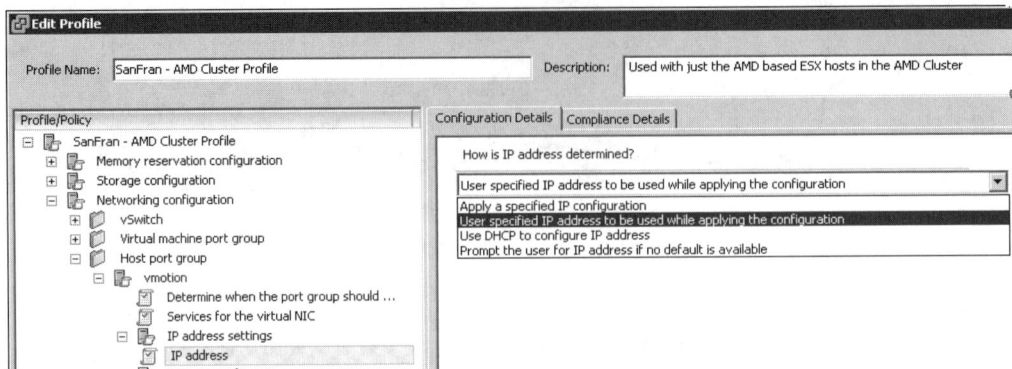

5. Repeat this for all the host port groups and Service Console port groups.

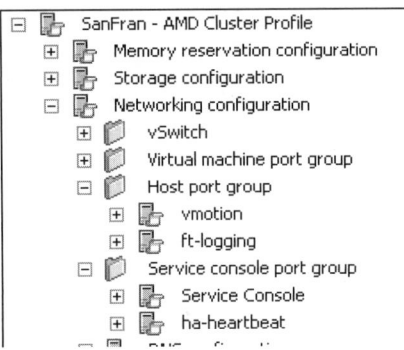

6. Click OK to save the changes to the profile.

Attaching and Applying a Host Profile

You can attach a profile to either an ESX host or a VMware cluster, from the Host Profiles location or from the Hosts and Clusters view. As an example, we will start by attaching the profile to an individual host to confirm that it works. Once we are satisfied that it functions correctly, we will use the host profile to create a new vSwitch on all the ESX hosts in a cluster to demonstrate how a new ESX host inherits the configuration of the cluster.

Attaching a Profile and Checking Host Compliance

Follow these steps to attach the host profile to an ESX host:

1. In the Host Profiles view, select the host profile and click the Attach Host/Cluster icon.

2. In the dialog box, select the target ESX host, and then click the Attach button. Notice how you cannot see the other vCenter in linked mode. This is because the host profile is associated with the vCenter you logged in to initially.

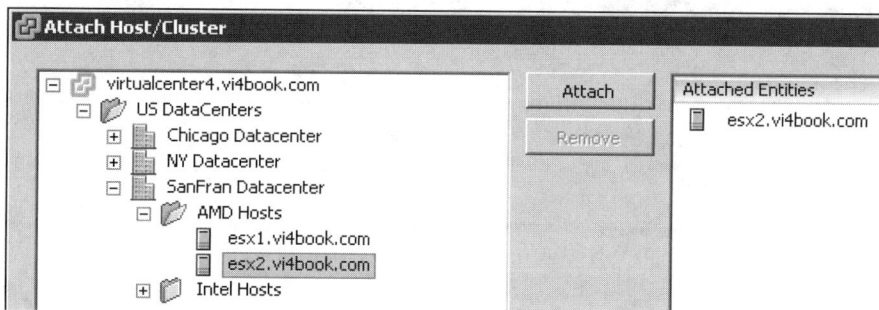

3. Click OK. This will make the selected ESX host appear in the Hosts and Clusters tab in the Host Profiles view with a status of Unknown. This is because it has never been checked to see if it has compliance or been applied.

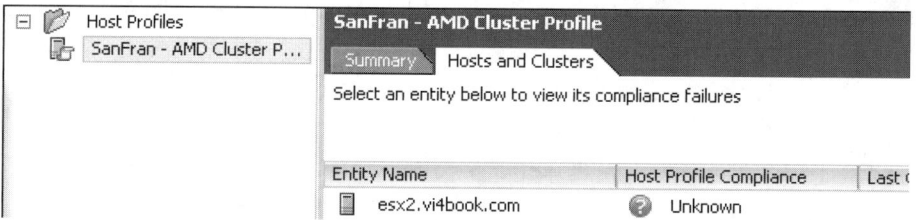

4. Right-click an ESX host and choose Check Compliance Now.

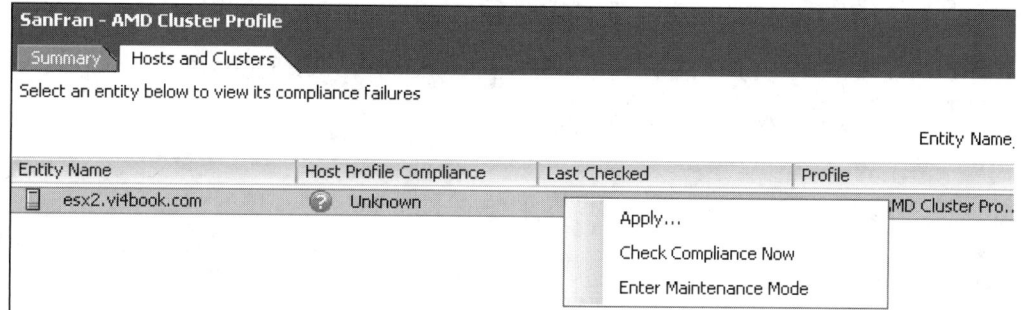

In my case, as esx2.vi4book.com is a cleanly installed ESX host without any settings, the check finds it to be noncompliant.

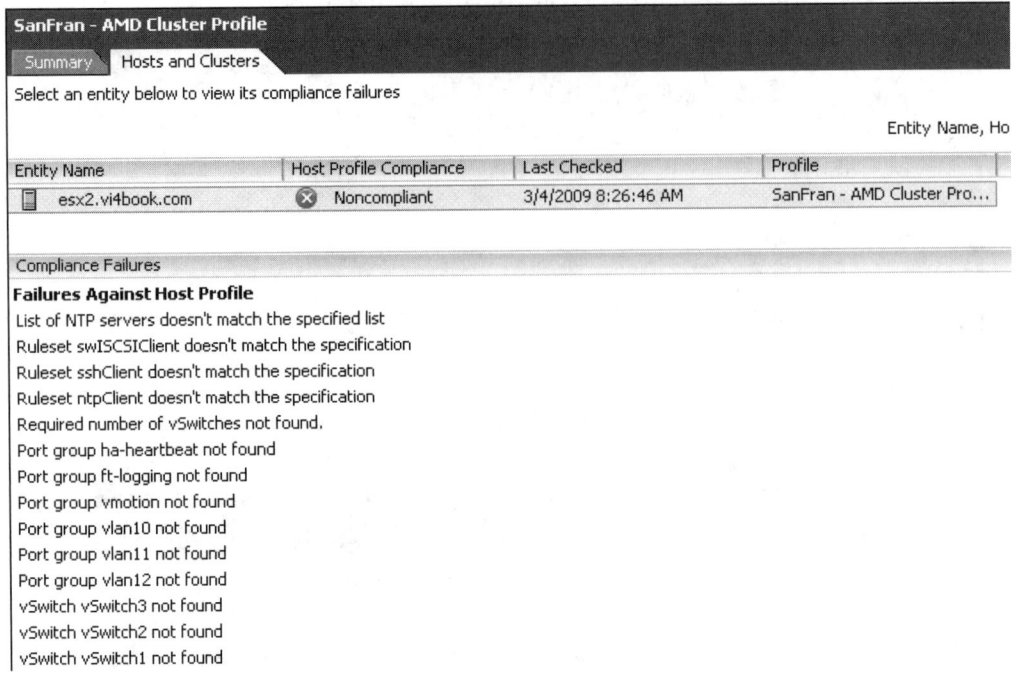

Applying a Host Profile to an ESX Host

Before you can apply a profile to an ESX host, it must be in maintenance mode. You can put it in maintenance mode from the Hosts and Clusters tab in the Host Profiles view. Right-click the ESX host and choose Enter Maintenance Mode. Then right-click the ESX host again and choose Apply. You will see a large dialog box, prompting you to enter the per-ESX host settings.

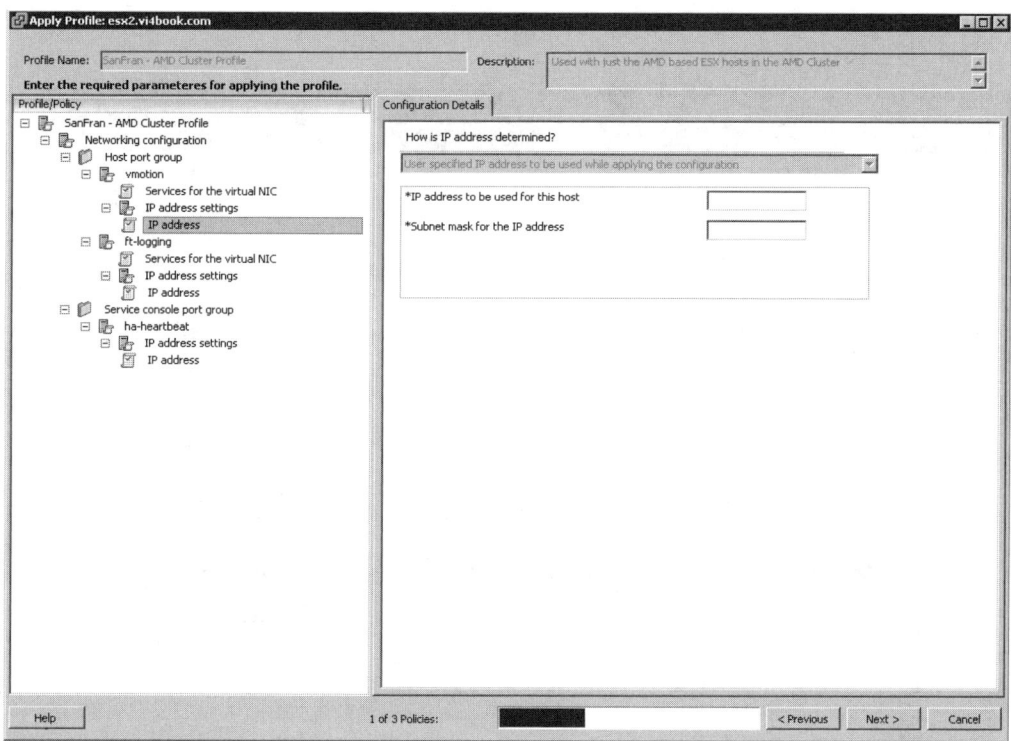

Notice how the bottom of the dialog box in this example says "1 of 3 Policies" and has Next and Previous buttons. This is because this example specified that the administrators must set a unique IP address for VMotion, HA heartbeat, and FT logging.

After entering the configuration details, you will see a summary of the changes applied by the host profile. If you have specified any duplicate IP addresses in this process, you will receive an error message, and the profile will not be applied, thus avoiding the consequences of an IP address conflict.

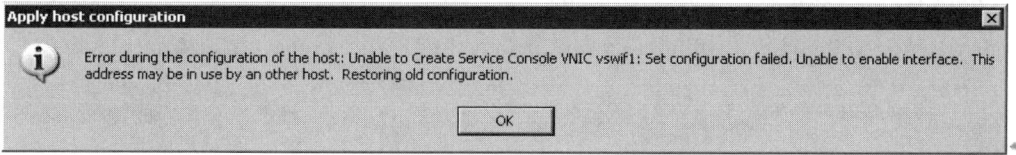

After you apply a host profile, a check compliance routine is automatically executed, and you are then able to exit maintenance mode.

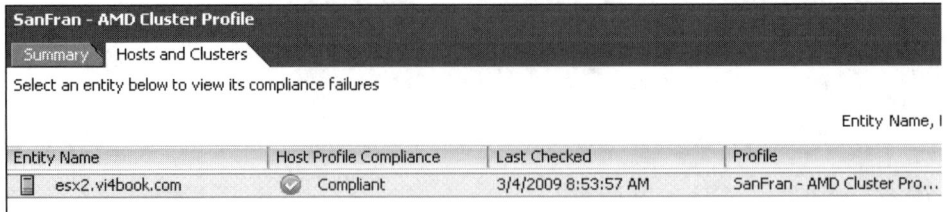

Applying a Host Profile to a Cluster and New ESX Host

It's at this point that host profiles become powerful.

1. In the Host Profiles view, select the host profile, and then click the Attach Host/ Cluster icon.

2. In the dialog box, select the target cluster, and then click the Attach button.

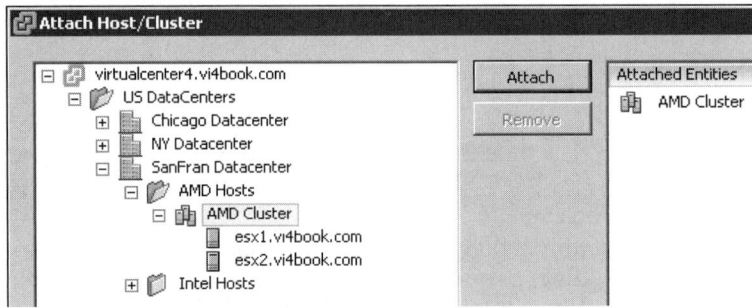

3. In the Hosts and Clusters view, right-click the cluster and choose Add New Host.

4. Right-click the ESX host and choose Enter Maintenance Mode.

5. Right-click the host again and select Apply Profile.

6. Enter the configuration details in the dialog box.

7. Return to the Host Profiles view and run a compliance check against the cluster.

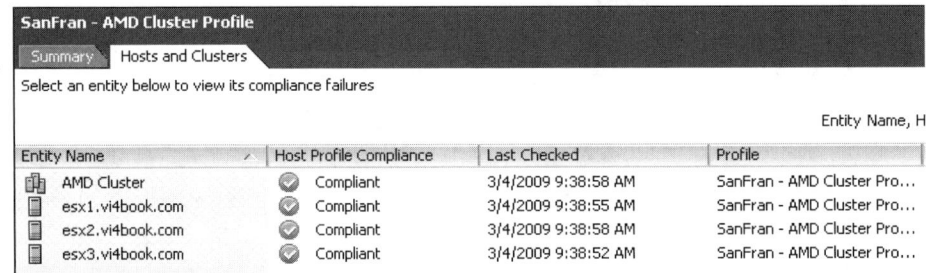

Well, that's the theory at least. In my experience, attaching the ESX host to the cluster directly with DRS/HA/FT enabled can cause more problems than it's worth. I would recommend adding the ESX host to vCenter, attaching and applying the host profile, and *then adding it to a cluster.* This appears to work without complications.

Using a Host Policy to Reconfigure a VMware Cluster

You can use host profiles to reconfigure an existing cluster in several ways, such as to create a new vSwitch, add a new VLAN tagged port group on an existing vSwitch, or add a new NFS mounting point. The downside is that for the host profile to be applied, you must first place the ESX host in maintenance mode, requiring a VMotion event in some cases. Other methods of carrying out this type of bulk administration do not require maintenance mode. Additionally, I've found adding components to an existing host profile can be quite slow sometimes, so you will need to be patient with the hourglass.

As an example, here is the procedure for adding a new VLAN to an existing vSwitch:

1. Edit the host profile.

2. Navigate to Networking Configuration, vSwitch.

3. Right-click Virtual Machine port group and choose Add Profile.

4. Type in the name of the new port group (vlan13 in this example).

5. Select the port group and navigate to VLAN ID Configuration and the VLAN ID policy setting. Enter the VLAN ID (13 in this example).

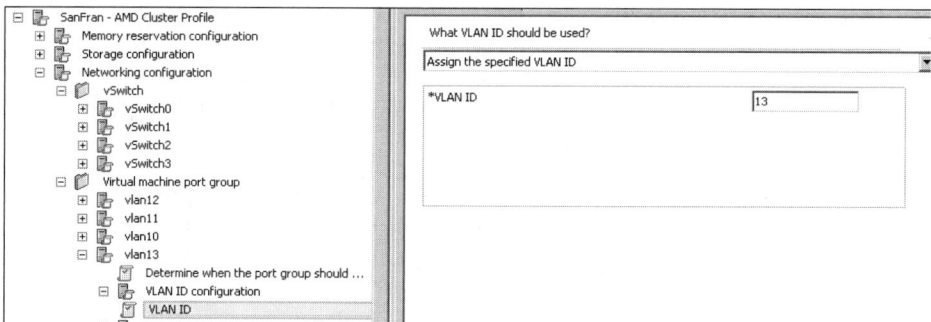

6. Select Switch Selection, and then select the "vSwitch to connect to" policy setting. Indicate on which switch this port group will be created.

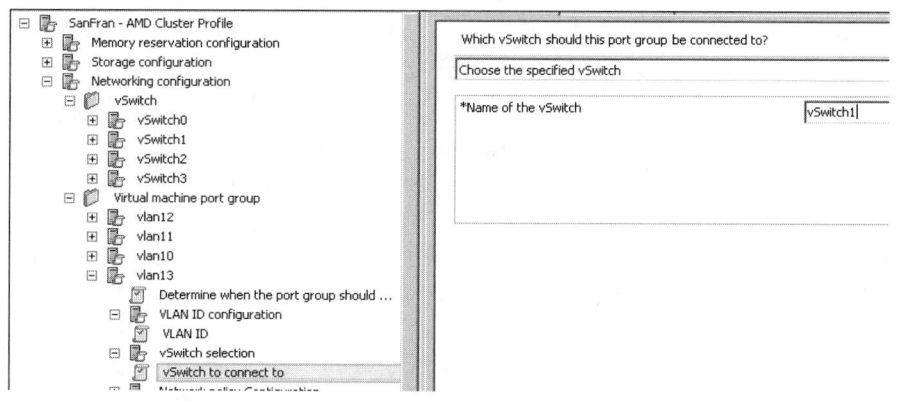

Updating and Exporting Host Profiles

It is possible to update the host profile from the original source ESX host from which it was created, and also to change to a different ESX host as your original source of the host profile. Additionally, host profiles created in one vCenter can be exported into the VMware Profile Format (.vpf) and imported to the destination vCenter environment with the Create New Profile wizard. You will find these options on the right-click menu of the host profile.

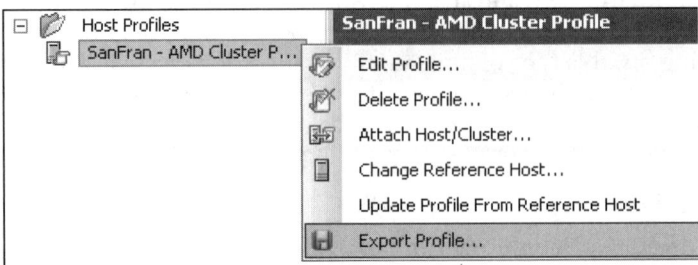

Using the vSphere CLI with ESX 4

I have tested the vSphere CLI against the ESX Classic version, and it works just fine. However, as I noted earlier, the vCLI does not duplicate all of the command-line tools of the Service Console. Therefore, there are some operations that you are unable to achieve with it, including adding a second Service Console port for the VMware iSCSI software initiator and VMware HA. You also cannot open the firewall ports for iSCSI, as the vCLI currently does not have an esxcfg-firewall equivalent.

As I mentioned in Chapter 12, the vCLI comes in three flavors: Windows installer, Linux installer, and a downloadable VM (called the VMware Management Appliance). They all use the Perl environment. The Windows version has ActivePerl installed, so it understands the .pl files that make up the vCLI. I tend to use the Windows version, mainly because my PC and management server (vCenter) run in Windows. The functionality of the different versions is much the same.

You can download the vSphere CLI and other scripting tools from this VMware Communites page:

http://communities.vmware.com/community/vmtn/vsphere/automationtools

After installing the vCLI, you will find that in the C:\Program Files\VMware\VMware VI VSphere CLI\bin directory, you have two main types of commands: ones beginning with esxcfg- expect to have an ESX host used with them, and ones beginning with vicfg- expect a valid name for vCenter and an ESX host. Both commands carry out the same function—it's just how you authenticate is different. I would recommend limiting yourself to the vicfg- commands, as VMware doesn't have a clear long term commitment to supporting the esxcfg- commands within the vCLI. As noted in VMware's PDF guide for the vCLI:

"VMware recommends that you use the command with the vicfg prefix. Commands with the esxcfg prefix are available mainly for compatibility reasons and might become obsolete."

The vCLI is useful for performing common configuration tasks after an installation has been completed or ESXi 4 has been enabled, such as the following:

- Creating vSwitches
- Setting up DNS
- Configuring NTP
- Enabling the VMware iSCSI software initiator
- Configuring NAS

NOTE *This section is meant as a tutorial and not a comprehensive demonstration or review of every single vCLI command and switch. If you want to learn more, consult the online documentation from VMware once you feel comfortable with this material.*

vCLI Frustrations

I find the vCLI can be quite frustrating when you first start using it, because each command can take some time to execute because of the authentication process. If your command has a syntax error, the command then scrolls an entire help page up the screen. This means you need to scroll back up the help page to find an error message that would help you with the syntax error. You then need to correct your error and repeat the command.

While the vCLI is quite well documented by VMware, it has limited detail on some commands, which forces you to use the sometimes obtuse command-line help to distinguish the required parameters from the optional ones. A case in point is the vicfg-swisci.pl script.

```
C:\Program Files\VMware\VMware VI Remote CLI\bin>vicfg-iscsi.pl --vihost=esx1.vi4book.com --parameter --lis
adapter_name is required.

Synopsis: C:\Program Files\VMware\VMware VI Remote CLI\bin\vicfg-iscsi.pl OPTIONS [<vmhba>]


Command-specific options:
   --adapter
   -H

        List iSCSI adapter(s).
```

Fortunately, there are resources (like forums and this book) to help you through the pain barrier! When VMware doesn't document things very well, I see that as an opportunity for Mr. RTFM to come to the rescue!

Authenticating to a Server

All vCLI commands require a host (ESX or vCenter), username, and password (HUP) to authenticate against the system prior to the command being executed. There are three ways to authenticate:

- Use a session file—a cookie that expires after 30 minutes of nonuse.
- Create a configuration file that holds your variables in a user account detailed in a file protected by file permissions.
- Pass-through the credentials of the current logon to the Microsoft Security Support Provider Interface (SSPI).

Creating a Session File to Store User Credentials

The following vCLI command creates a vSwitch. As you can see, the vast majority of this command is the specification of server names and user credentials.

```
vicfg-vswitch.pl --server=virtualcenter4.vi4book.com --
username=administrator  --password=vmware --vihost=esx1.vi4book.com -
a=vSwitch1
```

Using a session file reduces the amount of time spent specifying the names of servers and the user credentials. Using the vCLI toolkit, you can create a session file that stores all this information securely, and then you can call this file before executing commands.

To create a sample session file, open a command prompt at C:\Program Files \VMware \VMware VSphere CLI \Perl \apps \session and enter the following:

```
save_session.pl --savesessionfile c:\vc4
--server virtualcenter4.vi4book.com
--username administrator --password vmware
```

This will respond with the message "Session information saved" and create a file on drive C: called vc4, which will store your credentials in a cookie. This cookie looks like this if you view the contents of the file:

```
#LWP-Cookies-1.0
Set-Cookie3:vmware_soap_session="\"A1312BB4-3F79-45A4-BDE0-0AC267A69B58\"";
path="/"; domain=virtualcenter4.vi4book.com; path_spec; discard; version=0
```

Next, set the following variable:

```
set VI_SAVESESSIONFILE=c:\vc4
```

This `set` command saves you from having to specify the location of the session file every time you run a vCLI command, so you don't need to enter something like this:

```
vicfg-vswitch.pl -sessionfile=c:\vc4 --vihost=esx1.vi4book.com -a=vSwitch1
```

A session file is secure because it times out after a period of time. And you do need not specify the entire HUP to the vCLI; you just specify the ESX host on which you wish the command to execute.

Creating a Configuration File to Store User Credentials

One of the downsides of using a session file is that it does expire. If you want to keep your scripts and reuse them, you probably want to store your server names and credentials in a configuration file that is secured with NTFS permissions, rather than a cookie.

As an example, create a configuration file using Notepad by entering this command:

```
notepad c:\virtualcenter4.txt
```

And then add the following lines to the file:

```
VI_SERVER=vCenter.vi4book.com
VI_USERNAME=administrator
VI_PASSWORD=vmware
```

Make sure you secure this file with NTFS permissions in Windows so only your login account has access rights.

To ensure you don't need to specify the path to the configuration file every time you run a vCLI command, set the following variable:

```
set VI_CONFIG=c:\virtualcenter4.txt
```

Like the `set` command in the previous example, this saves you from needing to specify the location of the configuration file every time you run a vCLI command, so you don't need to enter something like this:

```
vicfg-vswitch.pl --config=c:\vCenter.txt --vihost=esx1.vi4book.com -
a=vSwitch1
```

To make this variable last beyond your current session, you would need to modify your default environmental variables in Windows by adding `VI_CONFIG` to your Windows session (open the System Control Panel, click the Advanced tab, and choose Environmental Variables).

Configuring Microsoft Windows Pass-Through Authentication

Another way of authenticating with the vCLI is with Windows pass-through authentication. This takes your current logged-on credentials (or the credentials of your scheduling agent) and uses them in the vCLI command. If the vCLI is installed locally to the vCenter, then local users can be used; if it is used remotely, you must use domain credentials.

By default, pass-through authentication is set to negotiate a common protocol through which to pass the username and password details. If necessary, in this configuration, you can set a variable called `VI_PASSTHROUGHAUTHPACKAGE`, which overrides this negotiated method, as in the following:

```
--passthroughauth --passthroughauthpackage "Kerberos"
```

Creating vSwitches

As noted earlier, one of the common tasks that you can perform using the vCLI is creating vSwitches, The next examples demonstrate how to create vSwitches using each of the authentication methods described in the previous section.

Creating an Internal vSwitch

Using a combination of `vicfg-vswitch` commands, together with the sample session file we created earlier, we can quickly build a vSwitch configuration for an ESX host.

Create a vSwitch using vCenter to authenticate, `vihost` to indicate which ESX host will create the switch, and the `-a` `switch`, as follows:

```
vicfg-vswitch.pl --vihost=esx1.vi4book.com -a=vSwitch1
```

Using `-A`, create a port group called esx1-internal0:

```
vicfg-vswitch.pl --vihost=esx1.vi4book.com -A=esx1-internal0 vSwitch1
```

Using –l, list the vSwitches on the ESX host and verify your work:

```
vicfg-vswitch.pl --vihost=esx1.vi4book.com -l
```

This will produce output as in the following example.

```
Switch Name      Num Ports    Used Ports         Configured Ports    MTU     Uplinks
vSwitch0         32           3                  32                  1500    vmnic0

   PortGroup Name               ULAN ID    Used Ports     Uplinks
   UM Network                   0          0              vmnic0
   Service Console              0          1              vmnic0

Switch Name      Num Ports    Used Ports         Configured Ports    MTU     Uplinks
vSwitch1         64           1                  64                  1500

   PortGroup Name               ULAN ID    Used Ports     Uplinks
   esx1-internal0               0          0
```

You will also see these commands are tracked in vCenter, as that is the system through which you are sending your vCLI commands. One of the great things about the new CLIs is, because they interact via vCenter, the result is a scripting solution that more closely integrates and logs against the management system.

Recent Tasks		
Name	Target	Status
Add Port Group	esx1.vi4book...	Completed
Add Virtual Switch	esx1.vi4book...	Completed

Creating a vSwitch with VLAN Tagging Support

In this example, we will use the sample configuration file we saved earlier and create a vSwitch with three port groups—called vlan10, vlan11, and vlan12—and set the VLAN tagging value accordingly. We will then attach two NICs to the vSwitch for load balancing and fault tolerance.

Create a new vSwitch using the –a switch, as in the previous example:

```
vicfg-vswitch.pl --vihost=esx1.vi4book.com -a=vSwitch2
```

Using –A, create port groups called vlan10, vlan11, and vlan12:

```
vicfg-vswitch.pl --vihost=esx1.vi4book.com -A=vlan10 vSwitch2
vicfg-vswitch.pl --vihost=esx1.vi4book.com -A=vlan11 vSwitch2
vicfg-vswitch.pl --vihost=esx1.vi4book.com -A=vlan12 vSwitch2
```

Using –v and –p, set the VLAN value on the properties of the correct port group:

```
vicfg-vswitch.pl --vihost=esx1.vi4book.com -v=10 -p vlan10 vSwitch2
vicfg-vswitch.pl --vihost=esx1.vi4book.com -v=11 -p vlan10 vSwitch2
vicfg-vswitch.pl --vihost=esx1.vi4book.com -v=12 -p vlan10 vSwitch2
```

Finally, using –L, link the relevant NICs to the vSwitch:

```
vicfg-vswitch.pl --vihost=esx1.vi4book.com -L=vmnic1 vSwitch2
vicfg-vswitch.pl --vihost=esx1.vi4book.com -L=vmnic2 vSwitch2
```

Creating a VMkernel Port for VMotion

In this example, using Windows pass-through authentication, we will create a third vSwitch with a port group called vmotion. Then we will set this to be a VMkernel port with a valid IP address for the VMotion network.

First, create a new vSwitch, as in the previous examples:

```
vicfg-vswitch.pl --passthroughauth --vihost=esx1.vi4book.com -a=vSwitch3
```

Next, create a port group called vmotion:

```
vicfg-vswitch.pl --passthroughauth --vihost=esx1.vi4book.com -A=vmotion
vSwitch3
```

Link the relevant NICs to the vSwitch:

```
vicfg-vswitch.pl --passthroughauth --vihost=esx1.vi4book.com -L=vmnic3
vSwitch3
```

Finally, using the `vicfg-vmknic.pl` command, add (`-a`) the IP address (`-i`) and subnet mask (`-n`) for the VMotion port group:

```
vicfg-vmknic.pl --passthroughauth --vihost=esx1.vi4book.com
-a -i 10.0.0.1 -n 255.255.255.0 -p vmotion
```

As with the `esxcfg-vmknic` command at the Service Console, this utility does *not* in itself enable VMotion on the VMkernel port.

Enabling the VMware iSCSI Software Initiator

Another common use of the vCLI is to enable the iSCSI software initiator (discussed in Chapter 6). Before enabling the initiator, set up the appropriate IP layer for iSCSI. The following commands demonstrate how to create a vSwitch with a valid port group for iSCSI communications:

```
vicfg-vswitch.pl --vihost=esx1.vi4book.com --a=vSwitch4
vicfg-vswitch.pl --vihost=esx1.vi4book.com --A=ipstorage vSwitch4
vicfg-vswitch.pl --vihost=esx1.vi4book.com -L=vmnic3 vSwitch4
vicfg-vswitch.pl --vihost=esx1.vi4book.com -L=vmnic4 vSwitch4
vicfg-vmknic.pl --vihost=esx1.vi4book.com -a -i 172.168.3.101 -n
255.255.255.0 -p ipstorage
```

Optionally, if your network supports this setting you can enable a larger MTU (also called jumbo frames) with the `vicfg-vswitch.pl -m` switch, like so:

```
vicfg-vswitch.pl --vihost=esx1.vi4book.com -m=9000 vSwitch4
```

CAUTION *Remember that arbitrarily changing the MTU value is not recommended without appropriate research and configuration of the physical network data layer. Unexpected and horrible events could occur if the value is set incorrectly.*

The following example shows how I have changed the MTU value for vSwitch4.

```
Switch Name      Num Ports     Used Ports        Configured Ports      MTU     Uplinks
vSwitch0         32            3                 32                    1500    vmnic0

    PortGroup Name             VLAN ID   Used Ports      Uplinks
    UM Network                 0         0               vmnic0
    Service Console            0         1               vmnic0

Switch Name      Num Ports     Used Ports        Configured Ports      MTU     Uplinks
vSwitch1         64            1                 64                    1500

    PortGroup Name             VLAN ID   Used Ports      Uplinks
    esx1-internal0             0         0

Switch Name      Num Ports     Used Ports        Configured Ports      MTU     Uplinks
vSwitch2         64            2                 64                    1500    vmnic1

    PortGroup Name             VLAN ID   Used Ports      Uplinks
    production                 0         0               vmnic1

Switch Name      Num Ports     Used Ports        Configured Ports      MTU     Uplinks
vSwitch3         64            3                 64                    1500    vmnic2

    PortGroup Name             VLAN ID   Used Ports      Uplinks
    vmotion                    0         1               vmnic2

Switch Name      Num Ports     Used Ports        Configured Ports      MTU     Uplinks
vSwitch4         64            4                 64                    9000    vmnic3

    PortGroup Name             VLAN ID   Used Ports      Uplinks
    ipstorage                  0         1               vmnic3
```

To enable the VMware iSCSI software initiator, use `vicfg-iscsi.pl` with the `-E` and `-e` switches. The uppercase `-E` indicates you are managing the iSCSI software initiator, rather than a hardware iSCSI adapter, and the lowercase `-e` indicates you are enabling it.

```
vicfg-iscsi.pl --vihost=esx1.vi4book.com -E -e
```

I prefer to use one-character switches, since I have less to type at the command line. Also, my text strings are not muddled up with the longer, although more meaningful, command-line switches. However, if you I think this `-E -e` syntax looks a bit strange and cryptic, you might prefer to use something less obtuse: `swiscsi`. The following command uses `swiscsi` instead of `-E`, and performs the same task as the previous example:

```
vicfg-iscsi.pl --vihost=esx1.vi4book.com -- swiscsi -e
```

To find out the virtual device HBA name of the VMware iSCSI software initiator, use the following command:

```
vicfg-iscsi.pl --vihost=esx1.vi4book.com -l -H
```

This should give you output such as the following:

```
vmhba34 - iSCSI Software Adapter
```

To find out your current IQN details, you can use –E (or --swiscsi) to indicate you are using the VMware iSCSI software initiator, -l to list, and –P to indicate you want to know the settings on the virtual HBA (vmhba34 in this example):

```
vicfg-iscsi.pl --vihost=esx1.vi4book.com -E -l -P vmhba34
```

The following example shows the output from the listing of the HBA.

```
=========PHBA Properties for Adapter vmhba34=========
VENDOR                        : VMware
MODEL                         : iSCSI Software Adapter
DESCRIPTION                   : VMware Software Initiator
SERIAL NUMBER                 :

=========Node Properties for Adapter vmhba34=========
NODE NAME VALID               : 1
NODE NAME                     : iqn.1998-02.com.vmware:esx1-d893hfdo
NODE ALIAS VALID              : 1
NODE ALIAS                    : esx1.vi4book.com
NODE NAME AND ALIAS SETTABLE  :
```

A less verbose output can be created using the command switches –E –l –I:

```
vicfg-iscsi.pl --vihost=esx1.vi4book.com -E -l -I vmhba34
```

Set the correct IQN for your VM HBA interface, using –I to set the iSCSI name, -n to set the name, and –k to set the alias:

```
vicfg-iscsi.pl --vihost=esx1.vi4book.com
-I -n=iqn.2008-11.com.vi4book:esx1 -k=esx1 vmhba34
```

NOTE *Due to their length, some of the commands have been wrapped here to make them fit more neatly on the page.*

Add the iSCSI target with –a to add, -D to discover, and –i to set the IP address:

```
vicfg-iscsi.pl --vihost=esx1.vi4book.com -a -D -i=172.168.3.99 vmhba34
```

This should respond with the message "Adding discovery address 172.168.3.99:3260 ..." Finally, issue a rescan and list the LUNs available on the target:

```
vicfg-rescan.pl --vihost=esx1.vi4book.com vmhba34
vicfg-iscsi.pl --vihost=esx1.vi4book.com -E -l -L vmhba34
```

The uppercase -L allows you to list (-l) LUNs on the VMware iSCSI software initiator (-E). The following example shows the output of this command.

```
Target: iqn.2003-10.com.lefthandnetworks:sanfran-management-group:11:citrix:
-------------------------------------------------
OS DEVICE NAME   : 02000000006000eb3363e59772000000000000000b695343534944
BUS NUMBER       : 0
TARGET ID        : 4
LUN ID           : 0
LUN SIZE         : 1048576 MB

-------------------------------------------------

Target: iqn.2003-10.com.lefthandnetworks:sanfran-management-group:18:web:
-------------------------------------------------
OS DEVICE NAME   : 02000000006000eb3363e5977200000000000000012695343534944
BUS NUMBER       : 0
TARGET ID        : 1
LUN ID           : 0
LUN SIZE         : 1048576 MB

-------------------------------------------------

Target: iqn.2003-10.com.lefthandnetworks:sanfran-management-group:14:sql:
-------------------------------------------------
OS DEVICE NAME   : 02000000006000eb3363e59772000000000000000e695343534944
BUS NUMBER       : 0
TARGET ID        : 3
LUN ID           : 0
LUN SIZE         : 1048576 MB

-------------------------------------------------

Target: iqn.2003-10.com.lefthandnetworks:sanfran-management-group:20:file:
-------------------------------------------------
OS DEVICE NAME   : 02000000006000eb3363e5977200000000000000014695343534944
BUS NUMBER       : 0
TARGET ID        : 0
LUN ID           : 0
LUN SIZE         : 1048576 MB

-------------------------------------------------

Target: iqn.2003-10.com.lefthandnetworks:sanfran-management-group:16:ad:
-------------------------------------------------
OS DEVICE NAME   : 02000000006000eb3363e5977200000000000000010695343534944
BUS NUMBER       : 0
TARGET ID        : 2
LUN ID           : 0
LUN SIZE         : 1048576 MB
```

If you are dealing with an iSCSI target that requires CHAP authentication, this can be configured with vicfg-iscsi.pl script, as follows:

```
vicfg-iscsi.pl --vihost=esx1.vi4book.com
-A -m=CHAP -c=chapRequired -u=iqn.2008-11.com.vi4book:esx1 -w=vmware
vmhba34
```

The -A switch sets the authentication, and the -m switch sets the method of authentication. The -c switch sets the type of CHAP authentication (chapProhibited, chapDiscouraged, chapPreferred, or chapRequired). The -u and -w switches set the username and password for the virtual vmhba iSCSI device.

NOTE *It took me most of the morning to work out the syntax of the darn vicfg-iscsi.pl script. Isn't that just the way in IT infrastructure—all that hard work, and no one bloomin' well notices or appreciates it, except you do, don't ya?*

Setting Your NTP Configuration

The time configuration utility is very easy to use. You can easily set multiple NTP servers and restart the service to allow these changes to take effect. The −a switch allows you to allocate a NTP service by name or IP address, and the −s and −r switches can be used to stop and start the NTP service on the ESX host.

```
vicfg-ntp.pl --vihost=esx1.vi4book.com -a=0.uk.pool.ntp.org
vicfg-ntp.pl --vihost=esx1.vi4book.com -a=1.uk.pool.ntp.org
vicfg-ntp.pl --vihost=esx1.vi4book.com -a=2.uk.pool.ntp.org
vicfg-ntp.pl --vihost=esx1.vi4book.com -s
vicfg-ntp.pl --vihost=esx1.vi4book.com -r
```

Configuring NAS

In contrast to the iSCSI configuration script, the script for configuring NAS, vicfg-nas.pl, is easy to use. The −a switch adds the NAS mount point into ESX, with the −o switch setting the name or IP address of the NAS service. The −s switch specifies the share name, indicated with a forward slash (/), followed by the friendly datastore name as used by the ESX host.

```
vicfg-nas.pl --vihost=esx1.vi4book.com -a -o=nfs1.vi4book.com -s=/iso nas-iso
```

Managing Files

You can use the vifs.pl script to manage the VMFS file system. It's important to know that this is one of the few commands that does not use the vihost= parameter. This command only works directly on the ESX host. It does not work via vCenter.

You can perform many actions with vifs.pl, including uploading and downloading files, listing directories, finding datastores, and copying files from one datastore to another. I recommend that you begin by listing the datastores available and experiment with uploading files from the system running the vCLI to the ESX host, just as you would with the vSphere Client and the Datastore Browser in the GUI. Using −S and providing the credentials as a parameter to the command will allow you to list the datastores available:

```
vifs.pl --server=esx1.vi4book.com --username=root --password=vmware –S
```

After gaining a list of accessible storage locations, you can think about uploading files via the ESX host. Use the −p switch to put files onto the datastore by first supplying the path to the local file, and then the destination, in the [datastorename] /directory form you saw in the SVMotion examples in Chapter 12:

```
vifs.pl --server=esx3.vi4book.com --username=root --password=vmware
-p=c:\w2k3.iso "[iso] /ms/w2k3.iso"
```

Notice how with vifs.pl you must specify the filename twice: once for the file to copy at the source, and again to specify the destination file you wish to create.

Creating a Snapshot of a VM and Exporting Its Files to Local Storage

This section provides a little demonstration of two utilities: vmware-cmd, a multipurpose command used to manipulate VMs at the command line, and vmkfstools, another multipurpose VM file and VMFS volume management tool. As an example, I will show how to use these tools together to archive a VM's virtual disk, in what is essentially a crude VM backup routine. I wouldn't recommend actually using these tools for this purpose, but this example does show you the syntax of these commands, how they differ significantly from the standard `vicfg-` commands, and how to use them together.

Locating a VM and Creating a Snapshot

To use the `vmware-cmd` command against a VM, you must know the path to the .vmx file. You can use `vmware-cmd` to retrieve a list of VMs on a given ESX host, as follows:

```
vmware-cmd.pl -H virtualcenter4.vi4book.com -U administrator -P vmware -T
esx1.vi4book.com -1
/vmfs/volumes/4919ab0b-878ebadc-159f-001560ace440/web02/web02.vmx
/vmfs/volumes/4919ab0b-878ebadc-159f-001560ace440/ctx02/ctx02.vmx
/vmfs/volumes/4919ab0b-878ebadc-159f-001560ace440/ctx01/ctx01.vmx
/vmfs/volumes/4919ab0b-878ebadc-159f-001560ace440/sql01/sql01.vmx
```

Notice how this command does not obey the conventions of the other vCLI commands you have seen so far from an authentication perspective. The HUP is used against the vCenter server to handle authentication, but the `-T` switch queries a specific ESX host (the target) to return the VMs currently registered on it together with `-1`. The `vmware-cmd` command does support the `[datastorename] /vmname/vnname.vmx` format for specifying the location of the .vmx file.

Once you have the full UUID path for the .vmx file, you can send instructions to take a snapshot of the VM in question with `vmware-cmd`:

```
vmware-cmd.pl -H virtualcenter4.vi4book.com -U administrator -P vmware -T
esx1.vi4book.com
/vmfs/volumes/4919ab0b-878ebadc-159f-001560ace440/web02/web02.vmx
createsnapshot "Before Export" "Taken before using vmkfstools to export the
VM to the 2gbsparse format" 1 1
```

First, you supply the HUP and `-T` values, together with the path to the .vmx file. Then you use the `vmware-cmd` switch `createsnapshot`, followed by the snapshot name and description, respectively. The two numbers at the end of the command, `1 1`, indicate you want to quiesce the VM during the snapshot period and take a snapshot of the contents of the VM's memory.

This snapshot process will be displayed in the GUI, and if you open the Snapshots window, you will see the snapshot with its description.

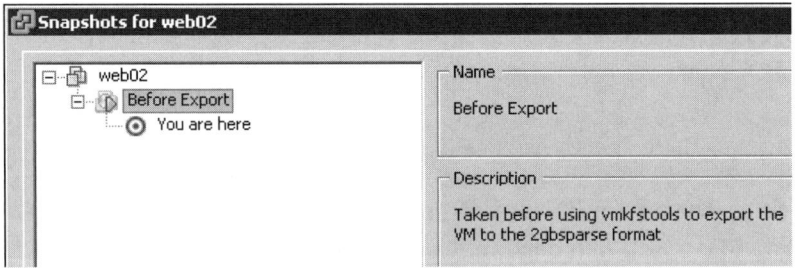

Exporting a VM to Local Storage

You can use the `vmkfstools.pl` script to export a virtual disk from the flat or monolithic format to the more archive-efficient format of 2gbsparse. Like the `vmware-cmd` script, `vmkfstools` does not comply with the authentication conventions of the `vicfg-` commands. This utility must be used directly against an ESX host, and for high-level actions such as formatting a VMFS volume, it may need root account access to work.

Use the following command to export a VM:

```
vmkfstools.pl --server esx1.vi4book.com --username root --password vmware
-i /vmfs /volumes /sanlun1 /web02 /web02.vmdk -d 2gbsparse /vmfs /volumes
/esx1_local /backup_web02.vmdk
```

The command begins with the HUP. Then it uses the `-i` switch to copy the virtual disk and the `-d` switch to set the destination disk format.

This export process is possible because, while a snapshot is engaged, it is possible to copy the VM's files. This is the bedrock of hot backups of the VM, which we will look at in more detail in the next chapter.

At the end of the export process, you should have a much smaller set of files. The format uses just the virtual disk space your files are consuming, rather than your files plus free unreserved virtual disk space.

You can view the exported version of the backup_web02.vmdk files with the `vifs.pl` command and the `-D` switch, which allows you to print a directory listing of the datastore:

```
vifs.pl --server=esx1.vi4book.com --username=root --password=vmware -D
[esx1_local]
```

```
C:\Program Files\VMware\VMware VI Remote CLI\bin>vifs.pl --server=esx1.vi4book.com --username=root --password=vmware -D [esx1_local
backup_web02-s002.vmdk
backup_web02-s003.vmdk
backup_web02-s004.vmdk
backup_web02-s005.vmdk
backup_web02-s006.vmdk
backup_web02.vmdk
esxconsole-48e51c2f-babd-c470-130e-001560ace440/
```

Commiting a Snapshot of a VM

Once the export process has completed, you no longer need the snapshot on the VM. You again use `vmware-cmd` to merge the changes accrued in the snapshot files into the virtual disk, and then delete unwanted snapshot data:

```
vmware-cmd.pl -H virtualcenter4.vi4book.com -U administrator -P vmware -T
esx1.vi4book.com
/vmfs/volumes/4919ab0b-878ebadc-159f-001560ace440/web02/web02.vmx
removesnapshots
```

Backing Up Your ESXi Configuration

It is possible to back up the configuration of the ESXi 4 host to a file, and restore it to the same host. This is especially useful if you intend to carry out a factory reset and you want to quickly restore your configuration. The command is not available via vCenter, and it is not intended for use with an ESX Classic host; it is supported only with ESXi 4.

You might want to consider moving all the VMs of the ESXi 4 host before triggering the backup, as the backup process does also include the list of VMs registered on the ESXi host.

It's safer not to have any registered VMs on the ESXi 4 host, to ensure you don't end up with two ESX hosts believing they both "own" the same VMs.

Use the following command to make the backup:

```
vicfg-cfgbackup.pl --server=esx3.vi4book.com --username=root --
password=vmware -s c:\esx3.bak
```

After executing this command, you will see this result:

```
Saving firmware configuration to c:\esx1.bak ...
```

The backup file (esx3.bak in this example) is a binary file, not a plain text file, and as such *cannot* be edited with a text editor or viewed with the Microsoft type command.

Before you test your backup, migrate all VMs off the ESXi host, and then perform a factory reset on the ESXi 4 host. To do this, you can use the management console of the ESXi 4 host. Alternatively, you can use the vicfg-cfgbackup.pl command, which contains the −r switch to trigger a factory reset. You can also add the −q switch, which will automate entering maintenance mode, a factory reset, and a reboot.

```
vicfg-cfgbackup.pl --server=esx3.vi4book.com --username=root --
password=vmware -r -q
```

The vCLI will report that it is entering maintenance mode and then exiting maintenance mode.

Once the system has rebooted, you will need to reconfigure your password and possibly your IP configuration. You will also probably need to communicate remotely with the ESXi 4 host to restore the backup configuration you created earlier. Alternatively, if you run DHCP in your server room, as I do to facilitate PXE booting for installations, then simply knowing the IP address assigned to the ESXi 4 system is enough to begin the restore process, as long as you have set some kind of password on the factory-reset ESXi 4 host. Whatever method you chose to temporarily allow network communication to the ESXi 4 host, you *must* set a password on the system in question, because vicfg-cfgbackup.pl does not support blank passwords for the authentication process.

To restore your ESXi 4 host configuration, at the vCLI prompt, type the following command:

```
vicfg-cfgbackup.pl --server=192.168.2.33 --username=root --password=vmware
-l c:\esx1.bak -f -q
```

The -l and -f switches force a reload of your backup file. The −q switch displays a prompt asking if you are sure you wish to carry out the task.

The vCLI will report the following:

```
Uploading config bundle to configBundle.tgz...
Performing restore...
```

Once the restore process has completed, the ESXi 4 host will automatically reboot itself. When it reboots, it is identical to the host that is still listed in vCenter. As such, it should exit maintenance mode and rejoin vCenter, and as a consequence, the cluster.

Using the vSphere Management Assistant

The vSphere Management Assistant (vMA) is yet another CLI environment, which is similar to the vCLI in terms of functionality and feel. vMA is actually a virtual appliance you can download from the VMware web site. It includes the vSphere CLI, VI Perl Toolkit, a logging component, and an authentication component that supports a noninteractive login. You can use vMA to perform many of the tasks commonly performed in the ESX Service Console, so if you are moving over to ESXi 4, you might find it a way of getting over the loss of your beloved COS.

I've heard many reports that users prefer vMA to the vCLI. I've found the CLI provided by vMA to be much more responsive than the vCLI, and I think this is because the way it handles authentication to the ESX is much quicker.

Downloading and Importing vMA

Download vMA from the VMware web site:

http://vmware.com/go/sysadmintools

Then extract the zip file to gain access to the .vmdk and .ovf files. You may wish to extract these files to the location of vSphere Client or a network share to facilitate the import process.

Follow these steps to import vMA:

1. From the File menu in the vSphere Client, select Deploy OVF Template.

2. In the wizard, select "Deploy from a file."

3. Click the Browse button and locate the extracted OVF file. Click Next. The wizard will report the name of the appliance, version, vendor, download size, and size of the virtual disk, with a brief description of the appliance.

4. Accept the EULA, and then click Next.

5. Select a VM folder location for vMA.

6. Select an ESX host or cluster to indicate where vMA will run.

7. Select a datastore to hold vMA, and then click Finish. vMA will be downloaded and imported into the vCenter environment.

8. Power on vMA. During the boot process, you will be asked if you would like it to be statically or DHCP configured. If you choose no, you can set a static configuration.

```
Starting network configuration ...
Configuring eth0...
Use DHCP to configure the network (yes/no) [yes]: no
Enter IP Address: 192.168.2.105
Enter Subnet Mask: 255.255.255.0
Enter Gateway Address: 192.168.2.199
Enter Primary DNS Address(Press Ctrl-D to clear existing value) [192.168.3.150]:

Enter Hostname [localhost.localdomain]: vma.vi4book.com_
```

9. After sorting out your IP configuration, you will be prompted to set the password for the vi-admin account.

You should now be able to SSH to vMA using an SSH client like PuTTY.

Adding Credentials and ESX Hosts

vMA has two user accounts called vi-admin and vi-user. The vi-user account is disabled until it is enabled by the vi-admin. Once both accounts are active, you can add ESX hosts into vMA. This is similar to adding ESX hosts into vCenter, which creates a vpxuser account. By using a vi-admin and vi-user account linked to every ESX host. you can authenticate against all the ESX hosts managed by vMA and run scripts against them, without additional authentication. vMA contains an authentication component called "Fast Pass," which allows this to happen.

The configuration of vMA involves enabling the vi-user for the first time, adding ESX hosts, and enabling "Fast Pass" for them.

To begin, SSH into your vMA, and log in as vi-admin with your password. Then set a password for the vi-user account, sending your instructions using sudo:

```
sudo passwd vi-user
```

The vi-admin is not root, and it receives all its privileges from the configuration of sudo, which is a delegation system that allows root to allow other users privileges above and beyond being merely a user. The response to this password reset is a rather humorous one, I think.

```
[vi-admin@vma ~]$ sudo passwd vi-user

We trust you have received the usual lecture from the local System
Administrator. It usually boils down to these three things:

    #1) Respect the privacy of others.
    #2) Think before you type.
    #3) With great power comes great responsibility.

Password:
Changing password for user vi-user.
New UNIX password:
Retype new UNIX password:
passwd: all authentication tokens updated successfully.
[vi-admin@vma ~]$ 
```

Next, use the vifp utility to add ESX hosts into vMA. This will create vi-admin and vi-user accounts on the ESX host. To add an ESX host (esx1.vi4book.com in this example), type the following:

```
sudo vifp addserver esx1.vi4book.com
```

You will be prompted for the vMA vi-admin password, then the ESX host's password.

```
login as: vi-admin
vi-admin@vma.vi4book.com's password:
Last login: Mon Mar  9 04:58:24 2009 from 192.168.3.191
[vi-admin@vma ~]$ sudo vifp addserver esx1.vi4book.com
Password:
root@esx1.vi4book.com's password:
[vi-admin@vma ~]$ 
```

Repeat this process for each ESX host vMA will manage.

To confirm your ESX hosts have been successfully added to the vMA's list, issue the following command:

```
vifp listservers
```

```
[vi-admin@vma ~]$ vifp listservers
esx1.vi4book.com          ESX
esx2.vi4book.com          ESX
esx3.vi4book.com          ESX
esx4.vi4book.com          ESX
[vi-admin@vma ~]$ ▮
```

The following command can be used to remove ESX hosts from the vMA ESX host list:

```
sudo vifp removeserver
```

Connecting to an ESX Host and Running Commands

When running commands after vi-fastpass has been set up, you have two options:

- Use the command `vifpinit` to select an ESX host.
- Use a statement in a Perl or Java script and call the `LoginByFastpass` option.

You will find examples of using these utilities in scripts in the /opt/vmware/vima/ samples directory.

If you have only one ESX host added to vMA, then there is no need to specify the ESX host. If you have multiple ESX hosts added, you *must* specify which ESX host should receive the command; otherwise vMA will just send it to the first ESX host on the list.

Set on which ESX host you wish the command to execute (esx1.vi4book.com in this example) with the following command:

```
vifpinit esx1.vi4book.com
```

Next, type an ESX command, such as the following:

```
esxcfg-vswitch -l
```

This should produce output like the following example.

```
[vi-admin@vma ~]$ vifpinit esx1.vi4book.com
[vi-admin@vma ~]$ esxcfg-vswitch -l
Switch Name      Num Ports      Used Ports      Configured Ports      MTU      Uplinks
vSwitch0         32             3               32                    1500     vmnic0

  PortGroup Name                 VLAN ID    Used Ports      Uplinks
  Service Console                0          1               vmnic0
```

As well as including all the standard vCLI commands like `esxcfg-vswitch` and `vi-cfg`, vMA has a number of unique commands. One worth looking at is `resxtop`, which creates an `esxtop` environment remotely, even for ESXi hosts.

Also of interest is the `vilogger` utility, which allows you to collect log files from the target ESX hosts according to the specified log policy. You might prefer this to setting up a Linux Syslog server, which some organizations use to maintain their log files in a central location.

Finally, vMA includes the `vima-update` utility, which updates the vMA software. This will be necessary to make sure its APIs, SDK, and utilities are in sync with the distribution of ESX you are currently running.

Using the Interactive Tech Support Mode in ESXi 4

As I've stated in previous chapters, in the long-term, the Classic edition of ESX is likely to be decommissioned, and vSphere 5 may be just the embedded ESXi edition. This will mean the end of the interactive logon on the ESX host, except when working with VMware Technical Support.

However, in ESXi 4, it is possible to generate an interactive command-line prompt at the physical console. The interactive CLI of ESXi is intended for use only when you are working with VMware Support. To generate this prompt, press ALT+F1, type **unsupported**, and press ENTER. You will be prompted for the root account password configured when ESXi was first booted to (memory) or installed (disk). After supplying the correct credentials, you will be in interactive Tech Support Mode.

```
        ESXi 4.0 http://www.vmware.com
        Copyright 2007-2008 VMware Inc.,

Password:

Tech Support Mode successfully accessed.
The time and date of this access have been sent to the system logs.

WARNING - Tech Support Mode is not supported unless used in
consultation with VMware Tech Support.
```

From this interactive CLI, you can issue many of the commands available in ESX Classic. Ideally, you should use one of the new CLI environments discussed in this chapter, such as the vSphere CLI, vMA, or PowerShell, rather than this interactive CLI.

Using the vSphere PowerCLI for Windows

To facilitate management and scripting tasks, VMware has developed its own cmdlets to use with Microsoft Windows PowerShell. This means you can use the same CLI to manage your virtual infrastructure as you do to manage your Windows environment. This section provides an introduction to using PowerShell with VMware.

TIP *Full coverage of using PowerShell with VMware would require a whole book in its own right. In fact, someone has written such a book. If you want to learn more about PowerShell, consider reading* Managing VMware Infrastructure with Windows PowerShell *by Hal Rottenberg (SAPIEN Technologies, 2009). It's certainly on my wish list.*

Installing Windows PowerShell and the vSphere PowerCLI

To get up and running with vSphere PowerCLI, you will need to download the Microsoft Windows PowerShell environment, and then download VMware's extensions.

I imagine that the very day this book is published, there will be a new version of PowerShell from Microsoft. So perhaps you should do a search for "MS PowerShell Download."

Currently, that search places Windows PowerShell 1.0 at the top of the list, and the download page for version 1.0, which ships in Windows Vista/XP/2003 format, is located here:

http://www.microsoft.com/windowsserver2003/technologies/management/powershell/download.mspx

Additionally, if you are installing Windows PowerShell to a clean copy of the OS, you may not have .NET 2.0 preinstalled. A search for "Microsoft .NET 2.0 Download" currently takes you to this download page:

http://www.microsoft.com/downloads/details.aspx?FamilyID=0856EACB-4362-4B0D-8EDD-AAB15C5E04F5&displaylang=en

Once you have downloaded and installed Windows PowerShell (it currently installs as if it were a hotfix or a service pack), you can then download the VMware vSphere PowerCLI for Windows from the VMware web site:

http://vmware.com/go/sysadmintools

The installation of the vSphere PowerCLI for Windows is generally a click Next, click Next affair. At the end, it will create a shortcut to start a PowerShell session. Despite this relatively innocuous installation, midway through you will be confronted with a somewhat cryptic warning.

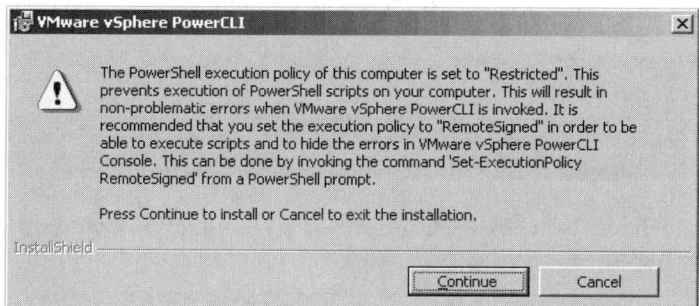

PowerShell uses certificate signing on software, and VMware uses one of its auto-generated certificates to facilitate this. This VMware certificate must be trusted before it is run. Additionally, you must adjust the security settings. By default, security settings are set to restricted, which limits the functionality of the PowerShell libraries to the system where they were installed. You can lower this security restriction to avoid dealing with unwanted and nonproblematic errors.

When you run PowerShell for the first time (by double-clicking the shortcut), you will receive a certificate prompt/warning.

Selecting A, for Always run, allows VMware's PowerShell libraries to function, trusting the auto-generated certificate, and stops this warning from appearing again. When you choose A, you will get an error message.

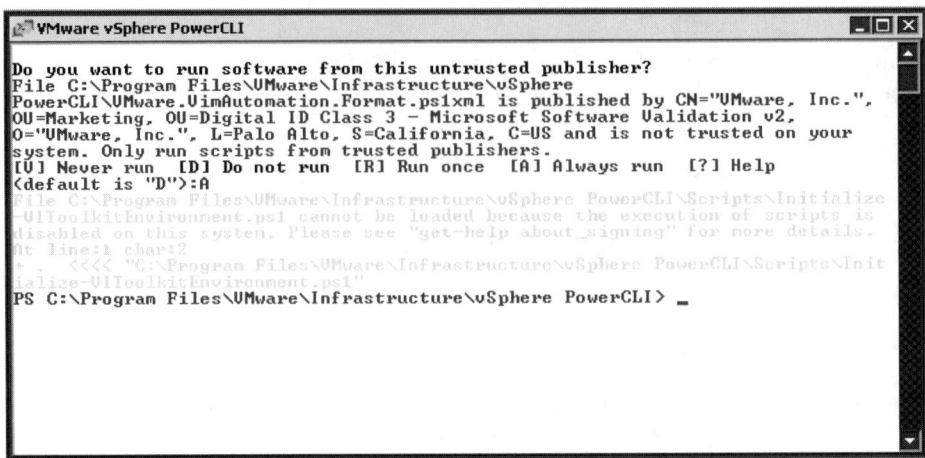

You need to input the variable mentioned in the installer to resolve this issue and allow unsigned and untrusted scripts to execute. Type the following:

```
Set-ExecutionPolicy RemoteSigned
```

***

CAUTION   *In VMware's warning dialog box, the space in this command isn't shown. There must be a space between* `Set-ExecutionPolicy` *and the policy setting of* `RemoteSigned`.

After doing this, the VMware PowerShell window should open without warnings or annoying red error messages.

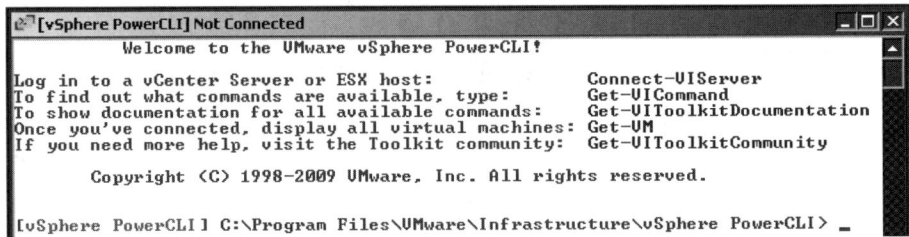

Using VMware PowerShell Cmdlets

To quickly test if VMware PowerShell is working, open a VMware PowerShell prompt by double-clicking the shortcut. Then type this command:

```
get-vc
```

Enter the name of the vCenter and log in with your vCenter administrator user account and your password. Next, type the following command:

```
get-vm
```

You should see a list of all the VMs currently being managed by vCenter.

```
[vSphere PowerCLI] Connected to virtualcenter4.vi4book.com as Administrator
             Welcome to the VMware vSphere PowerCLI!

Log in to a vCenter Server or ESX host:          Connect-VIServer
To find out what commands are available, type:   Get-VICommand
To show documentation for all available commands: Get-VIToolkitDocumentation
Once you've connected, display all virtual machines: Get-VM
If you need more help, visit the Toolkit community: Get-VIToolkitCommunity

      Copyright (C) 1998-2009 VMware, Inc. All rights reserved.

[vSphere PowerCLI] C:\Program Files\VMware\Infrastructure\vSphere PowerCLI> get-vc

cmdlet get-vc at command pipeline position 1
Supply values for the following parameters:
Server[0]: virtualcenter4.vi4book.com
Server[1]:
WARNING: There were one or more problems with the server certificate:

* The X509 chain could not be built up to the root certificate.

Name                        Port          User
----                        ----          ----
virtualcenter4.vi4book.com  443           Administrator

[vSphere PowerCLI] C:\Program Files\VMware\Infrastructure\vSphere PowerCLI> get-vm

Name        PowerState  Num CPUs  Memory (MB)
----        ----------  --------  -----------
file02      PoweredOn   1         384
web02       PoweredOn   1         384
ctx01       PoweredOn   1         384
sql02       PoweredOn   1         384
sql01       PoweredOn   1         384
```

Notice the top of the screen shows a list of commands to help you get started:

- `connect-viserver` connects to a ESX host or vCenter server (I used the shorter `get-vc` command in the example).

- `get-vicommand` lists cmdlets, or commands. This includes `get-host`, which lists all your ESX hosts in vCenter.

- `get-vitoolkitdocumentation` opens a VMware help file in a Microsoft Help format, which lists all the cmdlets available. This lists other `get-` cmdlets, which can be used to retrieve other information.

- `get-vm` lists all your VMs.

- `get-vitoolkitcommunity` opens a Web browser and takes you to the VMware Communities forum for the Windows VSphere PowerCLI.

NOTE *Although the commands are shown in camel case on the vSphere PowerCLI screen, cmdlets are not case-sensitive.*

The prompt created for the PowerShell window is `[VSphere PowerCLI] C:\Program Files\VMware\Infrastructure\VIToolkitForWindows>`, but you can still execute DOS commands, such as `dir` and `del`.

PowerShell First Principles

Objects, attributes, properties … eyes glaze over … fall asleep. As system administrators, we have all been there. During some training course or conference presentation, as some programmer type says, "objects, attributes, and properties," we promptly sigh and wonder when it will all be over. I've had that experience, and one of the major barriers I had with PowerShell is the object-orientedness of it all. Well, I'm here to say that PowerShell is for you and for me, and neither you nor I should glaze over and fall asleep.

My favorite piece of PowerShell came to me when I was using VI 3.5, and it is precisely one line long! When I first hit the ENTER key and saw the results in vCenter, a big smile came over my face, and I was convinced that PowerShell was for me—call it my holy grail. At last, I saw the point of all those presentations on objects, attributes, and properties.

VMware ESX with vCenter has never had a global way of getting the entire set of ESX hosts in a cluster to rescan their HBAs. Since I first started using VMware, we had to select each ESX host individually and click Rescan if a new LUN had been presented to the hosts. If the first rescan was unsuccessful because of a problem with LUN masking, we had to do it all over again. Granted, in vSphere 4, we do (finally) have the capability to do that from the vSphere Client. But here, I will use this simple example to show you the first principles of PowerShell.

Open a VMware PowerShell session and log in to vCenter with the `get-vc` cmdlet:

```
get-vc virtualcenter4.vi4book.com -user administrator -password vmware
```

You can use the cmdlet `get-vmhost` to list all the ESX hosts managed by the vCenter server to which you have just authenticated.

```
get-vmhost
```

```
[vSphere PowerCLI] Connected to virtualcenter4.vi4book.com as Administrator
[vSphere PowerCLI] C:\Program Files\VMware\Infrastructure\vSphere PowerCLI> get-vmhost

Name                          State            Id
----                          -----            --
esx1.vi4book.com              Connected        HostSys...
esx3.vi4book.com              Connected        HostSys...
esx2.vi4book.com              Connected        HostSys...


[vSphere PowerCLI] C:\Program Files\VMware\Infrastructure\vSphere PowerCLI>
```

If you use `get-vmhost` together with `get-vmstorage` and the action `-rescanallhba`, you can trigger a rescan across all ESX hosts managed by vCenter. This is achieved by passing on, or piping, the results of one cmdlet to another to fulfill the cmdlet's actions.

```
get-vmhost | get-vmhoststorage -rescanallhba
```

The pipeline symbol, |, causes the output objects of one cmdlet to be used as the input objects of another cmdlet. Normally, `get-vmstorage -rescanallhba` would need an ESX host to function, but by using `get-vmhost`, this pipelining can generate the list of ESX hosts to rescan.

If you follow this to its logical conclusion, one major benefit of PowerShell is being able to search for practically any value in vCenter—whether it's the attribute of an ESX host or a VM. So, for example, `get-vmhost | get-datastore` will list all datastores.

We are not limited to just `get-` style PowerShell commands. The PowerShell cmdlets from VMware fall into seven categories, which represent the main tasks carried out in vCenter:

- **Add**   Add an ESX host, for example.
- **Get**   Get a list of ESX hosts or VMs.

- **Move**   Move a VM a from one ESX host to another.
- **New**   Create a new vSwitch or port group.
- **Remove**   Remove a VM NIC,
- **Set**   Set a VM resource allocation.
- **Stop/Start**   Stop a VM or start an ESX host service.

Disconnecting CDs/Floppies

CD and floppy devices can cause a problem prior to a VMotion event. (This is not an issue if you have a cluster, as DRS now disconnects actively connected CD-ROM and floppy devices.) Additionally, as neither the floppy or CD-ROM are fully virtualized devices (their functionality is actually delivered via the Service Console), if they are left connected by accident, they can affect the performance of the VM.

You can use the `get-vm` cmdlet together with the `get-floppydrive` and `get-cdrom` cmdlets to set these devices as disconnected. Using the `set-floppydrive` and `set-cddrive` cmdlets, you can change the state of these devices to disconnected.

```
get-vm | get-floppydrive | set-floppydrive –connected:$false
get-vm | get-cddrive | set-cddrive –connected:$false
```

Here, I'm saying "List all the settings of the VMs and find the floppy drive settings, and then change them so they are not connected."

These bits of PowerCLI will disconnect a CD-ROM and floppy device, but will not clear the paths used to point to an ISO image. So you might prefer a method that sets the VM's CD-ROM and floppy device back to being a client device. You can do this by using the `–nomedia` option:

```
get-vm | get-cddrive | set-cddrive -nomedia
```

Renaming Port Groups and Correcting VM Settings

One of the tricky things to do in vSphere 4 (and VI3 and VI2 as well) is to correct the name of a port group without needing to manually correct each VM individually. One of the "features" of renaming port groups is that VMs become orphaned from the port group. While this problem has been fixed with distributed vSwitches, it may still be an issue if you are using standard vSwitches.

Let's say you are renaming a port group to fix a case-inconsistency issue. The following examples show the before and after effect in the GUI when the port group called Production is relabeled as production.

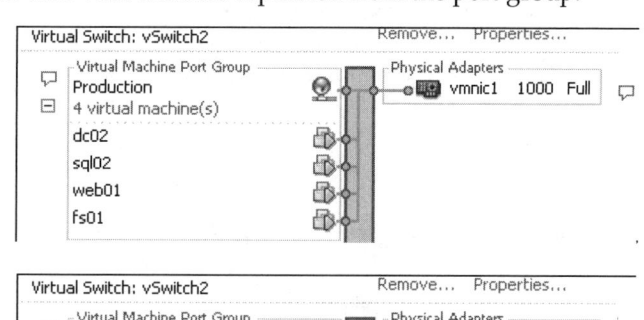

Additionally, on the properties of each and every VM, it will appear to have no port group set at all.

This problem remains a largely cosmetic one, as the renaming of the port group does not stop the VM from communication while it is powered on. If a VM is powered off and then powered on, the VM will start with its virtual NIC disconnected because it cannot connect to its port group, and as result, no users will be able to communicate with the VM.

At best, it is not pleasant to see this in the vSphere Client. At worst, it would take a lot of manual effort in the vSphere Client to correct each and every VM.

This issue can easily be fixed with PowerShell by a combination of `get-` cmdlets to find the information you are looking for, text sorting and filters on that information, and applying a `set-` cmdlet to the result, as follows.

Use the cmdlet `get-vm` piped with `get-networkadapter` to retrieve a list of port groups on all VM hosts managed within vCenter:

```
get-vm | get-networkadapter
```

Use the cmdlet `sort-object` to relist the output in alphabetical order:

```
get-vm | get-networkadapter | sort-object -property "NetworkName"
```

The `sort-object` cmdlet also supports the use of filtering text when used in conjunction with the `where` and `contains` options. This will allow you to filter just on a particular word—"Production" in this example:

```
get-vm | get-networkadapter | sort-object -property "NetworkName" | where
{'Production' -contains $_.NetworkName}
```

Now that you have filtered the results of all your `get-` cmdlets, you can pipe them out to `set-` commands to rename the port group on all the ESX hosts:

```
get-vm | get-networkadapter | sort-object -property "NetworkName" | where
{'Production' -contains $_.NetworkName} | set-networkadapter -NetworkName
'production'
```

Note how you are searching for the string "Production" and replacing it with "production." After typing this command, you will be asked if you wish to make this bulk change that will affect many VMs.

```
[vSphere PowerCLI] Connected to virtualcenter4.vi4book.com as administrator    _ □ ×
[vSphere PowerCLI] C:\Program Files\VMware\Infrastructure\vSphere PowerCLI> get-vm |
 get-networkadapter | sort-object -property "NetworkName" | where ('Production' -con
tains $_.NetworkName) | Set-NetworkAdapter -NetworkName "production"

Confirm
Are you sure you want to perform this action?
Performing operation "Setting NetworkName: production" on Target "Network adapter
1".
[Y] Yes  [A] Yes to All  [N] No  [L] No to All  [S] Suspend  [?] Help
(default is "Y"):A_
```

Select A, for Yes to All, and press ENTER to have every VM reconfigured. You will also see this task being processed in the vSphere Client.

Recent Tasks		
Name	Target	Status
Reconfigure Virtual Machine	dc01	In Progress
Reconfigure Virtual Machine	web02	In Progress
Reconfigure Virtual Machine	ctx01	In Progress
Reconfigure Virtual Machine	fs02	In Progress
Reconfigure Virtual Machine	ctx02	In Progress
Reconfigure Virtual Machine	fs01	Completed
Reconfigure Virtual Machine	sql02	Completed
Reconfigure Virtual Machine	dc02	Completed
Reconfigure Virtual Machine	sql01	Completed

Triggering Maintenance Mode
This small piece of PowerShell forces an ESX host to enter maintanance mode:

```
get-vmhost -name esx1.vi4book.com | set-vmhost -state maintenance
```

If used with DRS in fully automated mode, it should also trigger the evacuation of all VMs from the ESX host.

Listing All VMs and IP Addresses
The following PowerShell script can be used to generate a report of all the IP addresses used by the VMs in vCenter 4:

```
get-vm | select name, @{name="ip"; expression={foreach($nic in (get-view
$_.id).guest.net) {$nic.ipaddress}}}
```

Finding VMs on Local Storage

The following small piece of PowerShell can be used to create a report of VMs that are on local storage. It's useful to run on a daily or weekly basis (because, occasionally, folks don't engage the brain when creating a VM!).

```
get-datastore |where {$_.name -match "datastore|local|storage"} |get-vm
|get-harddisk |select filename |export-csv c:\localvms.csv
```

This uses the `get-datastore` cmdlet with the filter of `where` to match the volume name (datastore, local, or storage), which is then redirected into the `get-vm` and `get-harddisk` cmdlets to produce a list of VMs on the matched volume name. The result is output to a comma-separated values (CSV) file, which can be opened in an application like Microsoft Excel.

Creating Datacenters, Folders, and Clusters

In the next set of examples, I demonstrate how you can use PowerShell to create high-level objects in vCenter, including the whole process of creating datacenters, folders, clusters, and adding ESX hosts and resource pools. The goal is to create a new datacenter with DRS/HA clusters with resource pools and a folder structure as shown in the following screenshots.

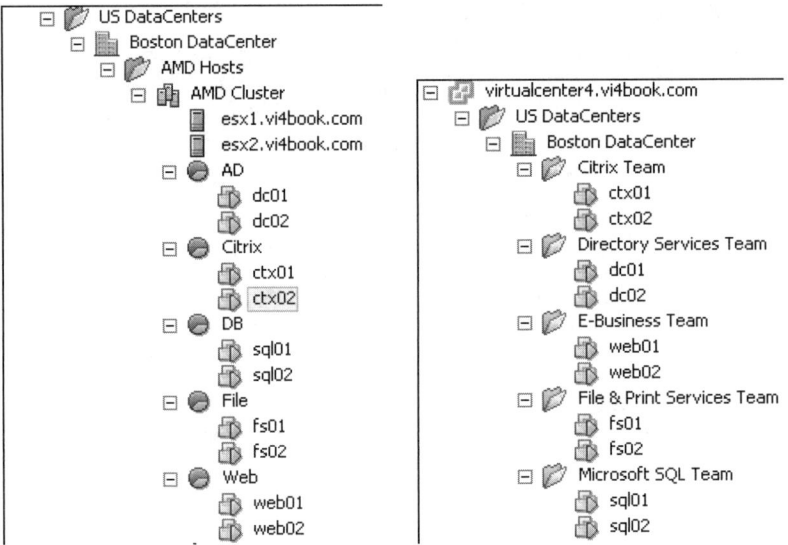

Creating a Datacenter with Folders   Most PowerShell commands that create a object will need the `–location` parameter, so if you are adding an ESX host or creating a vCenter object, you will need to indicate where you would like it to be created. In my experience, setting the `–location` parameter correctly takes the most time. Often, I will work on this part first to make sure my command has the correct focus.

For this example, I tried `get-folder –name 'US DataCenters'` first, to make sure I found the result I was looking for. Then I added the brackets around it (`get-folder –name 'US DataCenters'`), and then I added the task of creating a new datacenter.

Once you have located where the new vCenter object will be created, you will then need to set a name using the –name option. So here, we're saying "Create a new datacenter in the folder called US DataCenters and give it the name Boston DataCenter."

```
new-datacenter -location (get-folder -Name 'US DataCenters') -name 'Boston
DataCenter'
```

In some cases, PowerShell can be read almost as if it were English (it depends what part of planet Earth you come from whether this works for you!).

Next, add some folders in the new datacenter. First, create a new folder in the Boston DataCenter called AMD Hosts:

```
new-folder -location (get-datacenter -Name 'Boston DataCenter') -name 'AMD
Hosts'
```

Then repeat the command to create another new folder called Intel Hosts:

```
new-folder -location (get-datacenter -Name 'Boston DataCenter') -name
'Intel Hosts'
```

Creating Clusters   Now you can create clusters in your folders. Use the following command:

```
new-cluster -location (get-datacenter -name 'Boston DataCenter' | get-
folder -Name 'AMD Hosts') -name 'AMD Cluster' -HAEnabled
-HAAdmissionControlEnabled -HAFailoverLevel 2 -DRSEnabled
-DRSMode PartiallyAutomated
```

Here, we're saying, "Create a new cluster in the AMD Hosts folder in the Boston DataCenter. Call it AMD Cluster, and make sure that it's enabled for HA and DRS. And oh, by the way, can you make sure that HA is enabled to tolerate the loss of two ESX hosts before admission control kicks in? And, by the way, DRS should be enabled as well, but make sure it is only partially automated, rather than the default of fully automated. Cheers! Thanks, mate!"

Notice how the -location variable is getting longer and longer as you need to make sure to create an AMD cluster in the right location in the vCenter Inventory. Remember that you can use the name AMD Cluster as many times as you like, as long as it doesn't appear twice in exactly the same location in vCenter.

After creating the cluster, PowerShell should return your values accordingly.

Name	HAEnabled	HAFailover Level	DrsEnabled	DrsAutomationLevel
AMD Cluster	True	2	True	PartiallyAutomated

Adding an ESX Host to a Datacenter or Cluster   Using the cmdlets add-vmhost and get-datacenter, you can add an ESX host to a datacenter. add-vmhost is the main cmdlet carrying out the task, supplying the datacenter -location using the get-datacenter cmdlet. On its own, get-datacenter merely lists the datacenters owned and controlled by the vCenter server to which you authenticated.

```
add-vmhost esx2.vi4book.com -location (get-datacenter 'SanFran Datacenter')
-user root -password vmware
```

Here, we're saying, "Add esx2 to the datacenter called Boston DataCenter using the root account password."

If you wanted to add an ESX host directly into a cluster in a datacenter, you could use the `get-cluster` cmdlet in a very similar fashion, except being much more specific about the location. The –force command accept the default certificate presented by the ESX host when it is first added into the vCenter system.

```
add-vmhost esx1.vi4book.com -location (get-datacenter -name 'Boston
DataCenter' | get-folder -name 'AMD Hosts' | get-cluster -name 'AMD Cluster')
-user root –password vmware -force: $true
```

So, here we're saying, "Add esx1 to the AMD cluster held within a folder called AMD Hosts in the Boston DataCenter. And, by the way, the root account password is vmware."

The `ad-vmhost` cmdlet will display a progress bar to indicate that the ESX host is being added to vCenter.

```
Add Host
    percent complete: 80
    [oooooooooooooooooooooooooooooooooooooooooooooooooooooooooooooooooooooooooooooooooooooooo
```

Creating Resource Pools   While it is possible to create resource pools on the cluster before you add ESX hosts, they don't become visible until an ESX host is added to the cluster. That's why I prefer to add the ESX hosts to the cluster and then create the resource pools.

```
new-resourcepool -location (get-datacenter -name 'Boston DataCenter' | get-
folder -name 'AMD Hosts' | get-cluster -name 'AMD Cluster') -name Web
```

Here, we're saying, "Create a resource pool in the AMD Cluster held within a folder called AMD Hosts in the Boston DataCenter called Web."

As you can see, there's a pattern to the input, and it's becoming increasingly tedious to specify these full locations every time, isn't it? Keep this in mind when we come to look at storing your PowerShell in script files and setting variables!

It is possible to create resource pools with resource settings. For example, if you wanted you to create a resource pool called Production with a CPU share value of high, you would use the following command:

```
new-resourcepool -location (get-datacenter -name 'Boston DataCenter' | get-
folder -name 'AMD Hosts' | get-cluster -name 'AMD Cluster') -name Production
–cpushareslevel high
```

Creating VM Folders   So far, we have restricted ourselves to the main Hosts and Clusters view, but it is entirely possible to create folders in the Virtual Machines and Templates view as well. By default, the `new-folder` cmdlet creates folders in the Host and Clusters view (PowerShell uses the short name `hosts` to indicate this). Using the value `vm` forces the system to create a folder in the VMs and Templates view. Here's how to create a new folder structure for holding VMs:

```
new-folder -name 'Directory Services Team'  (get-datacenter -name 'Boston
Datacenter' | get-folder -name vm)
```

In this example, the grammar is somewhat different, which just goes to show that, as with English, in PowerShell there is more than one way of saying the same thing! Here, we're saying, "Create a new folder called Directory Services Team in the Boston DataCenter in the VMs and Templates view."

Moving VMs into a Resource Pool and VM Folder   Using the `move-vm` cmdlet, you can move VMs either from a logical location in the vCenter Inventory—say, from one folder or resource pool to another—or physically from one ESX host to another. The move can be done in bulk, as long as there is unique string via which you can search or filter.

In the case of moving a VM to a resource pool, you can use the `get-resourcepool` cmdlet to specify the destination, similar to how you use the `-location` variable.

```
move-vm -vm (get-vm -name dc*) -destination (get-datacenter -name 'Boston
DataCenter' | get-folder -name 'AMD Hosts' | get-cluster -name 'AMD
Cluster' | get-resourcepool -name 'AD')
```

Here, we're saying, "Move all the VMs that have the letters *DC* at the beginning of their name to a resource pool called AD in the Boston DataCenter in the folder called AMD Hosts containing a cluster called AMD Cluster."

You can take this same command and merely search for a different object to which to move the VM.

```
move-vm -vm (get-vm -name dc*) -destination (get-datacenter -name 'Boston
DataCenter' | get-folder -name 'Directory Services Team')
```

This completes the construction of the new datacenter, with DRS/HA clusters with resource pools and a folder structure as shown at the beginning of this demonstration.

Triggering VMotion

As noted in the previous section, you can also use `move-vm` to move a VM from one ESX host to another, as follows:

```
move-vm -vm (get-vm -name 'DC02') -destination (get-vmhost esx1.vi4book.com)
```

Here, we're saying, "Move the VM called DC02 to the ESX host called esx1.vi4book.com." You can move all the VMs from one ESX host to another, as follows:

```
move-vm -vm get-vmhost esx1.vi4book.com | get-vm | -destination (get-vmhost
esx2.vi4book.com)
```

Unfortunately, this method does not respect resource pool location, and unceremoniously dumps all the VMs on the root of the cluster. I recommend using maintenance mode with DRS, because this evacuates all the VMs from an ESX host without losing their resource pool location.

Taking a Snapshot of Many VMs

Using wildcards, you can take a snapshot of multiple VMs, as follows:

```
get-vm ctx* | ' foreach { '$_ | new-snapshot -name ($_.Name + "-Current")
'}
```

This searches for every VM that begins with *ctx*, and takes a snapshot of each one, naming them ctx01-current, ctx02-current, and so on.

Adding New Port Groups to Existing vSwitches

If you are not using distributed vSwitches, creating an additional port groups on an existing vSwitch when you have many ESX hosts can be a laborious process. The whole process can be easily carried out with a simple piece of PowerShell.

First, define your variables for the `new- virtualportgroup` cmdlet to create the port group, called vlan11 with the VLAN tag setting in this example.

```
$vlan = "vlan11"
$vlanvalue = "11"
$vmhosts = Get-VMHost | Sort-Object -Property Name
```

Then, using a `foreach` loop, search for every ESX host with a virtual switch called vSwitch2. Once this array (`$findvswitch`) has been created, it is used to create the port group on each ESX host.

```
foreach($hosts in $vmhosts){$findvswitch = get-virtualswitch -vmhost (get-
vmhost $hosts) | where-object { $_.Name -match "vSwitch2" } new-
virtualportgroup -name $vlan -virtualSsitch $findvswitch -vlanid $vlanvalue}
```

Using PowerShell Scripts

As noted earlier, PowerShell scripts can save you time in issuing PowerShell commands. PowerShell scripts have a filename extension of .ps1.

Creating and Executing a Simple Script File

A good example of a sample PowerShell script file is one that connects you to your vCenter server without having to type the entire `get-vc` command, and then carries out a task such as disconnecting all CD-ROMs without prompting for confirmation.

To create this sample script, at the PowerShell prompt, type the following:

```
notepad vc4.ps1
```

This will open Notepad, and Notepad will ask you if you want to create the file, as it was unable to retrieve it.

Type the `get-vc` command into the script:

```
get-vc virtualcenter4.vi4book.com –username administrator –password vmware
get-vm | get-cddrive | set-cddrive -nomedia -confirm:$false
```

`–confirm:$false` is an option on many cmdlets within the PowerCLI. It switches off the prompt that appears when you carry out a bulk action against many VMs or ESX hosts.

CAUTION *It's perhaps wise to run any cmdlet with the prompt in place and confirm your PowerShell code is correct before switching off warnings and prompts. They are intended to protect you from carrying out global tasks that could have unintended consequences.*

Save the .ps1 file and close Notepad.

To execute the script file type, the following:

```
./vc4
```

PowerShell already recognizes the .ps1 filename extension, so there is no need to specify it at the PowerShell prompt.

Creating and Executing a Script File with Variables

If you consider the earlier examples of creating datacenters, folders, and clusters, clearly, it would be more useful to have these PowerShell scripts in a single script file that you could just execute, rather than typing each command individually. The problem with this is that there would be a lot of repetition of the same information, although it would be easy to type this once and use the Clipboard to duplicate it. For example, the following three commands create a resource pool called AD, Web, and File, respectively.

```
new-resourcepool -location (get-datacenter -name 'Boston DataCenter' | get-folder -name 'AMD Hosts' | get-cluster -name 'AMD Cluster') -name AD
new-resourcepool -location (get-datacenter -name 'Boston DataCenter' | get-folder -name 'AMD Hosts' | get-cluster -name 'AMD Cluster') -name Web
new-resourcepool -location (get-datacenter -name 'Boston DataCenter' | get-folder -name 'AMD Hosts' | get-cluster -name 'AMD Cluster') -name File
```

Additionally, this script would be hard-coded to do just one task, and so would have a lot of unique strings, like Boston DataCenter and AMD Cluster, dotted throughout the script. It would be more sensible to use variables defined at the top of the script file, which could be adjusted by editing the .ps1 file, or by asking the user for input for the core information, such as the name of the datacenter folder or the name of the datacenter to be created. The following is an example of a script that reduces this repetition to the minimum.

Each part of the sample script begins with a description marked with a # (which indicates text that is not executed), followed by the PowerShell. I wrote this script, and I wouldn't call myself a scripting guru by any stretch of the imagination, and so perhaps you can think of a more efficient way of doing it. It's offered not as a sample of great scripting, but as just one way that it could be done. In this case, I wanted to do everything via PowerShell. There are examples on the PowerShell forums of using a Microsoft Excel spreadsheet to hold all the variables, rather than encoding them into the PowerShell .ps1 file, which I think is a lot neater.

```
# This list defines the plain text strings that are provided to the cmd-
lets. These are the friendly names I will see in vCenter. Variables are
declared by prefixing any string with the dollar sign ($) followed by what
you would like the value to hold.  You can do lists, which are useful in
foreach loops. I have a few lists that contain the ESX hosts, folders, and
resource pools I will be adding in the script.

$dcfoldername = 'US DataCenters'
$dcname = 'Atlanta DataCenter'
$hostfolder1 = 'AMD Hosts'
$hostfolder2 = 'Intel Hosts'
$cluster1 = 'AMD Cluster'
$cluster2 = 'Intel Cluster'
$hostlist = 'esx1.vi4book.com','esx2.vi4book.com'
$respoolist = 'AD','DB','File','Citrix','Web'
```

```
$vmfolderlist = 'Directory Services Team','Microsoft SQL Team','File &
Print Services Team','Citrix Team','E-Business Team'
$vmlist = 'dc*','sql*','fs*','ctx*','web*'
```

This is a location finder variable, which is often used in conjunction
with -location at the same time, expressing the fully qualified get-command
strings. This one locates a folder called US DataCenters. The –location
variable in a cmdlet is important because it's how we tell the cmdlet where
(location) we would like a virtual center object to be created or manipulated. The important thing to mention about the location variables in this
script is that, in this case, they cannot be defined at the very top of the
PowerShell script. This is because you cannot retrieve a positive result by
searching for an object that has yet to be created. The object must exist
before you can create a location variable for it; otherwise, all you will
receive is a null entry. A good way of testing location variables is just
to call them without any specific action. So if under the next line I had
on its own $dcfolderlocation, it should just return the piece of text "US
DataCenters," as long as the script finds that object somewhere in the
inventory to which we have authenticated.

```
$dcfolderlocation = get-folder -name $dcfoldername
$dcfolderlocation
```

Create a new datacenter in the US DataCenter folder called Atlanta Data-
Center using the $dcfoldername and $dcname variables.

```
new-datacenter -location $dcfolderlocation -name $dcname
```

This creates a new location variable to find in the US DataCenter folder
a datacenter called Atlanta DataCenter. If you compare the line of Power-
Shell above to the line of PowerShell below, you can see that they are VERY
similar. The only difference is the new-datacenter is now a get-datacenter
cmdlet, which is being made equal to another location variable called
$dcnamelocation. This is often a very quick way to create location vari-
ables. This location variable is very specific, filtering the results of
any cmdlet to just the US DataCenter folder, which contains a datacenter
called Atlanta DataCenter. This location variable must be defined after the
creation of the datacenter. After all, if we searched for the datacenter
before it was created, then it would always return a null or negative
answer.

```
$dcnamelocation = get-datacenter -location $dcfolderlocation -name $dcname
```

This creates two new folders in the US DataCenters\Atlanta DataCenter
called AMD Hosts and Intel Hosts using $hostfolder1 and $hostfolder2. To be
honest, I couldn't think of good names for these variables, and it does
seem rather pointless given the length of the text involved. But I feel
that using variables in this way offers more flexibility. It means if I
wanted to change the name of the folders, all I would have to do is change
the variables defined at the top of the script where they are easy to find,
rather them being embedded throughout the script and having to resort to
dangerous tools like Find and Replace to modify them.

```
new-folder -location $dcnamelocation -name $hostfolder1
new-folder -location $dcnamelocation -name $hostfolder2
```

This locates in the US DataCenter\Atlanta DataCenter a folder called AMD
Hosts & Intel Hosts. You might wonder why for every object I create, I am
also creating a location variable. Well, one of my worries is that I might
have two AMD Hosts folders held in two different datacenters in the same
vCenter. There would be a good chance of the script failing if it did not
state precisely where to find the objects. So see my location variables as
being a way of being very specific about where I want certain operations to
take place. Notice in the example below that I'm using one location variable $dcnamelocation together with $hostfolderN to define another location
variable called $hosfolderlocationN.

```
$hostfolderlocation1 = get-folder -location $dcnamelocation -name $hostfolder1
$hostfolderlocation2 = get-folder -location $dcnamelocation -name $hostfolder2
```

This creates a cluster located in the AMD/Intel Hosts folder called AMD
Cluster & Intel Cluster. Again it feels a bit silly to be using $cluster1
and $cluster2 when I could just have typed in the name of the new cluster.
But once again, I preferred to have these set as variables at the top of my
script to make them easy to modify if needed.

```
new-cluster -location $hostfolderlocation1 -name $cluster1 -HAEnabled -
DRSEnabled -DRSMode PartiallyAutomated
new-cluster -location $hostfolderlocation2 -name $cluster2 -HAEnabled -
DRSEnabled -DRSMode PartiallyAutomated
```

This locates in US DataCenters\Atlanta DataCenter\Intel or AMD folder a
cluster called AMD Cluster and Intel Cluster

```
$amdcluster = get-cluster -location $hostfolderlocation1 -name $cluster1
$intelcluster = get-cluster -location $hostfolderlocation2 -name $cluster2
```

This adds two ESX hosts into the AMD Cluster. For each ESX host in the
hostlist, use the add-vmhost command to join the ESX host to the AMD Cluster. Foreach loops are a handy way of dealing with repetitive "bulk" tasks.
For example, if I had 32 ESX hosts, I could have 32 lines of add-vmhosts.
It is much more efficient in a case like that to use a foreach loop.
Foreach loops have two parts: the condition is specified in brackets ($host
in @($hostlist)) and the second part in braces {add-vmhosts…} is the action
or command. So in my case what's being expressed is foreach hosts in the
hostlist, carrying out an add-vmhost task to add them into the cluster
called AMD Cluster located in the folder called US DataCenter, in a datacenter called Atlanta DataCenter in a folder called AMD Hosts. I think
there may be a better way of doing this, such as setting a variable for the
$hostname such as ESX, a variable for the $domainname, and another variable
for the number of ESX hosts you are adding, such that it would add esxN
.vi4book.com for esx1.vi4book.com, esx2.vi4book.com, and so on. I decided
that such a method would be overly complicated and being able to state
specifically which ESX hosts would be added via the $hostlist would be more
controlled.

```
foreach ($hosts in @($hostlist) ) { add-vmhost $hosts -location $amdcluster
-user root -password vmware }
```

```
# This adds resource pools into the AMD Cluster. For each resource pool in
the respoolist, use the new-respool cmdlet to create the resourcepools.
```

```
foreach ($respool in @($respoolist) ) { new-resourcepool -location
$amdcluster -name $respool }
```

```
# This locates the root VM folder name (vm) location in the US DataCenters\
Altanta DataCenters. This is so I can use this $vmrootfolder to create
virtual machine folders coming directly from the datacenter. Without this
location variable being set, I would be creating folders in the Hosts and
Clusters view.
```

```
$vmrootfolder = get-folder -name vm -location $dcnamelocation
```

```
# This creates a VM folder in the root VM folder. For each VM folder in the
vmfolderlist, use the new-folder cmdlet to create the VM folders.
```

```
foreach ($vmfolder in @($vmfolderlist) ) { new-folder -location
$vmrootfolder -name $vmfolder }
```

```
# This is a very crude move to the right folder. I was hoping to be able to
merge together $vmfolderlist and foreach statement using ctx*, dc*, and so
on to locate the right VMs and put them in the right folder. In the end, I
decided on a much simpler approach of searching for the VMs by a string
such as dc*, and then adding them to the right VM folder.
```

```
move-vm -vm (get-vm -name dc*) -destination (get-datacenter -name 'Atlanta
DataCenter' | get-folder -name 'Directory Services Team')
move-vm -vm (get-vm -name sql*) -destination (get-datacenter -name 'Atlanta
DataCenter' | get-folder -name 'Microsoft SQL Team')
move-vm -vm (get-vm -name fs*) -destination (get-datacenter -name 'Atlanta
DataCenter' | get-folder -name 'File & Print Services Team')
move-vm -vm (get-vm -name ctx*) -destination (get-datacenter -name 'Atlanta
DataCenter' | get-folder -name 'Citrix Team')
move-vm -vm (get-vm -name web*) -destination (get-datacenter -name 'Atlanta
DataCenter' | get-folder -name 'E-Business Team')
```

```
# Similarly, I was hoping to find a sophisticated way of doing a bulk move
of the right VMs into the right resource pools, but resorted to this method
instead.
```

```
move-vm -vm (get-vm -name dc*) -destination (get-datacenter -name 'Atlanta
DataCenter' | get-resourcepool  -name 'AD')
move-vm -vm (get-vm -name sql*) -destination (get-datacenter -name 'Atlanta
DataCenter' | get-resourcepool -name 'DB')
move-vm -vm (get-vm -name fs*) -destination (get-datacenter -name 'Atlanta
DataCenter' | get-resourcepool -name 'File')
move-vm -vm (get-vm -name ctx*) -destination (get-datacenter -name 'Atlanta
DataCenter' | get-resourcepool -name 'Citrix')
move-vm -vm (get-vm -name web*) -destination (get-datacenter -name 'Atlanta
DataCenter' | get-resourcepool -name 'Web')
```

```
# Power on every VM within the AMD Cluster within the US DataCenter's
Folder\Atlanta DataCenter\AMD Folder - the confirm:$false switches off the
confirmation question for whether this task should be allowed to continue.

get-vm -location $admcluster | start-vm -confirm:$false
```

TIP *You can find more sample scripts and utilities written with PowerShell at the VMware Communities forum library (http://communities.vmware.com/community/developer/) and the VMworld 2008 PowerShell Scripting Lab (http://blogs.vmware.com/vipowershell/files/vmworld_europe_2008_powershell_lab_7_manual.pdf).*

Scripted Installations of ESX 4 Classic

For the final topic in this chapter, we will move away from the high-level CLI tools discussed in the previous sections and look at something a little more prosaic—how to automate the installation of ESX Classic to a physical server. Essentially, an ESX scripted installation is nothing more than an unattended text file that answers all the questions normally confronted by the administrator. However, using the `%post` section in the scripted installation allows you to call `esxcfg-` commands to carry out postconfiguration tasks also.

There many methods of carrying out a scripted installation of ESX Classic. They basically fall into two distinct categories: over the network or from a custom ESX CD.

With PXE-based deployment, the physical host PXE boots, with the ESX source code and script file on a internal web server. The PXE boot server runs a DHCP, TFTP, and web service. Installations are as quick as the network, and no media is required. This method is ideal for remote datacenters, where you may not have physical access to the servers. All you need is an ILO/RAC board and access to F12 on the keyboard to trigger the PXE boot process.

A number of commercial tools provide PXE-based deployment, such as Altiris, HP Rapid Deployment Pack, and IBM's Rapid Deployment Manager. Free virtual appliances for this tasks are also available, including the Ultimate Deployment Appliance (UDA, created by Carl Thijssen, http://www.ultimatedeployment.org) and ESX Deployment Appliance (EDA, created by Herco van Brug, http://www.virtuall.nl). I've been using the UDA for some time with ESX 3, and I host the ESX version on the RTFM Education web site. Carl hosts the workstation version on his ultimatedeployment.org Web site.

NOTE *Both Carl Thijssen and Herco van Brug are clever Dutchmen, and it was my great pleasure to meet with both of them in February 2009 over dinner. My hope is that by facilitating that meeting, their two projects will merge together, or at the very least, they will share information.*

With CD-ROM–based installation, you boot from a customized boot CD, which contains both the ESX source code and the script that automates the installation process. A commercial product that wraps all this up in a neat bundle called V-Deployment. At the moment, this utility works only with ESX 3, but it may soon be updated to be compatible with ESX 4. This CD-ROM based installation is desirable when you cannot get approval for DHCP in the server room or datacenter, which is more common than you might think. Remember that for a PXE-based solution to work, you need only a small DHCP scope on the (V)LAN where the ESX Service Console NIC resides.

In this section, I will cover using the UDA for PXE-based scripted installations.

Downloading and Installing the UDA

As I noted, the UDA ships in two main formats: a workstation format available on ultimatedeployment.org web site, and an ESX format available on the RTFM Education Web site (http://www.rtfm-ed.co.uk). Many consultants prefer the workstation edition because they can carry the appliance on a laptop from one consultancy gig to another. If you're not a consultant, you may prefer to run the UDA on one of your ESX hosts.

I host the ESX version in two formats: a zip file containing an OVF file and a zip file with just the virtual disks. Here are the steps for importing the UDA in the OVF format:

1. Download the ESX version of the UDA from http://www.rtfm-ed.co.uk/ downloads/uda20-beta-ovf.zip to you management PC.

2. Right-click and extract the uda20-beta-ovf.zip file.

3. In vCenter, select Deploy OVF Template from the File menu.

4. Select "Deploy from file."

5. Click the Browse button and locate the OVF file.

6. Click Next to accept the description.

7. Set the UDA VM name and location in the Inventory.

8. Select a datastore location.

9. Select a network port group. Remember this appliance will be used to deploy ESX, so you must put it on the same network as the Service Console network.

Configuring the UDA

When you first power on the UDA, it will boot to Linux, and a small wizard runs to allow you to configure its various settings. Then you can run the UDA and configure your access storage and OS.

Configuring Network Settings

Through the UDA startup wizard, you set your host name, IP address, and DHCP configuration (if selected). Although you can use the TAB key to navigate the wizard, I've found using the cursor keys works the best.

1. Power on the UDA.

2. At the Welcome screen, press ENTER.

3. In the Hostname dialog box, type in the host name for your UDA. Notice how the interface clearly states that you should enter the host name only, not the FQDN.

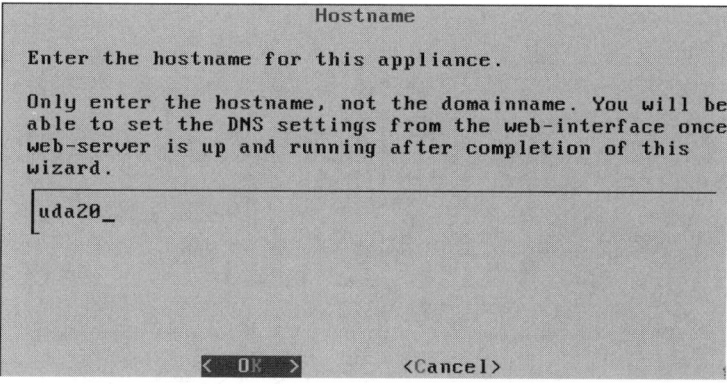

4. Set your IP address, subnet mask, and default gateway. As the UDA is both the boot source and source of the ESX media, I used the same network range as my ESX hosts.

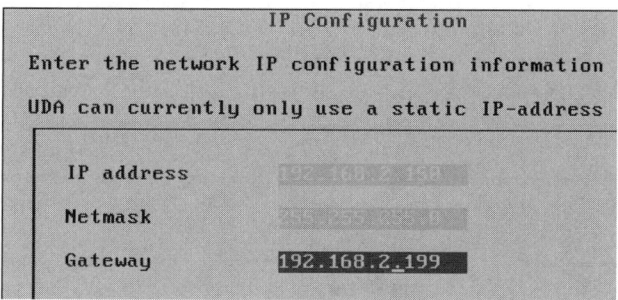

5. Enable DHCP in the Services list. If you already have a DHCP server, and merely wish the UDA server to be a PXE-boot server, skip this step. In the next section, I will describe how to make an existing Microsoft DHCP server issue the IP address to your ESX hosts and point to the UDA, as you may have corporate policies that enforce the use of authorized Active Directory DHCP servers.

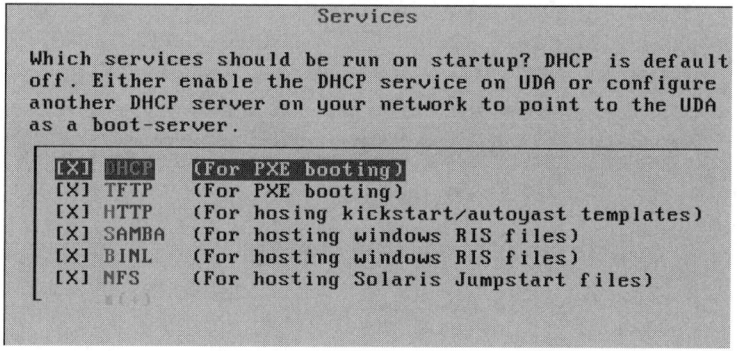

6. Set the network ID, subnet mask, and starting and ending range for your DHCP scope.

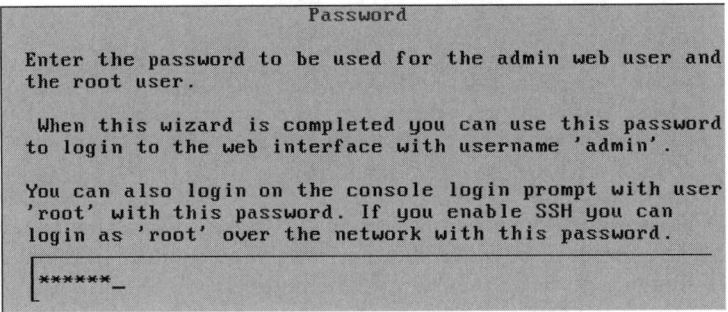

7. Set your password for root and admin accounts. The UDA uses the root account for SSH and console logins. It uses the more limited admin account to authenticate to the friendly Web page front end that allows for high-level postconfiguration.

8. Confirm your password and the summary of the settings you have provided.

9. Once the wizard completes, open a Web browser on the UDA and log in as admin with your password. You will see the UDA Welcome screen.

Ultimate Deployment Appliance

System	Services	Storage	OS	Templates

Welcome

Welcome to the Ultimate Deployment Appliance

for more information see:
www.ultimatedeployment.org

10. Optionally, click the System menu option, and then set your DNS server and DNS domain. This will allow you to use names, rather than IP addresses, when specifying storage access for the UDA.

Setting Up Access to Storage

After you have the UDA up and running, the next step is to give it access to storage where your main ISO images are held, which can be on a virtual disk, or on a Windows or NFS share.

NOTE *Before you begin, you may want to check that the UDA can ping the host name, make sure the user specified has rights to the share, and perform the other typical IP and authentication troubleshooting you would do for Windows. If that does not help, then you can resort to raw IP data, as the UDA will accept that as well.*

To define your storage, click the Storage menu option and click the New button.

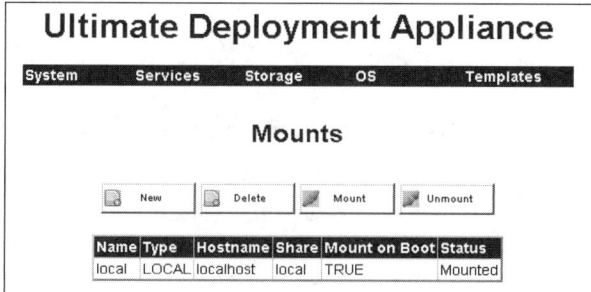

Select your storage from the Type pull-down list. If your ESX 4 ISO file resides on a Windows share, for example, select Windows Network Share, and then complete the dialog box. The Name field is for a friendly name that the UDA will use to refer collectively to all these settings.

Adding the OS

After you've set up the storage access, you can then mount the ESX 4 ISO file to the UDA. The UDA will automatically copy all the files required for a PXE boot from the disk to the UDA, without you needing to know anything about Linux, TFTP, DHCP, or PXE.

Next, you need to configure an OS for the UDA. It needs to know which OS you are using: Windows, ESX 3, ESX 4, or GentOS. Then you will indicate the flavor of that OS—ESX 4.0.0, ESX 4.0.1, ESX 4.5, and so on. This allows the UDA to mount any number of different distributions of a given OS. Once you have browsed and selected the ISO file in question, the UDA will then import the critical boot files required for PXE booting to be successful.

Follow these steps:

1. Click the OS menu option.

2. Click the New button.

3. Select your OS from the pull-down list (VMware ESX Server 4.X.X in this example).

4. Type in a unique flavor name (esx40 in this example). Flavor names can be anything you like, but you *must* set one for the UDA to work properly.

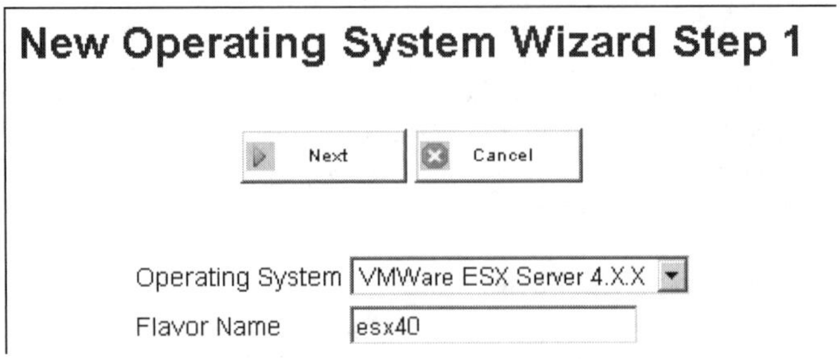

New Operating System Wizard Step 1

▶ Next   ⊗ Cancel

Operating System | VMWare ESX Server 4.X.X ▼
Flavor Name | esx40

---

5. Click Next, and then select the ESX ISO file in your mounting point.

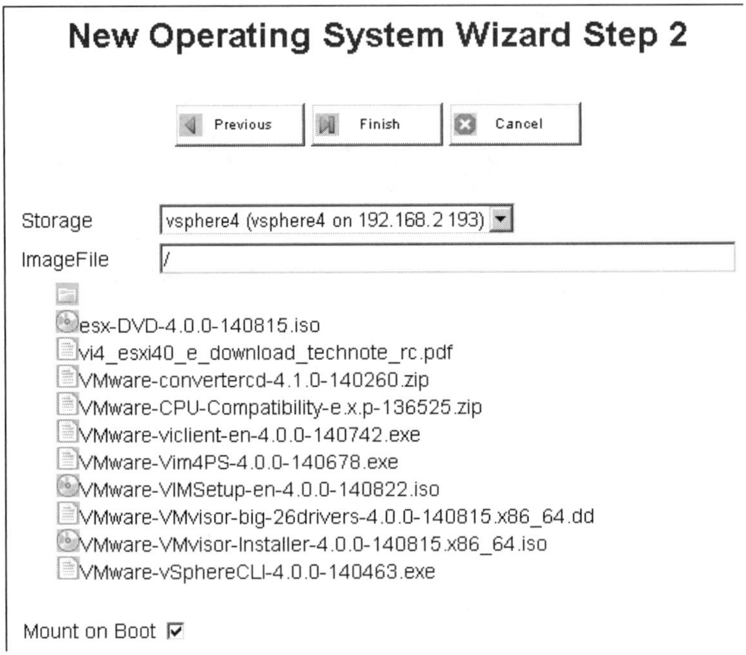

New Operating System Wizard Step 2

◀ Previous   ▶ Finish   ⊗ Cancel

Storage | vsphere4 (vsphere4 on 192.168.2 193) ▼
ImageFile | /

📁
🔵 esx-DVD-4.0.0-140815.iso
📄 vi4_esxi40_e_download_technote_rc.pdf
📄 VMware-convertercd-4.1.0-140260.zip
📄 VMware-CPU-Compatibility-e.x.p-136525.zip
📄 VMware-viclient-en-4.0.0-140742.exe
📄 VMware-Vim4PS-4.0.0-140678.exe
🔵 VMware-VIMSetup-en-4.0.0-140822.iso
📄 VMware-VMvisor-big-26drivers-4.0.0-140815.x86_64.dd
🔵 VMware-VMvisor-Installer-4.0.0-140815.x86_64.iso
📄 VMware-vSphereCLI-4.0.0-140463.exe

Mount on Boot ☑

---

6. Click the Finish button.

The UDA does *not* copy the entire CD from the network share; it copies just the files required for PXE booting. The share will still need to be online and available for the UDA to function.

Creating Templates

Each ESX host you have will need a text file to automate the installation—after all, it's a scripted installation. However, can you imagine having 30 to 40 different script files, each with IP addresses, subnet masks, and default gateways hard-coded into them? They would be a nightmare to maintain.

It would be so much better to have a single "master" template, which merely contains the installation instructions with variables, and a separate "subtemplate," which contains all those variables. And wouldn't it be great if you could define (within reason) any variable you like, and for the system to automatically build a menu to select from once the main PXE-boot process has completed? Well, I'm pleased to say that the UDA does all that for you! In fact, the ESX version of the UDA comes with a sample master template that does a complete scripted installation for you. All you need to do is change the variables.

Creating a Master Template

To create the master template, click the Template menu option to start the New Template Wizard. Type in the master template name (VI4BOOK in this example), select the OS (VMware ESX Server 4.X.X in this example), and then select the flavor used with this template (esx40 in this example).

New Template Wizard Step 1

	Next		Cancel

Template Name	VI4BOOK
Description	Used with the vi4book.com
Operating System	VMWare ESX Server 4.X.X
Flavor	esx40
Bind to MAC	
Publish	☑

The Sort button can be used to sort your templates by alphabetical order and reorder the list. The list will create a menu from which the operator can select a template.

In the second step of the New Template Wizard, select the hardware type you are using.

New Template Wizard Step 2

	Previous		Finish		Cancel

Template Name	VI4BOOK
Operating System	esx4
Flavor	esx40
Description	Used with the vi4book.com domain
MAC	
Publish	ON
Hardware Type	HP (cciss/c0d0)

HP (cciss/c0d0)
IBM (sda)
Dell (sda)
Generic SCSI (sda)

Caution *Remember HP servers with internal RAID controllers assume /dev/cciss/c0d0 for the first controller and the first disk. Dell and IBM servers will normally default to /dev/sda for local storage. The UDA will wipe any disks you set it to install ESX to, so it's important that /dev/sda isn't your Exchange mail store. Am I making myself clear here? If this worries you at all, then either disable the ESX host's HBAs in the BIOS or use the masking features of your storage array to make sure that the ESX host does not see any shared storage during the installation.*

I repeated this process to create a master template from my ESX hosts using the rtfm-ed.co.uk domain name.

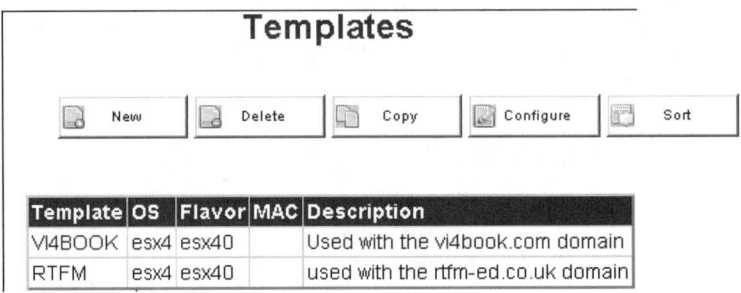

Template	OS	Flavor	MAC	Description
VI4BOOK	esx4	esx40		Used with the vi4book.com domain
RTFM	esx4	esx40		used with the rtfm-ed.co.uk domain

The names VI4BOOK and RTFM will build a menu system inside the UDA that will be displayed whenever you carry out a PXE boot. The following examples from an HP ILO card show what the end user will see.

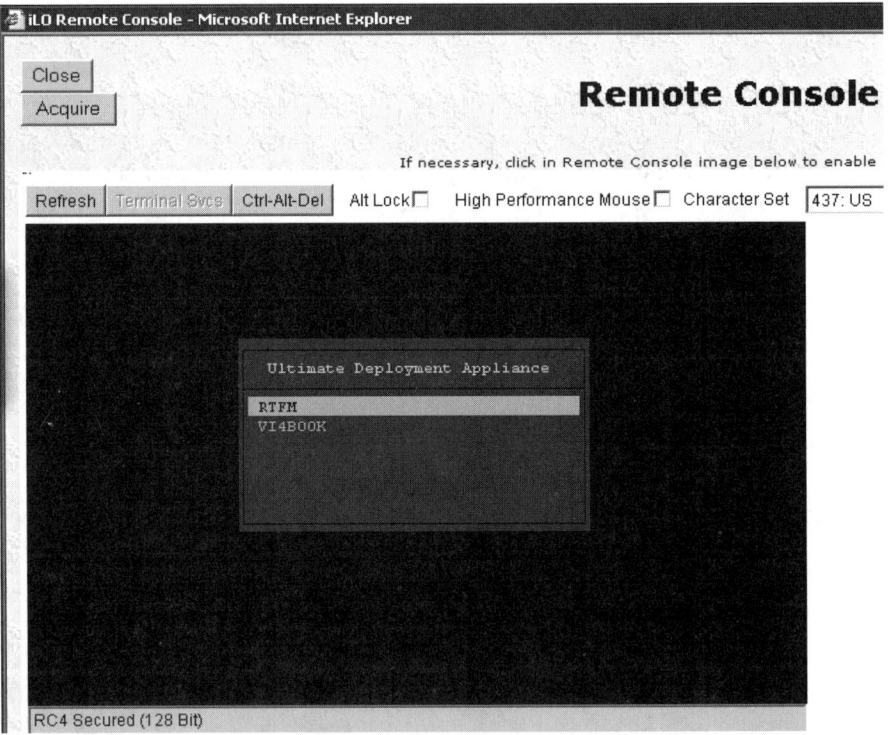

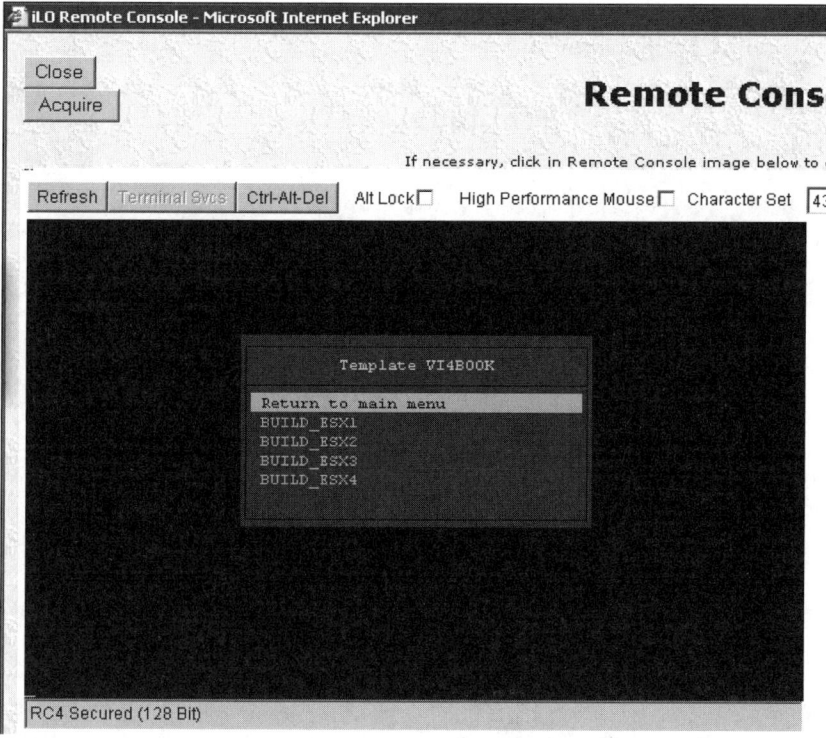

Adding Subtemplates

Subtemplates store the variables that make each ESX host different from the rest, such as its host name and IP address. The sample master template holds some variables, represented by square brackets, including the following:

- [DISKTYPE], which holds the variable of /dev/sda or /cciss/c0d0
- [IPADDR], which holds the variable for the ESX host's unique IP address
- [FQDN], which holds the variable for the ESX host's FQDN

By modifying the subtemplate file associated with each master template, you can quickly create configurations for many ESX hosts. You can make these changes by simply copying and pasting and modifying the variables.

To create a subtemplate, click the Template menu option, select the master template in the list, and click the Configure button.

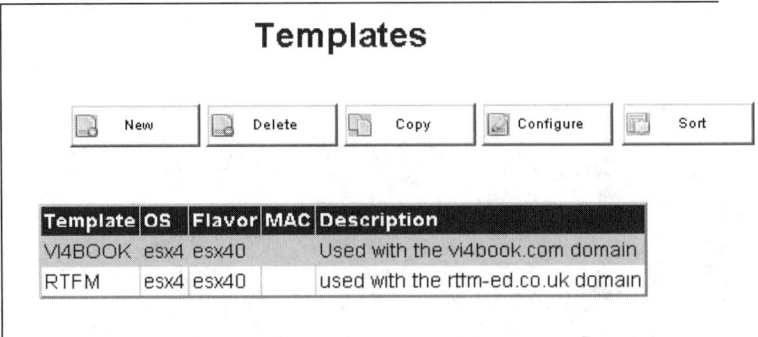

Select the Subtemplates option, and then click the Edit button. Input your variables using a semicolon as a separator.

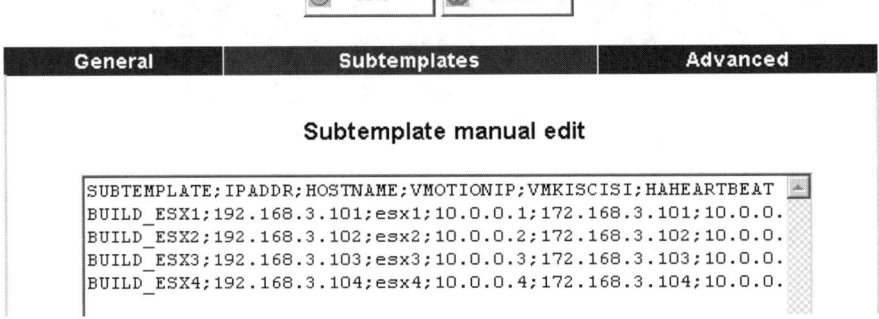

The variable SUBTEMPLATE is hard-coded. In this example, it will create a submenu inside my main menu of VI4BOOK with options to build_esx1 and so on.

Remember the sky is the limit here—you can create as many variables as you need for any purpose. In my live UDA environment, which I use to build either my rtfm-ed.co.uk hosts or my vi4book.com hosts, I use these variables:

```
SUBTEMPLATE;
IPADDR;
HOSTNAME;
VMOTIONIP;
VMKISCISI;
HAHEARTBEAT
FTLOGGING
```

The UDA is now good to go. You could jump in with both feet and give it a whirl. Alternatively, you could continue reading to learn more about the settings in the master template that automates the installation.

Scripted Installation File Overview with Advanced %post Scripting

This section contains a sample weasel script used by the UDA to automate the installation. A copy of this sample script can be downloaded from http://www.rtfm-ed.co.uk/downloads/esx4.cfg.

TIP *Even if you decide not to use the UDA, this script will work if you replace the variables (in square brackets) with actual values.*

I've added comments in *italics* in an in-line format to describe each part or add some explanation. Most of this stuff is common sense, so I will endeavor (believe it or not!) not to patronize you as we go through it.

```
# VMware ESX4 template Kickstart file
# Installation Method
install url http://[UDA_IPADDR]/[OS]/[FLAVOR]
```

This sets the install media is to be found on the UDA and delivered by its internal web server. It is possible to deliver the media to the ESX host using FTP or NFS as well as HTTP.

```
# VMware Specific Commands
vmaccepteula
```

You must include this or the script will fail.

```
# Timezone
timezone Europe/London
# Keyboard
keyboard uk
# Encrypted root password: password
auth --enableshadow --enablemd5
rootpw --iscrypted $1$5a17$In5zYe6YsCty76AycpGaf/
```

Md5sum represents a safe way of saving passwords in plain text files without disclosing the real password. There are a number of Web sites and software that can generate md5sum passwords for you. However, an easy method is to create a user and set a password, and then cat /etc/passwd to view the md5sum.

```
# Reboot after install
reboot
```

If you don't include this, the installer just stops prompting you to do a manual reboot.

```
# Network install type
network --device=vmnic0 --bootproto=static --ip=[IPADDR] --netmask=
255.255.255.0 --gateway=192.168.2.199 --nameserver=192.168.2.199 --
hostname=[HOSTNAME].vi4book.com --addvmportgroup=0
```

This is quite straightforward I think, with vmnic0 now replacing eth0 as a way of indicating both which network card to use during the install and also which network card will be mapped to vSwitch0. The --addvmportgroup=0 value prevents the installer from creating a virtual machine port group called VM Network on vSwitch0.

```
# Firewall settings
firewall -disabled
```

This controls the firewall of the installer, not the ESX firewall, which would be controlled by esxcfg-firewall.

```
#  Clear Partitions
clearpart --drives=[DISKTYPE] -overwritevmfs
```

This is quite dangerous as it destroys whatever is on the [DISKTYPE], which could be either cciss/c0d0 if it is a HP ProLiant Server or /dev/sda if it is an IBM or Dell server. Overwritevmfs forces the clearing of all partitions even if they are VMFS volumes. This is also quite dangerous if you touch the wrong disk/volume/LUN.

```
# BootLoader ( The user has to use grub by default )
bootloader --location=mbr --driveorder=[DISKTYPE]
```

This tells the installer where to put the MBR record. Without it, you will receive a benign warning that it will install GRUB to the disk selected for the partition table.

```
# Manual Partitioning
part /boot --fstype=ext3 --size=250 --ondisk=[DISKTYPE]
part None --fstype=vmkcore --size=100 --ondisk=[DISKTYPE]
part  [HOSTNAME]_local --fstype=vmfs3 --size=20000 --ondisk=[DISKTYPE]
-grow
```

This creates 3 partitions on [DISKTYPE]: the boot partition, vmkcore partition, and vmfs volume called local_[HOSTNAME]. The vmfs volume would not be 20MB but be the remainder of the volume.

```
virtualdisk vd1 --size=15000 --onvmfs=local_[HOSTNAME]
part swap --fstype=swap --size=1600 --onvirtualdisk=vd1|
part /opt --fstype=ext3 --size=2048 --onvirtualdisk=vd1
part /tmp --fstype=ext3 --size=2048 --onvirtualdisk=vd1
part /home --fstype=ext3 --size=2048 --onvirtualdisk=vd1
part / --fstype=ext3 --size=5120 --onvirtualdisk=vd1 -grow
```

This partitions the first virtual disk (vd1) of the Service Console. This virtual disk is created as 15GB on the local_[HOSTNAME]. So whatever the VMFS volume is called, it must have the correct name for the VMDK file to be created. We then proceed to create partitions within the virtual disk. The last partition / would not be 5120 but would grow to be the remainder of the virtual disk.

```
%packages
```

This allows you to install other packages aside from the base install. I don't use this in my scripted installation.

```
%post --interpreter=bash
```

%post is always at the end of the install process. Setting the –interpreter=bash prevents a benign warning, which would state if the installer is defaulting to BASH (Bourne Again SHell). If you don't include this, the commands below would still be processed, as long as they were recognizable by the BusyBox or the VMkernel.

```
cat << \EOF > /etc/rc3.d/S99postconf
#!/bin/sh
```

This creates a script called S99postconf, which is executed as part of the boot process once the installation has completed, and the ESX host boots for the first time. This is not unlike having an autoexec.bat in DOS with commands or other scripts that called in a "run-once" manner.

```
# Create vSwitch1 with a port group of internal
esxcfg-vswitch -a vSwitch1
esxcfg-vswitch -A internal-[HOSTNAME] vSwitch1
```

This uses the esxcfg-vswitch command to create a vSwitch and port group. Notice how esxcfg-vswitch –L is not being used, so network cards are NOT linked to the virtual switch.

```
# Create vSwitch2 with a port group of Production using vmnic1
esxcfg-vswitch -a vSwitch2
esxcfg-vswitch -A production vSwitch2
esxcfg-vswitch -L vmnic1 vSwitch2
```

This creates a simple virtual switch with one network card and therefore no fault tolerance.

```
# Create vSwitch3 with a port group of VMotion using vmnic2
esxcfg-vswitch -a vSwitch3
esxcfg-vswitch -A VMotion vSwitch3
esxcfg-vswitch -L vmnic2 vSwitch3
```

This creates a vSwitch valid for VMotion using the esxcfg-vmknic command to set the IP address and subnet mask valid for the network.

```
# Enable VMotion

service mgmt-vmware restart
sleep 60
esxcfg-vmknic -a VMotion -i [VMOTIONIP] -n 255.255.255.0
vmware-vim-cmd hostsvc/vmotion/vnic_set vmk0
vmware-vim-cmd hostsvc/net/refresh
```

On it is own, esxcfg-vswitch cannot enable the VMotion feature. We can do this with a high-level utility called vmware-vim-cmd. It is a supported utility and is actually a wrapper to an even more powerful utility called vimsh. Unfortunately, vimsh is not official supported by VMware; however, it is exceedingly powerful if you wish to do high-level changes. Both vmware-vim-cmd and vimsh have been well documented at the xtravirt.com Web site:

```
# Create add with a port group for iSCSI using vSwitch4

esxcfg-vswitch -a vSwitch4
esxcfg-vswitch -A ipstorage vSwitch4
esxcfg-vswitch -L vmnic3 vSwitch4
```

```
esxcfg-vswitch -L vmnic4 vSwitch4
esxcfg-vmknic -a ipstorage -i [VMKISCISI] -n 255.255.255.0

# HA Heartbeat Port on VMotion Switch
esxcfg-vswitch -A ha-heartbeat vSwitch3
esxcfg-vswif -a vswif2 -p ha-heartbeat -i [HAHEARTBEAT] -n 255.255.255.0
```

This creates a third Service Console port to allow an HA Heartbeat network to function.

```
# Set up iSCSI Software Emulator
esxcfg-swiscsi -e
vmkiscsi-tool -D -a 172.168.3.100 vmhba34
esxcfg-swiscsi -s
```

This enables the ESX iSCSI software initiator connecting to an iSCSI target with the IP of 172.168.3.100.

```
# Connect to a NAS...
esxcfg-nas -a nas-iso -o nfs.vi4book.com -s /iso
```

This mounts an NFS share to the ESX host. The name nas-iso is the friendly datastore name that users will see in the vSphere Client, whereas /iso is the actual name of the NFS share.

```
# VLAN Example
# esxcfg-vswitch -a vSwitch2
# esxcfg-vswitch -A accounts vSwitch2
# esxcfg-vswitch -A rnd vSwitch2
# esxcfg-vswitch -A sales vSwitch2
# esxcfg-vswitch -L vmnic4 vSwitch2
# esxcfg-vswitch -L vmnic5 vSwitch2
# esxcfg-vswitch -v 10 -p accounts vSwitch2
# esxcfg-vswitch -v 20 -p rnd vSwitch2
# esxcfg-vswitch -v 30 -p sales vSwitch2
```

This is a sample vSwitch with multiple port groups enabled for VLAN tagging and multiple network cards for fault tolerance. Accounts, rnd, and sales aren't great port group names, but I've used them to make sure it's clear that –v 10 sets the VLAN value, and that accounts, rnd, and sales are just friendly port group names.

```
# esxcfg-vswitch -A FT-Logging vSwitch3
# esxcfg-vmknic -a FT-Logging -i [FTLOGGING] -n 255.255.255.0
# service mgmt-vmware restart
# sleep 60
# vmware-vim-cmd hostsvc/advopt/update FT.Vmknic string vmk2
# vmware-vim-cmd hostsvc/net/refresh
```

This sample creates a vSwitch5 with two VMNics uplinked to it for VMware Fault Tolerence. It uses the vmware-vim-cmd command to enable the FT option on a VMKernel port.

```
# Add 2nd/3rd DNS settings
echo nameserver 192.168.3.200 >> /etc/resolv.conf
echo nameserver 192.168.3.201 >> /etc/resolv.conf
```

The installer does not accept more than one DNS server, so here I'm using the echo command to pass two IP addresses for my secondary and territory DNS servers.

```
# Create a local user for SSH Access - Default password is password
useradd -p '$1$Rg69B9QA$JUtqStBrjNFbyzyP9zTsf0' -c "Mike Laverick" lavericm
```

This creates a user called lavericm with a password of password and friendly name of Mike Laverick. There should be no real need to create users on an ESX host because you can use WinBind, which is part of the Samba Project, to allow users to log in using their LDAP credentials. Additionally, you can use sudo to prevent any need to disclose the ESX root password. In fact, there's only one time when you have to disclose the root account—when you add ESX into vCenter. If you intend not to use WinBind and instead use the esxcfg-auth to enable ESX to AD communication to allow for centralized password resets, you must remember that the name of the local ESX user account must match the name of the account in AD.

```
# DANGEROUS: Allow ROOT access using SSH
sed -e 's/PermitRootLogin no/PermitRootLogin yes/' /etc/ssh/sshd_config >
/etc/ssh/sshd_config.new
mv -f /etc/ssh/sshd_config.new /etc/ssh/sshd_config
service sshd restart
```

In production systems, I would not lower the security to allow the root to directly SSH (or PuTTY into) the ESX host. You would have no traceability of who did what and when. However, in certain lab environments where security concerns may be of less significance, you can weaken the security. SED is a text manipulation tool, which can search for and replace lines of text within a text file. It does that by searching an existing file and outputting the change to a new file. We can then take this new file and overwrite the original, using the service command to restart SSHD to have those changes take effect.

```
# Enable the SSH client (Out/From ESX hosts)
esxcfg-firewall -e sshClient
```

I quite like the ability to SSH and SCP from one ESX host to another, so on the firewall I enable the sshClient, which opens port 22 outbound. SSH on port 22 is already open inbound on the firewall.

```
# Enabling NTP Time Configuration
echo restrict 127.0.0.1 > /etc/ntp.conf
echo restrict default kod nomodify notrap noquery nopeer >> /etc/ntp.conf
echo server 0.uk.pool.ntp.org  >> /etc/ntp.conf
echo server 1.uk.pool.ntp.org  >> /etc/ntp.conf
echo server 2.uk.pool.ntp.org  >> /etc/ntp.conf
echo server 3.uk.pool.ntp.org  >> /etc/ntp.conf
echo fudge 127.127.1.0 stratum 10 >> /etc/ntp.conf
echo driftfile /var/lib/ntp/drift >> /etc/ntp.conf
# Create the Step-Tickers File
echo server 0.uk.pool.ntp.org >> /etc/ntp/step-tickers
echo server 1.uk.pool.ntp.org >> /etc/ntp/step-tickers
echo server 2.uk.pool.ntp.org >> /etc/ntp/step-tickers
echo server 3.uk.pool.ntp.org >> /etc/ntp/step-tickers
# Handle the Service Management
```

```
esxcfg-firewall -e ntpClient
service ntpd start
chkconfig --level 3 ntpd on
hwclock -systohc
```

As you can see, this enables time synchronization for the ESX host. This is well documented on many Linux forums and I have nothing to add that hasn't been said countless times before.

```
# SSH Legal Message...
echo  >> /etc/banner
echo This is a private system. >> /etc/banner
echo Do not attempt to login unless you are an authorised user. >>
/etc/banner
echo Any authorised or unauthorised access and use may be monitored >>

/etc/banner
echo and can result in criminal or civil prosecution under applicable law.
>> /etc/banner
echo  >> /etc/banner
echo The United Kingdown of England, Ireland, Scottland and Wales
>> /etc/banner
echo Computer Misuse Act 1990 >> /etc/banner
echo http://www.opsi.gov.uk/acts/acts1990/Ukpga_19900018_en_1.htm >>
/etc/banner
echo  >> /etc/banner
echo Banner /etc/banner >> /etc/ssh/sshd_config
```

Here I am creating a standard logon warning when anyone connects with SSH. I borrowed the disclaimer from a HP ILO Login Page, and looked up the legislation in the UK that governs the misuse of computers. I would recommend you consult your legal advisor for an appropriate legally binding message relative to your location in the world.

```
# Removes the Start-Up Script and Sets it executable

rm /etc/rc3.d/S99postconf
EOF
chmod +x /etc/rc3.d/S99postconf
```

Finally, the last part of S99postconf removes the S99postconf script as part of a cleanup routine that prevents the script from running more than once.

Enabling Microsoft Windows DHCP with UDA

In some environments, it may not be possible to use the UDA's built-in DHCP daemon. It is possible to disable the DHCP service on the UDA and configure a Microsoft DHCP server to take over the role. This is quite an easy configuration change.

To disable DHCP on the UDA, follow these steps:

1. Log on as admin on the UDA's Web admin tool.

2. Click the Services link.

3. Select the DHCP link.

4. Click the Configure button.

5. Disable the option for Start DHCP on boot.

6. Click the Apply button.

7. Click the Services link again.

8. Select the DHCP link again.

9. Click the Stop button.

To enable DHCP on the Windows DHCP server, configure the following scope options or server options:

- Enable the option 066 Boot Server Host Name, and set the empty string value to be the IP address of your UDA.

- Enable the option 067 Bootfile Name, and set the empty string to be **pxelinux.0**.

Interactive PXE Installation

It's not mandatory to have templates and subtemplates. It is possible to use the UDA just to provide the media, and carry out a manual graphical installation. This can be considerably quicker for manual installations because using RAC/ILO virtual media with a large DVD image can be very slow.

To set up for interactive PXE installation, create a new template, perhaps called GUI. Delete the default script in the advanced area, and modify the "Kernel option command line" from this:

```
ks=http://[UDA_IPADDR]/kickstart/GUI/[SUBTEMPLATE].cfg
initrd=initrd.[OS].[FLAVOR] mem=512M
```

to this:

```
initrd=initrd.[OS].[FLAVOR] mem=512M url=http://[UDA_IPADDR]/[OS]/[FLAVOR]
```

As you can see, merely by removing all reference to the kickstart file, you can simply load the installer over the network.

Summary

At the beginning of this chapter, I was careful not to pigeonhole the various tools and utilities together. Additionally, I didn't want to express my opinion on which is the best set of tools to use, for fear of being too biased. But now that you have been exposed to all the advanced configuration tools for vSphere 4, I will put forward which tools folks are most likely to use and why. Much depends on what your previous skills are and what flavor of ESX you are using. Remember that distributed vSwitches and host profiles are available only if you have an Enterprise Plus license, so you may well be limited to the tools that your organization is prepared to purchase.

Here are three scenarios:

- **New VMware guy using ESXi**   If you are new to VMware and you're using ESXi, I recommend using distributed vSwitches together with host profiles to automate as much of the postconfiguration process surrounding the ESX hosts as possible. If you are feeling adventurous, you could dip your toe into either the vMA or PowerShell. PowerShell is a good choice, because in the long-term, you would be learning a very rich and powerful CLI that would assist you in troubleshooting and generating reports.

- **New VMware guy using ESX Classic**   As with the previous scenario, I suggest sticking with distributed vSwitches and host profiles. This configuration is likely to work for you with little modification should you eventually switch to using ESXi. Invest sometime in learning PowerCLI from VMware to assist you in day to day management tasks.

- **Old-school ESX Classic guy**   If you are an old-school COS guy like me, and you're using ESX Classic, I would stick with using scripted installations and `esxcfg-` commands. You probably have scripts like this already in place, and I see no advantage in reinventing the wheel. That said, be aware that in the long-term, the comfort blanket of the Service Console will one day be removed. You need to start thinking about moving over to one of the more powerful tools like the vMA or PowerShell. Remember that the PowerCLI has hundreds of cmdlets compared to just twenty or thirty esxcfg- commands at the Service Console. PowerCLI is infinitely more functional compared to the old-school "Service Console."

As learning exercise I recently completely changed my environment to be ESXi and decided to switch all my post-configuration tasks in PowerCLI. I enjoyed the process so much I've now abandoned the use of %post in my VMware environment and everything is now carried out with PowerCLI. You can read more about my exploits and download sample PowerCLI scripts from my blog:

http://www.rtfm-ed.co.uk/?cat=21

http://www.rtfm-ed.co.uk/?p=1527

CHAPTER 18 | Virtual Machine Backup

This 	chapter covers VM backup techniques. First, I'll provide some insight into how hot backups work. Next, we'll look at the main backup strategies for VMs. The remainder of the chapter focuses on VMware's main technologies for backup: Consolidated Backup and the Data Recovery appliance.

What's New with VM Backup?

- The VMware Data Recovery appliance, a VM that facilitates backup and comes with the vSphere Client plug-in
- Improvements in VMware Consolidated Backup include new support for thinly provisioned disks and IDE disks; improved support for busy SAN and iSCSI links, vApps, and Windows Server 2008

How Do Hot Backups Work?

It is possible to back up the files that make up a VM while it is powered on and running—in other words, a hot backup. This is achieved either by VMware or a third-party backup vendor leveraging VMware's snapshot feature. In fact, with a few simple commands (`vmware-cmd` and `vmkfstools` or VMware's vCLI), you could cobble together your own "home-brewed" backup solution. But I wouldn't recommend that you do that, because others have got there before you and have been doing it longer.

As discussed in Chapter 7, when a snapshot is applied to a VM, the files that make up the VM become unlocked in the file system. When a file is unlocked, the possibility of backup becomes available. It's important to know that *all* vendors use VMware snapshots in this way. The quality of the backup vendor's software comes in the validation process—validating that the snapshot was successfully created prior to the backup starting and, critically, that the snapshot is deleted if or when the backup completes. And one of the most common reasons for VMware snapshots becoming excessively large is a backup process that did not successfully validate the snapshot process or alert the administrator when something went wrong.

By now, you might be pretty worried. After all, the previous paragraph wasn't especially reassuring, was it? Well, buddy, welcome to the real world! You need to be aware of the realities of hot backups of VMs, because forewarned is forearmed. This is not to say that they are not a good thing, but to remind you that bad things can happen, and you should be looking out for them.

First, let's take the quality of VMware snapshots in the context of backups. VMware snapshots in VI3.5 introduced a file system sync driver installed to the VM during the installation of VMware Tools. The job of this file system sync driver is to flush the file system cache, forcing a write-to-disk prior to the backup process. The intention is that you get the most complete backup you can have with live data still being in memory—that is to say, a consistent backup, rather than a crash-consistent backup.

This file system sync driver from VMware is pretty good, but in the early days of VI3, customers found it to be limited when it came to specific systems that store their data in modes beyond ordinary text or graphics files, such as Active Directory, Microsoft SQL Server, and Oracle. Essentially, the driver lacked the level of file system awareness required to back up these candidates reliably. The response to this was implementing hooks into Microsoft's Volume Shadow Copy Service. This came into the VI3.5 product at around the Update 1 or 2 period, and it has been maintained within vSphere 4. Interestingly, VMware appeared to be quite slow in taking up the Volume Shadow Copy Service; a number of third-party backup vendors such as Vizioncore offered this level of integration with Microsoft much earlier.

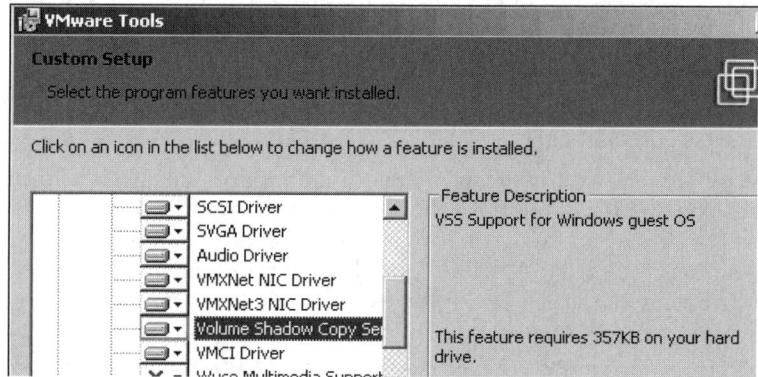

The second issue associated with VMware snapshots is that sometimes the snapshot is left behind after the backup process completes. This could be dangerous if left unchecked, as the VMware snapshot feature has at its heart a delta file, which grows incrementally in blocks of 16MB. One reason why VMware snapshots can be left behind after the backup has completed is simply sloppy coding (not one that goes down especially well). I've come across a number of home-brewed solutions where, because of poor scripting, the VM's snapshot has not been deleted at the end of the process.

Another factor is the fragility of your network. Most backup systems need communication with either the vCenter server or ESX host to function. The backup system might trigger the backup process without error, but midway through the backup job communication is lost to the ESX host or the vCenter server. This could be due to something VMware is responsible for, such as a failure of the vCenter service, or something as simple as some idiot in your environment creating an IP address conflict, or both. The net result of this lost communication is a backup that is successful, but fails to delete the snapshot at the end of the process.

Personally, I think we can accept that no network is perfect. While we strive to protect ourselves from mass network outages by teaming devices, when it comes to software or configuration, it becomes increasingly harder to offer the same level of redundancy. If we accept this as a reality, then the benchmark becomes how well the given backup solution detects, repairs, and logs this event, and how well it alerts the administrator to a potential problem.

Overview of Backup Strategies

There are a million ways of getting copied files to be the same in two different storage locations, which is as brief a description of backup as I can think of. The idea is that if the file in one location is lost, damaged, or deleted, the original data can be retrieved.

As a reader, you will be grateful that I won't bore you with lengthy descriptions of normal, differential, incremental, or synthetic backups, or extol the merits of disk-to-disk deduplication of data.

In my current role as an instructor, I'm often asked for a survey of backup options or strategies, together with an overview of different methods. These can be as crude or sophisticated as you like.

As an individual, my backup concerns are very modest: I back up my laptop data and I back up my nine critical VMs that make my life workable. None of these nine VMs are important to me; they could be rebuilt from scratch without any data loss. The only reason I back up those VMs is because I know what a royal pain in the butt it would be to carry out that rebuild.

You might be curious to know how I back up such a modest environment. Well, once a week, quarter, or year (depending on my mood), I power down those VMs and clone them as templates in the compressed format to an alternative removable drive. To me, a copy of a VM held in different location is a backup by any other name.

I recognize that the field of backup is immensely more complicated than what I have just described, and I am not by any means promoting or endorsing such an approach. However, it gives you an idea of the flexibility of backups in a virtual environment.

The holy grail of backup in the world of virtualization is to be able to back up a VM directly from its storage location (SAN, iSCSI, or NAS) without needing to install agents into the guest OS. This backup should offer all the features of conventional backups (normal, differential, and incremental). The backup should be quick, and even more important, so should the restore process. It should not take a degree in scripting languages to set up or use.

When it comes to backup solutions—an extremely important part of IT—the virtualization sector has taken some time to mature. Installing a backup agent inside a VM is still very common, because often the virtualization ecosystem has failed to deliver a solution that has approached anything near universal adoption by the VMware community. There is no one standardized way of backing up. What we have is many competing methods, which all come with advantages and disadvantages. Of course, one way of getting the best of all strategies is to use more than one method. However, this approach has the disadvantage of significantly increasing the cost of storing that backup data in multiple locations.

Essentially, the competing backup strategies can be broken down into four approaches:

- Install a backup agent inside the VM.
- Use free backup utilities.
- Buy a third-party virtualization-only solution.
- Use VMware technology: the Data Recovery appliance and Consolidated Backup.

Let's take a closer look at the advantages and disadvantages of each approach.

Backup Agents Inside the VM

It's entirely possible to back up individual files (.doc, .xls, and so on) inside the virtual disks, but it still remains common to install backup agents inside the VM and back up across the network. This strategy has the following advantages:

- **Mixed environments**   VMs and physical machines are backed up in a consistent way.
- **Very mature**   This backup method will reliably back up troublesome candidates like Microsoft Active Directory, SQL Server, Exchange, and Oracle, making sure your data is restored in a consistent state.
- **Easy adoption**   There is no need to re-rehearse your restore strategy or educate staff about new procedures and tasks.
- **Improved by virtualization**   If you lose an entire VM, you can very quickly deploy a new VM containing a backup agent preinstalled and start the restore process very easily.

However, using backup agents is not without disadvantages, such as the following:

- **Cost**   Most backup vendors charge a license fee for each backup agent. Some, like HP Data Protector, do not charge. Other vendors, like Symantec, have shifted the licensing policy to cancel out this disadvantage.

- **Throttled by network**   By definition, with an agent installed inside the VM, backup and restore operations will be constrained by the bandwidth from the backup storage location.

- **Performance hit**   During a backup, there will be increased I/O on the ESX host, to absorb the backup load.

- **Encapsulation, encapsulation, encapsulation**   One of the major benefits of virtualization is with your virtual disks, everything is already "just a file." When you use a backup agent inside a VM, you are effectively treating the VM as if it were physical. Some people think that this significantly reduces one of the advantages of virtualization; others don't see anything wrong with this approach.

Free Virtualization Backup Utilities

In the early days of virtualization (ESX 1 and ESX 2), there really was no backup solution beyond installing backup agents inside the VM. However, since the VM is really just a bunch of files, you could use command-line utilities to take a snapshot of a VM, and then export the VM's virtual disk to another location. Essentially, this represented a normal backup every time, and so the storage penalties were quite high. These solutions were also significantly dependent on the ESX Service Console as a scripting environment, and so would be unsuitable in an ESXi environment.

Over time, certain individuals developed these backup scripts in such a way that they almost became products, with the critical difference being that they were still free and supported only by the community. You might be surprised to know that despite the increased regulatory burden we live under, where corporate compliance is king, these methods were very popular in the VMware community. This was mainly because they were very good, and there was no alternative.

Some of these free utilities have passed into private hands and are no longer freely available. This leaves the granddaddy of them all: the vmbk.pl script, available from http://www.vmts.net. But whether it will continue to be improved and supported in vSphere 4 is unclear at this stage.

Third-Party Virtualization-Only Solutions

As you can see, there is plenty of scope for third parties to develop their own unique backup solutions. There are three main players currently in this virtualization-only space:

- PhD Virtual Technologies, esXpress product
- Veeam Backup & Replication
- Vizioncore, vRanger product (owned by Quest Software)

Vizioncore's vRanger (formerly esxRanger) is probably the most popular product in terms of units sold, and the product that has been around for some time.

These solutions have the following advantages:

- **Delivery of the holy grail**   All these vendors claim to deliver an agentless backup of VMs. Whether they do deliver this largely depends on the quality of their coding.

- **Unique features**   These solutions often include so-called "bleeding-edge" features. For example, these vendors delivered a delta backup of the entire VM (.nvram, .vmx, and so on) well before VMware's Consolidated Backup did this. With these delta backups, you back up all the files of the VM just once as with a normal copy, and then from that point, you are merely backing up the blocks of those files that have changed.

- **Simple to use**   Very often, these vendors have delivered point-and-click management tools that make virtualization backup and restore operations incredibly easy, and accessible to even small and medium-sized businesses (SMBs) whose administrators have modest data recovery skills. They also come with powerful scripting engines for the more able administrators to automate the backup process.

Of course, there are disadvantages as well:

- **IT politics**   The need to introduce a brand-new proprietary backup solution in addition to an existing backup solution—and one that might have its enterprise license agreement decided in a different continent—is often why these third-party solutions are not accepted. Basically, such a decision may be beyond your control.

- **Quality of regional support**   Some third-party backup vendors may have quite modest support teams. They may not operate in multiple time zones and in multiple languages.

- **Cost**   Although these third–party solutions are extremely competitive products, and the costs are not exorbitant for what they deliver, some might see acquiring them as yet another cost to the business. After all, you already have a backup solution—why can't you just use that?

Many third-party virtualization backup vendors will understandably wish to promote how their backup systems do not have an agent installed to the VM. They will endeavor to show how easy it is to back up an entire VM and restore an entire VM. They do this because this is what their technology usually does very well. However, I frequently find their ability to restore a cluster of individual files in different locations is less slick. As with VMware's Consolidated Backup, it will often involve copying files over the network to the hidden Windows shares.

VMware Technology

VMware has developed its own backup APIs, which the conventional third-party vendors can hook into. VMware Consolidated Backup (VCB) isn't actually a backup solution per se, but rather a collection of command-line tools, scripts, and drivers that allow an existing backup vendor to use its backup solution for Windows to access the VMFS volumes and files within the VMs. New to vSphere 4 is the VMware Data Recovery (vDR) appliance, which is a downloadable virtual appliance that assists in the backup process.

Of course, the VMware technologies also come with advantages and disadvantages. The new vDR appliance is very easy to set up. It provides a point-and-click interface that even someone with modest IT skills would find easy to use. It works with ESX Classic and ESXi to back up VMs, which allows for the backup of the VM's files. It includes support for advanced features such as compression of deduplicated data. There is no network hit when used with shared storage. After the first backup, all subsequent backups are merely the delta changes within the virtual disk using special change-block-tracking functionality (available only in VMs with hardware level 7).

However, vDR currently works only with vSphere 4, which will be an issue for those people who cannot upgrade quickly. Also, it currently allows for 100 VMs to be backed up, and the backup job process happens only once every 24 hours. For many larger companies, this lack of scalability will immediately discount its use, although these limitations may be removed soon. For now, I think that vDR will be popular in the SMB market, where virtualization is new and backup requirements are relatively modest.

VCB works with both vSphere 4 and VI3. It does not require any additional purchase or education investment, beyond becoming familiar with the VCB framework. You can continue using the same tools for backing up physical and virtual machines.

However, unlike vDR, it currently does not have deduplication functionality. It is also not capable of backing up a full VM, and then just recording the delta changes after the first normal backup.

With VCB, the backup load is removed from the network and the ESX hosts by means of a dedicated physical Windows server with a connection to your SAN, iSCSI, or NAS system. However, there have been reports that the VCB backup can become a bottleneck in its own right, especially when backing up large numbers of VMs (600+) and their VMDK files.

VCB is likely to remain popular in large enterprise environments, whose administrators cannot implement a third-party method for a variety reasons and need a solution that integrates with their corporate standards. Additionally, if these large corporations have a major commitment to VI3, the backward compatibility will be attractive to them.

A weakness of both VCB and vDR is their inability to back up snapshots generated by the end users. Therefore, any changes that have accrued in these snapshots are not included in the backup process. Theoretically, there is no reason why this isn't possible, but having to back up snapshots when the backup method itself uses snapshots does add complexity.

Using the VMware Data Recovery Appliance

The vDR appliance is built around the same APIs within vStorage that allow VCB to function. VMware does not intend (at this stage) for the vDR to replace VCB; the two will coexist. I've chosen to emphasize vDR because I think it's significantly easier to get up and running with it, and because it is new. And I like new, don't you?

vDR is a VM; in other words, it's a virtual appliance that assists in the backing up VMs. It backs up all of the VM files (.nvram, .vmx, .log, and .vmdk, including RDM files in virtual compatibility mode). Experimentally, it can also back up files within the VM, such as Word and Excel documents.

NOTE *In the early beta, vDR used a "helper" VM to allow SCSI-based hot-add backups, which are more efficient than network-based backups. This functionality was later integrated into the vDR appliance itself.*

You have the choice of backing up your VMs to virtual disks or RDM files (RDM files are currently only experimentally supported). It also supports the mounting of Windows shares (SMB/CIFS) for an over-the-network backup process. While vDR can utilize tape, you will need a third-party solution for this. (Although many businesses have moved over to disk-to-disk backups for performance and reliability, tape is still important to many organizations with large archive sets, especially those who must retain that data for auditing or compliance reasons.)

vDR works by placing a snapshot on the VMs to be backed up, and then mounts the target VM's files so it can be backed up. Once the backup is complete, the target's virtual disks are unmounted, and the snapshot is removed. Again, snapshots are used to unlock the files that make up the target VM.

How vDR's Data Deduplication Works

In conventional backups—even with normal, differential, and incremental strategies—many organizations back up the same data more than once because it is duplicated in many locations. For example, corporate logos might appear on multiple internal and external web servers.

Deduplication is a process that makes sure that you back up only genuinely unique data. A block-by-block comparison is made of the data so that the backup solution can spot these duplicates, regardless of storage location, file name, or date stamps.

To reduce the disk storage cost of backing up VMs, VMware has developed its own vendor-independent data deduplication process. VMware's deduplication process operates by analyzing the VM to be backed up and breaking it up into smaller, variable-block-sized chunks, which are anywhere from 2KB to 64KB. This support for a variable block size is important for performance. For each of these variable blocks, a SHA1 hash is generated and referenced to the block inside the virtual disk. This process eventually generates a list of SHA1 hashes, which collectively reference the entire data file. By analyzing these SHA1 values, vDR can recognize if a block has been backed up before and if it is has been modified.

This deduplication process is free and has been developed in house by VMware engineers. The deduplication process cannot be disabled, because the disk costs would make vDR unfeasible. The data is also encrypted to prevent malicious interception of the data.

While it is possible to use your storage vendor's deduplication process in addition to the VMware deduplication, the additional workload of deduplicating data that has already been deduplicated by VMware is, in most cases, not going to improve the utilization of the storage. If you forgive the pun, it would be an unnecessary duplication of the deduplication process!

What does pay dividends is backing up the *same type* of VM to the same destination, because, by definition, this increases the number of blocks that overlap, which increases the benefits of the deduplication process.

The deduplication data is stored as 1GB files in the VMwareDataRecovery folder in the virtual disk.

---

vDR Requirements

Currently, vDR is not backward-compatible with VI3.5, and you will require vCenter 4.*x* to run it. It must be placed on the network with the correct IP data to allow it to communicate with vCenter.

You will need vCenter and the vDR appliance to be running for backups to occur, but you do not need vCenter to carry out a restore process. If something goes wrong with vDR, you merely reimport the OVF file and point it to your backup destination.

NOTE VMware intends to rerelease the vDR appliance, rather than issue patches.

VMware recommends that you run the vDR appliance on an ESX host. It must be placed on an ESX host that has access to the datastores used by the VMs you wish to back up. Critically, the ESX host must have less than 80% CPU activity, and there must be 5GB free for each VM you back up.

The maximum number of VMs you can back up is 100 with a single vDR appliance. However, in practice, there is no limitation on the number of vDR appliances you can run simultaneously. VMware supports a maximum of eight backups and eight restorations as the same time.

vDR requires the new quiesced snapshot option, and therefore only VMs that have been upgraded or created using hardware level 7 qualify as valid target VMs.

vDR works with only one vCenter at a time, and does not integrate currently with the linked mode feature. Therefore, if you have multiple vCenters, you will need one vDR appliance per vCenter.

Installing and Configuring vDR

The vDR appliance is now being distributed on an ISO file together with the new vShield Zones feature, which allows for upgrades from the standard editions of vSphere 4 to the advanced and higher edition. The ISO file includes a small installer engine for the vDR plug-in used to extend the vSphere Client, as well as an OVF file that you can use to upload the appliance (using the vCenter's Deploy OVF Template option). The ISO image must be managed on a system running the vSphere Client, so you can then browse for the OVF file on the CD.

Once you have successfully imported the vDR appliance, you can optionally add a second virtual disk, which will act as your destination drive for backups. It is also possible to connect the vDR to SMB/CIFS (Windows) shares for backup across the network.

Importing vDR and Installing the vDR Plug-in

In this section, I will show you how to add a virtual disk to vDR, which will act as a storage location for backups. It is also possible to use RDM files. With either virtual disks or RDM files, if they are on an external array such as Fibre Channel SAN, your backup traffic will not be on the network. I will show you how to add Windows shares to vDR to back up your VMs across the network after discussing virtual disk setup. The vDR appliance is downloadable from the main vmware.com pages where you download the main product binaries. It is distributed as DVD .iso images together with VMware vShield Zones.

Follow these steps to import and install the vDR appliance:

1. From vCenter's File menu, select Deploy OVF Template.

2. Select "Deploy from file."

3. Browse for the OVF file on the CD-ROM. It is located at D:\DataRecovery\ VMwareDataRecovery-ovf\VMwareDataRecovery.ovf.

4. Click Next to accept the description.

5. Specify a name and location for the vDR appliance.

6. Select an ESX host/cluster/resource pool for the vDR appliance.

7. Select a datastore location for the vDR appliance.

8. Select a port group for the vDR appliance.

9. After the import process has completed, right-click the vDR appliance and choose Edit Settings.

10. Click the Add button.

11. Choose Hard Disk from the device list.

12. Choose "Create new virtual disk."

13. Specify a size and datastore location.

14. Power on the vDR and configure your networking using the Configure Network wizard.

After the vDR is powered on, from the same ISO file, you can install the vDR plug-in to extend the functionality of the vSphere Client. The plug-in is a small MSI file, about 5MB in size. You might want to just copy this MSI file to your management PC and run it from your desktop. The MSI file is located on the CD in the DataRecovery directory and is called VMwareDataRecoveryPlugin.msi. After installing the plug-in, you should find a VMware Data Recovery icon in the Home, Solutions and Applications location.

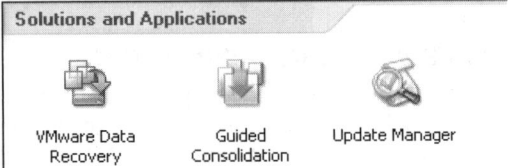

Connecting vDR to vCenter

The next step is to couple the vDR and vCenter systems together. This will allow the vDR appliance to enumerate the vCenter environment, so you can select VMs for backup.

Navigate to Home, then Solutions and Applications, and click the VMware Data Recovery icon. In the edit box on the Welcome page, type in the VM name of the vDR or its IP address. Then click Connect.

VMware Data Recovery - Not connected

Welcome to VMware Data Recovery

To deploy the VMware Data Recovery appliance, please go to File > Deploy OVF Template...

To manage VMware Data Recovery, please enter the IP address or name of the Data Recovery appliance virtual machine.

Virtual Machine Name / IP address: | vdr | ▼ | Refresh

Not connected

Connect

When prompted, enter your password to log in.

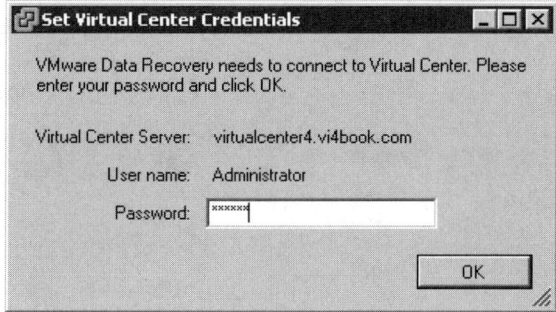

A Getting Started Wizard will now guide you through the process of preparing your backup destinations. If you cancel this wizard by mistake (as I did), you can restart it from the Getting Started Wizard link available on the Configuration tab.

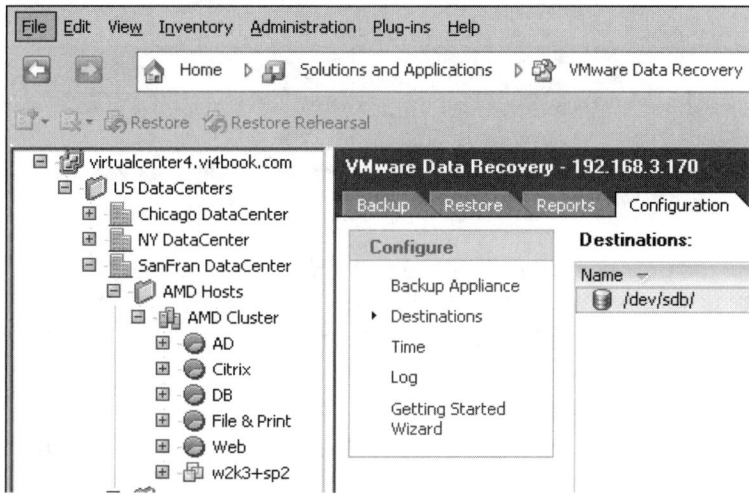

Formatting and Mounting a vDR Backup Disk

The virtual disk you added when importing the vDR appliance now needs to be formatted and mounted. This can be done from the Getting Started Wizard if you wish. I prefer to do it from the main options in the vCenter window.

Navigate to Home, then Solutions and Applications, and click the VMware Data Recovery icon. Select the Configuration tab. Then select the virtual disk that needs to be formatted and click the Format option. In this example, I have one backup destination drive (/dev/sdb), which is not mounted, as you can see by the status of Local Volume (Unmounted). It is 40GB in size and is blank because it has 40GB free.

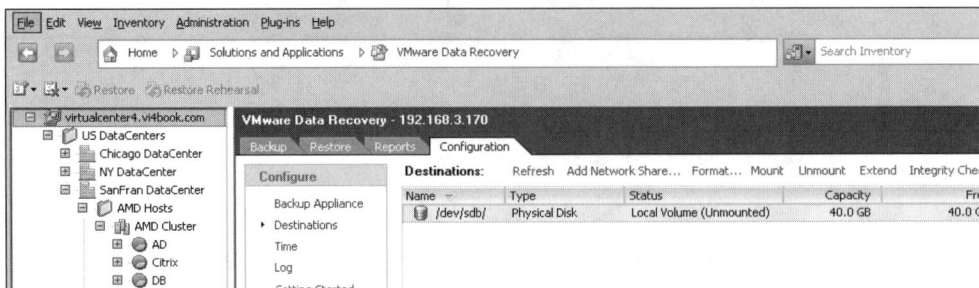

You'll need to confirm that you want this formatting to be carried out.

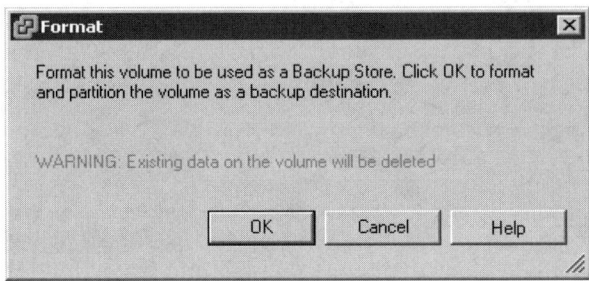

At the end of the process, the disk will be formatted and mounted for you. You can mount and unmount volumes at will using the options found on the Configuration tab. You may need to use these options if you want to add storage to the vDR appliance after its initial configuration.

Adding a Network Backup Location to vDR

In addition to using an internal mounted virtual disk, you can also mount Microsoft Windows network shares, commonly referred to as SMB/CIFS shares.

To add a network share, in the VMware Data Recovery Configuration tab, click Add Network Share.

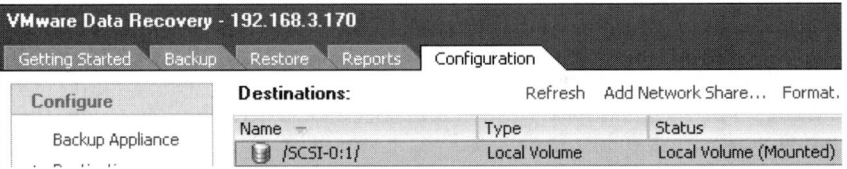

In the Add a Network Share dialog box, supply the UNC path, username, and password settings.

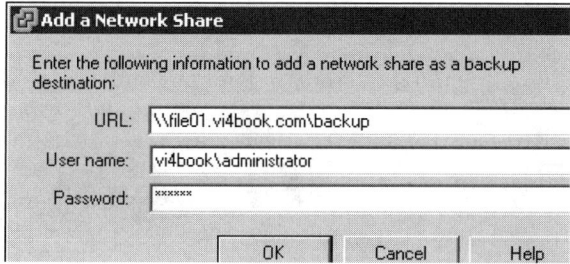

Backing Up a VM

There are two ways to back up a VM: right-click the VM in the Data Recovery inventory, or create a backup job from the Backup tab, which allows you to select multiple VMs in the tree.

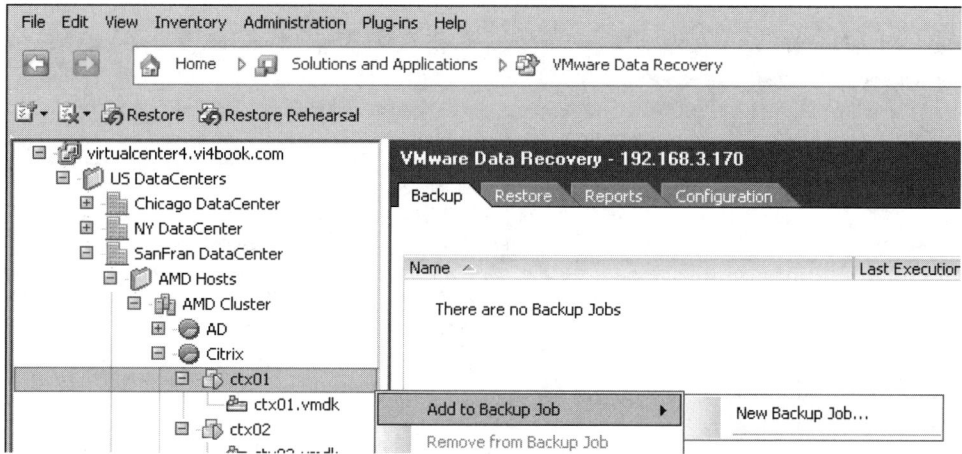

Creating a Backup Job

When you create a backup job, you set the retention policy, which controls how long your previous backups are kept. The built-in retention policies are Few, More, and Many, which progressively retain the backups for a longer and longer period. A custom retention policy option allows you to state how many backups from each period to retain. The longer the retention period, the more backups you will have, and the more options you will have to restore the VM. Despite the power of deduplication, these multiple backups are not free from a storage perspective. So as ever, your decisions are a compromise of the power of the recovery against the space consumed by the backup.

If the VM is referenced in more than one backup job, vDR uses the backup job that has the highest retention value. Additionally, if the backup destination is 80% full and has less than 250GB free, then the retention policy is applied daily in order to free up space by deleting stale restore points. If there is more than 250GB of space free and it is less than 80% full, the retention policy is applied weekly.

Follow these steps to create a new backup job:

1. Click the Backup tab and select the New option.

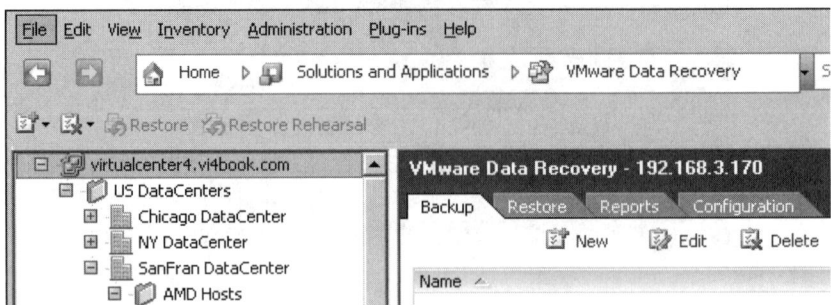

2. Select the VMs you wish to back up from the Inventory. In this example, I selected ctx01 and ctx02 by choosing the Citrix resource pool. Notice how you can search for VMs by a string using the "contains" option.

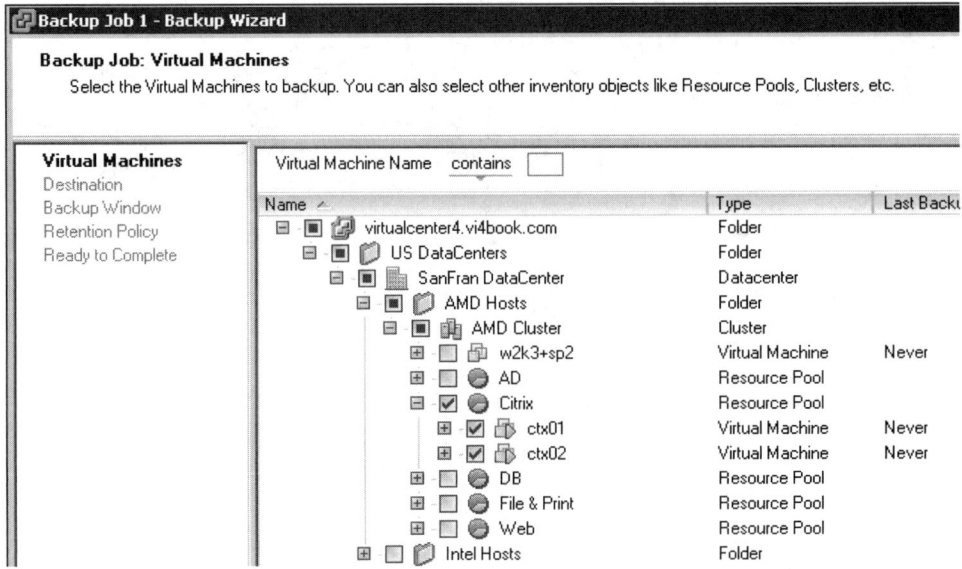

3. Select your backup destination from the list.

4. Select a backup window, which controls when a backup job is scheduled to run. The default is outside standard business hours, once a day.

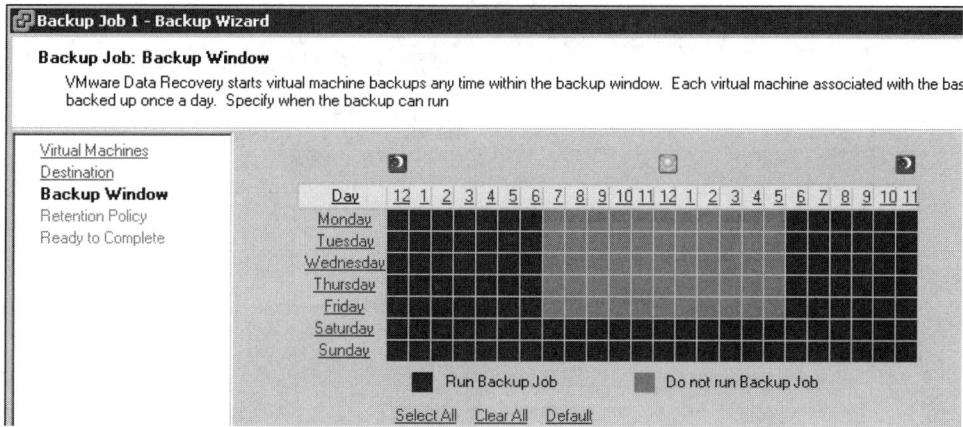

NOTE *vDR monitors the VM backup. If a backup fails or misses a backup window, it will be given the highest priority to be backed up next time the window becomes available.*

5. Set your retention policy.

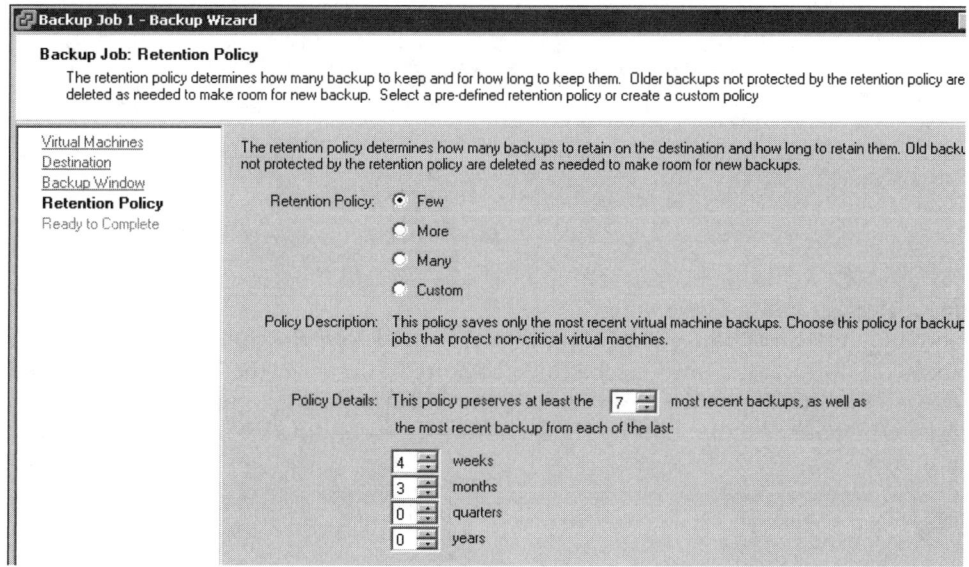

6. Complete the wizard, and it will create your backup job.

In this release, you cannot name your backup jobs when you create them in the wizard, but you may rename them after they have been created.

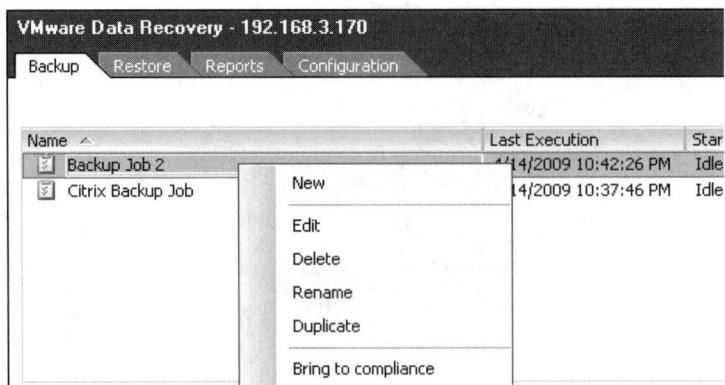

If your backup job was created using a VM container such as datacenter, cluster, or resource pool, the mere act of creating a VM in that container should automatically add it to the existing backup job. If this does not happen, you can manually add a VM to an existing job. Alternatively, if a VM has been added to a backup job accidentally, you can remove it with a simple right-click of the VM.

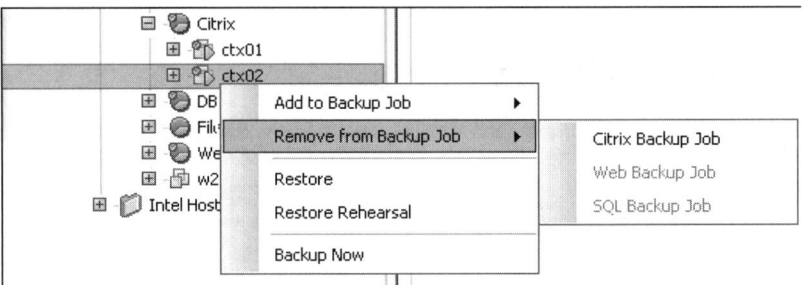

Bringing a Backup Job to Compliance

Occasionally, a backup job may not get processed and miss its schedule. Perhaps the vDR appliance was down at the time of scheduled backup. In this case, the VM will be flagged in dark red as "Not in compliance." You can trigger a manual backup and force the backup job to comply with your requirements by right-clicking the offending job and selecting "Bring to compliance."

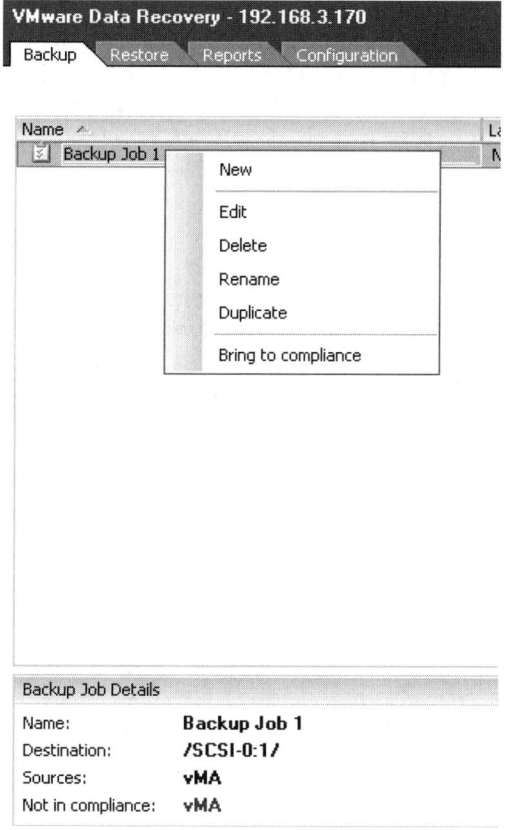

Starting an Integrity Check

It is possible to select either a disk or mounted network location and check it to see if the metadata and deduplication data it contains is in a good state. Integrity checks happen automatically, but you can trigger one manually. To do this, select the Configuration tab, and in the Configure pane, select the Destinations link. Choose the datastore, and then click the Integrity Check link.

VMware Data Recovery - 192.168.3.170				
Backup Restore Reports **Configuration**				

Configure	**Destinations:** Refresh Add Network Share... Format... Mount Unmount Extend Integrity Check...				
Backup Appliance	Name ▼	Type	Status	Capacity	Free
▸ Destinations	💾 /SCSI-0:1/	Local Volume	Local Volume (Mounted)	39.3 GB	35.5 GB
Time	💾 /192.168.3.171/backup/	Network Share	Local Volume (Mounted)	99.9 GB	92.2 GB

Extending a Backup Destination

If the size of the backup destination is increased, you can use the Extend option to force the vDR to extend the file system of the disk to take up the new space. To use this option, select the Configuration tab, and in the Configure pane, select the Destinations link. Choose the datastore, and then click the Extend link. This can take some time to complete and then refresh, so please be patient.

Restoring VMs

After you've made backups with the vDM appliance, you can restore an entire VM, an individual virtual disk, or individual files within a virtual disk.

Running a Restore Rehearsal

A simple way to test your restore process is to right-click the VM and choose Restore Rehearsal. When you use the Restore Rehearsal option, the wizard automatically renames the VM as *vm-name* Rehearsal. Additionally, the Reconnect NIC option is automatically set to No. This should prevent the administrator from overwriting the existing VM accidentally or creating IP address and NetBIOS name conflicts.

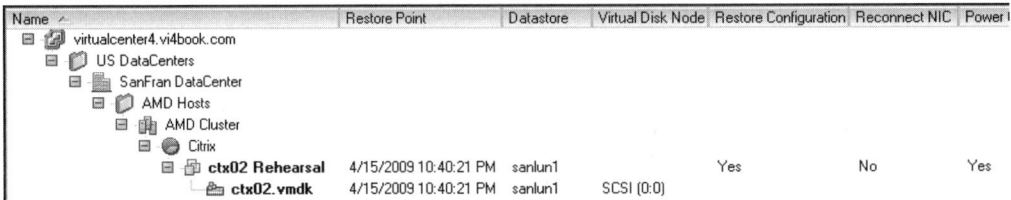

Restoring a VM to an Alternative Location

At some stage, you will want to carry out a test restore of a VM you have backed up to an alternative location, as a way of validating the backup process. And, of course, you may actually need to restore a VM. This is easy to do with vDR's Virtual Machine Restore Wizard.

For this example, I first created a resource pool called Backup and a VM folder called Backup as well. These will serve as the alternative Inventory locations for the VM. I will use local storage as the restore destination, as I am running a little low on Fibre Channel SAN space.

Here are the steps for restoring a VM:

1. Select the Restore tab and click the Restore icon.

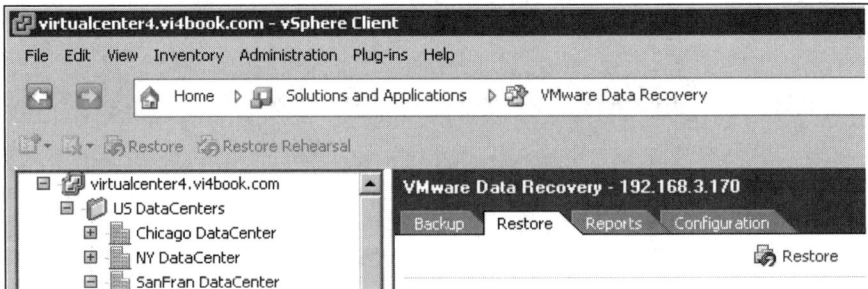

2. In the Virtual Machine Restore Wizard window, select the VM(s) you wish to restore. In this example, I have chosen to restore both disks that make up the VM called sql01. (As discussed in the next section, it is possible to select individual disks in this process.) You can see that this is the latest backup taken on the 4/15/2009, and there is an older backup taken on the same day. Notice also that the defaults show the last five restore points—whether these appear depend on the frequency of the backup and your retention policy.

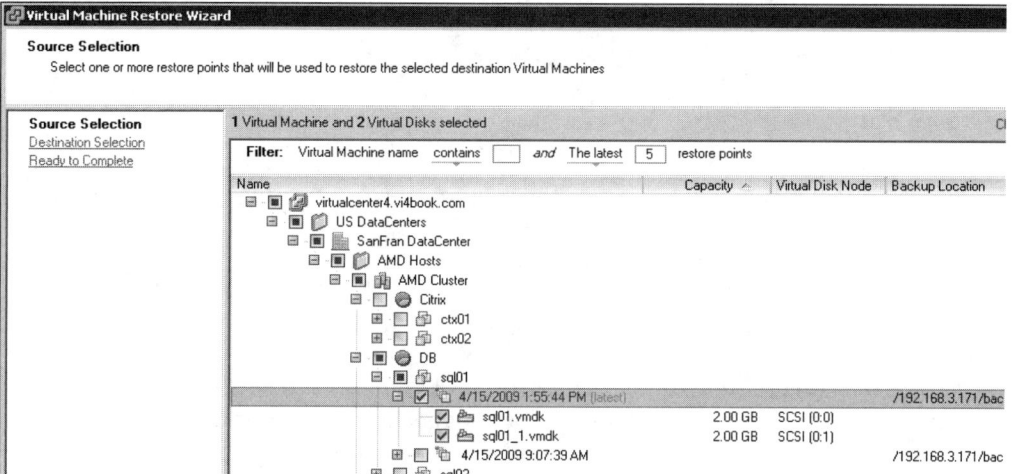

3. A red alert icon on the VM indicates that if you proceed with the restore, you would *overwrite* the original VM. Only by renaming it, and then relocating it, can you stop this from happening. Click in the edit box where the name of the VM is displayed and rename it.

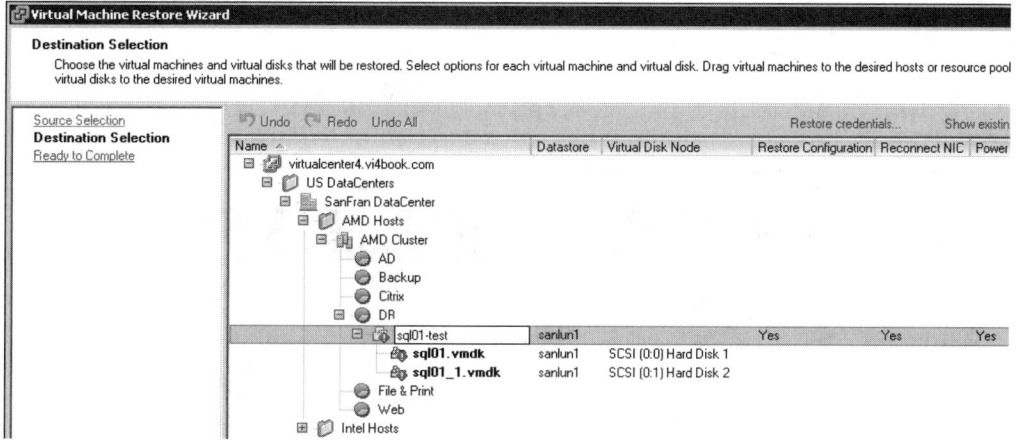

4. Relocate the VM to an alternative resource pool.

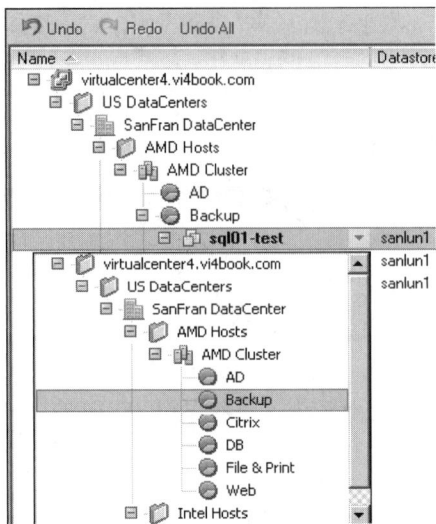

5. I also recommend setting Reconnect NIC and Power On to No. This will allow you to make sure your restored backup does not generate any IP address conflicts or Microsoft "Duplicate name exists on this network" errors.

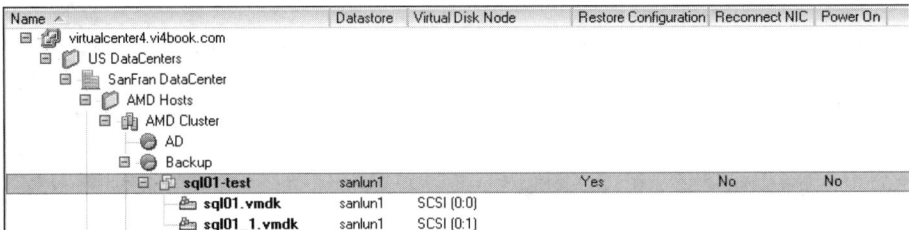

6. When you are finished, click Next, and then click Restore to trigger the restore process. The wizard will close, and you will be redirected to the Reports tab, where you may track the progress of the restore.

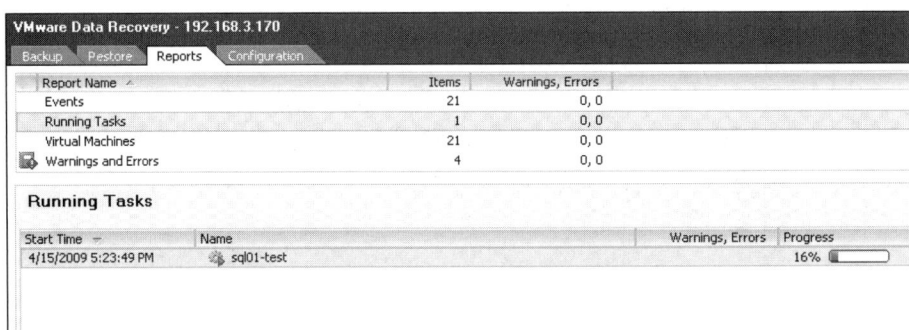

Restoring an Individual Virtual Disk

You might want to restore an individual virtual disk, for example, because you have lost a significant amount of data in it, but your guest OS is still in a fairly good shape. Or perhaps your data is fine, but your OS is damaged beyond simple repair, so you want to restore just the boot or system disk.

vDR does support the use of the restore process to overwrite an existing VM or virtual disk, but care must be taken to avoid a scenario where your VM is in a *worse* state after the restore process. That would rather defeat the objective.

CAUTION *You might be surprised to know how often overwriting a VM can result in a bad restore. I've seen it happen. In one notable case, I was a junior contractor and the bad restore was carried out by a senior IT manager. Unfortunately, no one was around to stop this "test" restore, which wiped out end users' data. I won't mention any company names. Just remember that a bad restore can cause as much damage as no backup strategy at all or infrequent backups.*

To restore an individual virtual disk, start the restore wizard and select the disk that needs be restored.

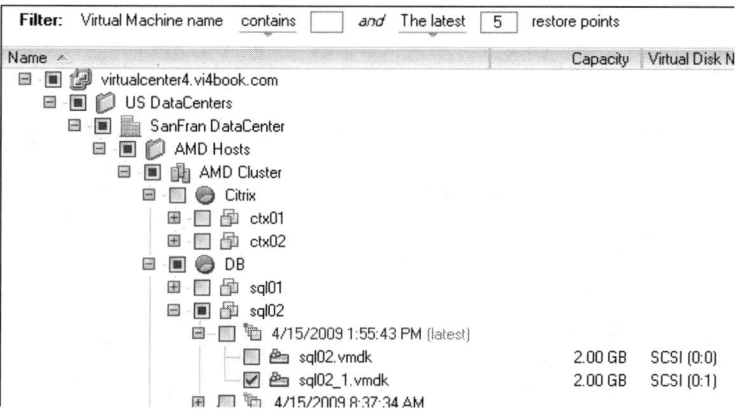

In the next part of the wizard notice the red exclamation mark. By continuing, you are agreeing to have the original virtual disk overwritten. Also, notice how the Restore Configuration and Reconnect NIC options are not available, because you are restoring only an individual virtual disk. Continuing in this manner is clearly quite dangerous.

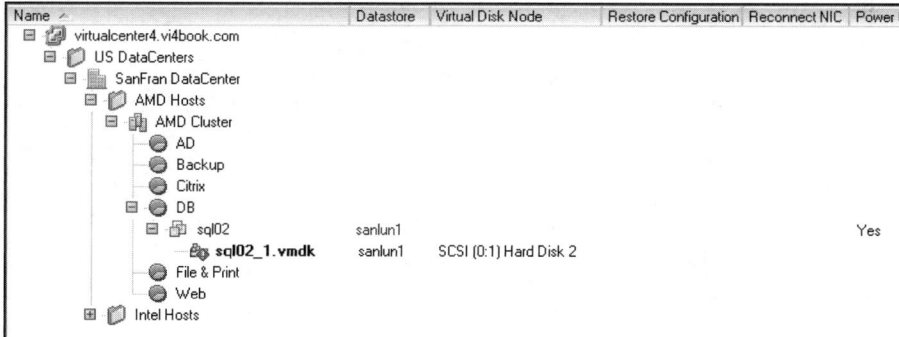

It is possible to restore the virtual disk to a different SCSI ID. This would modify the VM to have three virtual disks: the boot, the original data drive, and the restore data drive. This configuration can be achieved by clicking the pull-down arrow next to the SCSI disk reference in the Virtual Disk Node column. After you select a different SCSI ID (SCSI 0:2 in this example), the red exclamation mark is cleared on the VM.

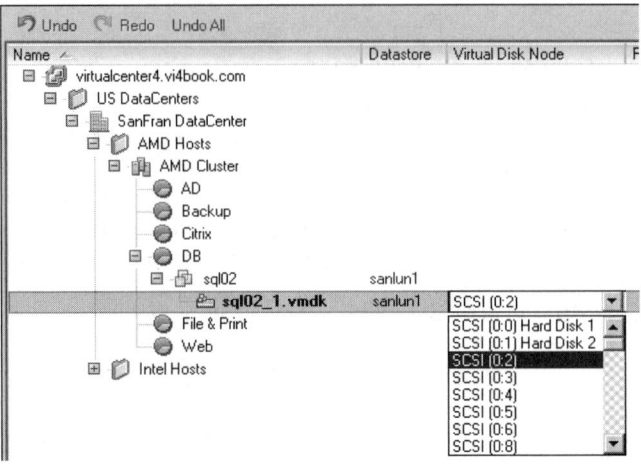

Click Next, and then click Restore. The VM will be powered off, and then the restore process will begin.

Currently, the vDR appliance does not power on the VM after the restore process has completed. Once you manually power on the VM, you will need to use Microsoft's Disk Management utility to get the restored virtual disk (SCSI0:2 in this example) to be visible, by assigning a drive letter to it.

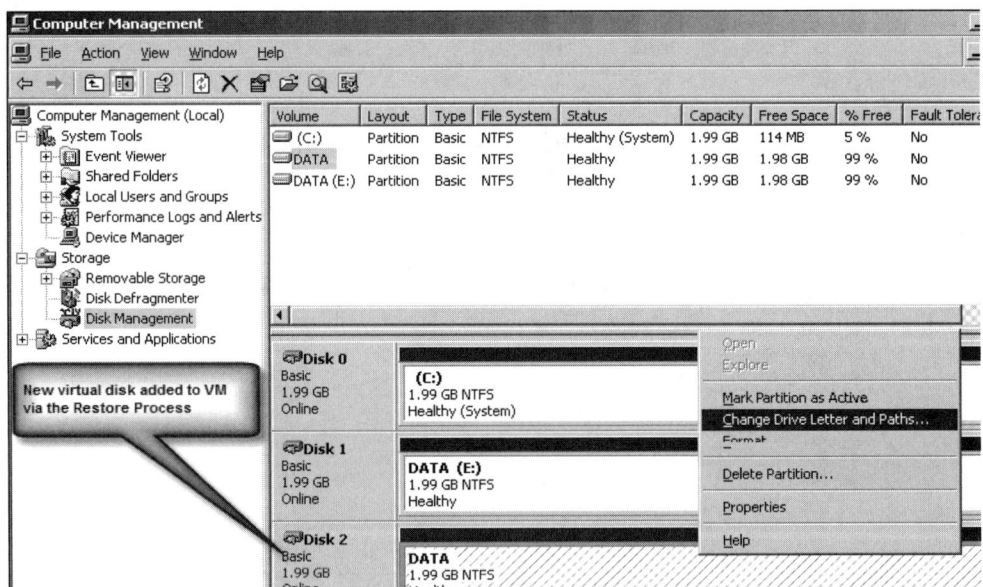

Caution *If you do not allocate a different SCSI ID, the restore process overwrites the original disk, and Windows will see the restored virtual disk as a brand-new device; as such, drive letter mappings are not restored. The Windows default allocates the next available drive letter to the restored disk.*

Restoring Individual Files Within a Virtual Disk

In this first release of vDR, VMware included, with experimental support, a method of mounting the restore points created by the appliance for the affected VM. This utility, vdrFileRestore.exe, links the restore points to the VM by using the unique BIOS identifier for the VM. This saves time in that, rather than restoring an entire virtual disk to pluck out a small number of files, the utility can access the restore points from vDR and allow you direct access to files.

Currently, the vdrFileRestore.exe utility is supported on Windows XP and later (including Windows Server 2008). In this release, vdrFileRestore.exe does not work with DNS. It available on the same download page as the ISO file that contains the vDR appliance and vShield software. The first time you execute vdrFileRestore.exe, it will unpack a number of files to make it work.

To use the utility, log in to the VM on which you wish to restore an individual file. On the C: drive, create a directory called C:\FLR and copy the vdrFileRestore.exe file.

To view all the restore points on vDR associated with this VM, type the following command:

```
vdrFileRestore.exe -a 192.168.3.170
```

Executing this command will produce a list of the restore points, with each one allocated a number. The restore point at the top of the list with the smallest number is the most recent version of the backup.

```
0: Restore point
Date: "Sat May 16 12:48:39 2009"
1: Restore point
Date: "Sun May 10 23:48:16 2009"
2: Restore point
Date: "Sat May 09 22:12:06 2009"
Please input restore point to mount from list above
```

Type in the number of the restore point you wish to mount, and the utility will mount the virtual disk data associated with the restore point. From Windows Explorer, you should be able to browse them. The utility will then list the virtual disks and allocate each one a drive letter from the restore point selected.

```
Mounting disk "ctx01.vmdk"...

All disks have been mounted, they are...
"\virtualcenter4.vi4book.com\US DataCenters\SanFran DataCenter\host\AMD Hosts\AM
D Cluster\Resources\Citrix\ctx01"
    "E" <- "ctx01.vmdk"

Please input "unmount" to terminate application and remove mount point
```

If you want to just access the latest restore point, you can issue this command:

```
vdrFileRestore.exe -l 192.168.3.170
```

When you are finished copying the files to the correct location, you can unmount the restore points by issuing the unmount command. Shortly before this book was released, VMware released a graphical version of the vdrFileRestore utility, which works in a very similiar way.

Managing Restore Points

As you saw earlier, it is possible to set a custom retention policy to govern how many restore points you can have and how long they are retained. Restore points are purged from the vDR appliance based on the rule set in the retention policy by the next backup or by an internal or manual integrity check. It is possible to manually delete restore points, or conversely, to lock restore points so they are not deleted automatically.

To force a restore point to be deleted, in the vDR view in vCenter, select the Restore tab, choose the restore point you wish to remove, and click the Mark for Delete icon.

A small red X will appear next to the restore point. At the next scheduled integrity check, the restore point will be deleted. However, if you wish to force that manually, you can run an integrity check from the Configuration tab, as described earlier.

To lock a restore point, select it on the Restore tab and click the Lock icon.

A small lock icon will appear next to the restore point. This will prevent it from being deleted by the retention policy.

Using VMware Consolidated Backup

Strictly speaking, VCB is not a backup solution but a collection of APIs and drivers that enable third-party vendor tools to back up a VM. With VCB, there is no network hit on the ESX host during the backup process. The backup traffic is offloaded to a physical Windows Server 2003 system, with SAN connectivity, on which the VCB software is installed. This software is referred to as the VCB proxy. It is even possible to run VCB within a VM, as you will learn in this section.

Two types of backup are supported with VCB:

- **File-level backups**   With a file-level backup, the virtual disk of the VM is mounted to a folder on the VCB proxy. The backup operator can select individual files inside the virtual disk. As you might expect, file-level backups are ideal for normal, differential, and incremental backups of data.

- **Full VM backups**   With a full VM backup, the virtual disk is backed up alongside all the other files that make up a VM, including the .nvram and log files. Full VM backups are ideal for archiving the operating system state of a VM. With a full VM backup, the virtual disks of a VM are exported into the 2GB sparse format to ensure that free space is not included in the backup process.

Both approaches support a hot backup of the VM. A special sync driver is installed to the VM during the installation of VMware Tools. This sync driver is able to reduce the activity generated in the file system within the VM.

Although the backup process is via the SAN, the restore process is across the network. This can slow the restore process significantly. Restoring from a full VM backup can be achieved quite neatly, but restoring an individual file means copying from the VCB proxy via Windows shares to the original destination.

CAUTION *The most common error with VCB is operator errors caused by mistyping of directory paths or job names. In most cases, the errors will arise from typing something like d:\backup, rather than d:\backups. Be sure to confirm that your backup and restore process works. The author of this book does not accept any liability for data loss.*

For full VM backups, VCB can be used independently of a third-party backup tool, but most people will want to use it in conjunction with such a tool. This is usually achieved with an integration module. Unfortunately, the help that is provided with the integration modules is not always very clear, or in some cases, accurate. The quality of the scripts can vary significantly, too. If you decide to use the integration modules that are shipped free with VCB, expect to spend some time on the VMware Communities forums reading posts and asking others for help.

Integration scripts are not available for some supported backup vendors, so you may be forced to create your own. In fact, some people prefer to write their own scripts, rather than debugging or reengineering scripts that have been written by others. On the other hand, some vendors have completely integrated VCB into their main backup products—a good example of this is NetBackup 6.5.

Installing VMware Consolidated Backup

Installing VCB is very easy; however, care must be taken with VCB proxy's connection to the SAN. By default, Windows Server 2003 will try to access hard disks and LUNs directly by writing a disk signature and mounting them as part of its system. This is potentially damaging to the VMFS file structure. Ideally, you want to build this server without connectivity to the SAN until you have turned off this automount feature.

If you have physical access to the server, you can disable the SAN connectivity by simply disconnecting the SAN cables. Alternatively, in the BIOS temporarily disable the Fibre Channel HBA. Once you have successfully installed Windows Server 2003, turn off automount using the DiskPart utility, as follows:

1. Log in to the proxy as administrator.

2. Open a command prompt by selecting Run from the Start menu and typing **cmd**.

3. Type the following command:

   ```
   diskpart
   ```

4. At this `diskpart` prompt, type the following command:

   ```
   automount
   ```

   As automount is enabled by a default, this command should disable automount and give you're the status information, "Automatic mounting of new volumes is disabled."

5. Exit DiskPart by typing this command:

   ```
   exit
   ```

You can now reenable the SAN connectivity. If you open the Disk Management console in Windows and are asked at any point to write a disk signature, the safest approach is to choose cancel and exit the wizard. Even safer still is to not open the Disk Management tool at all. However, you may need to do this to configure other storage devices.

Now you're ready to install VCB. Download the latest version of the VCB package from the VMware Web site and run the installation package. Acknowledge the prompt to install the VMware virtual volume storage bus driver. This VCB LUN driver gives the VCB proxy read-only access to the LUN and VMFS. Without this driver, Windows would not be able to access the file system to begin the backup process.

Using VCB on the Command Line

Most people who use VCB on a daily basis use an integration script provided by their vendor or VMware. This means they do not need to know how to use the VCB command-line utilities. However, having some familiarity with these command-line tools might assist you in troubleshooting and debugging scripts that have been provided by your backup vendor. Additionally. you may wish to write your own scripts.

To use the command-line tools, you will need to open a command prompt to the install directory of VCB. You may also wish to add this to the path entry of the environment variables of Windows. To do this, right-click My Computer, choose Properties, select the Advanced tab, and click the Environment Variables button. Under System Variables, select path, and then click the Edit button, Add a semicolon to the end of the current path and type **C:\Program Files\VMware\VMware Consolidated Backup Framework**.

You can confirm the path is correct by opening a new command prompt and running one of the VCB utilities, such as vcbMounter. The utility should run without error messages, such as "Bad command or file name."

You will notice that the commands on the following pages include some path settings and some variables. I've chosen to specify these on the command line directly. However, you can modify these variables from a configuration file called config.js, found on the VCB proxy in C:\Program Files\VMware\VMware Consolidated Backup Framework\config.

Some of the VCB commands are available on both the VCB proxy and the Service Console, as listed in Table 18-1, and some are available only on the Service Console, as listed in Table 18-2. One command, mountvm, which mounts virtual disks to a Windows folder, is available only on the VCB proxy. The commands at the Service Console are built into ESX for free, courtesy of VMware. As VMware moves toward supporting just the ESXi product, these commands may not always be available.

Command	Description
vcbVmName	Returns the identity of the VM
vcbSnapshot	Applies a snapshot
vcbMounter	Mounts virtual disks, and can trigger a full VM backup
vcbExport	Exports a virtual disk in other formats
vcbCleanup	Runs a generic script that cleans out mount points and snapshots
vcbSupport	Runs a generic script used when working with VMware Support

TABLE 18-1   VCB Utilities Available on the VCB Proxy and Service Console

Command	Description
`vcbResAll`	Restores all VMs on the ESX host
`vcbSnapAl`	Takes a snapshot of all VMs on the ESX host
`vcbUtil`	Lists all resource pools and VM folders
`vcbRestore`	Restores an individual VM across the network

TABLE 18-2 VCB Utilities Available Only on the Service Console

When executed on the Service Console, these commands *are* case-sensitive, but when executed on the VCB proxy, they are not. All the VCB commands have a similar syntax, which uses the following switches:

- `-h` to specify the name of an ESX host or vCenter system
- `-u` to specify the username
- `-p` to specify the password

In the following sections, I will demonstrate how the most useful commands are used: vcbVmName, vcbMounter, vcbRestore, vcbSnapshot, vcbExport, and mountvm.

***

NOTE *In all the upcoming examples, I use the administrator account with the VCB commands. However, there is a dedicated VCB role that you can use. This role has only four privileges, which are all that is required for the VCB proxy to work. I strongly recommend using this role.*

Viewing VM Unique Identifiers

To back up a VM, you need to be able to identify it in the vCenter or ESX host inventory. A VM has four identifiers:

- The VM's name as displayed in vCenter or ESX
- The VM's IP address
- The VM's UUID
- The VM's managed object reference (MOREF)

***

NOTE *The MOREF value is more commonly used by the vCenter SDK. It is generated at the first power on of the VM, and does not change after that.*

While the VM's name and IP address are friendly and easy to determine, they are also subject to change. The UUID and MOREF values are clearly less friendly but are guaranteed to be unique and unchanging.

To get this VM information, you can query vCenter using the `vcbVmName` command from the VCB proxy. All you need is one of the four values to find out the remaining three. At the command prompt, enter the following command (for a VM called ctx01 in this example):

```
vcbvmname -h virtualcenter4.vi4book.com -u administrator -p vmware
-s name:ctx01
```

This would produce the output like so:

```
Found VM
moref: vm-810
name: ctx01
uuid: 5034aae8-35c6-51a0-8f18-4264a177ee65
ipaddr:  192.168.3.14
```

TIP *As you can see, the UUID value is quite long. If I am using it, I will often imply the Windows command prompt copy-and-paste facility to capture this text to the Clipboard. I also use this function complete the very long paths that are sometimes typed into dialog boxes and configuration tools.*

As you've probably realized, you can use vcbVmName with -s to search by an identifier:

```
-s moref:vm-810
-s uuid:5034aae8-35c6-51a0-8f18-4264a177ee65
-s ipaddr:192.168.3.14
```

The IP address can be specified as a raw IP address, or by FQDN/host name if you have name resolution configured on the VCB proxy.

The vcbVmName command can also be used to check the power state of all the VMs in the vCenter environment:

```
vcbvmname -h virtualcenter4.vi4book.com -u administrator -p vmware
-s any:powerstate
```

Mounting and Unmounting VMs

The vcbMounter utility allows you to mount and unmount a VM's virtual disks from the command line. This is normally done prior to a backup. The process mounts the VM's virtual disks to a folder on the VCB proxy. These files can then be backed up as if they were local to the VCB proxy, when they are actually being remotely accessed using the VCB framework software through the HBA.

During the mounting process, vcbMounter applies a snapshot to the VM. This allows the virtual disks to be unlocked in the VMFS file system. The same principle works for RDM files as well, but only if you have them set with virtual compatibility mode. When vcbMounter unmounts the VM's file, this snapshot and its delta files are merged into the virtual disk, and then deleted. You can see this process in action if you have the vSphere Client open at the same time you run the vcbMounter command.

To mount a VM's files for a file-level backup by its name in vCenter, use this command:

```
vcbMounter -h virtualcenter4.vi4book.com -u administrator -p vmware
-a name:ctx01
-r d:\backups\ctx01 -t file
```

The –a switch allows you to set the attribute by which to identify the VM. The –r switch sets the mounting point. If d:\backups didn't exist, the command would return an error. You must specify some kind of path for vcbMounter to work correctly. The –t switch sets the type of backup. For Windows guests, you can use both file and fullvm as types; with all other guests, currently fullvm is the only option allowed.

The result of this command would look like something like this:

```
Opened disk: blklst://snapshot-861[sanlun1] ctx01/ctx01.vmdk@virtualcenter
xxxx/xxxx
Proceeding to analyze volumes
Done mounting
Volume 1 mounted at d:\backups\ctx01\digits\1 (mbSize=4086 fsType=NTFS )
Volume 1 also mounted on d:\backups\ctx01\letters\C
```

You can see the VM is mounted twice for one virtual disk: once by drive letter (\letters\C) and another time by a number representing the disk (\digits\1). The following examples show the activity generated in the vSphere Client by running the vcbMounter command.

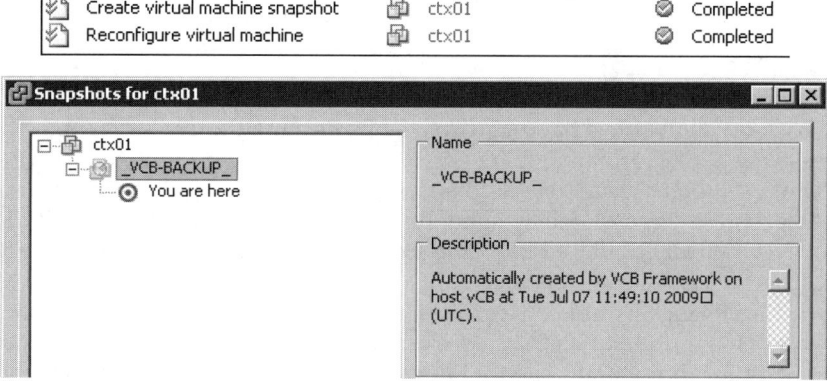

The next example shows the hard drive of my VCB proxy, listing the contents of the ctx01 virtual disk.

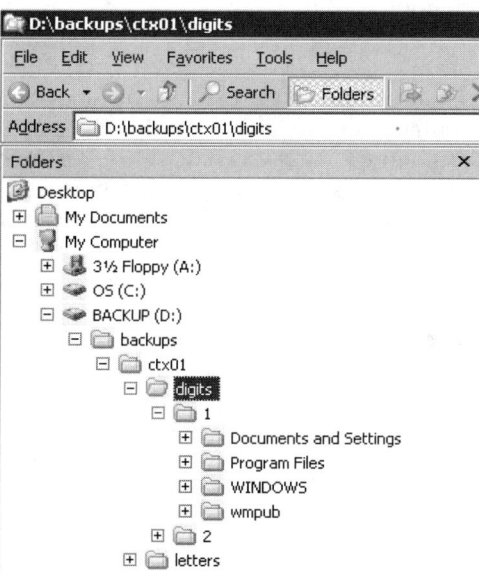

As you would expect, vcbMounter also allows you to unmount the VM's virtual disk:

```
vcbMounter -h virtualcenter4.vi4book.com -u administrator -p vmware -U
d:\backups\ctx01:
```

-U is a case-sensitive switch that directs vcbMounter to unmount the specified directory. This creates a new disk release and deletes the snapshot. The output merely shows the unmounting process:

```
Unmounted d:\backups\ctx01\digits\1\ (formatted)
Deleted directory d:\backups\ ctx01\digits\1\
Deleted directory d:\backups\ ctx01\digits\
Deleted directory d:\backups\ ctx01\letters\C\
Deleted directory d:\backups\ ctx01\letters\
Deleted directory d:\backups\ ctx01
```

Performing a Full VM Backup

If you wish to do full VM backup, the vcbMounter can achieve this for you. A full VM backup will back up all the files that make up a VM including the .nvram, .vmx, .vmdk in the 2gbsparse virtual disk format, and log files.

As noted in previous chapters, the 2gbsparse format is a special archive format that contains just the data of the virtual disk, rather than data plus the free space of the virtual disk.

So, if you have virtual disk that is 100GB in size with 5GB of data, the conversion process would produce a storage penalty of just 5GB. A total of 51 files would be created. The first three VMDK files would contain data, and the remaining .vmdk files would just be a 1KB in size. This is done to maintain the original disk geometries during the restore process. The first file is a metadata file that links all the 2gbsparse files together. Here's how you can calculate the number of files created during the conversion:

Size of disk in GB/2GB + 1 for the metadata file

In this example, the calculation is as follows:

100GB/2 + 1 = 51

Two additional files are created: the catalog file and the unmount.dat file. The unmount file is used to automate the unmount process. The catalog file is merely a text file which holds vCenter metadata information, so that when the VM is restored, the VM returns to the same ESX host, resource pool, and VMs and Templates location. The following is an example of a typical catalog file, with ctx01 being stored on VMFS volume called sanlun1:

```
version= esx-4.0
state= poweredOn
display_name= "ctx01"
uuid= "5034aae8-35c6-51a0-8f18-4264a177ee65"
disk.scsi0:0.filename= "scsi0-0-0-ctx01.vmdk"
disk.scsi0:0.diskname= "[sanlun1] ctx01/ ctx01.vmdk"
config.vmx= "[sanlun1] ctx01/ ctx01.vmx"
host= esx3.vi4book.com
timestamp= "Tue Jul 07 11:49:10 2009"
config.suspenddir= " sanlun1] ctx01/"
config.snapshotdir= "[ sanlun1] ctx01/"
config.file0= "ctx01.vmsd"
```

```
config.file1= "ctx01.vmxf"
config.file2= "ctx01.nvram"
config.logdir= "[sanlun1] ctx01/"
config.log0= "vmware-15.log"
config.log1= "vmware-16.log"
config.log2= "vmware-13.log"
config.log3= "vmware-14.log"
config.log4= "vmware-17.log"
config.log5= "vmware-12.log"
config.log6= "vmware.log"
folderpath= "/Datacenters/SanFran DataCenter/vm/Citrix Team"
resourcepool= "/Datacenters/ SanFran DataCenter/host/AMD Cluster/Resources"
```

The catalog file can be edited to change the default datastore and vCenter locations. This will allow you to carry out a test restore without destroying the original VM.

To perform the full backup, use the `vcbMounter` command and specify `fullvm` as the type using the `-t` switch:

```
vcbMounter -h virtualcenter4.vi4book.com -u administrator-p vmware
-a name:ctx01 -r d:\backups\ctx01 -t fullvm
```

In this case, d:\backups is both the mounting point and the destination of the backup of the VM.

You might notice that when `vcbMounter` runs, the format used is "compact," by which VMware means the 2gbsparse format. Rather than taking the virtual disk's name, it converts the name into a format that is more unique, such as scsi0-0-0-ctx01.vmdk. This information is used to identify the virtual disk on the SCSI bus.

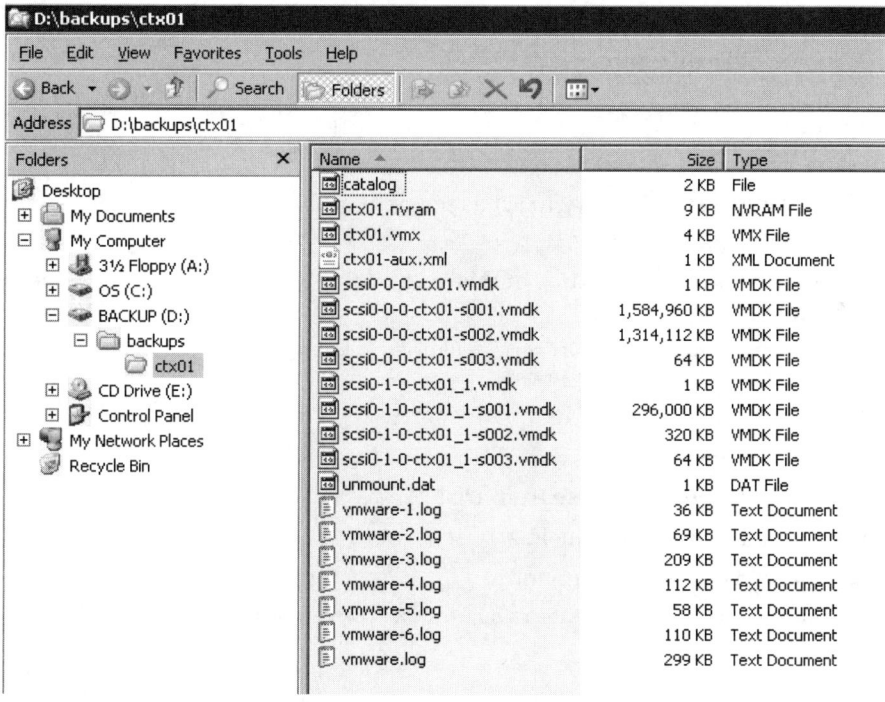

If you want to back up every running VM in the environment, you could use the `for` command in DOS. The following command basically states that for each VM that `vcbName` finds in a powered-on state, start a `vcbMounter` export of all the VMs to the D:\backup\ All directory.

```
for /f "tokens=2 delims=:" %%i in ('vcbvmname -h virtualcenter4.vi4book.com
-u administrator -p vmware -s powerstate:on ^| find "name:"') do @rd /s /q
"D:\Backups\All\%%i" &vcbmounter -h virtualcenter4.vi4book.com -u
administrator -p password -a name:"%%i" -r "D:\Backups\All\%%i" -t fullvm >
"D:\Backups\All\%%i.log
```

Thanks to Andrew Neilson (one of my former students), who works for Ericsson Services here in the UK, for providing this one-line batch file.

Performing a Full VM Restore

The restore process copies your backup to the ESX host and restores it from the 2gbsparse format to the monolithic or thick format. You could do this manually using WinSCP or the Veeam FastSCP utility, and then use the `vcbRestore` command at the Service Console. However, there is a more seamless way to complete this process.

Although Windows Server 2003 does only Windows file sharing (SMB/CIFS), and the VMkernel supports only NFS, the Service Console does support remote mounting of Windows shares. This means it is possible to share out the directory where your VMs have been backed up and restore them from the ESX host using the `vcbRestore` command. Another possibility is to share out the directory on the VCB proxy and import the VM using the VMware Converter utility. This allows for graphical front end and the ability to easily specify the destination of the restore process without modifying the catalog file. Here are the steps:

1. On the VCB proxy, share out the directory that contains your exported VMs (the d:\backups directory in this example).

2. Log in to the ESX host as root and open the firewall to allow the SMB client to function:

   ```
   esxcfg-firewall -e smbClient
   ```

3. Create a temporary directory to act as the network mounting point:

   ```
   mkdir /backups
   ```

4. Mount the directory (/backups in this example) using the `mount.cifs` command from Red Hat Linux:

   ```
   mount.cifs //vcb.vi4book.com/backups /backups
   -ouser=administrator,pass=vmware
   ```

5. Locate your backed-up VM in the Inventory.

6. Power off the VM.

7. Right-click and choose Delete from Disk.

8. Open a PuTTY session on the ESX host as root.

9. Issue the `vcbRestore` command:

   ```
   vcbRestore -h virtualcenter4.vi4book.com -u administrator -p vmware
   -s /backups/ctx01/
   -o on
   ```

-s specifies the subdirectory where the backup of VMs files are located. The -o on switch tells vcbRestore to power on the restored VM when the process has completed. Remember that in the Service Console, all commands are case-sensitive, so you must type vcbRestore with a capital R.

During the restore process, the vcbRestore tool reads the catalog file and registers the VM with the ESX host. At the Service Console, the vcbRestore utility will show a progress bar to indicate what is happening:

```
Converting "/vmfs/volumes/sanlun1/ctx01/ctx01.vmdk" (VMFS (flat)):
0%==================50%================100%
**************************************************
```

In this case, the utility is also converting the 2gbsparse disk back into a monolithic or thick disk.

Taking a Snapshot of a VM and Exporting a Virtual Disk

Although vcbMounter does a fine job of automating the snapshot and export process, it is bit of blunt stick, in the sense that it exports the whole VM. If you wish to export just a virtual disk, that can be done by bringing together two VCB commands: vcbSnapshot and vcbExport.

CAUTION *vcbExport does not currently support the* −m hotadd *or* −m nbd *switch. As such, it cannot be used with a virtualized VCB implementation.*

The vcbSnapshot command requires the use of the MOREF value. To find out the VM's MOREF value, use vcbname:

```
vcbvmname -h virtualcenter4.vi4book.com -u administrator -p vmware -s name:
ctx01
```

To take a snapshot of a VM, use vcbSnapshot:

```
vcbsnapshot -h virtualcenter4.vi4book.com -u administrator -p vmware -c
moref:vm-487 VCB_Snapshot "Manually created by Mike Laverick on 07/07/2009"
```

-c tells vcbSnapshot to create a snapshot for the ctx01 VM with the MOREF value of vm-487. The name of the snapshot will be VCB Snapshot, with its description in quotes.

When the command has completed, you will be told that the snapshot has been created and given its object reference number. You will need this snapshot number later when using vcbExport.

```
[2009-07-07 16:52:37.133 'CreateSnapshot' 3356 info] Creating snapshot
SsId:snapshot-491
```

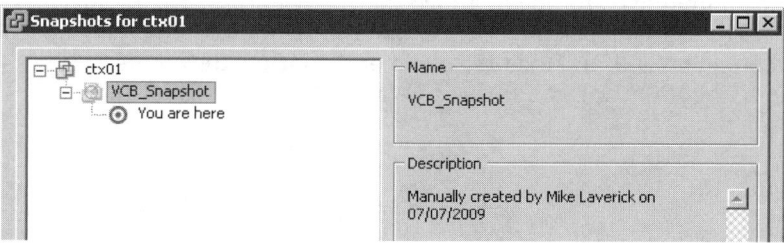

If you want to retrieve a list of virtual disks attached to the VM, use the −1 switch with vcbSnapshot:

```
vcbSnapshot -h virtualcenter4.vi4book.com -u administrator -p vmware -l
moref:vm-487 SsId:snapshot-491
```

This will give you a listing of the files that make up the VM:

```
scsi0.0:[sanlun1] ctx01/ctx01.vmdk
scsi0.1:[sanlun1] ctx01/ctx01_1.vmdk
vmx:[sanlun1] ctx01/ctx01.vmx
logdir:[sanlun1] ctx01/
suspenddir:[sanlun1] ctx01/
config0:ctx01.vmsd
config1:ctx01-aux.xml
config2:ctx01.nvram
config3:ctx01.vmxf
log0:vmware-7.log
log1:vmware-8.log
log2:vmware-3.log
log3:vmware-4.log
log4:vmware-5.log
log5:vmware-6.log
log6:vmware.log
```

Next, use the vcbExport command to export just the virtual disk you need:

```
vcbExport -s "blklst://snapshot-550[sanlun1]ctx01/ctx01.vmdk@virtualcenter4
.vi4book.com?administrator/vmware" -d d:\backups\ctx01.vmdk
```

Once the export of the virtual disk is completed, you can remove the snapshot from the VM using the vcbSnapshot utility:

```
vcbSnapshot -h virtualcenter4.vi4book.com -u administrator -p vmware -d
moref:vm-487 SsId:snapshot-550
```

Mounting a Virtual Disk to Retrieve an Individual File

The mountvm utility allows you to mount the backed-up version of the virtual disks to a folder such that you can navigate the file and folder structure within it. It has a very simple syntax:

```
mountvm -d d:\backups\ctx01\scsi0-0-0-ctx01.vmdk -cycleId d:\temp\ctx01
```

The −d switch indicates a path to the virtual disk you wish to use. The −cycleID switch generates a unique ID for the mounted disk in Windows, cycling this ID so it's always unique. The last path statement is the mounting location. If you navigate to the mounting location, you will find the file system of the virtual disk there. It is possible to then copy files to the VM using conventional Windows shares.

Once you are finished with the virtual disk, it can be unmounted with the `mountvm` command and the `-u` switch:

```
mountvm -u d:\tmp\ctx01
```

Virtualizing VCB

It is possible to run VCB in a VM. Of course, this means you do not benefit from the offloading of the backup to the proxy. Remember that a VM does not have a Fibre Channel card and cannot speak directly to the storage array.

To allow this functionality to work, add to your VCB commands a special mode option:

```
/m nbd
```

NBD stands for network block device, and it will allow the virtualized VCB proxy to use the network to transfer blocks via the ESX host that owns the VM to the VCB server. For this to work, the virtualized VCB needs to have name resolution to the ESX host and IP address visibility to it. NBD also comes in secure mode, which encrypts the data stream, which puts additional CPU burden on the host. It is enabled as follows:

```
/m nbdssl
```

The default mode is to use a SAN, where the VCB is a physical host with access to the shared storage via a dedicated HBA. Another mode available is COS, which is used if you running the utilities at the Service Console.

From VCB 1.5 onwards, a fifth mode has been introduced: hotadd. This method uses a VCB helper VM to automate the backup process. The VCB helper is used in the mounting of the virtual disks and always for a LAN-free backup, without using the network. This is similar to vDR, in that the virtual disks of the target VM are mounted to secondary VM to enable the backup process. This hotadd approach should allow for a more efficient backup process than NBD allows. The name of the helper VM is specific. It should be called *<name_ of_your_vcb*(VCB-HELPER). For example, if your virtualized VCB is called vCB, you would name your helper vCB(VCB-HELPER). The VCB helper is just a blank VM, but it does need a SCSI controller for virtual disks to be mounted correctly to it.

Using NBD or hotadd changes the VCB commands you have seen so far to look like this:

```
vcbMounter -h virtualcenter4.vi4book.com -u administrator -p vmware -a name:
ctx01 -r d:\backups\ctx01 -t file -m nbd
vcbMounter -h virtualcenter4.vi4book.com -u administrator -p vmware -a name:
ctx01 -r d:\backups\ctx01 -t file -m hotadd
```

Personally, I recommend using a dedicated physical host. However, you may find the NBD and hotadd modes useful in your development work or in product demonstrations.

Summary

This chapter covered VM backups with vDR and VCB. As you can see, new doors are opening in the world of backup triggered by virtualization. The problem is that those doors are not quite fully open at the moment. The holy grail will be both backup and restore via the SAN, off-loaded to a backup proxy similar to VCB.

As for my personal opinion, I'm not a fan of VCB. I find it too convoluted to configure, and the restore process is no better than any third-party product I have used. While I've been generally impressed by the third-party products. I still find their restore processes less than slick.

We are all looking for the most complete of backups possible. Neither VCB nor vDR back up the snapshot files, and for many, this limitation is a bitter pill to swallow. I hope this position will change as we progress to the next release of vSphere.

CHAPTER 19 | VMware Patch Management

This chapter covers VMware patch management with the VMware vSphere Host Update Utility and VMware Update Manager (VUM).

The vSphere Host Update Utility is used to patch ESX hosts and upgrade from ESXi 3 to ESXi 4. Personally, I think it's intended for those people who opt to download the free ESXi 4 software. Like any good software vendor, VMware allows the users of the free version to patch the ESX host software.

VUM, VMware's patch management system, is much meatier than the Host Update Utility. It comes in two main flavors: as a stand-alone application used for stand-alone ESX hosts and as a plug-in extension for vCenter. It patches and upgrades ESX hosts, and optionally can patch Windows-based VMs using the popular http://shavlik.com Web site as the source for Windows software updates.

NOTE *VMware will continue to support the older* esxupdate *command-line tool that has been used in the past to script the installation of individual patches. You can also use the* vihostupdate *utility in the RCLI or the vMA. You can get more information about these utilities in my free PDF guides, available from the RTFM Education Web site (http://www.rtfm-ed.co.uk/).*

What's New with VMware Patch Management?

- Staging patches to ESX hosts, which allows a pre-download of the patches locally to each ESX host prior to remediation, and should speed up the ESX host-patching process and reduce the amount of time spent in maintenance mode

- Baseline groups, which allow the administrator to group many different baselines together under a single name and apply the group to a vCenter object (ESX host or VM)

VMware Updates

In recent years, the rapidity of VMware updates has become quite dizzying; for example, for VI3.5, there were four major updates in a single year.

Like any good software vendor, VMware issues software updates to fix errors both in the management layer and at the ESX host. In the past, VMware has used three digits at the end of product names to indicate a change in the base build of the VI2 and VI3 products. For example, the change from ESX 3.0.1 to ESX 3.0.2 did not introduce major feature changes, and was regarded as a maintenance release to fix bugs and introduce better physical hardware support. The change from ESX 3.0.2 to ESX 3.5 was regarded as an important release that introduced new features. And, of course, the change from ESX 3 to ESX 4 is regarded as a brand-new product.

Since releasing VI3.5, a new numbering system has been adopted, using the labels Update 1, Update 2, and so on, commonly abbreviated as U1, U2, and so on. I treat these new releases, which roll up bug fixes, like Microsoft service packs, in that I generally wait some time before rolling them out in production environments.

On top of these releases, we receive intermediary patches as well, such as security updates that are released with the severity of critical and that cannot be left for a rollup period.

Using the vSphere Host Update Utility with ESXi 4

When you install the vSphere Client, you are asked whether you wish to install the VMware vSphere Host Update Utility. If you neglected to do this at install time, you can install this utility by using the following command:

```
VMware-viclient.exe /S /V"/qr INSTALL_VIUPDATE=1 /L*v %temp%\vim-viu-
launch.log"
```

Patching ESXi 4 with the Host Update Utility

The first time you run the Host Update Utility, you will be asked if you would like to download patches from the VMware repository. By default, patches are downloaded from the https://hostupdate.vmware.com web site to the C:\Documents and Settings\All Users\ Application Data\VMware\VMware VI Update location on the system where you run the Host Update Utility. You can change these default locations, and also configure options like proxy server settings, by modifying the settings.config file held in C:\Program Files\ VMware\Infrastructure\VIUpdate 4.0.

Follow these steps to use the utility:

1. From the Start menu, choose Programs, then VMware, then vSphere Host Update Utility 4.0.

2. Click Yes to accept the download.

3. Click the Add Host link.

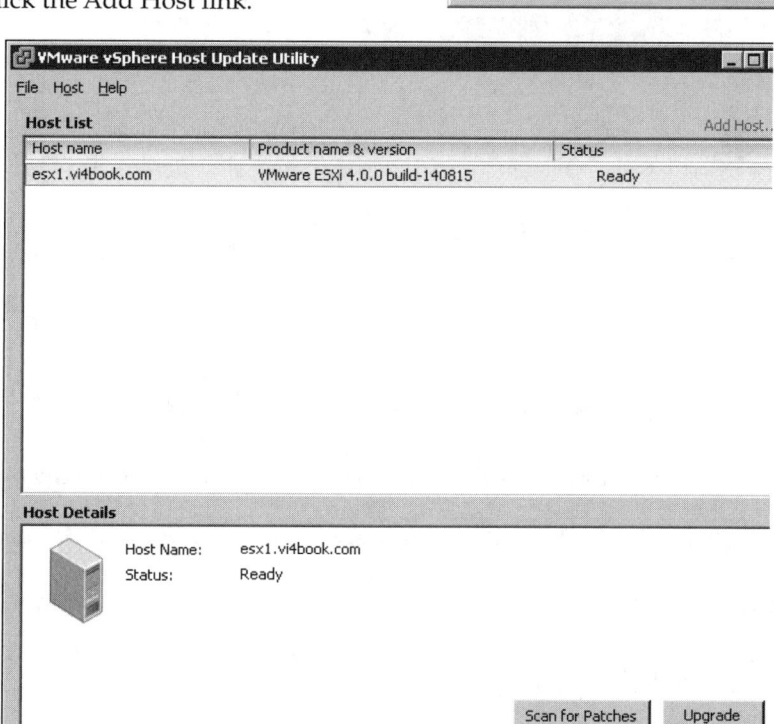

4. In the Add Host dialog box, enter the name or IP address of the ESXi 4 host.

5. Select the ESXi host from the list and click Scan for Patches.

6. Provide the root account and password to authenticate. After a scan, there may be patches ready to be applied.

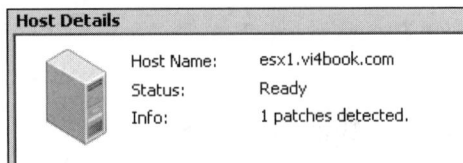

7. Click the Patch Host button to apply patches. You will see a dialog box listing the patches available. It also includes the option to not apply certain patches. Notice how even with the stand-alone utility, it will attempt to enter maintenance mode and perform a reboot, if possible.

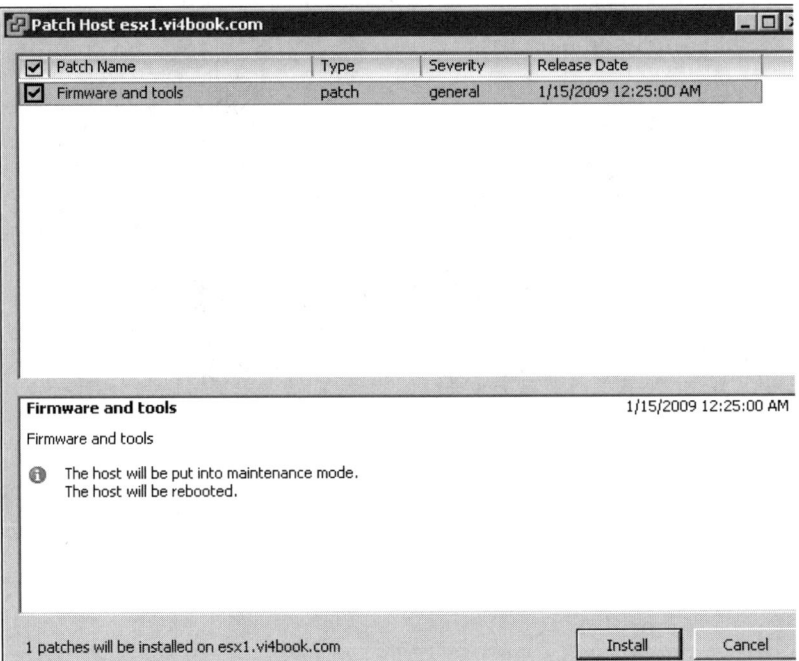

8. Click the Install button. You will see a progress bar outlining, well, the progress!

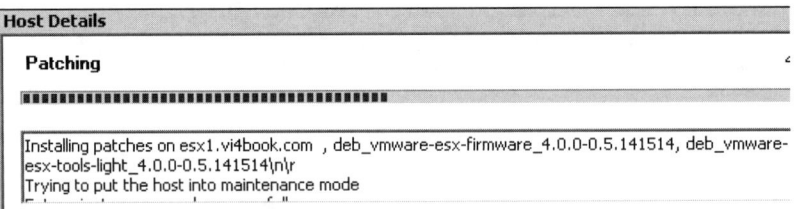

At the end of the process, you should see the Success status.

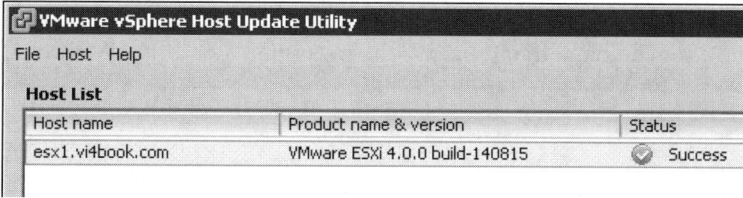

If you run another scan for patches, you will find that the build number has changed, and see the message "Host is up-to-date."

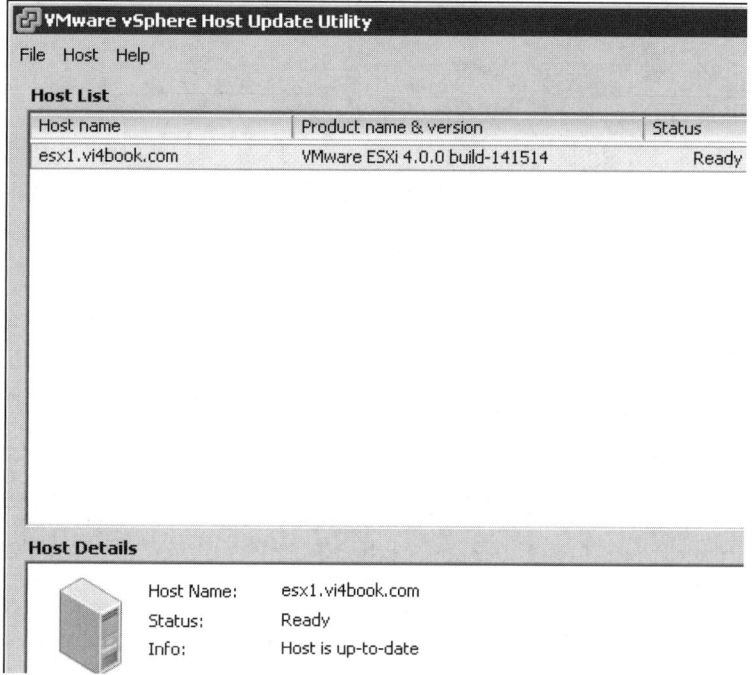

Rolling Back ESXi 4 Host Updates

ESXi 4 actually stores two builds: a boot build, which is the current one in use, and a standby build, to which you can roll back an update, should something go awry in the update process. After each successful update, a new standby build is created, so you always have a last-known-good build to which you can return.

For example, suppose the current boot build is 00002, and the current standby build is 00001. When you update the host to build 00003, the update process replaces build 00001 with build 00002, and makes build 00003 the standby build. If the update is successful, you continue to boot from build 00003 until the next update. For this reason, ESXi permits only one level of rollback. You can manually boot into the standby build instead of the current boot build; doing so destroys the current build and is a destructive process.

Here's how to roll back an update:

1. Reboot the ESXi 4 host.

2. When you see the page that displays the message, "Loading VMware Hypervisor," press SHIFT+R to select the standby build.

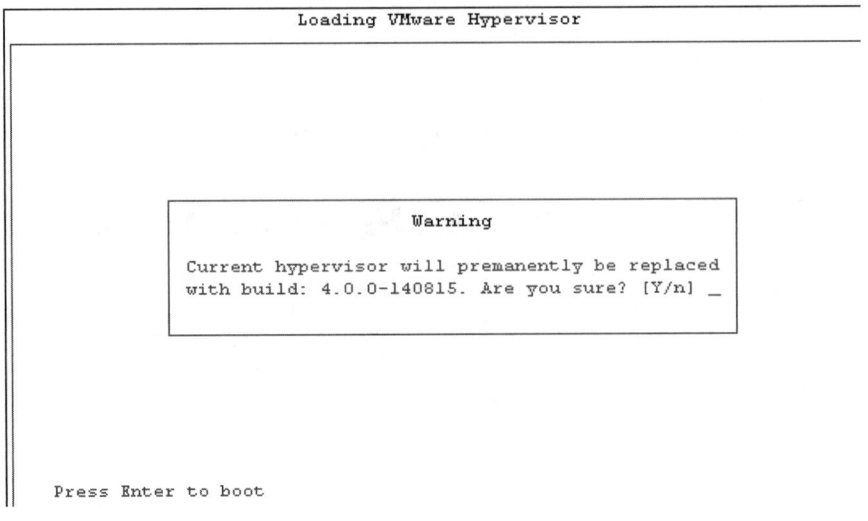

3. Press SHIFT+Y, and then press ENTER.

Using VMware Update Manager

VUM was introduced in VI3.5. Its main job is to patch ESX hosts and VMs. In its vCenter format, it allows you to set a baseline level for patches, and to scan the vCenter datacenter, cluster, or VM folder to see if the ESX hosts or the VMs meet this corporate baseline.

VUM can be set to manual or scheduled scanning, and this can be achieved with the VM being online or offline. Additionally, the system can be configured to offer a way of rolling back a VM, should the patch process itself introduce more problems than it remedies, using VMware's snapshot feature.

VUM integrates with DRS and can orchestrate the entire patch process. Working in conjunction with DRS, VUM will put the ESX host into maintenance mode, triggering the evacuation of the VMs from the ESX host. Next, VUM will patch the ESX host, and then force the ESX host to exit maintenance mode, triggering DRS to rebalance the cluster.

Updates are managed in a three-stage process:

- **Baseline**   Create a list of patches that form a "company standard" for ESX hosts and VMs.
- **Scan**   Check against the baseline for compliance.
- **Remediation**   Patch ESX hosts and VMs that fail to meet the baseline.

Installing VMware Update Manager

There are three main ways to run the VUM system. One way is to run the VUM service on the same Windows instances as your vCenter. Although this saves you money from a Windows licensing perspective, it does mean that the management system needs Internet access. Many big companies will frown at such a major component of their infrastructure being connected to the Internet in such a way. (I would agree with this philosophy, as I'm I'm one of those guys who doesn't understand why a Windows server needs a web browser, that that's another story.)

A second method essentially installs VUM to a separate Windows instance that is connected to the Internet.

The third method maintains the separation of the vCenter service and VUM services, but introduces a third component, which merely allows you to download patches. Then, using either a USB memory stick or a removable hard drive, you export the download patches to this removable media for uploading to your VUM system. This might be tricky if you have installed vCenter into a VM. A more practical solution might be to allow this download service to also be run inside a VM and download the patches to a second virtual disk. This second virtual disk can later be added to the VUM server to trigger the import process. In these two scenarios, your vCenter never directly has access to the Internet.

Another consideration is how to handle the VUM database. Like vCenter, VUM requires a back-end database to function. You have two choices: use the same database that vCenter uses or create a totally separate database. I recommend using a totally separate database, mainly because this will allow for separate backup and restore strategies should a problem occur with the vCenter or VUM database. So, I'll begin by explaining how to set up a Microsoft SQL Server database for VUM.

Creating a Database and Setting Permissions

The rights required for VUM to access the database are the same as those needed for vCenter. Here is the procedure for creating a Microsoft SQL Server 2005 database for use with VUM:

1. In Active Directory, create a user account for accessing the database, such as **vum1_dbuser**.

2. Open Microsoft SQL Server Management Studio.

3. Log in to SQL Server.

4. Right-click Databases and select New Database.

5. In the Database Name field, type a name for your database, such as **vum1-db**, and then click OK. You might wish to store the database in a different location. Remember that SQL Server defaults to saving databases on the C: drive.

6. Expand Security, right-click Logins, and choose New Login.

7. In the New Login dialog box, select the Windows Authentication radio button, and browse for the database user account you created at step 1. Set the default database to the database you created at step 5.

8. In the New Login dialog box, click the User Mapping tab, select the MSDB and vum1-db database, and enable the permission db_owner. Click OK.

9. Click OK, and then confirm the password again.

Configuring a DSN Connection

Next, configure a vCenter connection to the VUM database. As with the vCenter database, this requires the SQL Server Native Client to be installed on your vCenter server.

Before you begin, make sure your VUM database user account has local administrator rights to allow the installation routine to complete correctly.

1. Log in to the vCenter server using the account you created in Active Directory (vum1_dbuser in this example).

2. Open the ODBC Data Source Administrator (from Administrative Tools on the Start menu).

3. In the ODBC Data Source Administrator, choose the System DSN tab, and then click the Add button.

4. From the end of the list, choose SQL Server Native Client, and then click Finish.

5. In the Name field of the Create a New Data Source to SQL Server dialog box, type **VMware Update Manager**.

6. From the drop-down list, select your SQL Server 2005 server and click Next.

7. Select Windows Authentication and click Next.

8. Enable "Change the default database to" and select the vum1-db database you created earlier.

9. Click Next and Finish.

You should now be able to confirm all the dialog boxes associated with the ODBC setup and also test that you have connectivity to the database server. This test is nearly always successful. It does *not* test your user account credentials.

Installing VUM to vCenter with Internet Access

In this example, my vCenter has access to the Internet. Before I began the installation, I added a second virtual disk to the vCenter so that patches were not downloaded to the C: drive. I used the thinly provisioned format to make sure I used only the disk space occupied by the updates. VMware recommends that this disk be larger than 20GB. If it is smaller, you will receive a warning.

1. Start the autorun from the vCenter CD.

2. Select VMware Update Manager.

3. Complete the vCenter Server Information dialog box. The IP field defaults to the VMware vCenter IP address, but I prefer to use the FQDN of the vCenter server. The option exists so that VUM can run on a different Windows instance than that of vCenter.

CAUTION *The typical mistake made in the vCenter Server Information dialog box is to provide the username and password for the database. The account you should specify here is one that is valid for vCenter. This is required for VUM to extend vCenter with a plug-in at the end of the installation. Without the correct credentials, VUM cannot advertise or register this plug-in with vCenter. The database credentials for VUM come later in the installation routine. This does mean that the VUM server can be used on only one vCenter at a time. It is not possible to use one VUM server pointed at two different vCenter instances. Stated simply, there is a one-to-one relationship between each vCenter and VUM service.*

    4. In the Database Options dialog box, set the DSN used for the VUM database.

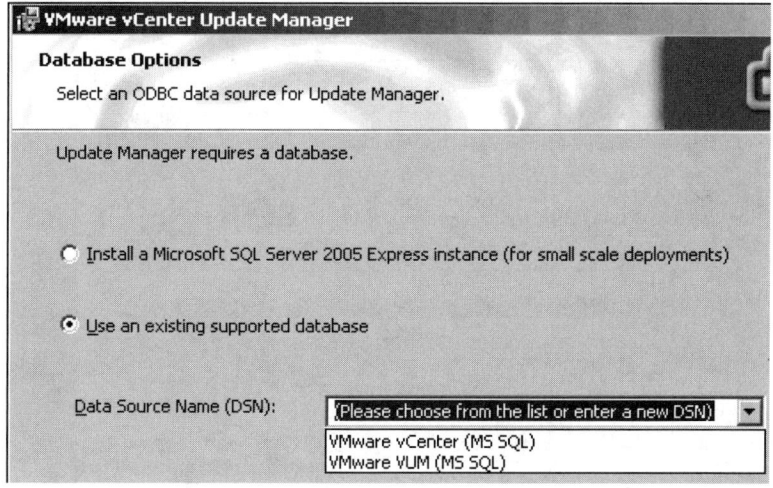

5. In the Database Information dialog box, you can set the credentials used for the VUM database. As you can see, if you are using Windows authentication in SQL Server, there is no need to set a username or password in this dialog box.

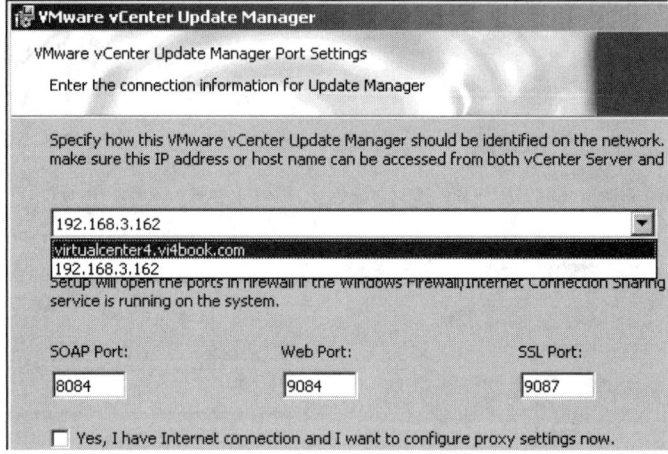

CAUTION *Early adopters of vSphere 4 have reported that occasionally the installation routine fails to grant the VUM database user account the "Right to logon as a service" privilege. If this happens, you can manually assign this privilege from the Services management console within Windows.*

6. In the VMware vCenter Update Manager Port Settings dialog box, set the communication ports for VUM, or accept the defaults. You can also set your proxy server settings (if needed) to allow the VUM service to communicate with the Internet for downloading patches. Again, the dialog box defaults to using an IP address to communicate with the vCenter service, but I prefer to use the FQDN.

7. Set the default locations for the VUM installation and where you would like to download the VUM files.

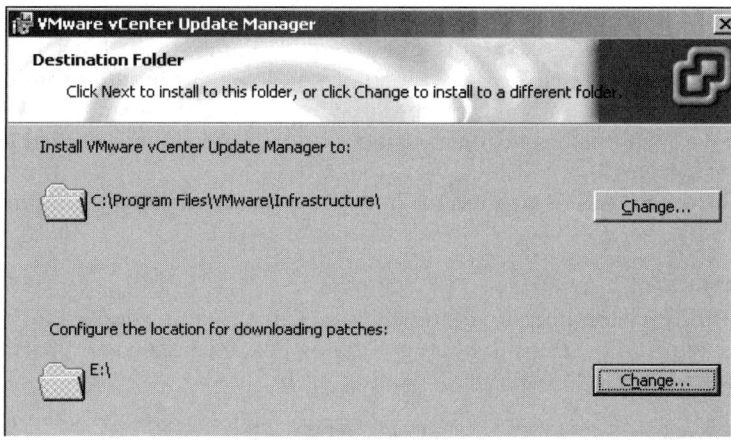

After VUM has started, you will see this progress bar in vCenter change as it downloads new signatures from the Internet. VUM checks both the VMware and Shavlik Web sites to find and download updates. Shavlik monitors a range of different guest OSs and the software they contain.

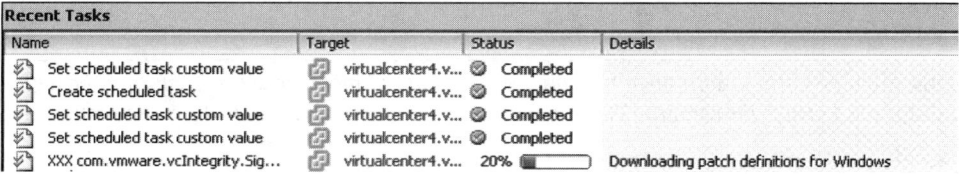

During this download process, you will see the kind of directory structure being created on the VUM server. In the example, the particular patch that has been downloaded for ESX includes a number of RPM files that will patch various drivers on the ESX host.

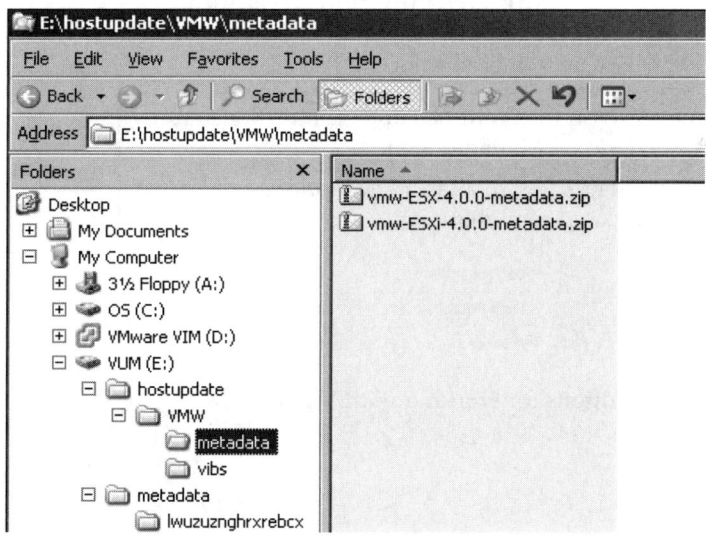

By default, VUM downloads ESX host updates, but does not download Windows or Linux updates. Instead it downloads tools that allow it to compare the latest bulletins to your Windows and Linux guests. The download of Windows or Linux patches takes place in the remediation phase, and only the patches that apply are downloaded. In other words, VUM does not download patches needlessly; it downloads the patches only at the time of fixing the relevant system.

While you're waiting for this process to complete, you can install and enable the VUM Extension plug-in.

Installing the VUM Client Plug-in

To install the VUM Extension plug-in, in the vSphere Client menu, choose Plug-ins, then Manage Plug-ins. Next, in the Plug-in Manager dialog box, click the Download and Install link for the VMware Update Manager Extension plug-in.

Plug-in Name	Vendor	Version	Status	Description	Progress
Installed Plug-ins					
vSphere Client Storage	VMware, Inc.	1.0.0.0	Enabled	vCenter Storage Information	
vCenter Service Status	VMware, Inc.	1.0.0.0	Disabled	vCenter Service Status	
Hardware Status	VMware, Inc.	1.0.0.0	Disabled	Hardware Status	
Available Plug-ins					
VMware vCenter Update Mana...	VMware, Inc.	4.0.0.2560	Download and Install...	VMware vCenter Update Manager extension	

CAUTION *Common errors with installing plug-ins are caused by incorrectly specifying the login details or the settings for communications between the vCenter and VUM that allow plug-ins to be added to the list.*

Quite a lot happens here. The progress bar goes by, and the MSI installation program cranks up. Eventually, you will be presented with a certificate Security Warning box.

When you enable the VUM plug-in, you will need to confirm another SSL certificate, which proves the identity of the VUM server. Additionally, you will receive a prompt from the vSphere Client about the untrusted nature of these certificates.

After installing and enabling the plug-in, you will have a number of graphical extensions to the vSphere Client user interface:

- In the Home view, on the Solutions and Applications tab, you will see an Update Manager icon.

- The right-click menus will display VUM options for scanning, staging, and remediation.

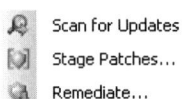

- The toolbar has buttons for working with VUM.

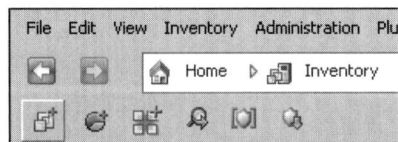

- The ESX host has an Update Manager tab.

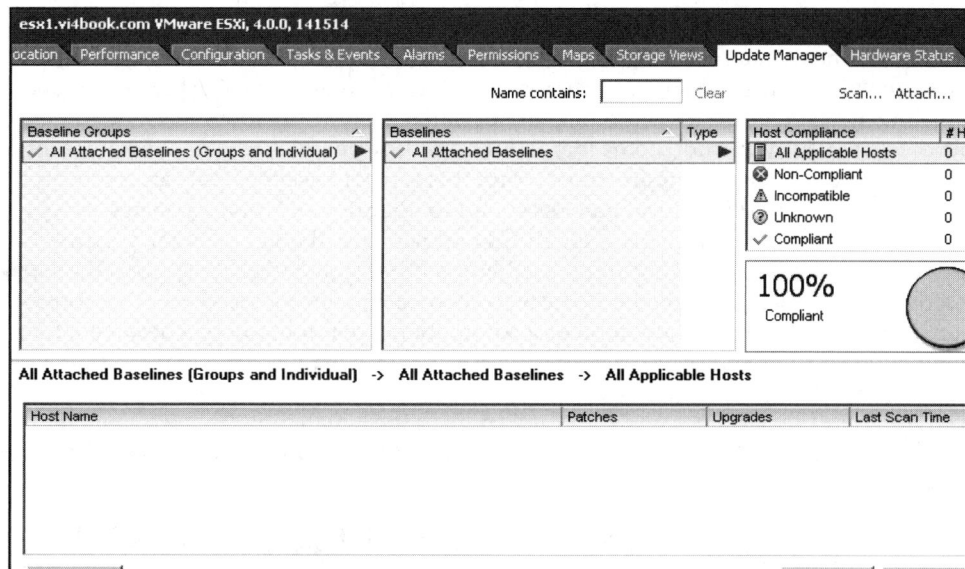

Creating Baselines and Baseline Groups

To see the default baselines created by the VUM installation procedure, click Home, then the Solutions and Applications tab, then the Update Manager icon. The view defaults to showing the two built-in baselines for use with ESX hosts. Clicking the VMs/VAs button shows you the built-in baselines for VMs and vApps.

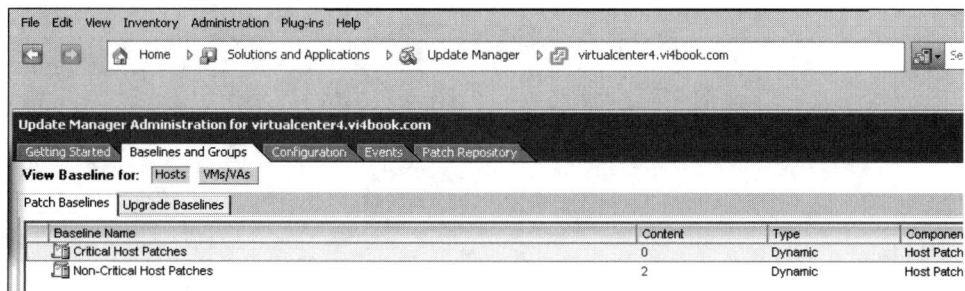

As you can see, the two main types of baselines you can have within an ESX host (or VM) are critical and noncritical. Additionally, baselines can be now placed into groups, which speed up the selection process when you have a lot of baselines.

Defining a Baseline

Baselines are basically lists of possible vulnerabilities and are used in the scanning process to see if an ESX host or a VM meets your requirements. It's possible that the default baselines will be good enough for your needs, depending on the ESX hosts and VMs for which your are managing patches.

You can have many different baselines, and attach those baselines to any number of datacenters, clusters, ESX hosts, VMs, or folders of VMs. So you might decide that baseline X is applied to folder A, but baseline Y is applied to folder B. ESX hosts or VMs that fail to meet these baselines can be fixed in a process that VMware calls *remediation*.

Additionally, baselines can either be dynamic or fixed. Dynamic baselines are automatically maintained by the update system, and they are updated as new vulnerabilities appear. It is possible to permanently exclude items manually from the dynamic baseline. Fixed baselines are manually specified by the administrator. With this type of baseline, you can create any combination of noncritical or critical patches suited to your organization's policies.

That all seems very simple. However, at first glance, the dialog boxes for creating baselines might not appear very intuitive, but with a little explanation, they do make sense.

As a quick example, I'll demonstrate how to create a custom VM baseline. I've chosen this type of baseline because, at the time of writing, there are not many patches available for ESX 4, which makes the dialog boxes a little sparse. Of course, there are plenty of patches for Windows and the software it contains!

To begin, from the Baselines and Groups Tab, click the Create link. In the Name field, type in a friendly name, such as **Custom Virtual Machine Baseline**. Next, under VM Baselines, select VM Patch.

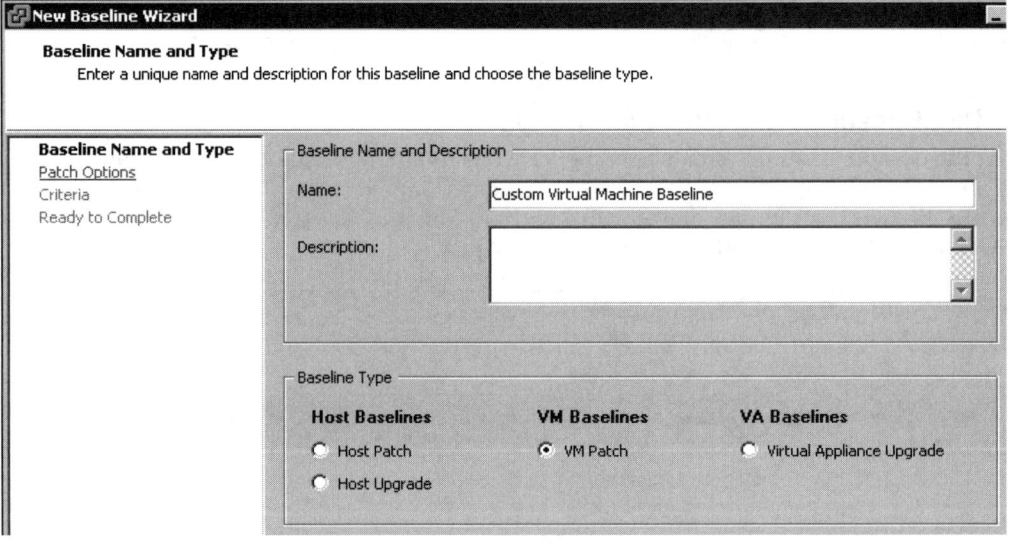

Now select whether you wish this baseline to be static or dynamic. Generally, I recommend dynamic baselines. As new patches and bug fixes are constantly being released, a baseline that requires manual intervention to update will be an administrative burden. Additionally, part of the agenda of all patch management systems is automation of the patching process, reducing the steps needed to be compliant to a minimum.

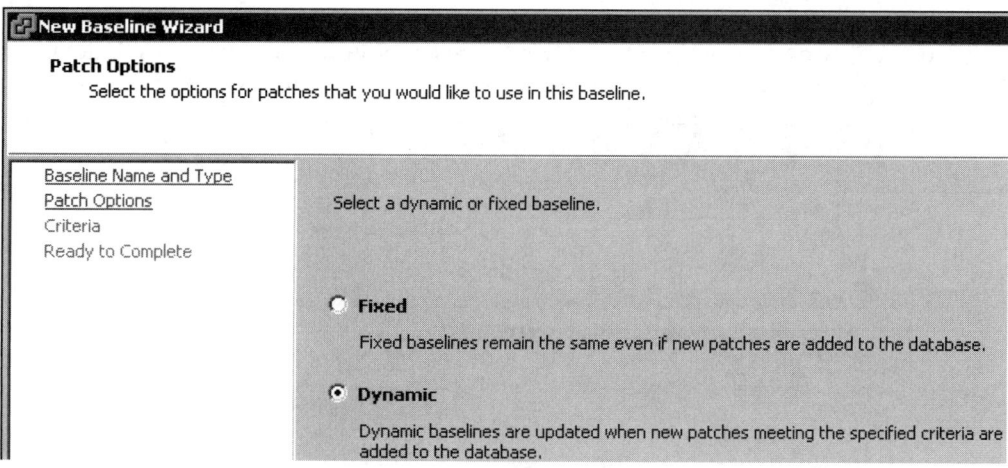

The next step in creating a baseline is either to include every patch or to reduce the number of patches. You can do this by simple filtering or by using the more powerful exclude/include option, which you can enable by selecting the "Add or remove specific patches to/from this baseline" option.

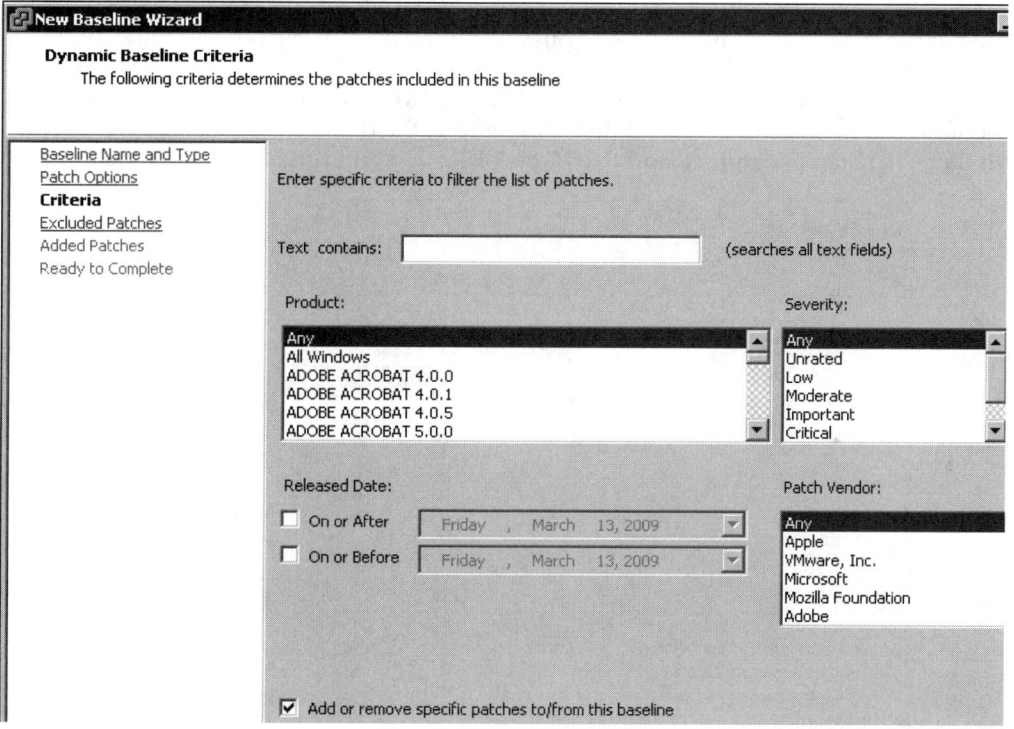

To just filter the patches, specify criteria using the lists in the dialog box. For example, if you wished to apply only critical updates from Microsoft, you would select All Windows in the Product list, Critical in the Severity list, and Microsoft in the Patch Vendor list.

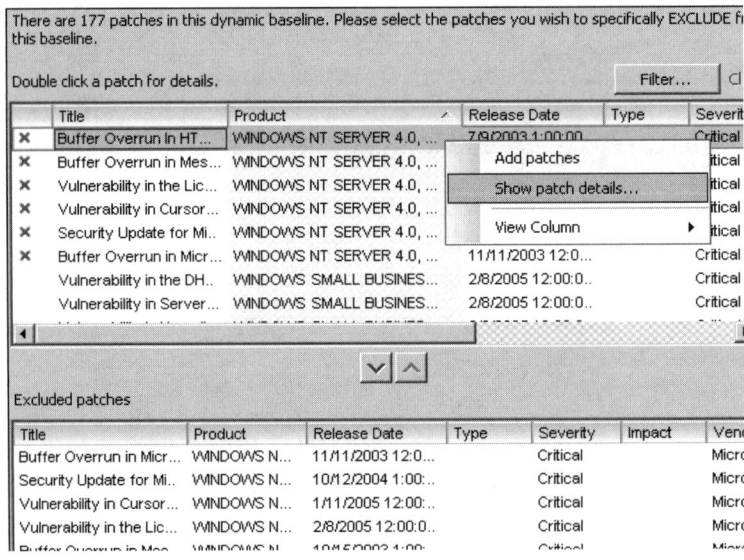

If you wished to do both, you could use a simple filter like the one in this example to reduce the list of patches to just Microsoft ones, and then use the exclude/include option to customize that list.

Enabling the "Add or remove specific patches to/from this baseline" option adds a picker-style dialog box to the wizard. In this example, the dialog box shows that there are 177 updates that can be applied, and that some of them could possibly be excluded.

Notice how they are all categorized as Critical. Ironically, despite the list being labeled "exclusions," these vulnerabilities would be used in a scan! The upper part of this dialog box is a list of patches that would be applied, and the lower part allows you to override this list and specifically exclude a critical patch.

The exclusion list provides a way of removing critical vulnerabilities that you do *not* wish to check your ESX host or VM against. The "Add patches" interface looks exactly same, and the decision about which to use depends on where the majorities lie. So, if you have 177 patches and you wish to apply only 3 of them, you would choose to *add* those 3 patches, which requires fewer clicks than excluding all the others. On the other hand, if you want to apply 170 of these patches, you would choose the exclude method.

In this example, I decided that the updates associated with the Windows NT Server 4 guest OS could be excluded, as I do not run Windows NT Server 4. As you can see, I sorted the patches by the Product column and used the downward-pointing arrow button to add them to the excluded list.

NOTE *Of course, VUM does not apply patches to the wrong system. So, in the example here, the Windows NT Server 4 patches would* not *be applied to Windows 2000 and later systems.*

If you are unsure of the purpose of a particular patch, you can right-click it and select "Show patch details." You will see a detailed advisory of the nature of the patch.

Remember that the number of updates does not categorically tell you how long the scan or remediation process will take. Some vulnerabilities can be patched with a 1KB file; others may need a 100MB file. That said, as a general rule of thumb, the more patches, the longer the scan/remediation process will take. As you would expect, scanning hundreds of VMs with thousands of updates takes considerably longer than scanning a much small number of ESX hosts with just a couple of vulnerabilities. The severest vulnerabilities generally lie within the scope of the guest OS, rather than with the VMware ESX server. You can substantially reduce the patch management of ESX by adopting ESXi, as most of the vulnerabilities in ESX Classic affect the Service Console piece of the platform.

The following example shows what appeared when I chose the "Add patches" option. My list includes a lot of patches—4330 in total. This list shows all the patches, including ones I didn't request, such as patches associated with Linux, which are noncritical. Here, you can *override* your initial filter to allow for exceptions to your general rule. For example, although I initially excluded updates for .NET Framework 3.0 SP2, many of the applications I run do require it, so I decided to include it in my list.

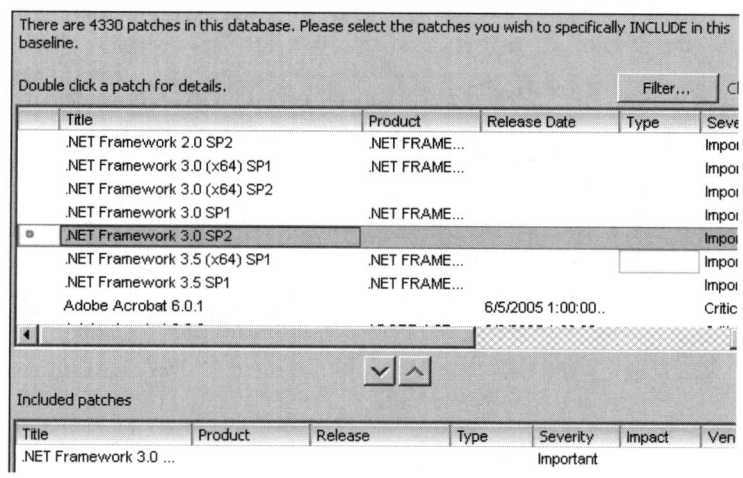

At the end of the wizard, review your selection process, and then click Finish. The baseline is added to the correct view for its type. In this example, clicking the VMs/VAs button shows the new VM baseline on the Patch Baselines tab.

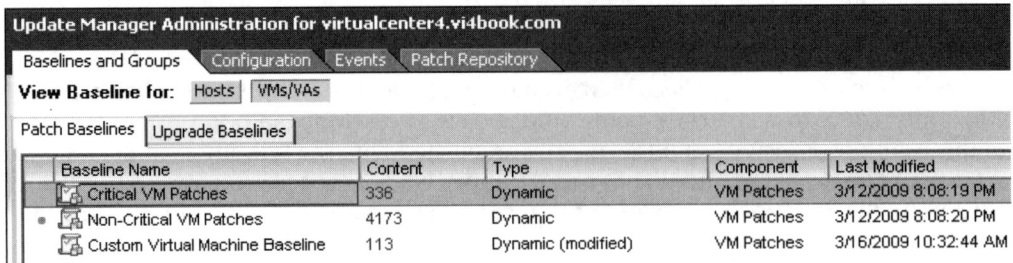

The Upgrade Baseline tab shows patches that can be used in the upgrade process from VI3.5 to vSphere 4 to update virtual hardware and VMware Tools on VMs. They can also be used after an upgrade to check the hardware and tools status of VMs, such as after you have upgraded from ESX 4.0.0 to ESX 4.0.1. Upgrade baselines are covered in the next chapter.

TIP *The VUM Repository tab shows which patches are available to be added or removed from the baseline. The Show button on the far right of this tab allows you to add a patch from this interface to the existing baseline.*

Creating Baseline Groups
Previous editions of VUM had only baselines, which were then attached to ESX hosts or VMs. This meant if you had a lot of baselines to attach, there would be some clicking to do. Now you can optionally create baseline groups, which allow you to attach bundles of baselines in many different combinations to an ESX host or VMs.

Creating a baseline group is easy, as it just involves using another picker utility, much like the one for excluding or adding patches. Follow these steps to create a baseline group:

1. On the Baselines and Groups tab, click the Create link next to Baseline Groups.

2. Type a friendly name for the baseline group.

3. Select a baseline type group. For this example, I chose the Virtual Machines and Virtual Appliances Baseline Group.

4. Optionally, select an upgrade baseline.

5. Select the baselines you wish to include. In this example, I added a second custom baseline for VMs to patch Adobe 8 vulnerabilities.

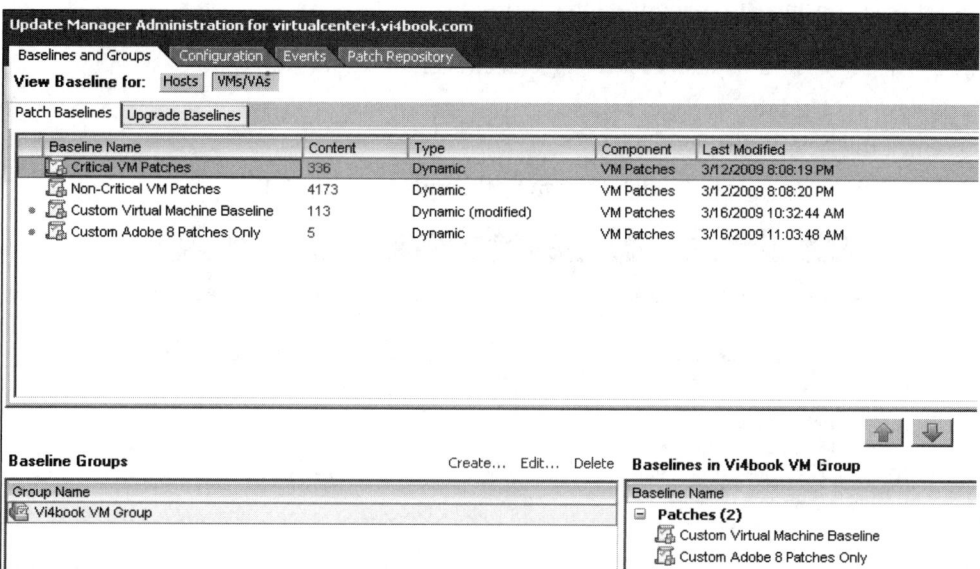

6. Click Next, and then click Finish. This will create a new baseline group.

Using the green up and down arrows, you can choose to remove or add baselines after the group has been created, or use the Edit link to modify the selected group.

Attaching Baselines and Scanning for Updates

Using your baselines, you can scan the inventory to produce a report on whether your ESX hosts or VMs meet those baselines. You can trigger a scan in nearly all the major nodes within vCenter. In the Hosts and Clusters view, you can start a scan from the following:

- On the Hosts and Clusters container itself, thereby scanning every datacenter, cluster, and ESX host
- Datacenters
- Clusters
- Hosts

If you wish to attach a baseline to a VM or a folder of VMs, you must switch to the VMs and Templates view. In the VMs and Templates view, you can start a scan from these items:

- On the VMs and Templates container itself, thereby scanning every VM and template
- Folders containing VMs
- Single VMs
- Templates (templates will be converted back to a VM format, powered on, and then scanned or remediated)

NOTE *You cannot attach a baseline to a resource pool object.*

Scanning All the ESX Hosts in a Cluster
To scan all the hosts in a cluster, follow these steps:

1. In the Hosts and Clusters view, select a cluster.
2. Select the Update Manager tab.
3. Click the Attach link.
4. Select the baselines you wish to scan with, and then click OK.

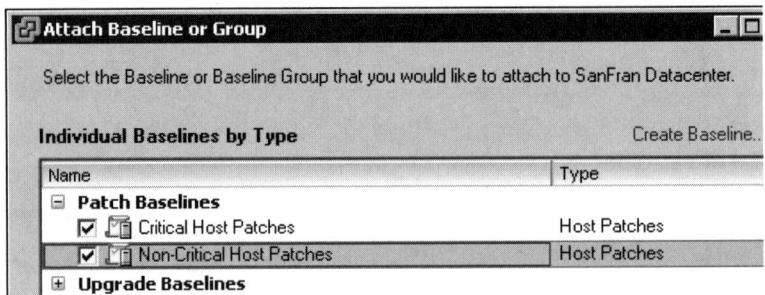

5. Click the Scan button on the toolbar, or right-click the datacenter and chose Scan for Updates.

6. In the Confirm Scan dialog box, choose to scan the ESX hosts for patches and/or upgrades. Checking the Upgrades box has VUM scan any ESX hosts that are older than ESX 4 to see if they qualify for an upgrade to the newer version.

After the scanning process completes, a report is generated at the point it was triggered—the datacenter view in this example.

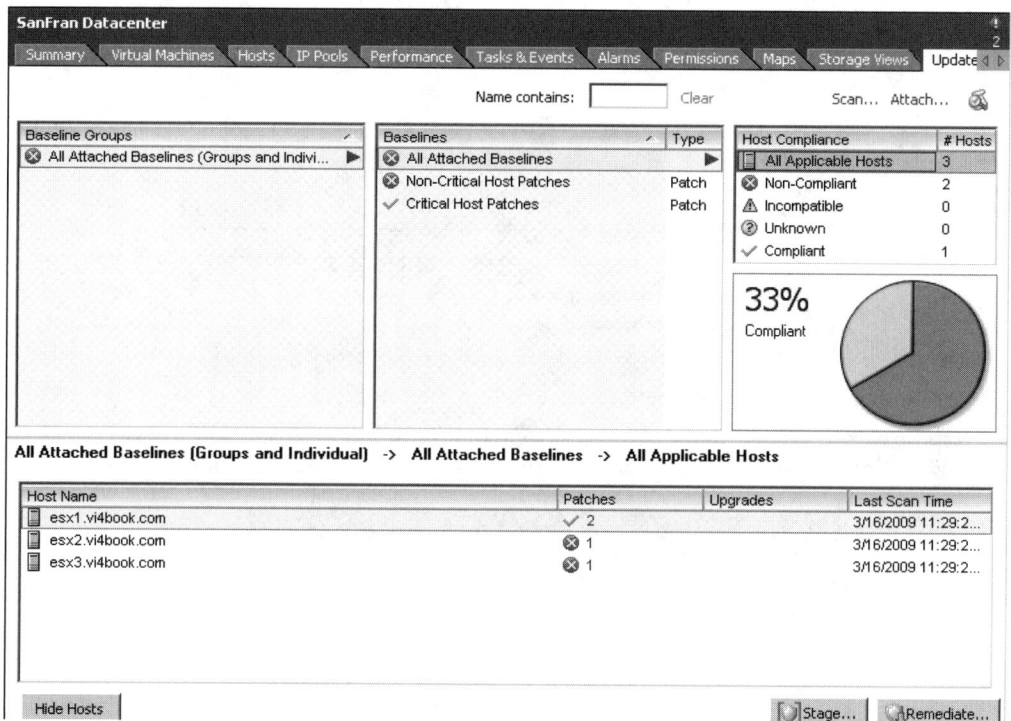

Here, out of my three ESX hosts, one met the baseline. The esx1 host passed, because it was recently patched using the stand-alone Host Update Utility. The two other ESx hosts failed, and they are flagged with red Xs indicating that they do not meet my baseline for ESX. This means my datacenter, which has three ESX hosts, is only 33% compliant.

Scanning All the VMs in a Datacenter

To scan all the VMs in a datacenter, follow these steps:

1. In the VMs and Templates view, select a datacenter.

2. Select the Update Manager tab.

3. Click the Attach link.

4. Select the baselines you wish to scan with, and then click OK.

Attach Baseline or Group

Select the Baseline or Baseline Group that you would like to attach to SanFran Datacenter.

Individual Baselines by Type   Create Baseline..

Name	Type
⊞ **Patch Baselines**	
⊞ **Upgrade Baselines**	

Baseline Groups   Create Baseline Group..

Name	Type
⊟ ☑ **Vi4book VM Group**	
☑ Custom Virtual Machine Baseline	VM Patches
☑ Custom Adobe 8 Patches Only	VM Patches

5. Right-click the datacenter and choose Scan for Updates.

6. In the Confirm Scan dialog box, choose whether to scan for patches, virtual appliance upgrades, VM hardware upgrades, and/or VMWare Tools upgrades.

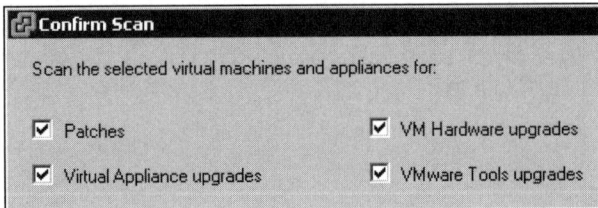

Confirm Scan

Scan the selected virtual machines and appliances for:

☑ Patches   ☑ VM Hardware upgrades

☑ Virtual Appliance upgrades   ☑ VMware Tools upgrades

As with ESX host scanning, VUM will generate a report showing compliant and noncompliant VMs.

NOTE *Occasionally, you might see in the Update Manager report window the word "unknown" and count of "unknowns." These are known unknowns, which are unknown because no scan has yet to take place. Once these unknowns are known, they are then known to the system, and these unknowns are removed. (How's that for Donald Rumsfeld–speak?)*

Staging and Remediation of ESX hosts

Remediation is a rather fancy term for applying a patch, and remediation can be initiated from the same levels as scanning in the vCenter Inventory.

One especially neat feature of remediation is the way that VUM is integrated with DRS. It can orchestrate the VMotion of VMs off an ESX host that is about to be patched and trigger entry/exit of maintenance mode. You can also configure what happens if maintenance mode cannot be achieved. This can be useful, for example, for VMs configured with local VMFS storage, which cannot be moved by DRS (because they fail to meet one of the main requirements of VMotion—shared storage).

The staging process is new to VUM. Staging an ESX host allows you to download patches from VUM to the ESX host but prevent the patching process from beginning. This allows VMware to have the patches downloaded locally to each ESX host, prior to triggering the patch installation process. The intention is to speed up the patching process and reduce the time that an ESX host is in maintenance mode.

Staging and Remediation of a Cluster

To stage a cluster, follow these steps:

1. Select the cluster and click the Update Manager tab.

2. Click the Stage button, or right-click the cluster and choose Stage Patches.

3. Select the baselines that will form the basis of your staging.

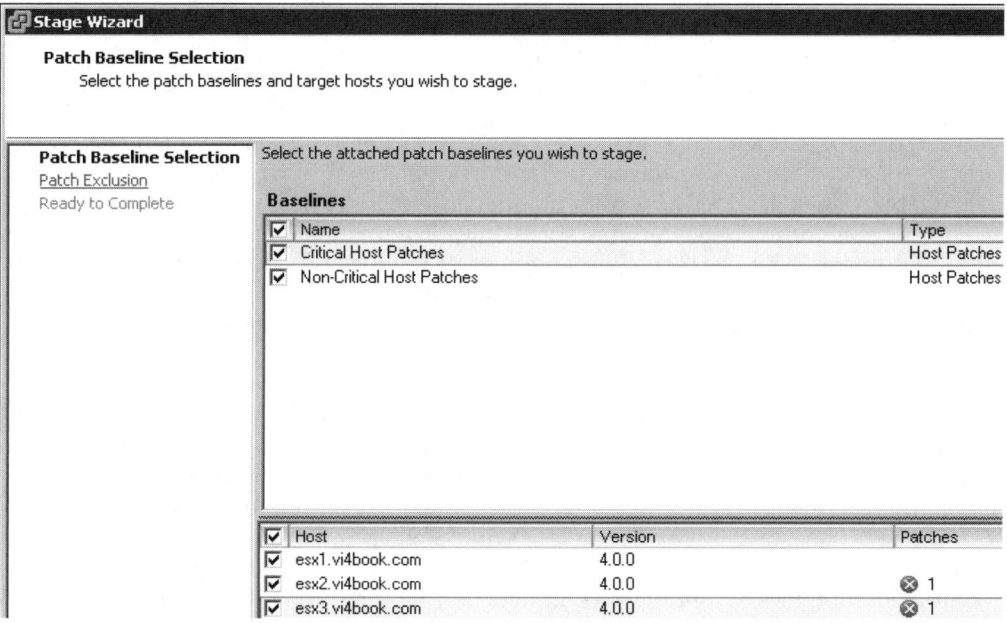

4. In the next dialog box, you will see again you are able to exclude certain patches from the staging process, Click Next, and then click Finish.

To begin the patching process (remediation), select the Remediate button, or right-click the cluster and choose Remediate.

The Remediate wizard looks and feels very much like the Stage wizard, but you can choose some additional options.

You can request that remediation happen immediately or set up a scheduled task, which will trigger the job at the time selected. The failure options control what should happen if VUM is unable to make an ESX host enter maintenance mode. The default is to keep trying the maintenance mode every 30 minutes, three times in a row until failing the task, and then move on to the next ESX hosts. The alternatives are to fail the task altogether or power off/ suspend VMs to make sure the maintenance mode completes.

If you have selected to start remediation immediately, the process will begin after you complete the wizard, and the Recent Tasks bar will show progress information. The Remediate Entity task gives you an entire view of the process, with each of the "Install" entries being a patch that has been applied. The Remediate Entity task will also include the time taken to reboot an ESX host and for maintenance mode to be exited. You should expect your ESX host to be flagged as "Not Responding" at some stage during the remediation process.

If you trigger remediation at a higher level than an ESX host (from the Hosts and Clusters view, datacenter view, or cluster view), VUM will patch each ESX host serially. This is to ensure as many ESX hosts are online as possible during the remediation process.

The remediation process should be seamless and require little intervention from the administrator, except in one situation. If you are running vCenter and VUM within VMs, and you remediate the ESX host on which they are running, you will receive a warning message, indicating that you must carry out a manual VMotion of the vCenter and VUM instances.

Task Details

Name: **Remediate Entity**   Target: esx4.vi4book.com   Initiated by: **Administrator**
Status: **There are errors during the remediation operation.**
Related Events:
7/14/2009 7:01:30 PM,   The host esx4.vi4book.com has a VM virtualcenter4 with VMware vCenter Update Manager or VMware vCenter installed. The VM needs to be moved to another host for the remediation to proceed.
7/14/2009 7:01:27 PM,   Task: Remediate Entity

After the remediation process is over, there is no need to manually rescan an ESX host to confirm that it now meets the baseline; this task is automated. On the Update Manager tab for a patched ESX host, its status will change from noncompliant to compliant.

Remediation of VMs

Remediation of a VM works in a similar way to remediation of an ESX host, except you have the chance to control when powered on, powered off, and suspended VMs are patched. With suspended VMs, VUM powers those VMs back on, patches them, and then resuspends them.

During the patching process, VMware will apply and retain a snapshot of the VM to allow the rollback of the VM prior to the patching process, in case a patch causes more problems than it fixes.

CAUTION *The remediation of VMs automatically creates a snapshot. Beware of simultaneously patching large numbers of VMs that have not been patch managed previously. You may run out of disk space for the delta files that make up a snapshot.*

To start the Remediate wizard, select a VM or folder of VMs, click the Update Manager tab, and click the Remediate button, or right-click the VM or folder and choose Remediate. Select the baselines that will form the basis of your remediation. Next, set your preferences for the schedule.

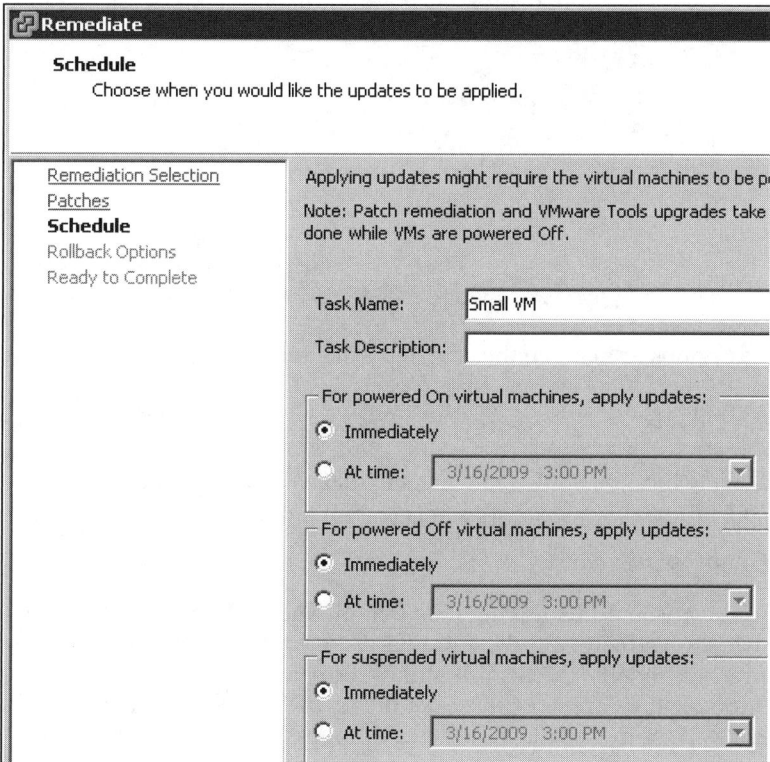

Notice how this dialog box is subtly different from the ESX host remediation dialog box, in that you can deal with the different power states of the VM. This can be useful if, for example, you are managing patches for a VDI environment.

The next step is to set your preferences for snapshots. As stated earlier, prior to remediation, you can let VUM apply a snapshot to each VM. This dialog box allows you to control that process.

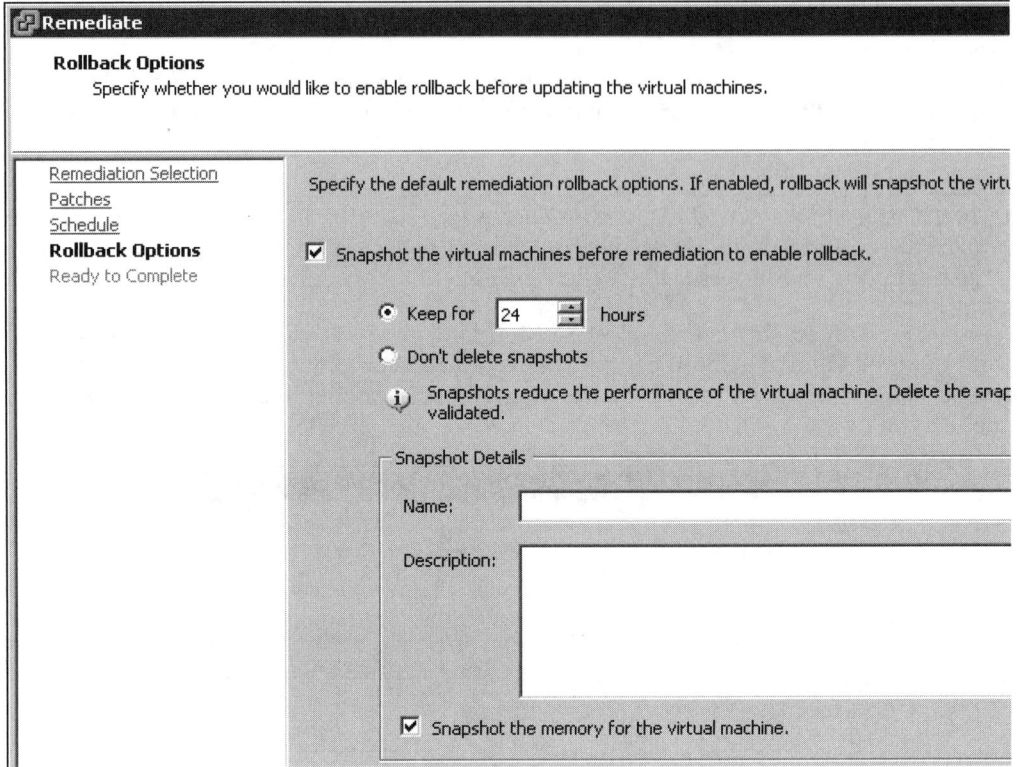

A number of options to manage the snapshots are available:

- Use a standard name and description for the snapshot that is applied to every VM affected.
- Do not delete the snapshot, so you can manage its removal manually.
- Retain the snapshot for a number of specified hours.
- Take a snapshot of memory.

The defaults may need adjusting here. By default, the VM's memory contents are not included in a snapshot, which would mean your VM would not be consistent, but merely crash-consistent. Additionally, the default allows the snapshot to be retained indefinitely, which could introduce the danger of the delta files growing (perhaps unchecked unless you search or set an alarm for them) and filling the volumes where they are created.

I found monitoring the progress of a large VM remediation tricky. Unlike the installation of ESX patches, where each update has an event entry of "install," no such progress information of that detail exists for VM patches. So unless you have VMs that are patched up to the hilt already, expect the Remediate Entity status to be on your screen for some time. In my case, with just Windows 2003 (SP1) and Windows 2000 Advanced Server (SP4), it took a long time to download all the patches and then apply them.

If you chose to take a snapshot of the VM before remediation, at the end of the process, you should find that snapshot in the Snapshots window.

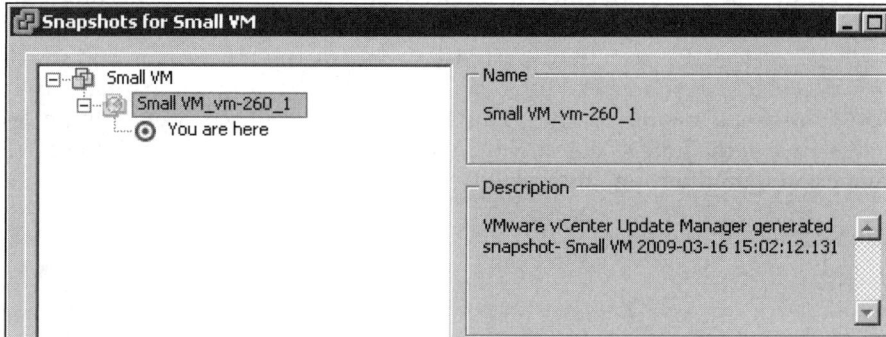

Configuring VMware Update Service Settings

You can configure some VUM settings, including those that control the remediation defaults, from its Configuration tab (click Home, then Solutions and Applications, then the Update Manager icon, and then Configuration).

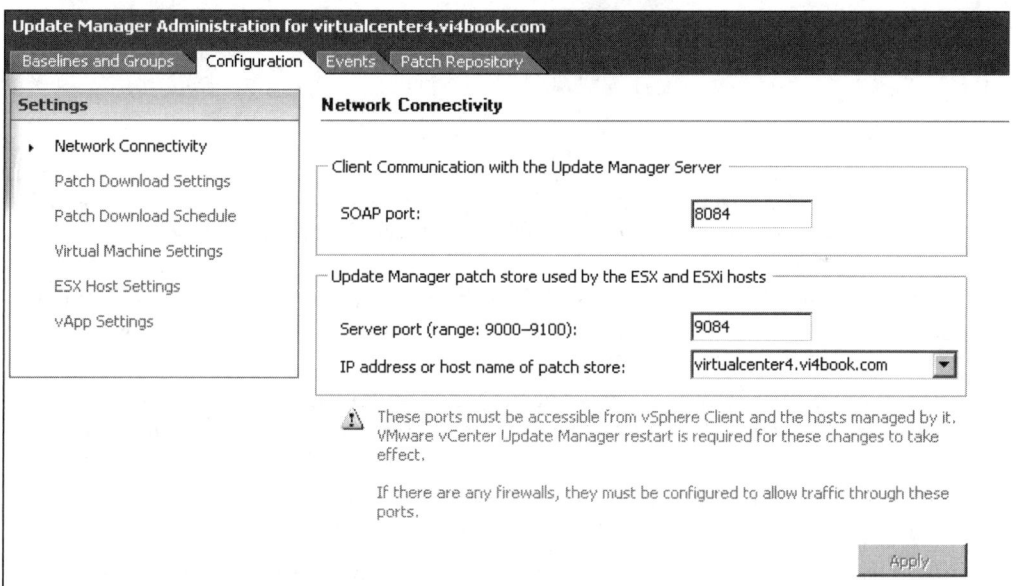

In the Settings list, you can select from the following categories:

- **Network Connectivity** Here, you can change the TCP SOAP port number used for client communication between the vSphere Client and the VUM server. Generally, this is used for downloading and installing the VUM plug-in that extends the vSphere Client. You can also set which port number (between 9000 and 9100) is used for the communications between the VUM server and vCenter.

- **Patch Download Settings** Here, you can control some patch-related settings. You can switch from being directly connected to the Internet or communicating via a proxy server. You can stop the download of ESX 3, ESX 4, Linux, and Windows patches. You can also set a third-party URL other than VMware.com and shavlik .com as a patching source. Additionally, from this page, you can manually trigger a download of available patches. This is useful, for example, if the Internet was unavailable at the time of the weekly scheduled download of the patch list (which can be configured through the Patch Download Schedule settings, described next).

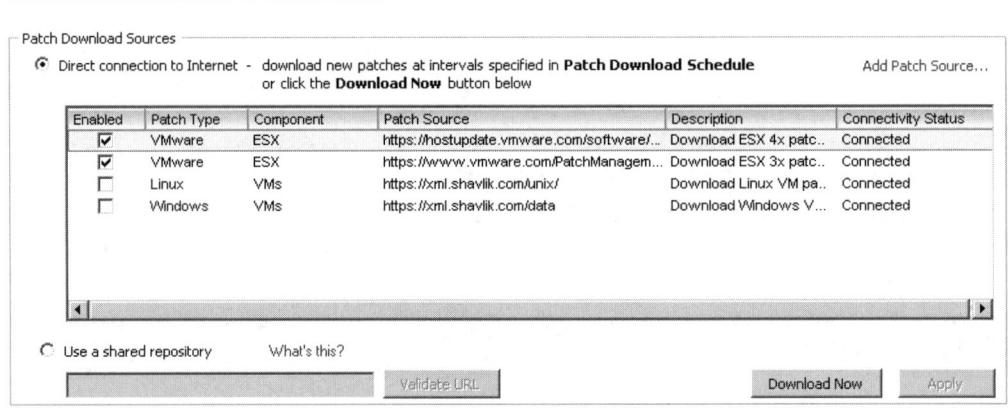

NOTE *Remember that downloading patches begins only at the staging or remediation process, and a Windows patch would be downloaded only if you remediated a Windows-based VM.*

- **Patch Download Schedule** This controls how frequently VUM checks for patches. By default, it checks once a week. Using these settings, you can change to any frequency that suits your purposes.

- **Virtual Machine Settings** This controls the default settings relating to whether VMs have a snapshot taken prior to the remediation and how long those snapshots are allowed to exist.

- **ESX Host Settings** This controls the response should an ESX host fail to enter maintenance mode.

- **vApp Settings** This allows you to disable smart reboot, which tries to reboot just the parts of the vApps that need to be rebooted after patching. It also reboots components that need to be rebooted to keep the overall vApp functioning.

NOTE *The Events tab in VUM is merely a filter system to show only events that specifically affect VUM.*

Summary

No software release is ever perfect, no matter how rigorous the testing by the software vendor or by end users of beta programs. That said, generally, VMware has a very good reputation for producing high-quality software that just works. In fact, sometimes VMware can be more conservative than other software vendors. By marking various features as being "experimental," it gives us a clear indication of the possible reliability of a given feature.

VUM is a very welcome addition to ESX and vCenter. Generally, people within the VMware community like VUM for patching ESX, and VUM represents a significant improvement on the methods we used to use in the past, which required scripting skills to automate. The VMware community is less enthralled by VUM's patching of VMs. I think this is mainly because folks don't want to manage two patch management systems—VUM for virtual Windows systems and Windows Update for physical Windows systems. Basically, people are looking for one patching system for an OS.

Critically, you should know that even VUM has an Achilles heel. The goal of VUM is to be able to patch the ESX host (which usually involves a reboot) without disrupting the operation of the VMs. To achieve this, it leverages VMotion and DRS. If you desire this high-level automation, care must be taken in validating that VMotion always works without errors and that an ESX host can successfully enter maintenance mode with stalling. If this is not the case, the administrator will need to manual intervene to correct these errors.

In the long-term, if you really wish to reduce the patching burden of ESX, a switch to ESXi is the way to go. As I stated earlier, most patches to ESX Classic are to the Service Console; in other words, they are Red Hat Linux patches. By removing this component, the ESX host becomes more and more just an appliance for running VMs.

One final thing to mention the VUM automation behavior does change if you try to patch an ESX hosts which has the vCenter running on it as a VM. The automatic move of VMs caused by VUM and DRS working together will still move VMs, except the VM that contains vCenter. If you do run vCenter in a VM it will have to be moved manually.

CHAPTER 20 | Upgrading from VI3.5 to vSphere 4

This chapter describes how to upgrade to vSphere 4. I left this topic to the very end of the book because I thought that most people would prefer to understand the product before upgrading to it. The most recent release of VI3.5 is Update 4, but VMware will continue to maintain the 3.5 release, so expect new patches and possibly even an Update 5.

Before attempting an upgrade, you need to consider your starting position and where you are trying to get to once the upgrade is completed. It's possible that a clean install will better suit your needs.

A Clean Install or an Upgrade?

I once attended a networking breakout session at VMworld in the same year that VI3 was released. At the end of the session, I outlined some problems I had with networking after upgrading from ESX 2 to ESX 3. I had resolved these problems, and as usual, documented them on a free PDF on my blog. But I was curious to know if there was a better way of resolving this in-place upgrade problem and the cause. The speaker suggested that perhaps a clean install was a better approach, and everyone in the audience laughed, because we already knew that would be the answer to this question.

The question of whether to perform a clean install or an upgrade is one that I've been asked since I started in IT in 1993. As ever, the answer is, "It depends."

In my experience, moving from one version of a product to another usually involves these key factors: How much of the current configuration do you need to retain, and what method will offer the smallest window of downtime with minimal impact on end users.

Consider the following in deciding between an upgrade and a clean install:

- **What is the state of your current VMware deployment?** It's not unusual for people to roll out a virtualization project in a week. Or perhaps their implementation is based on a proof-of-concept that was so successful that they decided to roll it out into production. These deployments are not ideal, but were left in place as "good enough" interim solutions. Clearly, if the existing implementation is unsatisfactory, then the release of vSphere 4 offers a legitimate reason to start again (and do a better job of it this time!).

- **Are you using ESX 2 and vCenter 1?** If you are using these releases of VMware virtualization technologies, I do not recommend trying to upgrade them. The main reason is that you would need to perform an intermediary upgrade from version 2 to version 3 before embarking on a second upgrade to version 4. If you have used automatic partitioning for the boot disk, you may find the /boot partition is too small to upgrade the host from ESX 2 to ESX 3, and then upgrade to ESX 4. Also, an upgrade from ESX 2 to ESX 4 would introduce a file system change from VMFS 2 to VMFS 3, or at the very least, a mass SVMotion of many VMs from one LUN to another. It's not unlike Microsoft stating that if you are on Windows NT 4, and you want to do an in-place upgrade to Windows 2003, you must upgrade to Windows 2000 first. Faced with the risks, complexities, and time involved, an upgrade would be more hassle than it would be worth.

NOTE *Personally, I've always been comfortable with upgrades within a release of software, say upgrading from version 8.1 to 8.2. I'm less comfortable with upgrades between releases, say from version 5 to 6. I'm totally hostile to an upgrade from a release that is two versions behind the current release, say from version 2 to 4. In my experience, the greater the gap from one release to another, that more intermediary steps there are, and the greater the chance that the upgrade will fail.*

- **Are you moving from ESX Classic to ESXi?**   If you think the time is right to move from ESX Classic to ESXi, then by definition, we are talking about a fresh "installation." In this case, take a long, hard look at the third-party software you currently use. Remember that ESXi is still quite new, and your third-party vendor might not support it. For example, some virtualization-only backup vendors may still require an agent to be installed on the ESX host. Additionally, you may have scripts that carry out tasks at the ESX hosts, and these may not function in ESXi. You may need to embrace one of the new scripting APIs in order to allow those processes to function after the switch.

- **How many changes have you made?**   Many vendors rigorously test their upgrade paths, but these tests are often made against a plain-vanilla installation of the previous release, without customization or the kind of real-world changes familiar to those who support the product in production. In my experience, the more heavily I have customized any vendor's product, the more likely the upgrade will fail (because an event for which no quality-assurance test was ever made is encountered), or the customization is lost altogether—which kind of negates the whole point of an upgrade. In my tests, the VMware upgrade process went relatively smoothly, but my upgrade was a clean install of VI3.5 Update 4 (the most recent release) to vSphere 4.

NOTE *The method of upgrading to vSphere4 using VUM documented in this chapter was actually broken in the Beta and Release Candidate phases. It was fixed at the time of general availability (GA). That does seem to be an indication that, like many software vendors, upgrading from one release to another might not be so rigorously tested and validated compared to other aspects of the vSphere 4 product. Of course, it is my job to confirm that these promises were made good at the time of the GA release. I'm pleased to say the issues I confronted have indeed been resolved.*

- **Are you using Microsoft SQL Server 2000 for vCenter 2?**   Remember that vCenter 4 no longer supports the use of Microsoft SQL Server 2000 as the back-end database for vCenter. This would make an in-place upgrade of vCenter difficult, as you would first need to migrate the SQL Server 2000 database to a new version, and then begin an in-place upgrade of vCenter 4. Of course, Microsoft and other database software vendors have their own migration tools for moving database files from one version to another. I think much depends on the size and scope of your vCenter implementation.

> *Tɪᴘ* *There are many articles on how to move databases from Microsoft SQL 2000 to Microsoft SQL Server 2005. One of the best is "Moving Data from SQL Server 2000 to SQL Server 2005," by Jayaram Krishnaswamy (http://www.aspfree.com/c/a/MS-SQL-Server/Moving-Data-from-SQL-Server-2000-to-SQL-Server-2005/).*

- **What other management products are using vCenter?**   You may have other management technologies from VMware that interact with vCenter, such as VMware View and VMware Site Recovery Manager. Many of the high-level management products communicate with vCenter as part of their day-to-day operations. Before embarking on an upgrade, you will need to fully research these products for their compatibilities with vCenter 4 and ESX 4, and ensure you have the supported releases of those products prior to the upgrade.

Taking into account these considerations, my recommendation is to carry out a clean install when possible, and perform an upgrade when the impact is minimal and you wish to preserve your existing configuration. For example, if I had a complicated vCenter environment with a lot of permissions and performance data, I would be very tempted by an upgrade. However, if I needed to migrate the database back end as well, it would give me pause for thought.

Upgrading existing VMs is highly desirable, as the tasks involved are not very intrusive and no one would want to start all over again, rolling out new VMs. However, I question the need to upgrade the ESX host software. Using VMotion, you could (if you have spare capacity in the cluster) completely clear the existing ESX host of VMs, and then remove it from an upgraded vCenter environment. It could be installed cleanly, perhaps using scripted installations, and added back into the cluster. I have often found that a clean install is actually quicker than an upgrade, especially if that installation is automated by scripts.

To me, the ESX host is just a block of CPU and memory, and there is nothing on the ESX hosts that I actually care about. By carrying out a clean install, I remove the anxiety about the stability and reliability of the platform caused by an in-place upgrade. (Of course, I speak from the position of having only 6 ESX hosts; I think my opinion would be tempered if I had 600 hosts.)

Finally, before we look at upgrading to vSphere4 using the VUM system it's perhaps worth mentioning that you can do a manual upgrade using the "esxupgrade.sh" script on the ESX 4.0 CD. Personally, I prefer to the upgrade using VUM as it's recommended by VMware. If you want to learn more about the manual method visit KB article 1009440 located here:

http://kb.vmware.com/selfservice/microsites/search.do?language=en_US&cmd=displayKC&externalId=1009440

Upgrading Using VMware Update Manager

Chapter 19 introduced the use of VUM for patch management. VUM also offers some unique features that make upgrading much easier:

- You can schedule tasks to occur at times that minimize the effect on end users.

- You can create baselines and run scans to confirm the upgrade was successful, and error-trap failures.

- You can take snapshots of VMs prior to upgrading VMware Tools and virtual hardware, offering an automated rollback method.

- You can select which components of ESX hosts or VMs are upgraded, without resorting to scripts or the Microsoft `msiexec` utility.

NOTE *If you have multiple installations of vCenter 2.5 and wish at the end of the process to have them in linked mode in vCenter 4, I recommend upgrading each of the independently. Once the upgrade has completed, use the vCenter Server Linked Mode Configuration Wizard to aggregate the vCenter implementations together.*

To demonstrate the upgrade process, I'm going to take you through the upgrade of an entire ESX 3 and vCenter 2 environment to an ESX 4 and vCenter 4 environment. The upgrade process is carried out in stages, and generally at the end of each stage, there is no going back. I recommend backing up your environment prior to starting any upgrade process.

There are six stages to the upgrade:

1. Upgrade vCenter and the vSphere Client.
2. Upgrade vCenter components: VUM, Converter, and Guided Consolidation.
3. Upgrade ESX hosts using VUM.
4. Upgrade VM Tools with VUM.
5. Upgrade virtual hardware using VUM.
6. Optionally, upgrade standard vSwitches to distributed vSwitches (covered in Chapter 5).

Between stages 4 and 5, I recommend that you create a record of the VM's IP configuration, as a precaution. Occasionally, an upgrade of virtual hardware can introduce a new PCI device or network adapter, and this may result in the original local area connection disappearing, along with your original IP settings. This will leave you with a new local area connection 2, which defaults to DHCP. This behavior seems to depend on the version of ESX and version of Windows within the guest OS.

Upgrading vCenter and the Client

If your existing vCenter environment runs in a VM (as mine does), you can take a snapshot of the existing state of the vCenter and database server, so you are able to roll back to a known-good state if the upgrade fails. If you want to be extra careful, you can even power down the virtual vCenter and database instance, and take a snapshot of them in a cold state.

The following example shows my existing vCenter 2.5 environment, before proceeding with the upgrade procedure described here.

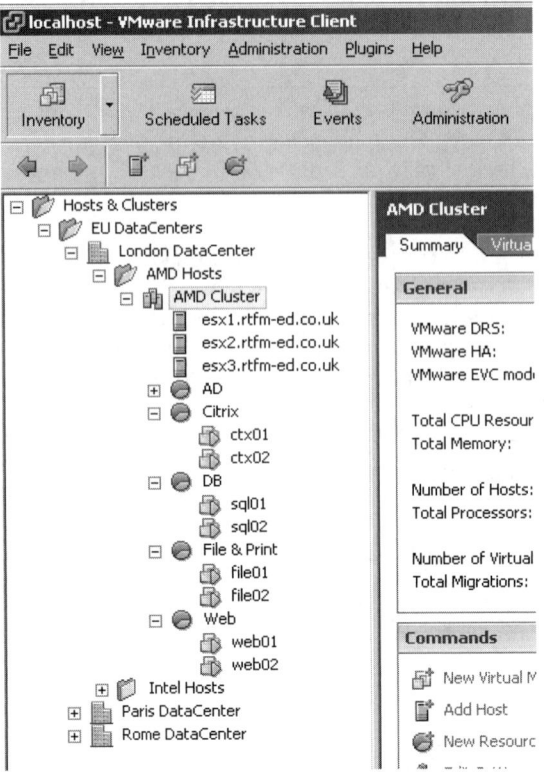

NOTE *vCenter 4 requires .NET Framework 3 SP1 to function, and you must have Windows 2003 SP 1 or higher on the vCenter server for .NET to be installed.*

1. Attach the vCenter CD to the system and initiate a vCenter 4 installation. During this time, you are likely to see the installation of the Microsoft Visual C++ 2005 package, if it has not already been installed. After a short time, you will be presented with a dialog box that indicates a previous installation has been found. Click Next to continue.

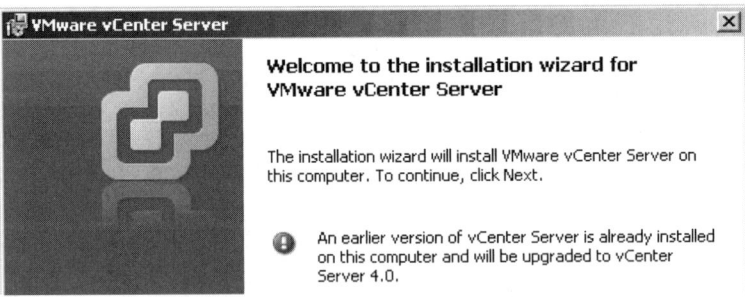

2. Provide your vCenter 4 license key and click Next.

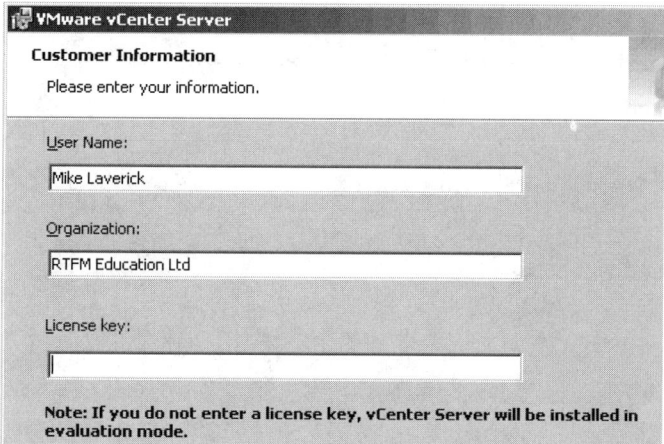

3. Provide the database credentials for the existing vCenter 2.5 database and click Next.

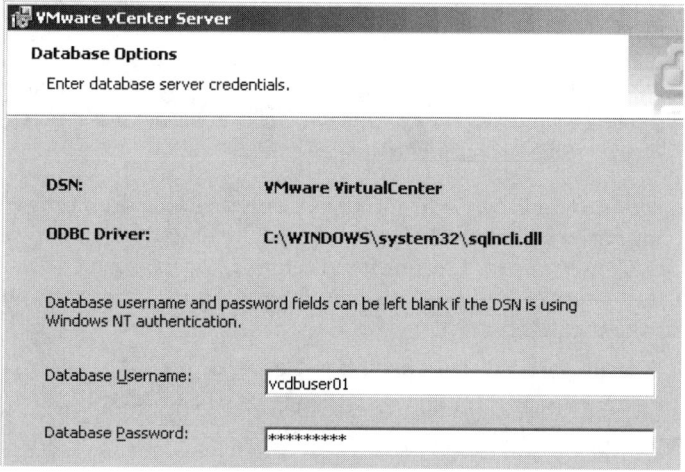

4. You will see a dialog box warning you that other plug-in services, such as the existing VUM installations that came with vCenter 2.5, are incompatible with vCenter 4, and will need upgrading as well. If you have installed the vCenter Converter or Guided Consolidation plug-ins, they also will be mentioned in this dialog box. Click OK to close the dialog box.

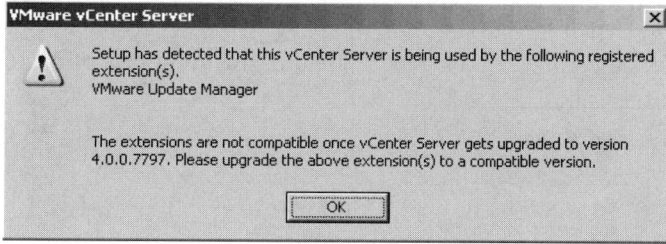

5. Choose the "Upgrade existing vCenter Server database," option, and check the box to confirm that you have taken a backup of the existing vCenter database.

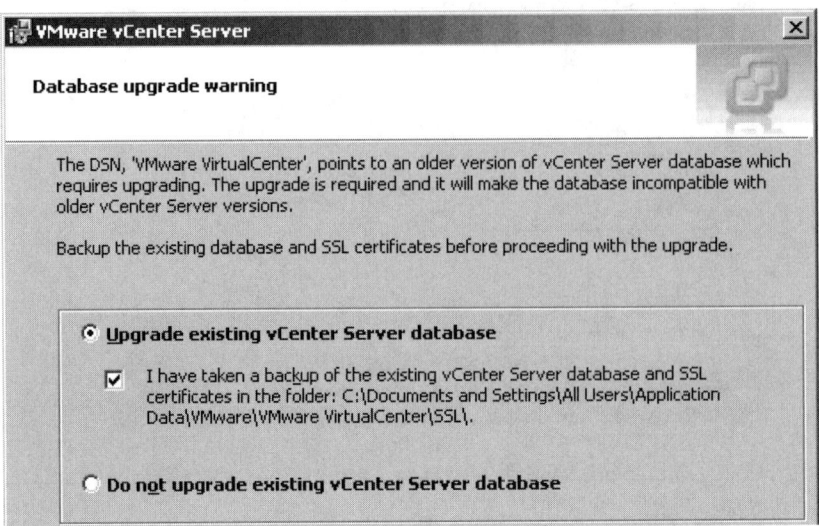

CAUTION *Choosing the "Do not upgrade existing vCenter Server database" option will reinitialize the database, which effectively wipes the existing data held in the database. If you chose this option, you may have done a clean installation of vCenter!*

6. Set which account will be used to run the vCenter service. Remember that the system account uses significantly high privileges, which, strictly speaking, are not required for vCenter to run. I recommend using a special service account. Note that this message appears only if you using SQL Server authentication rather than Windows authentication.

7. Accept the default port numbers used by vCenter 4.

8. Click Install to start the upgrade process. (Before the upgrade process begins, you may see that Microsoft .NET is installed.)

At the end of the upgrade process, you will see the database being upgraded, and then you will be asked to reboot the vCenter server.

Installing the vSphere Client

After the reboot, install the vSphere Client. This will cause the old VI Client to be removed.

When the vSphere Client loads, you may see the message "Exception has been thrown by target of an invocation." I believe this rather cryptic message (which can appear more than once) is due to an attempt to load the VUM and Converter plug-ins of the vSphere Client against an out-of-date VUM and Converter installation.

After the upgrade to vCenter 4, I was pleased to discover my ESX hosts were still connected, and the upgrade of the vCenter Agent was successfully triggered on all three of my ESX hosts.

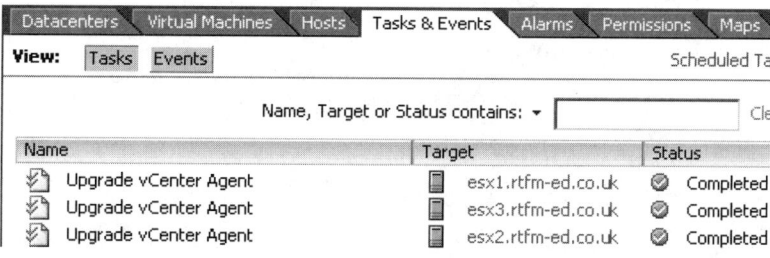

> **NOTE** *In previous upgrades of vCenter, sometimes ESX hosts were disconnected. This was usually caused by the vCenter Agent (.vpxd) that runs in ESX being out of date. Usually, right-clicking the ESX host and clicking Connect would trigger an installation of the new agent, and the ESX host would be reconnected.*

Confirm that your ESX servers are fully functional before going any further. For example, in my first attempt, I discovered I had problems with the VMware license server. This causes other issues, such as being unable to carry out VMotion and maintenance mode tasks.

Enabling SSL Checking

By default, an upgraded vCenter system retains the old method of adding ESX hosts, without validating their identity. This configuration is insufficient for features such as VMware FT, which requires ESX hosts to be joined to vCenter by confirming their SSL settings as well. (This is an important default, and I hope that VMware will change it in subsequent releases of vCenter 4.)

To reenable SSL checking, follow these steps:

1. In the vSphere Client, select the Administration menu and choose vCenter Server Settings.

2. Select the SSL Settings option.

3. In the dialog box, enable the option to make vCenter require verified host SSL certificates.

4. At the top of the Verified column, enable all ESX hosts to be verified.

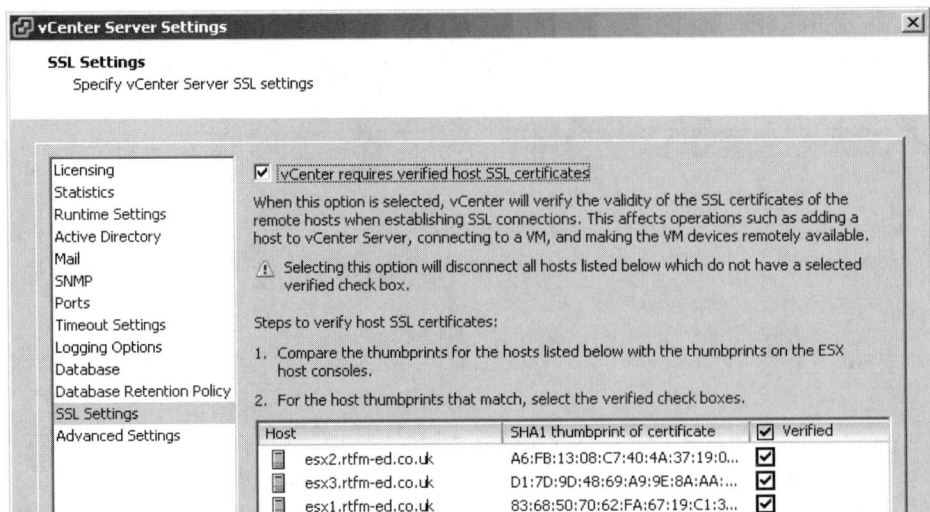

If you do not verify the existing ESX hosts in this way, they will become disconnected in vCenter, and they will not be manageable until you reconnect each and every one, and confirm their SSL thumbprint values.

Of course, probably very few people will be security conscious or diligent enough to actually confirm that SHA1 thumbprints match the ESX host. But if you do wish to confirm each SHA1 value, log in to each ESX host and run this command:

```
openssl x509 -sha1 -in /etc/vmware/ssl/rui.crt -noout -fingerprint
```

It should produce output like the following:

```
SHA1 Fingerprint=A6:FB:13:08:C7:40:4A:37:19:08:6D:4D:78:01:48:64:9A:4D:37:C3
```

This was taken from the esx2.rtfm-ed.co.uk server, and as you can tell, it matches the SHA1 value in my SSL Settings dialog box.

Upgrading vCenter Components

VUM is the recommended method of upgrading ESX hosts, VM hardware, and VMware Tools. So, the quicker you get VUM upgraded, the quicker you can upgrade those components. (If you prefer not to use VUM, there are other ways of upgrading the VM hardware and VMware Tools components, as described later in this chapter.)

Upgrading VUM

When you first start the upgrade of VUM, you will receive a warning that the previous version is installed. As with the vCenter upgrade, you will see the installation of the Microsoft Visual C++ 2005 package if it was not previously installed.

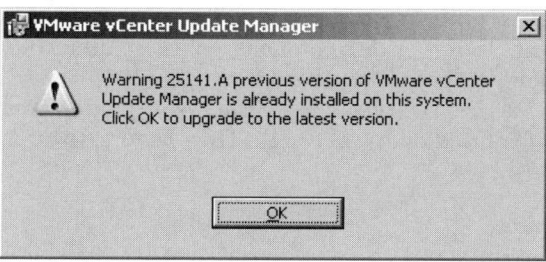

You will need to provide the username and password for your account for vCenter, as well as the database credentials for the VUM database.

VMware vCenter Update Manager   ×

vCenter Server Information

Enter vCenter Server IP address and credentials

Please provide the necessary information about vCenter Server below. VMware vCenter Update Manager will need this information to connect to the vCenter Server at startup.

VMware vCenter Server Information

IP: vc1.rtfm-ed.co.uk   HTTP Port: 80

Username: administrator   Password: ******

VMware vCenter Update Manager

Database Information

Enter additional database configuration information.

DSN: **VMware Update Manager**

ODBC Driver: **C:\WINDOWS\system32\sqlncli.dll**

Database username and password fields can be left blank if the DSN is using Windows NT authentication.

Database Username: vumdbuser01

Database Password: *********

After completing these two dialog boxes, you will see the standard warning about making sure you back up SQL Server if the database is set to full recovery mode. As with the upgrade of the vCenter database, a standard dialog box asks if you want to upgrade and to confirm that you have carried out a backup before the upgrade. Finally, you can set how the VUM server will be identified on the network. This defaults to using an IP address, but I prefer to use the FQDN.

Upgrading vCenter Converter

The vCenter Converter upgrade process is similar to the VUM upgrade process. When you choose to install vCenter Converter 4, as with the VUM upgrade, you will be asked to provide the vCenter username and password for the Converter utility to connect to vCenter, and to set the Converter TCP port numbers.

Upgrading Guided Consolidation

The upgrade of Guided Consolidation will request a user account and password for the collector service, which gathers information about your existing environment. It must have access to the local vCenter machine and access to the Active Directory domain to function. You will also need to specify which TCP ports the collector service listens on, and provide details of the vCenter server so the collector service can register the vCenter plug-ins.

Installing vSphere Client VUM and Converter Plug-ins

Once VUM and other components have been upgraded, you can download and install the plug-ins using the Plug-in Manager.

Plug-in Name	Vendor	Version	Status	Description
Installed Plug-ins				
vCenter Storage Monitoring	VMware Inc.	4.0	Enabled	Storage Monitoring and Reporting
vCenter Service Status	VMware, Inc.	4.0	Enabled	Displays the health status of vCenter services
vCenter Hardware Status	VMware, Inc.	4.0	Enabled	Displays the hardware status of hosts (CIM monitoring)
Available Plug-ins				
VMware Update Manager Exte...	VMware, Inc.	4.0.0....	Download and Install....	VMware Update Manager extension

After these have been upgraded, you should find the vSphere Client no longer creates any error messages. A security dialog box will appear to confirm the client's connection to the VUM server.

Upgrading ESX Hosts Using VUM

New to VUM is the ability to upgrade an ESX host from one release to another using the ESX Classic ISO file and a special ESXi-upgrade-release.zip file, which can be downloaded from VMware's web site and is also available using the free download version of ESXi.

Note that it is also possible to upgrade an ESXi 3.5 host using the Host Update Utility, as described later in this chapter.

The VUM method begins with defining an upgrade baseline, which you can then attach to the ISO file of ESX 4 and the zip file of ESXi.

Creating an Upgrade Baseline

Follow these steps to create an upgrade baseline:

1. Click Home, then the Solutions and Applications tab, then the Update Manager icon.

2. From the Baselines and Groups tab, select the Upgrade Baselines tab.

3. Click the Create link.

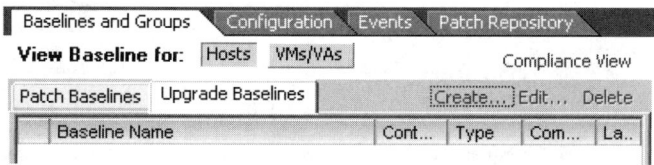

4. Type in a name and description for the upgrade baseline.

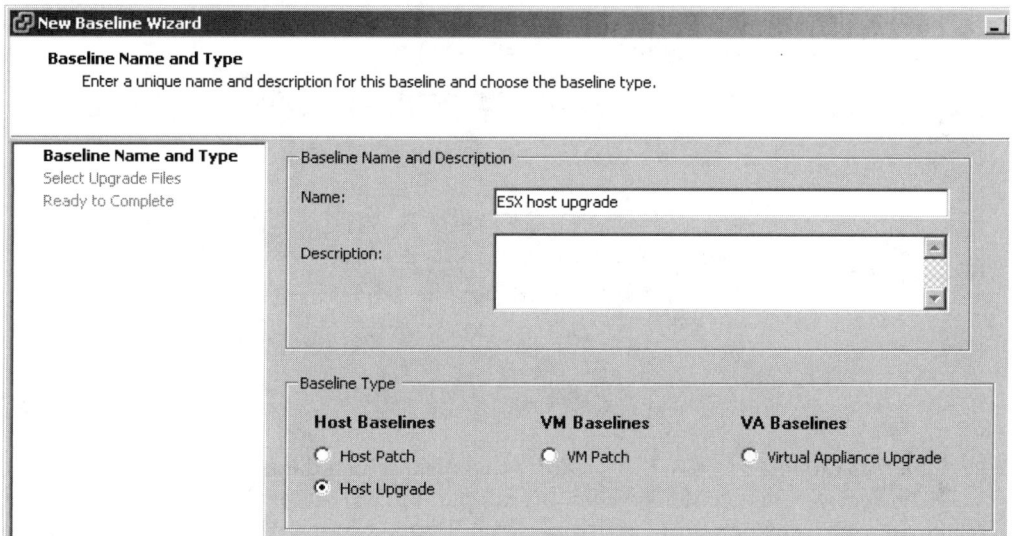

5. Browse for the ISO file on the ESX Classic DVD and the ESXi update zip file. VMware recommends that you add both types of files, and confirm that they are the same build number.

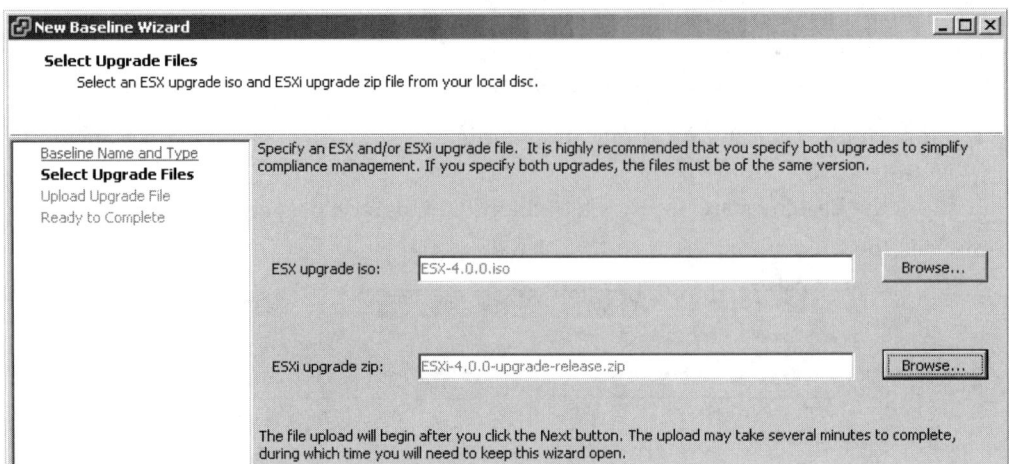

6. These files are copied to the partition you selected for VUM updates in the original vCenter 2.5 installation into a host_upgrade_packages directory. Click Next to trigger the upload process to the VUM server.

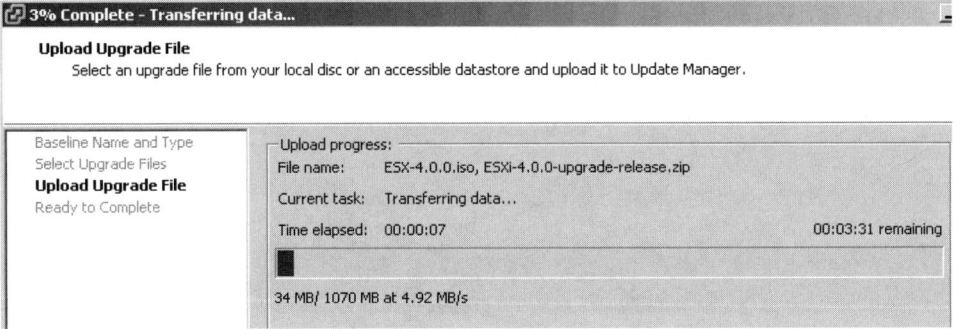

7. After this upload process, the wizard will ask on which datastore the virtual disk of the Service Console will be held. (Recall that the ESX 4 now holds the partitions of the Service Console within a virtual disk.) If you choose "Automatically select a datastore on the local host," the virtual disk will be located on a local VMFS volume; if there is insufficient space, the upgrade will fail. The "Select a datastore" option is used to store the Service Console virtual disk on a specified location for example a SAN based LUN. You might prefer this option if your ESX hosts already boot-from-SAN.

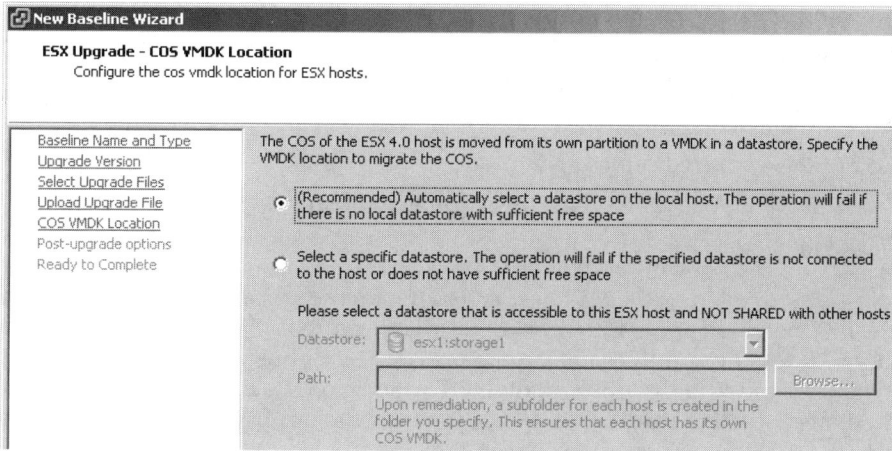

8. In the final part of the wizard, you can enable the rollback process, in case the upgrade process fails, and the postscripting process, which can be used to carry out secondary tasks. This script takes the format of a BASH shell script (.sh), which is akin to a .cmd or .bat file in Windows. It could be used to upgrade the hardware agents that you install to an ESX host, for example.

At the end of this process, you will have an upgrade baseline for the ESX host.

Updating an ESX Host

The next tasks are to attach your upgrade baseline and upgrade an ESX host. It is possible to attach a baseline to a high-level object, but I recommend applying it to just one ESX host initially, to make sure the upgrade works as expected.

Before triggering the remediate process, you might wish to manually move VMs from the ESX host using maintenance mode. If you have DRS enabled and configured as fully automated, this should happen automatically.

Follow these steps to apply the baseline and remediate the host:

1. In the Hosts and Clusters view, select an ESX host.

2. In the Update Manager tab, click the Attach link.

3. Select the upgrade baseline you created.

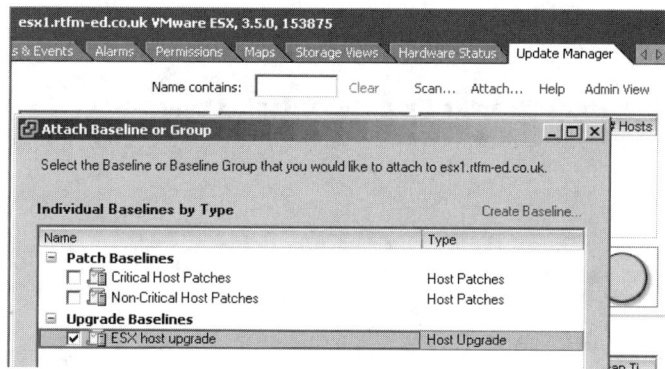

4. Click the Remediate button.

5. In the Remediation Selection dialog box, select the Upgrade Baselines type and the ESX host upgrade baseline you attached.

6. Accept the EULA.

7. Accept the upgrade options.

8. Select whether you want to start the upgrade immediately or set up a scheduled task.

9. Click Finish.

At around the 28% mark, the ESX host enters the reboot stage. After a certain amount of time, the ESX host will appear in vCenter as "disconnected." This is because it has been rebooted by VUM. VUM modifies the boot menu of the ESX host to add an ESX 4 Upgrade option. It makes it the default option, allowing five seconds to select a different boot. The server will then proceed to load the ESX upgrade files and apply the packages. You will see the status of the upgrade move to around 35% in vCenter, despite the fact that vCenter says the ESX host is disconnected. An IP stack is loaded during the installation, and it may be the case that vCenter is using some low-level method of monitoring the progress of the upgrade.

```
84% Complete - Installing package: net-snmp (329 of 335)
85% Complete - Installing package: rpm-python (330 of 335)
85% Complete - Installing package: smart (331 of 335)
85% Complete - Installing package: policycoreutils (332 of 335)
85% Complete - Installing package: man (333 of 335)
85% Complete - Installing package: net-snmp-utils (334 of 335)
85% Complete - Installing package: setools (335 of 335)
85% Complete - Installing Packages
85% Complete - Setup Module Loading
86% Complete - Migrating fstab
not migrating fstab entry: none /dev/pts devpts gid=5,mode=620 0 0
not migrating fstab entry: none /proc proc defaults 0 0
not migrating fstab entry: none /dev/shm tmpfs defaults 0 0
not migrating fstab entry: UUID=5ca6e239-9a74-42ab-8448-5df6f4e4919f
efaults 0 0
87% Complete - Migrating Configuration
88% Complete - Migrating Groups
88% Complete - Migrating Users
89% Complete - Updating Network Configuration
90% Complete - Setting License
91% Complete - Set Console Memory
92% Complete - Copying ESX Configuration
93% Complete - Writing Cleanup Script
94% Complete - Running "%post" Script
```

Rolling Back the ESX Host or Cleaning Up the ESX Boot Loader

After the upgrade, you will see that the option to boot to ESX 3 remains on the GRUB menu.

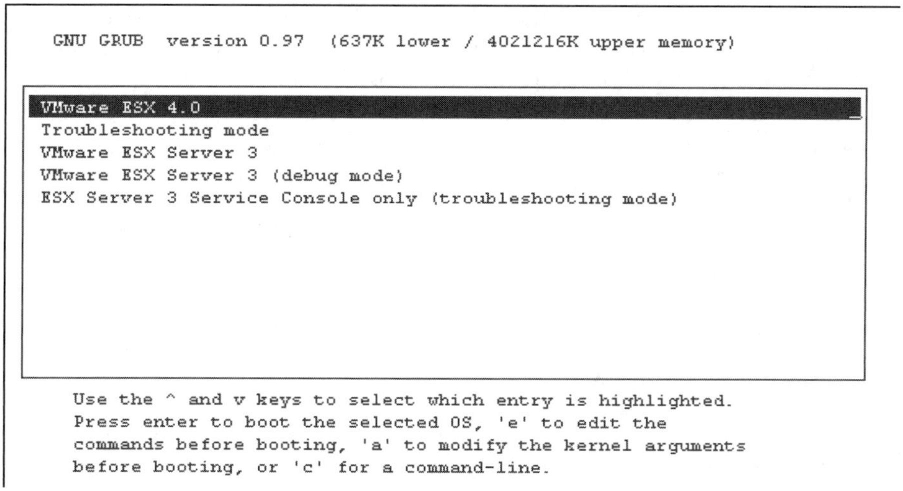

```
    GNU GRUB   version 0.97   (637K lower / 4021216K upper memory)


  VMware ESX 4.0
  Troubleshooting mode
  VMware ESX Server 3
  VMware ESX Server 3 (debug mode)
  ESX Server 3 Service Console only (troubleshooting mode)








      Use the ^ and v keys to select which entry is highlighted.
      Press enter to boot the selected OS, 'e' to edit the
      commands before booting, 'a' to modify the kernel arguments
      before booting, or 'c' for a command-line.
```

If you consider the upgrade to be unsuccessful, you can roll back to the ESX 3.5 installation using this Service Console script:

```
rollback-to-esx3
```

If the upgrade to ESX 4 has been successful, you can remove this option from the menu with the following:

```
cleanup-esx3 -f
```

The -f switch runs a forced cleanup, which doesn't prompt you during the cleanup process. The cleanup script removes any ESX 3.5 references held in /etc/fstab, deletes the ESX 3.5 boot files in the /boot partition, and cleans up the boot menu.

Relicensing the ESX Hosts

After the upgrade, you will need to license the ESX 4 hosts. During the upgrade process, you are using the older VMware license server to license the ESX hosts, while the vCenter 4 upgrade is licensed during the upgrade process itself. You will need to carry out two tasks: add the ESX host license key to vCenter, and then instruct the ESX 4 hosts to use it. Once all the ESX hosts are upgraded, the older VMware license server can be decommissioned.

As an ESX host is upgraded, it loses its license from the VI3.5 environment. You may wish to confirm that your hosts are fully licensed, and not in some evaluation mode instead. The following example shows the current state of my ESX hosts.

Licensing			
Report	View by: ⊙ Product ○ License key ○ Asset		
Product		Assigned	Capacity
⊟ License Server (vc01.vmeduc.local)			
VI3 ESX Server Standard		0 CPUs	8 CPUs
VI3 ESX_FULL_BACKUP		0 CPUs	8 CPUs
VI3 vCenter agent for ESX Server		0 CPUs	8 CPUs
VI3 vCenter Management Server		0 instances	1 instances
VI3 VMotion		0 CPUs	8 CPUs
VI3 VMware DRS		0 CPUs	8 CPUs
VI3 VMware HA		0 CPUs	8 CPUs
⊟ Evaluation Mode		3	Unlimited
⊞ (No License Key)		3	Unlimited
⊞ vCenter Server 4 Standard		1 instances	8 instances

Notice that my old VMware license server is still present, and that all my ESX hosts that were upgraded are in an evaluation mode. There is one vCenter server running, consuming one of my eight vCenter licenses.

Follow these steps to relicense an ESX host:

1. Navigate to Home, then Administration, then Licensing.

2. Click the Manage vSphere Licenses link.

3. Enter your vSphere license key(s). Then click the Add License Key button.

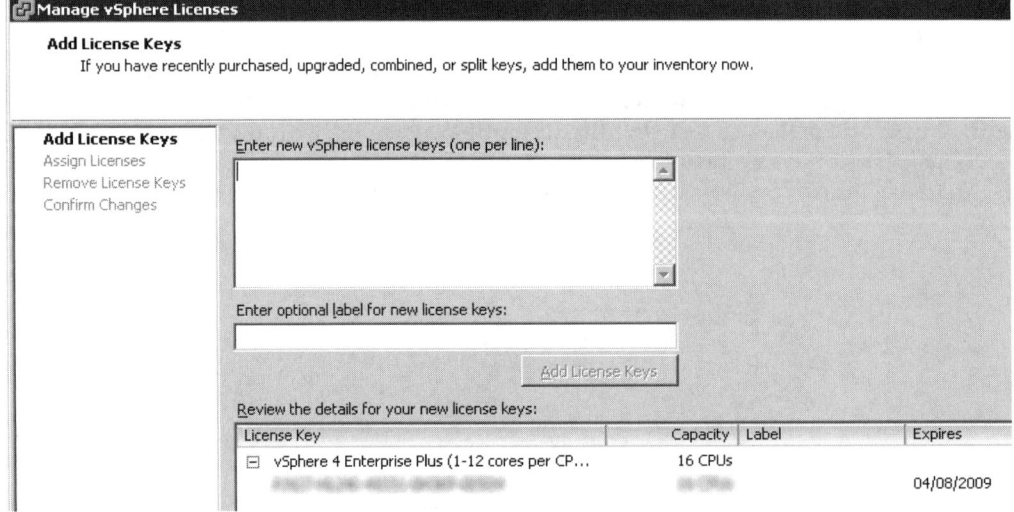

4. The next part of the wizard displays unlicensed assets by default (in my case, those unlicensed assets are the ESX hosts). Select the ESX host, and then select the new license.

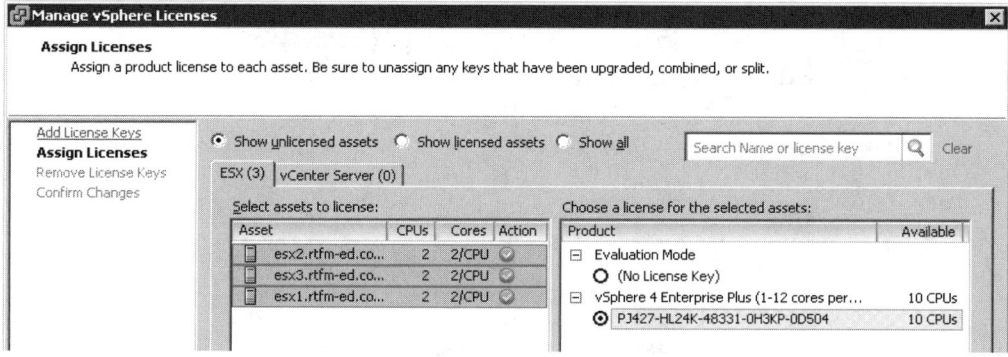

5. Click Next, and then click Finish.

Removing References to the Old License Server

Once all your ESX hosts are upgraded to ESX 4, you can remove references to the old VMware license server, as follows:

1. Disable the reference to the VMware license server by modifying the vCenter Server Settings. In the vSphere Client, select vCenter Server Settings from the Administraton menu. Then remove the check next to "Reconfigure ESX 3 hosts using license servers to use this server."

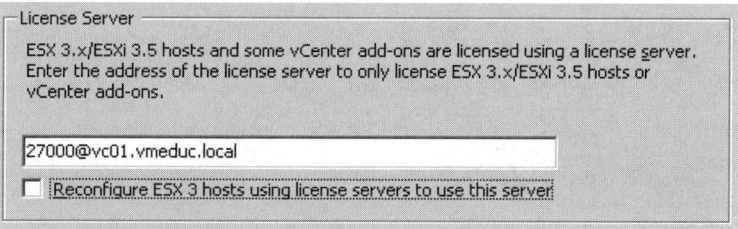

2. Log in to the license server and back up your vmware.lic file (located in C:\Program Files\VMware\VMware License Server\Licenses).

3. Use Add/Remove Programs to uninstall the VMware License Service.

Upgrading VMware Tools with VUM

You can easily tell if your VMs are up to date with VMware Tools by checking the VMware Tools Status column on the Virtual Machines tab.

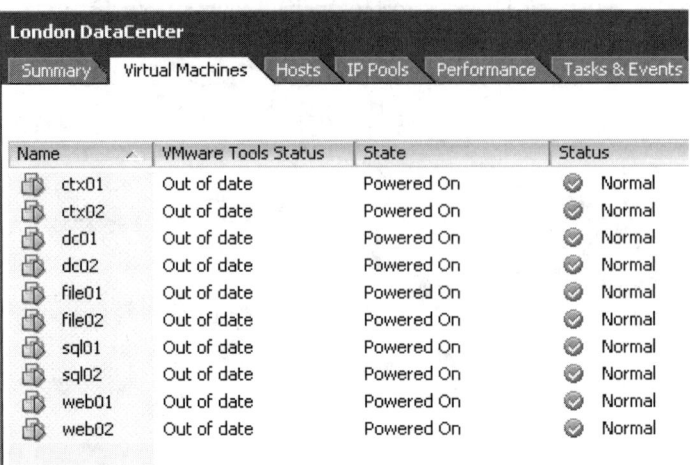

It is best to upgrade VMware Tools before you upgrade the VM hardware. The upgrade of the VM hardware does introduce the possibility of new drivers being installed. If you carry out a VMware Tools upgrade first, those drivers will already be there. In the case of changes that upgrade the VM's networking, failure to upgrade the VM's hardware can result in a loss of network settings. This can happen because a network device loses the old IP settings from the old network device inside the VM. If you attempt a VM virtual hardware upgrade before upgrading VMware Tools, you will receive a warning message.

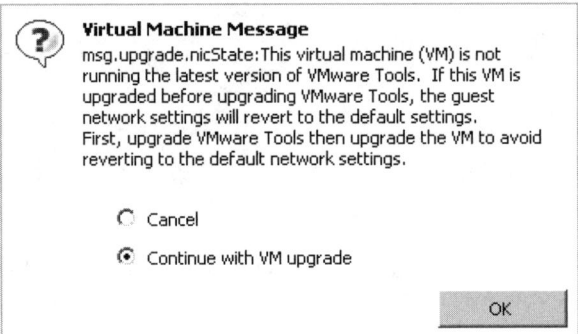

In most cases, the upgrade of VMware Tools is intrusive, as the installation of new drivers will generally trigger a reboot in Windows. Although running older versions of VMware Tools might not cause significant problems, it isn't recommended. Frequently, VMware Tools upgrades will fix and improve certain DLLs and other APIs that improve backup performance and reliability. Unless you persist in backing up the VM using conventional agents across the network, upgrading VMware Tools is highly recommended.

The upgrade of VMware Tools can be triggered in several ways:

- Through the GUI, either interacting with the upgrade via the Remote Console or automatically, without interaction. To perform the installation this way, right-click the VM and choose Guest, then Install/Upgrade VMware Tools.

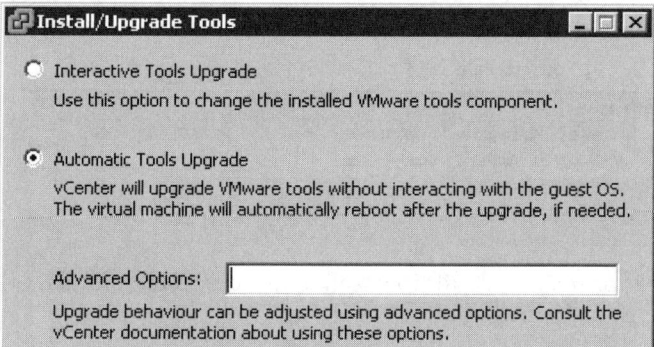

- By selecting more than one VM in the vCenter interface, which brings up a slightly different dialog box.

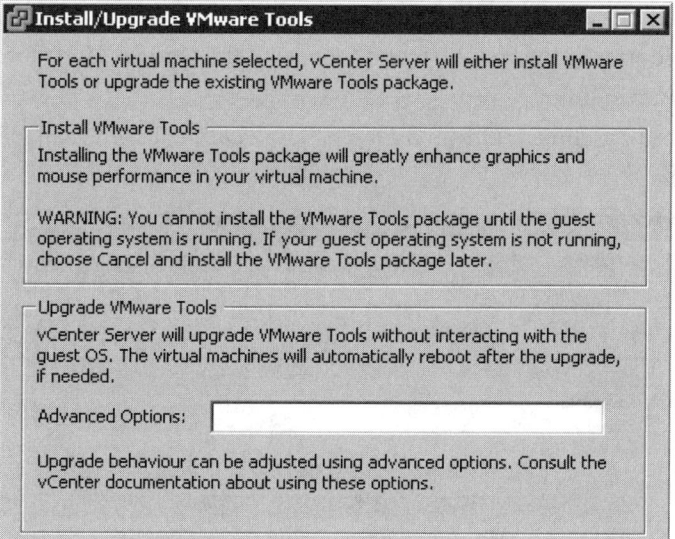

- Using the `vmware-vmupgrade` CLI utility on the vCenter server, as described in the "Upgrading VMs with CLI Tools" section later in this chapter.
- Using VUM, which is the recommended method.

VUM ships with built-in upgrade baselines to upgrade the VMware Tools and to upgrade virtual hardware, either for VMs or vApps. To see these baselines, click Home, then the Solutions and Applications tab, then the Update Manager icon. On the Baselines and Groups tab, click the View Baselines for VMs/VAs button, and then select the Upgrade Baselines tab.

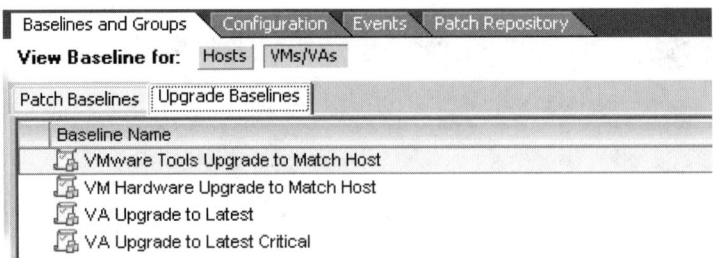

So, you just need to attach the built-in baseline to a datacenter, folder, or an individual VM, and then perform the remediation.

CAUTION *This task has a very good chance of rebooting your VMs.*

Follow these steps to use the built-in upgrade baseline to update VMware Tools:

1. Switch to the VMs and Templates view.
2. Select a folder or individual VM, and then click the Update Manager tab.
3. Click the Attach link.
4. In the Attach Baseline or Group dialog box, select the baseline called VMware Tools Upgrade to Match Host.

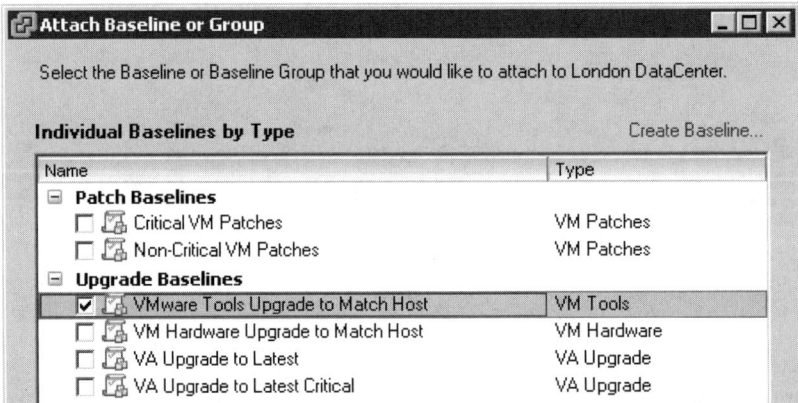

NOTE *Another option would be to select the Scan option, and in the Confirm Scan dialog box, check the current compliance against the ESX host by selecting the scan for VM hardware upgrades.*

5. Select the folder or VM, and click the Remediate button. If you are triggering the remediate process at a folder level, make sure you select all the VMs that require remediation.

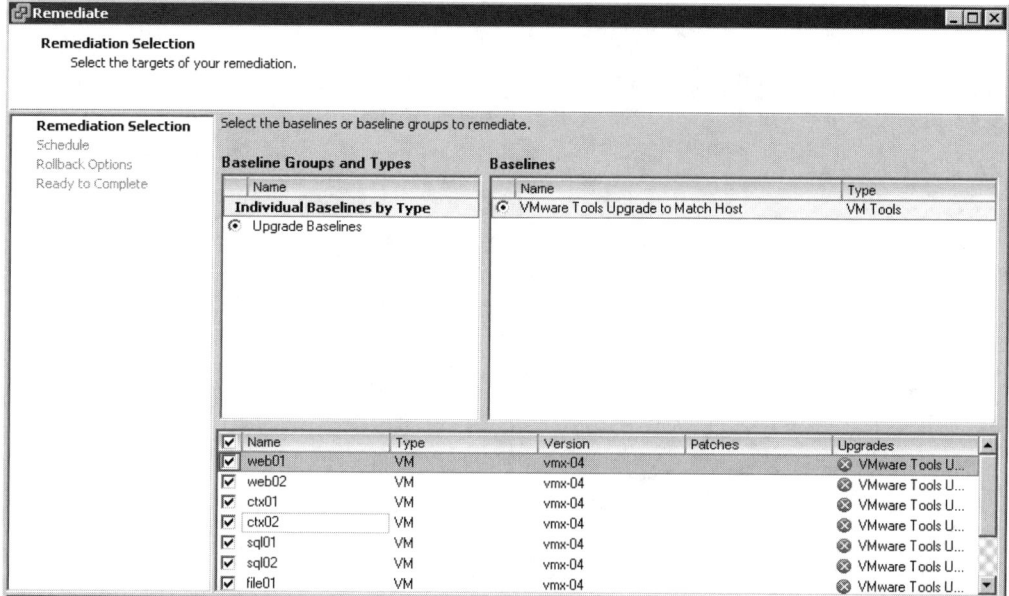

6. Set your options for when you would like the remediation to occur and where you would like to place the snapshots of the VMs prior to the upgrade.

You should see the remediation processes in the Recent Tasks bar.

Upgrading Virtual Hardware with VUM

You will be pleased to hear that upgrading virtual hardware is substantially easier than upgrading physical hardware, and does not require the use of screwdrivers or antistatic precautions.

Essentially, the upgrade of virtual hardware is a seamless one, in which the VM hardware level is updated to allow new functionality. For example, in VM hardware level 4, the VM is able to see only four vCPUs. When upgraded to VM hardware level 7, it can use up to eight vCPUs.

The upgrade of virtual hardware is an intrusive operation, in the sense that it requires that the VM be powered off at the time of the upgrade. So, even with features like DRS and VMotion, some downtime of the VM is inevitable.

The upgrade of the virtual hardware is an optional task, as it is by no means required for day-to-day functionality. You might consider this to be a "mixed-mode" scenario, where vCenter and ESX are running on the latest versions of the code, but the VM continues to have the same functionality as if it was running on ESX 3.*x*.

Note that once you upgrade the VM hardware, this will prevent VMotion from ESX 4 to ESX 3. This is why I recommend completing the upgrade of all the ESX hosts in a cluster before proceeding to upgrade the VMs.

There are several ways to upgrade the VM's hardware. One way is to right-click a VM when it is powered off and choose Upgrade Virtual Hardware. This may be useful to you if you wish to take a more ad hoc approach, upgrading virtual hardware on a case-by-case basis, possibly fitted around other maintenance tasks within the guest OS.

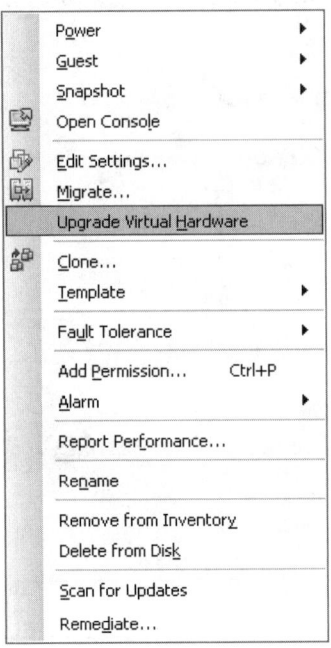

___

CAUTION *This task will definitely power down your VMs.*

As noted in the previous section, VUM comes with a built-in baseline for upgrading your VM hardware. Here's how to use it:

1. Switch to the VMs and Templates view.
2. Select a folder or individual VM, and then click the Update Manager tab.
3. Click the Attach link.
4. In the Attach Baseline or Group dialog box, select the baseline called VM Hardware Upgrade to Match Host.
5. Select the folder or VM, and then click the Remediate button. If you are triggering the remediate process at a folder level, make sure you select all the VMs that require remediation.
6. Set the options for when you would like the remediation to occur and where you would like to place the snapshots of the VMs prior to the upgrade.

Moving VMs to Directories

The option Move VMs to Directories appears on the right-click menu of ESX 4 hosts in vCenter.

I think this option should be regarded as a legacy, as its usage is legacy, to say the least. However, it is related to upgrades, and I want to take this opportunity to clarify why it exists.

The option to move VMs to directories first surfaced in the upgrade from ESX 2.*x* to ESX 3.*x*. As there is no direct path for upgrades from ESX 2 to ESX 4, it is unlikely ever to be used. But it was important for upgrades from ESX 2 to ESX 3.

In ESX 2, the VMs were frequently split between two locations, with the smaller files (.nvram, .vmx, and .log) of the VM being located on *local storage* in the /home/vmware location and the larger files (.vmdk) often located on shared Fibre Channel storage. This configuration design would have had dire consequences for features such as VMware HA, because if an ESX host crashed, the files that made up the VM would be inaccessible to the other hosts in the cluster. To remedy this, the Move VMs to

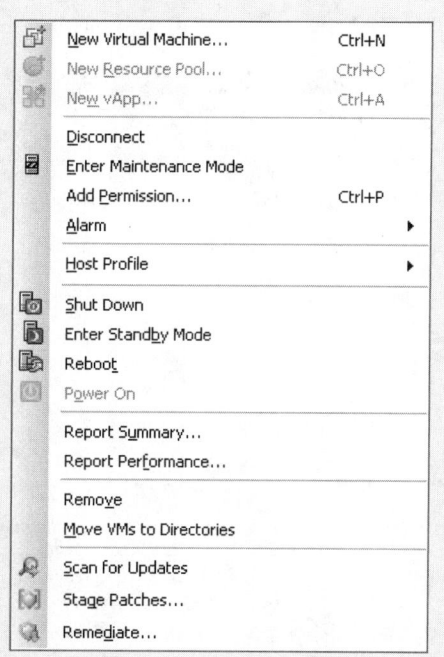

Directories option was used after an ESX 2 to ESX 3 upgrade to relocate all the files of the VM to a location available to all ESX hosts.

Upgrading ESXi Hosts Using the Host Update Utility

Upgrading an ESXi 3.5 host using the Host Update Utility is a very simple process—much simpler than using VUM, but also, as you might expect, with much reduced functionality. Remember that this utility is not recommended for large installations; it's really designed for people who are using the free ESXi product.

CAUTION *Before you begin the upgrade, the ESXi host must be in maintenance mode. Unlike VUM, the Host Update Utility does* not *integrate with DRS's fully automated mode and trigger maintenance mode for you.*

Before you begin, download the ESXi Upgrade zip file from VMware's Web site. Then follow these steps:

1. From the Start menu, load the Host Update Utility. When the Host Update Utility first runs, you will be asked if you want to download updates.

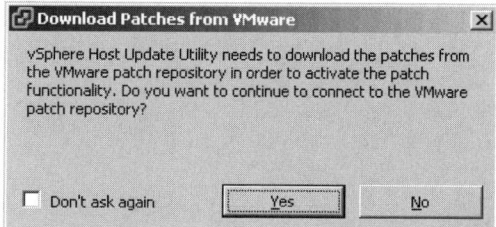

2. Click the Add Host link.

3. Type in the name or IP address of the ESXi 3.5 host.

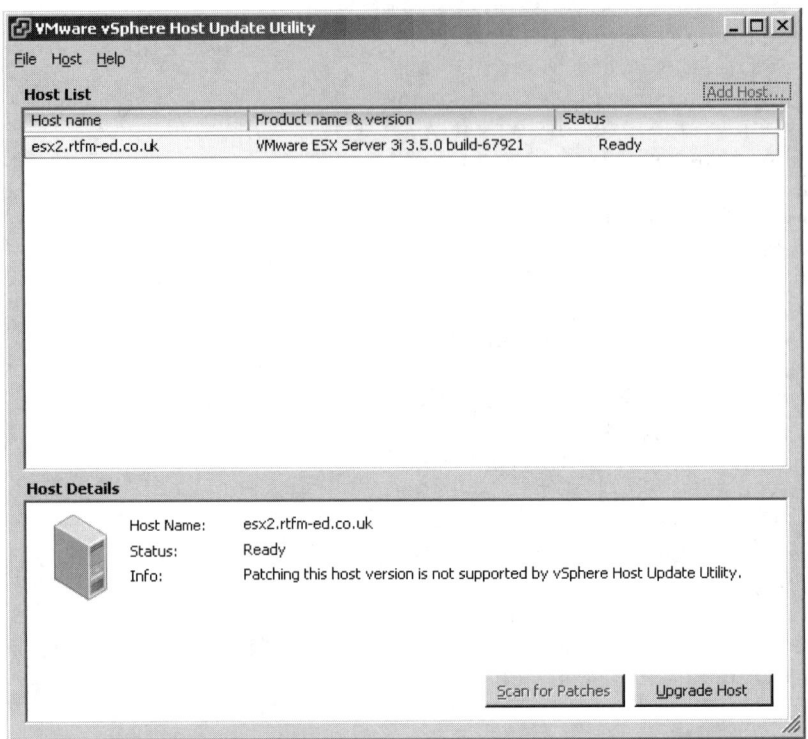

NOTE *Notice how the ESX host is not supported for patching, as this facility is only for ESX 4 hosts. However, the utility can upgrade the ESX 3.5 host.*

4. Click the Upgrade button.

5. In the next dialog box, click the Browse button and locate the ESXi Upgrade zip file. The package will be validated, which will take some time. Once this has completed, the wizard will continue.

6. In the ESXi Upgrade dialog box, accept the EULA.

7. Supply the password for the root account. At this stage, the utility will carry out a consistency check.

8. Click Finish to start the upgrade process. The remainder of the process is merely watching progress bars.

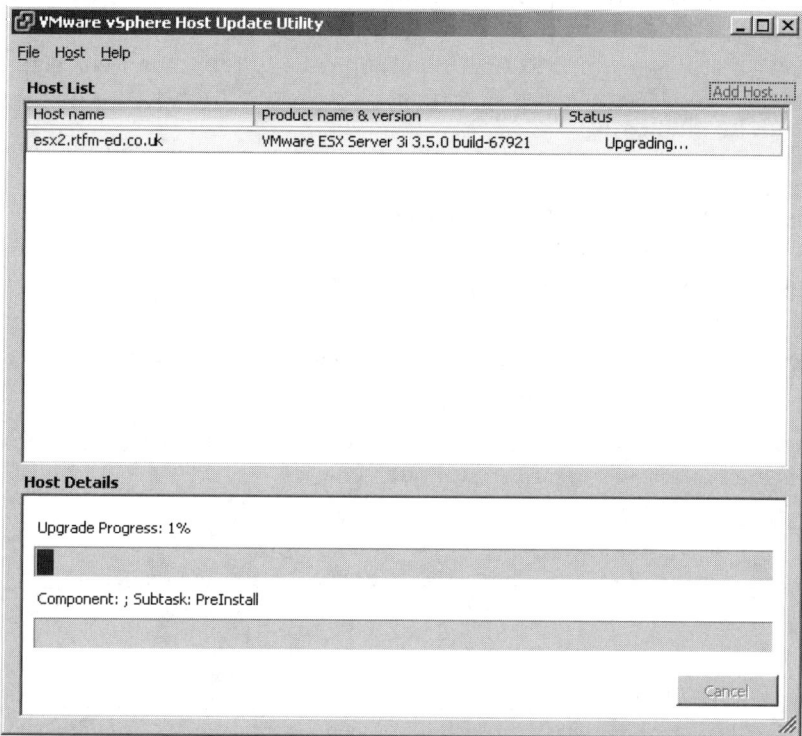

At the end of this process (which can take some time), you will see a message stating that the upgrade was successful.

You will need to reconnect the ESXi host to the vCenter server using the Connect option on the right-click menu. Additionally, you may wish to use the Host Update Utility to scan for patches for the ESXi host (once the ESXi host is upgraded, this update utility can then also patch it).

Upgrading VMs with CLI Tools

In this chapter, I've mainly emphasized the bulk method of upgrading using VUM. I recognize that some people prefer command-line utilities. Here, I will provide a brief overview of how to use the CLI to update virtual hardware and VMware Tools.

To update these components from the command line, you use the `vmware-vmupgrade` utility. The following are a few common errors that can occur with this utility:

- Remember that the VMs must be powered off first. If they are not, you will see an error message similar to "EU DataCenter/London DataCenter/AD/dc01: Cannot upgrade. VM is not powered-off."

- People often forget to input the slash (/) to indicate the end of one object in the vCenter Inventory and the start of another. If you do this, you will get this type of error message: "Failed to upgrade: failed to find object at EU DataCenter/London DataCenter\AD\dc01."

- The most common error is failing to authenticate with vCenter correctly. In this case, you'll see the message, "Failed to connect to VirtualCenter server: vim.fault.InvalidLogin."

Per-ESX Host Virtual Hardware and VMware Tools Update

To update virtual hardware and VMware tools from an ESX host, first power down the VMs you wish to update. Then log on to the vCenter server.

NOTE *It is possible to use Microsoft's Remote Desktop Connection software if you have enabled it on your vCenter server.*

Open a command prompt to C:\Program Files\VMware\Infrastructure\VirtualCenter Server and use the vmware-vmupgrade utility, as follows:

```
vmware-vmupgrade.exe
-u vi4book\administrator -p vmware
-h "EU DataCenters/London DataCenter/AMD Hosts/AMD Cluster/esx1"
-m 2
-t 10
```

NOTE *These lines have been wrapped for readability. When you type the command, it should be one continuous line of text.*

The switches –u and –p are required. They set the username and password to authenticate against vCenter. The –h switch is also required. It sets the path to an ESX host within the Inventory. In this example, all powered-off VMs running on esx1.vi3book.com will be updated.

The switches –m and –t are optional. They set how many VMs can simultaneously be updated and how long VMs are allowed to stay powered on (in minutes). This deals with the issue of VMs that will not power down gracefully.

You can also optionally use the –s switch to indicate that you wish to skip the upgrade of VMware Tools, and upgrade only virtual hardware.

Per VM Virtual Hardware and VMware Tools Update

To update virtual hardware and VMware tools from an ESX host, power down the VMs you wish to update, and then log on to the vCenter server. Open a command prompt to C:\Program Files\VMware\Infrastructure\VirtualCenter Server, and enter a command in the following form:

```
vmware-vmupgrade.exe
-u vi4book\administrator -p vmware
-n "EU DataCenters/London DataCenter/AD/dc01"
```

```
-n "EU DataCenters/London DataCenter/AD/dc02"
-n "EU DataCenters/London DataCenter/AD/dc03"
-n "EU DataCenters/London DataCenter/AD/dc04"
-n "EU DataCenters/London DataCenter/AD/dc05"
-n "EU DataCenters/London DataCenter/AD/dc06"
```

As you can see, with the –n switch, you can specify multiple VMs. And yes, you must specify –n each and every time!

NOTE *Unfortunately, in this release, it is not possible to simply specify a folder, and have vCenter assume that every VM in that folder (and subfolder) should be updated with a new version of VMware Tools.*

Summary

As you have seen, it is entirely possible to upgrade from a version of VMware Virtual Infrastructure to VMware vSphere. Critically, this upgrade can be achieved with almost minimal impact on your all-important VMs. Personally, I'm in favor of upgrades of vCenter, depending on whether you need to move to a new database platform. I see no particular need to upgrade ESX hosts, as long as you have an effective scripted installation of ESX 4 Classic, or host profiles with ESXi. Indeed, you might consider this to be a strategic time to move from ESX Classic to ESXi.

Upgrading VMware Tools and virtual hardware are the most intrusive updates you can make, depending on the number of VMs in vCenter. Personally, I prefer a more ad hoc approach to this upgrade. However, be aware that the new functionality and capabilities of vSphere 4 may be significantly reduced if this is deferred for too long. After all, what's the point of an upgrade if you don't take advantage of upgrading?

Keep in mind that this chapter covered only the immediate upgrade process. There are other steps to consider, such as migrating away from standard vSwitches to distributed vSwitches (covered in Chapter 5). Also, you may need to consider that after an upgrade, many of your VMs will not have the correct disk type for VMware FT.

Conclusion

Well, that's the end of this book. If you have read it from cover to cover, I'm extremely grateful that you took the time to do so. I do appreciate that we live in an age of overwhelming media. Some people will have dipped in and out of the book, and used it as a quick refresher or close study of a topic.

What's next? Well, you might use this book and other sources for training as part of the preparation for taking the VCP test. Although the goal of this book was to give you the knowledge and power you need to make the VMware software work for you, rather than as exam preparation, if you have read and absorbed the contents of this book, the exam should not be so daunting.

I also recommend adding my blog to your RSS feed. As I discover new features and information, I will be blogging about those.

My next big project after releasing this book will be to update my self-published work on Site Recovery Manager. Additionally, I am planning a video demo series, which shows every aspect of the vSphere 4 product. I will be taking the structure of this book as the framework for this series of videos. You might find these videos a useful visual aid.

I hope you have found that the high number of graphics have illustrated product functionality in a way that is almost like a real-time video, but on paper. Additionally, I hope that providing a book of this density within months of the product release marks a major step forward in delivering content at the very time it is most needed.

My long-term plan is to update this book at the next significant milestone in vSphere 4, when the product functionality has shifted significantly. My prediction is that there will probably be a vSphere 4.5 release in 2011.

Index

E

Cutting-Edge Virtualization Guides

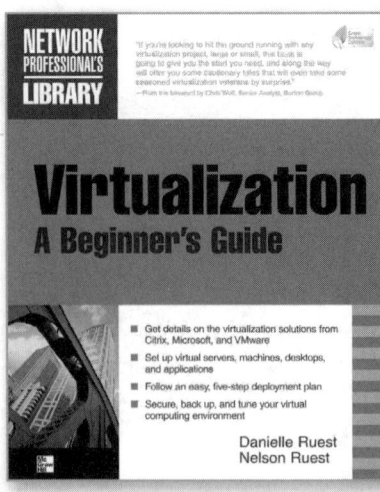

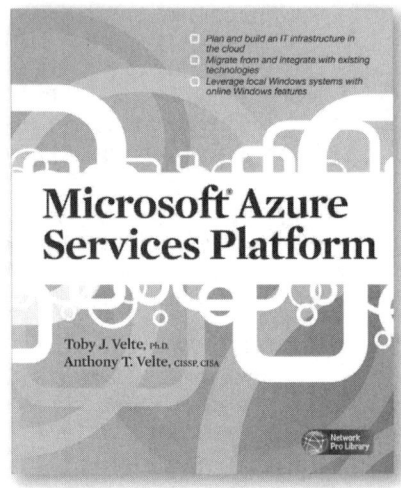